Identifying, Assessing, and Treating Dyslexia

Identifying, Assessing, and Treating Dyslexia

Editor: Aria Harris

AMERICAN
MEDICAL PUBLISHERS
www.americanmedicalpublishers.com

AMERICAN
MEDICAL PUBLISHERS
www.americanmedicalpublishers.com

Cataloging-in-Publication Data

Identifying, assessing, and treating dyslexia / edited by Aria Harris.
p. cm.
Includes bibliographical references and index.
ISBN 979-8-88740-199-7
1. Dyslexia. 2. Dyslexia--Diagnosis. 3. Dyslexia--Treatment. 4. Dyslexics. 5. Alexia. I. Harris, Aria.
RC394.W6 I34 2023
616.855 3--dc23

American Medical Publishers,
41 Flatbush Avenue,
1st Floor, New York,
NY 11217, USA

ISBN 979-8-88740-199-7 (Hardback)

Contents

Preface

Dyslexia is a learning disorder which is characterized by difficulty in reading due to problems with identifying speech sounds and learning to relate letters and words (decoding). Dyslexia is of two types, namely, developmental dyslexia and acquired dyslexia. Developmental dyslexia is used to describe an unanticipated difficulty in reading in children and adults who otherwise possess motivation, intelligence, and schooling considered necessary for accurate and fluent reading. Acquired dyslexia is a result of neurological factors such as traumatic brain injury or stoke. It causes problems with spelling words, reading quickly, writing words, pronouncing words, and understanding the meaning. The rate of attention deficit hyperactivity disorder (ADHD), developmental language disorders, and difficulties with numbers is higher in patients with this disorder. The interaction of genetic and environmental factors results in dyslexia. It can be diagnosed by a series of evaluations that includes examination of memory, spelling, vision, and reading skills. This book includes some of the vital pieces of works being conducted across the world, on various topics related to dyslexia. Its extensive content provides the readers with a thorough understanding of the identification, assessment and treatment of this condition. Researchers and students in this field will be assisted by this book.

The information shared in this book is based on empirical researches made by veterans in this field of study. The elaborative information provided in this book will help the readers further their scope of knowledge leading to advancements in this field.

Finally, I would like to thank my fellow researchers who gave constructive feedback and my family members who supported me at every step of my research.

Editor

Why do adults with dyslexia have poor global motion sensitivity?

Elizabeth G. Conlon*, Gry Lilleskaret, Craig M. Wright and Anne Stuksrud

Griffith Health Institute, School of Applied Psychology, Griffith University, Gold Coast, QLD, Australia

Correspondence:
Elizabeth G. Conlon, Griffith Health Institute, School of Applied Psychology, Griffith University, PMB 50 Gold Coast Mail Centre, Gold Coast, QLD 9726, Australia
e-mail: e.conlon@griffith.edu.au

Two experiments aimed to determine why adults with dyslexia have higher global motion thresholds than typically reading controls. In Experiment 1, the dot density and number of animation frames presented in the dot stimulus were manipulated because of findings that use of a high dot density can normalize coherence thresholds in individuals with dyslexia. Dot densities were 14.15 and 3.54 dots/deg^2. These were presented for five (84 ms) or eight (134 ms) frames. The dyslexia group had higher coherence thresholds in all conditions than controls. However, in the high dot density, long duration condition, both reader groups had the lowest thresholds indicating normal temporal recruitment. These results indicated that the dyslexia group could sample the additional signals dots over space and then integrate these with the same efficiency as controls. In Experiment 2, we determined whether briefly presenting a fully coherent prime moving in either the same or opposite direction of motion to a partially coherent test stimulus would systematically increase and decrease global motion thresholds in the reader groups. When the direction of motion in the prime and test was the same, global motion thresholds increased for both reader groups. The increase in coherence thresholds was significantly greater for the dyslexia group. When the motion of the prime and test were presented in opposite directions, coherence thresholds were reduced in both groups. No group threshold differences were found. We concluded that the global motion processing deficit found in adults with dyslexia can be explained by undersampling of the target motion signals. This might occur because of difficulties directing attention to the relevant motion signals in the random dot pattern, and not a specific difficulty integrating global motion signals. These effects are most likely to occur in the group with dyslexia when more complex computational processes are required to process global motion.

Keywords: coherent motion, dyslexia, temporal recruitment, perceptual contrast effect, attention

INTRODUCTION

Dyslexia is a neurobiological disorder that can affect multiple brain areas (Stein, 2001; Shaywitz et al., 2003; Vidyasagar and Pammer, 2010). Adults with dyslexia show evidence of poor phonological awareness (Wilson and Lesaux, 2001), slower processing speed (Laasonen et al., 2001; Conlon et al., 2011; Stenneken et al., 2011), poor spelling (Bruck, 1990) and reduced comprehension (Conlon and Sanders, 2011). Although researchers agree on the characteristics that distinguish adults with good and poor reading skills, there is less agreement found concerning the visual processes that are impaired in this group.

Evidence that some individuals with dyslexia have a sensory processing deficit isolated to the magnocellular (M) and/or dorsal visual streams has been reported over many years (Lovegrove, 1993; Habib, 2000; Stein, 2001). Groups with dyslexia have poorer temporal contrast sensitivity than controls but do not have poorer spatial contrast sensitivity, measured in the parvocellular visual stream (Lovegrove et al., 1986). Difficulties replicating these findings (Amitay et al., 2002; Williams et al., 2003) and evidence that poorer sensitivity is found only with use of methodologies that require either sequential processing (Ben-Yehudah et al., 2001) or prior adaptation to a stimulus (Johnston et al., 2008), indicates that groups with dyslexia have a visual sensory processing deficit only when performing tasks that use complex computational processes. The evidence indicates that these processes are particularly impaired in the medial temporal area (MT) of the dorsal stream (Cornelissen et al., 1995; Talcott et al., 2000; Hansen et al., 2001; Conlon et al., 2004, 2009, 2012; Wilmer et al., 2004; Roach and Hogben, 2007; Benassi et al., 2010).

Evidence supporting the hypothesis of poorer performance of groups with dyslexia on computationally complex tasks is obtained from studies that have used methodologies that require discrimination of speed or the direction of global motion at MT. Reduced sensitivity is found in groups with dyslexia than in typically reading controls on these tasks (Cornelissen et al., 1995; Demb et al., 1998a; Raymond and Sorensen, 1998; Talcott et al., 2000; Hansen et al., 2001; Conlon et al., 2004, 2009; Wilmer et al., 2004; Wright and Conlon, 2009; Benassi et al., 2010). Convergent evidence of poorer performance in groups with dyslexia on speed, contrast and direction discrimination tasks has been obtained using electrophysiological (Schulte-Körne et al., 2004; Schulte-Körne and Bruder, 2010; Jednoróg et al., 2011) and functional MRI technology in which reduced neural activation has been found in these groups compared to controls (Eden et al., 1996; Demb et al., 1998b; Ben-Shachar et al., 2007).

Although there is compelling evidence for reduced efficiency when processing these complex stimuli in individuals with dyslexia, there have also been failures to replicate the effects found (Amitay et al., 2002; Hill and Raymond, 2002; Ramus et al., 2003; Reid et al., 2007). One explanation of these inconsistent findings concerns the extent that individuals with dyslexia can capture or sample the relevant motion signals for further processing. Using the global motion task, the aim of the experiments conducted was to determine whether coherent motion thresholds in groups with dyslexia would systematically change with presentation of stimuli that either increase or decrease the probability that coherent motion will be detected in the stimulus used.

The perception of global motion is commonly assessed using an apparent motion task generated with a random dot kinematogram (RDK) containing signal and noise dots (Newsome and Paré, 1988). This process occurs in the MT area of the dorsal stream (Thakral and Slotnick, 2011). The signal dots move in a single direction while noise dots move randomly. The RDK contains a series of single animation frames in which apparent motion is generated by presenting the dots in different locations in the RDK, and then presenting the series of stimuli rapidly and sequentially. Signal dots must be extracted from the noise dots and then integrated to form a global perception of motion (Raymond, 2000). The minimum percentage of signal dots needed for accurate perception of global motion is defined as the "motion coherence threshold." The lower the proportion of signal dots needed to reach coherence threshold, the greater the sensitivity of the visual system to global motion.

Experimenters can systematically increase or decrease coherence thresholds by manipulating the stimulus parameters used to generate global motion. For example, increasing the number of animation frames presented on a single trial reduces coherence thresholds (McKee and Welch, 1985). This effect is known as temporal recruitment (Raymond and Isaak, 1998) and occurs because cell groups in the dorsal visual stream that are sensitive to direction of motion have increased opportunity to detect and integrate the signal dots across time with presentation of more animation frames. This allows for greater co-operation between stimulated motion analysers (Raymond and Isaak, 1998; Snowden and Braddick, 1989), which increases the probability that global motion will be detected.

Although there is evidence for temporal recruitment in good readers, the evidence for its influence on coherence thresholds in groups with dyslexia is limited. In one study, coherence thresholds were significantly lower in a group with dyslexia with presentation of ten animation frames (duration of 333 ms) when compared to four (duration of 133 ms; Hill and Raymond, 2002). However, in a second study, temporal recruitment had no influence on coherence thresholds in a group with dyslexia (Raymond and Sorensen, 1998). One important difference between the two studies was the dot density used to generate the RDK.

Dot density is the number of dots presented per degree of visual angle (dots/deg^2). This parameter has little influence on coherence thresholds in typical readers (Barlow and Tripathy, 1997). However, increasing the dot density can reduce coherence thresholds in groups with dyslexia (Talcott et al., 2000). In a previous study that manipulated the dot density in a RDK, Talcott et al. (2000) found that coherence thresholds were higher in a group with dyslexia than in controls when the dot density was 9 dots/deg^2 or less. No group differences in coherence thresholds were found when the dot density was 12.2 dots/deg^2. Increasing the dot density increases the number of motion signals that can be sampled in a limited area in space. Previous research has concluded that directionally selective cells in the dorsal stream are fewer and more sparsely distributed in individuals with dyslexia (Galaburda and Livingstone, 1993; Stein and Walsh, 1997; Talcott et al., 2000). In addition, visual evoked potentials (VEP) are attenuated with presentation of coherent motion, but not by presentation of noise only (Schulte-Körne et al., 2004). On this basis increasing the dot density in a RDK might increase the probability that these sparsely distributed cell groups can capture and integrate motion signals (Talcott et al., 2000). This might explain the reported findings of no reader group differences on global motion tasks that have used high dot densities (Hill and Raymond, 2002; Edwards et al., 2004).

In most studies that have investigated global motion processing in dyslexia, a single task has been conducted to determine whether the groups with and without dyslexia differ on coherence thresholds. Investigation of the influence of the stimulus parameters used has been limited. Experiment 1 aims to systematically manipulate the number of animation frames presented and the dot density in the RDK, thereby determining the influence of these parameters on coherence thresholds in groups with dyslexia and controls.

Additional parameters found to systematically influence global motion thresholds in groups with dyslexia are the contrast or color of the signal and noise dots presented in the RDK, and the use of a pre-cue as an attention aid. When the signal and noise dots are the same color and contrast, groups with dyslexia have higher coherence thresholds than controls (Cornelissen et al., 1995; Talcott et al., 1998, 2000). When the signal dots are of either a higher contrast or presented in a different color to the noise dots, no group differences in coherence thresholds are found (Sperling et al., 2006; Conlon et al., 2012). Using this methodology, the influence of the noise dots is reduced, therefore allowing more efficient sampling of the signal dots in the global stimulus. One explanation of this effect is that presentation of stimuli of higher contrast produce increased excitation in the cell groups stimulated, allowing automatic exclusion of the noise dots in the RDK (Edwards et al., 1996; Croner and Albright, 1997; Martinez-Trujillo and Treue, 2002). When the stimuli of higher contrast are the target motion signals, there is a greater probability that these stimuli will be sampled by the visual system, particularly when competing with lower contrast, lower energy stimuli for sampling.

Relative to conditions in which the signal and noise dots in the RDK are of equal contrast, individuals with dyslexia have higher coherence thresholds than controls when the signal dots are presented at a lower contrast than the noise dots (Conlon et al., 2012). This occurs because the high contrast, high energy noise dots mask the lower contrast, lower energy signal dots, reducing the capacity of the group with dyslexia to sample the available signal dots. However, if the signal dots are of a lower contrast than the noise dots and a pre-cue is presented alerting participants that the low contrast dots contain the coherent motion signals, no reader group differences in coherence thresholds are found. This occurred because the pre-cue resulted in lower coherence thresholds for the group with dyslexia but had no influence on the control group (Conlon et al., 2012). These findings are consistent with studies that have reported that the use of a pre-cue can also increase accuracy in visual search tasks that contain multiple stimuli in groups with dyslexia (Hawelka and Wimmer, 2008; Moores et al., 2011). One explanation of these findings is obtained from physiological data. Sensitivity to motion at MT in single cell recordings can be influenced by the attentional state of the receptive field (Treue and Maunsell, 1996; Treue and Trujillo, 1999). Using functional MRI technology, these findings have been extended to demonstrate an increased level of activation at MT in the human visual system on the basis of manipulations of attention to specific stimulus attributes (O'Craven et al., 1997; Buchel et al., 1998), for example, the speed changes in a motion stimulus. Behaviourally, directing attention in this way increases the length of the motion aftereffect, relative to passive viewing conditions (Buchel et al., 1998). The increased activity at MT occurs because of a top-down feedback loop from the posterior parietal cortex (PPC). This feedback loop acts to modulate sensory performance. In groups with dyslexia there is now substantial evidence of impairment in attention processing at the level (Vidyasagar, 1999; Lallier et al., 2010; Vidyasagar and Pammer, 2010).

A problem with the studies that have manipulated contrast or color or used a pre-cue is that the signal dots differed from noise in terms of motion, color and contrast. It may therefore have been the influence of contrast or color, rather than the availability of the target signal dots that led to systematic increases and decreases in coherence thresholds in groups with dyslexia.

The impact of stimulus parameters that can systematically influence coherence thresholds, while allowing the signal and noise dots to differ only on the direction of motion requires further investigation. One task that has been found to produce systematic changes in coherence thresholds by using motion alone is the perceptual contrast effect (Raymond and Isaak, 1998). Relative to a baseline condition in which coherence thresholds are obtained using a static prime, coherence thresholds are increased (i.e., sensitivity is reduced) in typical readers when a briefly presented, fully coherent motion prime is presented before a partially coherent test stimulus. This effect occurs provided the prime and test stimulus have the same direction of motion. When motion detectors responsive to the same direction of motion are stimulated by both the prime and test stimuli, the highly salient fully coherent prime reduces the visibility of the signal dots presented in the test stimulus because of the dramatic change in coherence of the prime and test. In fact, if presentation of the final two frames in a sequence of fully coherent motion is presented as partially coherent, these frames are not detected by participants (Raymond and Isaak, 1998). In contrast, coherence thresholds are reduced relative to the baseline condition when the prime and test have opposite directions of motion (Raymond and Isaak, 1998). The latter result might have occurred because the visibility of noise dots that matched the direction of motion in the prime was reduced, so decreasing the proportion of effective noise dots available for processing in the test RDK.

In explanation of their results, Raymond and Isaak (1998) argued that the prime was viewed as an object, so could disrupt processing of subsequently presented stimuli by reducing the efficiency of visual selection processes, if the prime and test had the same motion characteristics. These results cannot be explained by adaptation because the duration of the prime was less than 100 ms and the interstimulus interval (ISI) between the prime and test stimuli had no influence on thresholds (Raymond and Isaak, 1998; Glasser et al., 2011). Importantly, the only difference between the stimuli presented were the motion attributes of the prime. Experiment 2 will use the perceptual contrast effect to determine whether coherence thresholds can be systematically increased or decreased in individuals with dyslexia.

The overall aim of the experiments conducted in this study was to determine if using different methodologies can vary the strength of the motion signals used in a RDK, thus leading to subsequent systematic changes in coherence thresholds in groups with and without dyslexia. In the first experiment, the dot density and number of animation frames presented in a RDK were manipulated. In Experiment 2, coherence thresholds were obtained after brief exposure to a fully coherent prime moving in either the same or opposite direction of motion to the partially coherent test stimulus.

EXPERIMENT 1

The effect of dot density and temporal recruitment on coherence thresholds in groups of adults with or without dyslexia was investigated. Two dot densities, high (14.15 dots/deg^2) and low (3.54 dots/deg^2) were used. These dot densities were selected based on findings that no reader group differences in coherence thresholds are found at dot densities of 12.2 dot/deg^2 or greater (Talcott et al., 2000; Hill and Raymond, 2002). Temporal recruitment was manipulated by presenting each dot density condition for five (total duration, 83 ms) or eight (total duration, 133 ms) animation frames. These parameters were selected because Hill and Raymond (2002) found no reader group difference on a global motion processing task when dot density was high (45 dots/deg^2) and four animation frames (total duration, 133 ms) were presented.

If increasing dot density alone provides a sufficient increase in the capacity of the group with dyslexia when sampling the signal dots, no group difference in coherence thresholds were expected with presentation of a RDK with high dot density. This was expected to occur regardless of the number of animation frames presented. The group with dyslexia were expected to have higher coherence thresholds than the control group when dot density was low. If temporal recruitment effects are only found in the group with dyslexia in the high dot density condition, lower coherence thresholds were expected with presentation of the high dot density condition in which eight animation frames were presented. In the low dot density condition, no influence of the number of animation frames presented was expected.

MATERIALS AND METHODS

PARTICIPANTS

There were 21 individuals with dyslexia (M_{age} = 23.64 years; *SD* = 6.4) and 22 typically reading controls (M_{age} = 18.64 years; *SD* = 3.33). All participants had English as a first language and normal or corrected to normal visual acuity. Due to associations found in previous studies between visual discomfort and global motion processing, participants with a high score on the Visual Discomfort Scale were excluded (Conlon et al., 1999, 2009). Individuals with dyslexia were recruited from the University disability office, the laboratory register and from advertising. Typical readers were obtained from the student participant pool. All procedures were conducted in accordance with the University human research ethics committee that approved this project.

The criteria used to define adults with dyslexia were based on those used previously (Conlon et al., 2004, 2009, 2011, 2012; Conlon and Sanders, 2011). Individuals with dyslexia reported a history of reading difficulties and had standard word reading scores below average on the Wide Range Achievement Test – 3rd Edition (WRAT-3; Wilkinson, 1993). This test consists of 42 words of increasing difficulty and has internal consistencies of 0.90–0.95 for the age groups used in this study. A further criterion was that scores on the test of word reading efficiency (TOWRE; Torgesen et al., 1999) were below a standard score of 90.

Individuals with dyslexia also had scores at least two standard deviations (SD) below the mean of the control group on non-word and exception word reading tests. The non-word and exception word tests each had 25 items matched for word length. The internal consistencies for the non-word and exception word tests are .77 and .84 respectively. At least average ability as measured by the Block Design subtest from the WAIS-3 (Wechsler, 1998) was the final criterion.

Criteria for inclusion in the control group were word reading scores on the WRAT-3 and reading fluency scores on the TOWRE of at least a standard score of 105. Nonword and exception word reading test scores were at least 75%. At least average ability as measured by the Block Design subtest from the WAIS-3 (Wechsler, 1998) was the final criterion.

The group with dyslexia was significantly poorer than the control group on word reading, $t(41) = 13.24$, $p < 0.001$, non-word reading, $t(41) = 10.61$, $p < 0.001$, exception word reading, $t(41) = 11.23$, $p < 0.001$, and word reading fluency, $t(41) = 12.24$, $p < 0.001$ tests. No significant difference was found between groups on the measure of non-verbal ability used, $t(41) = 0.238$, $p = 0.81$. Both groups performed in the average range (see **Table 1**).

Table 1 | Performance of the control (*n* = 22) and dyslexia (*n* = 21) groups on the reading and ability measures. Experiment 1.

	Control	Dyslexia
	Mean (SD)	**Mean (SD)**
WRAT reading (standard)	110.82 (4.35)	91.67 (5.12)
Non-words/25	22.32 (1.8)	14.43 (2.9)
Exception words/25	19.5 (1.8)	10.57 (3.2)
TOWRE total (standard score)	112.4 (6.8)	83.48 (8.6)
Non-verbal ability (scaled)	12.54(3.0)	12.52(2.8)

STIMULI

Stimuli for the global motion task were generated using the Cambridge Research Systems hardware and Operating System Software, VSG Version 2/5. Stimuli were displayed on a 21 inch Hitachi HM-4721-D monitor with a resolution of 800 × 600 pixels, and a vertical screen refresh rate of 120 HZ.

The RDK contained either 100 (low dot density: 3.54 dots/deg^2) or 400 (high dot density: 14.15 dots/deg^2) white dots (luminance: 20 cd/m^2) presented on a black background (luminance: 0.54 cd/m^2) displayed within a borderless area subtending 6° × 6° presented in the middle of the computer screen. The display size was chosen to avoid pursuit eye movements (Hill and Raymond, 2002). The velocity of the stimuli was 10.5°/s and the dots had a diameter of one pixel (0.35 mm). The duration of a single animation was 16.67 ms, with a dot lifetime of two animation frames (33.34 ms), after which the signal dots disappeared before being regenerated at a randomly selected stimulus location within the panel. A standard wrap around technique was used for the signal dots as they reached the side of the screen. The noise dots randomly changed position in a Brownian fashion. Stimuli were presented for either five (84 ms) or eight animation frames (133 ms).

For each of the experimental conditions there were two blocks of trials. Separate coherence thresholds were obtained for each block. The adaptive psychophysical procedure used to estimate coherence thresholds was a three-down, one-up staircase with eight reversals. After three correct responses, coherence was halved, and after each incorrect response coherence was doubled. This allowed for an estimation of the coherence value needed to obtain a correct response on 79% of the trials (Kaernbach, 1991). Participants selected the direction of motion, left or right at the completion of each trial. Geometric mean thresholds were combined across both blocks of trials to obtain an overall estimate of coherence thresholds. The starting coherency was 50% in each condition.

Response bias was determined by presenting trials at 1% coherence at least once every five trials. Participants were expected to respond randomly to these trials, with about half the responses being to the left and half to the right. Response bias was evaluated by obtaining a percentage score for the proportion of left responses to these trials. No significant group differences in response bias were found (dyslexia, $M = 46\%$, $SD = 12.36$; control, $M = 44\%$, $SD = 11.07$), $t(42) = 0.676$, $p = 0.503$.

PROCEDURE

Each participant was assessed for reading ability. This assessment was followed by a separate session in a darkened laboratory in which coherence thresholds were obtained. Viewing was binocular with natural pupils and the viewing distance of 57 cm was controlled with a chin rest. A block of 20 practice trials was presented prior to each of the four conditions. Each trial began with presentation of a fixation cross which was replaced after 150 ms with the RDK. Participants responded to the direction of motion by depressing either the left or right button on the Cambridge

Research Systems CB-2 response box at the end of each trial. A new trial was automatically triggered after each response. The order of presentation of the experimental conditions was counterbalanced between and within groups.

RESULTS

The influence of dot density and the number of animation frames presented on coherence thresholds for the reader groups is shown in **Figure 1**. These data were analyzed using a 2 (group: dyslexia or control) × 2 (dot density: low or high) × 2 (animation frames: five or eight) mixed factorial ANOVA. The assumptions of the analysis were met. A significant main effects was found for reader group, $F(1, 41) = 15.80$, $p < 0.001$; $\eta_p^2 = 28$. Regardless of the condition, the group with dyslexia ($M = 47.09$; *95% CI* = 41.87–52.03) had higher coherence thresholds than controls ($M = 32.74$; *95% CI* = 27.65–37.84). Significant main effects were also found for dot density, $F(1, 41) = 18.81$, $p < 0.001$; $\eta_p^2 = 0.31$, and the number of animation frames presented, $F(1, 41) = 10.66$, $p = 0.002$; $\eta_p^2 = 0.21$. These were modified by a significant interaction between dot density and the number of animation frames presented, $F(1, 41) = 8.68$, $p = 0.005$, $\eta_p^2 = 0.17$. There were no other significant interactions found.

The influence of dot density and the number of animation frames presented on coherence thresholds was investigated with simple effects analysis. In the five-animation frame condition, dot density, high or low had no influence on coherence thresholds, $F(1, 41) = 3.97$, $p = 0.069$, $\eta_p^2 = 0.08$. Significantly lower coherence thresholds were found with presentation of the high compared to the low dot density stimuli for the eight animation frame condition, $F(1, 41) = 32.29$, $p < 0.001$, $\eta_p^2 = 0.44$. When dot density was low there was no evidence of temporal recruitment found, $F(1, 41) = 0.73$, $p = 0.396$, $\eta_p^2 = 0.02$. However, when dot density was high, coherence thresholds were significantly lower with presentation of eight than five animation frames, $F(1, 41) = 28.8$, $p < 0.001$, $\eta_p^2 = 0.41$, showing the influence of temporal recruitment. The percentage reduction in coherence thresholds in the high dot density condition with presentation of the higher number of animation frames was 7.5% for the group with dyslexia and 6.1% for the control group, indicating similar effects of temporal recruitment in each reader group.

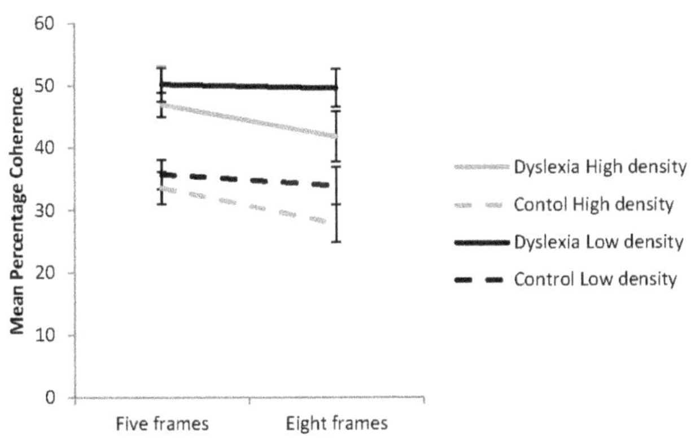

FIGURE 1 | Coherent motion thresholds for the effects of dot density and the number of animation frames presented for the groups with ($n = 21$) and without dyslexia ($n = 22$) in each of the four experimental conditions. Error bars represent ±1 standard error.

DISCUSSION

It was expected that manipulating the dot density and the number of animation frames presented in a single trial of the global motion task would systematically increase or decrease the capacity of the reader groups to efficiently sample the motion signals present in the RDK. The findings from the study were partially consistent with our hypotheses. Regardless of reader group, lower coherence thresholds were found with presentation of the high dot density condition when presented for eight animation frames, showing temporal recruitment effects. In the low dot density condition, temporal recruitment effects were not found. Across all conditions presented, the group with dyslexia had higher coherence thresholds than the control group. These findings are partially consistent with our hypotheses for the group with dyslexia only.

Previous studies have found that presentation of a RDK with a high dot density promotes increased processing efficiency in the group with dyslexia (Hill and Raymond, 2002; Edwards et al., 2004) because of the increased capacity to sample the signal dots presented within a limited area in space (Talcott et al., 2000). The findings of the current experiment indicate that the combination of high dot density and eight-animation frames used was not sufficient to normalize coherence thresholds in the group with dyslexia. The previous study that found no reader group differences in coherence thresholds when four animation frames (133 ms) were presented used a higher dot density (45 dots/deg^2; Hill and Raymond, 2002) than that used in the current study. In addition, when using a dot density of 12.2 dot/deg^2 one previous study found no reader group differences on the global motion task when stimulus durations of 900 ms were used (Talcott et al., 2000). These results indicate that dot density alone, unless very high, cannot normalize coherence thresholds in the group with dyslexia.

Lower coherence thresholds were found in the group with dyslexia in the high dot density condition and when the RDK was presented for eight animation frames. These results indicate that given sufficient signal dots captured when the higher dot density was used, normal temporal recruitment is found in the group with dyslexia. This result is consistent with the findings of Hill and Raymond (2002). The group with dyslexia can integrate motion signals over time, given sufficient motion samples from the high dot density condition. Findings that temporal recruitment did not occur in the low dot density condition support this conclusion, a result consistent with a previous study (Raymond and Sorensen, 1998).

Together these findings indicate that integration of the signal dots over time in the global motion task relies on the observer's capacity to extract sufficient signal dots from noise. A minimum level of energy in the motion signals may be required. This could be obtained with presentation of a high dot density, a greater number of animation frames or a combination of both. These findings might indicate that with sufficient signal energy to stimulate adequate neural activity in the less efficient dorsal stream of the group with dyslexia, the computation of the direction of global motion becomes more efficient.

There was no evidence of temporal recruitment in the low dot density condition for either reader group. Although these results were expected for the group with dyslexia, temporal recruitment effects were expected in the control group in this condition (Raymond and Sorensen, 1998; Talcott et al., 2000). These results indicate that presentation of the five frame stimulus in which the total stimulus duration was 84ms increased the perceptual difficulty of the stimulus beyond a level that even a well-functioning system could utilize when the dot density was low (Braddick, 1995). In addition, the duration of a single animation frame was short. Although the dot life-time of 33 ms was consistent with that used in previous studies (Raymond and Sorensen, 1998; Hill and Raymond, 2002), the frame duration was below 20 ms. In this case, a greater number of animation frames might have been needed to reach asymptotic motion thresholds (Snowden and Braddick, 1989).

The critical findings obtained from Experiment 1 are that coherent motion thresholds can be reduced in groups with and without dyslexia by increasing both dot density and the number of animation frames in a RDK. However, none of the experimental manipulations led to coherent motion thresholds being normalized in the group with dyslexia who had higher thresholds than controls in all conditions.

EXPERIMENT 2

Coherent motion thresholds in groups with dyslexia can be systematically increased by presenting signal dots at a lower contrast than the noise dots, and decreased by presenting signal dots at a higher contrast or different color to the noise dots (Sperling et al., 2006; Conlon et al., 2012). These effects are found because the higher contrast signals are the most salient so are preferentially processed in the human visual system (Edwards et al., 1996; Croner and Albright, 1997). In Experiment 2, manipulating motion only, we aimed to determine if coherence thresholds could be systematically increased and decreased in a group with dyslexia using a fully coherent prime presented in either the same or opposite direction of motion to the test stimulus.

It was expected that presentation of a fully coherent prime before the test stimulus would reduce the visibility of the signal dots in the partially coherence test stimulus in a similar way to that found when noise dots are presented at a higher contrast to the signal dots in the RDK. This would occur because of the reduced salience of the coherent motion in the partially coherent test, relative to the highly salient fully coherent prime. We expected that the threshold elevation found in a group with dyslexia would be greater than that found in the control group. However, if presenting a fully coherent prime in the opposite direction to the partially coherent test stimulus facilitates global motion processing in a group with dyslexia in a similar way to that found when presenting signal dots at a higher contrast to the noise dots, it was expected that no group difference in coherence thresholds would be found. In the baseline condition in which a stationary test stimulus was presented, higher coherence thresholds were expected in the group with dyslexia than for controls.

MATERIALS AND METHODS

PARTICIPANTS

There were 20 participants, 10 with dyslexia ($M_{age} = 22.11$ years, $SD = 3.49$) and 10 normally reading controls ($M_{age} = 21.9$ years; $SD = 4.12$). They were obtained using the same procedures as Experiment 1. No participant took part in both studies. All participants had a history of dyslexia, English as a first language and normal or corrected to normal visual acuity. The study had approval from the Human Research Ethics Committee. Group classification procedures were the same as Experiment 1 (see **Table 2**).

STIMULI AND APPARATUS

The apparatus and adaptive psychophysical procedure used were the same as those used in Experiment 1. In the global motion task, the RDK used as both the prime and the test had 300 white dots (luminance: 20 cd/m^2) presented on a dark background (luminance: 0.54 cd/m^2). The stimulus was displayed within a borderless area subtending 13.35° × 13.35° presented in the middle of the computer screen. Dot density was 3.83 dots/deg^2 and dot life time was three animation frames (50 ms). The dot life time was increased from Experiment 1 from the results of pilot testing. The motion primes were presented at 100% coherence, with one moving to the left and the other moving to the right. The baseline control stimulus was a stationary RDK with no dot displacement. Each of these stimuli was presented for 96 ms. When extinguished these were replaced with a blank low luminance field (0.54 cd/m^2) for 32 ms. This field was replaced with the partially coherent test stimulus, which was presented for 10 animation frames (160 ms). The method used is shown in **Figure 2**.

In each condition, the task was to determine whether the direction of coherent motion was to the left or to the right. Beginning coherence in all conditions was 25%. Two blocks of trials were presented for each condition. Threshold estimates were based on six threshold reversals for each block of trials.

Table 2 | Performance of the control ($n = 10$) and dyslexia ($n = 10$) groups on the reading measures. Experiment 2.

	Control	Dyslexia	
	Mean (SD)	**Mean (SD)**	***t*-test**
WRAT reading (standard)	115.6 (4.35)	94.1 (5.4)	$t(18) = 10.88, p < 0.001$
Non-words/25	24.0 (0.89)	15.5 (3.4)	$t(18) = 6.85, p < 0.001$
Exception words/25	21.9 (0.78)	11.4 (2.9)	$t(18) = 10.36, p < 0.001$
Non-verbal ability (scaled)	12.1 (0.87)	11.4(1.90)	$t(18) = 1.06, p = 0.303$

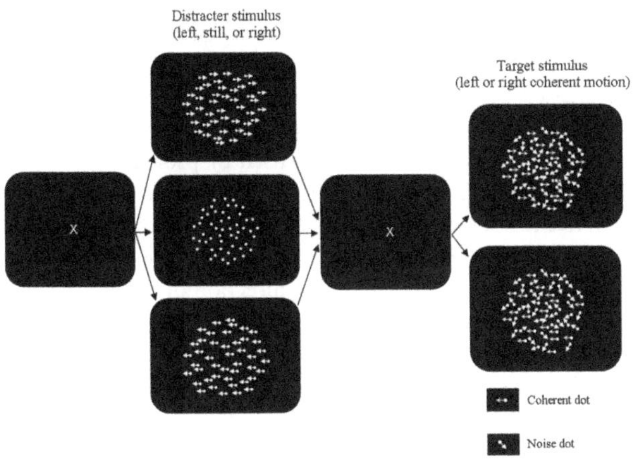

FIGURE 2 | Motion Segmentation Task used in Experiment 2. The fully coherent prime was presented in either the same or opposite direction to the partially coherent test. The stationary prime was used as a control condition. The blank stimulus between the prime and test was presented for 96 ms and the test stimulus was presented for 160 ms (10 animation frames).

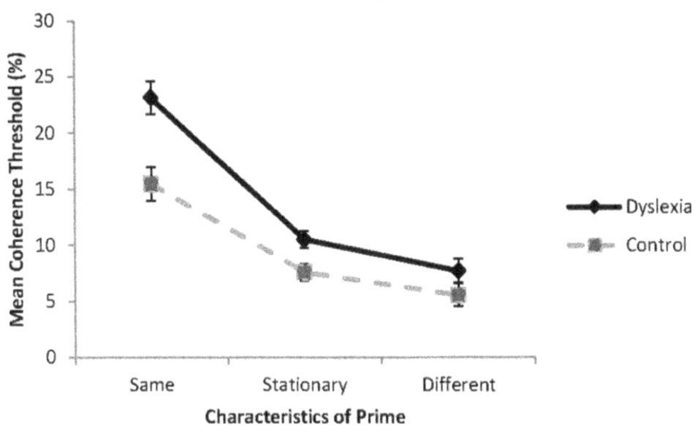

FIGURE 3 | Global motion coherence thresholds for group with dyslexia (n = 10) and controls (n = 10) when the probe and prime are presented in the same direction (same), in opposite directions (different) or when the prime is a stationary control stimulus. Standard error bars represent ±1 standard error.

The geometric mean coherence thresholds were obtained for each block of trials. These were averaged to determine coherence thresholds for each condition.

PROCEDURE

The global motion task was conducted in a separate session after assessment of reading ability. Testing took place in a darkened laboratory. Viewing distance of 57 cm was controlled with a chin rest. Viewing was binocular with natural pupils. Participants were instructed to judge whether the dots presented on the screen were moving to the left or the right. A block of 20 practice trials was followed by the experimental trials. Participants registered the direction of coherent motion by depressing the left or right keys on the response box at the end of each trial. A new trial began automatically after a response.

RESULTS

The results of the experiment are shown in **Figure 3**. The impact of the prime on threshold performance was analyzed using a 3 (condition: same, different, baseline) × 2 (group: dyslexia or control) mixed factorial ANOVA. All the assumptions of the analysis were met. Significant main effects were found for condition, $F(2, 36) = 113.8$, $p < 0.001$, $\eta_p^2 = 0.86$, and reader group, $F(1, 18) = 11.80$, $p = 0.003$, $\eta_p^2 = 0.40$. These effects were modified with a significant reader group by condition interaction, $F(2, 36) = 5.61$, $p = 0.008$, $\eta_p^2 = 0.24$.

Inspection of **Figure 3** shows that as expected, highest coherence thresholds were found when the prime and test were presented in the same direction of motion, and lowest coherence thresholds were found when the prime and test were presented in opposite directions of motion. Simple effects analysis revealed that the group with dyslexia had significantly higher coherence thresholds than the control group when the prime and test were presented in the same direction of motion, $F(1, 18) = 13.34$, $p = 0.002$, $\eta_p^2 = 0.43$, and in the baseline condition, when the prime was a stationary stimulus, $F(1, 18) = 7.69$, $p = 0.013$, $\eta_p^2 = 0.30$. No significant differences were found between reader groups when the prime and test were presented in opposite directions of motion, $F(1, 18) = 2.07$, $p = 0.167$, $\eta_p^2 = 0.10$. These results are consistent with the hypotheses of the study.

To determine to what extent the prime influenced coherence thresholds in each of the groups relative to the baseline condition, difference scores were obtained for each of the primed thresholds. Coherence thresholds were elevated by 12.63% ($SD = 3.81\%$) for the group with dyslexia and 7.87% ($SD = 3.60\%$) for the control group when the motion of the prime and the test was presented in the same direction. The increase in threshold was significantly greater for the group with dyslexia than for the control group, $t(18) = 2.86$, $p = 0.010$. When the prime and test were presented in opposite directions of motion, thresholds were enhanced by 2.76% ($SD = 1.74\%$) for the group with dyslexia, and by 2.03% ($SD = 1.48\%$) for the control group. The degree to which coherence thresholds were reduced, did not differ between the reader groups, $t(18) = 0.68$, $p = 0.513$, failing to support the hypothesis of greater facilitation in processing for the group with dyslexia. Although this change was sufficient for findings of a statistically significant threshold enhancement when compared to the baseline condition for the group with dyslexia, $t(18) = 4.78$, $p < 0.001$, the change was not sufficient to reveal reader group differences.

DISCUSSION

It was expected that presentation of a prime in the same or opposite direction of motion to the test would systematically increase or decrease the capacity of the group with dyslexia when sampling the signal dots in the partially coherent test stimulus. The results of the study are consistent with our hypotheses. Relative to the baseline condition, for both reader groups, higher coherence thresholds were found when the prime and test were presented with the same direction of motion and lower coherence thresholds were found when the prime and test were presented with opposite directions of motion. These results replicate the original findings of Raymond and Isaak (1998).

The significantly greater increase in coherence thresholds found in both reader groups when the prime and test were presented in the same direction of motion is consistent with our hypothesis that exposure to the highly salient fully coherent prime would reduce the visibility of the coherent motion signals in the test stimulus. This effect could have occurred because the visibility of the coherent motion signals was reduced, temporarily reducing their salience relative to the noise dots. This effect would have reduced the capacity of each reader group when excluding the noise dots in the test RDK. In this condition, the group with dyslexia had greater difficulty than the control group sampling the signal dots presented in the partially coherent test, producing a greater processing disadvantage. These findings are similar to those obtained in a previous study in which the signal dots were presented at a lower contrast than the noise dots in a RDK (Conlon et al., 2012). One explanation of these results is the capacity of the group with dyslexia to sample the available motion signals was reduced more than that found in the control group because of undersampling of the signal dots presented.

No significant reader group differences in coherence thresholds were found when the prime and test were presented in opposite directions of motion. These results are similar to those obtained when the signal dots presented in the RDK were a higher contrast or different color to the noise dots (Sperling et al., 2006; Conlon et al., 2012). This result occurred because of the higher energy in the target signal dots (Croner and Albright, 1997; Martinez-Trujillo and Treue, 2002) allowing greater sampling of these stimuli over the lower contrast noise dots. When the prime and test were presented in opposite directions of motion, similar facilitation of coherence thresholds was found. When the direction of motion in the test was in the opposite direction to the prime, the salience of a proportion of the noise dots would have been reduced, which might have increased the probability that signal dots would have been sampled. Evidence supporting this conclusion is obtained from the influence of presentation of a prime containing noise dots only. Higher coherence thresholds were found in the test because some of the directions of motion in the prime also masked the motion signals in the test stimulus (Raymond and Isaak, 1998).

The last important finding from the experiment was that the group with dyslexia had higher coherence thresholds than controls in the baseline control condition when the prime was a stationary stimulus. This result is consistent with many studies that have shown evidence of a global motion processing deficit in groups with dyslexia (Cornelissen et al., 1995; Raymond and Sorensen, 1998; Talcott et al., 2000; Conlon et al., 2004). Overall the findings from the experiment indicate that presentation of a fully coherent prime can influence the size of coherence thresholds, by increasing or decreasing the proportion of signal dots that can be easily sampled by individuals with dyslexia. While the perceptual processing explanation presented here can explain the systematic changes in coherence thresholds found, and provides a sensory explanation of the effects for the group with dyslexia, attention mechanisms might also be implicated. These will be discussed in the following section.

GENERAL DISCUSSION

The results of these experiments indicate that motion coherence thresholds in groups with dyslexia can be systematically increased or decreased when the capacity of these individuals to sample the signal dots in the RDK is manipulated. Increasing the dot density and number of animation frames used or presenting the prime and test stimulus in opposite directions of motion results in lower coherence thresholds for each reader group. Conversely, reducing the dot density and the number of animation used or presenting the prime and test in the same direction of motion produces higher coherence thresholds for each reader group. The efficiency of the computational processes needed when undertaking a global motion task in individuals with dyslexia will be discussed. The viability of explanations which include sensory processes only and those that include attention mechanisms will each be addressed.

When processing global motion two important computational processes are required, that of extracting signal from noise and integration of the extracted motion signals over space and time (Raymond, 2000). The results of the current study demonstrate that the efficiency with which individuals with dyslexia can sample the signal dots in the RDK and therefore efficiently perform these processes depends on the stimulus parameters and methodology used. The latent variable manipulated in both experiments was the strength or energy of the motion signals presented in the RDK. In Experiment 1, higher signal strength was produced by increasing the dot density and the number of animation frames over which the RDK was presented. In Experiment 2 signal strength in the test stimulus was manipulated by the direction of motion in the prime. In both experiments, lower coherence thresholds were obtained in the reader groups when stimuli producing the strongest motion signals were presented. Highest coherence thresholds were found in both experiments, when the strength of the signal dots in the RDK was weakest. In Experiment 1, this was presentation of stimuli with a low dot density, or presentation of stimuli presented for five animation frames and in Experiment 2, this was the condition in which the prime and test stimuli were presented in the same direction of motion.

Although the group with dyslexia had higher coherence thresholds than typical readers in all conditions of Experiment 1, evidence of normal temporal recruitment was found in the high dot density condition. Coherence thresholds for both reader groups were reduced by over 6% with presentation of the eight compared to the five frame condition. These results indicate normal temporal recruitment in the group with dyslexia when these individuals are able to sample sufficient motion signals. In a previous study that used a higher dot density than that used in the current study, normal temporal recruitment was found in the group with dyslexia. In addition, no significant reader group differences in coherence thresholds were found (Hill and Raymond, 2002). Together these results indicate two things. First, if dot density is sufficiently high, normal temporal recruitment occurs in the group with dyslexia because these individuals are able to sample sufficient motion signals to perform the integration process. Second, either a very high dot density or a combination of a high dot density and longer stimulus durations is needed to enable normal global motion processing in the group with dyslexia. In low dot density conditions, problems with temporal recruitment were found. This might occur because of the poorer capacity of individuals with dyslexia when sampling more motion signals presented more sparsely in space (Talcott et al., 2000; Stein, 2001, 2003). Electrophysiological studies in which lower activation was found with exposure to coherent motion but not to noise dots alone provides support for this explanation (Schulte-Körne et al., 2004; Jednoróg et al., 2011), indicating that the strength of the motion signals alone might be insufficient to promote efficient integration in the group with dyslexia.

Evidence that increased signal strength can normalize coherent motion processing in the group with dyslexia was also obtained in Experiment 2, where there were no significant group differences found when the prime and test stimuli were presented in opposite directions of motion. In this condition, the reduced salience of a proportion of the noise dots increased the efficiency of the signal extraction process, which in turn resulted in efficient integration of the extracted signals. These results are consistent with previous studies that have presented stimuli in which the noise dots were automatically excluded (Sperling et al., 2006; Conlon et al., 2012). It would be tempting to conclude that purely sensory processes are sufficient to potentially normalize coherent motion thresholds in groups with dyslexia, by facilitating noise exclusion. However, the impact of attention must also be considered.

Evidence that presentation of a fully coherent prime activates spatial attention has been found in an experiment similar to that conducted in Experiment 2, in which a transparent motion stimulus was used as the prime (Raymond et al., 1998). In a transparent motion task two fully coherent sheets of dots appear to move independently, each with orthogonal directions, for example motion moving leftward and upward. Prior to presentation of the prime a pre-cue alerted participants to the direction of motion in the transparent prime (horizontal or vertical) for which a judgment of motion direction was made. Presentation of the prime was followed by the partially coherent test stimulus, for which coherence thresholds were obtained. The results of the study found that for typical readers, if the attended direction of motion in the prime matched the direction of motion in the test, higher coherence thresholds were obtained. If the non-attended direction of motion of the prime matched the direction of motion of the test, lower coherence thresholds were found. These results were obtained only when the prime contained fully coherent motion, and not when arrows indicating the directions of motion were presented. These results indicate that selective attention is activated by the motion prime which influences coherence thresholds in the test, dependent on the allocation of attention to the prime (Raymond et al., 1998). These results are consistent with physiological data that has shown attention modulates activity in MT (O'Craven et al., 1997; Buchel et al., 1998). These results suggest that presentation of a single direction fully coherent prime also activated spatial attention when using the current methodology. Spatial attention may have modulated the response to the partially coherent test stimulus, dependent on the direction of motion in the prime. The time course of this activity might have been different for the group with dyslexia and the control group because of impaired attentional mechanisms in the group with dyslexia.

There is a growing body of research that has found groups with dyslexia have difficulties directing attention to rapidly presented stimuli (Vidyasagar and Pammer, 2010), shifting attention between stimulus sequences that are rapidly and sequentially presented (Hari and Renvall, 2001; Visser et al., 2004; Lallier et al., 2010) or orientating spatial attention (Facoetti et al., 2010). In the motion segmentation task (Experiment 2), two distinct stimulus events occurred rapidly and sequentially. First, the fully coherent prime was separated from the partially coherent test by an ISI of 32 ms. Spatial attention would have been automatically captured by the fully coherent prime, stimulating cell groups responsive to that direction of motion at MT (Martinez-Trujillo and Treue, 2002). With the rapid presentation of the test stimulus, attention had to be rapidly disengaged from the prime and directed at the test stimulus. If the group with dyslexia have difficulty rapidly disengaging attention from the prime and re-engaging attention on the test as suggested by Hari and Renvall (2001), the influence of the prime might be greater for the group with dyslexia than for the control group. When the prime and test were presented in the same direction of motion, difficulties disengaging attention from the prime might have added to the poor salience of the target motion signals in the test. This would have produced the much higher coherence thresholds found in this condition for the group with dyslexia than those found for the control group. Conversely, difficulties disengaging attention from the opposite direction prime might have increased the salience of the target motion signals in the test more for the group with dyslexia than for the control group, resulting in no significant group differences in coherence thresholds. This explanation raises the possibility that difficulties shifting attention are most apparent when stimuli to be processed stimulate cells groups in the same cortical area, so are task relevant. As no condition was presented using a blank prime, it is unknown if presentation of the stationary baseline condition also influenced thresholds. However, if difficulties shifting attention between the prime and test stimuli, partially account for the results obtained, presentation of longer ISIs between the prime and test, should reduce the processing disadvantage found when the prime and test are presented in the same direction. When the prime and test are presented in opposite directions, the amount of facilitation found should also be reduced. For a control group, presentation of ISIs up to 600 ms has no influence on coherence thresholds obtained (Raymond and Isaak, 1998).

Although difficulties shifting attention between the different objects (prime and test) presented in Experiment 2, could contribute to the results obtained, it is difficult to use this attentional process to explain the findings of Experiment 1 in which regardless of the stimulus parameters used, the group with dyslexia had higher coherence thresholds. However, when dot density was increased and longer stimulus duration used, normal temporal recruitment was found. These longer presentation times and high dot density might have allowed the group with dyslexia to orientate attention to the signal dots in the RDK more efficiently than in the conditions in which a low dot density and shorter stimulus duration was used. This would have allowed normal temporal recruitment. Findings of a larger effect size in between groups analysis when a low dot density is used in a global motion task provides some support for this conclusion (Benassi et al., 2010).

In addition, presentation of stimuli of a higher contrast or different color to the noise dots might also have captured attention, allowing normal processing of coherent motion (Sperling et al., 2006; Conlon et al., 2012). The use of a pre-cue to direct attention either to low contrast motion signals in the RDK or to direct attention to specific features in a visual search task (Moores et al., 2011) has also provided evidence that directing attention can normalize coherence thresholds and improve visual search in groups with dyslexia. Although speculative, these results do indicate that attentional processes at PPC might influence coherent motion sensitivity, particularly when the computational complexity of the task is high.

The presence of a sensory processing deficit in the M or dorsal streams in groups with dyslexia is controversial (Ramus et al., 2003), with many studies presenting evidence that supports the presence of such a deficit (e.g., Cornelissen et al., 1995; Talcott et al., 2000). There are also studies that have found no evidence that a deficit is present (Ramus et al., 2003; Edwards et al., 2004; White et al., 2006) or have reported that about 30% of the group with dyslexia have this type of deficit (Amitay et al., 2002; Conlon et al., 2009). Alternative explanations such as difficulties with noise exclusion (Sperling et al., 2006), inattention (Williams et al., 2003) or temporal integration (Raymond and Sorensen, 1998) have also been presented. The results of the current study could be explained within the controversial sensory processing framework of dyslexia. The findings are supported by physiological evidence that neurons in the M and dorsal stream of groups with dyslexia are fewer in number, presented more sparsely and in a more disorganized manner than those found in normal readers (Galaburda and Livingstone, 1993; Stein and Walsh, 1997; Talcott et al., 2000) and that reduced neural activation at MT is found when VEP activity is measured during exposure to coherent motion (Schulte-Körne et al., 2004; Jednoróg et al., 2011). These findings are consistent with problems sampling the available motion signals present in the RDK, particularly when the perceptual difficulty of the task is high. However, these results might also indicate that directing and shifting attention between the feature specific components of these complex stimuli also contributes. Further research should directly investigate the extent that groups with dyslexia can optimize the perceptual filters needed to process complex stimuli and exclude noise, processes that can be evaluated within the perceptual template model of attention (Lu and Dosher, 2008).

Reading is also a computationally complex process which requires the use of a combination of visual, auditory and linguistic processes. Some researchers have suggested that the attentional consequences of impaired processing in the M and dorsal streams, causes difficulties with attention processing at PPC (Hari and Renvall, 2001; Vidyasagar and Pammer, 2010). Attentional difficulties have been linked to the way that children and adults with dyslexia process the sequentially presented letters on pages of text (Vidyasagar, 1999). Due to the sample sizes used in the current experiments, particularly Experiment 2, the associations between the sub-skills of reading and coherence thresholds were not evaluated. The systematic increases and decreases in coherence thresholds found in the group with dyslexia when different methodologies are used indicates that the processes need to efficiently perform a coherent motion task in adults with dyslexia can be normalized under specific circumstances. The challenge for future research is to determine whether the motion processing deficit found in dyslexia occurs in some individuals because of a vulnerability that is independent of their reading difficulties, or whether the deficit found is associated with the development or maintenance of word reading difficulties in this group. To make causal associations prospective longitudinal studies are needed, which measure temporal processing prior to the development of reading skills.

ACKNOWLEDGMENTS

This work was supported by an Australian Research Postgraduate scholarship to the second author and a University research grant to the Elizabeth G. Conlon.

REFERENCES

Amitay, S., Ben-Yehudah, G., Banai, K., and Ahissar, M. (2002). Disabled readers suffer from visual and auditory impairments but not from a specific magnocellular deficit. *Brain* 125, 2272–2285. doi: 10.1093/brain/awf231

Barlow, H., and Tripathy, S. P. (1997). Correspondence noise and signal pooling in the detection of coherent visual motion. *J. Neurosci.* 17, 7954–7966.

Benassi, M., Simonelli, L., Giovagnoli, S., and Bolanzi, R. (2010). Coherence motion perception in developmental dyslexia: a meta-analysis of behavioural studies. *Dyslexia* 16, 341–357. doi: 10.1002/dys.412

Ben-Shachar, M., Dougherty, R. F., Deutsch, G. K., and Wandell, B. A. (2007). Contrast responsivity in MT+ correlates with phonological awareness and reading measures in children. *Neuroimage* 37, 1396–1406. doi: 10.1016/j.neuroimage.2007.05.060

Ben-Yehudah, G., Sackett, E., Malchi-Ginzberg, L., and Ahissar, M. (2001). Impaired temporal contrast sensitivity in dyslexics is specific to retain-and-compare paradigms. *Brain* 124, 1381–1395. doi: 10.1093/brain/124.7.1381

Braddick, O. (1995). Seeing motion signals in noise. *Curr. Biol.* 5, 7–9. doi: 10.1016/S0960-9822(95)00003-0

Bruck, M. (1990). Word recognition skills in adults with childhood diagnoses of dyslexia. *Dev. Psychol.* 26, 439–454. doi: 10.1037/0012-1649.26.3.439

Buchel, C., Joseph, O., Rees, G., Turner, R., Firth, C., and Friston, K. (1998). The functional anatomy of attention to visual motion. *Brain* 121, 1281–1294. doi: 10.1093/brain/121.7.1281

Conlon, E., Lovegrove, W. J., Chekaluk, E., and Pattison, P. (1999). Measuring visual discomfort. *Vis. Cogn.* 6, 637–663. doi: 10.1080/135062899394885

Conlon, E., Sanders, M., and Zapart, S. (2004). Temporal processing in poor adult readers. *Neuropsychologia* 42, 142–157. doi: 10.1016/j.neuropsychologia.2003.07.004

Conlon, E. G., Lilleskaret, G., Wright, C., M., and Power, G. F. (2012). The influence of contrast on coherent motion processing in dyslexia. *Neuropsychologia* 50, 1672–1681. doi: 10.1016/j.neuropsychologia.2012.03.023

Conlon, E. G., Sanders. M. A., and Wright, C. M. (2009). Relationships between global motion and global form processing, practice, cognitive and visual processing in adults with dyslexia or visual discomfort. *Neuropsychologia* 47, 907–915. doi: 10.1016/j.neuropsychologia.2008.12.037

Conlon, E. G., and Sanders, M. A. (2011). The reading rate and comprehension of adults with impaired reading skills or visual discomfort. *J. Res. Read.* 34, 193–214. doi: 10.1111/j.1467-9817.2009.01421.x

Conlon, E. G., Wright, C. M., Norris, K., and Chekaluk, E. (2011). Does a sensory processing deficit explain counting accuracy on rapid visual sequencing tasks in adults with and without dyslexia? *Brain Cogn.* 76, 197–205. doi: 10.1016/j.bandc.2010.10.014

Cornelissen, P., Richardson, A., Mason, A., Fowler, S., and Stein, J. (1995). Contrast sensitivity and coherent motion detection measured at photopic luminance levels in dyslexics and controls. *Vis. Res.* 10, 1483–1493. doi: 10.1016/0042-6989(95)98728-R

Croner, L. J., and Albright, T. D. (1997). Image segmentation enhances discrimination of motion in visual noise. *Vis. Res.* 37, 1415–1427. doi: 10.1016/S0042-6989(96)00299-4

Demb, J., Boynton, G., Best, M., and Heeger D. (1998a). Psychophysical evidence for a magnocellular pathway deficit in dyslexia. *Vis. Res.* 38, 1555–1599. doi: 10.1016/S0042-6989(98)00075-3

Demb, J. B., Boynton, G. M., and Heeger, D. J. (1998b). Functional magnetic imaging of early visual pathways in dyslexia. *J. Neurosci.* 18, 6939–6951.

Eden, G., VanMeter, J., Rumsey, J., Maisog, J., Woods, R., and Zeffiro, T. (1996). Abnormal processing of visual motion in dyslexia revealed by functional brain imaging. *Nature* 382, 66–69. doi: 10.1038/382066a0

Edwards, M., Badcock, D. R., and Nishida, S. (1996). Contrast sensitivity of the motion system. *Vis. Res.* 36, 2411–2421. doi: 10.1016/0042-6989(95)00321-5

Edwards, V. T., Giaschi, D. E., Dougherty, R. F., Edgell, D., Bjornson, B. H., Lyons, C., et al. (2004). Psychophysical indexes of temporal processing abnormalities in children with developmental dyslexia. *Dev. Neuropsychol.* 25, 321–354. doi: 10.1207/s15326942dn2503_5

Facoetti, A., Trussardi, A. N., Ruffino, M. K., Lorusso, M. L., Cattaneo, C., Galli, R., et al. (2010). Multisensory spatial attention deficits are predictive of phonological decoding skills in developmental dyslexia. *J. Cogn. Neurosci.* 22, 1011–1025. doi: 10.1162/jocn.2009.21232

Galaburda, A., and Livingstone, M. (1993). "Evidence for a magnocellular deficit in developmental dyslexia," in *Temporal Information Processing in the Nervous System: Special Reference to Dyslexia and Aphasia*, eds P. Tallal, A. M. Galaburda, R. R. Llinas, and C. von Euler (New York: New York Academy of Sciences), 82.

Glasser, D. M., Tsui, J. M., Pack, C. C., and Tadin, D. (2011). Perceptual and neural consequences of rapid motion adaptation. *Proc. Natl. Acad. Sci. U.S.A.* 108, 1080–1088. doi: 10.1073/pnas.1101141108

Habib, M. M. (2000). The neurological basis of developmental dyslexia. An overview and working hypothesis. *Brain* 123, 2373–2399. doi: 10.1093/brain/123.12.2373

Hansen, P. C., Stein, J. F., Orde, S. R., Winter, J. L., and Talcott, J. B. (2001). Are dyslexics' visual deficits limited to measures of dorsal stream function? *Neuroreport* 12, 1527–1530. doi: 10.1097/00001756-200105250-00045

Hari, R., and Renvall, H. (2001). Impaired processing of rapid stimulus sequences in dyslexia. *Trends Cogn. Sci.* 5, 525–532. doi: 10.1016/S1364-6613(00)01801-5

Hawelka, S., and Wimmer, H. (2008). Visual target detection is not impaired in dyslexic readers. *Vis. Res.* 48, 850–852. doi: 10.1016/j.visres.2007.11.003

Hill, G. T., and Raymond, J. E. (2002). Deficits of motion transparency perception in adult developmental dyslexics with normal unidirectional motion sensitivity. *Vis. Res.* 42, 1195–1203. doi: 10.1016/S0042-6989(02)00042-1

Jednoróg, K., Marchewka, A., Tacikowski, P., Heim, S., and Grabowska, A. (2011). Electrophysiological evidence for a magnocellular-dorsal pathway deficit in dyslexia. *Dev. Sci.* 14, 873–880. doi: 10.1111/j.1467-7687.2011.01037.x

Johnston, A., Bruno, A., Watanabe, A., Quansah, B., Patel, N., Dakin, S., et al. (2008). Visually based temporal distortion in dyslexia. *Vis. Res.* 48, 1852–1858. doi: 10.1016/j.visres.2008.04.029

Kaernbach, C. (1991). Simple adaptive testing with the weighted up-down method. *Percept. Psycophys.* 49, 227–229. doi: 10.3758/BF03214307

Laasonen, M., Service, E., and Virsu, V. (2001). Temporal order and processing acuity of visual, auditory, and tactile perception in developmentally dyslexic young adults. *Cogn. Affect. Behav. Neurosci.* 1, 394–410. doi: 10.3758/CABN.1.4.394

Lallier, M., Tainturier, M., Dering, B., Donnadieu, S., Valdois, S., and Thierry, G. (2010). Behavioral and ERP evidence of amodal sluggish attentional shifting in developmental dyslexia. *Neuropsychologia* 48, 4125–4135. doi: 10.1016/j.neuropsychologia.2010.09.027

Lovegrove, W. (1993). "Do dyslexics have a visual deficit?," in *Facets of Dyslexia and its Remediation*, eds S. F. Wright and R. Groner (Amsterdam: Elsevier Science Publishers), 33–49.

Lovegrove, W., Martin, F., and Slaghuis, W. (1986). A theoretical and experimental case for a visual deficit in specific reading disability. *Cogn. Neuropsychol.* 3, 225–267. doi: 10.1080/02643298608252677

Lu, Z.-L., and Dosher, B. A. (2008). Characterizing observers using external noise and observer models: assessing internal representations with external noise. *Psychol. Rev.* 115, 44–82. doi: 10.1037/0033-295X.115.1.44

Martinez-Trujillo, J. C., and Treue, S. (2002). Attentional modulation strength in cortical area MT depends on stimulus contrast. *Neuron* 35, 365–370. doi: 10.1016/S0896-6273(02)00778-X

McKee, S. P., and Welch, L. (1985). Sequential recruitment in the discrimination of velocity. *J. Opt. Soc. Am. A* 2, 243–251. doi: 10.1364/JOSAA.2.000243

Moores, E., Cassim, R., and Talcott, J. B. (2011). Adults with dyslexia exhibit larger crowding effects, increased dependence on cues, and detrimental effects of distractors on visual search tasks. *Neuropsychologia* 49, 3381–3390. doi: 10.1016/j.neuropsychologia.2011.10.005

Newsome, W. T., and Paré, E. B. (1988). A selective impairment of motion perception following lesions of the middle temporal visual area (MT). *J. Neurosci.* 8, 2201–2211.

O'Craven, K., Roden, B., Kwong, K., Triesman, A., and Savoy, R. (1997). Voluntary attention modulates fMRI activity in human MT-MST. *Neuron* 18, 591–598. doi: 10.1016/S0896-6273(00)80300-1

Ramus, F., Rosen, S., Dakin, S. C., Day, B. L., Catelotte, J. M., White, S., et al. (2003). Theories of developmental dyslexia: insights from a multiple case study of dyslexic adults. *Brain* 126, 841–865. doi: 10.1093/brain/awg076

Raymond, J. E. (2000). Attentional modulation of visual motion perception. *Trends Cogn. Sci.* 4, 42–50. doi: 10.1016/S1364-6613(99)01437-0

Raymond, J. E., and Isaak, M. (1998). Successive episodes produce direction contrast effects in motion perception. *Vis. Res.* 38, 579–589. doi: 10.1016/S0042-6989(97)00178-8

Raymond, J. E., O'Donnell, H. L., and Tripper, S. P. (1998). Priming reveals attentional modulation of human motion sensitivity. *Vis. Res.* 38, 2863–2867. doi: 10.1016/S0042-6989(98)00145-X

Raymond, J. E., and Sorensen, R. E. (1998). Visual motion perception in children with dyslexia: normal detection but abnormal integration. *Vis. Cogn.* 5, 389–404. doi: 10.1080/713756790

Reid, A. A., Szczerbinski, M., Iskierka-Kasperek, E., and Hansen, P. (2007). Cognitive profiles of adult developmental dyslexics: theoretical implications. *Dyslexia* 13, 1–24. doi: 10.1002/dys.321

Roach, N. W., and Hogben, J. H. (2007). Impaired filtering of behaviourally irrelevant visual information in dyslexia. *Brain* 130, 771–785. doi: 10.1093/brain/awl353

Schulte-Körne, G., Bartling, J., Deimel, W., and Remschmidt, H. (2004). Visual evoked potentials elicited by coherently moving dots in dyslexic children. *Neurosci. Lett.* 357, 207–210. doi: 10.1016/j.neulet.2003.12.098

Schulte-Körne, G., and Bruder, J. (2010). Clinical neurophysiology of visual and auditory processing in dyslexia: a review. *Clin. Neurophysiol.* 121, 1794–1809. doi: 10.1016/j.clinph.2010.04.028

Shaywitz, S. E., Shaywitz, B. A., Fulbright, R. K., Skudlarski, P., Mencl, W. E., Constable, T., et al. (2003). Neural systems for compensation and persistence: young adult outcome of childhood reading disability. *Biol. Psychiatry* 54, 25–33. doi: 10.1016/S0006-3223(02)01836-X

Snowden, R. J., and Braddick, O. J. (1989). The combination of motion signals over time. *Vis. Res.* 29, 1621–1630. doi: 10.1016/0042-6989(89)90143-0

Sperling, A. J., Lu, Z. L., Manis, F. R., and Seidenberg, M. S. (2006). Motion-perception deficits and reading impairment: it's the noise, not the motion. *Psychol. Sci.* 17, 1047–1053. doi: 10.1111/j.1467-9280.2006.01825.x

Stein, J., and Walsh, V. (1997). To see but not to read; the magnocellular theory of dyslexia. *Trends Neurosci.* 20, 147–152. doi: 10.1016/S0166-2236(96)01005-3

Stein, J. F. (2001). The magnocellular theory of developmental dyslexia. *Dyslexia* 7, 12–36. doi: 10.1002/dys.186

Stein, J. F. (2003). Visual motion sensitivity and reading. *Neuropsychologia* 41, 1785–1793. doi: 10.1016/S0028-3932(03)00179-9

Stenneken, P., Egetemeir, J., Schulte-Korne, G., Muller, H. H., Schnieder, W. X., and Finke, K. (2011). Slow perceptual processing at the core of developmental dyslexia: a parameter-based assessment of visual attention. *Neuropsychologia* 49, 3454–3465. doi: 10.1016/j.neuropsychologia.2011.08.021

Talcott, J., Hansen, P., Assoku, E., and Stein, J. (2000). Visual motion sensitivity in dyslexia: evidence for temporal and energy integration deficits. *Neuropsychologia* 38, 935–943. doi: 10.1016/S0028-3932(00)00020-8

Talcott, J. F., Hansen, P., Willis-Owen, C., McKinnell, I., Richardson, A., and Stein, J. (1998). Visual magnocellular impairment in adult developmental dyslexics. *Neuro Opthalmol.* 20, 187–201. doi: 10.1076/noph.20.4.187.3931

Thakral, P. P., and Slotnick, S. D. (2011). Disruption of MT impairs motion processing. *Neurosci. Lett.* 490, 226–230. doi: 10.1016/j.neulet.2010.12.057

Torgesen, J. K., Wagner, R. K., and Rashotte, C. A. (1999). *Test of Word Reading Efficiency (TOWRE)*. Austin, USA: Pro-Ed Inc.

Treue, S., and Maunsell, J. (1996). Attentional modulation of visual motion processing in cortical areas MT and MST. *Nature* 382, 539–541. doi: 10.1038/382539a0

Treue, S., and Trujillo, C. (1999). Feature-based attention influences motion processing gain in macaque visual cortex. *Nature* 399, 575–579. doi: 10.1038/21176

Vidyasagar, T. R. (1999). A neuronal model of attentional spotlight: parietal guiding the temporal. *Brain Res. Rev.* 30, 6–76. doi: 10.1016/S0165-0173(99)00005-3

Vidyasagar, T. R., and Pammer, K. (2010). Dyslexia: a deficit in visuo-spatial attention, not in phonological processing. *Trends Cogn. Sci.* 14, 57–63. doi: 10.1016/j.tics.2009.12.003

Visser, T. A. W., Boden, C., and Giaschi, D. E. (2004). Children with dyslexia: evidence for visual attention deficits in perception of rapid sequences of objects. *Vis. Res.* 44, 2521–2535. doi: 10.1016/j.visres.2004.05.010

Wechsler, D. (1998). *Wechsler Adult Intelligence Scale - Third Edition - Australian Adaptation.* USA: The Psychological Corporation, Adapted by Harcourt Brace & Company.

White, S., Milne, E., Rosen, S., Hansen, P. C., Swettenham, J., Frith, U., et al. (2006). The role of sensorimotor processing in dyslexia: a multiple case study of dyslexic children. *Dev. Sci.* 9, 237–255. doi: 10.1111/j.1467-7687.2006.00483.x

Wilkinson, G. S. (1993). *WRAT-3: Wide Range Achievement Test.* Delaware, USA: Jastak Associates.

Williams, M., Stuart, G., Castles, A., and McAnally, K. (2003). Contrast sensitivity in subgroups of developmental dyslexics. *Vis. Res.* 43, 467–477. doi: 10.1016/S0042-6989(02)00573-4

Wilmer, J. B., Richardson, A. J., Chen, Y., and Stein, J. F. (2004). Two visual motion processing deficits in developmental dyslexia associated with different reading skills. *J. Cogn. Neurosci.* 16, 528–540. doi: 10.1162/089892904323057272

Wilson, A. M., and Lesaux, N. K. (2001). Persistence of phonological processing deficits in college students with dyslexia who have age-appropriate reading skills. *J. Learn. Disabil.* 34, 394–400. doi: 10.1177/002221940103400501

Wright, C. M., and Conlon, E. G. (2009). Sensory processing in children with dyslexia. *Dev. Neuropsychol.* 34, 330–355. doi: 10.1080/87565640902801882

2

Influence of context-sensitive rules on the formation of orthographic representations in Spanish dyslexic children

Paz Suárez-Coalla*, Rrezarta Avdyli and Fernando Cuetos

Department of Psychology, University of Oviedo, Oviedo, Spain

****Correspondence:***
Paz Suárez-Coalla, Department of Psychology, University of Oviedo, Plaza Feijoo s/n, 33003 Oviedo, Spain
e-mail: suarezpaz@uniovi.es

Spanish-speaking developmental dyslexics are mainly characterized by poor reading fluency. One reason for this lack of fluency could be a difficulty in creating and accessing lexical representations, because, as the self-teaching theory suggest, it is necessary to develop orthographic representations to use direct reading (Share, 1995). It is possible that this difficulty to acquire orthographic representations can be specifically related to words that contain context-sensitive graphemes, since it has been demonstrated that reading is affected by this kind of graphemes (Barca et al., 2007). In order to test this possibility we compared a group of dyslexic children with a group of normal readers (9–13 years), in a task of repeated reading. Pseudo-words (half short and half long) with simple and contextual dependent rules were used. The length effect reduction on the reading speed, after repeated exposure, was considered an indicator of orthographic representation development, as the length effect is strong when reading unknown words, but absent when reading familiar words. The results show that dyslexic children have difficulties in developing orthographic representations, not only with context-sensitive graphemes, but also with simple graphemes. In contrast to the control children, in the dyslexic group differences between reading times for short and long stimuli remained without significant changes after six presentations. Besides, this happened with sensitive context rules and also with simple grapheme–phoneme conversion rules. On the other hand, response and articulation times were greatly affected by length in dyslexic children, indicating the use of serial reading. Results suggest that the problems related to storing orthographic representations could be caused by a learning deficit, independently of whether the word contained context-sensitive rules or not.

Keywords: dyslexia, orthographic representations, fluency, transparent orthography, context-sensitive rules

INTRODUCTION

Dyslexic children learning to read in transparent orthographic systems make relatively few errors in the reading of words when compared with dyslexics using opaque orthographic systems (Rack et al., 1992; Yap and Van der Leij, 1993; Sprenger-Charolles et al., 2000; De Jong and van der Leij, 2002; Nikolopoulos et al., 2003). Several cross-linguistic studies have shown that orthographic depth largely determines the reading skills of dyslexics, so that decoding problems are more evident in opaque orthographic systems, such as English, than in transparent orthographic systems (Wimmer and Goswami, 1994; Landerl et al., 1997). It appears that the high consistency between graphemes and phonemes facilitates learning of the alphabetic code, and consequently reading accuracy, even in dyslexic children.

Dyslexics in transparent orthographic systems, however, fail to achieve an acceptable level of reading speed (Wimmer, 1993; Spinelli et al., 2005); their reading is generally slow and laborious, similar to the reading of dyslexics in deep orthographic systems. (Oney and Goldman, 1984; Landerl, 2001; Zoccolotti et al., 2005; Suárez-Coalla and Cuetos, 2012). As the reading speed problems are more striking than the accuracy problems for these dyslexics (although they are also more error-prone than age-matched children), difficulty in acquiring reading speed is considered a marker of dyslexia in transparent orthographic systems such as Spanish, German, Italian, or Greek (Ziegler et al., 2003; Davies et al., 2007; Constantinidou and Stainthorp, 2009; Wimmer et al., 2010). In particular, dyslexics are much slower than normal children reading long words and non-words (Davies et al., 2007; De Luca et al., 2008; Suárez-Coalla and Cuetos, 2012).

Why don't dyslexic children develop reading fluency? Is it because they have difficulties learning and automating the grapheme–phoneme conversion rules? Probably, because differences between dyslexic and normal children are bigger in reading non-words (Yap and Van der Leij, 1993; Snowling, 1995), which indicate problems in using the sublexical route. Although in recent years, several authors have questioned this conclusion mostly based on methodological considerations (see Van den Broeck and Geudens, 2012, for a very thorough discussion). But dyslexics are also poorer in reading familiar words (Hatcher et al., 2002), which indicates difficulties to develop orthographic representations of the words. Then, what does prevent them from forming and accessing orthographic representations? According to the self-teaching theory, orthographic representations are developed through accurate and repeated reading (Reitsma, 1989; Share, 1995, 1999; Cunningham et al., 2002; De Jong et al., 2009). If dyslexics have difficulty developing orthographic representations, they should be even slower than normal individuals when reading frequent words, because they also have to read them by the sublexical route; indeed, some studies have confirmed this observation (Defior et al., 1998; Barca et al., 2006). The self-teaching hypothesis has been tested in different languages (Hebrew, English, and Dutch), with the findings suggesting that few exposures are required to form orthographic representations and pass from a sublexical to a lexical reading. However, this transition is more difficult for children with dyslexia (Manis, 1985; Reitsma, 1989). Additionally, it has been suggested that dyslexics are inefficient in learning graphemic materials because they were slower than controls in the learning rate of novel words when previous experience with texts was minimized (Pontillo et al., 2014).

Different methodologies have been proposed to investigate when the orthographic representations are formed (writing from dictation, choosing between several homophones of the target stimulus, reading latencies, etc.), but one widely recently used is based on the reduction of the length effect. From the study by Weekes (1997), it is well known that in typical readers, word length (number of letters) has a large influence on reading unfamiliar words and pseudowords, but has a small effect on low frequency words and no effect at all on high frequency words. The explanation, according to the dual route model, is that low frequency words and pseudowords are read in a serial or sublexical way, so the more graphemes, the larger the latencies. On the other hand, familiar words have a representation in the orthographic lexicon; so, when reading familiar words, all of the letters are identified in parallel, and the difference between the latencies of short and long words disappears (Coltheart et al., 2001). Therefore, the formation of orthographic representations will be reflected in a reduced length effect after repeated exposures to pseudowords (repeated reading). As a demonstration of this effect, Maloney et al. (2009) asked a group of participants to read the 100 Weeks study. They found that reading times were getting shorter, but more crucially, there was a reduction in the length effect: differences between long and short non-words became increasingly smaller.

In a recent study, Kwok and Ellis (2014) used this length effect methodology to study the formation of orthographic representations in dyslexic adults. Participants had to read a list of 24 non-words, half short and half long, repeated across ten blocks. Results showed a reduction in the difference in reading latencies between short and long words across blocks in normal readers, but dyslexics only showed convergence in the second session 7 days later. It seems that adult dyslexics need more exposures than control readers to create lexical representations.

With the same methodology, Suárez-Coalla et al. (2014) presented eight unfamiliar words, four long and four short, to a group of Spanish children with dyslexia and a control group to read in six different blocks. In a first experiment the unfamiliar words were presented within the context of a story and in a second experiment the words were presented in isolation. Reading and articulation times for the first and last block of the unfamiliar words were compared. In both experiments a decrease of the influence of length for the control group was found. However, for the dyslexic children, the influence of length remained unchanged after the repeated reading of the unfamiliar words. These results seem indicate that dyslexic children may be unable to develop orthographic representations, at least after six exposures, and that they may need to read each word more times.

Why do dyslexic children need more exposures to the words than normal children? It is quite possible that these results are a consequence of the difficulties they have in using grapheme–phoneme rules. Slow and inaccurate reading could prevent these children from developing orthographic representations. If so, the difficulties in forming orthographic representations will be higher for words associated with difficult rules, as for example those containing context-sensitive graphemes (Rastle and Coltheart, 1998; Rey and Schiller, 2005; Barca et al., 2007).

The Spanish orthographic system has 30 graphemes and is highly consistent; however, the pronunciation of "c" and "g"depends on the letter that follows (e.g., the letter "g" is pronounced as /γ/ when it is followed by "a," "o," "u"; but it is pronounced as /χ/ when followed by "e" and "i"). Therefore, the Spanish orthographic system is transparent, but contains some context-sensitive graphemes. Reading words and pseudowords is affected by graphemic complexity (complex GPC rules) in different languages (English: Rastle and Coltheart, 1998; French: Rey and Schiller, 2005; Italian: Barca et al., 2006). In Italian, a transparent language similar to Spanish, the graphemic complexity (contextuality) was tested in young Italian readers (third and fifth grades) using words with simple or contextual letter-sound conversion rules (Barca et al., 2007). In both groups, the words with contextual rules were read more slowly than words with simple rules. According to this result, we predict that it would be harder to build up orthographic representations for novel words that contain context-sensitive GPC rules than words that are made up of simple GPC rules only. We consider that this effect could be stronger for children with dyslexia than for normal readers because these rules are more difficult to learn and decode for dyslexics. So if these children have problems automating GPC rules, the context-sensitive GPC rules could entail an increased difficulty for them.

As a consequence, our goal in this study was to test, using the length effect reduction, if dyslexic Spanish children have problems in developing orthographic representations after repeated reading, and if these problems are greater when words include context-sensitive graphemes. Therefore, including context-sensitive graphemes would allow us testing whether dyslexics have poor learning of pseudowords because they have difficulties in learning and automating the grapheme–phoneme conversion rules.

In addressing that objective, we compared a group of Spanish dyslexic children with a group of normal readers on a task of repeated reading of pseudowords. Reading and articulation times were collected in order to discover if differences between short and long pseudowords decreased after repeated reading, and if this reduction of length effect was context-sensitive. In addition to reaction times (RTs), we have included articulation time (ATs), following previous studies (Davies et al., 2012; Suárez-Coalla and Cuetos, 2012), where ATs was a measure sensitive to the reader's ability and characteristics of the stimuli.

EXPERIMENT

PARTICIPANTS

A total of 50 children took part in the study, all native Spanish speakers with normal, or corrected to normal vision and without any known cognitive impairment (apart from dyslexia). Children did not have sensory disorders. They all had received adequate schooling. Twenty five were dyslexics: their ages ranged between 8 and 13 years ($M = 10.36$, SD = 1.5) and 25 were normal readers ($M = 10$, SD = 1.5). Both groups were matched by gender (13 female and 12 male) and age. The dyslexic children were attending a private center for individualized treatment and received special attention in school. Both groups shared the same social background (middle-class families in all cases). For the diagnosis of the dyslexic children, in addition to the Wechsler Intelligence Scale for Children (WISC; Wechsler, 2001), a Spanish reading process assessment battery – PROLEC-R (Cuetos et al., 2007) was used. The battery was administered individually and required the child to read aloud a list of 40 words and pseudowords as quickly and as accurately as they could. These words varied quite broadly in frequency (high or low) as well as in length (five and eight letters). Accuracy and reading speed (measured as the time taken to complete the task) were scored. Children in the control group were also assessed using the PROLEC-R battery and the WISC test. The average intelligence quotient (IQ) in the dyslexic group was 106, ranging from 90 to 116; in the control group the mean IQ was 115 ranging from 95 to 126. Both groups were matched regarding performance IQ; the dyslexic children differed significantly from the control group in verbal IQ ($p = 0.006$; common in people with dyslexia, and reported in other studies, e.g., Perea et al., 2014). Reading scores varied between the dyslexic and the control group; besides the dyslexic group scores were 1.5–2 SD below the average for each age category in the reading assessment battery (see **Table 1**). Furthermore, we confirmed significant differences between groups (dyslexics vs. controls) in reading accuracy of words [$t(48) = -5.18$; $p < 0.001$]; reading speed of words [$t(48) = 4.90$; $p < 0.001$]; reading accuracy of pseudowords [$t(48) = -7.62$; $p < 0.001$]; and reading speed of pseudowords [$t(48) = 5.88$; $p < 0.001$].

The study was approved by the Ethics Committee of the Department of Psychology, University of Oviedo. Before performing the experiments, informed written consent from all parents and teachers was obtained. A document was given to the parents describing the objectives of the study, the type of tasks to be performed and their duration. The study involved only children whose parents signed the informed consent forms. Additionally, before starting the experiment, tasks were explained to the children and they were asked if they agreed to participate in the study. All children agreed to participate in the tasks.

Table 1 | Summary of participants' characteristics.

Group	Dyslexics *M* (SD)	Controls *M* (SD)
Age	10.36 (1.50)	10.00 (1.50)
IQ	106.45 (6.92)	115.38 (7.41)
- verbal IQ	102.2 (9.08)	114.7 (11.61)
- performance IQ	107.6 (7.80)	109.05 (12.01)
Word accuracy (out of 40)	35.08 (4.01)	39.34 (0.83)
Word speed in sec (out of 40)	79.70 (47.26)	30.78 (7.41)
Word/sec	0.72 (0.32)	1.43 (0.35)
Pseudoword accuracy (out of 40)	29.37 (4.40)	36.47 (2.33)
Pseudoword speed in sec (out of 40)	101.25 (38.38)	53.60 (13.89)
Pseudoword/sec	0.46 (0.11)	0.85 (0.17)

IQ, intelligence quotient; M, mean; SD, standard deviation.

MATERIALS

Sixteen pseudowords in Spanish, half including consistent graphemes (d, t, m, or p), and half context dependent graphemes (g, j, z, or c), were used for this experiment. The pronunciations of contextual dependent graphemes varies according to the vowel that follows, as explained above. Half of the pseudowords were short (four letters, two syllables) and half long (six letters, three syllables); all had a consonant vocal (CV) syllabic structure (e.g., mepa, polato, zuge, gukato). According to the orthographic depth hypothesis, learning the alphabetic code is influenced by the orthographic consistency (Seymour et al., 2003); therefore, there would be more reading errors and lower reading fluency when stimuli are inconsistent, as opposed to when they are consistent. This would in turn cause difficulties in the formation of orthographic representations.

PROCEDURE

The participants were asked to read aloud the pseudowords which were presented in random order within each of six blocks. For each trial, this sequence was followed: an asterisk was placed as a fixation point for 500 ms; this was followed by a blank screen for another 500 ms, and then the pseudoword appeared on the screen for another 3500 ms. A pilot study was conducted to determine timing of this sequence. We found that a shorter time was insufficient for children with dyslexia, as they did not have time to read the entire stimulus; without being able to read the stimulus, it would have been impossible for them to form representations. After each block, a pause was marked and participants pressed the space bar to continue. Before conducting the experiment, six practice trials were run in order to familiarize the children with the reading task. Stimuli were presented through the DMDX software (Forster and Forster, 2003) in a laptop computer (12″) using a 24-point Arial font, colored black on a white background. Once the children were seated, the following instructions appeared on the screen: "Some invented words are going to appear in the screen; you must read them aloud as quickly as possible and without making any mistake." The task was performed individually in a quiet room at the children's school, or in the private center. The test lasted approximately 15 min. The children were not corrected if they misread pseudowords, thus trying to simulate the natural conditions of individual reading (self-teaching). Once the data were gathered, they were analyzed with the CheckVocal (Protopapas, 2007) software in order to obtain the correct responses, the reaction and articulation times.

ANALYSIS

Using the SPSS 19 statistical package, a mixed between-within subjects analysis of variance was conducted. Group (2: dyslexics *vs.* controls) was the between-subjects factor; and block (2: first *vs.* sixth), stimulus type (2: consistent vs. context dependent graphemes) and length (2: short *vs.* long) the within-subjects factors.

Two dependent variables were considered: RTs (the time from the stimuli appearing on the computer screen until the child began to read) and ATs (the time children spent reading the stimuli). The AT has not been widely used in the literature, although there are some studies that have used this measure (Davies et al., 2012; Suárez-Coalla and Cuetos, 2012). This measure seems interesting, as far as children are concerned, because the length effect in ATs could be an indicator (other than RTs) of serial reading. A length effect in the ATs of dyslexic children was found, which was interpreted as absence of orthographic representations and thus sequential reading (Suárez-Coalla and Cuetos, 2012). We used only the correct responses for the RTs and ATs analyses; these responses are important in enabling us to discover if the lack of automatization of phoneme–grapheme rules is the problem concerning orthographic representations.

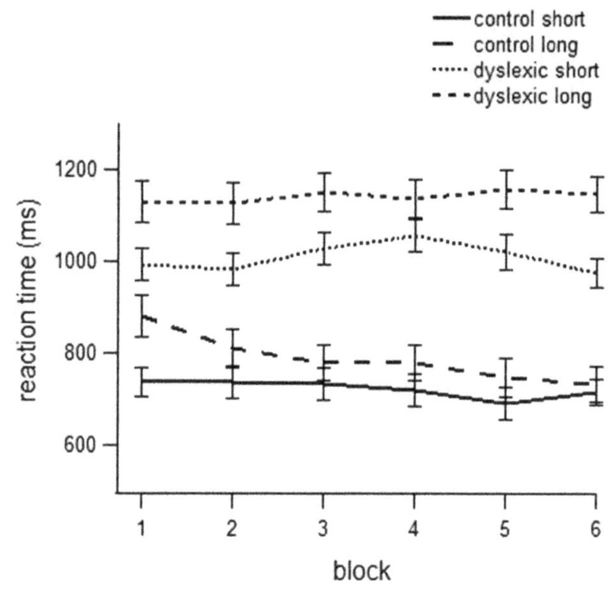

FIGURE 1 | Reading times to short and long pseudowords in dyslexics and controls across blocks.

RESULTS

A total of 4,800 responses were obtained from both groups, with 2,400 responses from each group. Considering the six blocks of stimuli, the dyslexic group committed a total of 465 errors (19.37%), and 73 non-responses (3.04%). Thirty (1.25%) responses were considered outliers (2 SDs above or below the mean). In contrast, the control group had a total of 207 errors (8.62%), three non-responses (0.12%), and 23 (0.96%) responses that were considered outliers. In the following analysis, only RTs and ATs to correct responses were used.

Reaction times

In the ANOVA we found a main effect of group [$F(1,48) = 46.400$, $p < 0.001$, partial $\mu^2 = 0.502$], with the dyslexic group slower than the control group; a block effect [$F(1,48) = 4.690$, $p = 0.036$, partial $\mu^2 = 0.093$], as a consequence of the reduction in the RTs across blocks; a stimulus type effect [$F(1,48) = 15.897$, $p < 0.001$, partial $\mu^2 = 0.257$], with longer RTs for pseudowords with context-dependent graphemes than pseudowords with consistent graphemes; and a length effect [$F(1,48) = 60.681$, $p < 0.001$, partial $\mu^2 = 0.569$], due to RTs being faster for short than for long stimuli. We also found a block by group interaction [$F(1,48) = 10.370$, $p = 0.002$, partial $\mu^2 = 0.184$], as the difference between RTs in first and last block was greater in the control than in the dyslexic group; a length by group interaction [$F(1,48) = 6.727$, $p = 0.013$, partial $\mu^2 = 0.128$], showing a larger difference between short and long stimuli in the dyslexic than in the control group; and a block by length by group interaction [$F(1,48) = 4.833$, $p = 0.033$, partial $\mu^2 = 0.095$]. This latter interaction indicates that differences between short and long pseudowords decrease after repeated reading in the control group, but not in the dyslexic group (see **Figure 1**). In a more detailed analysis (comparing the first block with the rest of the blocks) it was found that the reduction of the length effect was only significant for the last block.

In order to further explore the results and confirm the decrease of length effect in the control group, RTs were separately analyzed for control and dyslexic children. In the analysis of the control group, we found a block effect, [$F(1,24) = 17.927$, $p = 0.001$, partial $\mu^2 = 0.428$], indicating the decrease of RTs with the repeated reading in this group; a stimulus type effect, [$F(1,24) = 18.051$, $p < 0.001$, partial $\mu^2 = 0.429$], showing faster RTs in pseudowords with consistent graphemes than in pseudowords with context-dependent graphemes; and a length effect [$F(1,24) = 23.211$, $p < 0.001$, partial $\mu^2 = 0.492$], with longer RTs for long than short pseudowords.

We also found a stimulus type by length interaction [$F(1,24) = 6.488$, $p = 0.018$, partial $\mu^2 = 0.213$], as the length effect was smaller in pseudowords with consistent graphemes than in pseudowords with context-dependent graphemes; the block by stimulus type was close to significance [$F(1,24) = 3.571$, $p = 0.071$, partial $\mu^2 = 0.130$], indicating that RTs of pseudowords with consistent graphemes decreased more quickly with repeated reading; and a block by length interaction [$F(1,24) = 18.629$, $p < 0.001$, partial $\mu^2 = 0.437$], as the typical readers showed a length effect reduction with the repetitions.

By contrast, in the dyslexic group only a length effect was found [$F(1,24) = 36.220$, $p < 0.001$, partial $\mu^2 = 0.622$], indicating slower RTs for the longer pseudowords. The stimulus type effect was close to significance [$F(1,24) = 3.776$, $p = 0.065$, partial $\mu^2 = 0.146$], with longer RTs for pseudowords with context-dependent graphemes than for pseudowords with consistent graphemes. No effect of block was found indicating that reading times did not decrease after 6 exposures in the dyslexic group (see **Table 2** for the RTs in block 1 and block 6).

Table 2 | Summary of RTs, ATs, and % of errors by dyslexics and controls, in blocks 1 and 6.

			Dyslexics			Controls		
Block	**Stim. type**	**Length**	**RTs *M* (SD)**	**ATs *M* (SD)**	**% of errors**	**RTs *M* (SD)**	**ATs *M* (SD)**	**% of errors**
B1	Consistent	Short	955 (182)	550 (248)	0.21	689 (114)	425 (73)	0.08
		Long	1103 (274)	884 (356)	0.79	846 (201)	621 (98)	0.25
	Cont. dep.	Short	1015 (268)	656 (170)	1.25	784 (180)	536 (90)	0.96
		Long	1177 (287)	977 (362)	1.33	911 (229)	717 (119)	0.71
B6	Consistent	Short	964 (199)	541 (261)	0.08	673 (122)	435 (76)	0.00
		Long	1148 (250)	820 (298)	0.67	724 (138)	587 (89)	0.04
	Cont. dep.	Short	992 (198)	624 (194)	1.29	760 (167)	526 (80)	0.78
		Long	1148 (272)	933 (363)	0.92	740 (153)	678 (98)	0.12

Stim. type, stimulus type (consistent vs. context-dependent graphemes); Cont. dep., context dependent; B1, block 1; B6, block 6; RTs, reaction times; ATs, articulation times; M, mean; SD, standard deviation.

Articulation times

In the ANOVA on articulation times, we found a main effect of group [$F(1,48) = 13.166$, $p = 0.001$, partial $\mu^2 = 0.223$], with longer ATs in the dyslexic group; block [$F(1,48) = 6.267$, $p = 0.016$, partial $\mu^2 = 0.120$], with longer ATs were longer in the first than in the sixth block; stimulus type [$F(1,48) = 139.871$, $p < 0.001$, partial $\mu^2 = 0.753$], as pseudowords with context-dependent graphemes took more time than pseudowords with consistent graphemes; length [$F(1,48) = 356.407$, $p < 0.001$, partial $\mu^2 = 0.886$], with shorter ATs for short than long pseudowords. Moreover, we found a length by group interaction [$F(1,48) = 27.866$, $p < 0.001$, partial $\mu^2 = 0.377$], and a block by length interaction [$F(1,48) = 5.438$, $p = 0.024$, partial $\mu^2 = 0.106$], indicating that the length effect was more evident in the dyslexic than in the control group and decreaded in the last compared to the first block. A more detailed analysis (comparing the first block with the rest of blocks) showed that the reduction of the length effect already appeared in block 5 (block by length interaction) and was maintained in block 6 (see **Figure 2**).

As with the RTs, we conducted separate analyses for controls and dyslexics. In the analysis of the control group data, we found a stimulus type effect, [$F(1,24) = 278.345$, $p < 0.001$, partial $\mu^2 = 0.921$], with faster ATs in pseudowords with consistent graphemes than in pseudowords with context-dependent graphemes; and a length effect [$F(1,24) = 703.892$, $p < 0.001$, partial $\mu^2 = 0.967$]. Moreover, the block by length interaction was significant [$F(1,24) = 8.238$, $p = 0.008$, partial $\mu^2 = 0.256$], as the length effect decreased across blocks.

In the group with dyslexia, we found a length effect, [$F(1,24) = 144.292$, $p < 0.001$, partial $\mu^2 = 0.868$], with shorter ATs for short than in long stimuli; and a stimulus type effect [$F(1,24) = 45.494$, $p < 0.001$, partial $\mu^2 = 0.674$], with longer ATs for pseudowords with context-dependent graphemes than pseudowords with consistent graphemes. By contrast, the block by length interaction was not significant, indicating that length continued to affect the ATs after six repetitions.

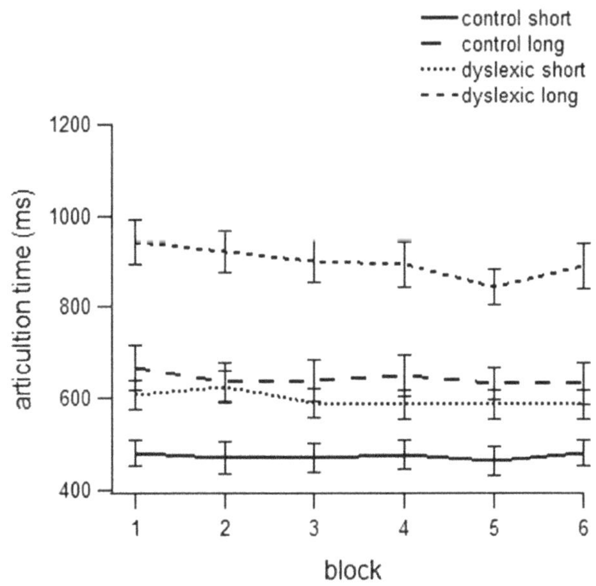

FIGURE 2 | Articulation times to short and long pseudowords in dyslexics and controls across blocks.

DISCUSSION

In this study, we addressed the difficulty of Spanish-speaking dyslexic children in developing orthographic representations and investigated whether this difficulty is related to words that contain context-sensitive graphemes. In order to test this hypothesis, we compared children with dyslexia and typical readers using pseudowords with or without contextual grapheme–phoneme rules. The length effect reduction on reading speed, after repeated exposure, was considered as an indicator of orthographic representation development.

The results showed that dyslexic children were significantly slower at reading (RTs and ATs) than controls in all blocks, especially with long pseudowords. Additionally, children in the control group reduced the RTs across blocks (83 ms difference between the first and the sixth block), while the RTs of dyslexics remained the same through repetitions (2 ms difference between the first and the sixth block).

A critical finding was that typical readers showed a significant reduction of the length effect in the sixth block after repeated reading, i.e., the difference between short and long pseudowords was not significant in the last block (only 16 ms difference), suggesting development of orthographic representations. By contrast, dyslexic children continued to manifest a length effect in the sixth block (174 ms difference between short and long stimuli). These results are consistent with studies in other orthographic systems reporting that dyslexics have difficulties in storing the orthographic representations of words (Hogaboam and Perfetti, 1978; Manis, 1985; Reitsma, 1989; Ehri and Saltmarsh, 1995; Martens and de Jong, 2008; Kwok and Ellis, 2014).They also confirm results recently obtained with Spanish dyslexic children using the same methodology (Suárez-Coalla et al., 2014).

Regarding the orthographic consistency (i.e., consistent vs. context-dependent rules), we found that pseudowords with context-dependent rules are associated with longer RTs, ATs, and greater number of reading errors, in both dyslexics and controls. Therefore, it seems that context-dependent rules were more difficult to learn and automate, even for typical readers, in accordance with other studies (Rastle and Coltheart, 1998; Rey and Schiller, 2005; Barca et al., 2006). Nevertheless, the influence of the context-dependent graphemes on the formation of the orthographic representations seems to be stronger on the control group than on the dyslexic children, since in the normal children the reduction of the length effect after repeated reading was smaller for the pseudowords with these graphemes than for the pseudowords composed of consistent rules. On the other hand, in the dyslexic children, the length effect was similar for both types of graphemes. This suggests that dyslexics may be having problems forming orthographic representations even for words with consistent rules. In fact, dyslexic children were not able to develop orthographic representations with six exposures and continue using sublexical reading for all new words. They probably need more exposures to achieve a direct reading, as suggested by Kwok and Ellis (2014) in their study with dyslexic adults. Overall, we conclude that dyslexic children show a selective learning deficit in forming orthographic representations, independent of whether stimuli contained consistent or not context-sensitive rules. This independence from context-sensitive rules suggests a lexical locus for the learning difficulty of children with dyslexia.

Notably, dyslexic children remained slower than controls for both short and long stimuli. This highlights the known difficulties of dyslexics to read new words or pseudowords (Rack et al., 1992; Grainger et al., 2003; Suárez-Coalla and Cuetos, 2012). Their reading speed was more or less constant throughout the task, even showing longer RTs in the last block than controls on the first exposure. There is a possibility that inaccuracy interferes with orthographic learning because the correct mastering of the alphabetic code seems crucial; more times a word is accurately read, the greater the chances to store the representation in memory (Share, 1995). In this study, we found that dyslexic children made more errors than children without dyslexia, although an improvement in reading accuracy along the blocks occurred for both groups of children.

Besides RTs, dyslexics were also slower than controls in ATs. This measure, similarly to the RTs, decreased along the blocks and was affected by orthographic consistency and length, with more time needed to pronounce context-dependent and long pseudowords, than consistent and short ones. These results are in keeping with Davies et al. (2012) proposal that cognitive processes continue after response onset when word pronunciations is still not yet fully prepared. We should underscore, however, that the length effect was stronger in dyslexics and, furthermore, it did not decrease across the blocks, as it did for the controls. This means that dyslexic children continue doing a serial reading, even after several repetitions.

Finally, considering these results and those of other studies (Kwok and Ellis, 2014; Suárez-Coalla et al., 2014), it will certainly be interesting to perform a study with a larger number of repetitions, and in different days, in order to know if dyslexic children are able to develop orthographic representations with more exposures (Kwok and Ellis, 2014).

In summary, this study addressed the formation of orthographic representations in dyslexic children and the possible influence of context-sensitive rules. Previous studies have investigated this issue, but this is the first time the possibility that the formation of orthographic representations depends on the presence of context-dependent rules has been studied. Our results indicate that Spanish dyslexic children have problems to form orthographic representations (independent of the presence of context dependent graphemes) and continue using sublexical reading even after several exposures.

ACKNOWLEDGMENT

This study was funded by Grant PSI2012-31913 from the Spanish Government.

REFERENCES

Barca, L., Burani, C., Di Filippo, G., and Zoccolotti, P. (2006). Italian developmental dyslexic and proficient readers: where are the differences? *Brain Lang.* 98, 347–351. doi: 10.1016/j.bandl.2006.05.001

Barca, L., Ellis, A. W., and Burani, C. (2007). Context-sensitive rules and word naming in Italian children. *Read. Writ.* 20, 495–509. doi: 10.1007/s11145-006-9040-z

Coltheart, M., Rastle, K., Perry, C., Langdon, R., and Ziegler, J. (2001). DRC: a dual route cascaded model of visual word recognition and reading aloud. *Psychol. Rev.* 108, 204–256. doi: 10.1037/0033-295X.108.1.204

Constantinidou, M., and Stainthorp, R. (2009). Phonological awareness and reading speed deficits in reading disabled Greek-speaking children. *Educ. Psychol.* 29, 171–186. doi: 10.1080/01443410802613483

Cuetos, R., Rodríguez, B., Ruano, E., and Arribas, D. (2007). *PROLEC-R. Batería de Evaluación de los Procesos Lectores, Revisada. [Battery for the Assessment of Reading Processes-Revised].* Madrid: TEA Ediciones.

Cunningham, A. E., Perry, K. E., Stanovich, K. E., and Share, D. L. (2002). Orthographic learning during reading: examining the role of the self-teaching. *J. Exp. Child Psychol.* 82, 185–199. doi: 10.1016/S0022-0965(02)00008-5

Davies, R., Cuetos, F., and González-Seijas, R. (2007). Reading development in a transparent orthography. *Ann. Dyslexia* 57, 179–198. doi: 10.1007/s11881-007-0010-1

Davies, R., Rodríguez-Ferrreiro, J., Suárez, P., and Cuetos, F. (2012). Lexical and sub-lexical effects on accuracy, reaction time and response duration: impaired and typical word and pseudoword reading in a transparent orthography. *Read. Writ.* 26, 721–738. doi: 10.1007/s11145-012-9388-1

De Jong, P. F., Bitter, D. J. L., van Setten, M., and Marinus, E. (2009). Does phonological recoding occur during silent reading, and is it necessary for orthographic learning? *J. Exp. Child Psychol.* 104, 267–282. doi: 10.1016/j.jecp.2009.06.002

De Jong, P. F., and van der Leij, A. (2002). Effects of phonological abilities and linguistic comprehension on the development of reading. *Sci. Stud. Read.* 6, 51–77. doi: 10.1207/S1532799XSSR0601_03

Defior, S., Justicia, F., and Martos, F. (1998). Desarrollo del reconocimiento de palabras en lectores normales y retrasados en función de diferentes variables lingüísticas. *Infancia y Aprendizaje* 21, 59–74. doi: 10.1174/021037098760403479

De Luca, M., Barca, L., Burani, C., and Zoccolotti, P. (2008). The effect of word length and other sublexical, lexical and semantic variables on developmental reading deficits. *Cogn. Behav. Neurol.* 21, 227–235. doi: 10.1097/WNN.0b013e318190d162

Ehri, L., and Saltmarsh, J. (1995). Beginning readers outperform older disabled readers in learning to read words by sight. *Read. Writ.* 7, 295–326. doi: 10.1007/BF03162082

Forster, K. I., and Forster, J. C. (2003). DMDX: a windows display program with millisecond accuracy. *Behav. Res. Methods Instrum. Comput.* 35, 116–124. doi: 10.3758/BF03195503

Grainger, J., Bouttevin, S., Truc, C., Bastien, M., and Ziegler, J. (2003). Word superiority, pseudoword superiority, and learning to read: a comparison of dyslexic and normal readers. *Brain and Lang.* 87, 432–440. doi: 10.1016/S0093-934X(03)00145-7

Hatcher, J., Snowling, M. J., and Griffiths, Y. M. (2002). Cognitive assessment of dyslexic: students in higher education. *Br. J. Educ. Psychol.* 72, 119–133. doi: 10.1348/000709902158801

Hogaboam, T. W., and Perfetti, C. A. (1978). Reading skill and the role of verbal experience in decoding. *J. Educ. Psychol.* 70, 717–729. doi: 10.1348/000709902158801

Kwok, R. K. W., and Ellis, A. W. (2014). Visual word learning in adults with dyslexia. *Front. Hum. Neurosci.* 8:264. doi: 10.3389/fnhum.2014.00264

Landerl, K. (2001). Word recognition deficits in German: more evidence from a representative sample. *Dyslexia* 7, 183–196. doi: 10.1002/dys.199

Landerl, K., Wimmer, H., and Frith, U. (1997). The impact of orthographic consistence on dyslexia: a German-English comparison. *Cognition* 63, 315–334. doi: 10.1016/S0010-0277(97)00005-X

Maloney, E., Risko, E. F., O'Malley, S., and Besner, D. (2009). Tracking the transition from sublexical to lexical processing: on the creation of orthographic and phonological lexical representations. *Q. J. Exp. Psychol.* 62, 858–867. doi: 10.1080/17470210802578385

Manis, F. R. (1985). Acquisition of word identification skills in normal and disabled readers. *J. Educ. Psychol.* 77, 78–90. doi: 10.1080/17470210802578385

Martens, V. E. G., and de Jong, P. F. (2008). Effects of repeated reading on the length effect in word and pseudoword reading. *J. Res. Read.* 31, 40–54. doi: 10.1111/j.1467-9817.2007.00360.x

Nikolopoulos, D., Goulandris, N., and Snowling, J. (2003). "Developmental dyslexia in Greek," in *Dyslexia in Different Languages*, ed. N. Goulandris (London: Whurr).

Oney, B., and Goldman, S. R. (1984). Recoding and comprehension skills in Turkish and English: effects of the regularity of grapheme–phoneme correspondences. *J. Educ. Psychol.* 76, 447–568.

Perea, M., Jiménez, M., Suárez-Coalla, P., Fernández, N., Viña, C., and Cuetos, F. (2014). Ability for voice recognition is a marker for dyslexia in children. *Exp. Psychol.* 24, 1–8. doi: 10.1027/1618-3169/a000265

Pontillo, M., De Luca, M., Ellis, A. W., Marinelli, C. V., Spinelli, D., and Zoccolotti, P. (2014). Failure to learn a new spatial format in children with developmental dyslexia. *Sci. Rep.* 4:4869. doi: 10.1038/srep04869

Protopapas, A. (2007). CheckVocal: a program to facilitate checking the accuracy and response time of vocal responses from DMDX. *Behav. Res. Methods* 39, 859–862. doi: 10.3758/BF03192979

Rack, J. P., Snowling, M. J., and Olson, R. K. (1992). The nonword reading deficit in developmental dyslexia: a review. *R. Res. Q.* 27, 29–53. doi: 10.2307/747832

Rastle, K., and Coltheart, M. (1998). Whammies and double whammies: the length effect on nonword reading. *Psychon. Bull. Rev.* 5, 277–282. doi: 10.2307/747832

Reitsma, P. (1989). "Orthographic memory and learning to read," in *Reading and Writing Disorders in Different Orthographic Systems,* eds P. G. Aaron and R. M. Joshi (New York: Kluwer), 31–44.

Rey, A., and Schiller, N. O. (2005). Graphemic complexity and multiple print-to-sound associations in visual word recognition. *Mem. Cogn.* 33, 76–85. doi: 10.3758/BF03195298

Seymour, P. H. K., Aro, M., and Erskine, J. M. (2003). Foundation literacy acquisition in European orthographies. *Br. J. Psychol.* 94, 143–174. doi: 10.1348/000712603321661859

Share, D. L. (1995). Phonological recoding and self-teaching: sine qua none of reading acquisition. *Cognition* 5, 151–218. doi: 10.1016/0010-0277(94)00645-2

Share, D. L. (1999). Phonological recoding and orthographic learning: a direct test of the self-teaching hypothesis. *J. Exp. Child Psychol.* 72, 95–129. doi: 10.1006/jecp.1998.2481

Snowling, M. J. (1995). Phonological processing and developmental dyslexia. *J. Res. Read.* 18, 132–138. doi: 10.1111/j.1467-9817.1995.tb00079.x

Spinelli, D., De Luca, M., Di Filippo, G., Mancini, M., Martelli, M., and Zoccolotti, P. (2005). Length effect in word naming in reading: role of reading experience and reading deficit in Italian readers. *Dev. Neuropsychol.* 27, 217–235. doi: 10.1207/s15326942dn2702_2

Sprenger-Charolles, L., Colé, P., Serniclaes, W., and Lacert, P. (2000). On subtypes of developmental dyslexia: evidence from processing time and accuracy scores. *Can. J. Exp. Psychol.* 54, 88–104. doi: 10.1037/h0087332

Suárez-Coalla, P., and Cuetos, F. (2012). Reading strategies in Spanish developmental dyslexics. *Ann. Dyslexia* 62, 71–81. doi: 10.1007/s11881-011-0064-y

Suárez-Coalla, P., Ramos, S., Álvarez-Cañizo, M., and Cuetos, F. (2014). Orthographic learning in dyslexic Spanish children. *Ann. Dyslexia* 64, 166–181. doi: 10.1007/s11881-014-0092-5

Van den Broeck, W., and Geudens, A. (2012). Old and new ways to study characteristics of reading disability: the case of the nonword-reading deficit. *Cogn. Psychol.* 65, 414–456. doi: 10.1016/j.cogpsych.2012

Wechsler, D. (2001). *Escala de Inteligencia para Niños-Revisión. [Intelligence Scale for Children-Revised].* New York, NY: Psychological Corporation.

Weekes, B. S. (1997). Differential effects of number of letters on word and nonword naming latency. *Q. J. Exp. Psychol. A* 50A, 439–456. doi: 10.1080/027249897392170

Wimmer, H. (1993). Characteristics of developmental dyslexia in a regular writing system. *Appl. Psycholinguist.* 14, 1–33. doi: 10.1017/S0142716400010122

Wimmer, H., and Goswami, U. (1994). The influence of orthographic consistency on reading development: word recognition in English and German children. *Cognition* 51, 91–103. doi: 10.1016/0010-0277(94)90010-8

Wimmer, H., Schurz, M., Strum, D., Richlan, F., Klackl, J., Kronbichler, M., et al. (2010). A dual route perspective on poor reading in a regular orthography: an fMRI study. *Cortex* 46, 1284–1298. doi: 10.1016/j.cortex.2010.06.004

Yap, R. L., and Van der Leij, A. (1993). Word processing in dyslexics: an automatic decoding deficit? *Read. Writ.* 5, 261–279. doi: 10.1016/j.cortex.2010.06.004

Ziegler, J. C., Perry, C., Ma-Wyatt, A., Ladner, D., and Schulte-Korne, G. (2003). Developmental dyslexia in different languages: language-specific or universal? *J. Exp. Child Psychol.* 86, 169–193. doi: 10.1016/S0022-0965(03)00139-5

Zoccolotti, P., De Luca, M., Di Pace, E., Gasperini, F., Judica, A., and Spinelli, D. (2005). Word length effect in early reading and in developmental dyslexia. *Brain Lang.* 93, 369–373. doi: 10.1016/j.bandl.2004.10.010

3

The contribution of discrete-trial naming and visual recognition to rapid automatized naming deficits of dyslexic children with and without a history of language delay

Filippo Gasperini*, Daniela Brizzolara, Paola Cristofani, Claudia Casalini and Anna Maria Chilosi

Department of Developmental Neuroscience, IRCCS Fondazione Stella Maris, Pisa, Italy

****Correspondence:***
Filippo Gasperini, Department of Developmental Neuroscience, IRCCS Fondazione Stella Maris, Viale del Tirreno 331, 56018 Calambrone, Pisa, Italy
e-mail: fgasperini@fsm.unipi.it

Children with Developmental Dyslexia (DD) are impaired in Rapid Automatized Naming (RAN) tasks, where subjects are asked to name arrays of high frequency items as quickly as possible. However the reasons why RAN speed discriminates DD from typical readers are not yet fully understood. Our study was aimed to identify some of the cognitive mechanisms underlying RAN-reading relationship by comparing one group of 32 children with DD with an age-matched control group of typical readers on a naming and a visual recognition task both using a discrete-trial methodology, in addition to a serial RAN task, all using the same stimuli (digits and colors). Results showed a significant slowness of DD children in both serial and discrete-trial naming (DN) tasks regardless of type of stimulus, but no difference between the two groups on the discrete-trial recognition task. Significant differences between DD and control participants in the RAN task disappeared when performance in the DN task was partialled out by covariance analysis for colors, but not for digits. The same pattern held in a subgroup of DD subjects with a history of early language delay (LD). By contrast, in a subsample of DD children without LD the RAN deficit was specific for digits and disappeared after slowness in DN was partialled out. Slowness in DN was more evident for LD than for noLD DD children. Overall, our results confirm previous evidence indicating a name-retrieval deficit as a cognitive impairment underlying RAN slowness in DD children. This deficit seems to be more marked in DD children with previous LD. Moreover, additional cognitive deficits specifically associated with serial RAN tasks have to be taken into account when explaining deficient RAN speed of these latter children. We suggest that partially different cognitive dysfunctions underpin superficially similar RAN impairments in different subgroups of DD subjects.

Keywords: dyslexia, RAN, discrete-trial naming, discrete-trial recognition, language delay

INTRODUCTION

One of the most robust research findings on the cognitive bases of developmental reading disorders (also known as Developmental Dyslexia, DD) is a deficit of children with DD on rapid serial naming tasks (for reviews see Wolf and Bowers, 1999 and Kirby et al., 2010). The most commonly used measure of this is the rapid automatized naming (RAN) task, in which subjects are presented with arrays of high frequency items (letters, digits, colors, or objects) and asked to name them as quickly as possible. Usually, children with DD perform this task accurately but slowly.

RAN speed deficits in children with DD have been first demonstrated in English speaking readers. However, since early English-based research in the 1970s and 1980s, a strong relation between RAN speed measures and reading acquisition has been documented in a wide array of languages, with both inconsistent (e.g., French: Plaza and Cohen, 2003) and consistent (e.g., German: Wimmer, 1993; Dutch: de Jong and van der Leij, 1999; Finnish: Holopainen et al., 2001; Italian: Di Filippo et al., 2005) alphabetic orthographies.

Despite this evidence, we are currently some way from obtaining a complete understanding of the reasons why RAN performance is related to reading.

Research aiming to reveal the nature of this relationship dates back to the early 80s (for a review see Bowers and Swanson, 1991); from then, many studies have investigated the issue, but evidence is mostly correlational (for reviews see Wolf et al., 2000 and Kirby et al., 2010). Only in the last decade there have been a few studies which experimentally manipulated factors that may account for RAN-reading relationship (Neuhaus and Swank, 2002; Jones et al., 2009; Georgiou et al., 2013; Zoccolotti et al., 2013). Although a consensus begins to emerge for some possible underlying mechanisms, the debate is still largely open for some others.

Substantial agreement exists that post-lexical access articulatory factors do not account for differences on RAN speed among children with different levels of reading ability. For example, when total time to complete RAN tasks is experimentally segregated into a *pause time*—namely the duration of pauses between items in sequenced articulations—and *articulation time*—namely the time to articulate each item—pause time and not articulation time significantly predicts reading ability, in both normal and DD readers (Georgiou et al., 2006; Araújo et al., 2011b). Hence, these results point to the inter-item processing—namely the processes intercurring from attentional disengaging from one stimulus to name retrieval for the next one—as the *locus* that drives RAN-reading association.

According to one influential view, RAN should be considered as part of a larger phonological construct together with phonological awareness (PA) and phonological short-term memory (PSTM), in that it primary reflects the rate of access to and retrieval of stored phonological information in long-term memory (Wagner et al., 1993; Pennington et al., 2001; Chiappe et al., 2002). Evidence supporting a role of phonological lexical access in mediating the RAN-reading relationship comes from studies using a discrete-trial methodology. These studies have often found that latency to name singularly presented highly familiar stimuli (the same used in the serial RAN tasks) is significantly correlated with reading measures, in both samples of children unselected for reading skill (Levy and Hinchley, 1990) and children with DD (Bowers and Swanson, 1991; Fawcett and Nicolson, 1994; Chiappe et al., 2002; Jones et al., 2009).

However, not all authors consider RAN performance as just another instance of phonological processing ability together with PA and PSTM. For example, Wolf and Bowers (1999) emphasize the multi-componential nature of serial RAN tasks, placing stronger emphasis on the efficiency with which multiple processes (attentional, visual, phonological, semantic and articulatory) are integrated through precise timing mechanisms, which in turn calls into question general processing speed. As a consequence, Wolf and Bowers (1999) state that phonological processes—which they index essentially through PA—and mechanisms underlying RAN performance represent two independent sources of variability in reading ability.

A good deal of evidence supports Wolf and Bowers' position. For example, RAN and PA are not strongly correlated (Swanson et al., 2003). Moreover, many cross-sectional and longitudinal studies have found that RAN speed contributes uniquely to the variance in reading ability when PA is controlled (Torgesen et al., 1997; Parrila et al., 2004; Kirby et al., 2009). However, PA does not end all of phonological processing; in their empirical model of phonological processing, Wagner et al. (1993) identified three significantly correlated but distinct factors: PA (blending and segmenting sounds from words), PSTM (digit span), and lexical access (naming speed). Therefore, the fact that RAN speed and PA are only modestly correlated and each predicts a unique proportion of variance in reading is not in conflict with the hypothesis that phonological processing abilities, in particular access to and retrieval of phonological codes from long-term memory, contribute substantially to RAN-reading relationship.

Other possible cognitive mechanisms underlying RAN speed and mediating its relationship with reading include early visual processes. RAN efficiency might reflect both the initial ability to visually analyze the stimuli's constituent features and the subsequent proficiency to integrate visual pattern information with stored representations. The role of visual processing in RAN-reading relationship has so far received minor attention and remains ill understood. Some indirect evidence seems consistent with the hypothesis of a contribution of low-level visual factors to RAN performance and its association with reading (Stainthorp et al., 2010; Araújo et al., 2011a). Using a visual naming task Araújo et al. (2011a) manipulated some variables related to early stages of visual processing of objects and found that, in contrast to control readers, naming performance of DD subjects did not improve with color or 3-dimensional object presentation compared with black-and-white or 2-dimensional object presentation respectively. These results lead the authors to state that "*processes involved in early visual feature analysis or in the integration of visual information stored in long-term memory might be affected in dyslexia*" (p. 224). However, directly comparing the contribution of a RAN task and a visual search task using the same stimulus materials, Di Filippo et al. (2006) found that the disadvantage of DD children with respect to controls on RAN tasks remained unchanged when the visual search performance was partialled out by covariance analysis. These latter findings are at odds with a significant role of early visual processing in driving RAN-reading relationship.

Further explanations of RAN-reading relationship arise from experimental evidence that serial RAN tasks are usually more closely correlated with reading than discrete-trial RAN paradigms (Bowers, 1995; Pennington et al., 2001; Jones et al., 2009; Logan et al., 2011). One interpretation emphasizes the importance of sequential requirements of RAN tasks as a way of explaining their relation with reading, as it is reasonable that speeded naming of multiple items in a matrix format requires both inhibition of previous (already named) stimuli and efficient processing of upcoming items (Jones et al., 2009). Actually, recent findings indicate that both foveal and peripheral processing occur while performing RAN tasks as well as in reading. Recent experimental evidence indicates that children with DD have difficulty not only distinguishing between multiple competing phonological representations at foveal stages of processing (when a verbal response is required), but also between multiple activated orthographic codes during parafoveal processing (Jones et al., 2013). More generally, RAN and reading could be related because several items are visible at once in both tasks, allowing subjects to pre-process some items in parafovea. Studies on text reading have shown that for typical readers the availability of upcoming words in the parafovea increases the speed with which the text is read (Sereno and Rayner, 2000); however, parafoveal information may in fact act as a source of interference for children with DD, in both reading (Chace et al., 2005; Pernet et al., 2006) and RAN tasks (Jones et al., 2009).

Overall, despite a growing number of studies in the last three decades, cognitive mechanisms underlying RAN-reading relationship are still a matter of considerable debate. It should also be considered that processes mediating RAN-reading relationship may at least partially change with reading development, when a progressive shift occurs from a serial grapheme-phoneme decoding strategy toward a parallel "sight-word" reading. Recent data on Greek speaking children (Protopapas et al., 2013) support this hypothesis by showing that the amount of common variance between serial RAN and reading was mostly explained by discrete-trial naming (DN) in 2nd graders, while a stronger contribution from sequential processing was evident among 6th graders. Based on these results, it is plausible to expect that processes driving RAN-reading relationship may also be different between normally developing and DD readers.

The general aim of the present study was to give a contribution in identifying cognitive mechanisms underlying RAN-reading relationship in children learning Italian, a language characterized by a transparent orthography. In a previous study, we obtained evidence that RAN and not phonological processing abilities (as assessed through PA and PSTM tasks) may represent the main cognitive marker of DD in Italian children (Brizzolara et al., 2006). This evidence is consistent with a growing body of studies in which RAN speed has been shown to be a strong predictor of reading ability in orthographically transparent languages, both in sample of children unselected for reading ability and in children with reading disability (e.g., for Finnish: Holopainen et al., 2001; for German: Landerl, 2001; for Dutch: de Jong and van der Leij, 2003; for Greek: Papadopoulos et al., 2009). Because of the relevance of cognitive processes underlying RAN speed for reading ability in transparent orthographies, a deeper understanding of mechanisms driving RAN-reading relationship seems of particular relevance.

In the present study, we focused on some of the cognitive processes underpinning RAN speed which may differentiate between children with DD and average readers, in particular, visual recognition of single items, lexical access and sequential processing of multiple items.

Firstly, we compared a group of DD children with an age-matched control group of typical readers on a DN paradigm in which items were digits or colors.

Secondly, children with DD and their controls were contrasted on a motor choice-reaction time task using the same stimuli as in the DN, in which subjects had to discriminate between a target stimulus and four distracters. Such experimental manipulation at the output stage of DN removes much if not all the name-retrieval component, allowing a direct test for the role of early visual processes involved in naming of isolated items. To our knowledge this is the first attempt to investigate the potential contribution of early visual factors to RAN-reading relationship using the same material as the serial RAN task, with specific focus on single-item processing level. Di Filippo et al. (2005, 2006) had previously made a similar experimental manipulation, using a visual search task with the same stimulus material as RAN; however, in Di Filippo et al.'s studies control on early visual processing was more wide-ranging (including scanning of the stimuli) and less specifically focused on single stimulus identification.

At the same time, investigating both DN and recognition in the same subjects using the same stimulus material allows testing the role of lexical access in differentiating RAN performance of DD and average readers, once potential differences at the stage of visual identification have been removed.

A further step of our study was to compare children with DD and controls on a serial RAN paradigm using the same stimuli as in the other two tasks, to verify if the expected differences in serial RAN survived after statistical control for the possible significant effects of both DN and discrete recognition (DR). If serial RAN continues to discriminate between children with DD and controls, then a further contribution to RAN-reading relationship has to be probably found in cognitive factors outside single-item processing (such as sequencing of multiple items and/or higher demands on precise timing mechanisms posed by serial RAN).

In our study children with DD were further assigned to two sub-groups according to whether or not they had a history of early language delay (LD) as determined retrospectively by parental report. In previous work we demonstrated a somewhat different cognitive profile in Italian DD children with and without a history of LD (Brizzolara et al., 2006; Chilosi et al., 2009; Pecini et al., 2011). In fact, while both groups shared a comparable RAN speed deficit, only DD children with a previous LD showed a moderate but widespread verbal deficit, extending from phonological processing (PA and PSTM) to other components of linguistic processing (lexical phonology, semantics and syntax). However, as the classification of LD in children with DD is based on a retrospective criterion (i.e., based on parents' report), in the present study a set of standardized behavioral and cognitive tests was also administered. These included measures of sub-lexical and lexical reading, written text comprehension, PSTM, verbal semantic knowledge and vocabulary. We expected to find lower scores among DD children with LD than among DD children without LD (LD-DD and noLD-DD, respectively) in all the oral verbal measures and in the test of reading comprehension, consistently with previous evidence indicating a moderate but widespread verbal deficit (i.e., not limited to phonological processing) among LD-DD children that does not affect noLD-DD subjects (Chilosi et al., 2009).

There is now mounting evidence that DD is an heterogeneous neurobiological condition (Eckert, 2004; Jednoróg et al., 2013) associated with multiple impairments in different cognitive domains (Bosse et al., 2007; Menghini et al., 2010), including phonological processing (Vellutino et al., 2004), early visual analyses (Stein, 2001; Martelli et al., 2009), skills automatization (Nicolson et al., 2001) and visual-spatial attention (Hari and Renvall, 2001; Franceschini et al., 2012). As a consequence, it would not be surprising if different cognitive deficits underpin impaired RAN performance in subgroups of DD children with distinct neurocognitive phenotypes.

On the basis of the reviewed evidence, we expected that children with DD considered as a group would be significantly slower than chronological age-matched controls on both serial RAN and DN tasks. We also expected that differences between DD and control groups on serial RAN tasks survived statistical control for differences in DN tasks. Both expectations seemed plausible in children learning a transparent orthography, as Italian, in which DD has been mainly characterized by a reading fluency deficit in the face of rather accurate decoding (for a review see Wimmer and Schurz, 2010; see also Zoccolotti et al., 1999 for evidence in Italian). The characteristic reading speed deficit of these children might be, in fact, equally well explained by a deficient orthography to phonology mapping at both sub-lexical and lexical level of reading, indexed by impaired DN (de Jong, 2011), as well as by a reduced ability to simultaneously process multiple adjacent items in the written text, tapped by the unique contribution of serial RAN to reading difficulties (Protopapas et al., 2013).

Predictions about DR tasks in our study were more open due to the variable results reported in the literature.

Hypotheses on possible different cognitive mechanisms underlying RAN-reading relationship in LD-DD and noLD-DD were more speculative, as to our knowledge this is the first study to address such topic. One possibility is that impaired lexical access is particularly relevant for RAN speed deficits in LD-DD children. Although name-retrieval deficits have often been described in both DD subjects without apparent previous or concurrent language difficulties (Wolf and Obregon, 1992; Swan and Goswami, 1997; Hanly and Vanderberg, 2010) and in children with specific oral language difficulties (also known as Specific Language Impairment, SLI; Kail and Leonard, 1986; Befi-Lopes et al., 2010; Coady, 2013), word finding difficulties might be more pronounced in LD-DD children in comparison with noLD-DD children: the two groups might share a common phonological lexical access deficit, while only the former would show an additional semantic deficit. Indeed, evidence exists for both a phonological (Coady, 2013) and a semantic (Kail and Leonard, 1986; Befi-Lopes et al., 2010) account of naming difficulties in children with oral language difficulties.

If impaired lexical access is particularly relevant for RAN speed deficits in LD-DD children, then slower performance on the DN tasks should be more evident in these subjects than in noLD-DD children. However, this might be true for the color more than for the digit condition. In fact, conceptual activation would mediate mainly color naming (Heurley et al., 2013), while more direct arbitrary mappings from visual stimuli to phonological labels occur for digits (Manis et al., 1999). Possibly, the unique contribution of serial RAN tasks over the one played by DN tasks would be smaller in LD-DD than in noLD-DD subjects.

MATERIALS AND METHODS

PARTICIPANTS

Informed consent was obtained from all the parents of participants in compliance with the Helsinki Declaration.

Participants with DD were selected on the basis of consecutive referrals to the Division of Child Neurology and Psychiatry of the University of Pisa from May 2009 to October 2010 for suspected specific learning disabilities. Criteria for inclusion in the DD sample were the following:

- non-verbal intelligence within normal limits, as assessed by Raven's Colored Progressive Matrices (Raven, 1984) for children from third to fifth grade and by Picture Completion and Block Design subtests of WISC-III (Wechsler, 1991) jointly considered for children from sixth to eighth grade (see below, for details);
- impaired score on a standardized single words reading test from the DDE-2 (Battery for the Evaluation of DD and Dysorthography), 2nd edition (Sartori et al., 2007) (see below);
- regular school attendance;
- absence of neurological abnormalities on a standard neurological examination;
- normal or corrected to normal visual acuity;
- no clinical evidence of oral language impairment at the time of assessment. Assessment of oral language was carried out by a child neuropsychiatrist with special expertise in speech and language disorders (A.C.) using a semi-structured interview. Normal fluency, well-formed sentences and the absence of phonological, semantic and grammatical errors in conversation were considered as signs of adequate language organization.

Thirty two (18 males and 14 females) children fulfilled these criteria. The mean age for children with DD was 11 years and 2 months, with a standard deviation (SD) of 1 year and 9 months. The youngest children were second graders and the oldest were eighth graders. More specifically, 15 children attended Primary school (from second grade to fifth grade) while 17 children attended Secondary school (from sixth to eighth grade). All DD participants were Italian native speakers. No child had been diagnosed as Attention Deficit Hyperactivity Disorder (ADHD) at the time of assessment.

Each child's clinical history was investigated by means of an assessment interview with his or her parents; this was carried out by the same child neuropsychiatrist with special expertise in speech and language disorders (A.C.) who assessed oral language abilities of children. The parents were also asked to fill out a questionnaire (Brizzolara et al., 2006; Chilosi et al., 2009) on motor, cognitive, and language developmental milestones. In order to encourage the parents to recall basic language milestones, examples of typical children's utterances were provided. A child was considered to have a positive history of LD if the analysis of his/her questionnaire revealed at least one of these signs: (1) no vocabulary burst before 24 months; (2) late combinatory use of words, that is, after 30 months; (3) persistence of grammatically incomplete sentences after 4 years of age; and (4) persistence of phonological mispronunciations after 4 years of age. On the basis of these criteria 18 children (11 males, 7 females) were considered as having had a LD. They had a mean age of 11 years and 1 month (SD = 2 years and 4 months). No language delay (noLD) was documented retrospectively in 14 children (7 males and 7 females). Their mean age was 11 years and 5 months. No significant difference for age ($F_{(1,30)} = 0.21$, *ns*) was present between LD and noLD DD groups.

One group of 32 Italian, native-speaking typical readers served as control for the children with DD. These participants were selected from several Primary and Secondary public schools and individually matched with DD subjects by sex and chronological age (± 3 months). For the children to be included, they also had to perform normally on the same standardized single word reading test (see below) and non-verbal intelligence tests used in children with DD. The mean age of the control group was 11 years and 2 months (SD = 1 year and 8 months), a value not significantly different from that of the DD group as expected on the basis of the selection criterion ($F_{(1,62)} = 0.01$, *ns*).

Control children were further subdivided into two groups, in which subjects were matched individually with DD children of LD and noLD group respectively. As expected, each DD group did not differ significantly from its own control group for age ($F_{(1,34)} = 0.06$ for the comparison involving the LD children and $F_{(1,26)} = 0.00$ for the comparison with the noLD children, both *ns*).

MATERIALS AND PROCEDURE

Non-verbal intelligence

Non-verbal intelligence was assessed by Raven's Colored Progressive Matrices (Raven, 1984; Italian standardization, Pruneti et al., 1996) for children from third to fifth grade and by Picture Completion and Block Design subtests of WISC-III (Wechsler, 1991; Italian standardization Orsini and Picone, 2006) jointly considered for children from sixth to eighth grade, in both the DD and control samples.

The cut-off for non-verbal intelligence within normal limits was set at one SD below the mean of the normative sample for the appropriate age level; for children from sixth to eighth grade the average between the Picture Completion and Block Design scaled scores was computed.

Mean *z* score (and SD) for non-verbal intelligence of the DD and control groups are reported in **Table 1**. The two groups did not differ significantly for non-verbal intelligence ($F_{(1,62)} = 0.16$, *ns*).

Likewise, no differences existed in non-verbal intelligence between the DD groups and their control subgroups ($F_{(1,34)} = 0.77$ for the comparison involving LD children and $F_{(1,26)} = 0.20$ for the comparison with the noLD children, both *ns*), as well as between the LD-DD and the noLD-DD subjects ($F_{(1,30)} = 0.83$, *ns*).

Mean *z* scores (and SDs) for non-verbal intelligence of the DD and control subgroups are reported in **Table 1**.

Reading assessment

Reading level for inclusion in the DD or in the control group was assessed using one subtest from the Battery for the Evaluation of DD and Dysorthography, 2nd Edition (Sartori et al., 2007). In this subtest subjects have to read aloud as quickly and accurately as possible four lists of 28 words with high or low frequency (4- to 8-letter long). Total number of errors and speed of reading (syllables/second) are computed. Raw scores were converted to *z* scores according to standard reference data; normative data are available separately for each grade from second to eighth grade.

A *z* score lower than 2 with respect to the mean of the normative sample for either accuracy or speed was taken as the cut-off criterion for inclusion in the DD group. This disjunctive criterion was used because it has been shown that subjects with DD can flexibly adapt their speed-accuracy rate (Hendriks and Kolk, 1997); consequently, a selection based on both parameters might fail to detect selective cases of pathological performance. At the same time, to limit overlaps between the DD and the control group, we adopted a conservative criterion: for children to be included in the control group the performance in the reading test could not be lower than one SD below the mean of the normative sample for either accuracy or speed.

Mean (and SD) *z* scores for the reading measures of both the DD and the control group are reported in **Table 1**. The control readers' performance was close to zero for both accuracy and speed. On the contrary, DD readers performed very poorly on both parameters. As expected on the basis of selection criteria, DD children scored significantly worse than control readers on both accuracy ($F_{(1,62)} = 10.05$, $p < 0.01$) and speed ($F_{(1,62)} = 22.18$, $p < 0.001$). Given the heterogeneity of age in our sample, we compared Primary with Secondary school children in both speed and accuracy raw scores of single-word reading. No significant difference emerged for both measures ($F_{(1,30)} = 1.49$, $p = 0.23$, $\eta^2 = 0.05$ for speed; $F_{(1,30)} = 1.64$, $p = 0.21$, $\eta^2 = 0.05$ for accuracy).

Table 1 also reports the mean (and SD) *z* scores for the reading measures of both LD- and noLD-DD children and the corresponding control children. No difference emerged between

Table 1 | Means and SDs (in brackets) of the whole DD sample, of the sub-groups of DD participants with (LD) and without (noLD) a history of language delay and the respective control groups on non-verbal intellective level and single word reading measures.

	DD subjects (whole sample, *n* = 32)	Controls (whole sample, *n* = 32)	LD-DD subjects (*n* = 18)	Controls for the LD-DD subjects (*n* = 18)	noLD-DD subjects (*n* = 14)	Controls for the noLD-DD subjects (*n* = 14)
Non-verbal intellective level (*z* scores)	0.12 (0.75)	0.19 (0.54)	0.02 (0.76)	0.22 (0.59)	0.26 (0.73)	0.15 (0.50)
Single word reading Accuracy (*z* scores)	−4.85 (8.99)	0.29 (0.73)	−6.33 (11.50)	0.45 (0.70)	−2.79 (2.68)	0.07 (0.74)
Single word reading Speed (*z* scores)	−6.27 (7.80)	0.36 (0.70)	−7.49 (10.05)	0.38 (0.78)	−4.57 (1.94)	0.33 (0.60)

z scores for both non-verbal intelligence level and reading measures were computed according to the corresponding normative data for age (non-verbal intelligence level) or grade level (reading measures; for details see the text).

LD and noLD groups on accuracy ($F_{(1,30)} = 1.59$, *ns*) and speed ($F_{(1,30)} = 1.46$, *ns*). On the contrary, as expected, both DD samples differed significantly from the corresponding control group on both the reading parameters (as regards LD children: $F_{(1,34)} = 6.25$, $p < 0.05$ and $F_{(1,34)} = 11.02$, $p < 0.01$ for accuracy and speed respectively; as regards noLD participants: $F_{(1,26)} = 13.90$, $p < 0.01$ and $F_{(1,26)} = 76.09$, $p < 0.001$ for accuracy and speed, respectively).

Other literacy measures

Reading decoding abilities were further investigated by means of a test of non-word reading, which is usually considered to tap the sub-lexical reading route. Non-word reading was assessed with a subtest from the same standardized battery of the word reading test (Sartori et al., 2007). In this subtest subjects have to read aloud as quickly and accurately as possible three lists of 16 non-words (5 to 9-letter long) in line with the phonotactic and phonographic rules of the Italian language. Total number of errors and speed of reading (syllables/second) are computed. Raw scores were converted to *z* scores according to standard reference data; normative data are available separately for each grade from second to eighth grade.

Text reading comprehension was also investigated, using a standardized test from the MT Reading battery (Cornoldi and Colpo, 1995, 1998). A meaningful passage is presented without a time limit. The participant has to read it silently and respond to multiple-choice questions. Stimulus materials, number of questions (10 to 15) and related reference norms vary from school level. Raw scores were converted to *z* scores according to standard reference data.

Mean (and SD) *z* scores for the non-word reading and written text comprehension measures of both the DD groups are reported in **Table 2**. The two groups did not differ significantly on non-word reading ($F_{(1,30)} = 2.03$, *ns* and $F_{(1,30)} = 1.07$, *ns* for accuracy and speed, respectively). A significant difference emerged for text reading comprehension ($F_{(1,30)} = 4.95$, $p < 0.05$), with a lower performance from LD-DD than noLD-DD children. In absolute terms, the mean performance of the former subgroup was more than one SD below the mean of the normative sample.

Oral verbal measures

Phonological short-term memory (PSTM). PSTM abilities were examined with a shortened version of a word span test (Ferretti et al., 2003), requiring the child to repeat two lists of Italian high-frequency, disyllabic words varying for phonological similarity. Stimulus presentation is controlled by a PC using a dedicated software. For each list (with or without phonological similar words), sequences of increasing length are presented (from two to seven words). The child is required to repeat the words in the correct order. The list presentation is interrupted when the child fails on three out of five series of the same length. For each list, memory span is the number of words of the longest sequence correctly repeated at least in three out of five presentations. The raw scores were converted to *z* scores according to standard reference data of the test, separately for each list, and then averaged to get a single *z* score for each subject.

Table 2 shows the means and SDs for the PSTM task of both LD-DD and noLD-DD group.

PSTM was significantly lower in the LD than in the noLD-DD children ($F_{(1,30)} = 7.44$, $p < 0.05$), falling more than one SD below the mean of the normative sample in the former.

Verbal semantics. Verbal semantic knowledge was investigated with the WISC-III Information sub-test (Wechsler, 1991; Orsini and Picone, 2006). Raw scores were transformed into scaled scores on a 1–19 scale, with mean = 10 and SD = 3. Data for this test were available for 28 children with DD of our sample (15 LD and 13 noLD; see **Table 2**). The two groups differed significantly on this subtest ($F_{(1,26)} = 5.86$, $p < 0.05$): LD-DD children performed worse than noLD-DD children, scoring as a group more than one SD below the population mean.

Vocabulary. Word knowledge (and also verbal concept formation) was examined using the WISC-III Vocabulary sub-test

Table 2 | Means and SDs (in brackets) of sub-groups of DD participants with (LD) and without (noLD) a history of language delay on literacy (non-word reading and written text comprehension) and oral verbal measures.

			LD-DD subjects (n = 18)	noLD-DD subjects (n = 14)
Literacy measures	Non-word reading (*z* scores)	Accuracy	−3.40 (2.96)	−2.14 (1.30)
		Speed	−2.96 (3.67)	−4.15 (2.11)
	Written text comprehension (*z* scores)		−1.17 (1.25)	−0.23 (0.90)
Oral verbal measures	Phonological STM (*z* scores)		−1.30 (0.84)	−0.50 (0.77)
	WISC-III Information (scaled scores)		6.30 (2.98)	9.00 (1.58)
	WISC-III Vocabulary (scaled scores)		8.42 (2.43)	9.70 (2.31)

z scores for the literacy and Phonological STM measures and scaled scores for the WISC-III subtests were computed according to corresponding normative data for grade level (reading measures) or age (Phonological STM and WISC-III subtests) (for details see the text).

(Wechsler, 1991; Orsini and Picone, 2006). Raw scores were transformed into scaled scores on a 1–19 scale, with mean = 10 and SD = 3. Data for this test were available for 28 children with DD of our sample (15 LD and 13 noLD; see **Table 2**). The LD children performed somewhat lower than the noLD-DD subjects on the Vocabulary sub-test, but the difference was not significant ($F_{(1,26)} = 1.59$, *ns*).

Experimental tasks

RAN test

Stimuli. For the RAN (or serial rapid naming) tasks, materials were adapted from Di Filippo et al. (2005, 2006). Stimuli were matrices of digits or colors on a white background. In each condition, five different stimuli were presented. The digits were 2, 4, 6, 7, and 9, generated with Helvetica font (size 24) and black typed. The colors were presented in small 1 by 1 cm squares; they were black, blue, red, yellow, and green. There were five rows of 10 stimuli in each matrix for a total of 50 stimuli. There was one matrix for each condition. A smaller matrix with two rows of five stimuli was also created for both digit and color condition to be used in a practice trial (see below). Target sequence was randomized within each matrix.

Procedure. Stimuli were displayed on a PC screen. The child was requested to name each stimulus in the matrix as quickly and accurately as possible, working from left to right and from top to bottom. A practice session with a small (10 stimuli) matrix was run for each condition; during this session, the examiner corrected any errors made by the child. For each condition (numbers or colors) time to complete the task was measured using a stopwatch and total time in seconds was used as the dependent measure. Naming errors were also recorded.

Discrete-trial naming (DN) test

Stimuli. Stimuli were the same as in the RAN test, except that in the DN tests both number and colors appeared singly on the PC screen on a white background. Target sequence was randomized for each condition. Similarly to the RAN task, for each condition (numbers or colors) a total of 50 stimuli were presented within a single block.

Procedure. For each condition (numbers and colors), stimuli were displayed singly in the center of a PC screen. Presentation was controlled by SuperLab Pro 2.0 package (Cedrus Corporation, 2002; San Pedro, California). The child was asked to name each digit or color as fast and accurately as possible. The stimulus remained on the screen until the subject responded or for a time limit of 6000 ms. Then a 500 ms blank followed before the next stimulus appeared. In order to avoid false responses, subjects were explicitly requested not to self-correct if they realized a naming error had occurred. For each condition, participants were given a practice session with 10 stimuli; at the end of this session children were corrected for any naming errors and taught to avoid self-corrections. Vocal latencies were recorded using the SuperLab Pro 2.0 package. Naming errors were also computed. In a few instances, trials were not valid due to technical failures or false responses; more generally, all latencies under 250 ms were counted as invalid trials. Only latencies for valid and correct trials were analyzed. For each condition the median response latency and the total number of naming errors were computed. Median latency was chosen as measure of central tendency to remove the influence of outlier values.

Discrete-trial recognition (DR) test

Stimuli. Stimuli and format presentation were the same as in the DN test. Target sequence was randomized for each condition, but the order of presentation was different than in the DN test.

Procedure. For each stimulus the trial sequence and temporal parameters were the same as in the DN test. The stimulus was singly displayed at the center of the PC screen and disappeared with the subject's response or after a time limit of 6000 ms. Then, a 500 ms blank followed before the next stimulus was presented. A motor choice-reaction time task was used to estimate efficiency of visual processing underpinning single-item naming. Participants were asked to press one of two keys on a response pad as fast and accurately as possible when the target stimulus appeared (number 7 for the digit condition and a green square for the color condition) and to press the other key when all the other stimuli were displayed. Responses to the target were made using the index finger of the dominant hand, while those to the other stimuli with the index finger of the non-dominant hand. Instructions were given to keep both index fingers on the corresponding keys for the entire session. For each condition, a practice session with 10 stimuli was given, in which participants' errors were corrected.

Both latency and accuracy of response were recorded by SuperLab Pro 2.0 for each stimulus. Latencies under 150 ms were considered as invalid trials, as they could be either technical failures or anticipations. Only latencies for valid or correct trials were analyzed. For each condition both median response latency and total number of recognition errors were computed.

General procedure

Participants were tested individually in a quiet room, located at the Division of Child Neurology and Psychiatry of Pisa University for children with DD or at their own school for control children. All the tests were administered in a single session. Each session started with the non-verbal intelligence tests, followed by the reading test and then by the experimental tasks. For each group, presentation sequence of the three experimental tasks was counterbalanced across participants according to a 3 × 3 Latin Square design. Likewise, for each experimental task the order of the two conditions (digits and colors) was counterbalanced across participants using a 2 × 2 Latin Square design.

DATA ANALYSIS

A first series of analyses compared the performances of control and DD subjects considered as one group on the RAN, DN and DR tests, separately for each condition (digits or colors).

Accuracy was very high for every task and condition, for both control and DD children. The mean percentages of errors are presented in **Table 3** for all three tasks according to condition (digits and colors) separately for control and DD subjects. Even in the DR tests where level of accuracy was slightly lower, percentage of errors was always below 5% and not statistically different between DD and control children ($F_{(1,62)} = 1.85$ for comparison on DR of digits and $F_{(1,62)} = 0.15$ for comparison on DR of colors, both *ns*). As a consequence, for each experimental task statistical comparisons were restricted to time measures. Mean total naming times in RAN tests and median response latencies in DN and DR tests were submitted to a one-way ANOVA with group (DD children, controls) as unrepeated factor. ANOVAs were carried out separately for digits and colors in each experimental task. In order to assess equality of variances between DD and control children the Levene's test was run for each comparison we made. In no case, variances differed significantly between groups (all $p > 0.05$).

For each comparison between DD and control groups effect size was also calculated by computing the Eta squared (η^2) value, which indicates the proportion of variance in the dependent variable explained by the independent variable (the reading group in our case).

As significant differences between the two groups on both RAN and DN tests emerged, an ANCOVA on mean RAN times using DN median latencies as covariates was carried out in order to determine the possible modulating role of the performance on the DN tests over the RAN tests. Two separate ANCOVAs were run for digit and color conditions.

In a second series of analyses the same statistical techniques were used to compare, separately, both LD- and noLD-DD children with their own control subgroups. As in the whole DD sample, percentages of errors (see **Table 3**) were very low for all three experimental tasks in both DD subgroups; it was slightly higher for the DR tasks, although always under 6% for both groups and with no significant differences from controls for both LD-DD group ($F_{(1,34)} = 0.41$ and $F_{(1,30)} = 1.24$ for digits and colors respectively, both *ns*) and noLD-DD group ($F_{(1,26)} = 1.57$ and $F_{(1,26)} = 2.97$ for digits and colors respectively, both *ns*). As a consequence, accuracy was not further examined. Time measures of each experimental task were submitted to two separate one-way ANOVAs with group (either LD- or noLD-DD *vs.* respective controls) as unrepeated factor. When the Levene's test for equality of variances between groups was applied, for only 1 out of 12 comparisons (the one on RAN of digits for LD-DD *vs.* control children) variances significantly differed between groups ($F = 5.19$, $p < 0.05$); in this case, violation of equality of variances was corrected using the Welch-Satterthwaite method. Effects sizes using η^2 value were also computed for the different comparisons between LD and noLD DD children and respective controls.

Again, as both RAN and DN time measures were significantly different in most cases, when necessary mean RAN times were submitted to ANCOVAs with group (either LD- or noLD-DD children *vs.* respective controls) as unrepeated factor and DN median latencies as covariates, separately for the digit and color condition, to determine if differences on RAN performance survived when DN performances were partialled out.

Finally, one-way ANOVAs were carried out to directly compare LD- and noLD-DD children on the three experimental tasks. Effects sizes using η^2 were calculated for each comparison.

For all statistical analyses significance level was set at $p < 0.05$.

RESULTS

WHOLE DD SAMPLE

Means (and SDs) for the three experimental tasks of both the whole DD sample and control group are reported in **Table 4** according to type of stimulus.

ANOVA on RAN times revealed a significant group effect, for both digits ($F_{(1,62)} = 27.95$, $p < 0.001$) and colors ($F_{(1,62)} = 8.96$, $p < 0.01$): DD children were significantly slower than controls in both RAN of digits and colors. Effect size was very large for digits ($\eta^2 = 0.31$, that is 31% of RAN times for digits explained by reading group) and medium-high for colors ($\eta^2 = 0.13$).

A significant group effect emerged also for DN response latencies, regardless of type of stimulus: latencies to respond were higher in DD group than in control group, for both digits ($F_{(1,62)} = 29.16$, $p < 0.001$) and colors ($F_{(1,62)} = 23.22$, $p < 0.001$). For both types of stimulus effect size was very large ($\eta^2 = 0.32$ and $\eta^2 = 0.27$ for digits and colors respectively).

Table 3 | Mean percentages of errors and SDs (in brackets) of the whole DD sample, of the sub-groups of DD participants with (LD) and without (noLD) a history of language delay and the respective control groups on the three experimental tasks as a function of type of stimulus (digits and colors).

	DD subjects (whole sample, $n = 32$)	Controls (whole sample, $n = 32$)	LD-DD subjects ($n = 18$)	Controls for the LD-DD subjects ($n = 18$)	noLD-DD subjects ($n = 14$)	Controls for the noLD-DD subjects ($n = 14$)
RAN of digits	1.69 (3.67)	0.19 (0.59)	1.00 (2.84)	0.34 (0.76)	2.58 (4.46)	0.00 (0.00)
RAN of colors	2.81 (4.06)	1.37 (2.06)	3.10 (5.00)	0.66 (1.68)	2.42 (2.50)	2.28 (2.20)
DN of digits	0.50 (1.61)	0.12 (0.71)	0.78 (2.08)	0.00 (0.00)	0.14 (0.54)	0.28 (1.06)
DN of colors	1.75 (2.58)	0.50 (1.13)	2.34 (3.16)	0.34 (0.76)	1.00 (1.30)	0.72 (1.48)
DR of digits	4.00 (2.69)	3.06 (2.83)	3.78 (2.36)	3.22 (2.84)	4.28 (3.12)	2.86 (2.90)
DR of colors	4.69 (3.58)	4.31 (4.04)	3.88 (2.70)	5.22 (4.30)	5.72 (4.36)	3.14 (3.48)

Table 4 | Means and SDs (in brackets) of whole DD sample, of the sub-groups of DD participants with (LD) and without (noLD) a history of language delay and the respective control groups on the three experimental tasks as a function of type of stimulus (digits and colors).

	DD subjects (whole sample, *n* = 32)	Controls (whole sample, *n* = 32)	LD-DD subjects (*n* = 18)	Controls for the LD-DD subjects (*n* = 18)	noLD-DD subjects (*n* = 14)	Controls for the noLD-DD subjects (*n* = 14)
RAN of digits (s)	32.72 (8.79)	22.50 (6.50)	33.39 (7.92)	21.39 (4.53)	31.86 (10.04)	23.93 (8.38)
RAN of colors (s)	43.69 (12.35)	35.44 (9.52)	46.00 (12.94)	34.44 (9.10)	40.71 (11.30)	36.71 (10.23)
DN of digits (ms)	686.5 (120.3)	544.2 (88.2)	713.7 (103.9)	529.2 (83.1)	651.5 (134.3)	563.4 (93.8)
DN of colors (ms)	804.6 (141.2)	650.0 (113.9)	818.5 (143.9)	627.4 (123.2)	786.6 (140.9)	679.1 (97.3)
DR of digits (ms)	452.5 (136.1)	420.5 (124.9)	448.7 (118.0)	403.4 (98.9)	457.4 (161.1)	442.5 (153.2)
DR of colors (ms)	449.9 (111.8)	432.9 (99.3)	443.9 (106.4)	407.2 (72.9)	457.7 (121.9)	466.0 (120.2)

On the contrary, no statistical difference resulted in DR response latencies between DD subjects and normal readers. This was true for both digits ($F_{(1,62)}$ = 0.96, *ns*) and colors ($F_{(1,62)}$ = 0.41, *ns*). Effect size was very small for both types of stimuli ($\eta^2 = 0.01$ in both conditions). It should be noted that DD and control participants did not differ also for number of errors on DR tasks (see above Section on Data Analyses); then a speed-accuracy trade-off on these tasks in the DD sample is to be excluded.

Results of ANCOVA on RAN times using DN response latencies as covariates gave different results for the two types of stimulus. When DN response latencies were partialled out, the group effect on RAN times remained statistically significant for digits ($F_{(1,62)} = 6.81$, $p = 0.01$) but not for colors ($F_{(1,62)} = 0.26$, *ns*), with effect size medium for the former ($\eta^2 = 0.10$) and negligible for the latter ($\eta^2 = 0.00$).

LD-DD SAMPLE

Table 4 shows means and SDs for all experimental tasks of both LD-DD children and respective controls according to type of stimulus.

LD-DD participants and their controls differed significantly on RAN speed for both digits ($F_{(1,34)} = 31.14$, $p < 0.001$) and colors ($F_{(1,34)} = 9.60$, $p < 0.01$) with large effect sizes of the group factor for both types of stimulus ($\eta^2 = 0.48$ and $\eta^2 = 0.22$ for digits and colors, respectively).

Significant differences between the groups were also evident on the DN response latencies, regardless of type of stimulus: mean response latencies in DN tasks were higher in LD-DD children than in typically developing readers for both digits ($F_{(1,34)}$ = 34.60, $p < 0.001$) and colors ($F_{(1,34)} = 18.32$, $p < 0.001$). In both conditions effect sizes were very large ($\eta^2 = 0.50$ and $\eta^2 = 0.35$ for digits and colors, respectively).

By contrast, no significant group effect was evident on DR response latencies. This applied to both digit ($F_{(1,34)}$ = 1.56, *ns*) and color condition ($F_{(1,34)}$ = 1.44, *ns*). Effect size was small for both types of stimuli ($\eta^2 = 0.04$ for both digits and colors). As already reported, also accuracy level did not differ between LD-DD children and their controls on DR tasks.

When the ANCOVA was performed on RAN times with DN latencies as covariates, a significant group effect was still evident in the digit condition ($F_{(1,34)} = 9.06$, $p < 0.01$), with effect size remaining large ($\eta^2 = 0.21$), but not in the color condition ($F_{(1,34)}$=1.77, *ns*) for which the effect size of group was small ($\eta^2 = 0.05$).

noLD-DD SAMPLE

Mean (and SDs) for the three experimental tasks of both noLD-DD participants and respective control group are reported in **Table 4** according to type of stimulus.

As for RAN times, a significant group effect was evident only in the digit condition ($F_{(1,26)} = 5.15$, $p < 0.05$): the noLD-DD group performed more slowly than control average readers on RAN of digits. Effect size for the group factor was large ($\eta^2 = 0.16$). RAN times for colors were not significantly different between the two groups ($F_{(1,26)}$ = 0.96, *ns*), the effect size being small ($\eta^2 = 0.04$).

ANOVA on DN response latencies showed significant differences between groups for both digits ($F_{(1,26)} = 4.06$, $p = 0.05$) and colors ($F_{(1,26)} = 5.52$, $p < 0.05$): noLD-DD children were slower than control children with both types of stimulus. Effect sizes were medium-high and large for digits ($\eta^2 = 0.13$) and colors ($\eta^2 = 0.17$), respectively.

Finally, DR latencies did not differ significantly between noLD-DD and controls, for both digits ($F_{(1,26)}$ = 0.06, *ns*) and colors ($F_{(1,26)}$ = 0.03, *ns*), with no appreciable effect size of group in both conditions ($\eta^2 = 0.00$ for both digits and colors). No difference emerged also for accuracy level (see Section on Data Analyses), ruling out the possibility of a speed-accuracy trade-off in the noLD-DD group.

When differences on DN latencies were partialled out by ANCOVA, differences between the two groups on RAN times for digits disappeared ($F_{(1,26)}$ = 1.47, *ns*), with a small effect size of group ($\eta^2 = 0.05$).

LD-DD VS. noLD-DD SAMPLE

No significant difference emerged between LD-DD and noLD-DD children, regardless of the experimental task and the type of stimulus ($F_{(1,30)} = 0.23$ and $F_{(1,30)} = 1.46$ for RAN of digits and colors respectively, $F_{(1,30)} = 2.18$ and $F_{(1,30)} = 0.39$ for DN of digits and colors respectively, $F_{(1,30)} = 0.03$ and $F_{(1,30)} = 0.12$ for DR of digits and colors, respectively).

Effect size of the group was small or absent for all comparisons, with the only exception of DN of digits in which a medium effect size was evident ($\eta^2 = 0.07$).

DISCUSSION

Children with DD were significantly slower than controls on serial RAN task, in both the digit and the color condition. By contrast, accuracy was quite high in both groups. These results are entirely consistent with those from a wide literature documenting deficient RAN speed in subjects with DD in spite of a very low incidence of naming errors (Wolf and Bowers, 1999; Kirby et al., 2010).

DD participants also showed significantly longer latencies than controls on naming items presented in a discrete form. Slowness of DD children on the DN task was evident for both digits and colors and emerged as a robust group effect in both the conditions. This finding confirms a substantial amount of evidence showing slowness of children with DD in naming familiar items even under the simple condition in which items are singularly presented (Bowers and Swanson, 1991; Fawcett and Nicolson, 1994; Chiappe et al., 2002; Jones et al., 2009; Zoccolotti et al., 2013). The typical interpretation offered for this result is in terms of impaired lexical access and/or retrieval from long-term memory (Walsh et al., 1988; Bowers and Swanson, 1991; Pennington et al., 2001). Such interpretation would also be consistent with results from another line of research documenting impaired performance of children with DD on both confrontation naming and naming to definition tasks (for a review see Snowling, 2000).

If a word-retrieval deficit is the reason for delayed vocal reaction times of children with DD on DN tasks, the same deficit could be easily identified as one factor underlying RAN difficulties of these subjects as serial RAN tasks necessarily involve single items naming. Indeed, this is one of the prominent explanations of such difficulties (Torgesen et al., 1997; Pennington et al., 2001; Chiappe et al., 2002). By this reasoning, RAN speed relates to reading performance as the former taps the same efficiency of accessing and retrieving phonological information the latter requires for accurately and effortlessly mapping orthography onto phonology at both lexical and sub-lexical level.

However, naming of single items not only requires lexical access, but also visual recognition of the item to be named. Thus, interpretation of impaired performance of children with DD on both DN and (at least partially) RAN tasks in terms of a name-retrieval deficit remains speculative, although plausible, until a deficit of visual processing on DN performance can not be excluded.

To this aim, in the present study we introduced a motor choice-reaction time task using the same singularly presented stimuli as in the DN task, where participants had to discriminate between a target stimulus and four distracters. Results on this task did not discriminate between children with DD and typical reader controls; response latencies in our DR task were almost the same in the two groups, regardless of type of stimulus. No statistical difference emerged also for level of response accuracy, so leaving out a speed-accuracy trade-off possibility in the performance of participants with DD. Then, our results do not support the hypothesis that some early visual deficit in single item recognition subtends deficient performance of DD subjects on DN tasks and consequently their reduced speed also on RAN tasks. To the best of our knowledge this is the first time a control on visual-perceptual factors underlying performance on DN task is made using the same stimulus materials as in such task.

Results discussed up to now support the role of a phonological-retrieval deficit in explaining slowed response latencies in the DN tasks, and possibly also reduced speed in RAN tasks, in subjects with DD. However results in our DD sample indicate that other mechanisms underpinning RAN performance contribute in mediating its relationship with reading. In fact, when influence of DN tasks latencies on RAN speed was controlled by covariance analysis, differences between DD and normal readers on RAN survived remaining robust for the digit condition, while disappearing for the colors condition. The unique contribution of serial RAN tasks to reading performance over that played by discrete-trial format of naming tasks is well documented in the literature (Bowers and Swanson, 1991; Jones et al., 2009; Logan et al., 2011; Georgiou et al., 2013; Zoccolotti et al., 2013).

Several aspects of serial RAN tasks might account for the greater differentiation of reader groups by this measure compared to that by discrete trial measures. One of these aspects refers to oculomotor requirements for efficient left-to-right visual scanning of stimuli presented in a matrix format, very similar to those necessary for efficient reading of texts. Another putative mechanism has been identified in attentional processes pertinent to the managing of serial information, especially those underlying parafoveal processing of upcoming items, consequent saccadic preparation, eye-movement execution and subsequent articulating of speech output. In a recent study where total response times (from the stimulus onset to the end of its pronunciation) were recorded, Zoccolotti et al. (2013) found that typical readers were significantly faster reading words arranged in rows than singly displayed words, at odds with participants with DD who had a disadvantage in reading multiple stimuli for long words. This last result is in line with other evidence documenting deficient parafoveal processing in subjects with DD (Chace et al., 2005; Jones et al., 2009, 2013). Interpretations of RAN deficits in terms of managing serial information are also reminiscent of another longstanding theory of RAN underpinnings proposed by Wolf, Bowers and colleagues (Bowers, 1995; Wolf and Bowers, 1999; Wolf et al., 2000). According to Bowers (1995) "*...although rapide/precise timing mechanisms may underpin performance on all the naming speed measures, the serial format for naming speed requires additional coordination of processes used to extract information from serial visual arrays*" (p. 211–212), thus making RAN tasks more similar to reading than DN naming tasks.

In our study, the unique contribution of serial RAN over that of DN in discriminating between DD and average readers was evident for the digits, but not for the colors, condition. Indeed, this pattern of results seems consistent with the interpretations which emphasize the role of processes pertaining to management and integration of multiple sub-processes in mediating RAN-reading relationship. A stronger predictive role of RAN of alphanumeric stimuli than non-alphanumeric stimuli over reading is not uncommon in the RAN literature (Walsh et al., 1988; McBride-Chang, 1996; Schatschneider et al., 2004). The usual explanation is that digits (like letters) constitute highly constrained categories that can be processed more "automatically" with practice than colors and figures (Wolf and Bowers, 1999). In turn, faster naming for alphanumeric than non-alphanumeric stimuli would let the integration of multiple sub-components involved in serial RAN to occur more efficiently with the former (Protopapas et al., 2013), also making RAN of letters and digits a closer approximation to fluent reading.

In the present study we treated RAN times as a unitary measure, not distinguishing between times to articulate each item and duration of pauses between subsequent articulations. As a consequence, another possible explanation for the unique contribution of serial RAN tasks to reading performance over that played by discrete-trial format might be that a lower articulation rate of participants with DD with respect to controls would selectively lengthen RAN times in the former without affecting response latencies in the DN tasks. However, various considerations make this hypothesis unlikely. First, although exceptions exist (e.g., Georgiou et al., 2008), recent investigations of the RAN components have mostly agreed that inter-item pauses and not articulation times are significantly related to reading (Neuhaus et al., 2001; Georgiou et al., 2006; Araújo et al., 2011b). Second, in a recent study where vocal reaction times and pronunciation times during a single-item reading task were measured, longer pronunciation times of DD with respect to control readers were found only for non-words and words exceeding six letters (Martelli et al., 2014). However, in our study words to be articulated for the naming tasks were all very high frequency words and shorter than six letters. Moreover, in a previous study on Italian second graders (unselected for reading ability) the association between articulation rate and reading speed of a text (which includes pronunciation times) was virtually absent; likewise, the contribution of RAN total times to reading speed of text remained significant and substantially unchanged after controlling for articulation rate (Gasperini et al., 2008).

The pattern of results described above refers to the whole sample of children with DD. Did this pattern hold when analyses were run separately on the two subgroups with (LD) or without (noLD) a history of previous LD? In the last years a number of studies has provided evidence for a partially different behavioral and neurocognitive profile between LD- and noLD-DD children (Brizzolara et al., 2006; Scuccimarra et al., 2008; Chilosi et al., 2009; Pecini et al., 2011). Consistently with such evidence, we expected a concurrent language weakness in the former group, which might have a particularly relevant impact on the DN performance of DD children with LD. Indeed, this is what we found. The LD-DD children scored significantly lower than the noLD-DD children in measures of phonological processing (PSTM), verbal semantic knowledge and written text comprehension, confirming our previous results. Moreover, although both DD groups were slower compared to typical readers on the DN task, naming single items proved to be more difficult for LD- than noLD-DD children, as indicated by the more marked effect size for in LD than in noLD participants DD (in the comparison with the control group) for both digits and colors. Indeed, a possible stronger lexical access deficit in the LD- than in noLD-DD group had been anticipated. However, such a deficit was not accounted for by a semantic retrieval impairment in the former group, in addition to a phonological retrieval deficit shared by both DD groups, as we had hypothesized. In fact, the DN deficit of the LD-DD children was not more evident for colors than for digits, as it would be expected if a semantic impairment would underlie the lexical access deficit of the LD-DD children. One possible explanation for the more marked lexical access difficulties of these subjects might well be only in terms of a phonological retrieval deficit, which would be more pronounced for the LD-DD children. Such an explanation would be consistent with data showing poorer phonological processing abilities in children with SLI than in children with DD without oral language problems (Kamhi and Catts, 1986; Tallal et al., 1997).

By contrast, both LD- and noLD-DD groups were indistinguishable from controls on the DR task, regardless of the type of stimulus, on both response latencies and accuracy.

Overall, these results indicate that children with DD have a discrete-item naming deficit which cannot be accounted for by a visual-perceptual impairment, but needs to be explained as a name-retrieval deficit. Such a deficit, is more marked in DD children with a previous LD and a concomitant verbal weakness.

Also other differences between LD- and noLD-DD children emerged in our study. A different pattern of results was in fact evident in the two groups when analyzing data of the RAN task. First, while for LD-DD children differences from controls were present regardless of the type of stimulus, for noLD-DD children impaired RAN speed occurred only for digits. Moreover, while a significant slowness of LD-DD children with respect to controls on RAN task survived for digits (but non for colors) after controlling for differences in DN response latencies, no significant difference was still evident on RAN of digits between noLD-DD and control readers when DN speed was controlled.

The absence of a "specific" serial RAN deficit for colors in both DD groups is consistent with the hypothesis of a general reduced role of processes pertaining to the managing of multiple activities in RAN of non-alphanumeric stimuli (Protopapas et al., 2013). However, a "non-specific" RAN deficit for colors was still evident in LD-DD children, possibly as a consequence of their marked name-retrieval deficit for this type of stimuli, which would "propagate" to the serial condition. The same would not occur in the noLD-DD group, who showed a much smaller deficit of lexical access for colors with respect to LD children, with the result that noLD-DD children did not differ significantly from controls on RAN of colors.

The difference between the two DD groups was however more relevant on RAN of digits, in which both samples were impaired, but only in the LD children significant slowness with respect to controls survived after controlling for differences in response latencies in the DN task. This finding seems indicative of a greater difficulty of LD- with respect to noLD-DD children in rapidly and precisely integrating different cognitive and linguistic processes underlying RAN performance with digits. On the basis of our data reasons for a different involvement of "synchronization" deficits in the two DD subtypes cannot be much more than speculative. It might be that the larger name-retrieval deficit of LD- than noLD-DD children is responsible for a greater impairment of precise/timing mechanisms in the former than in the latter. When lexical access severely taxes the processing capacity of the child, in fact, integrating such a process with other activities is also severely affected. However, also a specific deficit with a precise/timing mechanism and/or sequential processing *per se* might affect LD DD children, accounting for the unique contribution of serial RAN over the one by discrete naming in differentiating this group from controls.

It remains unclear why noLD-DD subjects showed a "non-specific" RAN deficit for digits, but not for colors; their lexical access deficit was in fact very similar for the two types of stimulus. An explanation for such difference in terms of a reduced efficiency of noLD-DD children in simultaneously performing multiple activities, which would mainly occur for digits rather than colors, seems unlikely; not only a statistically significant difference of these subjects from controls on RAN of digits was not more evident once differences on DN of the same material was controlled for, but the group effect size *per se* (as resulted from the covariance analysis) was small.

Results of our study were obtained on groups of subjects widely ranging in school grade (from second to eighth). Such heterogeneity might raise some doubts on the interpretation of results concerning cognitive underpinnings of RAN speed deficit in children with DD. However, when we compared absolute speed of reading (syllables/s in reading of lists of single words) between the subgroup of Primary school children (from second to fifth grade) and the subgroup of Secondary school children (from sixth to eighth grade) no significant difference emerged. The absolute reading speed level of both subgroups was comparable with that of Italian second grade typical readers, as provided by the norms of the standardized reading test employed (Sartori et al., 2007). At such level, Italian normal readers are in a stage in which they are shifting from sub-lexical (serial) to lexical (holistic) written word processing (Zoccolotti et al., 2005; Orsolini et al., 2006) and, consequently, the need for a rapid access to lexical phonology becomes crucial. Indeed, according to some authors, the characteristic reading speed deficit of Italian children with DD would mainly reflect a problem in acquiring efficient use of a lexical strategy in reading (Zoccolotti et al., 1999; Orsolini et al., 2009). However, recently Zoccolotti et al. (2013) highlighted a further *locus* for the impaired reading fluency of Italian DD in a reduced advantage with multiple over single words in reading of these subjects with respect to average readers. Both of these impairments (lexical-reading and simultaneous processing of multiple items) are consistent with deficits in lexical access and in managing the sequential information in serial RAN for DD children, as suggested by our results.

One limitation of the present study is that evidence of LD in the pre-school years is retrospective, but this was unavoidable as the children with DD were referred to us for assessment of academic achievements at school age. Such limitation might raise some doubts as to the reliability of classification of participants with DD according to whether or not they had a history of previous LD. However, we also found *concomitant* weaker verbal abilities of the LD- than the noLD-DD group, not limited to deficient oral phonological processing but also encompassing impaired verbal semantic knowledge and text reading comprehension, despite absence of differences in reading decoding abilities.

Another weakness of our study is the relatively small size of each group with DD, when DD participants were subdivided according to the presence or absence of a previous LD. In these conditions significant, but not strong enough, effects of both reading group and type of stimulus on performance in the different experimental tasks might not emerge because of low statistical power. Then, future studies should address issue of cognitive deficits underpinning RAN impaired performance of different categories of DD subjects using larger sample sizes for each subgroup. It should be noted, however, that in our study analyses of the group effect size on the experimental measures turned out to be small at best for those comparisons which were not statistically significant. Then, a substantial change of our results with larger samples does not seem very likely.

Despite the above limitations, we think our study offers a contribution to a better understanding of the reasons why RAN speed discriminates between DD and typical readers, as well as in pointing out possible different cognitive mechanisms at the basis of RAN impairment in different subgroups of children with DD. Recently, there has been a growing interest for potential differences in cognitive processes underpinning RAN performance in different populations of subjects. However, up to now this interest has mainly concentrated on identifying possible developmental differences in the pattern of interrelations among different naming paradigms and/or measures and reading in samples of mostly typically developing readers in different school grades (e.g., Georgiou et al., 2006; de Jong and Messbauer, 2011; Protopapas et al., 2013). In the present study we expanded such aim by comparing different subtypes of children with DD, classified according to whether or not they had a history of previous language delay, which represent two partially different neurocognitive phenotypes. Results from this comparison indicate that this is a worth pursuing goal and a potentially fruitful area of research, as superficially similar RAN impairments in different populations of subjects with DD may obscure at least partially different underlying cognitive deficits.

AUTHORS' CONTRIBUTION

Filippo Gasperini, Child Neuropsychologist, PhD, contributed to the design of the work, acquisition, analysis, and interpretation of the data, to writing the paper and final approval of the version to be published.

Daniela Brizzolara, Child Neuropsychologist, contributed to the design of the work, to interpretation of the data and to writing the paper, revising the paper critically for intellectual content and final approval of the version to be published.

Paola Cristofani, Child Psychologist, contributed to acquisition and analysis of experimental data and final approval of the version to be published.

Claudia Casalini, Child Psychologist, contributed to acquisition of clinical data, revising the final manuscript and final approval of the version to be published.

Anna Maria Chilosi MD, PhD, Specialist in Child Neurology and Psychiatry, contributed to acquisition of anamnestic data of all children with DD, to writing, revising the paper critically for intellectual content and final approval of the version to be published.

ACKNOWLEDGMENTS

We would like to thank Irene Fioretti for collecting some of the cognitive, reading and experimental data on typically developing readers of the study at their schools.

We are also grateful to Claudia Brancati, who helped in creating digital stimulus materials for experimental tasks of the study.

REFERENCES

Araújo, S., Faísca, L., Bramão, I., Inácio, F., Petersson, K. M., and Reis, A. (2011a). Object naming in dyslexic children: more than a phonological deficit. *J. Gen. Psychol.* 138, 215–228. doi: 10.1080/00221309.2011.582525

Araújo, S., Inácio, F., Francisco, A., Faísca, L., Petersson, K. M., and Reis, A. (2011b). Component processes subserving rapid automatized naming in dyslexic and non-dyslexic readers. *Dyslexia* 17, 242–255. doi: 10.1002/dys.433

Befi-Lopes, D. M., Pereira, A. C., and Bento, A. C. (2010). Phonological representation of children with Specific Language Impairment (SLI). *Pro Fono* 22, 305–310.

Bosse, M. L., Tainturier, M. J., and Valdois, S. (2007). Developmental dyslexia: the visual attention span deficit hypothesis. *Cognition* 104, 198–230. doi: 10.1016/j.cognition.2006.05.009

Bowers, P. G. (1995). Tracing symbol naming speed's unique contributions to reading disabilities over time. *Read. Writ.* 7, 189–216. doi: 10.1007/bf01027185

Bowers, P. G., and Swanson, L. B. (1991). Naming speed deficits in reading disability: multiple measures of a singular process. *J. Exp. Child Psychol.* 51, 195–219. doi: 10.1016/0022-0965(91)90032-n

Brizzolara, D., Chilosi, A. M., Cipriani, P., Di Filippo, G., Gasperini, F., Mazzotti, S., et al. (2006). Do phonologic and rapid automatized naming deficits differentially affect dyslexic children with and without a history of language delay? A study of Italian dyslexic children. *Cogn. Behav. Neurol.* 19, 141–149. doi: 10.1097/01.wnn.0000213902.59827.19

Cedrus Corporation. (2002). *Super Lab Pro 2.0 Package.* San Pedro California.

Chace, K. H., Rayner, K., and Well, A. D. (2005). Eye movements and phonological parafoveal preview: effects of reading. *Can. J. Exp. Psychol.* 59, 209–217. doi: 10.1037/h0087476

Chiappe, P., Stringer, R., Siegel, L. S., and Stanovich, K. E. (2002). Why the timing deficits hypothesis does not explain reading disability in adults. *Read. Writ.* 15, 73–107. doi: 10.1023/A:1013868304361

Chilosi, A. M., Brizzolara, D., Lami, L., Pizzoli, C., Gasperini, F., Pecini, C., et al. (2009). Reading and spelling disabilities in children with and without a history of early language delay: a neuropsychological and linguistic study. *Child Neuropsychol.* 15, 582–604. doi: 10.1080/09297040902927614

Coady, J. A. (2013). Rapid naming by children with and without specific language impairment. *J. Speech Lang. Hear. Res.* 56, 604–617. doi: 10.1044/1092-4388(2012/10-0144)

Cornoldi, C., and Colpo, G. (1995). *Nuove Prove MT per la scuola Media Inferiore.* Firenze: OS.

Cornoldi, C., and Colpo, G. (1998). *Prove di lettura MT per la scuola elementare - 2.* Firenze: O.S.

de Jong, P. F. (2011). What discrete and serial rapid automatized naming (RAN) can reveal about reading. *Sci. Stud. Read.* 15, 314–337. doi: 10.1080/10888438.2010.485624

de Jong, P. F., and Messbauer, V. C. (2011). Orthographic context and the acquisition of orthographic knowledge in normal and dyslexic readers. *Dyslexia* 17, 107–122. doi: 10.1002/dys.427

de Jong, P. F., and van der Leij, A. (1999). Specific contributions of phonological abilities to early reading acquisition: results from a Dutch latent variable longitudinal study. *J. Educ. Psychol.* 91, 450–476. doi: 10.1037//0022-0663.91.3.450

de Jong, P. F., and van der Leij, A. (2003). Developmental changes in the manifestation of a phonological deficit in dyslexic children learning to read a regular orthography. *J. Educ. Psychol.* 95, 22–40. doi: 10.1037/0022-0663.95.1.22

Di Filippo, G., Brizzolara, D., Chilosi, A., De Luca, M., Judica, A., Pecini, C., et al. (2005). Rapid naming, not cancellation speed or articulation rate, predicts reading in an orthographically regular language (Italian). *Child Neuropsychol.* 11, 349–361. doi: 10.1080/09297040490916947

Di Filippo, G., Brizzolara, D., Chilosi, A. M., De Luca, M., Judica, A., Pecini, C., et al. (2006). Naming speed and visual search deficits in readers with disabilities: evidence from an orthographically regular language (Italian). *Dev. Neuropsychol.* 30, 885–904. doi: 10.1207/s15326942dn3003_7

Eckert, M. (2004). Neuroanatomical markers for dyslexia: a review of dyslexia structural imaging studies. *Neuroscientist* 10, 362–371. doi: 10.1177/1073858404263596

Fawcett, A., and Nicolson, R. (1994). Naming speed in children with dyslexia. *J. Learn. Disabil.* 27, 641–646. doi: 10.1177/002221949402701004

Ferretti, G., Brizzolara, D., and Casalini, C. (2003). Phonological working-memory test. Computerized test produced and standardized within the research project "Neuropsicologia e Neurolinguistica" financed by Italian Ministry of Health, IRCCS Stella Maris, Pisa.

Franceschini, S., Gori, S., Ruffino, M., Pedrolli, K., and Facoetti, A. (2012). A causal link between visual spatial attention and reading acquisition. *Curr. Biol.* 22, 814–819. doi: 10.1016/j.cub.2012.03.013

Gasperini, F., Brizzolara, D., and Fatighenti, A. (2008). "Denominazione rapida seriale (RAN) e denominazione rapida di stimoli singoli in bambini non selezionati per abilità di lettura: un contributo all'identificazione dei fattori sottostanti l'associazione tra RAN e lettura," in Paper presented at *17th annual meeting of the AIRIPA (Associazione Italiana per la Ricerca e l'Intervento nella Psicopatologia dell'Apprendimento).* Piacenza, Italy.

Georgiou, G. K., Parrila, R., and Kirby, J. (2006). Rapid naming speed components and early reading acquisition. *Sci. Stud. Read.* 10, 199–220. doi: 10.1207/s1532799xssr1002_4

Georgiou, G. K., Parrila, R., and Liao, C. H. (2008). Rapid naming speed and reading across languages that vary in orthographic consistency. *Read. Writ.* 21, 885–903. doi: 10.1007/s11145-007-9096-4

Georgiou, G. K., Parrila, R., Cui, Y., and Papadopoulos, T. C. (2013). Why is rapid automatized naming related to reading? *J. Exp. Child Psychol.* 115, 218–225. doi: 10.1016/j.jecp.2012.10.015

Hanly, S., and Vanderberg, B. (2010). Tip-of-the-tongue and word retrieval deficits in dyslexia. *J. Learn. Disabil.* 43, 15–23. doi: 10.1177/0022219409338744

Hari, R., and Renvall, H. (2001). Impaired processing of rapid stimulus sequences in dyslexia. *Trends Cogn. Sci.* 5, 525–532. doi: 10.1016/s1364-6613(00)01801-5

Hendriks, A. W. C. J., and Kolk, H. H. J. (1997). Strategic control in developmental dyslexia. *Cogn. Neuropsychol.* 14, 321–366. doi: 10.1080/026432997381510

Heurley, L. P., Brouillet, T., Chesnoy, G., and Brouillet, D. (2013). Color perception involves color representations firstly at a semantic level and then at a lexical level. *Cogn. Process.* 14, 19–29. doi: 10.1007/s10339-012-0527-z

Holopainen, L., Ahonen, T., and Lyytinen, H. (2001). Predicting delay in reading achievement in a highly transparent language. *J. Learn. Disabil.* 34, 401–413. doi: 10.1177/002221940103400502

Jednoróg, K., Gawron, N., Marchevka, A., Heim, S., and Grabovska, A. (2013). Cognitive subtypes of dyslexia are characterized by distinct patterns of grey matter volume. *Brain Struct. Funct.* 18. doi: 10.1007/s00429-013-0595-6. [Epub ahead of print].

Jones, M. W., Ashby, J., and Branigan, H. P. (2013). Dyslexia and fluency: parafoveal and foveal influences on rapid automatized naming. *J. Exp. Psychol. Hum. Percept. Perform.* 39, 554–567. doi: 10.1037/a0029710

Jones, M. W., Branigan, H. P., and Kelly, M. L. (2009). Dyslexic and nondyslexic reading fluency: rapid automatized naming and the importance of continuous lists. *Psychon. Bull. Rev.* 16, 567–572. doi: 10.3758/pbr.16.3.567

Kail, R., and Leonard, L. B. (1986). Word-finding abilities in language-impaired children. *ASHA Monogr.* 25, 1–39.

Kamhi, A. G., and Catts, H. W. (1986). Toward an understanding of developmental language and reading disorders. *J. Speech. Hear. Disord.* 51, 337–347. doi: 10.1044/jshd.5104.337

Kirby, J. R., Geier, B. K., and Deacon, S. H. (2009). "Predictors of reading: phonological awareness, naming speed, orthographic processing and morphological awareness," Paper presented at the *16th Annual Meeting of the Society for the Scientific Study of Reading, Boston.*

Kirby, J., Georgiou, G., Martinussen, R., and Parrila, R. (2010). Naming speed and reading: from prediction to instruction. *Read. Res. Q.* 45, 341–362. doi: 10.1598/rrq.45.3.4

Landerl, K. (2001). Word recognition deficits in German: more evidence from a representative sample. *Dyslexia* 7, 183–196. doi: 10.1002/dys.199

Levy, B. A., and Hinchley, J. (1990). "Individual and developmental differences in the acquisition of reading skills," in *Reading and its Development: Component Skills Approaches*, eds T. H. Carr and B. A. Levy (New York: Academic Press), 81–128.

Logan, J. A. R., Schatschneider, C., and Wagner, R. K. (2011). Rapid serial naming and reading ability: the role of lexical access. *Read. Writ.* 24, 1–25. doi: 10.1007/s11145-009-9199-1

Manis, F. R., Saidenberg, M. S., and Doi, L. M. (1999). See dick RAN: rapid naming and the longitudinal prediction of reading subskills in first and second graders. *Sci. Stud. Read.* 3, 129–157. doi: 10.1207/s1532799xssr0302_3

Martelli, M., De Luca, M., Lami, L., Pizzoli, C., Pontillo, M., Spinelli, D., et al. (2014). Bridging the gap between different measures of the reading speed deficit in developmental dyslexia. *Exp. Brain Res.* 232, 237–252. doi: 10.1007/s00221-013-3735-6

Martelli, M., Di Filippo, G., Spinelli, D., and Zoccolotti, P. (2009). Crowding, reading and developmental dyslexia. *J. Vis.* 9, 1–18. doi: 10.1167/9.4.14

McBride-Chang, C. (1996). Models of speech perception and phonological processing in reading. *Child Dev.* 67, 1836–1856. doi: 10.2307/1131735

Menghini, D., Finzi, A., Benassi, M., Bolzani, R., Facoetti, A., Giovagnoli, S., et al. (2010). Different underlying neurocognitive deficits in developmental dyslexia: a comparative study. *Neuropsychologia* 48, 863–872. doi: 10.1016/j.neuropsychologia.2009.11.003

Neuhaus, G. E., Foorman, B. R., Francis, D. J., and Carlson, C. D. (2001). Measures of information processing in rapid automatized naming (RAN) and their relation to reading. *J. Exp. Child Psychol.* 78, 359–373. doi: 10.1006/jecp.2000.2576

Neuhaus, G. E., and Swank, P. R. (2002). Understanding the relations between RAN letter subtest components and word reading in first-grade students. *J. Learn. Disabil.* 35, 158–174. doi: 10.1177/002221940203500206

Nicolson, R. I., Fawcett, A. J., and Dean, P. (2001). Developmental dyslexia: the cerebellar deficit hypothesis. *Trends Neurosci.* 24, 508–511. doi: 10.1016/s0166-2236(00)01896-8

Orsini, A., and Picone, L. (2006). *WISC-III. Contributo alla taratura italiana.* Firenze: O.S.

Orsolini, M., Fanari, R., Cerracchio, S., and Famiglietti, L. (2009). Phonological and lexical reading in Italian children with dyslexia. *Read. Writ.* 22, 933–954. doi: 10.1007/s11145-008-9134-x

Orsolini, M., Fanari, R., Tosi, V., De Nigris, B., and Carrieri, R. (2006). From phonological-recoding to lexical reading: a longitudinal study on reading development in Italian. *Lang. Cogn. Process.* 21, 576–607. doi: 10.1080/01690960500139355

Papadopoulos, T. C., Georgiou, G. K., and Kendeou, P. (2009). Investigating the double-deficit hypothesis in Greek: findings from a longitudinal study. *J. Learn. Disabil.* 42, 528–547. doi: 10.1177/0022219409338745

Parrila, R., Kirby, J. R., and Mc Quarrie, L. (2004). Articulation rate, naming speed, verbal short-term memory and phonological awareness: longitudinal predictors of early reading development. *Sci. Stud. Read.* 8, 3–26. doi: 10.1207/s1532799xssr0801_2

Pecini, C., Biagi, L., Brizzolara, D., Cipriani, P., Di Lieto, M. C., Guzzetta, A., et al. (2011). How many functional brains in developmental dyslexia? When the history of language delay makes the difference. *Cogn. Behav. Neurol.* 24, 85–92. doi: 10.1097/wnn.0b013e318222a4c2

Pennington, B. F., Cardoso-Martins, C., Green, P. A., and Lefly, D. L. (2001). Comparing the phonological and double deficit hypotheses for developmental dyslexia. *Read. Writ.* 14, 707–755. doi: 10.1023/A:1012239018038

Pernet, C., Valdois, S., Celsis, P., and Démonet, J. F. (2006). Lateral masking, levels of processing and stimulus category: a comparative study between normal and dyslexic readers. *Neuropsychologia* 44, 2374–2385. doi: 10.1016/j.neuropsychologia.2006.05.003

Plaza, M., and Cohen, H. (2003). The interaction between phonological processing, syntactic awareness and naming speed in the reading and spelling performance of first-grade children. *Brain Cogn.* 53, 287–292. doi: 10.1016/s0278-2626(03)00128-3

Protopapas, A., Altani, A., and Georgiou, G. K. (2013). Developmental of serial processing in reading and rapid naming. *J. Exp. Child Psychol.* 116, 914–929. doi: 10.1016/j.jecp.2013.08.004

Pruneti, C. A., Fenu, A., Freschi, G., Rota, S., Cocci, D., Marchionni, M., et al. (1996). Aggiornamento della standardizzazione italiana del test delle Matrici Progressive Colorate di Raven (CPM). *Boll. Psicol. Appl.* 217, 51–57.

Raven, J. C. (1984). *CPM. Coloured Progressive Matrices.* Firenze: O.S.

Sartori, G., Job, R., and Tressoldi, P. E. (2007). *DDE-2. Batteria per la valutazione della dislessia e della disortografia evolutiva.* 2nd Edn.. Firenze: O.S.

Schatschneider, C., Fletcher, J. M., Francis, D. J., Carlson, C. D., and Foorman, B. R. (2004). Kindergarten prediction of reading skills: a longitudinal comparative study. *J. Educ. Psychol.* 96, 265–282. doi: 10.1037/0022-0663.96.2.265

Scuccimarra, G., Cutolo, L., Fiorillo, P., Lembo, C., and Cossu, G. (2008). Is there a distinct form of developmental dyslexia in children with specific language impairment ? Findings from am orthographically regular language. *Cogn. Behav. Neurol.* 21, 221–226. doi: 10.1097/WNN.0b013e31818a5caf

Sereno, S. C., and Rayner, K. (2000). Spelling-sound regularity effects on eye-fixations in reading. *Percept. Psychophys.* 62, 402–409. doi: 10.3758/bf03205559

Snowling, M. J. (2000). *Dyslexia.* 2nd Edn. Oxford: Blackwell.

Stainthorp, R., Stuart, M., Powell, D., Quinlan, P., and Garwood, H. (2010). Visual processing deficits in children with slow RAN performance. *Sci. Stud. Read.* 14, 266–292. doi: 10.1080/10888431003724070

Stein, J. (2001). The magnocellular theory of developmental dyslexia. *Dyslexia* 7, 12–36. doi: 10.1002/dys.186

Swan, D., and Goswami, U. (1997). Picture naming deficits in developmental dyslexia: the phonological representations hypothesis. *Brain Lang.* 56, 334–353. doi: 10.1006/brln.1997.1855

Swanson, H. L., Trainin, G., Necoechea, D. M., and Hammill, D. D. (2003). Rapid naming, phonological awareness and reading: a meta-analysis of the correlational evidence. *Rev. Educ. Res.* 73, 407–440. doi: 10.3102/00346543073004407

Tallal, P., Allard, L., Miller, S., and Curtiss, S. (1997). "Academic outcomes of language impaired children," in *Dyslexia: Biology, Cognition and Intervention*, eds C. Hulme and M. Snowling (London: WhurrPress), 167–181.

Torgesen, J. K., Wagner, R. K., Rashotte, C. A., Burgess, S., and Hecht, S. (1997). Contributions of phonological awareness and rapid automatic naming ability to the growth of word-reading skills in second-to fifth-grade children. *Sci. Stud. Read.* 1, 161–195. doi: 10.1207/s1532799xssr0102_4

Vellutino, F. R., Fletcher, J. M., Snowling, M. J., and Scanlon, D. M. (2004). Specific reading disability (dyslexia): what have we learned in the past four decades? *J. Child Psychol. Psychiatry* 45, 2–40. doi: 10.1046/j.0021-9630.2003.00305.x

Wagner, R. K., Torgesen, J. K., Laughon, P. L., Simmons, K., and Rashotte, C. A. (1993). Development of young readers' phonological processing abilities. *J. Educ. Psychol.* 85, 83–103. doi: 10.1037/0022-0663.85.1.83

Walsh, D. J., Price, G. G., and Gillingham, M. G. (1988). The critical but transitory importance of letter naming. *Read. Res. Q.* 23, 108–122. doi: 10.2307/747907

Wechsler, D. (1991). WISC III, wechsler intelligence scale for children—Third Edition.

Wimmer, H. (1993). Characteristics of developmental dyslexia in a regular writing system. *Appl. Psycholinguist.* 14, 1–33. doi: 10.1017/s0142716400010122

Wimmer, H., and Schurz, M. (2010). Dislexia in regular orthographies: manifestation and causation. *Dyslexia* 16, 283–299. doi: 10.1002/dys.411

Wolf, M., and Bowers, P. G. (1999). The double-deficit hypothesis for the developmental dyslexias. *J. Educ. Psychol.* 91, 415–438. doi: 10.1037//0022-0663.91.3.415

Wolf, M., Bowers, P. G., and Biddle, K. (2000). Naming-speed processes, timing and reading: a conceptual review. *J. Learn. Disabil.* 33, 387–407. doi: 10.1177/002221940003300409

Wolf, M., and Obregon, M. (1992). Early naming deficits, developmental dyslexia and a specific deficit hypothesis. *Brain Lang.* 42, 219–247. doi: 10.1016/0093-934x(92)90099-z

Zoccolotti, P., De Luca, M., Di Pace, E., Gasperini, F., Judica, A., and Spinelli, D. (2005). Word length effect in early reading and in developmental dyslexia. *Brain Lang.* 93, 369–373. doi: 10.1016/j.bandl.2004.10.010

Zoccolotti, P., De Luca, M., Di Pace, E., Judica, A., Orlandi, M., and Spinelli, D. (1999). Markers of developmental surface dyslexia in a language (Italian) with high grapheme-phoneme correspondence. *Appl. Psycholinguist.* 20, 191–216. doi: 10.1017/s0142716499002027

Zoccolotti, P., De Luca, M., Lami, L., Pizzoli, C., Pontillo, M., and Spinelli, D. (2013). Multiple stimulus presentation yields larger deficits in children with developmental dyslexia: a study with reading and RAN-type tasks. *Child Neuropsychol.* 19, 639–647. doi: 10.1080/09297049.2012.718325

4

Impaired auditory sampling in dyslexia: further evidence from combined fMRI and EEG

Katia Lehongre[1], Benjamin Morillon[2], Anne-Lise Giraud[3] and Franck Ramus[4]*

[1] *Research Center of the Brain and Spine Institute (CRICM), Hôpital de la Pitié-Salpêtrière, Paris, France*
[2] *Department of Psychiatry, Columbia University Medical Center, New York, NY, USA*
[3] *Department of Neuroscience, University of Geneva, Geneva, Switzerland*
[4] *Laboratoire de Sciences Cognitives et Psycholinguistique, Ecole Normale Supérieure, EHESS, CNRS, Paris, France*

Correspondence:
Franck Ramus, Laboratoire de Sciences Cognitives et Psycholinguistique, Ecole Normale Supérieure, 29 rue d'Ulm, 75005 Paris, France
e-mail: franck.ramus@ens.fr

The aim of the present study was to explore auditory cortical oscillation properties in developmental dyslexia. We recorded cortical activity in 17 dyslexic participants and 15 matched controls using simultaneous EEG and fMRI during passive viewing of an audiovisual movie. We compared the distribution of brain oscillations in the delta, theta and gamma ranges over left and right auditory cortices. In controls, our results are consistent with the hypothesis that there is a dominance of gamma oscillations in the left hemisphere and a dominance of delta-theta oscillations in the right hemisphere. In dyslexics, we did not find such an interaction, but similar oscillations in both hemispheres. Thus, our results confirm that the primary cortical disruption in dyslexia lies in a lack of hemispheric specialization for gamma oscillations, which might disrupt the representation of or the access to phonemic units.

Keywords: dyslexia, auditory sampling, phonemic processing, gamma oscillation, theta oscillation, delta oscillation, EEG-fMRI

INTRODUCTION

Developmental dyslexia is a specific difficulty in the acquisition of reading skills that is not accounted for by mental age, visual acuity deficit or inadequate schooling (WHO, 2011). It is thought to affect between 3 and 7% of the population (Lindgren et al., 1985), although estimates vary widely depending on cut-off criteria on reading performance scales.

While there remains a great diversity of theoretical outlooks on dyslexia (Ramus and Ahissar, 2012), it is now widely agreed that the majority of dyslexic individuals share difficulties in one or several aspects of phonological processing, including paying attention to and mentally manipulating speech sounds (phonological awareness), storing phonological material for a few seconds (verbal short-term memory), and rapidly retrieving long-term phonological representations (Wagner and Torgesen, 1987; Vellutino et al., 2004). Debates persist on whether this phonological deficit (i) follows from an underlying primary auditory processing deficit (Tallal, 1980; Goswami et al., 2011), (ii) arises from a degradation of phonological representations or in difficulties accessing them (Ramus and Szenkovits, 2008), and (iii) is sufficient by itself to account for learning disability or merely a risk factor (Pennington, 2006).

At the anatomo-functional level, while the issue remains debated (Richlan et al., 2011), the vast majority of findings from functional and structural brain imaging and post-mortem dissection converge on a disruption of left perisylvian cortical networks, which are involved in speech processing and recruited for reading acquisition (Galaburda et al., 1985; Eckert, 2004; Richardson and Price, 2009; Linkersdorfer et al., 2012). Genetic variations associated with dyslexia further point to structural and functional variations in the perisylvian language network (Darki et al., 2012; Pinel et al., 2012; Giraud and Ramus, 2013).

A new theoretical framework for the cortical organization of speech processing sheds a new light on the neural basis of developmental dyslexia. According to "asymmetric sampling in time" (AST) theory (Poeppel, 2003), left and right auditory cortices show cortical oscillations at different preferred rates: low gamma (25–45 Hz) in the left hemisphere and delta-theta (1–7 Hz) in the right. Gamma and theta oscillations are assumed to play a role in the segmentation of the sound stream into units of the corresponding sizes, which may be optimal for the analysis of phonemes by the left auditory cortex and syllables and prosodic cues by the right one (around 25 and 200 ms, respectively). While this hypothesis has received empirical support from neuroimaging and neurophysiological studies (Giraud et al., 2007; Abrams et al., 2008; Telkemeyer et al., 2009; Morillon et al., 2010), its implications for developmental dyslexia are not so clear. On the one hand, Giraud and Poeppel (2012) have hypothesized that dyslexic individuals might not show the typical left-hemisphere specialization for the gamma rate, which would explain their specific difficulties with the processing of phonemic units. On the other hand, Goswami (2011) has hypothesized that dyslexic individuals might rather show atypical cortical oscillations in the theta

(4–7 Hz) or in the delta (1–4 Hz) frequency band, thereby leading to processing deficits at the syllable and more generally at the prosodic level, which are also proposed to be causally linked to reading disability (Goswami et al., 2010).

In a previous study, we used magnetoencephalography (MEG) to measure auditory steady-state responses (ASSRs) to an amplitude-modulated white noise in dyslexic and control individuals. We found the expected left dominance of ASSRs in the *planum temporale* in the gamma range (25–35 Hz) in controls, but not in dyslexic participants who displayed no or a reversed asymmetry (Lehongre et al., 2011). These results, that are supported by another study that also measured ASSRs [using electroencephalography (EEG)] and found group differences at 20 Hz in the left hemisphere (Poelmans et al., 2012), were consistent with the hypothesis of a left-hemisphere-based gamma oscillation disruption, but did not explicitly test the delta/theta alteration hypothezis. In the delta/theta range, one study found no group difference at 4 Hz using EEG-ASSR (Poelmans et al., 2012), and another one exploring MEG-ASSRs at 2, 4, 10 and 20 Hz found a right-hemisphere dominance at 2 Hz in controls but not in dyslexic participants and no further group difference at any other frequency (Hamalainen et al., 2012). Using more naturalistic speech stimuli, an EEG study found that poor readers, in contrast to good readers, did not present the natural dominance of the right hemisphere to follow the speech envelope. They presented a more bilateral pattern, but this was the case only when speech was compressed to 50% of its original duration (Abrams et al., 2009). Finally, anomalies in the alpha rhythm have also been found in children with dyslexia or with language impairments (Heim et al., 2011; Babiloni et al., 2012; Han et al., 2012).

In the context of these conflicting results, the goals of the present study were twofold: Firstly, to replicate and extend the results of our previous study, using more naturalistic stimuli and an entirely different methodology; secondly, to directly compare the predictions of the two main theories by testing cortical oscillations in the gamma, theta and delta ranges in auditory cortices. For this purpose, rather than using a simple amplitude-modulated noise, we exposed participants to an audiovisual documentary movie featuring more ecological conversational speech, thereby including the whole range of amplitude modulations relevant to language.

We used simultaneous EEG and functional magnetic resonance imaging (fMRI) to measure the activity of the auditory cortex at both high temporal (millisecond) and spatial (millimeter) resolution. Changes in Blood-oxygen-level-dependent (BOLD) are associated with changes in the spectral profile of neuronal activity (Rosa et al., 2010b), and EEG and fMRI do not capture exactly the same signals. Only a small fraction of the BOLD signal reflects synaptic activity involving pyramidal cells (Lee et al., 2010; Logothetis, 2010), which we hypothesize here to work as a sampling device. By combining delta, theta and low-gamma power variations and BOLD activity we expect to capture the part of the BOLD activity that is explained out by circuits involving pyramidal cells, which generate these rhythms. Furthermore, simultaneous EEG/fMRI recordings are well suited to study oscillations in continuous recordings with uncontrolled states as it has been demonstrated in several studies [see for review: (Herrmann and Debener, 2008; Rosa et al., 2010a; Laufs, 2012)].

MATERIALS AND METHODS

PARTICIPANTS

Thirty-two normal-hearing, French–native-speakers participated in a simultaneous EEG and fMRI experiment (with approval of the local ethics committee; biomedical protocol C08–39). Seventeen participants reported a history of reading disability, scored at or below the expected level for ninth graders in a standardized reading test, and at least 90 in non-verbal IQ. The remaining 15 participants were normal readers matching dyslexic participants with respect to age, gender, handedness, and non-verbal IQ, but scoring above the ninth grade reading level. Demographic and psychometric data, as well as the results of a larger battery (Soroli et al., 2010) of literacy and phonological tests are reported in **Table 1**.

BEHAVIORAL TEST BATTERY

Non-verbal intelligence was assessed in all participants using Raven's matrices (Raven et al., 1998). Their receptive vocabulary was assessed with the EVIP test (Dunn et al., 1993), a French adaptation of the Peabody picture vocabulary scale. They were included on the basis of performance on the Alouette test (Lefavrais, 1967), a meaningless text that assesses both reading accuracy and speed, yielding a composite measure of reading fluency. Orthographic skills were assessed using a computerized orthographic choice task, and a spelling-to-dictation test. Phonological tests: we used the WAIS digit span as a measure of verbal working memory (Wechsler, 2000). Phonological awareness was assessed using a computerized spoonerism task, in which participants heard pairs of words, and had to produce them swapping the initial phonemes. Finally, rapid automatized naming was assessed using the object and digit sheets from the PhAB (Frederickson et al., 1997) and two custom-made color sheets modeled on the object sheets, with five different colors repeated 10 times each, one replacing each object. The dependent variable is the total time taken to name all items on each sheet, irrespective of errors.

MRI ACQUISITION

Subjects were either asked to rest with closed eyes or to pay attention to an audiovisual movie (Morillon et al., 2010). The movie, a scientific documentary on an ecological topic, included three speakers (2 men). Data were acquired in three sessions with session 1: 10 min of rest; sessions 2 and 3: 10 min of movie followed by 11 min of rest. The scanner produced a constant auditory signal during data acquisition presumed not to interfere with our analyzes, given that its modulation frequencies are outside our frequencies of interest (See supplemental data p. 1, Morillon et al., 2010).

The three sessions yielded 1560 echoplanar fMRI image volumes (Tim-Trio; Siemens, 40 transverse slices, voxel size = $3 \times 3 \times 3$ mm; repetition time = 2 s; echo time = 50 ms; field of view = 192). A 7-min anatomical T1-weighted magnetization-prepared rapid acquisition gradient echo sequence (176 slices, field of view = 256, voxel size = $1 \times 1 \times 1$ mm) was acquired at the end of scanning.

Table 1 | Summary of behavioral tests.

	Controls (15 subjects)			Dyslexics (17 subjects)		
	n	Mean	sd	*n*	Mean	sd
Males	7			9		
Right handed	10			12		
Age	15	24.09	3.54	17	23.79	4.04
Non-verbal IQ	15	112.07	13.43	17	111.35	10.73
EVIP Vocabulary	15	123.07	2.94	15	120.67	5.26
Reading fluency (nb of correct words/min)***	15	196.16	36.98	17	113.53	24.70
Spelling (%)**	15	94.22	4.67	12	81.25	11.81
Orthographic choice accuracy (%)	14	95.07	5.47	15	89.60	9.82
RAN of objects (sec)**	15	61.80	10.23	17	78.37	17.85
RAN of digits (sec)***	15	31.87	6.56	17	44.78	12.34
RAN of colors (sec)**	15	54.33	9.15	17	71.21	18.80
Spoonerisms accuracy**	15	0.75	0.10	15	0.50	0.26
Digit span (%)***	15	10.73	1.58	17	7.35	2.85

As indicated by the number of participants, some values were missing for some tests.
*Sec: seconds; Stars indicate significant differences between controls and dyslexics (independent t-test, ** for $p < 0.01$, *** for $p < 0.001$, uncorrected).*

MRI PREPROCESSING

We used statistical parametric mapping (SPM8; Wellcome Department of Imaging Neuroscience, UK; www.fil.ion.ucl.ac.uk) for fMRI standard preprocessing, which first involved realignment of each subject's functional images and coregistration with structural images. Structural images were segmented, spatially normalized to Montreal Neurological Institute stereotactic space to 3 × 3 × 3 mm and finally spatially smoothed with a 10-mm full-width half-maximum isotropic Gaussian kernel to compensate for residual variability after spatial normalization.

EEG ACQUISITION

Continuous EEG data were recorded at 5 kHz from 62 scalp sites (Easycap electrode cap) using MR compatible amplifiers (BrainAmp MR and Brain Vision Recorder software; Brainproducts). Two additional electrodes (electro-oculograph, EOG and electrocardiograph, ECG) were placed under the right eye and on the collarbone. FCz was set as reference for the acquisition of all electrodes. Impedances were kept under 10 kΩ and EEG was time-locked with the scanner clock, which helps to have a very reproducible, more easily removed MRI artifact, thus resulting in higher EEG quality in the gamma band (Mandelkow et al., 2006).

EEG PREPROCESSING

Gradient and pulse artifacts were first detected and marked using in-house software (wiki.cenir.org/doku.php/datahandler). Detection was achieved by correlating the data with automatically (for gradient) or manually (for pulse) defined templates. We used the raw signal of channel FC2 for gradient artifacts, and the raw ECG signal filtered between 0.5 and 10 Hz for pulse artifacts. In a second step, artifacts were corrected using two software: FASST v111017 (www.montefiore.ulg.ac.be/~phillips/FASST.html) for gradient artifacts and EEGlab v.9 (sccn.ucsd.edu/eeglab) for pulse artifacts. In both cases we used the principal component analyses methods implemented in the software. Blinks and vertical eye movements were corrected using independent component analyses as described in EEGlab's tutorial. Data were subsequently down-sampled to 250 Hz and re-referenced to a common average reference. The original reference electrode was recalculated as FCz, generating a total of 63 cortical electrodes.

For each subject, periods with head movement artifacts were detected by visual inspection, for rejection purposes as described below. As our interest was in auditory activity, we focused the analyses described below on the temporal channels that best captured the activity of our ROIs, i.e., where we observed the highest correlation between EEG and BOLD: T7, T8, FT7, FT8, TP7, TP8, TP9, and TP10.

ANALYZES

Analyzes are reported for the movie condition, as our interest was to explore brain oscillation properties during natural speech processing. Analyzes were also conducted on rest sessions but did not yield any significant result, in particular no group effect.

TIME-FREQUENCY ANALYZIS

For each movie session, we performed time-frequency (TF) analyzes with a Morlet wavelets approach using Fieldtrip (Oostenveld et al., 2011) at each channel for frequencies from 1 to 48 Hz bands, with a frequency step of 1 Hz and a time step of 0.1 s. For each frequency and channel, the previously detected periods of movement were rejected by replacing values by NaNs (Not A Number). The power time courses were converted to Z-scores, which, when larger than 4, were replaced by NaNs to remove residual artifacts. The transformed signal was then averaged over the eight temporal channels, Z-transformed a second time and averaged across frequency bands of interest: 1–3 Hz (delta), 4–7 Hz (theta) and 25–35 Hz (gamma). Finally NaNs were replaced by zeros. We removed (on average across all subjects) around 40 s of signal per movie condition (mean +/− s.e.m: controls: 36 +/− 8 s; dyslexics: 45 +/− 18 s; independent *t*-test: $t = -0.44$, $p = 0.65$).

REGIONS OF INTEREST (ROI)

In accordance with AST theory we focused our analysis on the auditory cortex. We used three regions of interest (ROI) within Heschl's gyrus (Te1.0, Te1.1, and Te1.2), and the *planum temporale*: Te3 (**Figure 1**), all defined from cytoarchitectonic criteria using the SPM anatomy toolbox v.1.6. BOLD time courses were averaged over voxels using MarsBar (Brett et al., 2002).

CORRELATION BETWEEN BOLD TIME COURSE OF ROIs AND EEG POWER SPECTRUM

For each ROI and frequency band (delta, theta and gamma), we built a design matrix to perform a partial correlation between the BOLD time course of the ROI and the EEG power. The EEG time courses (averaged across all eight electrodes) of each frequency band were convolved with the hemodynamic response function (HRF) and downsampled to 0.5 Hz, i.e., the fMRI sampling rate. This analyzis was meant to capture the degree to which each ROI oscillates in each frequency band. A positive correlation indicates that the EEG power fluctuations in any given frequency band are reflected in the modulations of local synaptic activity as detected with fMRI (Laufs et al., 2003). Such correlations allow us to exploit the spatially detailed BOLD effect to precisely localize widespread EEG effects, resulting in a finer localization of oscillatory activity than with EEG only (Rosa et al., 2010a). We averaged over the whole set of temporal electrodes (left and right hemisphere) to avoid hemispheric biases in the EEG. Using this approach, asymmetries arise from specific correlations with the BOLD effect (Giraud et al., 2007). Our statistical model also included the motion parameters, their derivatives, the averaged signal of three brain compartments (white-matter gray-matter and CSF), and of all out-of-brain voxels, as nuisance covariates, as well as a regressor modeling the sessions. For normalization purposes the entire matrix was Z-transformed in time.

GROUP LEVEL STATISTICS

A repeated-measures ANOVA (with Greenhouse-Geisser corrections when appropriate) was performed with SPSS (IBM Corp. Released 2012. IBM SPSS Statistics for Windows, Version 21.0. Armonk, NY), with the Fisher transformed partial correlation coefficients between EEG power and BOLD time courses as dependent variables, the 4 areas, 3 frequency bands and 2 hemispheres as within-subject factors, and group, sex and handedness as between-subject factors. All factors were entered as main effects in the model, as well as the 2nd, 3rd, and 4th order interactions of the 3 within-subject factors and group. Effect sizes were estimated for some measures of within or between group differences with Cohen's formula: $d = (M_1 - M_2)/SD_{pooled}$, with M_1 = mean of group 1, M_2 = mean of group 2, $SD_{pooled} = \sqrt{[(SD_1^2 + SD_2^2)/2]}$, SD_1 = standard deviation of group 1, SD_2 = standard deviation of group 2. All other analyses were done using Matlab (version 2011/2012) (The MathWorks Inc., Natick, Massachusetts, USA).

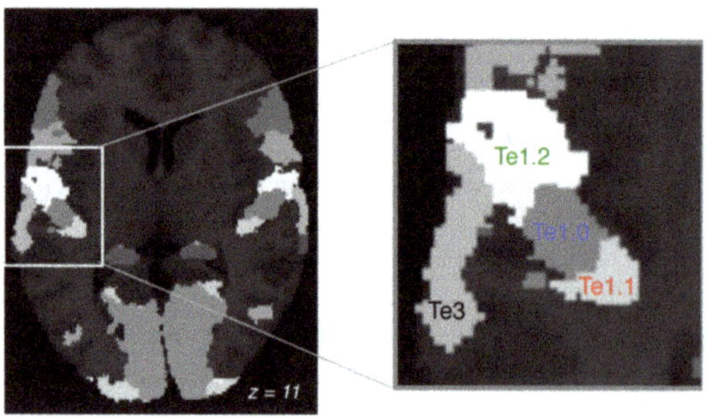

FIGURE 1 | Regions of interest. Cortical cytoarchitectonic areas defined by the anatomy toolbox (axial plane, MNI: z = +11). Focus on the left auditory cortex and the four ROIs: Te1.1, Te1.0, Te1.2, Te3. Te1 is Heschl's gyrus and Te3 is the *planum temporale*.

RESULTS

The repeated-measures ANOVA yielded significant main effects of area and hemisphere, and a group × frequency × hemisphere interaction.

Across groups, frequencies and hemispheres, there was a main effect of area [$F_{(2.2, 26.8)} = 7.45$, $p = 0.001$]. Correlations between EEG and fMRI were overall strongest in area Te1.2 and weakest in area Te1.1. This suggests that different regions of the auditory cortex show differential strength of responses in the frequency bands of interest, however, the specific correlation pattern observed here does not suggest any obvious interpretation. We also observed a main effect of hemisphere, with overall higher correlations in the right than in the left hemisphere [$F_{(1, 28)} = 8.28$, $p = 0.008$], an effect that seems to be carried by the delta and theta bands [$F_{(1,28)} = 10.15$, $p = 0.004$ and $F_{1,28} = 7.04$, $p = 0.013$ respectively, see **Figure 2**].

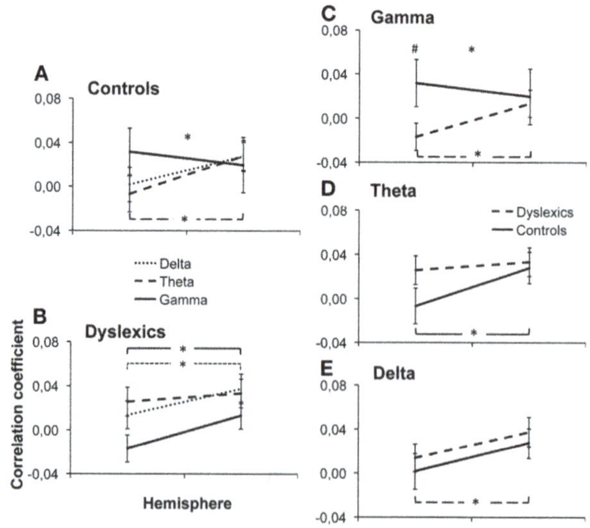

FIGURE 2 | Group × Frequency × Hemisphere interaction. Individual beta values were averaged over ROIs and plotted along the different dimensions of the interaction: Frequency × Hemisphere interaction in controls **(A)** and dyslexics **(B)** and Frequency × Group interaction in the gamma **(C)**, delta **(D)** and theta **(E)** bands. Error bars represent the s.e.m. *indicates a significant interaction or difference with $p < 0.05$. #indicates a marginally significant difference, $p = 0.066$.

Table 2 | Mean values of partial correlations.

	Controls ($n = 15$)				Dyslexics ($n = 17$)			
	Left		Right		Left		Right	
	Mean	sd	Mean	sd	Mean	sd	Mean	sd
Gamma	0.03	0.08	0.02	0.10	−0.02	0.06	0.01	0.05
Theta	0.00	0.06	0.03	0.06	0.03	0.05	0.03*	0.05
Delta	0.01	0.06	0.03*	0.05	0.01	0.05	0.04*	0.06

Averaged partial correlation over areas in left and right hemispheres of both groups.
Stars indicate values significantly different from 0 ($p < 0.05$).

Most interestingly, we observed a group × hemisphere × frequency band interaction [$F_{(1.90, 27.10)} = 6.56$, $p = 0.003$, **Figure 2**, **Table 2**. Controls presented a frequency × hemisphere interaction [$F_{(1.76, 11.24)} = 5.21$, $p = 0.017$, **Figure 2A**], with right dominance for theta [$F_{(1, 12)} = 8.71$, $p = 0.012$]. The delta and gamma bands showed no significant asymmetry [$F_{(1, 12)} = 3.10$, $p = 0.104$; $F_{1, 12} = 0.51$, $p = 0.487$, respectively]. Conversely, dyslexics showed the same correlation patterns across frequencies [frequency × hemisphere: $F_{(1.93, 13.07)} = 1.32$, $p = 0.288$; **Figure 2B**], but overall stronger correlations in the right than in the left hemisphere [$F_{(1, 14)} = 6.83$, $p = 0.020$], carried mostly by the gamma and delta bands [$F_{(1, 14)} = 5.16$, $p = 0.039$; $F_{(1, 14)} = 8.94$, $p = 0.010$ respectively]. Thus, the control group presented a hemispheric division of labor consistent with that predicted by Poeppel (2003) and observed by Giraud and collaborators (Giraud et al., 2007; Morillon et al., 2010), while the dyslexic group did not.

To further interpret this triple interaction, we first compared the neural organization for each frequency band between groups by testing group × hemisphere interactions for each frequency band. For the gamma band (**Figure 2C**), there was a hemisphere × group interaction [$F_{(1, 28)} = 5.30$, $p = 0.029$], with a marginally significant group difference in the left [Controls > Dyslexics, $F_{(1)} = 3.66$, $p = 0.066$, effect size: $d = 0.71$] but not in the right hemisphere [$F_{(1)} = 0.29$, $p = 0.867$]. However, the theta and delta bands (**Figures 2D,E**) showed no significant group × hemisphere interaction [$F_{(1, 28)} = 2.80$, $p = 0.105$ and $F_{1, 28} = 0.001$, $p = 0.937$, respectively]. Thus, the difference between the two groups lies primarily in the lateralization of cortical responses to the gamma band.

Finally, in order to fully describe the triple interaction, we tested the group × frequency interaction, hemisphere by hemisphere. In the left hemisphere, we observed a group × frequency interaction [$F_{(1.43, 27.57)} = 4.39$, $p = 0.030$], with marginally stronger correlations for the gamma band in controls than in dyslexics as described in the paragraph above. However, in the right hemisphere we observed no group × frequency interaction [$F_{(1.52, 27.48)} = 0.17$, $p = 0.781$]. This suggests that the cortical disorganization of the auditory cortex in dyslexia affects the left more than the right hemisphere.

Because hand preference is to some extent linked with language laterality, we also investigated hand preference effects. We found an area × hemisphere × hand preference interaction [$F_{(2.20, 26.80)} = 6.035$, $p = 0.003$), reflecting over both groups stronger right than left correlations between EEG power and the BOLD signal for right-handers in area Te1.0 and Te1.2 [$F_{(1, 19)} = 8.35$, $p = 0.009$; $F_{(1, 19)} = 13.87$, $p = 0.001$, respectively], and stronger right than left correlations for left-handers in area Te1.1 and Te3 [$F_{(1, 7)} = 5.67$, $p = 0.049$; $F_{(1, 7)} = 10.06$, $p = 0.016$, respectively]. There was also a hemisphere × hand preference interaction in Te1.2 [$F_{(1, 28)} = 9.12$, $p = 0.005$], with a trend in the left hemisphere for stronger correlations in left handed than in right handed subjects [$F_{(1)} = 3.56$, $p = 0.069$].

Finally, because of the suspicion that males and females might have partly different brain bases for dyslexia (Humphreys et al., 1990; Altarelli et al., 2013; Evans et al., 2013) we checked whether there was any sex effect. No main effect of sex and no significant interaction involving this factor were observed, whether groups were considered together or apart. Thus, the results obtained seem to hold equally across males and females.

DISCUSSION

In a previous study (Lehongre et al., 2011) we observed that dyslexic subjects had disrupted ASSRs at phoneme-relevant rates (low gamma around 30 Hz). While controls presented a left dominance in low-gamma range oscillations, in accordance with AST theory (Poeppel, 2003), dyslexic individuals showed no asymmetry or a right dominance. However, that study relied on the processing of an unnatural sound, a white noise that was modulated in amplitude. Furthermore, that the noise was modulated from 10 to 80 Hz made it impossible for us to test brain responses in frequency bands beyond this range. In particular, we could not test Goswami (2011) hypothesis that oscillations at syllable-relevant rates (delta and theta, 1–7 Hz) were disrupted. In the current study, we used more ecological audiovisual stimuli in which sounds were essentially natural conversational speech that better reflects situation outside the laboratory, and we were able to analyze at once the whole range of frequencies that are suspected to be altered in dyslexia, in Heschl's gyrus and the *planum temporale*. By using natural speech we preferentially induce those oscillations that are prominent in speech envelope (delta/theta), and periodically reset by speech onsets. As gamma power is both evoked by speech edges and controlled by theta modulations, it also follows speech modulations in primary auditory cortex (Giraud and Poeppel, 2012).

While our results do not show a clear-cut group difference in all of the conditions examined, they do show significant interactions that, in our view, constitute stronger results than a group difference in a single hand-picked condition. Our main finding is a group × hemisphere × frequency interaction, indicating that dyslexics differ from controls in the way the processing of the three target frequency bands is distributed across the two hemispheres. While control subjects show a frequency × hemisphere interaction, with a right dominance only for theta oscillations, dyslexic subjects show the same correlation patterns across the three bands, with a global dominance of the right hemisphere, suggesting a different pattern of hemispheric specialization.

With respect to the two target hypotheses on dyslexia, we find that dyslexic individuals' auditory cortical function differs from controls more in the left than in the right auditory cortex (group × frequency interaction in the left hemisphere only), and more for the gamma than for the delta and theta bands (group × hemisphere interaction for the gamma band only). The present results hence are consistent with our previous conclusion (Lehongre et al., 2011), that dyslexia reflects a primary disruption of left-hemisphere based gamma band oscillations.

Exploring low frequency oscillations in the delta (1–3 Hz) and theta ranges (4–7 Hz), we confirmed a right dominance for delta-theta oscillations in the auditory cortex of both controls and dyslexics (Poeppel, 2003). However, as there was neither a group × hemisphere interaction for the delta and theta bands, nor any hint of a group difference in the right hemisphere, the present results do not lend much support to the hypothesis of a right-hemisphere based, delta or theta oscillation disruption (Goswami, 2011).

One possibility to explain the conflicting results between studies might be a language difference. Indeed studies reporting group differences in delta-theta frequency bands were carried out in English only (Abrams et al., 2009; Hamalainen et al., 2012). It might be that speakers of a stress-timed language like English acquire stronger sensitivity to delta and theta rhythms than those of a syllable-timed language like French. However, this hypothesis is not consistent with the results obtained in (stress-timed) Dutch speakers by Poelmans et al. (2012). Another parameter to take into account is that the BOLD signal is described as mostly driven by oscillations in the beta/gamma band (Magri et al., 2012). This might induce both greater EEG/BOLD correlations and a better signal/noise ratio for this frequency band than for the delta/theta range, and therefore increase our statistical power to detect group differences in the gamma band. However, we do not find in our data any evidence of greater correlations in the gamma than in the delta-theta bands.

Our study also differs from the other EEG/MEG studies, as we did not analyze simple EEG power spectrum. The reason is that our stimulus being conversational speech, there is no multiply-repeated stimulus that enables a well-defined spectro-temporal analyzis of the evoked response. We did not analyze the phase locking with the speech envelope either, because this would provide information about low frequencies (Howard and Poeppel, 2012), but not the gamma band, and we wanted to compare both frequency bands. Our analysis of correlations between the EEG power time course and the BOLD signal allowed us to estimate the degree to which activations in specific brain regions reflect cortical oscillations in given frequency bands. The EEG signal alone lacks spatial resolution, and the BOLD signal alone reflects much more than cortical oscillations. Here we were able to interrogate auditory cortex very precisely, as variations in EEG/BOLD correlations presumably reflect variations in cortical oscillations in the specific areas of interest, that are probably related to the fluctuations in amplitude of the speech envelope modulations.

To what extent do our results depend on the naturalistic audio-visual stimuli used here, as opposed to amplitude-modulated sounds used in previous studies? Our exclusive focus on primary and secondary auditory cortex makes it unlikely that we should observe direct responses to either the higher-level linguistic information, or the visual information. However, it is plausible that the access to semantic information and the presence of synchronized visual information (lip movements) may have served to enhance the responses to the auditory stimuli, thereby improving the signal/noise ratio.

As described by other functional and anatomical studies, many measures highlight a weak or reversed brain lateralization related to language in dyslexics, including in the *planum temporale*, labeled Te3 here (Galaburda et al., 1985, 1987; Altarelli et al., submitted). The lack of hemispheric specialization for delta, theta, and gamma oscillations could affect the efficiency of the auditory processing based on a dual-scale temporal integration (Poeppel, 2003). One possible consequence of this deficit of low gamma oscillations in dyslexics' left hemisphere is to lead them to segment the auditory input into non-standard phonemic units, hence distorting the very format of their phonological representations. This would be consistent with the general understanding of the phonological deficit in dyslexia (Mody et al., 1997; Adlard and Hazan, 1998; Serniclaes et al., 2004; Vellutino et al., 2004). Another possibility would be that such cortical oscillations do not directly affect the format of phonological representations, but their salience or their availability for downstream cognitive processes. Thus, the disruption of phoneme-relevant cortical oscillations is also compatible with the view that dyslexics' phonological representations are essentially normal, but that phonemic units are more difficult to rapidly access, to pay attention to, and to manipulate for dyslexic individuals (Ramus and Szenkovits, 2008; Ramus and Ahissar, 2012; Giraud and Ramus, 2013).

CONCLUSION

In this study, we used a combined EEG-fMRI paradigm to measure the oscillations of auditory cortical areas in response to speech stimuli in dyslexic and in control adult participants, in three frequency bands of interest: gamma (25–35 Hz), theta (4–7 Hz) and delta (1–3 Hz). We first confirmed the presence of an auditory sampling impairment in dyslexia, using natural speech listening conditions. Secondly, we further confirmed that this impairment consisted mainly in a in a reduced responsiveness of left auditory cortex to gamma oscillations. On the other hand, we found little evidence for a disruption in auditory sampling in the delta and theta rates. Our results are consistent with a large literature showing the difficulties of dyslexic individuals with the representation, processing, or access to phonemic units, and provide a possible brain basis for this phenomenon.

ACKNOWLEDGMENTS

This work has been supported by the European Commission, the Fondation pour la Recherche Médicale, the Neuropôle de Recherche Francilien, the Fondation Bettencourt-Schueller, and the Agence Nationale de la Recherche. We would like to thank Nadège Villiermet for conducting the behavioral test battery on the participants.

REFERENCES

Abrams, D. A., Nicol, T., Zecker, S., and Kraus, N. (2008). Right-hemisphere auditory cortex is dominant for coding syllable patterns in speech. *J. Neurosci.* 28, 3958–3965. doi: 10.1523/JNEUROSCI.0187-08.2008

Abrams, D. A., Nicol, T., Zecker, S., and Kraus, N. (2009). Abnormal cortical processing of the syllable rate of speech in poor readers. *J. Neurosci.* 29, 7686–7693. doi: 10.1523/JNEUROSCI.5242-08.2009

Adlard, A., and Hazan, V. (1998). Speech perception in children with specific reading difficulties (dyslexia). *Q. J. Exp. Psychol.* A 51, 153–177.

Altarelli, I., Monzalvo, K., Iannuzzi, S., Fluss, J., Billard, C., Ramus, F., et al. (2013). A functionally guided approach to the morphometry of occipito-temporal regions in developmental dyslexia: evidence for differential effects in boys and girls. *J. Neurosci.* doi: 10.1523/JNEUROSCI.5854-12.2013

Babiloni, C., Stella, G., Buffo, P., Vecchio, F., Onorati, P., Muratori, C., et al. (2012). Cortical sources of resting state EEG rhythms are abnormal in dyslexic children. Clin. Neurophysiol. 123, 2384–2391. doi: 10.1016/j.clinph.2012.05.002

Brett, M., Anton, J.-L., Valabregue, R., and Poline, J.-B. (2002). "Region of interest analysis using an SPM toolbox," in Presented at the 8th International Conferance on Functional Mapping of the Human Brain, Vol. 16 (Sendai). Available on CDROM in NeuroImage, abstract 497.

Darki, F., Peyrard-Janvid, M., Matsson, H., Kere, J., and Klingberg, T. (2012). Three dyslexia susceptibility genes, DYX1C1, DCDC2, and KIAA0319, affect temporoparietal white matter structure. *Biol. Psychiatry* 72, 671–676. doi: 10.1016/j.biopsych.2012.05.008

Dunn, L. M., Thériault, C. M., and Dunn, L. M. (1993). Echelle de vocabulaire en images Peabody (EVIP). Toronto, ON: Psycan.

Eckert, M. (2004). Neuroanatomical markers for dyslexia: a review of dyslexia structural imaging studies. Neuroscientist 10, 362–371. doi: 10.1177/1073858404263596

Evans, T. M., Flowers, D. L., Napoliello, E. M., and Eden, G. F. (2013). Sexspecific gray matter volume differences in females with developmental dyslexia. *Brain Struct. Funct.* doi: 10.1007/s00429-013-0552-4. [Epub ahead of print].

Frederickson, N., Frith, U., and Reason, R. (1997). *Phonological Assessment* Battery. Windsor: nferNelson.

Galaburda, A. M., Corsiglia, J., Rosen, G. D., and Sherman, G. F. (1987). Planum temporale asymmetry: reappraisal since Geschwind and Levitsky. *Neuropsychologia* 25, 853–868. doi: 10.1016/0028-3932(87)90091-1

Galaburda, A. M., Sherman, G. F., Rosen, G. D., Aboitiz, F., and Geschwind, N. (1985). Developmental dyslexia: four consecutive patients with cortical anomalies. Ann. Neurol. 18, 222–233. doi: 10.1002/ana.410180210

Giraud, A. L., Kleinschmidt, A., Poeppel, D., Lund, T. E., Frackowiak, R. S., and Laufs, H. (2007). Endogenous cortical rhythms determine cerebral specialization for speech perception and production. Neuron 56, 1127–1134. doi: 10.1016/j.neuron.2007.09.038

Giraud, A. L., and Poeppel, D. (2012). Cortical oscillations and speech processing: emerging computational principles and operations. Nat. Neurosci. 15, 511–517. doi: 10.1038/nn.3063

Giraud, A. L., and Ramus, F. (2013). Neurogenetics and auditory processing in developmental dyslexia. Curr. Opin. Neurobiol. 23, 37–42. doi: 10.1016/j.conb.2012.09.003

Goswami, U. (2011). A temporal sam-pling framework for developmental dyslexia. Trends Cogn. Sci. 15, 3–10. doi: 10.1016/j.tics. 2010.10.001

Goswami, U., Gerson, D., and Astruc, L. (2010). Amplitude envelope perception, phonology and prosodic sensitivity in children with developmental dyslexia. Read. Writ. 23, 995–1019. doi: 10.1007/s11145-009-9186-6

Goswami, U., Wang, H. L.S., Cruz, A., Fosker, T., Mead, N., and Huss, M. (2011). Language-universal sensory deficits in developmental dyslexia: English, Spanish, and Chinese. J. Cogn. Neurosci. 23, 325–337. doi: 10.1162/jocn.2010.21453

Hamalainen, J. A., Rupp, A., Soltesz, F., Szucs, D., and Goswami, U. (2012). Reduced phase locking to slow amplitude modulation in adults with dyslexia: an MEG study. *Neuroimage* 59, 2952–2961. doi: 10.1016/j.neuroimage.2011.09.075

Han, J., Mody, M., and Ahlfors, S.P. (2012). Gamma phase locking modulated by phonological contrast during auditory comprehension in reading disability. Neuroreport 23, 851–856. doi: 10.1097/WNR.0b013e32835818e1

Heim, S., Friedman, J.T., Keil, A., and Benasich, A. A. (2011). Reduced sensory oscillatory activity during rapid auditory processing as a correlate of language-learning impairment. *J. Neurolinguistics* 24, 538–555. doi: 10.1016/j.jneuroling.2010.09.006

Herrmann, C. S., and Debener, S. (2008). Simultaneous recording of EEG and BOLD responses: a historical perspective. Int. J. Psychophysiol. 67, 161–168. doi: 10.1016/j.ijpsycho.2007.06.006

Howard, M. F., and Poeppel, D. (2012). The neuromagnetic response to spoken sentences: co-modulation of theta band amplitude and phase. *Neuroimage* 60, 2118–2127. doi:10.1016/j.neuroimage. 2012.02.028

Humphreys, P., Kaufmann, W. E., and Galaburda, A. M. (1990). Developmental dyslexia in women: neuropathological findings in three patients. Ann. Neurol. 28, 727–738. doi: 10.1002/ana.410280602

Laufs, H. (2012). A personalized history of EEG-fMRI integration. *Neuroimage* 62, 1056–1067. doi: 10.1016/j.neuroimage.2012.01.039

Laufs, H., Krakow, K., Sterzer, P., Eger, E., Beyerle, A., Salek-Haddadi, A., et al. (2003). Electroencephalographic signatures of attentional and cognitive default modes in spontaneous brain activity fluctuations at rest. Proc. Natl. Acad. Sci. U.S.A. 100, 11053–11058. doi: 10.1073/pnas.1831638100

Lee, J. H., Durand, R., Gradinaru, V., Zhang, F., Goshen, I., Kim, D. S., et al. (2010). Global and local fMRI signals driven by neurons defined optogenetically by type and wiring. Nature 465, 788–792. doi: 10.1038/nature09108

Lefavrais, P. (1967). Test de l'Alouette, 2nd Edn. Paris: Editions du Centre de Psychologie Appliquée.

Lehongre, K., Ramus, F., Villiermet, N., Schwartz, D., and Giraud, A. L. (2011). Altered low-gamma sampling in auditory cortex accounts for the three main facets of dyslexia. Neuron 72, 1080–1090. doi: 10.1016/j.neuron.2011.11.002

Lindgren, S. D., De Renzi, E., and Richman, L. C. (1985). Cross-national comparisons of developmental dyslexia in Italy and the United States. Child Dev. 56, 1404–1417. doi: 10.2307/1130460

Linkersdorfer, J., Lonnemann, J., Lindberg, S., Hasselhorn, M., and Fiebach, C. J. (2012). Grey matter alterations co-localize with functional abnormalities in developmental dyslexia: an ALE meta-analysis. PLoS ONE 7:e43122. doi: 10.1371/journal.pone.0043122

Logothetis, N. K. (2010). Bold claims for optogenetics. Nature 468, E3–4; discussion: E4–E5.

Magri, C., Schridde, U., Murayama, Y., Panzeri, S., and Logothetis, N. K. (2012). The amplitude and timing of the BOLD signal reflects the relationship between local field potential power at different frequencies. *J. Neurosci.* 32, 1395–1407. doi: 10.1523/JNEUROSCI.398511.2012

Mandelkow, H., Halder, P., Boesiger, P., and Brandeis, D. (2006). Synchronization facilitates removal of MRI artefacts from concurrent EEG recordings and increases usable bandwidth. *Neuroimage* 32, 1120–1126. doi: 10.1016/j.neuroimage.2006.04.231

Mody, M., Studdert-Kennedy, M., and Brady, S. (1997). Speech perception deficits in poor readers: auditory processing or phonological coding? J. Exp. Child Psychol. 64, 199–231. doi: 10.1006/jecp.1996.2343

Morillon, B., Lehongre, K., Frackowiak, R. S. J., Ducorps, A., Kleinschmidt, A., Poeppel, D., et al. (2010). Neurophysiological origin of human brain asymmetry for speech and language. Proc. Natl. Acad. Sci. U.S.A. 107, 18688–18693. doi: 10.1073/pnas.1007189107

Oostenveld, R., Fries, P., Maris, E., and Schoffelen, J. M. (2011). FieldTrip: open source software for advanced analysis of MEG, EEG, and invasive electrophysiological data. Comput. *Intell. Neurosci.* 2011, 156869. doi: 10.1155/2011/156869

Pennington, B. F. (2006). From single to multiple deficit models of developmental disorders. Cognition 101, 385–413. doi: 10.1016/j.cognition.2006.04.008

Pinel, P., Fauchereau, F., Moreno, A., Barbot, A., Lathrop, M., Zelenika, D., et al. (2012). Genetic variants of FOXP2 and KIAA0319/TTRAP/THEM2 locus are associated with altered brain activation in distinct language- related regions. J. Neurosci. 32, 817–825. doi: 10.1523/JNEUROSCI.5996-10.2012

Poelmans, H., Luts, H., Vandermosten, M., Boets, B., Ghesquiere, P., and Wouters, J. (2012). Auditory steady state cortical responses indicate deviant phonemicrate processing in adults with dyslexia. Ear Hear. 33, 134–143. doi: 10.1097/AUD.0b013e31822c26b9

Poeppel, D. (2003). The analysis of speech in different temporal integration windows: cerebral lateralization as "asymmetric sampling in time." Speech Commun. 41, 245–255. doi: 10.1016/S0167-6393(02)00107-3

Ramus, F., and Ahissar, M. (2012). Developmental dyslexia: the difficulties of interpreting poor performance, and the importance of normal performance. Cogn. Neuropsychol. 29, 104–122. doi: 10.1080/02643294.2012.677420

Ramus, F., and Szenkovits, G. (2008). What phonological deficit? Q. J. Exp. Psychol. 61, 129–141. doi: 10.1080/17470210701508822

Raven, J., Raven, J. C., and Court, J. H. (1998). Advanced Progressive Matrices. Oxford: Oxford Psychologists Press.

Richardson, F. M., and Price, C. J. (2009). Structural MRI studies of language function in the undamaged brain. Brain Struct. Funct. 213, 511–523. doi: 10.1007/s00429-009-0211-y

Richlan, F., Kronbichler, M., and Wimmer, H. (2011). Meta- analyzing brain dysfunctions in dyslexic children and adults. *Neuroimage* 56, 1735–1742. doi: 10.1016/j.neuroimage.2011.02.040

Rosa, M. J., Daunizeau, J., and Friston, K. J. (2010a). EEGfMRI integration: a critical review of biophysical modeling and data analysis approaches.

J. Integr. Neurosci. 9, 453–476. doi: 10.1142/S0219635210002512

Rosa, M. J., Kilner, J., Blankenburg, F., Josephs, O., and Penny, W. (2010b). Estimating the transfer function from neuronal activity to BOLD using simultaneous EEG-fMRI. *Neuroimage* 49, 1496–1509. doi: 10.1016/j. neuroimage.2009.09.011

Telkemeyer, S., Rossi, S., Koch, S. P., Nierhaus, T., Steinbrink, J., Poeppel, D., et al. (2009). Sensitivity of newborn auditory cortex to the temporal structure of sounds. *J. Neurosci.* 29, 14726–14733. doi: 10.1523/JNEUROSCI.1246-09.2009

Serniclaes, W., Van Heghe, S., Mousty, P., Carre, R., and Sprenger-Charolles, L. (2004). Allophonic mode of speech perception in dyslexia. J. Exp. Child Psychol. 87, 336–361. doi: 10.1016/j.jecp.2004.02.001

Soroli, E., Szenkovits, G., and Ramus, F. (2010). Exploring dyslexics' phonological deficit III: foreign speech perception and production. *Dyslexia* 16, 318–340. doi: 10.1002/dys.415

Tallal, P. (1980). Auditory temporal perception, phonics, and reading disabilities in children. *Brain Lang.* 9, 182–198. doi: 10.1016/0093-934X(80)90139-X

Vellutino, F. R., Fletcher, J. M., Snowling, M. J., and Scanlon, D. M. (2004). Specific reading disability (dyslexia): what have we learned in the past four decades?

J. Child Psychol. Psychiatry 45, 2–40. doi: 10.1046/j.0021-9630. 2003.00305.x

Wagner, R. K., and Torgesen, J. K. (1987). The nature of phonological processing and its causal role in the acquisition of reading skills. Psychol. Bull. 101, 192–212. doi: 10.1037/0033-2909.

101.2.192

Wechsler, D. (2000). *WAIS-III: Echelle de l'intelligence de Wechsler pour adultes. Troisième Edn.* Paris: Editions du Centre de Psychologie Appliquée.

World Health Organization. (2011). *International Statistical Classification of Diseases and Related Health Problems—10th revision. Geneva:* World Health Organization.

5

Age, dyslexia subtype and comorbidity modulate rapid auditory processing in developmental dyslexia

Maria Luisa Lorusso *, Chiara Cantiani and Massimo Molteni

Unit of Neuropsychology of Developmental Disorders, Department of Child Psychopathology, Scientific Institute IRCCS "E. Medea", Bosisio Parini, Italy

Correspondence:
Maria Luisa Lorusso, Unit of Neuropsychology of Developmental Disorders, Department of Child Psychopathology, Scientific Institute IRCCS "E. Medea", Via Don Luigi Monza 20, Bosisio Parini, 23842, Italy
e-mail: marialuisa.lorusso@bp.lnf.it

The nature of Rapid Auditory Processing (RAP) deficits in dyslexia remains debated, together with the specificity of the problem to certain types of stimuli and/or restricted subgroups of individuals. Following the hypothesis that the heterogeneity of the dyslexic population may have led to contrasting results, the aim of the study was to define the effect of age, dyslexia subtype and comorbidity on the discrimination and reproduction of non-verbal tone sequences. Participants were 46 children aged 8–14 (26 with dyslexia, subdivided according to age, presence of a previous language delay, and type of dyslexia). Experimental tasks were a *Temporal Order Judgment* (TOJ) (manipulating tone length, ISI and sequence length), and a *Pattern Discrimination Task*. Dyslexic children showed general RAP deficits. Tone length and ISI influenced dyslexic and control children's performance in a similar way, but dyslexic children were more affected by an increase from 2 to 5 sounds. As to age, older dyslexic children's difficulty in reproducing sequences of 4 and 5 tones was similar to that of normally reading younger (but not older) children. In the analysis of subgroup profiles, the crucial variable appears to be the advantage, or lack thereof, in processing long vs. short sounds. Dyslexic children with a previous language delay obtained the lowest scores in RAP measures, but they performed worse with shorter stimuli, similar to control children, while dyslexic-only children showed no advantage for longer stimuli. As to dyslexia subtype, only surface dyslexics improved their performance with longer stimuli, while phonological dyslexics did not. Differential scores for short vs. long tones and for long vs. short ISIs predict non-word and word reading, respectively, and the former correlate with phonemic awareness. In conclusion, the relationship between non-verbal RAP, phonemic skills and reading abilities appears to be characterized by complex interactions with subgroup characteristics.

Keywords: developmental dyslexia, subgroups, rapid auditory processing, language impairment, dyslexia subtypes

INTRODUCTION

Developmental Dyslexia (DD) is defined as a specific disability in learning to read adequately despite at least normal intelligence, adequate instruction and socio-cultural opportunities, and the absence of sensory defects in vision and hearing (American Psychiatric Association, 1994). The prevailing views concerning the etiology of DD point to a deficit in encoding, representing and processing speech sounds (Snowling, 2001; Ramus et al., 2003; Ramus and Szenkovits, 2008). However, the question whether these difficulties reveal the core deficit of dyslexia or whether they are manifestations of a more general and basic auditory deficit is controversial.

According to Tallal's (1980) hypothesis, children with DD would be impaired in their ability to perceive auditory stimuli that have short duration and occur in rapid succession. Such a deficit at the auditory level could compromise the temporal analysis of speech at the phoneme level, and thus the building of correct phoneme representations. With such constraints, the development of language skills, both oral and written, would be difficult. Tallal and Piercy (1973a,b) revealed that children with Specific Language Impairment (SLI) have difficulties in discriminating between rapidly presented non-speech auditory stimuli, and in reproducing their order (discrimination and repetition tasks). Later, this hypothesis has been generalized to children with DD (Tallal, 1980). The procedure usually employed involves tasks that require discriminating between, or reproducing the order of, complex tones of varying frequency, manipulating both Inter-Stimulus Interval (ISI) and sound length. The difficulty in performing these tasks was interpreted by Tallal and colleagues as a deficit in extracting temporal information from short and rapid auditory stimuli, and it was referred to as deficient Temporal Auditory Processing (ATP) (Tallal, 1980). This interpretation was questioned by several researchers, who brought controversial evidence as to the exact nature of the deficit being linked to timing issues or rather to the analysis of complex stimuli (Rosen, 2003), spectral analysis and discrimination (Studdert-Kennedy and Mody, 1995), processing of stimulus streams and sluggish attentional shifting (Hari and Renvall, 2001; Lallier et al., 2012) or perceptual learning (Banai and Ahissar, 2009). As suggested by Mauk and Buonomano (2004), it is possible that in these tasks learning occurs as a result of interval-specific cognitive processes other than temporal processing *per se*; "for example, because interval discrimination tasks require comparing the test interval and a standard interval, improvement could rely on better representation of the standard interval or improved storage or retrieval from working or short-term memory" (Mauk and Buonomano, 2004, pp. 318). A prominent role of short-term memory in producing the results has also been proposed by Share et al. (2002), Tallal and Piercy (1973a,b). Heiervang et al. (2002) for instance, found that in longer trials (requiring to reproduce 3, 4, and 5 tones) children with DD made more errors compared to normally reading children. The temporal nature of the tasks has been subsequently toned down, and the hypothesis has been reworded as Rapid Auditory Processing (RAP), a definition leaving more space to different interpretations of the deficit. Despite extensive research effort, however, the specific nature of RAP problems remains ill-defined.

A first controversial point concerns the *speech-specific nature* of the deficits, as claimed by Studdert-Kennedy and Mody (1995), and Mody et al. (1997). Nowadays, the growing number of studies showing deficits concerning also the discrimination and reproduction of non-speech stimuli points toward a more general and basic auditory problem. Vandermosten et al. (2010, 2011) recently found a clear pattern in children and adults with DD, showing a temporal-specific deficit in both speech and non-speech categorization tasks. Nonetheless, the relationship between RAP deficits, phonemic awareness and reading is still a matter of debate (see Johnson et al., 2009; Malenfant et al., 2012).

A second controversy concerns the *selectivity* of the auditory processing deficit i.e., its being restricted to brief and rapidly presented stimuli. Tallal (1980) employing the Temporal Order Judgment task (TOJ) showed that children with DD performed worse than the control group in the identification of brief sounds (75 ms), but only for short Inter-Stimulus Intervals (ISIs) (8–305 vs. 428 ms). In support of the selectivity of the deficit in DD, Gaab et al. (2007) brought evidence of a disruption of cerebral regions specifically devoted to rapid auditory processing. Several results unequivocally consistent with the "restricted" RAP hypothesis have been reported, though the emphasis alternates between ISI and tone length, or both (Tallal, 1980; Reed, 1989; Heiervang et al., 2002; Cohen-Mimran and Sapir, 2007). On the other side, the findings of a second group of researchers support the hypothesis of a general auditory deficit, not restricted to short and rapid sounds (Marshall et al., 2001; Waber et al., 2001; Share et al., 2002; Bretherton and Holmes, 2003; Cantiani et al., 2010). As pointed out by Rosen (2003), group differences at long ISIs do not often emerge only because of ceiling performance. Other types of auditory processing have also been called into play, including processing of dynamic features of auditory stimuli, such as amplitude and frequency modulations (AM, FM) in the speech signal (Witton et al., 1998; Talcott et al., 2000) or sensitivity to longer time-scale patterns of intonation, rhythm and stress (Goswami et al., 2002; Pasquini et al., 2007; Thomson and Goswami, 2008; see Hämäläinen et al., 2012 for a review).

A last issue concerns the *predictive value* of measures of RAP with respect to reading and reading-related skills. Several studies found general correlations between different measures of impaired auditory processing and reading and/or phonological difficulties (Tallal, 1980; Witton et al., 1998; Ahissar et al., 2000; Marshall et al., 2001; Share et al., 2002; Hood and Conlon, 2004; Cohen-Mimran and Sapir, 2007). In many studies, however, correlations and/or predictive power were weak (Marshall et al., 2001; Share et al., 2002; Hood and Conlon, 2004) or non-significant (Reed, 1989; Heiervang et al., 2002). A recent study (Johnson et al., 2009) found that phonemic awareness predicts later RAP performance to a greater degree than the reverse. On the other hand, longitudinal studies in which behavioral and ERP responses to auditory stimuli had been recorded in newborn children with and without familial risk for language and reading disorders (Benasich and Tallal, 2002; Benasich et al., 2002; Leppänen et al., 2010) show that the infants' ability to discriminate temporal characteristics of the stimuli differs in the two groups (with and without risk) and predicts later language and reading-related skills: these findings at the very least rule out the hypothesis that RAP deficits are a consequence of reduced phonemic awareness. As a viable compromise, based on data from a longitudinal study, Boets et al. (2011) suggest a bidirectional relationship between auditory processing of non-speech stimuli and speech perception.

HOW SHOULD THIS WIDE HETEROGENEITY OF RESULTS BE EXPLAINED?

Although the exact nature of the processes tapped by RAP tasks is a primary issue for research, the origin of the extreme variability in research findings, as described above, remains an interesting and still unanswered question. Various hypotheses have been proposed pointing to differences within the dyslexic population (McArthur and Bishop, 2001). In fact, only a subgroup of children with DD has often been found to be impaired in RAP tasks: Tallal (1980) found that only 8 (out of 20) children with DD had a clear deficit on the TOJ task. Similar within-group differences were found by Marshall et al. (2001; 4 of 17), Bretherton and Holmes (2003; 20 of 42), Ramus et al. (2003; 9 of 16), Banai and Ahissar (2004; 15 of 46), and Cohen-Mimran and Sapir (2007; 4 of 12).

First, *Age* has often been suggested to provide variability within the dyslexic group. Tallal (2000) claimed that only younger children with DD have RAP deficits, which may be explained by a maturational lag in the development of the auditory system (McArthur and Bishop, 2001; Wright and Zecker, 2004). The magnitude of this deficit is expected to diminish as children grow older: older children with dyslexia could have compensated the deficit, but only after it has compromised in a permanent way the quality of phoneme representations. Results in line with this hypothesis were found by Hautus et al. (2003), through a test of auditory temporal acuity (a gap-detection task).

Second, the *presence of language impairments* was hypothesized by several authors to be related to RAP performance (Tallal and Stark, 1982; Heath et al., 1999; Joanisse et al., 2000). In particular, Tallal and Stark (1982) did not find any tone processing deficits in reading-impaired children without concomitant oral language delay. Similarly, Heath et al. (1999) compared disabled readers with and without concomitant oral language delay in a TOJ task, and found a deficit only in the first group.

Finally, it was supposed that the RAP deficit affects only a subgroup of children with DD, based on *type of dyslexia*. Several studies suggest the existence of various subtypes of DD characterized by different cognitive and neuropsychological profiles and by different reading strategies (e.g., Bakker, 1973; Boder, 1973; Castles and Coltheart, 1993). More recently, the existence of markedly different cognitive profiles within the dyslexic population has been further confirmed (Ramus et al., 2003; Heim et al., 2008; Menghini et al., 2010). The main classification systems distinguish between dyslexic individuals with predominant difficulties in non-word reading and phonological tasks (these subtypes may be classified as L-types, phonological, dysphonetic dyslexics in Bakker's, Coltheart's and Boder's taxonomies, respectively), and dyslexic individuals who are mostly impaired in the access to the visual lexicon, as shown by their difficulties in whole-word recognition needed for reading irregular words (classified as P-types, surface or dyseidetic dyslexics). Consistent with Tallal's findings of a correlation between tone processing and non-word reading, it was assumed that only (or especially) phonological dyslexics would have a deficit in RAP (Cestnick, 2001). However, not all reports are consistent with this hypothesis: Lachmann et al. (2005) even found greater anomalies in children with dyseidetic DD compared to children with dysphonetic DD in a temporal processing task using event-related brain potentials (ERP).

Aim of the present study was to test the hypothesis that differences in age, dyslexia subtype and comorbidity with language impairments can be linked to different patterns of performance on RAP tasks. Although any subgrouping procedure may be seen as a reductive simplification of a complex, multi-factor picture (with much variability due to the specific tests and cut-offs used), our hypothesis was that a number of distinctions can highlight some crucial differences in the population. Specifically, based on previously reported findings, we expected that (a) the level of difficulty and thus of sensitivity of the different tasks would be modulated by age for children with DD in a possibly different way as compared to control children; (b) the presence of an additional language impairment would further hamper RAP performance, and (c) children with a phonological type of dyslexia would have worse RAP performance as compared to children with non-phonological dyslexia. The study is the first one, to our knowledge, to take into account all these variables in the same sample of dyslexic children. In order to avoid introducing new sources of variability in the results, only tasks that have been previously employed and well-described in the literature were used.

MATERIALS AND METHODS

PARTICIPANTS

Forty-six children aged between 8 and 14 years participated in the study: 26 children with DD and 20 normally reading control children. The participants in the two groups were matched for gender and age. Parental consent was obtained after the purpose and procedures of the study had been explained. The study had been approved by the Ethics Committee of the Institute according to standards of the Helsinki Declaration (1964).

Children with DD included in the sample had been referred to the Unit of Cognitive Psychology and Neuropsychology of the institute because of learning difficulties. All children had been diagnosed as dyslexic based on standard inclusion and exclusion criteria (ICD-10; World Health Organization, 1992). Their performance in reading was two (or more) standard deviations below the mean in at least one of the age-standardized Italian reading tests included in the battery (word, non-word and text reading), and their non-verbal or performance IQ was above 85. Performance IQ was estimated by the Italian adaptation of the Wechsler Intelligence Scale for Children-revised (WISC-R; Wechsler, 1994) ($n = 15$), or Cattell's "Culture Free" test (Cattell, 1979) ($n = 11$). All children attended mainstream schools (as is usual in the Italian educational system), and none of them had started remediation programs at the time of participation in the study. Comorbidity with ADHD or other psychopathological conditions was excluded, based on standard diagnostic criteria (DSM-IV; American Psychiatric Association, 1994).

Control children were recruited in local schools. They all performed normally in a text reading task, and their performance IQ (Cattell's "Culture Free" test) was above 85. Participants' characteristics compared with unpaired t-tests are shown in **Table 1**. No group difference emerged in age, but there was a significant difference in performance IQ.

Subgroups

Within the dyslexic sample, two subgroups based on the presence or absence of a previous language delay were created, after an accurate analysis of clinical records: all children had been diagnosed at the Institute following the same diagnostic protocols; thus, a detailed anamnestic record was available including in-depth information about language development. Inclusion criteria were previous diagnoses of Language Impairment (LI) (a diagnosis of LI is made when at least two scores on a standardized battery of receptive and expressive language are below 2 SDs with respect to age norms) and/or reports of significant delays (reported delays were considered significant if the main linguistic milestones were acquired with at least one year delay with respect to normal development) in early vocabulary and syntactic development, in addition or not to a history of speech and language therapy. Transient phonetic/articulatory difficulties without any additional linguistic problem were not considered sufficient for inclusion in the DD-LI group, even if speech therapy had been

Table 1 | Participant characteristics (p-values indicating significant group differences are marked in bold).

Group	DD ($N = 26$) Mean (SD)	Control ($N = 20$) mean (SD)	Group comparison $F(df)$, p
Male	21	15	
Female	5	5	
Age in months	128.58 (23.04)	133.20 (22.27)	0.468 (1.45), 0.497
Performance IQ[a]	102.96 (8.29)	112.00 (11.36)	9.737 (1.45), **0.003**
READING: accuracy[b]	−2.94 (1.68)	0.09 (0.57)	59.604 (1.45), < **0.001**
READING: speed[b]	−1.89 (1.74)	0.31 (0.29)	31.241 (1.45), < **0.001**

[a]*Scores at WISC-R or Cattell's "Culture Free" test;* [b]*Scores are expressed as Z-scores in the text reading task.*

delivered. Based on these elements, it was ascertained that 10 children had had a clear previous language impairment (LI) and 11 children had never presented linguistic difficulties (noLI). For five of the children, available information was not sufficient to decide on the presence of a previous linguistic impairment, so they were not classified and not included in the analysis. Hearing tests had been performed for all children with a former diagnosis of SLI as part of the diagnostic procedure. For dyslexic participants, hearing tests were performed anytime there was a reason to suspect that a hearing problem may be present (based on parents' reports or on the clinicians' assessment). Only children for whom no report of a hearing loss was recorded were included in the study.

Further, two subgroups based on type of dyslexia were created. This division was based on the difference in accuracy (z-scores) between word and non-word reading (with at least 0.5 difference in z-scores)[1]. This procedure is similar, although not identical, to the regression procedure suggested by Castles and Coltheart (1993) and followed by Ziegler et al. (2008) and Peterson et al. (2013), to select "relative phonological" and "relative surface" dyslexics. Children with "phonological DD" performed worse when reading non-words, while children with "surface DD" performed worse when reading words. Accordingly, a total of 10 children were assigned to the subgroup of phonological DD, 12 were assigned to the subgroup of surface DD and 4 could not be classified.

Table 2 shows the combinations of z-scores expressing accuracy and speed in reading words and non-words, for each participant. It can be easily seen that the great majority of children had difficulties with both kinds of stimuli, and that a "relative" rather than a "pure" subtype classification is the best choice. As to accuracy vs. speed scores as the basis for classification, it can be seen that both variables would allow to identify (largely but not completely overlapping) subgroups with similar numbers of participants. It was decided to use accuracy rather than speed scores based on previous studies in which a subdivision according to accuracy scores highlighted strong and reliable differences in visual and auditory attention (Facoetti et al., 2010; Franceschini et al., 2012), i.e., in low-level processing skills.

Subgroup characteristics and one-way ANOVA comparisons are shown in **Table 3**. Subgroup comparisons reflected the inclusion criteria in each subgroup (see comparison for non-word reading accuracy in the type-of-dyslexia subgroups). All subgroups resulted comparable for IQ. Generally, children with DD-noLI had lower performances in reading and reading-related tasks than children with DD+LI (these differences reached significance for reading accuracy and short-term memory scores). No significant differences emerged in overall reading and reading-related tasks when comparing subgroups based on type of dyslexia (except for the difference in word reading accuracy scores). However, an interesting pattern emerged for the phonemic awareness scores, that was further explored. A repeated-measure ANOVA was performed, entering type of phonemic awareness task (see following section for a description) as within-subject factor (phoneme deletion vs. phonemic blending) and type of dyslexia as between-subject factor. A significant interaction between type of phonemic awareness task and type of dyslexia was found, $F_{(1, 20)} = 5.36$, $p < 0.05$; $\eta_p^2 = 0.211$, suggesting different phonemic awareness difficulties in the two subgroups. Namely, children with phonological dyslexia had similar performances in the two phonemic awareness tasks, whereas children with surface dyslexia were more impaired in phonemic blending than in phoneme deletion [$F_{(1, 11)} = 21.47$, $p = 0.001$; $\eta_p^2 = 0.661$].

The distribution of dyslexia subtypes in the two groups with/without previous language delay was not significantly different, $\chi^2(1, N = 19) = 1.269$, $p > 0.05$.

TASKS

Reading and reading-related tasks

Reading skills were assessed through two different tasks:

- "Prove di lettura MT per la scuola elementare-2" (Reading tests for primary school, Cornoldi et al., 1998) and "Nuove prove di lettura MT per la scuola media inferiore" (New reading tests for secondary school, Cornoldi and Colpo, 1995), widely used Italian tests providing accuracy and speed scores in reading aloud age-normed texts.
- "Batteria per la valutazione della dislessia e disortografia evolutiva" (Battery for the assessment of Developmental reading and spelling disorders, Sartori et al., 1995). In particular, speed and accuracy z-scores were computed for single word (4 lists of 28 words) and non-word reading (3 lists of 16 non-words).

Two *phonemic awareness* tests were taken from an unpublished battery (Cossu et al., 1988):

- "Phoneme deletion": canceling the first two phonemes of orally given words
- "Phonemic blending": integrating sequentially presented phonemes into words

Scores for each test are expressed as number of errors on 20 words. Only age means and cut-off scores are provided as normative data.

Short-term memory was assessed by a digit span subtest, comprising Digits Forwards and Digits Backwards. For the children who had undergone intelligence testing with the WISC-R, the weighted score of the Digit Span subtest was recorded. For the other participants, digit span was assessed by a subtest of TEMA (Test di Memoria e Apprendimento, an Italian adaptation of TOMAL, Reynolds and Bigler, 1994), and recorded as z-scores.

Experimental tasks

The experimental tasks were created based on well-established protocols described in the literature. Moreover, they had already been used in a previous study by the authors (Cantiani et al., 2010). Only nonspeech processing skills were addressed, in order

[1]Although it is sometimes argued that mistakes are very rare in transparent orthographies (e.g., Landerl et al., 1997), it was clearly shown that children with DD do make mistakes (though less numerous than is described for opaque languages), even in a language with a very consistent orthography as Italian (Brizzolara et al., 2006; Menghini et al., 2010).

Table 2 | z-scores for word and nonword reading for each participant (DD group).

				Word reading accuracy	Word reading speed	Nonword reading accuracy	Nonword reading speed
Subtype	Surface	1		−4.78	−3.50	−3.86	−1.83
		2		−6.21	−4.73	−4.69	−2.45
		3		−4.88	−1.48	−3.51	−2.33
		4		−6.90	−1.81	−4.97	−0.22
		5		−8.71	−8.18	−3.53	−5.77
		6		−4.50	−4.20	−2.17	−2.14
		7		−3.50	−1.02	−0.68	−0.34
		8		−5.20	−5.60	−3.60	−3.36
		9		−4.86	−1.40	−2.21	−0.85
		10		−3.11	−1.45	−0.48	−1.14
		11		−1.44	−3.39	−0.82	−2.48
		12		−2.60	−4.70	−0.40	−5.00
		Total	*N*	12	12	12	12
			Mean	−4.7242	−3.4550	−2.5767	−2.3258
	Phonological	1		−2.64	−1.05	−4.97	−0.62
		2		−3.66	−1.40	−4.28	−2.06
		3		−0.92	−1.80	−2.71	−1.04
		4		−0.14	−6.63	−2.47	−5.40
		5		−0.69	−2.14	−1.28	−0.52
		6		−1.68	−2.59	−2.92	−4.89
		7		−2.18	−5.76	−3.36	−7.50
		8		−1.88	0.09	−3.36	0.50
		9		0.24	−0.43	−4.07	−0.18
		10		−0.86	0.44	−5.81	0.63
		Total	*N*	10	10	10	10
			Mean	−1.4410	−2.1270	−3.5230	−2.1080
	Total	*N*		22	22	22	22
		Mean		−3.2318	−2.8514	−3.0068	−2.2268

to avoid direct influences from linguistic or phonological deficits. All stimuli were digitally generated using Praat software (www.praat.org) and were presented to each child on an ASUS computer by means of E-prime Experiment Generator and Controller software (Schneider et al., 2002).

The *Temporal Order Judgment (TOJ) task* (Tallal and Piercy, 1973a,b; Tallal, 1980) was constructed using two complex tones composed of frequencies within the speech range. The two tones differed in the fundamental frequency (Fo = 100 Hz for the low tone and Fo = 305 Hz for the high one), and tone duration for both tones was either 75 or 250 ms. Children were instructed to indicate the order of the tones after each trial by pressing a yellow key for the "low" tone and a blue key for to the "high" tone. The same experimental paradigm was used in two different tasks: a Rapid Temporal Order Judgment (Rapid-TOJ) task, in which ISI was manipulated, and a Temporal Order Judgment Memory (TOJ-Memory) task, in which the number of elements to keep in memory was manipulated.

In the *Rapid Temporal Order Judgment (Rapid-TOJ) task*, stimulus pairs were created by pairing the two stimuli in all four possible combinations (AA, AB, BB, BA) with different inter-stimulus intervals: 8, 15, 30; 60, 150, 305, and 428 ms, and presented randomly. A short training with visual and verbal feedback was given to familiarize the children with the task. First, each tone was demonstrated separately seven times, and participants had to answer by pressing the corresponding key. Then, single tones were presented in random order. This training was continued for a maximum of 48 trials or until a criterion of 20 correct responses in a series of 24 consecutive stimuli was reached ($p < 0.001$ Binomial Test). In the last phase of training, participants were trained to respond to each of the four possible stimulus patterns by pressing the keys in the correct order. There were four demonstrations by the experimenter, followed by eight trials in which participants responded independently. An inter-stimulus interval (ISI) of 428 ms was employed during training. After the training session, 24 similar trials were given without feedbacks. Children were then tested on two-element stimulus patterns with ISIs of 8, 15, 30, 60, 150, and 305 ms. Each subject received a total of 24 two-element patterns, four for each ISI, with random presentation order. This training and testing procedure was carried out twice, once for each of the two stimulus durations: 75 and 250 ms (presentation order for the two blocks was balanced across participants).

In the *Temporal Order Judgment Memory (TOJ-Memory) task*, stimulus sequences consisted of four and five elements created as random combinations of the two complex tones, with a fixed ISI of 428 ms. Two different blocks were presented in

Table 3 | Subgroup characteristics (*p*-values indicating significant group differences are marked in bold).

Grouping Criteria				Comparison between dyslexic subgroups
Presence/absence of previous language impairment		**DD+LI**	**DD-no LI**	***F(df), p***
	N	10	11	
	AGE[a]	130.2 (23.90)	122.6 (20.19)	0.62 (1.20), 0.442
	IQ[b]	107.2 (7.24)	101.0 (8.73)	3.01 (1.20), 0.099
	READING: accuracy[c]	−2.14 (0.69)	−3.67 (1.42)	9.53 (1.20), **0.006**
	READING: speed[c]	−1.74 (1.61)	−2.72 (2.08)	1.44 (1.20), 0.244
	SHORT–TERM MEMORY[d]	−0.48 (0.62)	−1.078 (0.45)	6.01 (1.19), **0.025**
	PHONEME DELETION[e]	1.50 (1.43)	3.27 (2.49)	3.88 (1.20), 0.064
	PHONEMIC BLENDING[e]	3.50 (2.63)	5.36 (3.44)	1.91 (1.20), 0.183
Type of dyslexia		**"Phonological" DD**	**"Surface" DD**	***F(df), p***
	N	10	12	
	AGE[a]	128.3 (17.88)	133.2 (27.71)	0.236 (1.21), 0.632
	IQ[b]	102.3 (9.02)	102.2 (8.07)	0.00 (1.21), 0.989
	READING: accuracy[c]	−2.66 (0.85)	−3.51 (1.50)	2.505 (1.21), 0.129
	READING: speed[c]	−1.92 (2.32)	−2.76 (1.43)	1.075 (1.21), 0.312
	NON–WORD READING: accuracy[f]	−3.52 (1.30)	−2.57 (1.67)	2.115 (1.21), 0.161
	WORD READING: accuracy[f]	−1.44 (1.19)	−4.72 (1.96)	21.225 (1.21), < **0.001**
	SHORT–TERM MEMORY[d]	−1.03 (0.51)	−0.91 (0.39)	0.331 (1.20), 0.572
	PHONEME DELETION[e]	3.00 (2.45)	1.67 (1.87)	2.09 (1.21), 0.163
	PHONEMIC BLENDING[e]	4.00 (2.87)	5.33 (3.23)	1.03 (1.21), 0.323

[a]Age in months; [b]Scores on WISC-R or Cattell's "Culture Free" test: [c]Global scores were created considering both scores on word and non-word reading and on text reading. Mean scores expressed as Z-scores were calculated separately for accuracy and speed; [d]Z-scores; [e]raw scores (number of errors); [f]Z-scores in the word and non-word reading tasks.

a counterbalanced order: one included 10 four-tone sequences and one included 10 five-tone sequences. Both blocks were preceded by training including one trial demonstrated by the experimenter, and three trials in which children responded independently and feedback was given. The whole training and testing procedure was carried out twice, once for each of the two stimulus durations: 75 and 250 ms (order counterbalanced across participants). Data from 2-stimulus series with 428 ms ISI from the Rapid-TOJ task were included in the analyses of the TOJ-Memory task, so as to increase the range of sequence lengths and analyze memory effects on performance (stimulus sequences of two, four and five elements).

In the *Pattern Discrimination Task* (adapted from Kujala et al., 2000) a simple behavioral procedure was adopted, requiring the children to discriminate four-tone rhythmic patterns. The stimulus patterns consisted of four synthetically generated tones (500 Hz in frequency and 30 ms in duration) separated by different ISIs (50 ms; 150 ms; 200 ms). Two different stimulus patterns (rhythms) were created by changing the order of the ISIs, and separately recorded on audio files:

- Rhythm A: sound—200 ms ISI—sound—50 ms ISI—sound—150 ms ISI—sound
- Rhythm B: sound—200 ms ISI—sound—150 ms ISI—sound— 50 ms ISI—sound

The two rhythms were paired in all four possible combinations (AA, AB, BB, BA) with 700-ms intervals. The children listened to the pairs of rhythms and were requested to say whether the two rhythms were equal (50%) or different (50%). The answers were recorded by the experimenter by pressing different keys on the computer keyboard. During the testing phase a fixation point was shown on the computer screen. The task, composed of 24 trials, was preceded by two different training phases: a passive training including 8 trials (two for each combination) demonstrated by the experimenter, and an active training including 4 trials (one for each combination), in which participants responded independently and feedback was given.

Apparatus and procedures

All testing was conducted individually in a quiet room. Experimental and reading tasks were presented in a single session, with a total duration of about 1 h and a half. Task sequence was counterbalanced within participants to control for fatigue effects. The stimuli of the RAP tasks were presented binaurally through headphones

(Sennheiser HD270) with an intensity of approximately 60 dB. All the responses were recorded via the computer keyboard.

RESULTS

DATA ANALYSES

In the first part of this section, the results of the whole sample of dyslexic participants on the three tasks are compared with those of control participants. Two separate ANOVAs (repeated measures GLM) were performed for the two different TOJ tasks (Rapid-TOJ, TOJ-Memory), and a univariate ANOVA was performed for the Pattern Discrimination task, considering the mean percentage of correct answers. In all ANOVAs, Group (dyslexic vs. control participants) was entered as between-subject factor and Age as a covariate, while within-subject factors differed according to the specific task. For the Rapid-TOJ task, accuracy on trials with short ISIs (from 8 to 30 ms inclusive) were compared with accuracy on trials with longer ISIs (60–428 ms inclusive). The cut-off was set at 40 ms as this time frame was suggested to be crucial for speech discrimination (Fitch et al., 1997). This subdivision was similar to that used in previous studies (e.g., Heath et al., 1999; Cohen-Mimran and Sapir, 2007). The adequacy of this 40 ms cut-off was empirically confirmed by a preliminary analysis on the single ISI values. Due to the significant difference in performance IQ between groups (control children had higher IQs), Pearson's bivariate correlations were first computed between performance-IQ measures and all experimental variables. Since significant correlations ($p_s < 0.05$) were found for the TOJ-Memory task, IQ was entered as a covariate for this task. The "Delancy-Maxwell" method was applied to both IQ-scores and Age, in order to center the mean of the covariates, thus avoiding distortions of the main effects (Delaney and Maxwell, 1981). Specifically, the measure used as a covariate was the deviation of each individual score with respect to the mean score in the whole sample.

The second part of this section will focus on the dyslexic group, subdivided according to the presence/absence of a previous language impairment, and to type of dyslexia. Again, separate ANOVAs were performed for the three tasks, considering the mean percentage of correct answers. For each task, two different ANOVAs were performed, first with Language (presence vs. absence of language delay) and then with Type of Dyslexia (surface vs. phonological dyslexia) as between-subject factors. The results of control participants will be shown in the graphs as a reference point, but will not be included in the analyses. Due to the high correlations between the three tasks (all $p_s < 0.001$), no statistical corrections were employed to adjust for multiple analyses. One-tailed p-values are reported (as specified in the text) when clearly unidirectional hypotheses were considered. Two-tailed p-values are to be intended when not otherwise specified. Due to the limited number of participants in each subgroup, all analyses showing significant differences were repeated with nonparametric statistics, and only the results that were confirmed by nonparametric tests are reported here.

Finally, correlations between measures of RAP variables and reading, phonemic awareness and short-term memory scores will be illustrated, both concerning the whole sample and the dyslexic group.

COMPARING CHILDREN WITH/WITHOUT DYSLEXIA

Rapid-TOJ task

In addition to the described between-subject factor Group and the covariate Age, two within-subject factors were considered: Stimulus Length (75 vs. 250 ms) and Interstimulus Interval (ISI) (short ISIs: 8–30 ms vs. long ISIs: 60–428 ms). The main effect of Group reached statistical significance, $F_{(1,42)} = 6.13$, $p < 0.01$ [1-tailed]; $\eta_p^2 = 0.127$, with fewer correct responses for the dyslexic group compared to the control group. Significant effects were found for Stimulus Length, $F_{(1,42)} = 18.80$, $p < 0.001$; $\eta_p^2 = 0.309$, and ISI, $F_{(1,42)} = 29.77$, $p < 0.001$; $\eta_p^2 = 0.415$. A close-to-significance interaction (Stimulus Length × ISI: $F_{(1,42)} = 3.97$, $p = 0.053$; $\eta_p^2 = 0.086$) indicated a general greater difficulty associated with the processing of short and rapid sounds. Finally, an interaction ISI × Group × Age emerged, $F = 6, 70$, $p < 0.05$, $\eta_p^2 = 0.138$. This interaction is illustrated in **Figure 1**. No further interactions were found of any variable with either Group or Age (all $p_s > 0.05$).

TOJ-Memory task

In addition to Group and Age, two within-subject factors were considered: Stimulus Length (75 vs. 250 ms) and Sequence Length (2 vs. 4 vs. 5 elements). A significant main effect emerged for Group, $F_{(1,41)} = 14.93$, $p < 0.001$ [1-tailed]; $\eta_p^2 = 0.267$. Moreover, a significant interaction between Group and Sequence Length was found, $F_{(2,82)} = 5.53$, $p < 0.005$ [1-tailed]; $\eta_p^2 = 0.119$, due to a worse drop in performance from the 2-tone-sequences to the 5-tone-sequences for children with DD as compared to control children. A further interaction with Age [Group × Age × Sequence Length, $F_{(2,82)} = 2.78$, $p < 0.05$ [1-tailed]; $\eta_p^2 = 0.064$), indicates different performance patterns within the dyslexic group, as shown in **Figure 2**.

Pattern discrimination task

Similarly to the results obtained in the TOJ tasks, the main effects of Group, $F_{(1,45)} = 28.42$, $p < 0.001$ [1-tailed]; $\eta_p^2 = 0.404$, and Age, $F_{(1,45)} = 5.25$, $p < 0.05$, $\eta_p^2 = 0.111$, but not the interaction between Group and Age, reached statistical significance.

COMPARING SUBGROUPS OF CHILDREN WITH DD

No main effects of the subgroup divisions (Language and Type of Dyslexia) emerged in any task (all $p_s > 0.2$). However, significant interactions were found, that will be presented separately for the Rapid-TOJ task and the TOJ-Memory task. **Figure 3** shows the distribution of the main variables in the subgroups, and outliers for each group.

Rapid-TOJ task

Concerning the subdivision *Presence/absence of a previous language delay*, a significant interaction emerged between Language and Stimulus Length, $F_{(1,19)} = 4.85$, $p < 0.05$; $\eta_p^2 = 0.204$. As **Figure 4** shows, children with DD+LI, similarly to control children, performed worse when sounds were shorter ($M = 0.585$;

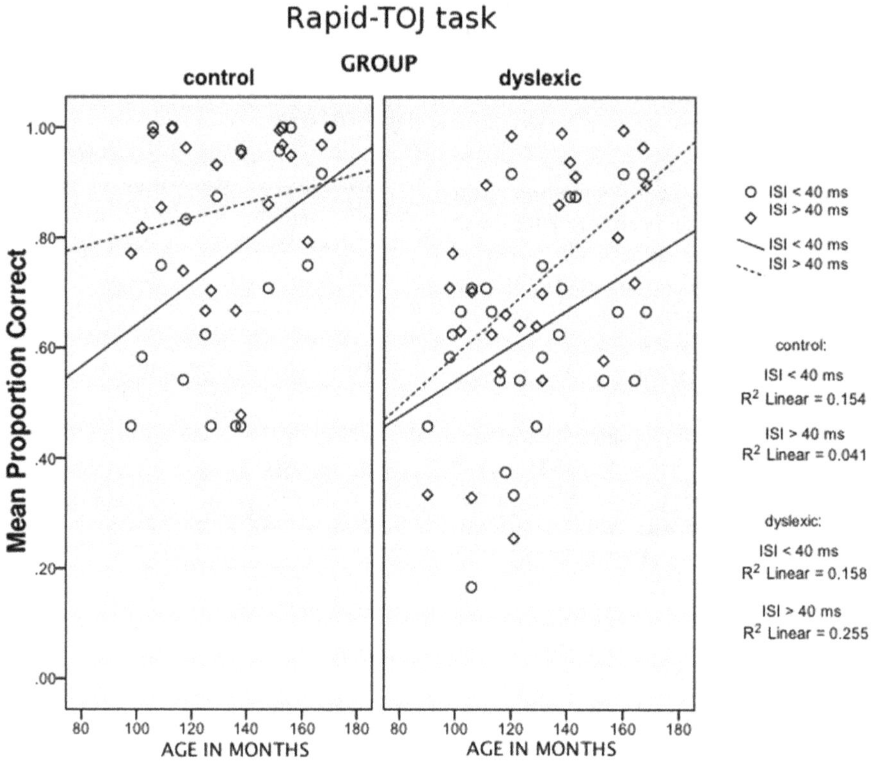

FIGURE 1 | Scatter plots of Age (in months, x-axis) against the mean proportion of correct answers in the Rapid-TOJ task (y-axis), for short and long-ISI conditions, for the two groups (control children and children with DD).

$SD = 0.188$) and better when sounds were longer ($M = 0.755$; $SD = 0.208$), $F_{(1, 9)} = 7.09, p < 0.05$; $\eta_p^2 = 0.441$, while children with DD-noLI had similar performances in the two conditions (shorter sounds: $M = 0.708$; $SD = 0.226$; longer sounds: $M = 0.717$; $SD = 0.213$), $F_{(1, 10)} = 0.062$, $p > 0.05$. As compared to controls, a difference approaching statistical significance was found for children with DD+LI in the 75-ms-tone condition, $F_{(1, 30)} = 3.919, p = 0.058, \eta_p^2 = 0.123$ while a significant difference for children with DD-noLI was found only in the long-tone condition, $F_{(1, 31)} = 6.803, p < 0.05$ ($\eta_p^2 = 0.190$). No other significant interactions emerged. Concerning the subdivision *Type of dyslexia*, no significant interactions were found (all $p_s > 0.1$).

TOJ-Memory task

Concerning the subdivision *Presence/absence of a previous language delay*, a significant interaction between Language and Stimulus Length was found, $F_{(1, 19)} = 9.00$, $p < 0.01$; $\eta_p^2 = 0.321$. As **Figure 5** shows, children with DD+LI, comparably to control children, performed worse when sounds were shorter ($M = 0.365$; $SD = 0.218$) and better when sounds were longer ($M = 0.517$; $SD = 0.218$), $F_{(1, 9)} = 9.58$, $p < 0.05$ ($\eta_p^2 = 0.516$), while children with DD-noLI had similar performances in the two conditions (shorter sounds: $M = 0.562$; $SD = 0.206$; longer sounds: $M = 0.538$; $SD = 0.208$), $F_{(1, 10)} = 0.51$; $p > 0.05$. Compared to the control children, significant differences were found in both conditions for children with DD+LI [75-ms-tone condition, $F_{(1, 30)} = 15.239, p = 0.001, \eta_p^2 = 0.352$; 250-ms-tone condition, $F_{(1, 30)} = 12.90, p = 0.001, \eta_p^2 = 0.315$), while a significant difference for children with DD-noLI was found only in the long-tone condition, $F_{(1, 31)} = 12.15, p < 0.01$, $\eta_p^2 = 0.295$. No other significant interactions emerged. As shown in **Figure 3**, two outliers may be identified in the DD-noLI subgroup processing short sounds. Yet, after excluding these subjects in the main ANOVA, the interaction Language × Stimulus Length remains significant, $F_{(1, 17)} = 8.45, p = 0.01; \eta_p^2 = 0.332$.

Concerning the subdivision *Type of dyslexia*, the only significant interaction concerned Type of Dyslexia and Stimulus Length, $F_{(1, 20)} = 4.49$, $p < 0.05$; $\eta_p^2 = 0.184$. In this case, children with surface DD (similarly to children with DD+LI and to controls) performed worse with shorter ($M = 0.449$; $SD = 0.193$) than with longer tones [$M = 0.572$; $SD = 0.210$, $F_{(1, 11)} = 7.041$, $p < 0.05$, $\eta_p^2 = 0.390$], while children with phonological DD performed similarly in the two conditions (shorter sounds: $M = 0.470$; $SD = 0.277$; longer sounds: $M = 0.453$; $SD = 0.229$), $F_{(1,9)} = 0.127$, $p > 0.05$, as **Figure 6** shows. Although *post-hoc* analyses do not show any significant differences between subgroups, both subgroups differ significantly from controls in both conditions (all $p_s < 0.05$, η_p^2 ranging between 0.189 and 0.401). Also in this case, two outliers may be identified in the subgroup of children with surface DD in the processing of long sounds (see **Figure 3**). Again though, when repeating the main ANOVA without these participants, the interaction Type of Dyslexia x Stimulus Length keeps its significance, $F_{(1, 18)} = 5.69$, $p < 0.05$; $\eta_p^2 = 0.240$.

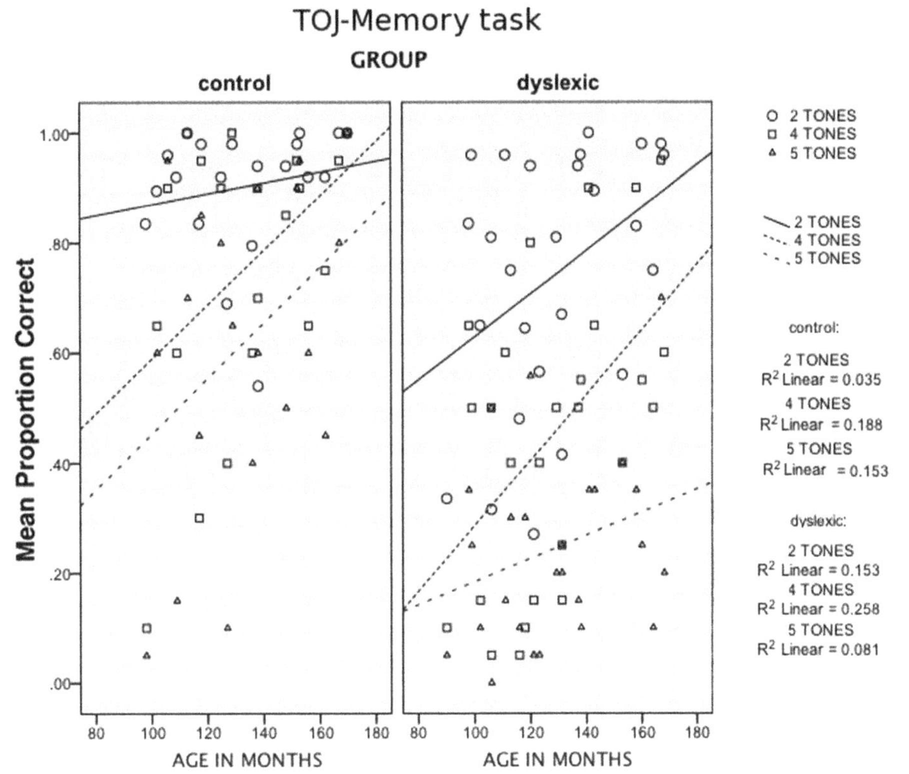

FIGURE 2 | Scatter plots of Age (in months, x-axis) against the mean proportion of correct answers in the TOJ-Memory task (y-axis), for the different Sequence Length conditions (2, 4, and 5-tone conditions) for the two groups (control children and children with DD).

CORRELATIONS BETWEEN MEASURES OF RAP AND READING/READING-RELATED VARIABLES

Calculation of correlations was performed for the two groups of dyslexic and normally reading children separately, in order to avoid spurious effects of reading ability (see also Rosen, 2003). To reduce the number of correlations to be computed, compound scores were considered for the RAP variables, including: average of all Rapid-TOJs; average of all Memory-TOJs; average of all TOJs (irrespective of sequence length), average of all TOJs subdivided for length (75 and 250). Considering the results of the previous analyses, two new variables were purposely computed, expressing the difference between accuracy scores with 250 and with 75 ms tones (i.e., the advantage for processing long tones) in all the TOJ tasks (Long-short tones) and the difference between long and short ISIs (Long-short ISIs)[2]. Pattern discrimination scores were also included in the analysis. A first interesting result is the absence of correlations in the control group between RAP variables and age, whereas strong correlations emerged in the group with dyslexia. Since no correlation was found in the DD group between RAP variables and IQ, nor did any correlations emerge between age or IQ and reading scores expressed as z-scores (all $r_s < 0.3$), Pearson's bivariate correlations were computed including z-scores. The "Long-short tones" difference variable showed the strongest correlations with reading variables (but no correlations with age and IQ), namely with Text and Nonword reading accuracy ($r = 0.402$ and 0.399 respectively, $p < 0.05$) and with overall Nonword reading ability (average of speed and accuracy z-scores) ($r = 0.554$, $p < 0.005$). This variable also showed a correlation with Phoneme deletion (raw score, $r = -0.438$, $p < 0.05$), which was confirmed also when partialling out the effect of Age ($r = -0.413$, $p < 0.05$). Phoneme deletion, in turn, correlated with Pattern discrimination scores, albeit at a very moderate level ($r = -0.380, p = 0.07$). Significant correlations emerged also between phonemic blending and word reading speed and accuracy ($r = 0.451$, $p < 0.05$ and $r = 0.507$, $p < 0.01$, respectively) and between phoneme deletion and nonword reading speed and accuracy ($r = 0.445$, $p < 0.05$ and $r = 0.433$, $p < 0.01$, respectively). Correlations with the ISI-related variable (Long-short ISIs) did not reach significance, but it is noteworthy that almost all correlations with reading variables are negative ones, i.e., contrary to what happens with tone length, high sensitivity to differences in ISI predicts lower reading performances. A moderate correlation between the two differential variables was found only for control children ($r = 0.446$, $p = 0.048$).

Multiple linear regressions were additionally performed to further explore the relationship between RAP, reading and reading related measures. A regression analysis (backward method) based on the results of the correlation analysis allowed to predict

[2]This variable was computed within each subject by regressing ln(ISI) onto performance and using predicted performance for the maximum and the minimum ISI. Then, the score related to the minimum ISI was subtracted from the score related to the maximum ISI.

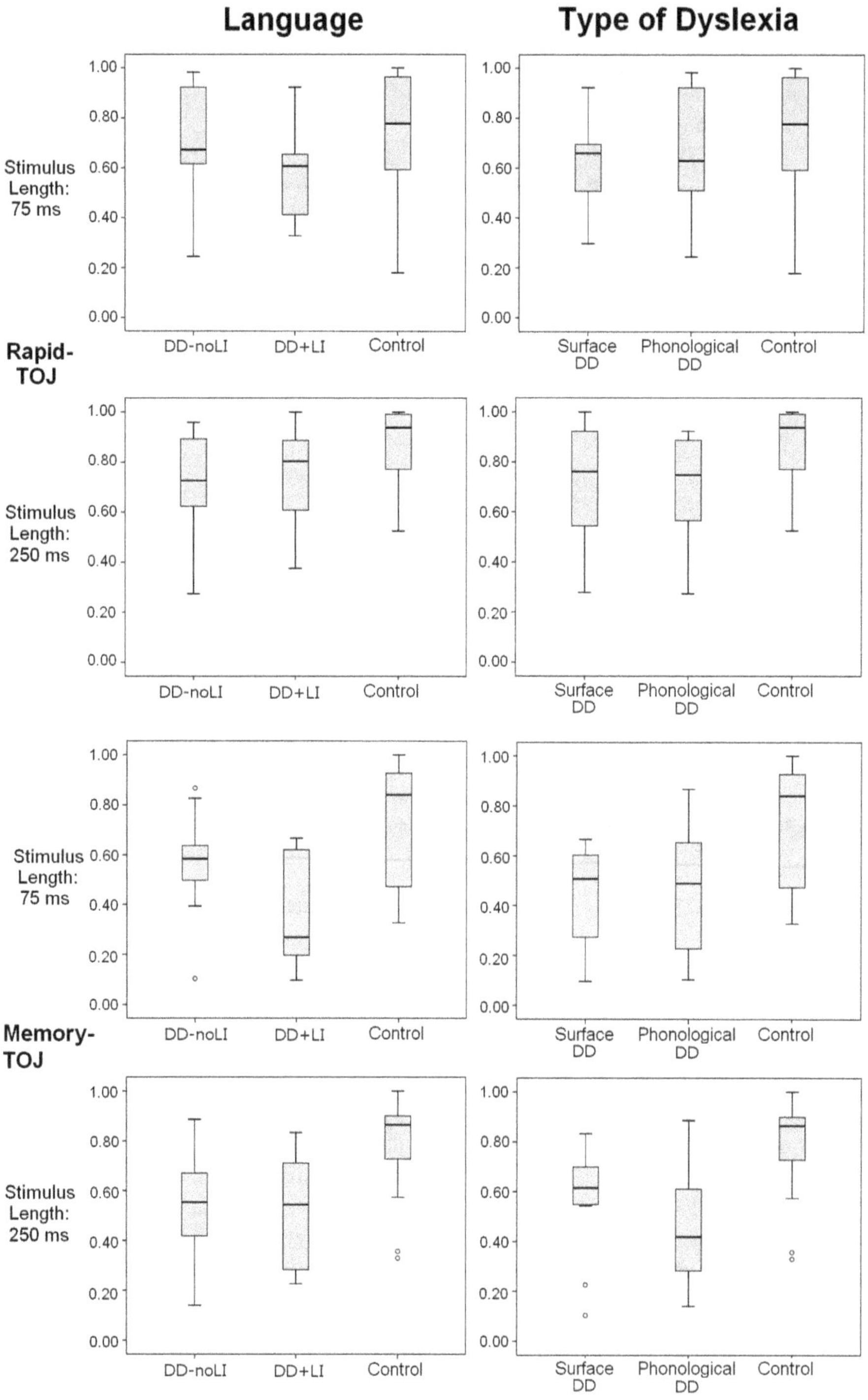

FIGURE 3 | Box plots displaying the distribution of individual scores in different subgroups (based on Language and Type of Dyslexia) for the Rapid-TOJ and the Memory-TOJ tasks. Empty circles correspond to outliers.

Nonword reading ability (average of speed and accuracy z-scores) through Phoneme deletion, total Pattern discrimination and the "Long-short tones" difference (entered together with Age and Phonemic blending, which showed no effect on the depending variable). The model was highly significant, $F_{(3, 22)} = 5.583$, $p = 0.006$ and explained 42% of the variance (30% was explained by the "Long-short tones" difference, 12% by Phoneme deletion, and 1% by Pattern discrimination scores). The best predictive model ($F = 3.506$, $p = 0.047$, $R^2 = 0.234$) for Word reading scores included phonemic blending and the difference between short and long ISIs (both with negative coefficient), that explained, respectively, 14.5 and 8.9%, of the variance. A general reading

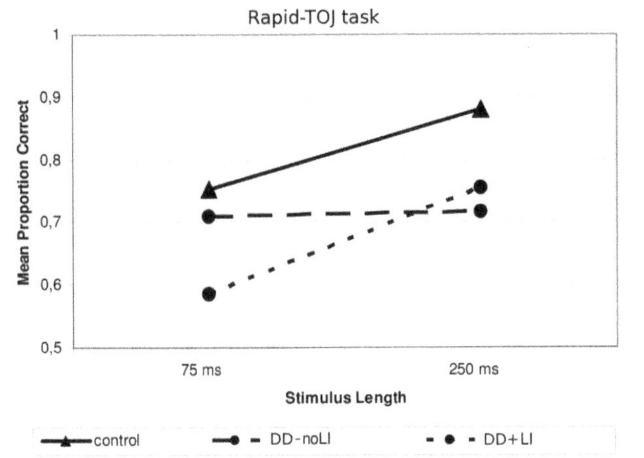

FIGURE 4 | Mean proportion of correct answers in the Rapid—TOJ task for the subgroups divided according to Language.

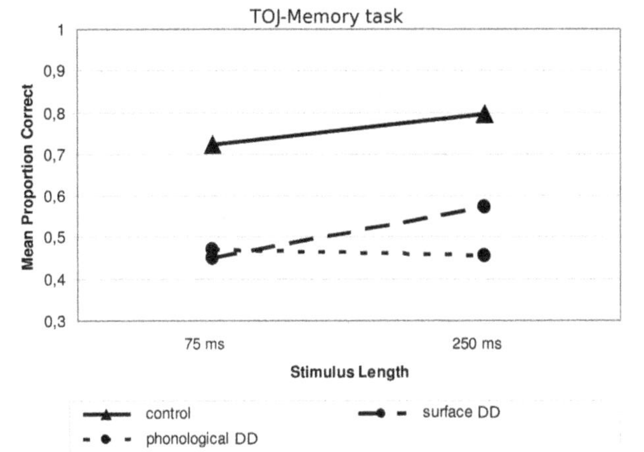

FIGURE 6 | Mean proportion of correct answers in the TOJ—Memory task for the subgroups divided according to Type of Dyslexia.

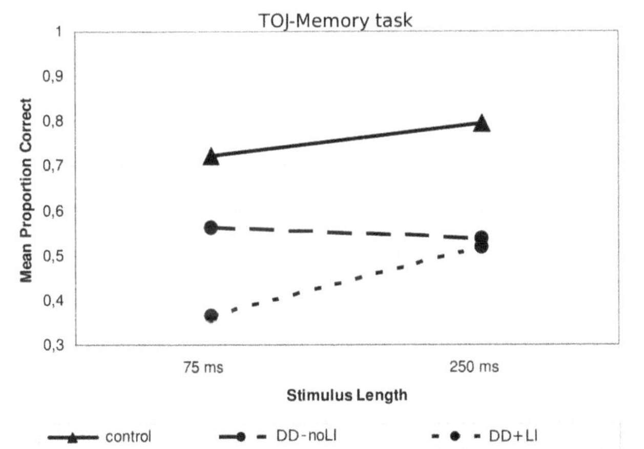

FIGURE 5 | Mean proportion of correct answers in the TOJ—Memory task for the subgroups divided according to Language.

score expressing the average of word, nonword and text reading, including speed and accuracy, was best predicted ($F = 5.346$, $p = 0.012$, $R^2 = 0.317$) by both differential scores concerning ISIs (15.8%) and stimulus length (15.9%). Phonemic blending was nonsignificant and added less than 4% to the variance. On the other hand, Phoneme deletion scores could be predicted by "Long-short tones" difference (accounting for 19% of variance) and Pattern discrimination scores (accounting for 13% of variance) - whereas Age had no effect on the model—$F_{(2, 23)} = 5.195$, $p = 0.014$, $R^2 = 0.31$. No predictive model was found for Phonemic blending scores.

DISCUSSION

The aim of the present study was to investigate Rapid Auditory Processing (RAP) abilities in Italian children (reading a regular orthography) with DD, subdivided according to age, presence/absence of a previous language delay, and subtype of dyslexia, following the hypothesis that differences in performance among subgroups could explain part of the heterogeneity of results described in the literature concerning RAP.

First of all, the presence of a general auditory processing deficit concerning non-verbal stimuli in Italian children with DD was confirmed, extending the finding obtained in a smaller sample of Italian children with DD (Cantiani et al., 2010), and replicating recent findings concerning other languages with consistent orthographies (Georgiou et al., 2010; Landerl and Willburger, 2010). Children with DD performed worse than their matched controls both in reproducing the order of pairs and sequences of tones, and in judging the equality of 4-tone rhythms. The task that seems to better discriminate between control children and children with DD is the Pattern Discrimination task. In order to exclude that the reading difficulties themselves could be the cause of a suboptimal development of these skills (see Rosen, 2003; Ziegler et al., 2009), a further comparison with a Reading Level (based on Text reading speed) matched group was performed, confirming the presence of a significant difference between children with DD ($n = 9$) and (younger) control children ($n = 9$), $F_{(1, 17)} = 5.40$, $p < 0.05$ [2-tailed]; $\eta_p^2 = 0.268$ (with IQ as covariate).

Specifically concerning the TOJ-Memory task, all participants showed a drop in performance with sequences of 5 sounds compared to sequences of 4 sounds, but children with DD performed worse with the longest sequences, compared to controls. A similar result was obtained by Heiervang et al. (2002), and might point to the role of auditory short-term memory. The influence of short-term memory on reading acquisition is largely supported (Ackerman et al., 1990; Kibby et al., 2004). Moreover, some authors consider short-term memory, and in particular working memory, as a crucial factor influencing performance in RAP tasks (Banai and Ahissar, 2004), also when only two sounds are presented.

Age plays a relevant role in the Rapid-TOJ task (see **Figure 1**). Its effects can be seen in control children only for the most difficult condition, i.e., with the shortest ISIs. By contrast, in children with DD performance improves with age in both conditions, but particularly so in the easier one (longer ISIs) where children with DD finally reach the level of control children. Similarly, in the TOJ-Memory task (see **Figure 2**) control children show improvements with age in the most difficult conditions (with 4 and 5-tones), but not in the easiest condition (2-tones), probably due to a ceiling effect. Conversely, in children with DD age affects performance in the 2 and 4-tone conditions, but not in the most difficult one (5 tones), which shows a relative floor effect. These results, similar to those found by Hautus et al. (2003) and Tallal (2000), may suggest a relative compensation of RAP deficits in children with DD, with difficulties appearing only when the complexity of the task increases, either through short-term memory load or through faster presentation rates. This may reflect an anomalous or slowed development of short-term memory functions in children with DD. For instance, Nicolson et al. (1992) found in 15-year-old children with DD only a lack of fluency in articulation and slight deficits in memory span, while deficits in phonological processing were no longer detectable.

The results obtained by subdividing children with DD on the basis of the *presence/absence of a language delay* are partly in line with previous findings such as those reported by Tallal and Stark (1982), Heath et al. (1999), and Joanisse et al. (2000), who found auditory processing deficits only in reading-impaired children with a concomitant oral language delay. Indeed, in our sample children with DD and a previous language delay did obtain the lowest scores in RAP measures. However, they showed a pattern of performance similar to that of normally reading children, yielding lower accuracy scores with shorter stimuli. On the other hand, children with DD-only had a more mildly impaired, but more anomalous performance pattern, not showing the advantage for longer stimuli found in the other subgroups. A possible explanation calls into play the effect of language impairment on the use of cognitive strategies during RAP tasks. Indeed, children with DD and a previous language impairment are often characterized by problems with lexical access (Bishop et al., 2009; Chilosi et al., 2009). Following Bretherton and Holmes (2003), performance on RAP tasks may be facilitated by the use of verbal labels to characterize and more easily distinguish or recognize the different sequences, but children with impaired lexical access may have difficulties in establishing and retrieving verbal labels for the tone sequences quickly and accurately. By contrast, dyslexic-only children seem to be characterized by a phonemic awareness deficit—indeed, their performance in phoneme deletion is almost significantly worse than that of children with a previous language impairment (see **Table 2**). This hypothesis is in line with the findings in English-speaking children with DD with and without oral language impairments, showing that the latter are characterized by more severe phonological deficits and the former by impairment in broader language abilities (Bishop and Snowling, 2004). Nonetheless, the greater impairments in phonemic awareness and verbal memory found in DD-only children does not produce greater impairments in RAP tasks (the hypothesis that RAP deficits are simply a consequence of phonemic awareness deficits also contrasts with data from longitudinal studies such as Benasich and Tallal, 2002; Leppänen et al., 2010). This suggests that other deficits, not related to phonemic awareness and to verbal memory, and also not expressing an effect of worse reading skills (DD+LI children have better reading scores than DD-noLI) must constitute the basis for the significantly lower performance on RAP tasks. Such abilities might have to do with lexical skills, which are a characteristic of SLI children, with and without dyslexia, as shown in many studies (e.g., Chilosi et al., 2009; Nation, 2014).

The present results from children subdivided according to presence/absence of a previous language delay need further explanation. First of all, the language-impaired subgroup does not show lower performances in phonemic awareness and reading scores as usually described in the literature concerning opaque languages such as English (Catts et al., 2005; Ramus et al., 2013). Instead, these children show similar or even better performances with respect to the subgroup without previous language delay. This finding is consistent with other studies on Italian children (Brizzolara et al., 2006; Scuccimarra et al., 2008; Chilosi et al., 2009) where language-impaired children with DD showed no clear disadvantage in reading measures compared to dyslexic-only children, and it may suggest a reduced impact of linguistic deficits on learning regular orthographies. As to the relationship with RAP, it may be hypothesized that a milder but more pervasive deficit as that observed in dyslexic-only children has a greater impact on reading (possibly—as shown by correlation scores—through its effects on phonemic awareness) than a more severe but more "normally modulated" deficit as is observed in children with DD and a previous language delay. Also the inclusion of children for whom a language disorder was present in the past but was then resolved or compensated may have led to unexpected results. Indeed, the presence of early delays in language development that are compensated or resolved before school age is a common report for many children with dyslexia (e.g., Scarborough and Dobrich, 1990; Stothard et al., 1998), and it may well be associated to less severe reading impairment as compared to children with persistent (and probably more pervasive) language disorders. Additionally, published studies on RAP deficits in children with language impairment mostly fail to distinguish children with/without a concomitant reading disorder (e.g., Tallal and Piercy, 1973a,b), and the same is true for studies investigating dyslexic children (e.g., Marshall et al., 2001; Bretherton and Holmes, 2003, etc.), without extending the analysis to (previous and/or concomitant) language abilities—so that previous characterizations of the various subgroups may have been confounded.

Results from the subdivision according to *type of dyslexia* partially support Tallal's findings of a correlation between tone processing and non-word reading (Tallal, 1980). However, we did not find that RAP impairment was specific of children with phonological DD, as was reported by Cestnick (2001). In our sample, the main difference between children with phonological and surface DD relates to sound length (processing longer vs. shorter sounds). In fact, only children with surface DD (similarly to children with DD and previous language delay, and to a certain extent to controls) improved their performance with longer stimuli, showing a more severe difficulty with short sounds. By contrast, children with phonological DD performed similarly in the two conditions. The lack of advantage in recognizing words—which was the criterion for defining these children as "surface" dyslexic—may thus be related to less efficient lexical access, similar to what was suggested for dyslexic children with previous language impairment. In both cases, generally reduced performance on RAP tasks with an otherwise "normal" performance pattern may result from impaired use of cognitive, lexical strategies to facilitate the task. What remains to be explained is the anomalous performance pattern in so-called "phonological dyslexic" children, who have more difficulties in reading nonwords.

Indeed, the interaction found in the present sample between type of phonemic awareness task and type of dyslexia (see the paragraph on the characterization of the subgroups) suggests that the equation between impaired nonword reading and low phonemic awareness skills is a too simplistic one. The direct link between RAP scores and nonword reading (correlations and regression models), and the indirect correlations emerging between nonword reading and phoneme deletion, and between phoneme deletion and pattern discrimination point to a specific bridge between RAP (the advantage in processing long over short tones and rhythmic pattern analysis), the ability to analyze and manipulate (but not to blend) phonemic strings, and nonword reading ability, the latter ability being relatively preserved in surface dyslexic children. In spite of the label of Phonological dyslexia, thus, poor nonword reading does not imply lower performance on phonemic awareness tasks [overall performance on phonemic awareness tasks in this group does not differ at all from that of surface dyslexic children, $p > 0.99$; see (Ziegler et al., 2008) and (Sprenger-Charolles et al., 2000) for similar findings] but rather a *different* type of impairment on phonemic tasks. The role of phoneme deletion as opposed to phonemic blending and its relationship with nonword reading is an interesting one: the ability to analyze and manipulate single phonemes producing nonwords from words (the result of the deletion process) is more relevant to the possibility to handle non-lexical phonemic sequences such as nonwords. Phoneme blending, by contrast, appears more strictly related to the ability to recognize strings of sounds as meaningful units, namely as lexical entries such as words. The importance of phoneme deletion in explaining nonword reading had already been highlighted by (e.g., Pasquini et al., 2007). Nonetheless, one could have expected phonemic blending to predict nonword reading as well, being one of its constituent processes: the absence of such effect calls into play the twofold nature of nonword reading as a phonological and visual task. Indeed, strong relationships have been demonstrated between visual-spatial attentional deficits and nonword reading in Italian children with DD (Facoetti et al., 2006, 2010; Franceschini et al., 2012) suggesting that reading ordered strings of letters not only requires phonological ability, but also visual-spatial attentional skills. Furthermore, attentional deficits in the visual and auditory modality seem to follow similar pathways (Facoetti et al., 2003, 2010). It may be thus be hypothesized that the children showing more problems in the auditory modality correspond to DD+LI (language-impaired, here showing the lowest scores on RAP tasks), while children with phonological dyslexia (who show both the lowest scores and the most anomalous pattern on RAP tasks) may suffer from problems involving both the auditory and the visual modality (thus possibly more pervasive and with a more severe expression).

As a conclusion, the present findings are best interpreted within a multifactor model of dyslexia (see Pennington, 2006; Boets et al., 2007), which takes into account the effects of variables related to developmental trends and specific neuropsychological profiles. Further, it may suggest that other variables, especially related to verbal memory, lexical processing and attentional functions play a role in modulating the relationship between auditory temporal processing of nonverbal stimuli, phonemic skills and reading abilities. Since lexical access and attention have not been directly measured in the present study, their involvement follows from more speculative reasons and deserves further investigation. The lack of advantage for processing longer stimuli seems to be a very crucial issue, possibly indicating a more pervasive deficit in RAP (whatever the exact nature of this process and the mechanisms implied), which can produce detrimental effects on reading—especially when interacting with concomitant impairments at the visual-attentional level. Last but not least, the correlations between RAP variables, phonemic awareness skills and reading support the idea that processing auditory stimuli is not simply an associated problem, but concurs in determining both the quality and quantity of the reading deficit, in strict interplay with other variables. These findings thus do not support simplified versions of the RAP deficit, just focusing on deficits in processing short and rapid sounds, and rather depict a far more complex model of the interrelations between the different variables. Very crucial is the finding that RAP variables, not expressing absolute performance levels but rather differential scores describing the level of sensitivity to changes in tone length or ISI, are the best predictors of reading abilities in their various aspects, and better predictors than phonemic awareness and verbal memory skills. Even further, such differential variables contribute to the prediction of specific forms of phonemic awareness itself. Interestingly, while higher sensitivity to changes in tone length is associated to better reading performance, higher sensitivity to ISI changes are associated with worse reading performance. A closer inspection of correlation patterns in DD children suggests, in fact, that increased ISI-related differences depend on better performance with the longest ISIs ($r = 0.630$, $p = 0.001$, i.e., they express greater ability to take advantage from increases in ISI) whereas increased differences with respect to tone length depend on lower performances with short tones ($r = -0.371$, $p = 0.062$, i.e., they express more severe impairments).

The limited number of participants in each of the various subgroups calls for caution in generalizing its results. Further limitations of the study are the absence of concomitant language and attention measures, and the use of previous clinical reports (in a few cases, parents' reports) to identify children with comorbid language impairments. Nonetheless, the relatively homogeneous profiles within each group and the replication of some of the results in reading-level matched comparisons support their validity, and may offer stimulating hints as to the range and type of variables that need to be taken into account when investigating sensory processing in developmental disorders and their relationship with reading skills. The crucial role played by RAP variables (related to length of the stimuli, ISI, and to sensitivity to their modulations) in predicting specific aspects of reading performance (with differential effects on word and nonword reading) suggests that addressing such skills in intervention programs and choosing specific RAP targets according to the specific reading patterns may be an effective and innovative rehabilitation strategy. Furthermore, the present results suggest that linguistic variables (possibly at the lexical level) different from memory and phonemic awareness influence RAP and reading performance in children with comorbid DD and (even if compensated) LI. Further research seems to be necessary for the identification and characterization of such variables, that could shed better light on the complex relationships between low- and high-level processing of language.

REFERENCES

Ackerman, P. T., Dykman, R. A., and Gardner, M. Y. (1990). Counting rate, naming rate, phonological sensitivity, and memory span: major factors in dyslexia. *J. Learn. Disabil.* 23, 325–327. doi: 10.1177/002221949002300514

Ahissar, M., Protopapas, A., Reid, M., and Merzenich, M. M. (2000). Auditory processing parallels reading abilities in adults. *Proc. Natl. Acad. Sci. U.S.A.* 97, 6832–6837. doi: 10.1073/pnas.97.12.6832

American Psychiatric Association. (1994). *Diagnostic and Statistical Manual of Mental Disorders, 4th Edn.* Washington, DC: American Psychiatric Association.

Bakker, D. J. (1973). Hemispheric specialization and stages in the learning to read process. *Ann. Dyslexia* 23, 15–27.

Banai, K., and Ahissar, M. (2004). Poor frequency discrimination probes dyslexics with particularly impaired working memory. *Audiol. Neuro-Otol.* 9, 328–340. doi: 10.1159/000081282

Banai, K., and Ahissar, M. (2009). Perceptual learning as a tool for boosting working memory among individuals with reading and learning disability. *Learn. Percept.* 1, 115–134. doi: 10.1556/LP.1.2009.1.9

Benasich, A. A., and Tallal, P. (2002). Infant discrimination of rapid auditory cues predicts later language impairment. *Behav. Brain Res.* 136, 31–49. doi: 10.1016/S0166-4328(02)00098-0

Benasich, A. A., Thomas, J. J., Choudhury, N., and Leppänen, P. H. (2002). The importance of rapid auditory processing abilities to early language development: evidence from converging methodologies. *Dev. Psychobiol.* 40, 278–292. doi: 10.1002/dev.10032

Bishop, D. V. M., Hayiou-Thomas, M. E., McDonald, D., and Bird, A. (2009). Children who read words accurately despite language impairment: Who are they and how do they do it? *Child Dev.* 80, 593–605. doi: 10.1111/j.1467-8624.2009.01281.x

Bishop, D. V. M., and Snowling, M. J. (2004). Developmental dyslexia and specific language impairment: Same or different? *Psychol. Bull.* 130, 858–886. doi: 10.1037/0033-2909.130.6.858

Boder, E. (1973). Developmental dyslexia: a diagnostic approach based on three atypical reading-spelling patterns. *Dev. Med. Child Neurol.* 15, 663–687. doi: 10.1111/j.1469-8749.1973.tb05180.x

Boets, B., Vandermosten, M., Poelmans, H., Luts, H., Wouters, J., and Ghesquière, P. (2011). Preschool impairments in auditory processing and speech perception uniquely predict future reading problems. *Res. Dev. Disabil.* 32, 560–570. doi: 10.1016/j.ridd.2010.12.020

Boets, B., Wouters, J., van Wieringen, A., and Ghesquiere, P. (2007). Auditory processing, speech perception and phonological ability in preschool children at high-risk for dyslexia: a longitudinal study of the auditory temporal processing theory. *Neuropsychologia* 45, 1608–1620. doi: 10.1016/j.neuropsychologia.2007.01.009

Bretherton, L., and Holmes, V. M. (2003). The relationship between auditory temporal processing, phonemic awareness, and reading disability. *J. Exp. Child. Psychol.* 84, 218–243. doi: 10.1016/S0022-0965(03)00023-7

Brizzolara, D., Chilosi, A., Cipriani, P., Di Filippo, G., Gasperini, F., Mazzotti, S., et al. (2006). Do phonologic and rapid automatized naming deficits differentially affect dyslexic children with and without a history of language delay? A study of Italian dyslexic children. *Cogn. Behav. Neurol.* 19, 141–149. doi: 10.1097/01.wnn.0000213902.59827.19

Cantiani, C., Lorusso, M. L., Valnegri, C., and Molteni, M. (2010). Perception of non-verbal auditory stimuli in Italian dyslexic children. *Dev. Neuropsychol.* 35, 115–123. doi: 10.1080/87565640903335955

Castles, A., and Coltheart, M. (1993). Varieties of developmental dyslexia. *Cognition* 47, 149–180. doi: 10.1016/0010-0277(93)90003-E

Cattell, R. B. (1979). *Culture Free, Scale 2 – Forma A e B.* Firenze: Organizzazioni Speciali.

Catts, H. W., Adlof, S. M., Hogan, T. P., and Weismer, S. E. (2005). Are specific language impairment and dyslexia distinct disorders? *J. Speech Lang. Hear. Res.* 48, 1378–1396. doi: 10.1044/1092-4388(2005/096)

Cestnick, L. (2001). Cross-modality temporal processing deficits in developmental phonological dyslexics. *Brain Cogn.* 46, 319–325. doi: 10.1006/brcg.2000.1273

Chilosi, A. M., Brizzolara, D., Lami, L., Pizzoli, C., Gasperini, F., Pecini, C., et al. (2009). Reading and spelling disabilities in children with and without a history of early language delay: a neuropsychological and linguistic study. *Child Neuropsychol.* 15, 582–604. doi: 10.1080/09297040902927614

Cohen-Mimran, R., and Sapir, S. (2007). Auditory temporal processing deficits in children with reading disabilities. *Dyslexia* 13, 175–192. doi: 10.1002/dys.323

Cornoldi, C., and Colpo, G. (1995). *Nuove Prove di Lettura MT Per la Scuola Media Inferiore.* Firenze: Organizzazioni Speciali.

Cornoldi, C., Colpo, G., and Gruppo, M. T. (1998). *Prove di Lettura MT Per la Scuola Elementare-2.* Firenze: Organizzazioni Speciali.

Cossu, G., Shankweiler, D., Liberman, I. Y., Katz, L., and Tola, G. (1988). Awareness of phonological segments and reading ability in Italian children. *Appl. Psycholinguist.* 9, 1–16. doi: 10.1017/S0142716400000424

Delaney, H. D., and Maxwell, S. E. (1981). On using analysis of covariance in repeated measures designs. *Multivar. Behav. Res.* 17, 117–130.

Facoetti, A., Lorusso, M. L., Paganoni, P., Cattaneo, C., Galli, R., Umiltà, C., et al. (2003). Auditory and visual automatic attention deficits in developmental dyslexia. *Cogn. Brain Res.* 16, 185–191. doi: 10.1016/S0926-6410(02)00270-7

Facoetti, A., Trussardi, A. N., Ruffino, M., Lorusso, M. L., Cattaneo, C., Galli, R., et al. (2010). Multisensory spatial attention deficits are predictive of phonological decoding skills in developmental dyslexia. *J. Cogn. Neurosci.* 22, 1011–1025. doi: 10.1162/jocn.2009.21232

Facoetti, A., Zorzi, M., Cestnick, L., Lorusso, M. L., Molteni, M., Paganoni, P., et al. (2006). The relationship between visuo-spatial attention and nonword reading in developmental dyslexia. *Cogn. Neuropsychol.* 23, 841–855. doi: 10.1080/02643290500483090

Fitch, R. H., Miller, S., and Tallal, P. (1997). Neurobiology of speech perception. *Ann. Rev. Neurosci.* 20, 331–353. doi: 10.1146/annurev.neuro.20.1.331

Franceschini, S., Gori, S., Ruffino, M., Pedrolli, K., and Facoetti, A. (2012). A causal link between visual spatial attention and reading acquisition. *Curr. Biol.* 22, 814–819. doi: 10.1016/j.cub.2012.03.013

Gaab, N., Gabrieli, J. D. E., Deutsch, G. K., Tallal, P., and Temple, E. (2007). Neural correlates of rapid auditory processing are disrupted in children with developmental dyslexia and ameliorated with training: An fMRI study. *Restor. Neurol. Neurosci.* 25, 295–310.

Georgiou, G. K., Protopapas, A., Papadopoulos, T. C., Skaloumbakas, C., and Parrila, R. (2010). Auditory temporal processing and dyslexia in an orthographically consistent language. *Cortex* 46, 1330–1344. doi: 10.1016/j.cortex.2010.06.006

Goswami, U., Thomson, J., Richardson, U., Stainthorp, R., Hughes, D., Rosen, S., et al. (2002). Amplitude envelope onsets and developmental dyslexia: a new hypothesis. *Proc. Natl. Acad. Sci. U.S.A.* 99, 10911–10916. doi: 10.1073/pnas.122368599

Hämäläinen, J. A., Salminen, H. K., and Leppänen, P. H. T. (2012). Basic auditory processing deficits in dyslexia: systematic review of the behavioral and event-related potential/field evidence. *J. Learn. Disabil.* 46 413–427. *doi: 10.1177/0022219411436213*

Hari, R., and Renvall, H. (2001). Impaired processing of rapid stimulus sequences in dyslexia. *Trends. Cogn. Sci.* 5, 525–532. doi: 10.1016/S1364-6613(00)01801-5

Hautus, M. J., Setchell, G. J., Waldie, K. E., and Kirk, I. J. (2003). Age-related improvements in auditory temporal resolution in reading-impaired children. *Dyslexia* 9, 37–45. doi: 10.1002/dys.234

Heath, S. M., Hogben, J. H., and Clark, C. D. (1999). Auditory temporal processing in disabled readers with and without oral language delay. *J. Child Psychol. Psychol.* 40, 637–647. doi: 10.1111/1469-7610.00480

Heiervang, E., Stevenson, J., and Hugdahl, K. (2002). Auditory processing in children with dyslexia. *J. Child Psychol. Psychol.* 43, 931–938. doi: 10.1111/1469-7610.00097

Heim, S., Tschierse, J., Amunts, K., Wilms, M., Vossel, S., Willmes, K., et al. (2008). Cognitive subtypes of dyslexia. *Acta Neurobiol. Exp.* 68, 73–82.

Hood, M., and Conlon, E. (2004). Visual and auditory temporal processing and early reading development. *Dyslexia* 10, 234–252. doi: 10.1002/dys.273

Joanisse, M. F., Manis, F. R., Keating, P., and Seidenberg, M. S. (2000). Language deficits in dyslexic children: speech perception, phonology, and morphology. *J. Exp. Child Psychol.* 77, 30–60. doi: 10.1006/jecp.1999.2553

Johnson, E. P., Pennington, B. F., Lee, N. R., and Boada, R. (2009). Directional effects between rapid auditory processing and phonological awareness in children. *J. Child Psychol. Psychol.* 50, 902–910. doi: 10.1111/j.1469-7610.2009.02064.x

Kibby, M. Y., Marks, W., Morgan, S., and Long, C. J. (2004). Specific impairment in developmental reading disabilities: a working memory approach. *J. Learn. Disabil.* 37, 349–363. doi: 10.1177/00222194040370040601

Kujala, T., Myllyviita, K., Tervaniemi, M., Alho, K., Kallio, J., and Näätänen, R. (2000). Basic auditory dysfunction in dyslexia as demonstrated by brain activity measurements. *Psychophysiology* 37, 262–266. doi: 10.1111/1469-8986.3720262

Lachmann, T., Berti, S., Kujala, T., and Schroger, E. (2005). Diagnostic subgroups of developmental dyslexia have different deficits in neural processing of tones and phonemes. *Int. J. Psychophysiol.* 56, 105–120. doi: 10.1016/j.ijpsycho.2004.11.005

Lallier, M., Thierry, G., and Tainturier, M. J. (2012). On the importance of considering individual profiles when investigating the role of auditory sequential deficits in developmental dyslexia. *Cognition* 126, 121–127. doi: 10.1016/j.cognition.2012.09.008

Landerl, K., and Willburger, E. (2010). Temporal processing, attention, and learning disorders. *Learn. Individ. Differ.* 20, 393–401. doi: 10.1016/j.lindif.2010.03.008

Landerl, K., Wimmer, H., and Frith, U. (1997). The impact of orthographic consistency on dyslexia: a German-English comparison. *Cognition* 63, 315–334. doi: 10.1016/S0010-0277(97)00005-X

Leppänen, P. H., Hämäläinen, J. A., Salminen, H. K., Eklund, K. M., Guttorm, T. K., Lohvansuu, K., et al. (2010). Newborn brain event-related potentials revealing atypical processing of sound frequency and the subsequent association with later literacy skills in children with familial dyslexia. *Cortex* 46, 1362–1376. doi: 10.1016/j.cortex.2010.06.003

Malenfant, N., Grondin, S., Boivin, M., Forget–Dubois, N., Robaey, P., and Dionne, G. (2012). Contribution of temporal processing skills to reading comprehension in 8Year-olds: evidence for a mediation effect of phonological awareness. *Child Dev.* 83, 1332–1346. doi: 10.1111/j.1467-8624.2012.01777.x

Marshall, C. M., Snowling, M. J., and Bailey, P. J. (2001). Rapid auditory processing and phonological ability in normal readers and readers with dyslexia. *J. Speech Lang. Hear. Res.* 44, 925–940. doi: 10.1044/1092-4388(2001/073)

Mauk, M. D., and Buonomano, D. V. (2004). The neural basis of temporal processing. *Annu. Rev. Neurosci.* 27, 307–340. doi: 10.1146/annurev.neuro.27.070203.144247

McArthur, G. M., and Bishop, D. V. (2001). Auditory perceptual processing in people with reading and oral language impairments: current issues and recommendations. *Dyslexia* 7, 150–170. doi: 10.1002/dys.200

Menghini, D., Finzi, A., Benassi, M., Bolzani, R., Facoetti, A., Giovagnoli, S., et al. (2010). Different underlying neurocognitive deficits in developmental dyslexia: a comparative study. *Neuropsychologia* 48, 863–872. doi: 10.1016/j.neuropsychologia.2009.11.003

Mody, M., Studdert-Kennedy, M., and Brady, S. (1997). Speech perception deficits in poor readers: auditory processing or phonological coding? *J. Exp. Child Psychol.* 64, 199–231. doi: 10.1006/jecp.1996.2343

Nation, K. (2014). Lexical learning and lexical processing in children with developmental language impairments. *Philos. Trans. R. Soc. Lond. B Biol. Sci.* 369:20120387. doi: 10.1098/rstb.2012.0387

Nicolson, R. I., Fawcett, A. J., and Baddeley, A. D. (1992). *Working Memory and Dyslexia.* Report LRG 3/91, Department of Psychology, University of Sheffield.

Pasquini, E. S., Corriveau, K. H., and Goswami, U. (2007). Auditory processing of amplitude envelope rise time in adults diagnosed with developmental dyslexia. *Sci. Stud. Read.* 11, 259–286. doi: 10.1080/10888430701344280

Pennington, B. F. (2006). From single to multiple deficit models of developmental disorders. *Cognition* 101, 385–413. doi: 10.1016/j.cognition.2006.04.008

Peterson, R. L., Pennington, B. F., and Olson, R. K. (2013). Subtypes of developmental dyslexia: testing the predictions of the dual-route and connectionist frameworks. *Cognition* 126, 20–38. doi: 10.1016/j.cognition.2012.08.007

Ramus, F., Marshall, C. R., Rosen, S., and van der Lely, H. K. (2013). Phonological deficits in specific language impairment and developmental dyslexia: towards a multidimensional model. *Brain* 136, 630–645. doi: 10.1093/brain/aws356

Ramus, F., Rosen, S., Dakin, S. C., Day, B. L., Castellote, J. M., White, S., et al. (2003). Theories of developmental dyslexia: insights from a multiple case study of dyslexic adults. *Brain* 126, 841–865. doi: 10.1093/brain/awg076

Ramus, F., and Szenkovits, G. (2008). What phonological deficit? *Q. J. Exp. Psychol.* 61, 129–141. doi: 10.1080/17470210701508822

Reed, M. A. (1989). Speech perception and the discrimination of brief auditory cues in reading disabled children. *J. Exp. Child Psychol.* 48, 270–292. doi: 10.1016/0022-0965(89)90006-4

Reynolds, C. R., and Bigler, E. D. (1994). *Test of Memory and Learning: Examiner's manual.* Austin, TX: Pro-ed.

Rosen, S. (2003). Auditory processing in dyslexia and specific language impairment: is there a deficit? What is its nature? Does it explain anything? *J. Phonetics* 31, 509–527. doi: 10.1016/S0095-4470(03)00046-9

Sartori, G., Job, R., and Tressoldi, P. E. (1995). *Batteria per la Valutazione della Dislessia e Della Disortografia Evolutiva.* Firenze: Organizzazioni Speciali.

Scarborough, H. S., and Dobrich, W. (1990). Development of children with early language delay. *J. Speech Lang. Hear Res.* 33, 70.

Schneider, W., Eschman, A., and Zuccolotto, A. (2002). *E-prime User's Guide.* Pittsburg, CL: Psychology Software Tools Inc.

Scuccimarra, G., Cutolo, L., Fiorillo, P., Lembo, C., Pirone, T., and Cossu, G. (2008). Is there a distinct form of developmental dyslexia in children with specific language impairment? Findings from an orthographically regular language. *Cogn. Behav. Neurol.* 21, 221–226. doi: 10.1097/WNN.0b013e31818a5caf

Share, D. L., Jorm, A. F., Maclean, R., and Matthews, R. (2002). Temporal processing and reading disability. *Read. Writ.* 15, 151–178. doi: 10.1023/A:1013876606178

Snowling, M. J. (2001). From language to reading and dyslexia. *Dyslexia* 7, 37–46. doi: 10.1002/dys.185

Sprenger-Charolles, L., Cole, P., Lacert, P., and Serniclaes, W. (2000). On subtypes of developmental dyslexia: evidence from processing time and accuracy scores. *Can. J. Exp. Psychol.* 54, 87–104. doi: 10.1037/h0087332

Stothard, S. E., Snowling, M. J., Bishop, D. V. M., Chipchase, B. B., and Kaplan, C. A. (1998). Language-impaired preschoolers: a follow-up into adolescence. *J. Speech Lang. Hear Res.* 41, 407.

Studdert-Kennedy, M., and Mody, M. (1995). Auditory temporal perception deficits in the reading impaired: a critical review of the evidence. *Psychon. Bull. Rev.* 2, 508–514. doi: 10.3758/BF03210986

Talcott, J. B., Witton, C., McLean, M. F., Hansen, P. C., Rees, A., Green, G. G. R., et al. (2000). Dynamic sensory sensitivity and children's word decoding skills. *Proc. Natl. Acad. Sci. U.S.A.* 97, 2952–2957. doi: 10.1073/pnas.040546597

Tallal, P. (1980). Auditory temporal perception, phonics, and reading disabilities in children. *Brain Lang.* 9, 182–198. doi: 10.1016/0093-934X(80)90139-X

Tallal, P. (2000). "Experimental studies of language impairments: from research to remediation," in *Speech and Language Impairments in Children: Causes, Characteristics, Intervention and Outcome*, eds D. V. M. Bishop and L. B. Leonard (Hove: Psychology Press Publishers), 131–155.

Tallal, P., and Piercy, M. (1973a). Defects of non-verbal auditory perception in children with developmental aphasia. *Nature* 241, 468–469.

Tallal, P., and Piercy, M. (1973b). Developmental aphasia: impaired rate of non-verbal processing as a function of sensory modality. *Neuropsychologia* 11, 389–398.

Tallal, P., and Stark, R. E. (1982). Perceptual/motor profiles of reading impaired children with or without concomitant oral language deficit. *Ann. Dyslexia* 32, 163–176. doi: 10.1007/BF02647960

Thomson, J. M., and Goswami, U. (2008). Rhythmic processing in children with developmental dyslexia: auditory and motor rhythms link to reading and spelling. *J. Physiol.* 102, 120–129. doi: 10.1016/j.jphysparis.2008.03.007

Vandermosten, M., Boets, B., Luts, H., Poelmans, H., Golestani, N., Wouters, J., et al. (2010). Adults with dyslexia are impaired in categorizing speech and non-speech sounds on the basis of temporal cues. *Proc. Natl. Acad. Sci. U.S.A.* 107, 10389–10394. doi: 10.1073/pnas.0912858107

Vandermosten, M., Boets, B., Luts, H., Poelmans, H., Wouters, J., and Ghesquière, P. (2011). Impairments in speech and nonspeech sound categorization in children with dyslexia are driven by temporal processing difficulties. *Res. Dev. Disabil.* 32, 593–603. doi: 10.1016/j.ridd.2010.12.015

Waber, D. P., Weiler, M. D., Wolff, P. H., Bellinger, D., Marcus, D. J., Ariel, R., et al. (2001). Processing of rapid auditory stimuli in school-age children referred for evaluation of learning disorders. *Child Dev.* 72, 37–49. doi: 10.1111/1467-8624.00264

Wechsler, D. (1994). *WISC-R Scala di Intelligenza Wechsler per Bambini (Riveduta)* Firenze: Organizzazioni Speciali.

Witton, C., Talcott, J. B., Hansen, P. C., Richardson, A. J., Griffiths, T. D., Rees, A., et al. (1998). Sensitivity to dynamic auditory and visual stimuli predicts nonword reading ability in both dyslexic and normal readers. *Curr. Biol.* 8, 791–797. doi: 10.1016/S0960-9822(98)70320-3

World Health Organization. (1992). *The ICD 10 Classification of Mental and Behavioural Disorders: Clinical Descriptions and Diagnostic Guidelines.* Geneva: author.

Wright, B. A., and Zecker, S. G. (2004). Learning problems, delayed development, and puberty. *Proc. Natl. Acad. Sci. U.S.A.* 101, 9942–9946. doi: 10.1073/pnas.0401825101

Ziegler, J. C., Castel, C., Pech-Georgel, C., George, F., Alario, F. X., and Perry, C. (2008). Developmental dyslexia and the dual route model of reading: Simulating individual differences and subtypes. *Cognition* 107, 151–178. doi: 10.1016/j.cognition.2007.09.004

Ziegler, J. C., Pech-Georgel, C., George, F., and Lorenzi, C. (2009). Speech-perception-in-noise deficits in dyslexia. *Dev. Sci.* 12, 732–745. doi: 10.1111/j.1467-7687.2009.00817.x

6

Visual processing of multiple elements in the dyslexic brain: evidence for a superior parietal dysfunction

Muriel A. Lobier[1,2]*, Carole Peyrin[1,3], Cédric Pichat[1,3], Jean-François Le Bas[4] and Sylviane Valdois[1,3]

[1] *Laboratoire de Psychologie et NeuroCognition, Université Grenoble Alpes, Grenoble, France*
[2] *Neuroscience Center, University of Helsinki, Helsinki, Finland*
[3] *CNRS, Laboratoire de Psychologie et NeuroCognition, UMR5105, Grenoble, France*
[4] *INSERM U836/Université Joseph Fourier – Institut des Neurosciences, Grenoble, France*

Correspondence:
Muriel A. Lobier, Neuroscience Center, P. O. Box 56, FI-00014 University of Helsinki, Finland
e-mail: muriel.lobier@gmail.com

The visual attention (VA) span deficit hypothesis of developmental dyslexia posits that impaired multiple element processing can be responsible for poor reading outcomes. In VA span impaired dyslexic children, poor performance on letter report tasks is associated with reduced parietal activations for multiple letter processing. While this hints towards a non-specific, attention-based dysfunction, it is still unclear whether reduced parietal activity generalizes to other types of stimuli. Furthermore, putative links between reduced parietal activity and reduced ventral occipito-temporal (vOT) in dyslexia have yet to be explored. Using functional magnetic resonance imaging, we measured brain activity in 12 VA span impaired dyslexic adults and 12 adult skilled readers while they carried out a categorization task on single or multiple alphanumeric or non-alphanumeric characters. While healthy readers activated parietal areas more strongly for multiple than single element processing (right-sided for alphanumeric and bilateral for non-alphanumeric), similar stronger multiple element right parietal activations were absent for dyslexic participants. Contrasts between skilled and dyslexic readers revealed significantly reduced right superior parietal lobule (SPL) activity for dyslexic readers regardless of stimuli type. Using a priori anatomically defined regions of interest, we showed that neural activity was reduced for dyslexic participants in both SPL and vOT bilaterally. Finally, we used multiple regressions to test whether SPL activity was related to vOT activity in each group. In the left hemisphere, SPL activity covaried with vOT activity for both normal and dyslexic readers. In contrast, in the right hemisphere, SPL activity covaried with vOT activity only for dyslexic readers. These results bring critical support to the VA interpretation of the VA Span deficit. In addition, they offer a new insight on how deficits in automatic vOT based word recognition could arise in developmental dyslexia.

Keywords: developmental dyslexia, visual attention, reading, superior parietal lobes

INTRODUCTION

Developmental dyslexia is a severe, persistent reading disability: dyslexic children and adults do not acquire efficient, fluent reading despite adequate schooling and intelligence. A large body of research has supported difficulties with language processing (Bishop and Snowling, 2004) and more specifically with phonological processing of oral language as the core deficit in dyslexia (Ramus, 2003; Vellutino et al., 2004; Ramus and Szenkovits, 2008). Accordingly, numerous studies have reported links between phonological deficits and left hemisphere language areas neural dysfunction in developmental dyslexia (see Démonet et al., 2004; Maisog et al., 2008; Richlan et al., 2009, 2011 for reviews). In addition, developmental dyslexia has been associated with disrupted activity in the left ventral occipito-temporal (vOT) cortex (Richlan et al., 2009, 2011; Van der mark et al., 2011) thought to subserve visual processing of letter strings (Dehaene and Cohen, 2011). However, in accordance with multifactorial accounts of dyslexia (Pennington, 2006; Menghini et al., 2010; Vidyasagar and Pammer, 2010), recent research has hinted towards a possible visual component to the core deficit in dyslexia. Various deficits in visual attention (VA) and visual processing have been identified in dyslexic individuals as supporting different visual-attentional models of developmental dyslexia (Hari and Renvall, 2001; Facoetti et al., 2006, 2008; Boden and Giaschi, 2007; Bosse et al., 2007; Vidyasagar and Pammer, 2010). Most of these models assume the co-occurrence of VA and phonological deficits in dyslexic individuals except the VA span model which posits that a deficit in multi-element (ME) visual processing can account for reading acquisition problems in a subset of dyslexic individuals who otherwise have preserved phonological skills (Valdois et al., 2004, 2014b; Bosse et al., 2007).

Indeed, according to both case studies (Valdois et al., 2003; Dubois et al., 2010) and group studies (Bosse et al., 2007; Lassus-Sangosse et al., 2008), a subset of dyslexic children suffers from a selective deficit in multiple letter report tasks, independently from any phonological deficit. Performance on report tasks is interpreted as indexing the number of individual elements that can be processed in parallel, i.e., the VA Span. Impaired performance is thus viewed as a consequence of a reduced VA Span: dyslexic children cannot process as many letters in parallel as normal reading children. Furthermore, within the theoretical framework of the MultiTrace Memory (MTM) model (Ans et al., 1998), a reduced VA Span also results in impaired reading performance. According to the MTM model, letters of a word are processed in parallel through a visual-attention window. In expert readers, the size of this window adapts to the length of the to-be-read word in order to encompass all of its letter string. If the to-be-read word is unfamiliar, the window's size is subsequently reduced to cover fewer letters and focus on the word orthographic units (letters, graphemes, or syllables). Reading then switches from a fast, parallel procedure to a slow, serial identification of successive orthographic units. If a deficit in visual processing capacity limits the ability of the visual-attention window to spread over a whole word, then words cannot be identified by a fast, parallel procedure resulting in impaired reading ability (for a more detailed and complete theoretical overview of the role of VA Span in impaired reading, see Valdois et al., 2004).

The VA Span definition places no constraints on the visual elements to which it refers: they may be letters or other visual elements. In turn, the VA Span deficit hypothesis posits that the ME processing deficit it evidences extends to any type of visual element, independently of its lexical nature. However, it has been suggested that low performance in letter report tasks using both verbal report and verbal stimuli (letters or digits) follows not from a deficit in visual processing but from impaired mapping of visual codes onto phonology (Hawelka and Wimmer, 2008; Ziegler et al., 2010). This hypothesis is supported by data suggesting that normal readers' performance on a two alternative forced choice partial report task is higher than dyslexic readers' for letters and digits but not symbols (Ziegler et al., 2010). However, other studies have brought forward evidence for a ME deficit that extends to non-verbal tasks and stimuli. Dyslexic adults and children are impaired on a symbol-string matching task requiring no verbal report (Pammer et al., 2004; Jones et al., 2008). A recent study used a non-verbal ME visual processing task to explore visual processing performance on non-verbal character strings in dyslexic children chosen to have a VA span disorder (Lobier et al., 2012b). In this task, a five element string made up of characters belonging to two different categories (e.g., pseudo-letters/unknown geometrical shapes, letters/digits) was displayed for 200 ms and then masked. Participants were asked to identify how many characters in the displayed string belonged to a previously designated target category. VA span impaired dyslexic children showed lower performance than age-matched controls, regardless of target character category. Since this categorization task required no verbal response and since no visual to phonological code mappings exist for novel target characters, these results argue strongly for an underlying visual processing impairment in the VA Span deficit (see Valdois et al., 2012, for converging evidence against the visual to phonological code mapping hypothesis). The prevalence of the VA Span deficit in the dyslexic population has been previously estimated in cohorts of dyslexic children. Around a third of dyslexic children were found to exhibit an isolated VA Span deficit in either French (Bosse et al., 2007; Zoubrinetzky et al., 2014), British (Bosse et al., 2007), or Brazilian Portuguese (Germano et al., submitted).

Abnormal neural activity in brain areas associated with VA in VA Span impaired children has brought forward additional evidence for VA as a constraining factor of VA Span performance in dyslexia. Neural correlates of the VA Span deficit were first explored in an functional magnetic resonance imaging (fMRI) study comparing neural activity for a flanked letter categorization task between normal reading and VA Span impaired dyslexic children (Peyrin et al., 2011). VA mechanisms involved in multi-letter processing were assessed using a task that minimized verbal report and phonological processing. Results showed that superior parietal lobule (SPL) activity was reduced bilaterally in dyslexic children compared to controls. Importantly, a recent case report (Peyrin et al., 2012) suggested that this SPL dysfunction is specific to the VA span deficit rather than to dyslexia. Neural activity for the same visual categorization task was assessed in two dyslexic adults with distinct neurocognitive profiles. SPL activity was normal for the patient with a phonological deficit but preserved VA span performance whereas it was decreased for the patient with a VA span deficit but preserved phonological performance.

The co-occurrence of poor multiple letter report performance and SPL dysfunction is consistent with a visuo-attentional account of the VA span disorder. SPL activity has not only been associated with visuo-spatial attention (Wojciulik and Kanwisher, 1999; Corbetta and Shulman, 2002; Behrmann et al., 2004) but also, more specifically, with ME processing (Mitchell and Cusack, 2008; Xu and Chun, 2009; Scalf and Beck, 2010). Closer to the cognitive demands of reading, SPL activity relates to length effects in pseudo-word reading (Valdois et al., 2006) and is observed in proficient readers when word letter parallel identification is compromised (Cohen et al., 2008 see also Gaillard et al., 2006). If SPL plays a role in reading acquisition, it should show different patterns of activation for different levels of reading proficiency. Indeed, less proficient readers have stronger bilateral (children vs. adults, see Church et al., 2008), right lateralized (Adult ex-illiterates vs. literates, see Dehaene et al., 2010) posterior parietal activity than more proficient readers. In addition, activity in left SPL and right IPL/SPL clusters is negatively correlated with reading proficiency (Jobard et al., 2011). In line with this putative role of SPL in reading acquisition, Brem et al. (2010) report activity peaks in right SPL for visual word processing in learning to read children. In Chinese, Cao et al. (2010) shows developmental increases in bilateral SPL during visuo-orthographic processing and stronger involvement of the right SPL during the visual comparison of two-character words than during phonological processing of the same words.

We recently showed stronger SPL involvement for pre-orthographic processing of multiple character strings than of single flanked characters, for both alphanumeric (AN) and non-alphanumeric (nAN) characters (Lobier et al., 2012a). However, this reduced SPL activity has only been reported for multiple letter processing, which cannot disentangle between a general ME impairment or a more specific letter processing impairment. A stronger argument for a VA dysfunction as the underlying factor in VA Span impairment would be made by showing a similar SPL dysfunction in dyslexic participants on a non-verbal ME task using both verbal and non-verbal stimuli.

The main aim of this study is to use non-verbal categorization tasks to isolate the underlying neural dysfunction in the VA Span disorder in dyslexia using fMRI. VA span impaired dyslexic adults and healthy skilled adult readers carried out a visual categorization with either alphanumeric, familiar characters or non-alphanumeric, unfamiliar characters. In order to isolate neural correlates specific to parallel processing of MEs, the task had two conditions: a ME categorization condition of interest and a single-element (SE) categorization control condition. Both conditions were carried out with either AN or nAN characters. While both the experimental and control conditions required visual categorization of the attended stimuli, only the experimental condition required processing of several elements. Contrasts between these conditions should highlight neural activations that are specific to ME processing demands.

Our central hypothesis is that the VA span deficit is associated with disrupted SPL activity for pre-orthographic multiple character processing regardless of character type. In line with previous studies, we expect to find abnormal parietal activations for multiple-element processing for the dyslexic group. More importantly, these abnormal brain activations should be found regardless of stimuli type. We first contrasted whole-brain neural activity between VA span impaired dyslexic adults and control normal-reading adults. In addition, we used regions of interest (ROIs) to compare more specifically activity in inferior parietal and superior parietal cortices between groups. Finally, since abnormal activity in the vOT cortex is commonly reported for dyslexic readers, we also used ROIs to test whether SPL activity was correlated with vOT activity.

MATERIALS AND METHODS

PARTICIPANTS

Twelve dyslexic (mean age 21.6 ± 4.2 years) and twelve healthy, skilled adult readers (mean age 23.8 ± 2.6 years) took part in this study. They were all right-handed and had normal or corrected to normal vision. All participants had given informed consent and received 60 Euros for their participation. Dyslexic participants were recruited through the university disabilities office. They had previously undergone a complete neuropsychological assessment to establish the diagnosis of developmental dyslexia and the presence of a VA span disorder while ruling out any co-morbid attentional disorders (e.g., ADHD). The diagnosis of developmental dyslexia was established using both inventories and testing procedures in accordance with the guidelines of the ICD-10 classification of Mental and Behavioral disorders. Reading speed was estimated for all participants, using the "Alouette" text (Lefavrais, 1965) that required reading a 265 word text as quickly and as accurately as possible during 3 min. Control participants had no reported learning or reading disability. Reading speed for dyslexic participants was significantly lower than for control participants (Dyslexic: Mean = 119wpm, 95%CI = [103–135], Controls: Mean = 202wpm, 95%CI = [185–219], $t(22) = 7.9$, $p < 0.0001$). This study was approved by the local ethics committee.

VISUAL ATTENTION SPAN ASSESSMENT

All participants carried out a global letter report task in order to assess their VA span abilities. Ceiling effects are often observed for adults on the 5-letter report task used in previous studies with children (Valdois et al., 2003; Bosse et al., 2007). For this reason, a 6-letter report task was developed for testing adults (Peyrin et al., 2012). Stimuli were random 6-consonant strings presented in black upper-case letters on a white background. At the start of each trial, a central fixation point was displayed for 1000 ms followed by a 50 ms blank screen. A horizontal 6-letter string was then presented for 200 ms, centered on fixation. Participants were asked to report all the letters they had seen with no time pressure. Ten training and 24 experimental trials were carried out. Experimental stimuli were 24 consonant strings built-up from 10 consonants (BPTFLMDSRH). An additional 10 different letter strings were used for training. Score was the number of accurately reported letters, regardless of order (maximum score: 144).

The VA span performance of the participants was compared to normative data from the EVADYS diagnostic tool (Valdois et al., 2014a). Every control participant scored within 1 SD of the norm on the VA span task. The dyslexic participants' VA Span abilities were at least 1.65 standard deviations below adult norms. Performance on the 6-letter whole report task indexing ME processing capacity (VA Span) was significantly lower for dyslexic (3.5 letters per trial on average) than for control (5.3 letters) participants (Dyslexic: Mean score = 84, 95%CI = [74–94], Control: Mean score = 128, 95%CI = [123–133], $t(16.4) = 9.0$, $p < 0.0001$).

fMRI STUDY

Stimuli

Four different character categories were used: letters, digits, Japanese Hiragana, and pseudo-letters, with five different characters in each category. While participants had extensive multiple character processing experience with two categories (letters and digits), the other two were completely novel. The font used for letters and digits was Arial. Letters were drawn from the following set of five consonants: D, F, K, M, and V. Digits were drawn from the following set of five digits 3, 5, 6, 8, and 9. Pseudoletters were taken from a set created by Hawelka and Wimmer (2008) by cutting and rearranging letter visual features. The five characters created from consonants D, F, K, M, and V made up the pseudo-letter set. The five Hiragana characters were chosen amongst the 48 possible characters of the Hiragana syllabary so that their mean visual complexity as defined by Majaj et al. (2002), was similar to that of the other character sets. Character perimetric complexity is a reliable predictor of character recognition efficiency (Pelli et al., 2006): characters sets with similar average perimetric complexity are recognized with similar efficiency.

For the ME condition, strings of five characters were built-up from these sets. There were 48 AN strings and 48 nAN strings. Out of the 48 AN strings, 24 were consistent and 24 were inconsistent. Consistent strings were made up exclusively of letters and digits. Twelve of the consistent strings contained three letters and two digits and the other 12 contained two letters and three digits. Inconsistent strings were made up of letters, digits and one distractor character, either Hiragana or pseudo-letter. Twelve of the inconsistent strings contained two letters, two digits and one distractor character and the other 12 contained three letters, one digit and one distractor character. The position and choice of the distractor character was controlled across trials. Similarly, individual character positions were counterbalanced across consistent and inconsistent trials. The 48 nAN strings were built up the same way as the AN ones, with pseudo-letters and Hiragana replacing letters and digits. Distractor characters were then letters and digits. For the SE condition, stimuli were made up of one central character surrounded by four pound (#) signs. There were 48 strings: 24 with a central AN character (12 letters, 12 digits) and 24 with a central nAN character (12 pseudo-letters, 12 Hiragana). For all stimulus strings, characters subtended a visual angle of 0.7°. To minimize visual crowding, the distance between adjacent characters was of 0.57°. The entire string subtended a visual angle of 5.4° and was drawn in white on a black background.

Procedure

A task requiring visual categorization of characters was carried out in two conditions: ME and SE (see **Figure 1**). Stimuli were displayed for 200 ms to avoid useful ocular saccades and serial visual processing. Stimuli display was driven by E-Prime software (E-Prime Psychology Software Tools, Inc., Pittsburgh, USA). Synchronization between scanner and paradigm was ensured by a trigger pulse sent from the scanner to the computer on which E-Prime was running. The paradigm was presented using a video projector (Epson EMP 8200), a projection screen situated behind the magnet and a surface mirror centered above the participant's eyes. A response key was used to collect participant responses. Response accuracy and reaction times (RT, in milliseconds) were recorded.

In the ME condition, visual categorization of individual characters of a ME string was required. Performance was monitored by asking participants to report the number of target category characters present in the stimulus string. For AN strings, participants were asked to report the number of letters present in a letter and digit 5-character string. For nAN strings, participants were asked to report the number of Hiragana characters in a Hiragana and pseudo-letter character string. Participants pressed the index finger button for two target-category characters and the middle finger button for three target-category characters. They carried out 48 trials for each condition, half with two target characters and half with three target characters. Trial order was pseudo-randomized.

In the SE condition, visual categorization of a single character flanked by pound signs was required. Performance was monitored by asking participants to report whether or not the stimulus character belonged to either one of two target categories (AN: letters or digits, nAN: Hiragana or pseudo-letters). If the stimulus character belonged to a target category, participants pressed the index finger button. If it did not, they pressed the middle finger button. They carried out 48 trials for each condition, half of which contained a target category character. Trial order was pseudo-randomized. This condition was designed to control for three important task characteristics. First, low-level visual stimulation was similar to the ME condition: five characters were displayed (four pound signs and a central stimulus character). Second, motor response was the same for both tasks. Last, both conditions required character categorization, controlling for higher-order categorization processing.

Immediately before the scanning session, participants took part in a 45 min training session. Participants first performed two character-identification tasks in order to familiarize themselves with the two unfamiliar character types. During the second part of training, participants were familiarized with the experimental task. For each condition (ME and SE) and each character type (AN and nAN), they first carried out five training trials followed by a sequence of 48 trials with the same timing as the experimental sequence (but different stimulus strings).

EVENT-RELATED fMRI EXPERIMENTAL DESIGN

Each participant carried out four event-related-fMRI sessions: two to assess ME processing (one for AN and one for nAN characters)

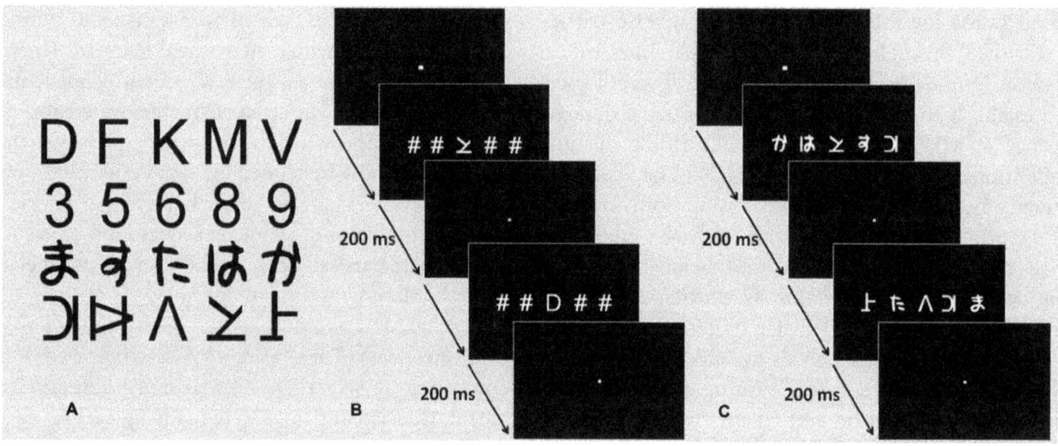

FIGURE 1 | Character sets and fMRI task procedure. (A) Character sets (letters, digits, Hiragana, pseudo-letters). **(B)** Procedure screens for the single element task. **(C)** Procedure screens for the multiple element task.

and the other two to assess SE processing (one for AN and one for nAN characters). FMRI session order was counterbalanced across participants. Stimuli onsets were optimized using pseudo-randomized ER-fMRI paradigms (Friston et al., 1999). For each session, 48 stimulus strings were displayed: 24 consistent and 24 inconsistent. In order to provide an appropriate baseline measure (Friston et al., 1998), 27 null-events (three of them at the end of the session) were included in each session. These null-events comprised a black screen and a fixation dot displayed at the center of the screen. SOA between events was set to 3 s. SOAs between trial events were of 3, 6, or 9 s, depending on the presence of null-events. To reduce eye movements, participants were asked to fixate the fixation dot during null-events. In order to stabilize the magnetic field, each functional run started with five dummy scans that were discarded before analysis. After these dummy scans, 90 functional volumes were acquired for each run. Each functional session lasted 3 min 45 s.

MR ACQUISITION

A whole-body 3T MR scanner was used (Bruker MedSpec S300) with 41 mT/m maximum gradient strength and 120 mT/m/s maximum slew rate. For functional scans, the manufacturer-provided gradient-echi/T2* weighted EPI method was used. Thirty-nine adjacent axial slices parallel to the bi-commissural plane were acquired in interleaved mode. Slice thickness was 3.5 mm. The in-plane voxel size was 3 mm × 3 mm (216 × 216 field of view acquired with a 72 × 72 pixels data matrix; reconstructed with 0 filling to 128 × 128 pixels). The main sequence parameters were: TR = 2.5 s, TE = 30 ms, flip angle = 80°. To correct images for geometric distortions induced by local B0-inhomogeneity, a B0 fieldmap was derived from two gradient echo data sets acquired with a standard 3D FLASH sequence ΔTE = 9.104 ms). The fieldmap was subsequently used during data processing. Finally, a T1-weighted high-resolution three dimensional anatomical volume was acquired, by using a sagittal magnetization-prepared rapid acquisition gradient echo (MP-RAGE) sequence (field of view = 256 × 224 × 176 mm; resolution = 1.333 × 1.750 × 1.375 mm; acquisition matrix: 192 × 128 × 128 pixels; reconstruction matrix = 256 × 128 × 128 pixels).

DATA PROCESSING

Both preprocessing and statistical analyses of the data were performed using the Statistical Parametric Mapping software (SPM5, Wellcome Department of Imaging Neuroscience, London, UK; http://www.fil.ion.ucl.ac.uk/spm; Friston et al. (1994). Functional volumes were time corrected using the 20th slice as reference. All volumes were then realigned using rigid body transformations to correct for head movement, using the first ER-fMRI session as the reference volume. The T1-weighted anatomical volume was co-registered to the realigned mean images and normalized to MNI space using a trilinear interpolation. The anatomical normalization parameters were then used for functional volume normalization. Finally, each functional volume was smoothed by an 8-mm FWHM (Full Width at Half Maximum) Gaussian kernel. Time series for each voxel were high-pass filtered (1/128 cut-off) to remove low-frequency noise and signal drift.

STATISTICAL ANALYSES

Whole-brain analyses

Statistical analyses were performed on the pre-processed functional images for each one of the four sessions. For each session (ME AN and nAN, SE AN and nAN), consistency (consistent and inconsistent character strings) was modeled as a regressor convolved with a canonical hemodynamic function. Movement parameters computed during the realignment corrections (three translations and three rotations) were included in the design matrix of each session as additional parameters. Parameter estimates of activity in each voxel were generated using the general linear model at each voxel for each condition and each participant. Linear contrasts between the HRF estimates for the different experimental sessions were used to generate statistical parametric maps. All analyses were carried out with consistent and inconsistent trials separately as well as together. Results did not differ qualitatively between analyses; however all results presented here (behavioral and fMRI) were computed using consistent trials only.

At the individual level, statistical parametric maps were computed for several contrasts of interest. The entire cerebral network associated with ME processing was assessed by contrasting the ME condition to baseline (fixation point) conjointly for both character types (AN and nAN). The cerebral network associated with SE processing was assessed by contrasting the SE condition to baseline conjointly for both character types (AN and nAN). We identified brain regions involved more specifically in attention demanding simultaneous processing by contrasting the multiple to the SE condition for each character type. We then performed separate random-effect group analyses for control and dyslexic participants on the contrast images from individual analyses (Friston et al., 1998), using one-sample t-tests. Clusters of activated voxels were identified for each group, based on the intensity of the individual responses (Contrasts against baseline: voxel-wise threshold: $p < 0.001$ uncorrected for multiple comparisons, $T > 4.0$, with an cluster extent threshold correction of $p < 0.05$, Contrasts between conditions: voxel-wise threshold: $p < 0.001$ uncorrected for multiple comparisons, $T > 4$, with a cluster extent threshold of 20 voxels) Finally, two-sample t-tests were performed in order to statistically compare brain activity between controls and dyslexics on the relevant contrasts. Significance thresholds for between-group comparisons (voxel-wise threshold: $p < 0.001$ uncorrected for multiple comparisons, $T > 3.5$, with a cluster extent threshold of 20 voxels) were chosen by reference to previous studies reporting activation differences between skilled and dyslexic readers (Hoeft et al., 2007; van der Mark et al., 2009; Wimmer et al., 2010). For all analyses, brain regions were reported according to the Automated Anatomical Labelling SPM toolbox (Tzourio-Mazoyer et al., 2002).

A priori ROIs

Analysis was finally completed by statistically comparing activity for skilled and dyslexic readers within *a priori* anatomical ROIs. A first set of four ROIs was defined using predefined masks from the Wake Forest University (WFU) PickAtlas (Maldjian et al., 2003). ROI masks were created with the automated anatomical labeling atlas, which uses an anatomical parcellation of the MNI MRI single-subject brain and sulcal boundaries to define each anatomical volume. In order to assess neural activity in the part of the vOT cortex usually associated with character string processing, a second set of two *a priori* ROIs was defined by rectangular boxes. These ROIs were designed in reference to previous research (Jobard et al., 2003; Cai et al., 2010) within the bilateral fusiform and inferior temporal gyri rather than by anatomical boundaries. Parameter estimates (percent signal change) of event-related responses were then extracted from all ROIs for each participant. We both compared ROI activity between groups and tested whether activity levels in SPL covaried with activity levels in vOT. All ROIs were constructed using the SPM Marsbar toolbox (http://marsbar.sourceforge.net).

To investigate the presence of neural dysfunction in dyslexic participants, we first compared ROI activity between groups across different task conditions. To investigate putative links between neural activity in superior parietal cortex and in ventral occipital cortex for ME processing, we used multiple regression analyses to test whether percent signal change for the ME condition in SPL ROIs significantly predicted percent signal change in vOT ROIs while taking into account the putative effect of stimulus type. We ran separate regressions for each group (Dyslexic/Control) and hemisphere (Right/Left). The regression models tested were vOT $\sim$ SPL + stimulus Type [stimulus Type was numerically coded as 0 (AN) or 1 (nAN)].

RESULTS

fMRI BEHAVIORAL RESULTS

Reaction times and accuracy for consistent trials during the fMRI task are presented in **Table 1**. For each condition, RTs and accuracy were entered in a 2 × 2 mixed design ANOVA with Group (Dyslexic vs. Control) as a between-subjects factor and character type (AN vs. nAN) as a within-subject factor. ME condition accuracy data were transformed in order to meet parametric assumptions. For the SE condition, there were no significant main effects or interaction (Group: $F(1,22) = 4.1$, $p = 0.054$, $\eta^2 = 0.11$, Type: $F(1,22) = 1.4$, n.s., $\eta^2 = 0.02$, Group × Type: $F(1,22) = 0.08$, n.s., $\eta^2 = 0.00$). For ME RTs, the Type main effect was significant [$F(1,22) = 7.5$, $p < 0.05$, $\eta^2 = 0.05$], as well as the Group × Type interaction [$F(1,22) = 9.1$, $p < 0.01$, $\eta^2 = 0.05$] Type: [$F(1,22) = 16.5$, $p < 0.001$, $\eta^2 = 0.19$]. The main effect of Group was not significant [$F(1,22) = 2.9$, n.s., $\eta^2 = 0.10$]. Contrasts corrected for multiple comparisons showed that dyslexic participants are slower than control participants for AN character strings ($t(22) = 2.8$, $p < 0.05$) but not for nAN strings ($t(22) = 0.5$, n.s.). Accuracy for the SE condition was near ceiling for both groups. There were no significant main effects of Group [$F(1,22) = 4.1$, $p = 0.053$, $\eta^2 = 0.11$] or Type [$F(1,22) = 1.4$, n.s., $\eta^2 = 0.02$] and no significant Group × Type interaction [$F(1,22) = 0.8$, n.s., $\eta^2 = 0.00$]. For accuracy in the ME condition, control participants were significantly more accurate than dyslexic participants [$F(1,22) = 8.3$, $p < 0.01$, $\eta^2 = 0.21$], and participants were more accurate for AN strings than for nAN strings [$F(1,22) = 16.5$, $p < 0.001$, $\eta^2 = 0.19$]. The Group × Type interaction was not significant [$F(1,22) = 2.0$, n.s., $\eta^2 = 0.03$], suggesting that the accuracy difference between dyslexic and control participants is the same regardless of character type.

fMRI RESULTS

Within-group brain networks

First, we used contrasts between our task and baseline to identify the main networks of brain regions involved in multiple or SE processing in each group separately for AN and nAN character strings. Brain activations are illustrated in **Figure 2**. Relative to baseline (fixation) ME processing activated a broad and bilateral cortical network in control participants regardless of stimulus type. Visual areas included occipital extra-striate cortex bilaterally as well as fusiform and inferior temporal gyri bilaterally. Parietal activations extended over SPL and IPL bilaterally. Finally, cortical activations included the pre-supplementary motor area for AN characters as well as the right superior and middle frontal gyri for nAN characters. Dyslexic participants activated a more limited network. For AN characters; visual areas included the lingual gyrus. Parietal areas were limited to left IPL and postcentral gyrus. As with control participants, cortical activations included pre supplementary cortex. In addition, activation was present in the left rolandic operculum and supramarginal gyrus. The activation pattern was similar for nAN characters, save for the left rolandic operculum and supramarginal gyrus activity that was absent. Relative to baseline, SE processing activated a mostly ventral cortical network in control participants. For AN characters, a very limited network included the left calcarine, lingual gyrus, and cuneus as well as the right fusiform gyrus. For nAN characters; visual areas included occipital gyri and fusiform gyri bilaterally. Activated parietal areas were limited to the left postcentral and precentral gyri. For dyslexic participants, there were no significant activations at our chosen threshold for AN characters (Lowering the threshold revealed activation patterns similar to control participants). For nAN characters, activated visual areas included the right fusiform and bilateral lingual gyri.

For each group, brain regions specific to ME processing were identified by contrasting ME and SE conditions for each stimuli type (AN and nAN) separately. Brain areas showing stronger activations for the ME than the SE condition are listed in **Table 2** and illustrated in **Figure 3**. For control participants, the [$ME > SE$] contrast for AN strings activated a single right hemisphere parietal cluster. This cluster extended over parts of the superior and inferior parietal lobule as well as angular, superior occipital and mid occipital gyri. For nAN strings, control participants had stronger ME activations bilaterally in parietal cortex. A left hemisphere parietal cluster extended mainly over SPL (and over limited parts of precuneus and IPL) while the right hemisphere cluster extended exclusively over SPL. Increased activity was also found in the pre supplementary motor area. For dyslexic participants, the [$ME > SE$] contrast for AN and nAN characters revealed pre-supplementary motor area clusters in both conditions. Neither contrast revealed any parietal activation at the chosen threshold. No brain areas showed significantly stronger activity for the ME condition than for the SE condition in either group:..

Between-group differences in activation

Two-sample *t*-tests were then performed to statistically compare brain activation in control and dyslexic readers on relevant contrasts. To identify brain areas significantly more activated in normal readers than in dyslexic participants in ME processing,

Table 1 | fMRI task performance of dyslexic and control participants for consistent trials.

	Dyslexics ($n = 12$)				Controls ($n = 12$)			
	Reaction time		Accuracy		Reaction time		Accuracy	
	Mean	95%CI	Mean	95%CI	Mean	95%CI	Mean	95%CI
Single element AN	772	689–857	0.95	0.89–1.0	690	637–743	0.99	0.98–0.1.0
Single element nAN	945	795–1095	0.95	0.92–0.99	812	729–894	0.98	0.96–1.0
Multiple element AN	1197	1040–1353	0.75	0.61–0.89	956	855–1057	0.94	0.90–0.97
Multiple element nAN	1187	1018–1356	0.66	0.58–0.73	1144	1030–1257	0.76	0.70–0.86

Reaction times are reported in ms, accuracy in proportion correct.

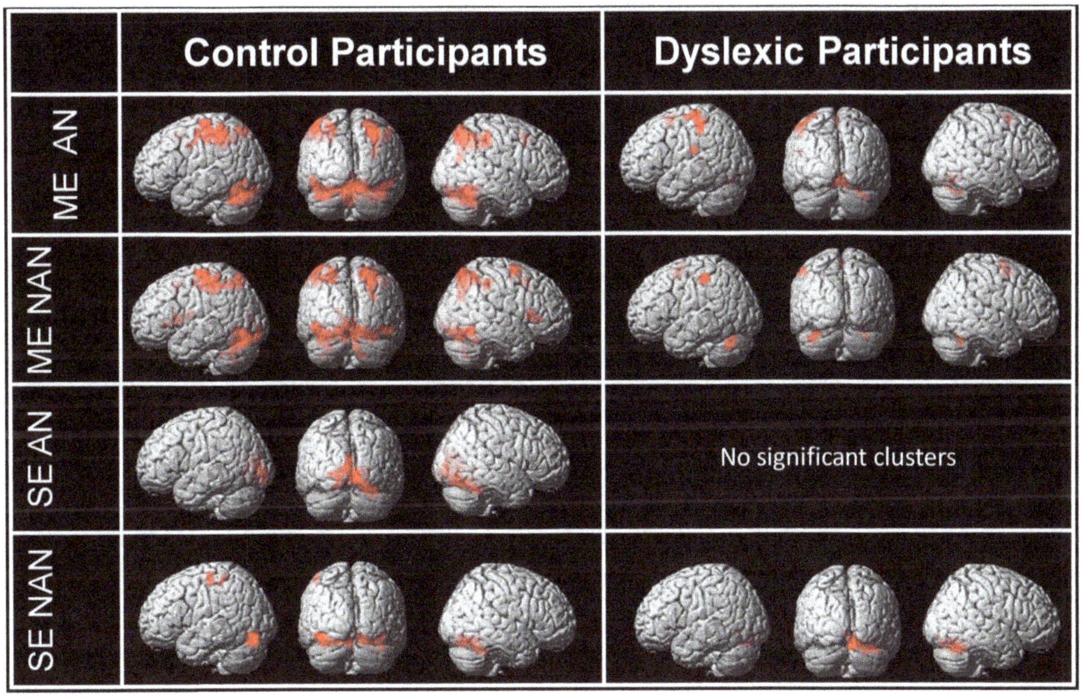

FIGURE 2 | Whole-brain activations induced by multiple and single element processing for AN and nAN conditions for control and dyslexic participants, overlaid on a surface-rendered single subject brain normalized to MNI template. Top two rows: BOLD activation for the contrast [ME > Baseline] for each condition (AN and nAN) in control and dyslexic participants. Bottom two rows: BOLD activation evoked for the contrast [ME > Baseline] for each condition (AN and nAN) in control and dyslexic participants. For all contrasts: voxel-wise threshold of $p < 0.001$ uncorrected with an extent threshold correction of $p < 0.05$ at the cluster level.

we compared activations for the ME condition between each group for each character type separately. Brain areas showing stronger activations for the control group than for the dyslexic group are listed in **Table 3** (ME and SE conditions) and illustrated in **Figure 4** (ME condition). For AN characters, the right parietal cortex (including SPL and extending to the superior part of the occipital cortex and precuneus) and the left vOT cortex (including the inferior temporal and fusiform gyri) were more strongly activated in control than dyslexic readers. For nAN characters, there were stronger activations for control than dyslexic participants in the right parietal cortex (including SPL and precuneus) as well as in the right vOT cortex (including inferior temporal and inferior occipital gyri). The opposite comparison ([Dyslexic > Control]) revealed no areas more activated for dyslexic than for control participants for either character type.

We then compared activations for SE processing between each group by contrasting activations maps ([Control > Dyslexic]) for the SE condition separately for each character type (AN and nAN) There were no brain areas significantly more activated in control than in dyslexic participants for either character type. The opposite contrasts ([Dyslexic > Control]) showed that for AN characters, a single left middle/superior frontal gyri cluster was more strongly activated in dyslexic than control participants (see **Table 3**). For

Table 2 | Cerebral regions significantly more activated for multiple element than for single element processing.

	Control group			Dyslexic group		
	x, y, z	*k*	*z*	*x, y, z*	*k*	*z*
[ME>SE] – AN	–	–	–	–	–	–
Parietal cortex	–	–	–	–	–	–
Right precuneus/superior parietal lobule	30, –60, 50	109	4.4	–	–	–
Bilateral pre-supplementary motor area	–	–	–	0, 12, 53	20	4.0
[ME>SE] – nAN	–	–	–	–	–	–
Parietal cortex	–	–	–	–	–	–
Right superior parietal lobule	21, –69, 56	24	3.6	–	–	–
Left superior parietal lobule/precuneus	–27, –60, 56	21	3.4	–	–	–
Insular cortex	–	–	–	–	–	–
Right insula/putamen	27, 24, 0	26	4.9	–	–	–
Bilateral pre supplementary motor area	12, 9, 49	34	3.9	6, 21, 46	26	3.9

The statistical significance voxel-wise threshold of $p < 0.001$ uncorrected ($T > 4.02$) with an extent threshold correction of $p < 0.05$ at the cluster level. For each cluster, peak MNI coordinates (x,y,z), cluster spatial extent k and peak z-value are indicated. Anatomical labels are based on the automated anatomical labeling (AAL) atlas. Labels represent anatomical regions with the largest percentages of overlap with the activation cluster.

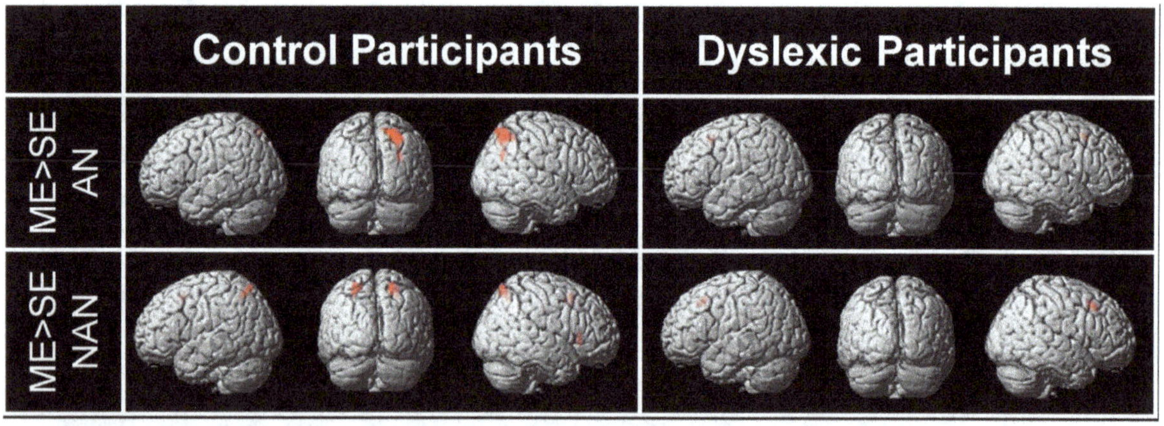

FIGURE 3 | BOLD activation for the contrast [ME > SE] for each condition (AN and nAN) and group (Control and Dyslexic), overlaid on a surface-rendered single subject brain normalized to MNI template. For all contrasts: voxel-wise threshold of $p < 0.001$ uncorrected with a cluster threshold of 20 voxels.

nAN characters, there were no brain areas significantly more activated in dyslexic than in control participants.

Regions of interest

Previous research has linked behavioral deficits in simultaneous visual processing in dyslexia to lower activation in parietal brain areas, and more specifically in the SPL bilaterally and the left inferior parietal lobule (Peyrin et al., 2011; Reilhac et al., 2013). We compared parietal activations in dyslexic and skilled readers in four predefined and standardized neuro-anatomical ROIs using predefined masks from the WFU PickAtlas (Maldjian et al., 2003). The first two ROIs were defined as right and left SPL intersected with BA7 and the next two as right and left IPL intersected with BA 40 (as defined by the automated labeling atlas which uses an anatomical parcellation of the MNI single subject brain and sulcal boundaries to define anatomical volumes). The SPL/BA7 ROI sizes were, respectively, of 139 (R) and 136 (L) voxels. The IPL/BA40 ROI sizes were, respectively, of 333 (R) and 367 (L) voxels (ROIs are illustrated in **Figure 5**). Parameter estimates (percent signal change) were extracted for each ROI and entered in a 2 × 2 × 2 mixed ANOVA with Condition (ME vs. SE) and Character Type (AN vs. nAN) as within-subject factors as well as Group (Dyslexic vs. Control) as a between-subject factor (see **Figure 5**). Concerning right SPL, there were significant main effects of Condition [$F(1,22) = 21.3$, $p < 0.0001$, $\eta^2 = 0.13$] and Group [$F(1,22) = 12.5$, $p < 0.01$, $\eta^2 = 0.22$] as well as a significant Group × Condition interaction [$F(1,22) = 7.5$, $p < 0.05$, $\eta^2 = 0.05$]. There was neither a significant main effect of character

Table 3 | Overview of clusters significantly more activated for one group compared to the other [control > dyslexic and control > dyslexic; voxel-wise threshold of $p < 0.001$ uncorrected ($T > 3.5$) with a cluster extent $k > 20$].

	Control > Dyslexic		
	x, y, z	*k*	*z*
[ME – AN > Baseline]			
Parietal cortex			
Right superior parietal lobule/superior occipital gyrus	33, −69, 46	100	4.4
Temporo-occipital cortex			
Left inferior temporal/fusiform gyri	−45, −57, −21	59	4.2
[ME – nAN > Baseline]			
Parietal cortex			
Right superior parietal lobule/precuneus	15, −72, 63	23	3.5
Temporo-occipital cortex			
Right inferior temporal/inferior occipital gyri	48, −63, −11	23	3.8
	Dyslexic > Control		
[SE– AN > Baseline]			
Frontal cortex			
Left frontal middle/superior gyri	−24, 24, 32	23	4.4

For each cluster, peak MNI coordinates (x,y,z), cluster spatial extent k and peak z-value are indicated. Anatomical labels are based on the AAL [(automated anatomical labeling) atlas (Tzourio-Mazoyer et al., 2002)]. Labels represent anatomical regions with the largest percentages of overlap with the activation cluster. Contrasts with no significant clusters are not presented.

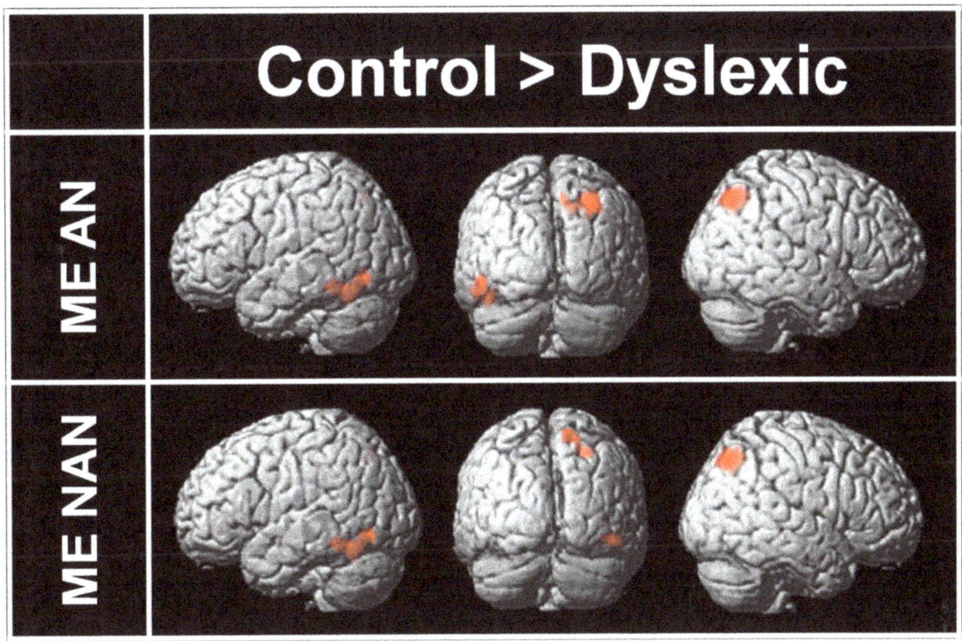

FIGURE 4 | Brain areas more strongly activated in control participants than in dyslexic participants for ME processing and AN or nAN characters, overlaid on a surface-rendered single subject brain normalized to MNI template. For all contrasts: voxel-wise threshold of $p < 0.001$ uncorrected with a cluster threshold of 20 voxels.

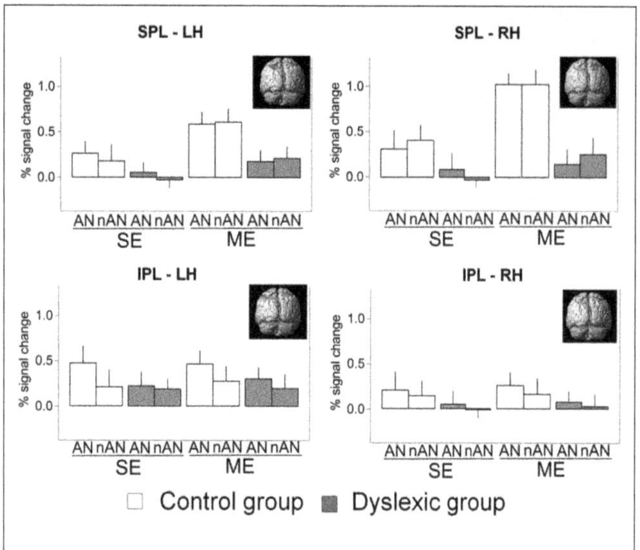

FIGURE 5 | Mean percent signal change for *a priori* SPL and IPL ROIs. Error bars indicate standard error.

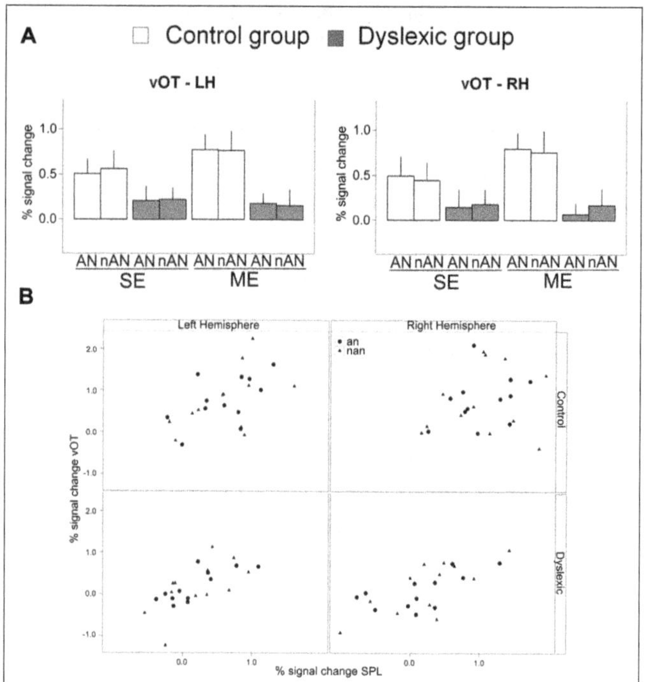

FIGURE 6 | (A) Mean percent signal change for *a priori* vOT ROIs. Error bars indicate standard error. **(B)** Scatterplots of vOT mean percent signal change as a function of SPL mean percent signal change for multiple element processing. Each combination of Hemisphere (Left/Right) and Group (Control/Dyslexic) is represented.

type nor any other significant interaction. The difference in activation between groups was affected by the number of elements to be processed. Contrasts indicated that the interaction was driven by a different effect of Group in each Condition. The effect of Group was significant for the ME condition [$F(1,22) = 20.4$, $p < 0.001$], but non-significant in the SE condition [$F(1,22) = 3$, n.s.]. Concerning left SPL, there were significant main effects of Condition [$F(1,22) = 11.9$, $p < 0.01$, $\eta^2 = 0.09$] and Group [$F(1,22) = 8.4$, $p < 0.05$, $\eta^2 = 0.11$]. No other effects were significant. The difference in activity between groups in left SPL is not affected by condition demands. Concerning IPL, results were similar for right and left hemisphere. There were no significant main effects for either Group [RH: $F(1,22) = 1.1$, n.s.; LH: $F(1,22) = 0.7$, n.s.], Condition [RH: $F(1,22) = 0.1$, n.s.; LH: $F(1,22) = 0.1$, n.s.] or Character Type [RH: $F(1,22) = 0.6$, n.s.; LH: $F(1,22) = 3.2$, n.s.], suggesting that IPL is not specifically implicated in ME processing in either healthy or dyslexic readers.

Abnormal brain activity for letter strings in the left vOT cortex in dyslexia is well documented (see Richlan et al., 2011 for a recent meta-analysis). We built a ROI covering the fusiform and inferior temporal gyri using a coordinate-delimited box (RH: $X = -34$ to -55, $Y = -34$ to -68, $Z = -4$ to -26, mirror-reversed for LH). This ROI was defined by Cai et al. (2010) according to activation peaks reported in meta-analysis of normal word reading by Jobard et al. (2003). Parameter estimates were extracted and analyzed similar to SPL and IPL ROIs (See **Figure 6A**). In the right hemisphere ROI, there was a significant main effect of Group [$F(1,22) = 7.5$, $p < 0.05$, $\eta^2 = 0.13$] and no other effects were significant [Condition: $F(1,22) = 1.5$, n.s., $\eta^2 = 0.01$; Type: $F(1,22) = 0.01$, n.s., $\eta^2 = 0.00$]. The result pattern was similar in the left hemisphere with a significant main effect of Group [$F(1,22) = 7.5$, $p < 0.05$, $\eta^2 = 0.14$] and no other significant effects [Condition: $F(1,22) = 1.3$, n.s., $\eta^2 = 0.01$; Type: $F(1,22) = 0.01$, n.s., $\eta^2 = 0.00$]. Reduced brain activity in the vOT cortex for dyslexic participants is present for single or ME processing as well as for AN or nAN character strings.

To investigate putative links between neural activity in superior parietal cortex and in ventral occipital cortex, we ran regressions for each group and hemisphere with percent signal change in vOT ROIs as the dependent variable and percent signal change in SPL ROIs as well as stimulus type as regressors (Scatterplots of the data are shown in **Figure 6B**). The effect of stimulus type was non-significant in all regressions, suggesting that a putative link between vOT and SPL is independent of character type. In the right hemisphere, SPL predicted vOT for the dyslexic group [Full regression: $F(2,21) = 10.1$, $R^2 = 0.49$, $p < 0.001$, SPL regressor: $\beta = 0.6$, $t = 4.5$, $p < 0.0001$], but, not for the control group [Full regression: $F(2,21) = 0.5$, $R^2 = 0.05$, n.s., SPL regressor: $\beta = 0.3$, $t = 1.0$, n.s.]. In the left hemisphere, SPL predicted vOT for the dyslexic group [Full regression: $F(2,21) = 8.9$, $R^2 = 0.46$, $p < 0.01$, SPL regressor: $\beta = 0.8$, $t = 4.2$, $p < 0.0001$], as well as for the control group [Full regression: $F(2,21) = 4.3$, $R^2 = 0.29$, $p < 0.05$, SPL regressor: $\beta = 0.6$, $t = 3.0$, $p < 0.01$].

DISCUSSION

The present fMRI study compared character string processing in VA Span impaired dyslexic readers and healthy skilled readers. Reduced performance of dyslexic participants on a 6-letter global report compared to control participants is posited to index a general impairment of parallel ME processing. This VA Span impairment has been associated with reduced SPL activation for multiple letter processing in dyslexic children (Peyrin et al., 2011). The main purpose of this study was to extend these results to nAN character processing. We hypothesized that abnormal parietal activations should be found in dyslexic individuals with a VA span disorder regardless of character type for ME processing. In addition, we hypothesized that if parietal cortex is involved in visual processing and information extraction from multiple character strings, then parietal activity should correlate with vOT activity for character string processing. Participants carried out a visual categorization task in two conditions: SE or MEs. The task was carried out with alphanumeric, familiar characters and non-alphanumeric, unfamiliar characters in order to investigate the stimulus specificity of the putative parallel ME processing deficit.

Dyslexic participants for this study were selected to present a VA Span deficit at the individual level. VA Span abilities were assessed outside the scanner, using a 6-letter whole report paradigm similar to the 5-letter paradigm used with children (Bosse et al., 2007; Bosse and Valdois, 2009). Dyslexic participants were not able to report as many letters from a briefly presented array of letters as normal-reading adults. This behavioral impairment is taken as indexing a reduced ability to attend to and process MEs simultaneously. Dubois et al. (2010) showed that a reduced VA Span co-occurred with reduced VA capacity for MEs in dyslexic children while Stenneken et al. (2011) provide similar evidence for reduced VA capacity in high achieving dyslexic adults. In our experimental fMRI task, dyslexic participants were expected to perform as well as control participants for the SE condition, but to perform significantly worse for the ME condition, in line with a specific ME processing deficit. Furthermore, the ME processing behavioral impairment has been associated with abnormal brain activations in the parietal cortex, and more specifically in SPL. Comparisons between activations for ME processing in control and dyslexic participants were expected to highlight abnormal parietal neural activity in dyslexia, regardless of to-be-processed character type.

Behavioral results are consistent with a specific ME processing deficit regardless of character type. Both groups performed at ceiling for SE categorization, although RTs were slower for nAN characters than for AN characters for both groups. For the ME condition, dyslexic participants were less accurate than control participants regardless of character type, but were slower only for AN characters. Reduced accuracy for both character types argues for a general inability to attend to and process all displayed elements in VA Span impaired dyslexics. The different pattern of results for RTs could be explained by accuracy and RTs indexing different processes in character recognition for short exposure durations (Santee and Egeth, 1982). While accuracy could be sensitive to early perceptual effects, RTs could be more sensitive to later processes such as response interference. Within such a framework, poor VA capacity (an early process) would lead to poorer accuracy for dyslexic participants regardless of character type. Interference by later processes could be stronger when the task is not performed at ceiling performance levels, resulting in slowed RTs for dyslexic participants for both character types and in slowed RTs for control participants only for nAN characters.

NEURAL CORRELATES OF SINGLE AND MULTIPLE ELEMENT PROCESSING IN HEALTHY, SKILLED READERS

In control participants, ME processing recruited additional regions from a broad occipito-parietal network compared to SE processing (see **Figure 2**). ME processing activated vOT cortex, as expected for processing single (Flowers et al., 2004) or multiple letters and symbols (Tagamets et al., 2000; Turkeltaub et al., 2003; Brem et al., 2006). However, patterns of parietal activation differed. In SE processing, there were no significant parietal activations. In contrast, ME processing activated a broad parietal network, including SPL, IPL, and precuneus bilaterally. Involvement of IPL and SPL in VA processes is well documented (Behrmann et al., 2004), and could be related to the attentional demands of attending to several characters. Furthermore, activations of SPL and IPL for multiple character processing are consistent with reports of similar activations in adult healthy skilled readers for letter string processing (Levy et al., 2008; Valdois et al., 2009), a flanked character categorization task (Peyrin et al., 2008) or a visual matching task (Reilhac et al., 2013), and in typically reading children for the same flanked character categorization task (Peyrin et al., 2011).

Brain areas specifically involved in ME processing in healthy readers were identified by contrasting ME to SE conditions for each stimuli type (AN and nAN) separately. ME processing activated parietal cortex more strongly than SE processing for both character types. For nAN characters, additional increased activation were located in the right insula, as have been previously reported in VA tasks (Hahn et al., 2006), and in the pre supplementary motor area consistent with that area's putative role in cognitive processes (Picard and Strick, 2001). Increased SPL activity for ME processing was limited to the right hemisphere for AN characters while bilateral for nAN characters. Similar recruitment of left-side homologues for VA tasks with high cognitive demands has been previously reported (Nebel et al., 2005). SPL activations are broadly consistent with our team's previous studies investigating neural correlates of ME processing (Peyrin et al., 2008, 2011), albeit specific activity seems to be more right lateralized in this study. As parietal activity has consistently been associated with visuo-spatial attention (Corbetta and Shulman, 2002; Behrmann et al., 2004), increased parietal activations for both conditions (AN and nAN) could index increased demands on VA for the processing of MEs.

NEURAL CORRELATES OF SINGLE AND MULTIPLE ELEMENT PROCESSING IN DYSLEXIC READERS

Neural networks associated with single and ME processing were more limited in dyslexic participants. For SE processing, visual processing activity was limited to the occipital and occipito-temporal cortices. ME processing in dyslexic readers failed to elicit the broad parietal network present for control participants. Although similar pre-supplementary motor area activations were present for both groups, parietal activations for dyslexics were limited to the left supramarginal gyrus and post-central gyrus. This relative absence of parietal activation is consistent with previous assessments of neural activity for multiple letter processing in dyslexic participants with poor VA Span performance (Peyrin et al., 2008, 2011, 2012; Reilhac et al., 2013; Valdois et al., 2014b).

Further assessment of neural networks subserving ME processing was carried out by contrasting multiple and SE processing for each character type. Similarly to control participants, ME processing led to increased pre-supplementary motor area activations in both conditions (AN and nAN). This pre-supplementary motor area activity, present for more demanding task conditions (ME > SE AN and nAN for dyslexic participants, but also ME > SE nAN for control participants) could reflect higher cognitive demands (Picard and Strick, 2001). However, a complete absence of parietal activation in either hemisphere, for either character type, is to be noted. This absence of parietal activations could reflect a failure to engage appropriate attentional mechanisms for processing MEs, failure that would then lead to impaired behavioral performance.

MODULATION OF MULTIPLE ELEMENT PARIETAL ACTIVATIONS BY READING ABILITY

To identify brain areas significantly more activated in normal readers than in dyslexic participants in ME processing, we compared activations for the ME condition between each group for each character type separately. For both character types (AN and nAN), control participants had larger activations in broadly similar areas in both ventral and dorsal cortices. Reduced activity in vOT cortex was present in the left hemisphere for AN characters and in the right hemisphere for nAN characters. Consistent with the difference in ME processing activity patterns between groups, dyslexic participants exhibit reduced activation in right hemisphere SPL regardless of character type. While previous studies have hinted towards a left SPL dysfunction in VA Span impaired dyslexics (Peyrin et al., 2008, 2011), the current findings seem to point to right SPL as the critical area subserving successful ME processing.

Taken together, results from these whole-brain analyses point towards a right hemisphere superior lobule dysfunction in VA Span impaired dyslexic adults. This functional impairment of parietal cortex seems to be condition-related (present in multiple but not in SE processing) but not stimuli-type related (equally large for NA and nAN characters). Furthermore, this pattern of dysfunction is localized to SPL. This account is supported by our *a priori* ROI analyses. For right hemisphere SPL, the difference in activation between groups was affected by the number of elements to be processed (the activation difference was present for ME processing but absent for SE processing). Interestingly, although whole-brain comparisons between groups did not reveal any left hemisphere activation differences, ROI analyses of left SPL showed stronger activations for normal readers for both ME and SE processing.

A possible confounding factor in these results is the difference in behavioral performance between groups. Differences in neuronal activity could reflect lower accuracy for dyslexic participants within a functional parietal network rather than a dyslexic parietal dysfunction. It, however, seems unlikely that between-group differences in neuronal activation only resulted from between-group differences in RTs, since between-group neuronal activity differences were present for the ME-nAN condition in the absence of between-group RTs differences.

The critical result of this study is that this parietal dysfunction is present regardless of character type. Whole-brain comparisons between groups for the ME-nAN condition revealed dyslexic under-activation in right hemisphere SPL clusters. Indeed, result patterns in SPL ROIs suggested that activations did not differ between character types, and this was true for both dyslexic and control participants. The activation difference between control and dyslexic participants is the same for AN, familiar, verbal characters, and nAN, unfamiliar, non-verbal characters. This strongly suggests the existence of abnormal neural function in dyslexia in non-language related processes.

Finally, this pattern of condition sensitive/stimuli non-sensitive deficit seems to be circumscribed to right SPL. Activation patterns in other parietal (left SPL, bilateral IPL) or upper visual areas (bilateral vOT) were explored in our *a priori* ROI analyses. Bilateral IPL is equally activated for ME or SE conditions, suggesting it plays no specific role in ME processing. This is supported by the absence of activation strength differences between dyslexic and control participants for either the ME or SE conditions. There were also stronger activations for control participants than dyslexic participants in vOT and left SPL. However, this activation difference between groups was similar for (1) SE and ME conditions and (2) for AN and nAN character strings. Within the constraints of our experimental paradigm, VOT BOLD activity seems to be sensitive to neither VA demands nor character type.

IMPLICATIONS FOR THE VA SPAN HYPOTHESIS OF DYSLEXIA

While previous studies had reported decreased activations in SPL for ME processing in VA Span impaired dyslexia (Peyrin et al., 2011, 2012; Reilhac et al., 2013; Valdois et al., 2014b), this is the first study to do so by using a non-verbal task requiring verbal and non-verbal stimuli processing. Our results bring forward new evidence for a visual-attention account of the VA Span deficit. Indeed, these data speaks against two alternative explanations of poor dyslexic performance on the VA Span letter report tasks: impaired print tuning and impaired object-to-phonological code mapping. While our results do not rule out impaired print tuning as one of the contributing factors to poor letter report performance, they argue against it being the sole cause. If poor letter report performance only indexed reduced perceptual specialization for letter (Nazir et al., 2004) or letter-like character (Szwed et al., 2012) strings in dyslexia (Maurer et al., 2007; van der Mark et al., 2009), we would expect poor performance on our ME categorization task to be associated with activation differences in visual rather than parietal cortex. If poor letter report performance were a consequence of impaired visual-to-phonological code mapping (Hawelka and Wimmer, 2008; Ziegler et al., 2010 but see Valdois et al., 2012), we would expect dyslexic participants to perform as well as control participants on a non-verbal categorization task, even more so for non-verbal stimuli. In contrast and in line with similar behavioral results previously reported with typical reading children (Lobier et al., 2012b), dyslexic participants performed worse than control participants in the ME condition. Furthermore, impaired visual-to-phonological code mapping would not result in abnormal brain activity for dyslexic individuals for visual processing of non-verbal character strings, as is present in our data. In contrast, decreased activation of right hemisphere SPL, a brain area consistently associated with space-based (Vandenberghe et al., 2001; Yantis et al., 2002) and object-based (Yantis and Serences, 2003) attention, could index impaired ability to properly attend to MEs simultaneously. SPL could subserve two necessary attentional mechanisms: chunking character strings into appropriate individual elements and allocating spatial attention to each individual element to allow further processing. This could be done by modulating lower level visual responses to spatial locations or features (Corbetta and Shulman, 2002). If all visual elements cannot be attended to in our ME categorization condition, target characters may be missed, leading to poor performance. Similarly, if dyslexic participants can attend to fewer letters than control participants in the VA Span letter report task, their performance will be worse. Poor performance or neurobiological dysfunction cannot be ascribed to different amounts of lifelong experience with characters between dyslexic and control participants. First, all participants had the same amount of limited experience with the nAN characters. Second, SPL parietal dysfunction is of similar magnitude regardless of stimuli type, consistent with similar parietal activation patterns for letter and non-letter stimuli (Nebel et al., 2005). In sum, abnormal parietal activations in VA Span impaired dyslexic participants for ME processing of both AN and nAN character strings supports a ME visual processing disorder as the underlying cause of the VA Span deficit.

IMPLICATIONS FOR NEUROBIOLOGICAL MODELS OF DYSLEXIA

Neurobiological accounts of dyslexia, in line with classic models of reading usually highlight neural dysfunction of the left hemisphere reading network as a hallmark of dyslexia. These functional deficits are present in brain areas thought to subtend phonological processing (left inferior frontal, and parieto-temporal gyri) and orthographic word processing (vOT cortex; see Shaywitz and Shaywitz, 2005 for a review). These abnormal brain activations are identified using reading or reading related tasks (e.g., rhyming) and verbal visual stimuli, in line with a phonological account of dyslexia. The overwhelming developmental model of this disruption of reading neural circuits is one where the vOT neural dysfunction systematically follows from frontal and temporo-parietal dysfunction (McCandliss and Noble, 2003): impaired phonological processing impedes the acquisition of orthographic knowledge and the development of appropriate neural tuning for print (Maurer et al., 2007; van der Mark et al., 2009). However, this model fails to account for a number of empirical findings. First, there is mounting evidence that while a number of dyslexic children do in fact have a phonological deficit, a non-negligible number do not (White et al., 2006; Bosse et al., 2007; Vidyasagar and Pammer, 2010). In line with these behavioral results, a recent case study has reported not only normal phonological behavioral performance but also normal activation of the fronto-temporo-parietal network associated with phonological processing (Peyrin et al., 2012). Second, a recent meta-analyses of brain imaging studies of dyslexic children and adults has failed to find unilateral evidence for a contrasted pattern of predominant left temporo-parietal dysfunction in children and predominant left vOT dysfunction in adults (Richlan et al., 2011). These results suggest that reduced print tuning and orthographic specificity of left vOT cortex in dyslexia could follow from alternative disruption in the learning to read process.

Two aspects of our data are noteworthy. As expected from our hypotheses and appropriately highlighted earlier, VA Span impaired dyslexic adults display reduced parietal activations in tasks requiring visual processing of multiple characters, AN or not. More unexpectedly, task related activations were also reduced in vOT cortex bilaterally and for both character types. Previous accounts of reduced vOT in dyslexia have been associated with processing of letter strings (word or non-words) and restricted to LH vOT (Helenius et al., 1999; Maurer et al., 2007; van der Mark et al., 2009; Wimmer et al., 2010). Indeed, neural responses for non-alphabetic strings have usually been similar in dyslexic and control readers (Helenius et al., 1999; van der Mark et al., 2009 but see Maurer et al., 2007). However, an important caveat of these studies is that their experimental tasks required no explicit processing of individual elements of the non-alphabetic strings. In contrast, in our study, explicit processing of the individual characters composing strings is necessary for both character type. Therefore, if visual processing of individual elements in vOT is influenced by top-down VA related parietal activity, then a parietal dysfunction should result is abnormal vOT activity regardless of character type. In addition, while the difference in vOT activity between letter and non-letter string processing is present only in left vOT in expert readers, visual processing of both string types recruits vOT bilaterally (Tagamets et al., 2000; Vinckier et al., 2007). If at least part of this vOT activity is top-down driven by parietal cortex, then abnormal parietal function will result in abnormal vOT activity bilaterally. The presence of consistent correlations between SPL and vOT activity in each hemisphere further argues for this interpretation of our data. We posit that not only these two co-occuring neural dysfunctions (SPL and VOT) are related but that this relationship can explain disrupted vOT function in dyslexic readers independently from any phonological deficit.

How can impaired parietal function lead to decreased vOT activity in a ME processing task? Parietal areas are responsible for feature and spatial attention focus and shifts (Kanwisher and Wojciulik, 2000). Dorsal areas are thus involved in a fast feedforward/feedback loop with visual areas: early visual signals trigger parietal attention mechanisms and global analysis which then guides further processing in the ventral stream (Bullier, 2001). If attentional processes fail, the downstream ventral processing is also disrupted. In our task, failure to allocate attention appropriately to each element of the character string reduces feedback to ventral areas responsible for character recognition (Szwed et al., 2011) and thus leads to reduced occipito-temporal activations. How does this relate to impaired vOT specificity for print in dyslexia? When children learn to read, they cannot at first rely on fast, parallel processing of words as supported by vOT in expert readers (Dehaene and Cohen, 2011). Letter string processing is supported by attention-based processes as supported by parietal cortex. Development of orthographic knowledge in vOT is therefore dependent on appropriate attentional feedback from parietal areas for proper letter identification. Similar involvement of parietal areas in reading is seen when spatial layout of words is modified in order to disrupt automatic vOT processing (Mayall et al., 2001; Pammer et al., 2006; Cohen et al., 2008; Rosazza et al., 2009). If parietal function fails, vOT specialization cannot take place and fast, automatic visual word processing cannot be achieved. In line with such a model, Richlan (2012) has proposed that impaired general attention processes in dyslexic readers, indexed by abnormal left IPL activity, could result in lack of vOT specialization for print.

Recent connectivity studies in normal and dyslexic readers offer support for this account. Both resting-state and functional connectivity between parietal areas and vOT have been reported, and this connectivity is modulated by reading efficiency. Vogel et al. (2011) investigated resting state connectivity between the specific part of vOT cortex thought to subserve orthographic reading, namely the visual word form area (VWFA; Cohen and Dehaene, 2004; Dehaene and Cohen, 2011) and the dorsal attentional network. They not only found significant connectivity between the VWFA and superior parietal cortex bilaterally, but this connectivity was significantly correlated to reading ability. Better readers had stronger connectivity between SPL and VWFA. Van der mark et al., 2011 investigated functional connectivity between five different seed regions of left vOT cortex (including the VWFA) and other brain regions in normal-reading and dyslexic children. In normal-reading children, bilateral SPL was significantly correlated to the middle, VWFA proper, seed area. This correlation between bilateral SPL and the VWFA seed area did not reach significance in dyslexic children (In that study, however, that the difference in functional connectivity between normal reading and dyslexic children did not reach significance for SPL-VWFA but did for left IPL-VWFA). Taken together, these results speak strongly for an important role of SPL in efficient reading.

In line with the VA span hypothesis of dyslexia (Bosse et al., 2007), VA Span impaired dyslexic adults are impaired in a non-verbal ME processing task. This impairment is associated with reduced specificity of SPL for ME processing, in support of a visual account of the VA span deficit. Co-occurring reduced vOT activation could be related to reduced connectivity between dorsal and ventral visual areas, in line with recent accounts of reduced SPL-vOT connectivity in dyslexia. Further research is needed to (1) investigate if and how the time-course of parietal and vOT activity in ME processing tasks deviates in dyslexic participants and (2) assess connectivity between SPL and vOT in both normal-reading and dyslexic readers with a VA span disorder.

REFERENCES

Ans, B., Carbonnel, S., and Valdois, S. (1998). A connectionist multiple-trace memory model for polysyllabic word reading. *Cereb. Cortex* 105, 678–723. doi: 10.1037/0033-295X.105.4.678-723

Behrmann, M., Geng, J. J., and Shomstein, S. (2004). Parietal cortex and attention. *Curr. Opin. Neurobiol.* 14, 212–217. doi: 10.1016/j.conb.2004.03.012

Bishop, D. V. M., and Snowling, M. J. (2004). Developmental dyslexia and specific language impairment: same or different? *Psychol. Bull.* 130, 858–886. doi: 10.1037/0033-2909.130.6.858

Boden, C., and Giaschi, D. (2007). M-stream deficits and reading-related visual processes in developmental dyslexia. *Psychol. Bull.* 133, 346–366. doi: 10.1037/0033-2909.133.2.346

Bosse, M.-L., Tainturier, M. J., and Valdois, S. (2007). Developmental dyslexia: the visual attention span deficit hypothesis. *Cognition* 104, 198–230. doi: 10.1016/j.cognition.2006.05.009

Bosse, M.-L., and Valdois, S. (2009). Influence of the visual attention span on child reading performance: a cross-sectional study. *J. Res. Read.* 32, 230–253. doi: 10.1111/j.1467-9817.2008.01387.x

Brem, S., Bach, S., Kucian, K., Guttorm, T. K., Martin, E., Lyytinen, H., et al. (2010). Brain sensitivity to print emerges when children learn letter-speech sound correspondences. *Proc. Natl. Acad. Sci. U.S.A.* 107, 7939–7944. doi: 10.1073/pnas.0904402107

Brem, S., Bucher, K., Halder, P., Summers, P., Dietrich, T., Martin, E., et al. (2006). Evidence for developmental changes in the visual word processing network beyond adolescence. *Neuroimage* 29, 822–837. doi: 10.1016/j.neuroimage.2005.09.023

Bullier, J. (2001). Integrated model of visual processing. *Brain Res. Rev.* 36, 96–107. doi: 10.1016/S0165-0173(01)00085-6

Cai, Q., Paulignan, Y., Brysbaert, M., Ibarrola, D., and Nazir, T. A. (2010). The left ventral occipito-temporal response to words depends on language lateralization but not on visual familiarity. *Cereb. Cortex* 20, 1153–1163. doi: 10.1093/cercor/bhp175

Cao, F., Lee, R., Shu, H., Yang, Y., Xu, G., Li, K., et al. (2010). Cultural constraints on brain development: evidence from a developmental study of visual word processing in Mandarin Chinese. *Cereb. Cortex* 20, 1223–1233. doi: 10.1093/cercor/bhp186

Church, J. A., Coalson, R. S., Lugar, H. M., Petersen, S. E., and Schlaggar, B. L. (2008). A developmental fMRI study of reading and repetition reveals changes in phonological and visual mechanisms over age. *Cereb. Cortex* 18, 2054–2065. doi: 10.1093/cercor/bhm228

Cohen, L., and Dehaene, S. (2004). Specialization within the ventral stream: the case for the visual word form area. *Neuroimage* 22, 466–476. doi: 10.1016/j.neuroimage.2003.12.049

Cohen, L., Dehaene, S., Vinckier, F., Jobert, A., and Montavont, A. (2008). Reading normal and degraded words: contribution of the dorsal and ventral visual pathways. *Neuroimage* 40, 353–366. doi: 10.1016/j.neuroimage.2007.11.03

Corbetta, M., and Shulman, G. L. (2002). Control of goal-directed and stimulus-driven attention in the brain. *Nat. Rev. Neurosci.* 3, 201–215. doi: 10.1038/nrn755

Dehaene, S., and Cohen, L. (2011). The unique role of the visual word form area in reading. *Trends Cogn. Sci.* 15, 254–262. doi: 10.1016/j.tics.2011.04.003

Dehaene, S., Pegado, F., Braga, L. W., Ventura, P., Nunes Filho, G., Jobert, A., et al. (2010). How learning to read changes the cortical networks for vision and language. *Science* 330, 1359–1364. doi: 10.1126/science.1194140

Démonet, J.-F., Taylor, M. J., and Chaix, Y. (2004). Developmental dyslexia. *Lancet* 363, 1451–1460. doi: 10.1016/S0140-6736(04)16106-0

Dubois, M., Kyllingsbaek, S., Prado, C., Musca, S. C., Peiffer, E., Lassus-Sangosse, D., et al. (2010). Fractionating the multi-character processing deficit in developmental dyslexia: evidence from two case studies. *Cortex* 46, 717–738. doi: 10.1016/j.cortex.2009.11.002

Facoetti, A., Zorzi, M., Cestnick, L., Lorusso, M. L., Molteni, M., Paganoni, P., et al. (2006). The relationship between visuo-spatial attention and nonword reading in developmental dyslexia. *Cogn. Neuropsychol.* 23, 841–855. doi: 10.1080/02643290500483090

Facoetti, A., Ruffino, M., Peru, A., Paganoni, P., and Chelazzi, L. (2008). Sluggish engagement and disengagement of non-spatial attention in dyslexic children. *Cortex* 44, 1221–1233. doi: 10.1016/j.cortex.2007.10.007

Flowers, D. L., Jones, K., Noble, K., VanMeter, J., Zeffiro, T. A, Wood, F. B., et al. (2004). Attention to single letters activates left extrastriate cortex. *Neuroimage* 21, 829–839. doi: 10.1016/j.neuroimage.2003.10.002

Friston, K. J., Fletcher, P., Josephs, O., Holmes, A., Rugg, M. D., and Turner, R. (1998). Event related fMRI: characterizing differential responses. *Neuroimage* 7, 30–40. doi: 10.1006/nimg.1997.0306

Friston, K. J., Holmes, A. P., Worsley, K. J., Poline, J. P., Frith, C. D., and Frackowiak, R. S. (1994). Statistical parametric maps in functional imaging: a general linear approach. *Hum. Brain Mapp.* 2, 189–210. doi: 10.1002/hbm.460020402

Friston, K. J., Zarahn, E. O. R. N. A., Josephs, O., Henson, R. N. A., and Dale, A. M. (1999). Stochastic designsin event-related fMRI. *Neuroimage* 10, 607–619. doi: 10.1006/nimg.1999.0498

Gaillard, R., Naccache, L., Pinel, P., Clémenceau, S., Volle, E., Hasboun, D., et al. (2006). Direct intracranial fMRI and lesion evidence for the causal role of left infero temporal cortex in reading. *Neurons* 50, 191–204. doi: 10.1016/j.neuron.2006.03.031

Hahn, B., Ross, T. J., and Stein, E. A. (2006). Neuroanatomical dissociation between bottom-up and top-down processes of visuospatial selective attention. *Neuroimage* 32, 842–853. doi: 10.1016/j.neuroimage.2006.04.177

Hari, R., and Renvall, H. (2001). Impaired processing of rapid stimulus sequences in dyslexia. *Trends Cogn. Sci.* 5, 525–532. doi: 10.1016/S1364-6613(00)01801-5

Hawelka, S., and Wimmer, H. (2008). Visual target detection is not impaired in dyslexic readers. *Vision Res.* 48, 850–852. doi: 10.1016/j.visres.2007.11.003

Helenius, P., Tarkiainen, A., Cornelissen, P. L., Hansen, P., and Salmelin, R. (1999). Dissociation of normal feature analysis and deficient processing of letter-strings in dyslexic adults. *Cereb. Cortex* 9, 476. doi: 10.1093/cercor/9.5.476

Hoeft, F., Meyler, A., Hernandez, A., Juel, C., Taylor-Hill, H., Martindale, J. L., et al. (2007). Functional and morphometric brain dissociation between dyslexia and reading ability. *Proc. Natl. Acad. Sci. U.S.A.* 104, 4234–4239. doi: 10.1073/pnas.0609399104

Jobard, G., Crivello, F., and Tzourio-Mazoyer, N. (2003). Evaluation of the dual route theory of reading: a metanalysis of 35 neuroimaging studies. *Neuroimage* 20, 693–712. doi: 10.1016/S1053-8119(03)00343-4

Jobard, G., Vigneau, M., Simon, G., and Tzourio-Mazoyer, N. (2011). The weight of skill: interindividual variability of reading related brain activation patterns in fluent readers. *J. Neurol.* 24, 113–132. doi: 10.1016/j.jneuroling.2010.09.002

Jones, M. W., Branigan, H. P., and Kelly, M. L. (2008). Visual deficits in developmental dyslexia: relationships between non-linguistic visual tasks and their contribution to components of reading. *Dyslexia* 14, 95–115. doi: 10.1002/dys

Kanwisher, N., and Wojciulik, E. (2000). Visual attention: insights from brain imaging. *Nat. Rev. Neurosci.* 1, 91–100. doi: 10.1038/35039043

Lassus-Sangosse, D., N'Guyen-Morel, M. A., and Valdois, S. (2008). Sequential or simultaneous visual processing deficit in developmental dyslexia? *Vision Res.* 48, 979–988. doi: 10.1016/j.visres.2008.01.025

Lefavrais, P. (1965). *Test de l'Alouette.* Paris: Editions du centre de psychologie appliquée.

Levy, J., Pernet, C., Treserras, S., Boulanouar, K., Berry, I., Aubry, F., et al. (2008). Piecemeal recruitment of left-lateralized brain areas during reading: a spatio-functional account. *Neuroimage* 43, 581–591. doi: 10.1016/j.neuroimage.2008.08.008

Lobier, M., Peyrin, C., Le Bas, J. F., and Valdois, S. (2012a). Pre-orthographic character string processing and parietal cortex: a role for visual attention in reading? *Neuropsychologia* 50, 2195–2204. doi: 10.1016/j.neuropsychologia.2012.05.023

Lobier, M., Zoubrinetzky, R., and Valdois, S. (2012b). The visual attention span deficit in dyslexia is visual and not verbal. *Cortex* 48, 768–773. doi: 10.1016/j.cortex.2011.09.003

Maisog, J. M., Einbinder, E. R., Flowers, D. L., Turkeltaub, P. E., and Eden, G. F. (2008). A meta-analysis of functional neuroimaging studies of dyslexia. *Ann. N. Y. Acad. Sci.* 1145, 237–259. doi: 10.1196/annals.1416.024

Majaj, N. J., Pelli, D. G., Kurshan, P., and Palomares, M. (2002). The role of spatial frequency channels in letter identification. *Vision Res.* 42, 1165–1184. doi: 10.1016/S0042-6989(02)00045-7

Maldjian, J. A., Laurienti, P. J., Kraft, R. A., and Burdette, J. H. (2003). An automated method for neuroanatomic and cytoarchitectonic atlas-based interrogation of fMRI data sets. *Neuroimage* 19, 1233–1239. doi: 10.1016/S1053-8119(03)00169-1

Maurer, U., Brem, S., Bucher, K., Kranz, F., Benz, R., Steinhausen, H.-C., et al. (2007). Impaired tuning of a fast occipito-temporal response for print in dyslexic children learning to read. *Brain* 130, 3200–3210. doi: 10.1093/brain/awm193

Mayall, K., Humphreys, G. W., Mechelli, A., Olson, A., and Price, C. J. (2001). The effects of case mixing on word recognition: evidence from a PET study. *J. Cogn. Neurosci.* 13, 844–853. doi: 10.1162/08989290152541494

McCandliss, B. D., and Noble, K. G. (2003). The development of reading impairment: a cognitive neuroscience model. *Ment. Retard. Dev. Disabil. Res. Rev.* 9, 196–204. doi: 10.1002/mrdd.10080

Menghini, D., Finzi, A., Benassi, M., Bolzani, R., Facoetti, A., Giovagnoli, S., et al. (2010). Different underlying neurocognitive deficits in developmental dyslexia: a comparative study. *Neuropsychologia* 48, 863–872. doi: 10.1016/j.neuropsychologia.2009.11.003

Mitchell, D. J., and Cusack, R. (2008). Flexible, capacity-limited activity of posterior parietal cortex in perceptual as well as visual short-term memory tasks. *Cereb. Cortex* 18, 1788–1798. doi: 10.1093/cercor/bhm205

Nazir, T. A., Ben-Boutayab, N., Decoppet, N., Deutsch, A., and Frost, R. (2004). Reading habits, perceptual learning, and recognition of printed words. *Brain Lang.* 88, 294–311. doi: 10.1016/S0093-934X(03)00168-8

Nebel, K., Wiese, H., Stude, P., de Greiff, A., Diener, H.-C., and Keidel, M. (2005). On the neural basis of focused and divided attention. *Cogn. Brain Res.* 25, 760–776. doi: 10.1016/j.cogbrainres.2005.09.011

Pammer, K., Hansen, P., Cornelissen, P. L., and Holliday, I. (2006). Attentional shifting and the role of the dorsal pathway in visual word recognition. *Neuropsychologia* 44, 2926–2936. doi: 10.1016/j.neuropsychologia.2006.06.028

Pammer, K., Lavis, R., Hansen, P., and Cornelissen, P. L. (2004). Symbol-string sensitivity and children's reading. *Brain Lang.* 89, 601–610. doi: 10.1016/j.bandl.2004.01.009

Pelli, D. G., Burns, C. W., Farell, B., and Moore-Page, D. C. (2006). Feature detection and letter identification. *Vision Res.* 46, 4646–4674. doi: 10.1016/j.visres.2006.04.023

Pennington, B. F. (2006). From single to multiple deficit models of developmental disorders. *Cognition* 101, 385–413. doi: 10.1016/j.cognition.2006.04.008

Peyrin, C., Démonet, J. F., N'Guyen-Morel, M. A., Le Bas, J. F., and Valdois, S. (2011). Superior parietal lobule dysfunction in a homogeneous group of dyslexic children with a visual attention span disorder. *Brain Lang.* 118, 128–138. doi: 10.1016/j.bandl.2010.06.005

Peyrin, C., Lallier, M., Baciu, M., and Valdois, S. (2008). "Brain mechanisms of the visual attention span in normal and dyslexic readers," in *Behavioural, Neuropsychological and Neuroimaging Studies of Spoken and Written Language*, ed. M. Bacxiu (Trivandrum: Signpost Edition).

Peyrin, C., Lallier, M., Démonet, J.-F., Pernet, C., Baciu, M., Le Bas, J. F., et al. (2012). Neural dissociation of phonological and visual attention span disorders in developmental dyslexia: fMRI evidence from two case reports. *Brain Lang.* 120, 381–394. doi: 10.1016/j.bandl.2011.12.015

Picard, N., and Strick, P. L. (2001). Imaging the premotor areas. *Curr. Opin. Neurobiol.* 11, 663–672. doi: 10.1016/S0959-4388(01)00266-5

Ramus, F. (2003). Developmental dyslexia: specific phonological deficit or general sensorimotor dysfunction? *Curr. Opin. Neurobiol.* 13, 212–218. doi: 10.1016/S0959-4388(03)00035-7

Ramus, F., and Szenkovits, G. (2008). What phonological deficit? *Q. J. Exp. Psychol.* 61, 129–141. doi: 10.1080/17470210701508822

Reilhac, C., Peyrin, C., Démonet, J. F., and Valdois, S. (2013). Role of the superior parietal lobules in letter-identity processing within strings: fMRI evidence from skilled and dyslexic readers. *Neuropsychologia* 51, 601–612. doi: 10.1016/j.neuropsychologia.2012.12.010

Richlan, F. (2012). Developmental dyslexia: dysfunction of a left hemisphere reading network. *Front. Hum. Neurosci.* 6:120. doi: 10.3389/fnhum.2012.00120

Richlan, F., Kronbichler, M., and Wimmer, H. (2009). Functional abnormalities in the dyslexic brain: a quantitative meta-analysis of neuroimaging studies. *Hum. Brain Mapp.* 30, 3299–3308. doi: 10.1002/hbm.20752

Richlan, F., Kronbichler, M., and Wimmer, H. (2011). Meta-analyzing brain dysfunctions in dyslexic children and adults. *Neuroimage* 56, 1735–1742. doi: 10.1016/j.neuroimage.2011.02.040

Rosazza, C., Cai, Q., Minati, L., Paulignan, Y., and Nazir, T. A. (2009). Early involvement of dorsal and ventral pathways in visual word recognition: an ERP study. *Brain Res.* 1272, 32–44. doi: 10.1016/j.brainres.2009.03.033

Santee, J. L., and Egeth, H. E. (1982). Do reaction time and accuracy measure the same aspects of letter recognition? *J. Exp. Psychol. Hum. Percept. Perform.* 8, 489–501. doi: 10.1037//0096-1523.8.4.489

Scalf, P. E., and Beck, D. M. (2010). Competition in visual cortex impedes attention to multiple items. *J. Neurosci.* 30, 161–169. doi: 10.1523/JNEUROSCI.4207-09.2010

Shaywitz, S. E., and Shaywitz, B. A. (2005). Dyslexia (specific reading disability). *Biol. Psychiatry* 57, 1301–1309. doi: 10.1016/j.biopsych.2005.01.043

Stenneken, P., Egetemeir, J., Schulte-Körne, G., Müller, H. J., Schneider, W. X., and Finke, K. (2011). Slow perceptual processing at the core of developmental dyslexia: a parameter-based assessment of visual attention. *Neuropsychologia* 49, 3454–3465. doi: 10.1016/j.neuropsychologia.2011.08.021

Szwed, M., Dehaene, S., Kleinschmidt, A., Eger, E., Valabrègue, R., Amadon, A., et al. (2011). Specialization for written words over objects in the visual cortex. *Neuroimage* 56, 330–344. doi: 10.1016/j.neuroimage.2011.01.073

Szwed, M., Ventura, P., Querido, L., Cohen, L., and Dehaene, S. (2012). Reading acquisition enhances an early visual process of contour integration. *Dev. Sci.* 15, 139–149. doi: 10.1111/j.1467-7687.2011.01102.x

Tagamets, M., Novick, J., and Chalmers, M. (2000). A parametric approach to orthographic processing in the brain: an fMRI study. *J. Cogn. Neurosci.* 12, 281–297. doi: 10.1162/089892900562101

Turkeltaub, P. E., Gareau, L., Flowers, D. L., Zeffiro, T. A, and Eden, G. F. (2003). Development of neural mechanisms for reading. *Nat. Neurosci.* 6, 767–773. doi: 10.1038/nn1065

Tzourio-Mazoyer, N., Landeau, B., Papathanassiou, D., Crivello, F., Etard, O., Delcroix, N., et al. (2002). Automated anatomical labeling of activations in SPM using a macroscopic anatomical parcellation of the MNI MRI single-subject brain. *Neuroimage* 15, 273–289. doi: 10.1006/nimg.2001.0978

Valdois, S., Bosse, M.-L., Ans, B., Carbonnel, S., Zorman, M., David, D., et al. (2003). Phonological and visual processing deficits can dissociate in developmental dyslexia: evidence from two case studies. *Read. Writ.* 16, 541–572. doi: 10.1023/A:1025501406971

Valdois, S., Bosse, M.-L., and Tainturier, M.-J. (2004). The cognitive deficits responsible for developmental dyslexia: review of evidence for a selective visual attentional disorder. *Dyslexia* 10, 339–363. doi: 10.1002/dys.284

Valdois, S., Guinet, E., and Embs, J. L. (2014a). *EVADYS: logiciel d'évaluation de l'empan visuo-attentionnel chez les personnes dyslexique (EVADYS: a software for the assessment of visual attention span abilities in dyslexic individuals).* Isbergues: Ortho-Editions.

Valdois, S., Peyrin, C., Lassus-Sangosse, D., Lallier, M., Démonet, J. F., and Kandel, S. (2014b). Dyslexia in a French–Spanish bilingual girl: behavioural and neural modulations following a specific visual-attention span intervention program. *Cortex* 53, 120–145. doi: 10.1016/j.cortex.2013.11.006

Valdois, S., Juphard, A., Baciu, M., Ans, B., Peyrin, C., Segebarth, C., et al. (2006). Differential length effect in reading and lexical decision: convergent evidence from behavioural data, connectionist simulations and functional MRI. *Brain Res.* 1085, 149–162. doi: 10.1016/j.brainres.2006.02.049

Valdois, S., Lassus-Sangosse, D., and Lobier, M. (2012). Impaired letter-string processing in developmental dyslexia: what visual-to-phonology code mapping disorder? *Dyslexia* 18, 77–93. doi: 10.1002/dys.1437

Valdois, S., Peyrin, C., and Baciu, M. (2009). "The neurobiological correlates of developmental dyslexia," in *Some Aspects of Speech and the Brain*, eds S. Fuchs, H. Loevenbruck, D. Pape, and P. Perrier (Berlin: Verlag Publishers), 141–162.

Vandenberghe, R., Gitelman, D. R., Parrish, T. B., and Mesulam, M. M. (2001). Functional specificity of superior parietal mediation of spatial shifting. *Neuroimage* 14, 661–673. doi: 10.1006/nimg.2001.0860

van der Mark, S., Bucher, K., Maurer, U., Schulz, E., Brem, S., Buckelmüller, J., et al. (2009). Children with dyslexia lack multiple specializations along the visual word-form (VWF) system. *Neuroimage* 47, 1940–1949. doi: 10.1016/j.neuroimage.2009.05.021

Van der mark, S., Klaver, P., Bucher, K., Maurer, U., Schulz, E., Brem, S., et al. (2011). The left occipitotemporal system in reading: disruption of focal fMRI connectivity to left inferior frontal and inferior parietal language areas in children with dyslexia. *Neuroimage* 54, 2426–2436. doi: 10.1016/j.neuroimage.2010.10.002

Vellutino, F. R., Fletcher, J. M., Snowling, M. J., and Scanlon, D. M. (2004). Specific reading disability (dyslexia): what have we learned in the past four decades? *J. Child Psychol. Psychiatry* 45, 2–40. doi: 10.1046/j.0021-9630.2003.00305.x

Vidyasagar, T. R., and Pammer, K. (2010). Dyslexia: a deficit in visuo-spatial attention, not in phonological processing. *Trends Cogn. Sci.* 14, 57–63. doi: 10.1016/j.tics.2009.12.003

Vinckier, F., Dehaene, S., Jobert, A., Dubus, J. P., Sigman, M., and Cohen, L. (2007). Hierarchical coding of letter strings in the ventral stream: dissecting the inner organization of the visual word-form system. *Neuron* 55, 143–156. doi: 10.1016/j.neuron.2007.05.031

Vogel, A. C., Miezin, F. M., Petersen, S. E., and Schlaggar, B. L. (2011). The putative visual word form area is functionally connected to the dorsal attention network. *Cereb. Cortex* 22, 537–549. doi: 10.1093/cercor/bhr100

White, S., Milne, E., Rosen, S., Hansen, P., Swettenham, J., Frith, U., et al. (2006). The role of sensorimotor impairments in dyslexia: a multiple case study of dyslexic children. *Dev. Sci.* 9, 237–255; discussion 265–269. doi: 10.1111/j.1467-7687.2006.00483.x

Wimmer, H., Schurz, M., Sturm, D., Richlan, F., Klackl, J., Kronbichler, M., et al. (2010). A dual-route perspective on poor reading in a regular orthography: an fMRI study. *Cortex* 46, 1284–1298. doi: 10.1016/j.cortex.2010.06.004

Wojciulik, E., and Kanwisher, N. (1999). The generality of parietal involvement in visual attention. *Neuron* 23, 747–764. doi: 10.1016/S0896-6273(01)80033-7

Xu, Y., and Chun, M. M. (2009). Selecting and perceiving multiple visual objects. *Trends Cogn. Sci.* 13, 167–174. doi: 10.1016/j.tics.2009.01.008

Yantis, S., Schwarzbach, J., Serences, J. T., Carlson, R. L., Steinmetz, M. A., Pekar, J. J., et al. (2002). Transient neural activity in human parietal cortex during spatial attention shifts. *Nat. Neurosci.* 5, 995–1002. doi: 10.1038/nn921

Yantis, S., and Serences, J. T. (2003). Cortical mechanisms of space-based and object-based attentional control. *Curr. Opin. Neurobiol.* 13, 187–193. doi: 10.1016/S0959-4388(03)00033-3

Ziegler, J. C., Pech-Georgel, C., Dufau, S., and Grainger, J. (2010). Rapid processing of letters, digits and symbols: what purely visual-attentional deficit in developmental dyslexia? *Dev. Sci.* 13, F8–F14. doi: 10.1111/j.1467-7687.2010.00983.x

Zoubrinetzky, R., Bielle, F., and Valdois, S. (2014). New insights on developmental dyslexia subtypes: heterogeneity of mixed reading profiles. *PLoS ONE* 9:e99337. doi: 10.1371/journal.pone.0099337

7

Reading into neuronal oscillations in the visual system: implications for developmental dyslexia

Trichur R. Vidyasagar [1,2]*

[1] *Visual and Cognitive Neuroscience Laboratory, Department of Optometry and Vision Sciences, University of Melbourne, Parkville, VIC, Australia*
[2] *Melbourne Neuroscience Institute, University of Melbourne, Parkville, VIC, Australia*

***Correspondence:**
Trichur R. Vidyasagar, Department of Optometry and Vision Sciences, The University of Melbourne, Alice Hoy Building, Room 429, Parkville, VIC 3010, Australia
e-mail: trv@unimelb.edu.au

While phonological impairments are common in developmental dyslexia, there has recently been much debate as to whether there is a causal link between the phonological difficulties and the reading problem. An alternative suggestion has been gaining ground that the core deficit in dyslexia is in visual attentional mechanisms. If so, the visual aetiology may be at any of a number of sites along the afferent magnocellular pathway or in the dorsal cortical stream that are all essential for a visuo-spatial attentional feedback to the primary visual cortex. It has been suggested that the same circuits and pathways of top-down attention used for serial visual search are used for reading. Top-down signals from the dorsal parietal areas to primary visual cortex serially highlight cortical locations representing successive letters in a text before they can be recognized and concatenated into a word. We had shown in non-human primates that the mechanism of such a top-down feedback in a visual attention task uses synchronized neuronal oscillations at the lower end of the gamma frequency range. It is no coincidence that reading graphemes in a text also happens at the low gamma frequencies. The basic proposal here is that each cycle of gamma oscillation focuses an attentional spotlight on the primary visual cortical representation of just one or two letters before sequential recognition of letters and their concatenation into word strings. The timing, period, envelope, amplitude, and phase of the synchronized oscillations modulating the incoming signals in the striate cortex would have a profound influence on the accuracy and speed of reading. Thus, the general temporal sampling difficulties in dyslexic subjects may impact reading not necessarily by causing phonological deficits, but by affecting the spatio-temporal parsing of the visual input within the visual system before these signals are used for letter and word recognition.

Keywords: developmental dyslexia, neuronal oscillations, posterior parietal cortex, primary visual cortex, top-down attention, reading

INTRODUCTION

For nearly three decades, the dominant model to explain the reading difficulties experienced by those with developmental dyslexia (DD) was one that was phonologically based (Bradley and Bryant, 1983; Goswami and Bryant, 1990; Stanovich, 1998; Shaywitz and Shaywitz, 2005; Ziegler and Goswami, 2005; Goswami, 2011). This was supported not only by the profound deficits in phonological skills and in phonemic awareness commonly found to be associated with dyslexia, but also by the findings of temporal processing difficulties in the auditory system that provided a possible neuronal basis for the phonological theory (Tallal, 1980; Ahissar et al., 2000; Temple et al., 2000; Breier et al., 2001). Recently, these findings were integrated with a host of studies on neuronal oscillatory mechanisms that are relevant for temporal sampling of speech and were applied to DD in a model termed the "temporal sampling framework" (TSF) by Goswami (2011). This was a fresh new approach in the field and brought a sound neurophysiological perspective to the phonological model of dyslexia. In essence, in line with the new understanding of the possible role of neuronal oscillations in speech perception (Luo and Poeppel, 2007; Poeppel et al., 2008), Goswami (2011) suggests that deficits in syllabic perception at delta/theta (4–10 Hz) frequencies form the critical basis for the reading impairment in DD. However, the TSF could be applied to the various stages of processing within the visual system as well, prior to the information entering the phonological processing stage. This leads one to consider how oscillatory activity may influence visual processing. The following account proposes a mechanism that underpins reading, based upon recent neurophysiological demonstrations of how visual cortical areas communicate with each other and the biophysical limitations surrounding such communication. It leads with an introduction to how these factors influence a function long established in phylogeny, namely visual attention, which could hold the key for our ability to read.

THE ROLE OF TOP-DOWN FEEDBACK SIGNALS FROM PARIETAL CORTEX IN SERIAL VISUAL SEARCH

An alternative to the phonological basis for dyslexia has been the suggestion that the core deficit is in visuo-spatial attentional mechanisms that may be crucial to reading (Ans et al., 1998; Vidyasagar, 1999, 2001; Facoetti et al., 2000; Valdois et al., 2004; Pammer and Vidyasagar, 2005; Vidyasagar and Pammer, 2010). A number of studies have shown significant impairments in visual attention in children with DD (Casco and Prunetti, 1996; Hari et al., 1999; Vidyasagar and Pammer, 1999; Facoetti et al., 2000, 2008; Facoetti and Molteni, 2001; Bednarek et al., 2004; Kinsey et al., 2004; Valdois et al., 2004; Strasburger, 2005; Bosse et al., 2007; Roach and Hogben, 2007; Solan et al., 2007; Dhar et al., 2008; Jones et al., 2008; Kevan and Pammer, 2008; Bosse and Valdois, 2009; Facoetti et al., 2010; Ruffino et al., 2010). However, why should such a deficit in spatial attention cause dyslexia? This leads one to consider what may be the neural processes that nature has evolved that humans exploit in reading and what may be the neurophysiological constraints that these processes impose on our reading abilities. It has been proposed (Vidyasagar, 1999) that reading uses a circuit that the visual system had evolved to deal with the common problem of recognizing a target in a cluttered world. The visual system faces two major challenges in real visual scenes that are usually populated by myriad objects of different sizes, forms, colors, etc. These are:

1. Neurons in the ventral cortical stream that mediate object recognition exhibit progressively larger receptive fields (**Figure 1**) but yet display position invariance, i.e., they respond to the optimum stimulus, say a face, a car, or a letter, irrespective of their location within the large receptive field (Boussaoud et al., 1991). This and the various other invariances such as for retinal size and angle of view constitute an essential property for any object recognition system, so as to avoid the combinatorial problem of having neurons specific for a feature or object for every possible location, viewpoint, etc. However, the loss of location information will be an impediment in a number of situations, including that of reading a text, since the spatial sequence of letters within a word is vital for word recognition.
2. Different attributes of an object, such as color, form, depth, movement, etc are processed in separate cortical areas and there are over 30 of these in the primate cerebral cortex (Felleman and van Essen, 1991). How can these attributes be bound together so that the objects can be correctly identified?

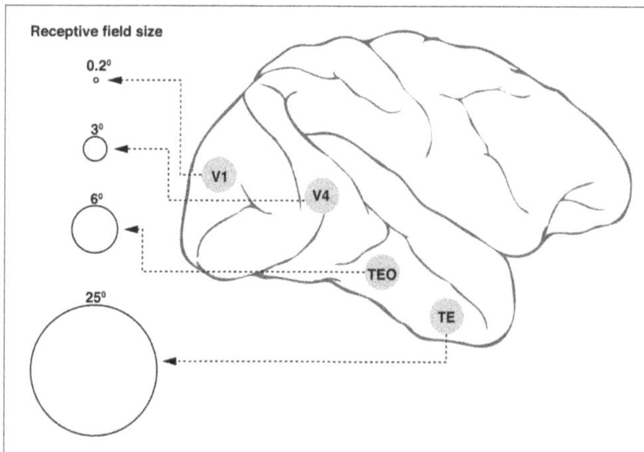

FIGURE 1 | Receptive field (RF) sizes along the ventral cortical stream in the primate. While the degree of complexity of processing may increase, the RF size at any one eccentricity also increases dramatically along the various cortical areas from V1 into the temporal pole. The circles shown in the figure are not drawn to scale, but the numbers above the circles indicate approximate relative sizes of the RF diameters.

One widely accepted solution to this double conundrum, supported by a long and continuing series of experiments using *visual search* paradigms, is that a spotlight of attention highlights one location at a time and the attributes of each object get bound by the coincident processing of its features (Treisman and Gelade, 1980; Treisman, 1988). The neuronal basis of this solution is likely to be a feedback from the parietal cortical region back to earlier visual areas, area V5/MT and still further back to V1, from where the two cortical streams originate (Vidyasagar, 1999). Many studies have now identified attentional facilitation of discrete locations in area MT (Saalmann et al., 2007) and the primary visual cortex (Vidyasagar, 1998; Brefzynski and DeYoe, 1999; Gandhi et al., 2001; McAdams and Reid, 2005; Simola et al., 2009). When only a small location of the visual scene on the primary visual cortex, pertaining to say one object, gets preferentially highlighted for a short period, the signals from this area will lead to unambiguous object identification despite the large receptive fields of neurons in the ventral stream; also, the different attributes of the object get bound together due to the coincidence of activation in different areas that process each of these attributes.

VISUAL SEARCH AND READING

The earliest scripts in recorded history are only about 6000 years old and many human communities did not have any written language until recently but all have the capacity to read and write. For this reason, it has been repeatedly pointed out that, during reading, we are using or "recycling" neural circuits that evolved over hundreds of thousands of years for other reasons (e.g., Vidyasagar, 1999; Dehaene and Cohen, 2007). What could these circuits be? It is now well established that the Visual Word Form area (VWFA), that shows specific activation during reading and dubbed the "letterbox area" of the brain (Cohen and Dehaene, 2004; Dehaene, 2009; Dehaene and Cohen, 2011), is one of the subdivisions in the ventral occipitotemporal region involved in object recognition (Puce et al., 1996; Kanwisher et al., 1997; Ishai et al., 1999; Haxby et al., 2001; Malach et al., 2002). This happens to be an area that codes for visual images of a particular spatial scale and when humans learn to read, the VWFA seems to be responsible for stringing letters together into words. In fact, literacy training in childhood even causes this area to expand at the cost of adjoining areas of the ventral visual cortex that code for objects at other spatial scales (Dehaene et al., 2010). Given such impressive plasticity of this ventral region, the core deficit in DD is unlikely to be a lesion here, unless one finds comparable deficits in object recognition of all types, which is not the case. However, prior to the stage of word recognition at VWFA, there are many steps in visual processing which are all critical for reading. Beyond the stage of initial processing of elementary contours such as lines and edges, a vital hurdle to be overcome is the conundrum described in the previous section. Written text such as the one you are reading now is almost certainly the most frequent and crowded visual scene at a fine spatial scale that we are confronted with in modern civilization. How do we manage to identify each letter and combine them in the appropriate sequence to form words despite the limitations mentioned earlier? One solution that has been proposed (Vidyasagar, 1999, 2001; Vidyasagar and Pammer, 1999, 2010) was that during reading we exploit the same circuits and processes that we had evolved for visual search and object identification in a cluttered world. It was hypothesized that during the periods of eye fixation in reading a text, each lasting approximately 250 ms, feedback signals to V1 sweep a spotlight of covert attention across the letters of individual words and this temporal sequence of identified letters leads to their concatenation into the spatial sequence subsequent to their serial recognition in the ventral stream. Given this scenario, reading may well be the most challenging task for the visuo-spatial attentional mechanisms in a visual world dominated by the printed text and any deficit of these attentional resources can lead to the impairment in what is possibly one of the most sensitive of all our brain functions, namely reading.

Many studies had implicated a deficit in the magnocellular pathway in dyslexia (e.g., Lovegrove et al., 1980; Livingstone et al., 1991; Cornelissen et al., 1995; Eden et al., 1996; Stein and Walsh, 1997; Pammer and Wheatley, 2001; Solan et al., 2004). Such a deficit can potentially be the basis of the attentional impairment (Vidyasagar and Pammer, 1999), since the visual inputs to the dorsal stream, the putative driver of the attentional feedback, is dominated by magnocellular signals. However, the magnocellular deficit has not always been found to be associated with dyslexia as reviewed by Skoyles and Skottun (2004). This discrepancy in the literature is not entirely surprising, for two reasons: (1) A visuo-spatial attentional deficit and consequent reading impairment can be caused not only by a lesion in the visual magnocellular pathway, but also in the dorsal stream structures themselves or in the feedback pathways to the striate cortex. (2) For a magnocellular deficit to manifest as dyslexia, it needs to be at the critical visual field site, namely a small region near the center of the fovea where covert attention is used for letter identification as described above. Unless a magno deficit involves this region, a reading difficulty need not be expected. That almost none of the studies have paid attention to this confounder, could be a contributory factor to the discrepancy in the literature on the relationship between magnocellular dysfunction and the reading impairment.

THE ROLE OF NEURONAL OSCILLATIONS IN VISUAL SEARCH AND READING

If, as suggested above, top-down feedback is essential for serial letter recognition in reading, what could be the neuronal mechanism that makes such feedback modulation and parsing of letters possible? The answer to this question may come from the recent realization that oscillatory activity of neurons is fundamental for organizing and integrating information in the brain (for review, Buzsáki, 2006). Recent studies into the role of synchronized oscillations in visual attention (Saalmann et al., 2007; Gregoriou et al., 2009; Miller and Buschman, 2013), and speech perception (Giraud and Poeppel, 2012) provide an insight into how neuronal oscillations might also mediate the top-down feedback process in visual search and reading.

Humans analyze speech in essentially two integration windows: one at ~150 ms and above, i.e., at delta-theta band for syllabic segmentation and one at ~30 ms and below, i.e., at low gamma range for phonemic segmentation (Giraud et al., 2007; Abrams et al., 2009; Lehongre et al., 2011; Giraud and Poeppel, 2012). Processing of human speech indicates that weak gamma oscillation at rest (30–40 Hz) gets stronger with auditory input and individual neurons tuned for specific acoustic frequencies tend to fire more at a particular phase at each cycle (Giraud and Poeppel, 2012). In this scenario, acoustic energy concentrated in formants in the feedforward input at delta-theta range is itself conceived to lead to nesting of the higher gamma frequencies.

These sampling principles in the time domain with acoustic speech signals can be applied also to the visual system, which has to perform a spatiotemporal sampling of the visual input. While modulation frequencies in the delta-theta (3–10 Hz) band are crucial in speech perception for syllabic segmentation of the amplitude envelope, there is no reason at all for segmentation at these rates to be crucial for the visual system in deciphering individual letters or for that matter concatenating them into a word. There is no actual physical modulation at the syllabic level in the visual input arising from a text. The critical visual segmentation is primarily at the level of graphemes, which in English, are the alphabetic letters. Regular, periodic, segmentation at the word level is impractical since word lengths vary considerably. This is not the case with letters which usually occupy approximately the same physical space and can be sampled in a nearly periodic fashion by a spatiotemporal sampling process.

The one naturally occurring process in the brain that could be exploited for parsing the neuronal signals related to letters in a text that arrive at the primary visual cortex is in fact the top-down signals that are usually used for serially highlighting items in a visual search task. Such modulation of early areas is now known to be mediated by synchronized neuronal oscillations (Fries, 2005; Saalmann et al., 2007). In visual search, one can envisage a small group of cells in the posterior parietal cortex (PPC) oscillating in synchrony when they mediate focal spatial attention (Saalmann et al., 2007), either due to the relative saliency of the sensory input or in response to top-down signals from the prefrontal executive regions (Buschman and Miller, 2009). The frequency of the neuronal synchrony of the top-down signals from PPC have been identified to be 25–45 Hz (Saalmann et al., 2007) and the ones from prefrontal cortex to PPC to be 22–34 Hz (Buschman and Miller, 2007).

Oscillations can potentially either define the periods when and how often a set of post-synaptic neurons would fire in response to inputs that otherwise are too weak to reach threshold or enhance responses to a specific set of input signals, or do both. By the same token, the lack of oscillatory modulation of the membrane potential may by default act as suppression, since it would require a much stronger input to lift the membrane potential to threshold. The feedback pathways are known to be excitatory in nature (Anderson et al., 2011), but local inhibitory connections could cause suppression of unattended stimuli (Miller and Buschman, 2013).

It is not unlikely that the top-down signals from the PPC to MT and further to V1 (Vidyasagar, 1998; Brefzynski and DeYoe, 1999; Gandhi et al., 2001; McAdams and Reid, 2005) that are essential for serial visual search might also be exploited for reading. The same oscillatory nature of the modulation can be used for scanning the printed text during reading and process one letter (or two) at a time. One could conceive of each cycle of an oscillating wavelet in the low gamma range highlighting one of the salient locations on the visual field representation (**Figure 2**). This permits discrete chunks of information, just from one location or object, to be processed concurrently in the ventral stream for perceptual binding and object identification. For this to work in serial visual search, one would expect the salient locations on the parietal priority map to be activated in sequence with each cycle of a gamma wavelet switching to a different spatial location. There is evidence for this from the work of Buschman and Miller in macaques (2009; 2010), which showed spatial attention in a serial search task being directed by FEF in the frontal cortex with the fronto-parietal synchrony serially activating object locations in LIP. In fact, monkeys were found to shift their covert attention every 40 ms and the neural correlate of such shifts were observed in the oscillations of local field potentials in the FEF synchronized to 25 Hz. In learning to read, I suggest that the fronto-parietal network gets trained to do a similar serial, but *spatially sequential*, switching of top-down focal attention signals.

A consequence of the above framework is that any sampling process that humans use for reading an alphabetic text such as English is likely to have a temporal frequency roughly related to the rate at which readers sample individual letters or small groups of letters (say, in twos or threes as most words have upwards of two or three letters in them). I propose that if reading exploits the same mechanisms that we employ for visual search, both reading speed, and print sizes would fall within limits that are ultimately determined by the low gamma frequency range used by the visual search mechanism for top-down gating of visual signals arriving

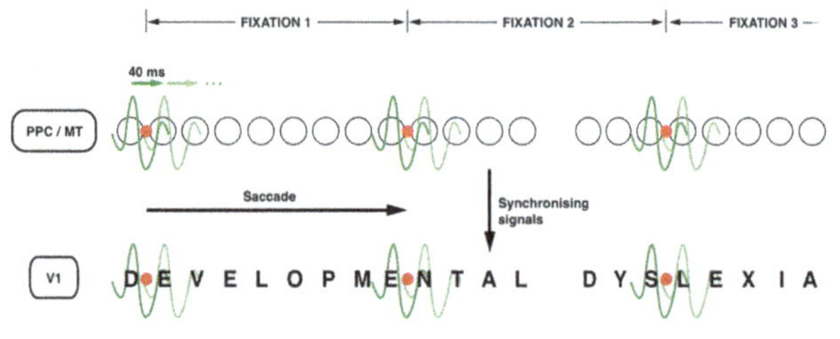

FIGURE 2 | Neuronal oscillations underlying the spotlight of attention that enables sequential letter processing during reading. A wavelet of low gamma frequency (say around 25 Hz, i.e., with a period of 40 ms) sweeps across the retinotopic map in posterior parietal cortex and MT leading to sequential shift of the locus of top-down facilitation in V1 through interareal synchrony. The letters in the bottom row (DEVELOPMENTAL DYSLEXIA) represent the bottom-up sensory signals in V1 corresponding to each letter of the text that is being read. The fine grain representation of the visual world in V1 preserves the form of each letter, even though they are not coded as "letters" in V1. The circles in the middle row represent the loci of activities in LIP and MT that code for letter locations in the text. The letter representations highlighted by each subsequent cycle of the gamma wavelet are hypothesized to be processed and recognized individually and in sequence in the ventral stream. Only two cycles are shown for each fixation but they are presumed to sweep across the letters away and to the right of the fixation point to cover 7–8 letter-spaces during each fixation. The red dot represents the point of eye fixation. The top row indicates the periods of fixation, each lasting 250–300 ms.

at V1. Thus, the speed of both these processes—visual search and reading—measured as items or characters (alphabets) processed in unit time—will be within the major frequency band of the synchrony between these areas during periods of focal spatial attention. Most common visual search paradigms yield a slope of 20–45 ms/item depending upon task demands (e.g., Wolfe et al., 1998; Wolfe and Horowitz, 2004), whose reciprocal, namely frequency, in cycles per second is between 22.2 and 50 Hz. This is in fact very similar to the range (25–45 Hz) of low gamma frequencies that the parietal cortex has been shown to use for top-down modulation of early visual areas (Saalmann et al., 2007).

With most instances of visual search, the main immediate task may be only object identification, but in the case of reading, the cognitive load is considerably beyond simple identification of letters and words. After the letters are concatenated into words, the words need to be semantically interpreted, strung together in to a sentence and the overall meaning of sentences and the passage comprehended. Furthermore, there is the necessity of having to proceed along a specific spatial gradient (left to right in the horizontal direction in English) to the exclusion of all other directions. Therefore, for a function such as reading that is forced to use an evolutionarily older process (visual search) whose sampling bandwidth is limited to a range of 22.2–50 Hz, it would be best to use the slowest possible speed within that range, thus, parsing letters at the lower end of this range to prevent the subsequent cognitive processing stages from being overloaded.

How well are these predictions borne out by data on reading speeds? In a major study (Rubin and Turano, 1992), the average reading speed was found to be in fact a maximum of 303 words/min. This translates, in English which has an average of 4.5 letters to a word, to about 23 alphabetic characters per second (23 Hz) or nearly 44 ms per letter. This is almost precisely the lower end of the neuronal oscillation range for the top-down signals from PPC that mediate focal spatial attention (Saalmann et al., 2007). A further testable prediction from the above framework is that the variation in reading speed seen in the population may roughly reflect the variation between individuals in the speed of visual search. In fact, recent experiments (Verghese et al., under review) indicate a significant positive correlation between these two variables. Valdois and colleagues, investigating further their earlier finding that reading performance was influenced by visual attention span (Bosse and Valdois, 2009), also found that reading speed was affected by only one component of visual attention capacity, namely visual processing speed (Lobier et al., 2013). These observations follow directly from the above theory that the speed determined by the gamma frequency oscillation is the essential rate-limiting step in reading.

PHYSIOLOGICAL CONSTRAINTS ON OSCILLATIONS, VISUAL SEARCH AND READING

If visual search and reading are dependent on oscillating signals that mediate the essential cortical interactions, they are inevitably locked into a narrow range of speeds that are related to the low gamma range of the neural synchrony that underpins the interactions. In turn, there are compelling biophysical and physiological reasons why the frequency of oscillations themselves fall within a particular range (Buzsáki, 2006). Frequency of rhythmically discharging GABAergic neurons and the resonance properties of pyramidal cells determined by their time constants allow only a relatively narrow window of frequencies of oscillations that could facilitate within-area and between-areas synchrony (Hutcheon and Yarom, 2000; Markram et al., 2004; Economo and White, 2012). This may be the reason why the commonly encountered neuronal oscillations are in the gamma frequency range, 20–70 Hz, which resonate best with neurons, which all tend to have integration times between 15 and 50 ms. While within-area synchrony may be largely driven by relatively higher gamma frequencies, typically in the 35–85 Hz range, as for example for stimulus driven synchrony of V1 cells (Eckhorn et al., 1988), between-area synchronization is usually slower, being 25–45 Hz for the LIP (an area within the macaque PPC) to MT feedback (Saalmann et al., 2007). This may be related to the type of post-synaptic cells that receive the feedback, the local circuitry that could influence the active properties of the cells and their time constants. While the frequency of the feedback to V1 from area MT mediating focal attention has not yet been directly measured, we already know that the MT cells fire at 25–45 Hz during focal spatial attention (Saalmann et al., 2007).

The intrinsic properties of neurons—some of them subject to dynamic changes, such as conductance of ion channels and others not subject to changes such as the size of the cell itself that sets the outer limits to input resistance—can potentially play a fundamental role in the emergence of neuronal oscillations and to what frequencies in the input signals that the neuron will resonate most. These variables are reflected in the range of low gamma oscillations seen in interareal synchrony. **Figure 3** is a putative model of the top-down modulation of V1 activity by a feedback from area MT at low gamma frequencies, whose range is determined by the resonance properties of the post-synaptic V1 cells and the circuitry they are embedded in.

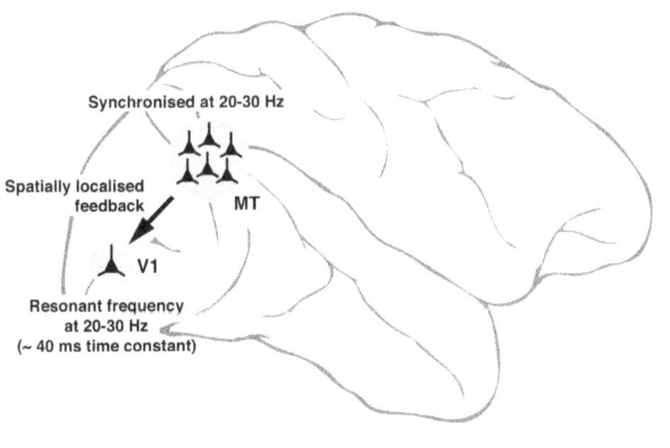

FIGURE 3 | Schematic diagram, explaining the neuronal basis of feedback oscillations. Local network properties and biophysical parameters such as time constants of neurons determine the synchronizing frequencies of neurons in MT that provide feedback to V1 and the resonant properties of neurons in V1. It is suggested that a group of neurons representing a single location (of say, an object) in the parietal saliency map sending its signals via the corresponding group of neurons in MT can set the membrane potential of the spatially equivalent group of neurons in V1 (only 1 shown) to oscillate at its resonant frequency. Such an oscillation would facilitate the V1 neurons to respond to a sensory input more readily as the input signals ride on the top of the depolarizing crests in membrane potential.

While there are a number of cortical areas involved in reading such as the VWFA in the ventral cortex (for reviews, Dehaene, 2009; Wandell, 2012), there have been few electrophysiological studies so far that have identified the frequencies that mediate cortical interactions between these areas. The account presented in this paper has largely concentrated on the feedback within the dorsal stream for two reasons. First, there is relevant electrophysiological data available that provide us with some real numbers. Second, since the neural process mediating visual search is essential for parsing of letters in a text and determines reading speed, the neuronal oscillations in the dorsal feedback are likely to have a more decisive influence on the speed of orthographic processes than the oscillatory activities within the ventral stream.

SYNCHRONIZED OSCILLATIONS AND DEVELOPMENTAL DYSLEXIA

There has been much controversy recently whether the core deficit in dyslexia is in phonological processing or in visuo-spatial attention (for reviews, see Ramus, 2003; Vidyasagar and Pammer, 2010; Goswami, 2011). Though there are profound phonological deficits in most cases of DD, the causality has not been established (Castles and Coltheart, 2004; Vidyasagar and Pammer, 2010; Vidyasagar, 2012), whereas there are now many studies claiming visual attentional deficits as the critical causative factor (e.g., Vidyasagar and Pammer, 1999; Facoetti et al., 2000, 2008; Facoetti and Molteni, 2001; Valdois et al., 2004; Bosse et al., 2007; Kevan and Pammer, 2008; Bosse and Valdois, 2009). In an attempt to anchor the aetiology of dyslexia in basic neurophysiology, Goswami (2011) attributed the phonological deficits and by inference the reading impairment to possible alteration of the syllabic sampling of speech (Goswami, 2011). The nesting of phonemic sampling at the low gamma rates of around 20–30 Hz within the low delta/theta syllabic frequency of around 4 Hz implies that altered sampling at syllabic rates could be the basis of the poor sensitivity of dyslexic children to low frequencies in the amplitude modulated acoustic input (Lorenzi et al., 2000). However, in a recent study of auditory steady state cortical responses (ASSR) to an amplitude modulated noise spectrum measured using magnetoencephalography and MRI (Lehongre et al., 2011), a significant deficit was seen in dyslexic subjects only for low gamma (phonemic) frequencies (20–30 Hz) in the left planum temporale. This appears at odds with the idea of a core deficit in syllabic (delta/theta) frequencies suggested by Goswami (2011), unless the low frequency transitions reset the neuronal activity occurring at gamma frequencies as suggested for selective attention by Schroeder and Lakatos (2009).

The sensory stimulus for the study by Lehongre et al. (2011) was acoustic, but I suggest that the deficit may be one that is more general across other modalities as well and the use of visual stimuli might expose deficits in visual areas, particularly those involved in visuo-spatial attention. As mentioned earlier, the critical sampling rate for visual search is indeed in the same range of low gamma frequencies and not the much slower delta/theta rate, which in fact shows no deficit in the study by Lehongre et al. (2011). The sampling rate that is used by the visuo-spatial attentional process for sequential reading of letters in a word is also the low gamma rate. The core deficit in DD may thus be an impairment in sampling at this rate. The deficits in speech perception and phonological processing may be a consequence of poorer sampling of the acoustic signals, but the reading deficit itself may be a consequence of similar impaired sampling at low gamma frequencies in the visual domain. In this scheme, the essential deficit in dyslexia is entirely within the visual system. The phonological deficits occur in parallel and to some extent they could also be partially the result of poor orthographic processing.

It should be noted that the sampling rate that we generally use for reading is not one that evolution had selected for reading but one that had possibly been selected for visual search and as noted above, this range is itself under certain constraints. However, reading comprehension, unlike reading speed, depends upon the working memory and cognitive capacities of the individual and the demands placed on them by the semantic content of the text. It is thus, most likely that as one learns to read, the brain uses the speed at the low end of the gamma range used for visual search (namely around 20–25 Hz), so that sufficient time can be spent on each grapheme and the subsequent processing stages. It is possible that due to the biophysical and network parameters that determine the limited range of frequencies for neuronal oscillations, the rate that one uses for reading may differ between individuals and this may explain the variance seen in reading speeds. Every reader ultimately gets "locked" into a particular narrow range of speeds, which makes slower or faster parsing of letters in a text inefficient. For complex material, the sampling rate one is locked into may turn out to be "too fast" for some. In fact, adult dyslexics, who are "compensated" may actually have a better reading comprehension scores even though their reading speeds will be slower than controls. On the flip side, fast readers (and hyperlexics), who are essentially "locked" into this higher speed, may have a gamma range for top-down modulation that is shifted toward higher frequencies, as indeed seen in their faster visual search (Verghese et al., under review). This shifted range will enable faster reading, but reading comprehension will be compromised due to overloading of the subsequent working memory and semantic stages.

The basic deficit in DD may be either an impairment (e.g., lower amplitude of oscillation) of the sampling at low gamma frequencies that affects visual search and reading and/or a slowing down of this rate. A change in amplitude or frequency of the synchronized oscillations is likely to affect the efficiency of modulation of V1 by the top-down feedback. Lower power will lead to poorer facilitation of sensory signals arriving in V1 and alteration in frequency would lead to a mismatch with the resonant frequencies of the V1 cells with subsequently poorer oscillations of the membrane potential. In either case, reading speed will be affected, but when there is some slowing down of the sampling rate, reading comprehension may in fact be better.

One interesting observation made by Lehongre et al. (2011) was that the dyslexics do not always show a general slowing of temporal processing as originally proposed by Tallal (1980). In fact the dyslexic subjects also show an increase in the 40 Hz activity in the right hemisphere to the acoustic stimuli. However, in the scheme proposed here, both slower and faster sampling would have consequences—slower by reducing reading speed and faster by overloading the working memory capacity and the time needed for semantic interpretation of the text.

Buzsáki (2006) has argued that the oscillating frequency of a cluster of neurons will be slower when the spatial extent of the group is larger. This has implications for the framework proposed here that involves a discrete moving spotlight of attention that is represented by a spatial sequence of small groups of neurons on the parietal priority map, that each fire in synchrony. Thus, if the spotlight of attention is larger and spans more than one letter at a time (as it could happen with experienced readers who may identify sets of two or even three letters at each gamma cycle), the rhythm may be slower. Thus, the reading speed may not be very much faster with a larger span, leading to a fairly narrow range of optimum font sizes in print. In fact, the distribution of print sizes in many types of publications all fall within a range that was indeed found optimal for reading (Legge and Bigelow, 2011).

It should not, however, be interpreted that the above scheme discounts the role of delta and theta frequencies that have been suggested as being critically important in reading and for speech recognition (Goswami, 2011; Power et al., 2012). In fact, the saccadic eye movements in reading occur on average at about 4 Hz, i.e., a saccade approximately every 250 ms (Rayner, 1998). One could argue that the sensory inputs get parsed at this rate, which is close to the word and syllabic reading speeds, a frequency range that has been implicated in the aetiology of DD (Goswami, 2011). However, the critical information processing essential for decoding a printed text is the parsing and identification of letters, which for most readers occurs at low gamma rates. In fact, this process may itself determine the saccade frequency. The decreasing strength of covert attention at increasing distance from the center of the fovea and the individual's preferred gamma frequency will limit in time and space the number of letters that can be sequentially identified during a single period of fixation and can even trigger the subsequent saccade. That the efferent oculomotor signals lead to saccades at the delta/theta frequency during reading does not imply that the afferent stream also gets segmented at the same rate for purposes of detailed sensory processing. Thus, the critical parsing of the afferent signals for grapheme recognition may be restricted largely to the low gamma range.

Low frequency oscillations in human cortical areas have also been reported in a number of other situations, for example with regard to sustained visual attention (Busch and VanRullen, 2010), speech recognition (Giraud and Poeppel, 2012; Power et al., 2012), auditory syntactic processing (Schmidt-Kassow and Kotz, 2008), and modulation of visual awareness (Mathewson et al., 2012). Taken together, these studies suggest the existence of a number of different time scales at which neural oscillations are linked to cognitive processes, ranging from the delta frequencies in decoding speech (Giraud and Poeppel, 2012) to the 12 Hz seen with visual awareness (Mathewson et al., 2012). As remarked earlier, the range of oscillating frequencies depend upon the network dynamics of the respective circuitry and the resonance properties of the cells in the network. Unlike the above instances, in the case of reading, the critical frequency used in specific decoding of the text may be the low gamma frequencies. These frequencies are known to be used in shifting the loci of attention in visual search tasks (Buschman and Miller, 2009, 2010) and are also impaired in DD (Lehongre et al., 2011).

It is worth stressing that reading a text is a very different process from speech recognition. Speech decoding is dictated by external inputs and has to be dynamic and flexible, occurring not only at multiple time scales (syllabic and phonetic), but also at the different frequencies that the speaker outputs, with the listeners having little choice in the sampling required of them. In reading this is not a problem, since the rate that is most optimal for the reader's perceptual and cognitive systems can be employed by every individual reader without any external constraint. Thus, the temporal characteristics associated with speech recognition need not necessarily determine the processing speeds of the visual system in the case of reading.

PREDICTIONS OF THE SCHEME

A few testable predictions that specifically follow from the scheme outlined in this paper are summarized below:

1) Reading speed will show a positive correlation with the speed of visual search.
2) Reading speed will also show a positive correlation with the frequency of interareal synchrony between the dorsal stream and primary visual cortex.
3) Those with slower reading speeds, including many compensated adult dyslexics, will have better reading comprehension than faster readers.
4) As each individual is locked into a narrow range of sampling, one cannot force oneself to a slower reading speed by parsing letters more slowly, without seriously affecting reading comprehension.
5) In DD, the use of periodic visual stimuli will reveal an impairment in the low gamma frequencies in the visual cortical areas, similar to that seen in auditory areas with acoustic stimuli.

At this juncture, one might attempt to predict the consequences of the scheme for non-alphabetic languages such as Chinese. Even though in Chinese, there are only 1.5 characters per word on average (Sun et al., 1985), as against 4.5 letters to a word in English, it does not follow that the reading speed would be three times faster and it is not. The approximately 6000 Chinese characters cannot be taken as equivalent to the set of 26 alphabetic characters in English. A more appropriate level of parsing is by radicals which constitute a smaller set of 214 elemental units that go to form any one of the 6000 characters. As there are on average 2.6 radicals to a character (Shi et al., 2003) and the reading rate in horizontally written Chinese is 580 characters per minute (Sun et al., 1985), the speed of parsing would be ca. 40 ms/radical (25 Hz). This is in the same ballpark as in English (44 ms/letter on average).

The above argument can be extended also to difficult visual searches, where search speeds can be much slower, i.e., much longer than the 40–44 ms/item indicated above for reading. When searching for targets that are more complex than conjunction of elementary features such as lines and colors as in the case of a face in a crowd, a car in parking lot, or a book on a cluttered desk, the situation is more akin to that of reading Chinese characters. Thus, a process of parsing at low gamma frequencies across the details of each complex object would yield larger slopes per object. Unless there is a unique feature in the target that can lead to pop-out, complex objects would yield larger search slopes proportionate to the number of elementary features that they are composed of. However, parsing of these elementary features would *always* occur at the same low gamma frequency. This is a strong and testable prediction from the scheme proposed here.

CONCLUSION

The development of writing and reading was a cultural programme in human history that happened to exploit a mechanism that had evolved for covert serial visual search. Top-down signals from a fronto-parietal network that uses neuronal synchrony for interareal attentional gating have been found to function at low gamma frequencies, with each cycle of the oscillation shifting to a different location during serial search. It is proposed here that this same mechanism is used for sequential scanning of individual letters during reading. This explains the fact that the reading speed of graphemes in a text is also in the same gamma range. This is consistent with the findings that with acoustic stimuli, there is an impairment of oscillations in the low gamma range in DD (Giraud and Poeppel, 2012).

Most genetic markers of DD seem to be involved in development of cortical laminae and migration of neurons (for review, Paracchini et al., 2007) and consistent with these, morphological changes in sizes of neurons and cytoarchitecture have been found in many regions of the brain including the visual system (for review, Galaburda and Livingstone, 1993; Galaburda, 1994). One important consequence of such changes in cell morphology and circuitry will be a change in the resonance properties of neurons and thus, the frequency and amplitudes of neuronal oscillations in the brain. Mild impairments of such brain rhythms may not affect most behavioral functions except those that are most sensitive to the disruption. As argued earlier, reading is one of the most challenging tasks in present civilization for visual attentional mechanisms, as the parsing of the text is done within a narrow spatiotemporal range. Thus, with any mild impairment of the attentional mechanisms, reading may be compromised, while for most other cognitive functions which also use top-down attentional processes, the deficit may not be so disabling.

ACKNOWLEDGMENTS

I thank Ashika Verghese for helpful discussions and Sivaram Viswanathan for help with the illustrations. I also thank one of the referees whose query about non-alphabetic languages such as Chinese led me to the serendipitous observation that the parsing of elementary features in every language may be at the low gamma range. My experimental work cited in this paper was supported by grants from the Australian National Health and Medical Research Council and the Australian Research Council.

REFERENCES

Abrams, D. A., Nicol, T., Zecker, S., and Kraus, N. (2009). Abnormal cortical processing of the syllable rate of speech in poor readers. *J. Neurosci.* 29, 7686–7693. doi: 10.1523/JNEUROSCI.5242-08.2009

Ahissar, M., Protopapas, A., Reid, M., and Merzenich, M. M. (2000). Auditory processing parallels reading abiloities in adults. *Proc. Nat. Acad. Sci. U.S.A.* 97, 6832–6837. doi: 10.1073/pnas.97.12.6832

Anderson, J. C., Kennedy, H., and Martin, K. A. C. (2011). Pathways to attention: sdynaptic relationships of frontal eye field to V4, lateral intraparietal cortex and area 46 in macaque monkey. *J. Neurosci.* 31, 10872–10881. doi: 10.1523/JNEUROSCI.0622-11.2011

Ans, B., Carbonnel, S., and Valdois, S. (1998). A connectionist multiple-trace memory model for polysyllabic word reading. *Psychol. Rev.* 105, 678–723. doi: 10.1037/0033-295X.105.4.678-723

Bednarek, D. B., Saldana, D., Quintero-Gallego, E., Garcia, I., Grabowska, A., and Gomez, C. M. (2004). Attentional deficit in dyslexia: a general or specific impairment. *Neuroreport* 15, 1787–1790. doi: 10.1097/01.wnr.0000134843.33260.bf

Bosse, M. L., Tainturier, M. J., and Vadois, S. (2007). Developmental dyslexia: the visual attention span deficit hypothesis. *Cognition* 104, 198–230. doi: 10.1016/j.cognition.2006.05.009

Bosse, M.-L., and Valdois, S. (2009). Influence of the visual attention span on child reading performance: a cross-sectional study. *J. Res. Read.* 3, 230–253. doi: 10.1111/j.1467-9817.2008.01387.x

Boussaoud, D., Desimone, R., and Ungerleider, L. G. (1991). Visual topography of area TEO in the macaque. *J. Comp. Neurol.* 306, 554–575. doi: 10.1002/cne.903060403

Bradley, L., and Bryant, P. E. (1983). Categorizing sounds and learning to read: a causal connection. *Nature* 301, 419–421. doi: 10.1038/301419a0

Brefzynski, J. A., and DeYoe, E. A. (1999). A physiological correlate of the spotlight of visual attention. *Nat. Neurosci.* 2, 370–374. doi: 10.1038/7280

Breier, J. I., Gray, L., Fletcher, J. M., Dhel, R. L., Klaas, P., Foorman, B. R., et al. (2001). Perception of voice and tone onset timecontinua in children with dyslexia with and without attention deficit/hyperactivity disorder. *J. Exp. Child Psychol.* 80, 245–270. doi: 10.1006/jecp.2001.2630

Busch, N. A., and VanRullen, R. (2010). Spontaneous EEG scillations reveal periodic sampling of visual attention. *Proc. Natl. Acad. Sci. U.S.A.* 107, 16048–16053. doi: 10.1073/pnas.1004801107

Buschman, T. J., and Miller, E. K. (2007). Top-down and bottom-up control of attention in the prefrontal and posterior parietal cortices. *Science* 315, 1860–1862. doi: 10.1126/science.1138071

Buschman, T. J., and Miller, E. K. (2009). Serial covert shifts of attention during visual search are reflected by the frontal eye fields and correlated with population oscillations. *Neuron* 63, 386–396. doi: 10.1016/j.neuron.2009.06.020

Buschman, T. J., and Miller, E. K. (2010). Shifting the spotlight of attention: evidence for discrete computations in cognition. *Front. Hum. Neurosci.* 4:194. doi: 10.3389/fnhum.2010.00194

Buzsáki, G. (2006). *Rhythms of The Brain.* New York, NY: Oxford University Press. doi: 10.1093/acprof:oso/9780195301069.001.0001

Casco, C., and Prunetti, E. (1996). Visual search of good and poor readers: effects with targets having single and combined features. *Percept. Mot. Skills* 82, 1155–1167. doi: 10.2466/pms.1996.82.3c.1155

Castles, A., and Coltheart, M. (2004). Is there a causal link from phonological awareness to success in learning to read. *Cognition* 91, 77–111. doi: 10.1016/S0010-0277(03)00164-1

Cohen, L., and Dehaene, S. (2004). Specialization within the ventral stream: the case for the visual word form area. *Neuroimage* 22, 466–476. doi: 10.1016/j.neuroimage.2003.12.049

Cornelissen, P., Richardson, A., Mason, A., Fowler, S., and Stein, J. (1995). Contrast sensitivity and coherent motion detection measured at photopic luminance levels in dyslexics and controls. *Vision Res.* 35, 1483–1494. doi: 10.1016/0042-6989(95)98728-R

Dehaene, S. (2009). *Reading in The Brain: The Science and Evolution of a Human Invention.* New York, NY: Viking.

Dehaene, S., and Cohen, L. (2007). Cultural recycling of cortical maps. *Neuron* 56, 384–398.

Dehaene, S., and Cohen, L. (2011). The unique role of the visual word form area in reading. *Trends Cogn. Sci.* 15, 254–262. doi: 10.1016/j.tics.2011.04.003

Dehaene, S., Pegado, F., Barga, L. W., Ventura, P., Nunes Filho, G., Jobert, A., et al. (2010). How learning to read changes the cortical networks for vision and language. *Science* 330, 1359–1364. doi: 10.1126/science.1194140

Dhar, M., Been, P. H., Minderaa, R. B., and Althaus, M. (2008). Distinct information processing charactristics in dyslexia and ADHD during a covert orienting task: an event-related potential study. *Clin. Neurophys.* 119, 2011–2025. doi: 10.1016/j.clinph.2008.05.027

Eckhorn, R., Bauer, R., Jordan, W., Brosch, M., Kruse, W., Munk, M., et al. (1988). Coherent oscillations: a mechanism feature linking in the visual cortex. Multiple electrode and correlation analyses in the cat. *Biol. Cybern.* 60, 121–130. doi: 10.1007/BF00202899

Economo, M. N., and White, J. A. (2012). Membrane properties and the balance between excitation and inhibition control gamma-frequency oscillations arising from feedback inhibition. *PLoS Comput. Biol.* 8:e1002354. doi: 10.1371/journal.pcbi.1002354

Eden, G. F., VanMeter, J. W., Rumsey, J. M., Maisog, J. M., Woods, R. P., and Zeffiro, T. A. (1996). Abnormal processing of visual motion in dyslexia revealed by functional brain imaging. *Nature* 382, 66–69. doi: 10.1038/382066a0

Facoetti, A., Corradi, N., Ruffino, M., Gori, S., and Zorzi, M. (2010). Visual attention and speech segmentation are both impaired in preschoolers at familial risk for developmental dyslexia. *Dyslexia* 16, 226–239. doi: 10.1002/dys.413

Facoetti, A., and Molteni, M. (2001). The gradient of visual attention in developmental dyslexia. *Neuropsychologia* 39, 352–357. doi: 10.1016/S0028-3932(00)00138-X

Facoetti, A., Paganoni, P., Turatto, M., Marzola, V., and Mascetti, G. G. (2000). Visual-spatial attention in developmental dyslexia. *Cortex* 36, 109–123. doi: 10.1016/S0010-9452(08)70840-2

Facoetti, A., Ruffino, M., Peru, A., Paganoni, P., and Chelazzi, L. (2008). Sluggish engagement and disengagement of non-spatial attention in dyslexic children. *Cortex* 44, 1221–1233. doi: 10.1016/j.cortex.2007.10.007

Felleman, D. J., van Essen, D. C. (1991). Distributed hierarchical processing in the primate cerebral cortex. *Cereb. Cortex.* 1, 1–47. doi: 10.1093/cercor/1.1.1

Fries, P. (2005). A mechanism for cognitive dynamics: neuronal communication through neuronal coherence. *Trends Cogn. Sci.* 9, 474–480. doi: 10.1016/j.tics.2005.08.011

Galaburda, A. M. (1994). Developmental dyslexia and animal studies: at the interface between cognition and neurology. *Cognition* 50, 133–149. doi: 10.1016/0010-0277(94)90025-6

Galaburda, A. M., and Livingstone, M. (1993). Evidence for a magnocellular defect in developmental dyslexia. *Ann. N.Y. Acad. Sci.* 682, 70–82. doi: 10.1111/j.1749-6632.1993.tb22960.x

Gandhi, S. P., Heeger, D. J., and Boynton, G. M. (2001). Spatial attention affects brain activity in human primary visual cortex. *Proc. Natl. Acad. Sci. U.S.A.* 96, 3314–3319. doi: 10.1073/pnas.96.6.3314

Giraud, A. L., Kleinschmidt, A., Poeppel, D., Lund, T. E., Frackowiak, R. S. J., and Laufs, H. (2007). Endogenous cortical rhythms determine cerebral specialization for speech perception and production. *Neuron* 56, 1127–1134. doi: 10.1016/j.neuron.2007.09.038

Giraud, A. L., and Poeppel, D. (2012). Cortical oscillations and speech processing: emerging computational principles and operations. *Nat. Neurosci.* 15, 511–517. doi: 10.1038/nn.3063

Goswami, U. (2011). A temporal sampling framework for developmental dyslexia. *Trends Cogn. Sci.* 15, 3–10. doi: 10.1016/j.tics.2010.10.001

Goswami, U., and Bryant, P. (1990). *Phonological Skills and Learning to Read.* London: Erlbaum.

Gregoriou, G. G., Gotts, S. J., Zhou, H., and Desimone, R. (2009). High-frequency, long-range coupling between prefrontal and vsual corex during attention. *Science* 324, 1207–1210. doi: 10.1126/science.1171402

Hari, R., Valta, M., and Uutela, K. (1999) Prolonged attentional dwell time in dyslexic adults. *Neurosci. Lett.* 271, 202–204. doi: 10.1016/S0304-3940(99)00547-9

Haxby, J. V., Gobbini, M. I., Furey, M. L., Ishai, A., Schouten, J. L., and Pietrini, P. (2001). Distributed and overlapping representations of faces and objects in ventral temporal cortex. *Science* 293, 2425–2430. doi: 10.1126/science.1063736

Hutcheon, B., and Yarom, Y. (2000). Resonance, oscillation and the intrinsic frequency preference of neurons. *Trends Neurosci.* 23, 216–222. doi: 10.1016/S0166-2236(00)01547-2

Ishai, A., Ungerleider, L. G., Martin, A., Schouten, J. L., and Haxby, J. V. (1999). Distributed representation of objects in human ventral visual pathway. *Proc. Natl. Acad. Sci. U.S.A.* 96, 9379–9384. doi: 10.1073/pnas.96.16.9379

Jones, M. W., Branigan, H. P., and Kelly, M. L. (2008). Visual deficits in developmental dyslexia: relationships between non-linguistic visual tasks and their contribution to components of reading. *Dyslexia* 14, 95–115. doi: 10.1002/dys.345

Kanwisher, N., McDermott, J., and Chun, M. M. (1997). The fusiform face area: a module in human extrastriate cortex specialized for face perception. *J. Neurosci.* 17, 4302–4311.

Kevan, A., and Pammer, K. (2008). Visual processing deficits in preliterate children at familial risk for dyslexia. *Vision Res.* 48, 2835–2839. doi: 10.1016/j.visres.2008.09.022

Kinsey, K., Rose, M., Hansen, P., Richrdson, A., and Stein, J. (2004). Magnocellular mediated visual-spatial attention and reading ability. *Neuroreport* 15, 2215–2218. doi: 10.1097/00001756-200410050-00014

Legge, G. E., and Bigelow, C. A. (2011). Does print size matter for reading? A review of findings from vision science and typography. *J. Vision* 11. doi: 10.1167/11.5.8

Lehongre, K., Ramus, F., Villiemet, N., Schwartz, D., and Giraud, A. L. (2011). Altered low-gamma sampling in auditory cortex accounts for three main facets of dyslexia. *Neuron* 72, 1080–1090. doi: 10.1016/j.neuron.2011.11.002

Livingstone, M. S., Rosen, G. D., Drislane, F. W., and Galaburda, A. M. (1991). Physiological and anatomical evidence for a magnocellular defect in developmental dyslexia. *Proc. Natl. Acad. Sci. U.S.A.* 88, 7943–7947. doi: 10.1073/pnas.88.18.7943

Lobier, M., Dubois, M., and Valdois, S. (2013). The role of cisual processing speed in reading speed development. *PLoS ONE* 8:e58097. doi: 10.1371/journal.pone.0058097

Lorenzi, C., Dumont, A., and Füllgrabe, C. (2000). Use of temporal envelope cues by children with developmental dyslexia. *J. Speech Lang. Hear. Res.* 43, 1367–1379.

Lovegrove, W. J., Bowling, A., Badcock, D., and Blackwood, M. (1980). Specific reading disability: differences in contrast sensitivity as a function of spatial frequency. *Science* 210, 439–440. doi: 10.1126/science.7433985

Luo, H., and Poeppel, D. (2007). Phase patterns of neuronal responses reliably discriminate speech in human auditory cortex. *Neuron* 54, 1001–1010. doi: 10.1016/j.neuron.2007.06.004

Malach, R., Levy, I., and Hasson, U. (2002). The topography of high-order human object areas. *Trends Cogn. Sci.* 6, 176–184. doi: 10.1016/S1364-6613(02)01870-3

Markram, H., Toledo-Rodriguez, M., Wang, Y., Gupta, A., Silberberg, G., and Wu, C. (2004). Interneurons of the neocortical inhibitory system. *Nat. Rev. Neurosci.* 5, 793–807. doi: 10.1038/nrn1519

Mathewson, K. E., Prudhomme, C., Fabiani, M., Back, D. M., Lleras, A., and Gratton, G. (2012). Making waves in the stream of consciousness: entraining oscillations in eeg alpha and fluctuations in visual awareness with rhythmic visual stimulation. *J. Cogn. Neurosci.* 24, 2321–2333. doi: 10.1162/jocn_a_00288

McAdams, C. J., and Reid, R. C. (2005). Attention modulates the responses of simple cells in monkey primary visual cortex. *J. Neurosci.* 25, 11023–11033. doi: 10.1523/JNEUROSCI.2904-05.2005

Miller, E. K., and Buschman, T. J. (2013). Cortical circuits for the control of attention. *Curr. Opin. Neurobiol.* 23, 216–222. doi: 10.1016/j.conb.2012.11.011

Pammer, K., and Vidyasagar, T. R. (2005). Integration of the visual and auditory networks in dyslexia: a theoretical perspective. *J. Res. Read.* 3, 320–331. doi: 10.1111/j.1467-9817.2005.00272.x

Pammer, K., and Wheatley, C. (2001). Isolating the M(y)-cell response in dyslexia using the spatial frequency doubling illusion. *Vision Res.* 41, 2139–2147. doi: 10.1016/S0042-6989(01)00092-X

Paracchini, S., Scerri, T., and Monaco, A. P. (2007). The genetic lexicon of dyslexia. *Ann. Rev. Genomics Hum. Genet.* 8, 57–79. doi: 10.1146/annurev.genom.8.080706.092312

Poeppel, D., Idsardi, W. J., and Wassenhove, V. (2008). Speech perception at the interface of neurobiology and linguistics. *Philos. Trans. R. Soc. Lond. B Biol. Sci.* 363, 1071–1086. doi: 10.1098/rstb.2007.2160

Power, A. J., Mead, N., Barnes, L., and Goswami, U. (2012). Neural entrainment to rhythmically presented auditory, visual and auditory-visual speech in children. *Front. Psychol.* 3:216. doi: 10.3389/fpsyg.2012.00216

Puce, A., Allison, T., Asgari, M., Gore, J. C., and McCarthy, G. (1996). Differential sensitivity of human visual cortex to faces, letterstrings and textures: a functional magnetic resonance imaging study. *J. Neurosci.* 16, 5205–5215.

Ramus, F. (2003). Developmental dyslexia: specific phonological deficit or general sensorimotor dysfunction. *Curr. Opin. Neurobiol.* 13, 212–218. doi: 10.1016/S0959-4388(03)00035-7

Rayner, K. (1998). Eye movements in reading and information processing: 20 years of research. *Psychological. Bull.* 124, 372–422. doi: 10.1037/0033-2909.124.3.372

Roach, N. W., and Hogben, J. H. (2007). Impaired filtering of behaviourally irrelevant visual information in dyslexia. *Brain* 130, 771–785. doi: 10.1093/brain/awl353

Rubin, G. S., and Turano, K. (1992). Reading without saccadic eye movements. *Vision Res.* 32, 895–902. doi: 10.1016/0042-6989(92)90032-E

Ruffino, A., Trussardi, A. N., Gori, S., Finzi, A., Giovagnoli, S., Menghini, D., et al. (2010). Attentional engagement deficits in dyslexic children. *Neuropsychologia* 48, 3793–3801. doi: 10.1016/j.neuropsychologia.2010.09.002

Saalmann, Y. B., Pigarev, I. N., and Vidyasagar, T. R. (2007). Neural mechanisms of visual attention: how top-down feedback highlights relevant locations. *Science* 316, 1612–1615. doi: 10.1126/science.1139140

Schmidt-Kassow, M., and Kotz, S. A. (2008). Entrainment of syntactic processing. ERP responses to predictable time intervals during syntactic reanalysis. *Brain Res.* 1226. 144–155. doi: 10.1016/j.brainres.2008.06.017

Schroeder, C. E., and Lakatos, P. (2009). Low-frequency neuronal oscillations as instruments of sensory selection. *Trends Neurosci.* 32, 9–18. doi: 10.1016/j.tins.2008.09.012

Shaywitz, S. E., and Shaywitz, B. A. (2005). Dyslexia (specific reading disability). *Biol. Psychiatry* 57, 926–933. doi: 10.1016/j.biopsych.2005.01.043

Shi, D., Damper, R. I., and Gunn, S. R. (2003). Offline handwritten Chinese character recognition by radical cmpoistion. *ACM Trans. Asian Lang. Inform. Process.* 2, 27–48. doi: 10.1145/964161.964163

Simola, J., Stenbacka, L., and Vanni, S. (2009). Topography of attention in the primary visual cortex. *Eur. J. Neurosci.* 29, 188–196. doi: 10.1111/j.1460-9568.2008.06558.x

Skoyles, J., and Skottun, B. C. (2004). On the prevalence of magnocellular deficits in the visual system of non-dyslexic individuals. *Brain Lang.* 88, 79–82. doi: 10.1016/S0093-934X(03)00162-7

Solan, H. A., Shelley-Tremblay, J., Hansen, P. C., Silverman, M. E., Larson, S., and Ficarra, A. (2004). M-cell deficit and reading disability: a preliminary study of the effects of temporal vision-processing therapy. *Optometry* 75, 640–650. doi: 10.1016/S1529-1839(04)70211-0

Solan, H. A., Shelley-Tremblay, J., Hansen, P. C., and Larson, S. (2007). Is there a common linkage among readimg comprhesion, visual attention and magnocellular processing? *J. Learn Disabil.* 40, 270–278.

Stanovich, K. E. (1998). Explaining the differences between the dyslexic and the garden-variety poor reader: the phonological-core variable-difference model. *J. Learn. Disabil.* 21, 590–604. doi: 10.1177/002221948802101003

Stein, J. F., and Walsh, V. (1997). To see but not to read: the magnocellular theory of dyslexia. *Trends Neurosci.* 20, 147–152. doi: 10.1016/S0166-2236(96)01005-3

Strasburger, H. (2005). Unfocussed spatial attention underlies the crowding effect in indirect form vision. *J. Vis.* 5, 1024–1037. doi: 10.1167/5.11.8

Sun, F., Morita, M., and Stark, L. W. (1985). Comparative patterns of reading eye movement in Chinese and English. *Percept. Pyschophys.* 37, 502–506. doi: 10.3758/BF03204913

Tallal, P. (1980). Auditory temporal perception, phonics, and reading disabilities in children. *Brain Lang.* 9, 182–198. doi: 10.1016/0093-934X(80)90139-X

Temple, E., Poldrack, R. A., Protopapas, A., Nagarajan, S., Salz, T., Tallal, P., et al. (2000). Disruption of the neural response to rapid acoustic stimuliin dyslexia: evidence from functional MRI. *Proc. Natl. Acad. Sci. U.S.A.* 97, 13907–13912. doi: 10.1073/pnas.240461697

Treisman, A. M. (1988). Features and objects: the fourteenth Bartlett memorial lecture. *Q. J. Exp. Psychol. A* 40, 201–237. doi: 10.1080/02724988843000104

Treisman, A. M., and Gelade, G. (1980). A eature integration theory of attention. *Cogn. Psychol.* 12, 97–136. doi: 10.1016/0010-0285(80)90005-5

Valdois, S., Bosse, M.-L., and Tainturier, M.-J. (2004). The cognitive deficits responsible for developmental dyslexia: review of evidence for a selective visual attentional disorder. *Dyslexia* 10, 339–363. doi: 10.1002/dys.284

Vidyasagar, T. R. (1998). Gating of neuronal responses in macaque primary visual cortex by an attentional spotlight. *Neuroreport* 9, 1947–1952. doi: 10.1097/00001756-199806220-00006

Vidyasagar, T. R. (1999). A neuronal model of attentional spotlight: parietal guiding the temporal. *Brain Res. Rev.* 30, 66–76. doi: 10.1016/S0165-0173(99)00005-3

Vidyasagar, T. R. (2001). From attentional gating in macaque primary visual cortex to dyslexia in humans. *Prog. Brain Res.* 134, 297–312. doi: 10.1016/S0079-6123(01)34020-7

Vidyasagar, T. R. (2012). "Aetiology of dyslexia: a visual perspective on a phonological marker," in *Visual Aspects of Dyslexia*, eds J. F. Stein and Z. Kapoula (Oxford: Oxford University Press), 151–170. doi: 10.1093/acprof:oso/9780199589814.003.0010

Vidyasagar, T. R., and Pammer, K. (1999). Impaired visual search in dyslexia relates to the role of the magnocellular pathway in attention. *Neuroreport* 10, 1283–1287. doi: 10.1097/00001756-199904260-00024

Vidyasagar, T. R., and Pammer, K. (2010). Dyslexia: a deficit in visuo-spatial attention, not in phonological processing. *Trends Cogn. Sci.* 14, 57–63. doi: 10.1016/j.tics.2009.12.003

Wandell, B. A. (2012). The neurobiological basis of seeing words. *Ann. N.Y. Acad. Sci.* 22234, 63–80. doi: 10.1111/j.1749-6632.2010.05954.x

Wolfe, J. M., and Horowitz, T. S. (2004). What attributes guide the deployment of visual attention and how do they do it. *Nat. Rev. Neurosci.* 5, 1–7. doi: 10.1038/nrn1411

Wolfe, J. M., Palmer, E. M., and Horowitz, T. S. (1998). Reaction time distributions constrain models of visual search. *Vision Res.* 50, 1304–1311. doi: 10.1016/j.visres.2009.11.002

Ziegler, J. C., and Goswami, U. (2005). Reading acquisition, developmental dyslexia and skilled readingacross languages: a psycholinguistic grain size theory. *Psychological. Bull.* 131, 3–29. doi: 10.1037/0033-2909.131.1.3

8

Impaired extraction of speech rhythm from temporal modulation patterns in speech in developmental dyslexia

Victoria Leong* and Usha Goswami

Department of Psychology, Centre for Neuroscience in Education, University of Cambridge, Cambridge, UK

****Correspondence:***
Victoria Leong, Department of Psychology, Centre for Neuroscience in Education, University of Cambridge, Downing Street, Cambridge CB2 3EB, UK
e-mail: vvec2@cam.ac.uk

Dyslexia is associated with impaired neural representation of the sound structure of words (phonology). The "phonological deficit" in dyslexia may arise in part from impaired speech rhythm perception, thought to depend on neural oscillatory phase-locking to slow amplitude modulation (AM) patterns in the speech envelope. Speech contains AM patterns at multiple temporal rates, and these different AM rates are associated with phonological units of different grain sizes, e.g., related to stress, syllables or phonemes. Here, we assess the ability of adults with dyslexia to use speech AMs to identify rhythm patterns (RPs). We study 3 important temporal rates: "Stress" (~2 Hz), "Syllable" (~4 Hz) and "Sub-beat" (reduced syllables, ~14 Hz). 21 dyslexics and 21 controls listened to nursery rhyme sentences that had been tone-vocoded using either *single* AM rates from the speech envelope (Stress only, Syllable only, Sub-beat only) or *pairs* of AM rates (Stress + Syllable, Syllable + Sub-beat). They were asked to use the acoustic rhythm of the stimulus to identity the original nursery rhyme sentence. The data showed that dyslexics were significantly poorer at detecting rhythm compared to controls when they had to utilize multi-rate temporal information from *pairs* of AMs (Stress + Syllable or Syllable + Sub-beat). These data suggest that dyslexia is associated with a reduced ability to utilize AMs <20 Hz for rhythm recognition. This perceptual deficit in utilizing AM patterns in speech could be underpinned by less efficient neuronal phase alignment and cross-frequency neuronal oscillatory synchronization in dyslexia. Dyslexics' perceptual difficulties in capturing the full spectro-temporal complexity of speech over multiple timescales could contribute to the development of impaired phonological representations for words, the cognitive hallmark of dyslexia across languages.

Keywords: amplitude modulation, envelope, speech rhythm, dyslexia, oscillations

INTRODUCTION

SPEECH RHYTHM AND PHONOLOGICAL AWARENESS IN DYSLEXIA

Dyslexia is characterized across languages by difficulties in phonological processing (e.g., Snowling, 2000; Ziegler and Goswami, 2005). Phonological processing encompasses the encoding and representation of speech at a range of grain sizes, both segmental (i.e., phoneme) and supra-segmental (e.g., rime, syllable and stress). As simple decoding (word reading) requires the acquisition of phonology-orthography correspondences at different grain sizes (segmental for alphabetic languages, syllabic for some character-based scripts), this cognitive "phonological deficit" affects reading acquisition in dyslexia across languages. While an impairment in segmental processing in dyslexia has long been noted (e.g., Tallal and Piercy, 1974; Snowling, 1981), supra-segmental sensitivity has only recently been a focus of study, and then mainly in English (e.g., Wood and Terrell, 1998; Goswami et al., 2002, 2010). This is surprising, as children's phonological sensitivity to supra-segmental features of speech develops early in all languages, well before the onset of formal literacy instruction. Indeed, EEG studies reveal sensitivity to the dominant stress patterns in the native language within the first months of life (Friederici et al., 2007; Ragó et al., 2014).

For English-learning infants, this early sensitivity toward dominant syllable stress patterns such as the "Strong-weak" (S-w) trochaic motif has been shown to be important for word learning (Jusczyk et al., 1993; Echols et al., 1997). By the age of 7.5 months, English-learning infants are capable of using the trochaic stress pattern as a template for segmenting words from continuous speech (Jusczyk et al., 1999). During early childhood, pre-literate children across languages already exhibit an awareness for rime and syllable units in speech. Pre-readers are able to identify pairs of words that rhyme (e.g., "mat" rhymes with "hat" but not with "cut"), and to clap out the number of constituent syllables in a word (Bradley and Bryant, 1983; Treiman and Zukowski, 1991; Ziegler and Goswami, 2005). In fact, children's phonological awareness of rhyme, syllables and stress predicts their later success in learning to read (Bradley and Bryant, 1983; de Bree et al., 2006; Whalley and Hansen, 2006).

Sensitivity to supra-segmental features of speech, particularly speech rhythm and syllable stress, also appear to be impaired in children and adults with developmental dyslexia (e.g., Wood and Terrell, 1998; Kitzen, 2001; Goswami et al., 2010; Holliman et al., 2010, 2012; Leong et al., 2011; Mundy and Carroll, 2012). Acoustically, prosodic rhythm and stress in the speech signal are cued by a combination of amplitude, duration and frequency changes (Hirst, 2006). The amplitude-based cues to rhythm are contained within the slow-varying "amplitude envelope" of speech (Plomp, 1983; Howell, 1984, 1988a,b; Greenberg et al., 2003; Tilsen and Johnson, 2008; Leong, 2012; Tilsen and Arvaniti, 2013). These slowly-varying amplitude patterns also cue the location of the rhythmic "perceptual (P)-center" or *moment of occurrence* of a sound (Allen, 1972; Morton et al., 1976; Scott, 1993, 1998; Villing, 2010). The P-center forms the basis for the deliberate rhythmic timing of speech and for synchronization of speech between speakers (Cummins and Port, 1998; Cummins, 2003). The P-center is related perceptually to a particular rhythmic marker within the speech amplitude envelope: the envelope onset rise time. Perceptual sensitivity to rise time is impaired in children and adults with dyslexia in a range of languages (Goswami et al., 2002; Hämäläinen et al., 2005, 2009; Surányi et al., 2009; Poelmans et al., 2011; Goswami et al., 2011a; see Goswami, 2011, for a recent summary). The rise time or "attack" time of a sound refers to the rate at which its amplitude increases during its initial onset, and is closely related to its P-center and rhythmic "beat strength." For example, a trumpet note with a fast rise time and early P-center will typically be perceived as having a stronger beat than a bowed violin note with a slower rise time and later P-center (Gordon, 1987). In speech, envelope onset rise times distinguish between stressed and unstressed syllables (Leong et al., 2011; Goswami and Leong, 2013), and provide phonetic cues to voice onset time and manner of articulation, for example aiding in phonetic distinctions such as between /b/ and /w/ (Goswami et al., 2011b). Dyslexics' difficulties in perceiving amplitude envelope rise times across languages has led to the theoretical suggestion that a deficit in neural rhythmic entrainment to amplitude modulation (AM) patterns in speech could underlie the phonological deficit in developmental dyslexia (Goswami, 2011; "temporal sampling theory").

NEURONAL OSCILLATORY ENTRAINMENT IN DYSLEXIA

The speech amplitude envelope contains a spectrum of AM at different temporal rates, with certain key rates of AM associated with characteristic timescales of speech information. For example, the envelope is dominated by modulations that occur at around 3–5 Hz, corresponding to the average duration of the syllable (Greenberg et al., 2003; Greenberg, 2006). AMs at a slower rate of ~2 Hz are associated with inter-stress intervals in speech, which have an average duration of 493 ms (Dauer, 1983). Toward the other end of the modulation spectrum, faster modulations immediately above the 'classic' syllable rate of 3–5 Hz correspond to more quickly-uttered unstressed syllables (~10 Hz, Greenberg et al., 2003). Faster modulations up to 50 Hz are thought to provide phonemic cues to manner of articulation, voicing, and vowel identity (Rosen, 1992). Although the amplitude envelope has been the focus of many speech intelligibility studies (e.g., Drullman et al., 1994a,b; Shannon et al., 1995), the spectral fine structure also makes an important contribution to speech intelligibility, particularly under adverse listening conditions (Qin and Oxenham, 2003; Xu et al., 2005; Obleser et al., 2012).

Recently, Poeppel and colleagues have proposed a neural account of speech processing based on multi-time resolution of the modulation patterns in the speech envelope (multi-time resolution models, e.g., Poeppel, 2003; Giraud and Poeppel, 2012). In multi-time resolution models, the brain is thought to track speech information at different timescales using neuronal oscillations at different frequencies. These neuronal oscillations *entrain* ("phase-lock") to speech modulation patterns on equivalent timescales, so that peaks and troughs in oscillatory activity align with peaks and troughs in modulations in the signal. According to Giraud and Poeppel (2012), neuronal oscillatory activity in the Theta band (3–7 Hz) tracks syllable patterns in speech, while slower oscillatory activity in the Delta band (1–3) Hz tracks phrasal and intonational patterns, such as stress intervals. Fast oscillatory activity in the Gamma band (25–80 Hz) is thought to track quickly-varying phonetic information, such as formant transitions and voice-onset times, which have timescales in the order of tens of milliseconds. This convergence between characteristic timescales in speech and the dominant neuronal oscillatory bands in auditory cortex has been used to argue that oscillatory entrainment ("phase locking") may be an important neural mechanism for parsing the speech signal into appropriately-sized linguistic units for further lexical processing (Ghitza and Greenberg, 2009; Schroeder and Lakatos, 2009; Giraud and Poeppel, 2012; Zion Golumbic et al., 2012).

In line with dyslexics' difficulties in rise time perception, which are particularly evident for slower rise times (Richardson et al., 2004; Stefanics et al., 2011). Goswami (2011) proposed a "temporal sampling" framework to explain why the development of accurate phonological representation of speech is impaired across languages in developmental dyslexia. The temporal sampling framework proposed that impaired phonological representation in dyslexia could arise in part from impaired oscillatory entrainment to *slow* AMs (<10 Hz) that carry stress and syllable patterning in speech (i.e., involving delta and theta oscillations, see Goswami, 2011; Power et al., 2012, 2013; Soltész et al., 2013). As neuronal oscillations in the cortex exhibit hierarchical nesting across slow and fast timescales (e.g., theta-gamma phase-amplitude coupling; Lakatos et al., 2005), an impairment in slow oscillatory activity (e.g., delta, stressed syllable rate; theta, syllable rate) could also have consequences for speech encoding at faster timescales, such as the Gamma or other phonetic rate timescales. Indeed, recent studies using non-speech stimuli have indicated that the hemispheric lateralization of Gamma-rate oscillations (~30 Hz) may be altered in dyslexia (Lehongre et al., 2011, 2013).

AM PERCEPTION IN DYSLEXIA

Consistent with Goswami's (2011) proposal, several AM perception studies based on non-speech stimuli and psychoacoustic modulation thresholds indicate that dyslexics show poor AM sensitivity below 10 Hz (e.g., Lorenzi et al., 2000; Amitay et al., 2002; Rocheron et al., 2002; although note that Poelmans et al., 2012 observed no deficit at 4 Hz). Studies reporting on modulation thresholds for faster AM rates vary in whether they report dyslexic deficits. For example, while McAnally and Stein (1997), Witton et al. (1998), and Menell et al. (1999) all observed deficits in dyslexics' AM detection at ~20 Hz, Hämäläinen et al. (2009) failed to find a deficit at the same rate. Meanwhile, while no dyslexic deficit at 80 Hz was reported by (Hari et al., 1999), a study by Poelmans et al. (2012) found atypical laterality effects in EEG for 20 Hz AM speech-weighted noise, and a study by Lehongre et al. (2011) found atypical laterality effects in MEG for 35 Hz AM white noise. Similarly mixed results have been observed for dyslexics' perception of very slow "stress rate" AMs. While an early study by Witton et al. (1998) found that the perception of 2 Hz AMs was unimpaired in dyslexia, subsequent studies by Stuart et al. (2006) and Hämäläinen et al. (2012) have reported significant group differences in AM sensitivity at the 1 Hz and 2 Hz rates respectively. From the non-speech studies, it is currently unclear whether dyslexics have a *general* deficit in AM perception that affects all modulation rates, or whether their deficit is *specific* to the AM rates <10 Hz that are identified in temporal sampling theory (Goswami, 2011). It is also possible that a single auditory anomaly, impaired phonemic sampling in left auditory cortex, accounts for the impaired phonological processing found in dyslexia (Lehongre et al., 2011).

While AM studies are important for studying phase-locking, their implications for real-life speech perception are limited because the AM patterns used in these studies are artificial sinusoids and not real speech AMs. Real-speech AMs differ from artificial sinusoids in several important ways. First, unlike sinusoids, speech AMs are not perfectly periodically regular, but contain phase-advancements or delays that reduce their temporal predictability. Secondly, real-speech AMs differ in patterning at different acoustic frequencies. These temporal differences in modulation patterning across different "spectral channels" are crucial for speech intelligibility (e.g., Shannon et al., 1995). Finally, in real speech, AM patterns at all timescales (e.g., stress, syllable and phoneme) are *concurrently transmitted* to the listener, unlike artificial AM studies in which only one AM rate is presented at a time. During real-life speech processing, listeners probably extract speech information using *combinations* of AMs at different rates. For example, we have recently reported that listeners detect prosodic RPs by computing the *phase relationship* between two concurrent rates of speech AM: the "Stress" rate (~2 Hz) and the "Syllable" rate (~4 Hz, see Leong, 2012). This proposal is summarized in **Figure 1**. Dyslexics' ability to use such AM *combinations* in real speech has, to our knowledge, not been tested.

One obvious difficulty is that the complexity of the speech signal makes the extraction of specific features like cross-frequency AM phase alignment at pre-determined rates very difficult. Accordingly, studies using "vocoded" (envelope-only) real speech are useful. In vocoder studies, the speech signal is split into different frequency channels (e.g., typically 2, 4, 8 or 16 channels), the envelopes from each channel are used to modulate noise or tone carriers, and are then recombined. The resulting speech sounds like a harsh whisper, and is initially difficult to recognize. Speech vocoder studies with dyslexic children consistently suggest that their ability to use envelope cues for speech perception is impaired (e.g., Lorenzi et al., 2000; Johnson et al., 2011; Nittrouer and Lowenstein, 2013). For example, Lorenzi et al. (2000) used 4-channel noise-vocoded VCV syllables (e.g., /aCa/) as stimuli, and found that both typically-developing and dyslexic 11-year-old children performed more poorly than adults when using envelope cues (<500 Hz) for speech intelligibility. However, while the speech recognition performance of control children improved significantly over the course of five training sessions during the experiment, the performance of dyslexic children did *not* improve with training. Johnson et al. (2011) and Nittrouer and Lowenstein (2013) found more direct evidence for impaired speech envelope perception in dyslexia. In their study using 4- and 8-channel semantically-unpredictable noise-vocoded monosyllabic sentences (e.g., "dumb shoes will sing"), Johnson et al. (2011) found that 10–11 year-old children with reading difficulties showed significantly poorer word recognition of vocoded speech than control children, for both 4- and 8-channel stimuli. Similarly, Nittrouer and Lowenstein (2013) used 4-channel noise-vocoded sentences and found that there were consistent differences in speech perception performance between typically-developing and dyslexic children, for both age groups tested (8–9 years and 10–11 years).

In each of these studies, the vocoded stimulus typically contained a very wide range of envelope AM rates rather than a single AM rate (e.g., the envelope was low-pass filtered under 500 Hz). Thus, a complication of these experiments is that a deficit in perceiving speech modulations at a *specific* rate (e.g., 4 Hz) would be masked if the dyslexic children were able to extract redundant speech information at other modulation rates (e.g., 20 Hz) to compensate for a slow AM deficit (see Drullman, 2006). Conversely, if a difference in performance is observed (as was the case in these studies), it is not clear whether this is caused by a general deficit in AM processing that affects all modulation rates, a specific deficit at certain AM rates (e.g., pertaining to stress, syllable or phoneme-rate information), or a deficit in combining AM information across different temporal rates. Therefore, to assess speech AM perception in dyslexia more closely, a combination of the two approaches (from AM studies and vocoding studies) is needed. Ideally, the stimuli should be created from the envelopes of real speech, but AMs at specific modulation rates (or combinations of modulation rates) should be systematically isolated from these real envelopes. Here, we present one such study.

EXPERIMENTAL RATIONALE AND HYPOTHESES

Given the prior literature on the relationship between rhythmic awareness and reading (e.g., Thomson et al., 2006; Thomson and Goswami, 2008; Goswami and Leong, 2013; Tierney and Kraus, 2013), we were specifically interested in assessing dyslexics' ability to use different AM rates in speech for *rhythm perception* (rather than speech intelligibility *per se*). Accordingly, we devised a rhythm perception task using rhythmic sentences (nursery rhymes) that had been tone-vocoded using different AM rates. For normal adult listeners, speech rhythm perception relies on sensitivity to the phase-relationship between 2 key AM rates (stress ~2 Hz and syllable ~4 Hz; Leong, 2012). Furthermore, in prior work on rhythmic entrainment, we have shown that children and adults with dyslexia show "tapping to the beat" impairments at 2 Hz (Thomson et al., 2006; Thomson and Goswami, 2008), while when tapping to speech rhythms adults with dyslexia show impairment at the syllable rate (~4 Hz; Leong and Goswami, 2014). Accordingly, here we presented dyslexic and

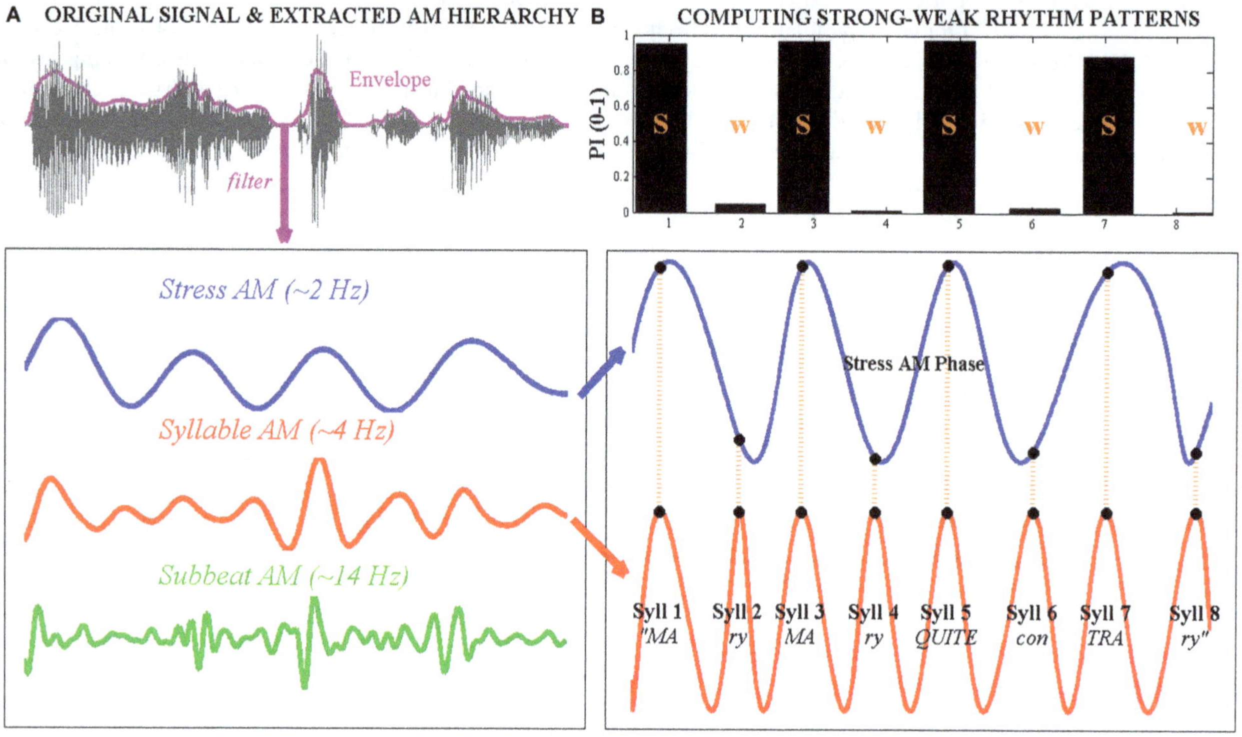

FIGURE 1 | Computation of strong-weak (s-w) syllable stress patterns using the phase-relationship between "Stress"- and "Syllable"-rate amplitude modulations (AMs) in the speech envelope, illustrated with the trochaic (s-w) nursery rhyme sentence "Mary Mary quite contrary." Left, **(A)** the original waveform of the speech signal is shown at the top, with the whole-band amplitude envelope superimposed as a bold line. The envelope is band-pass filtered at three different rates to produce a Stress AM (~2 Hz), a Syllable AM (~4 Hz) and a Sub-beat AM (~14 Hz) respectively. Right, **(B)** to compute the syllable stress pattern of the sentence, the oscillatory phase series of the Stress AM and the Syllable AM are extracted. Here, AM phase values are projected onto a cosine function for ease of visualization. Note that the 8 Syllable AM cycles correspond to the 8 spoken syllables in the sentence. The concurrent Stress AM phase at Syllable AM peaks (indicated with vertical dotted lines) is transformed into a prominence index (PI), shown in the bar graph at the top. Syllable AM peaks that occur near the oscillatory peak of the Stress AM achieve PI values of ~1, while Syllable AM peaks that occur near the oscillatory trough of the Stress AM achieve PI values of ~0. Here, syllables with a high PI (near 1) are considered "strong" while syllables with a low PI (near 0) are considered "weak." Note that this Stress-Syllable AM phase relationship accurately reflects the trochaic syllable stress pattern of the sentence.

control adult listeners with tone-vocoded (envelope-only) sentences that contained only a narrow range of AM rates under 20 Hz. In order that the modulation patterns in our stimuli would be realistically speech-like, these modulation bands did not contain only a single AM rate (i.e., a "4 Hz" sinusoid). Rather each AM band contained a narrow range of AM rates centered around a target rate (e.g., 2.3–7 Hz, centered around 4 Hz), each of which we refer to in shorthand by the center rate (e.g., here as "~4 Hz" or "Syllable-rate AMs").

Our dependent variable was the accuracy of speech rhythm perception. We created stimuli that contained modulations from either a single narrow AM band (i.e., Stress only ~2 Hz, Syllable only ~4 Hz, Sub-beat only ~14 Hz), or from *paired combinations* of AM bands (Stress + Syllable and Syllable + Sub-beat). On the basis of the temporal sampling framework (Goswami, 2011), we predicted no dyslexic impairment at the sub-beat band rate of ~14 Hz (included as a control frequency band), but significant impairment at both rates <10 Hz (Syllable and Stress rates). On the basis of our prior data on rhythmic entrainment to speech rhythms (Leong and Goswami, 2014), we also predicted that dyslexics would have difficulty in *combining* speech information across different temporal modulation rates. As Leong's modeling work (Leong, 2012) has shown that rhythm perception depends critically on the Stress + Syllable AM combination, it may be that particular dyslexic difficulty is found for this combination.

Note that in this experiment we used the 'Sub-beat' rate (~14 Hz) as a control AM band, not the "phoneme rate" (~30 Hz) that is the theoretical focus of AM work by Lehongre et al. (2011, 2013). Our decision was motivated by the classic psychophysical studies of Drullman et al. (1994a,b). These studies indicated that AM rates up to 16 Hz are the most important for speech intelligibility, and that the inclusion of faster AM rates *above 16 Hz* result in little improvement to intelligibility. Furthermore, in a rhythmic context, we noticed that unstressed syllables are often compressed to a "sub-beat" length in order to fit within the standard "beat" length of one ordinary syllable. For example, in the nursery rhyme sentence "Humpty Dumpty sat on the wall," the syllables "sat" and "on" are compressed together, or reduced, to fit the space of one regular syllable like "Hum." Consequently, the overall trochaic rhythm of the sentence is not disrupted. Thus, the "Sub-beat" rate (~14 Hz) is likely to correspond to speech modulations that are important for intelligibility, but which contribute little toward the overall rhythmic patterning of "Strong" and "weak" beats in a sentence, making this an ideal control modulation band. As the cited "phoneme" rate (~30 Hz) commonly refers to the timescale of formant transition patterns in speech (e.g., Giraud and Poeppel, 2012), we plan to examine this rate in the context of frequency modulation (FM) perception in future studies.

METHODS

PARTICIPANTS

Twenty-one adults (9 M, 12 F) with developmental dyslexia and 26 control adults (7 M, 19 F) participated in the study. All dyslexic participants had received a formal diagnosis of developmental dyslexia and also showed significant reading and phonological deficits according to our own test battery. All participants had no other diagnosed auditory or learning difficulties, spoke English as a first language, and were aged under 40 years. As shown in **Table 1**, dyslexic and control participants were matched on IQ [2 subscales of the Wechsler Abbreviated Scale of Intelligence (WASI), Wechsler, 1999: A non-verbal subscale (Block Design) and a verbal subscale (Vocabulary)]. However, there was a significant age difference between dyslexic and control groups, where controls were slightly older on average [dyslexic mean age = 22.9 years; control mean age = 25.5 years; $F_{(1, 45)} = 5.66$, $p < 0.05$]. To account for this age difference, all our subsequent statistical analyses include age as a covariate. As this statistical solution is impartial, we felt that it would be preferable to manually excluding certain participants on the basis of their age, which would entail subjectivity as to how many and which participants to exclude.

Table 1 | Group performance on standardized ability, literacy and phonological tests.

Task	Dyslexic	Controls	$F_{(1, 45)}$
Age	22.9	25.5	5.66*
(SE)	(0.6)	(0.8)	
IQ	129.6	129.8	0.01
(SE)	(1.0)	(1.5)	
- Non-Verbal IQ T score	70.6	70.7	0.01
	(0.7)	(0.8)	
- Verbal IQ T score	62.0	62.0	0.00
	(1.0)	(1.5)	
Auditory STM score (out of 16)	10.3	13.0	22.91***
(SE)	(0.4)	(0.4)	
Reading standard score	110.8	115.8	8.81**
(SE)	(1.4)	(1.0)	
Spelling standard score	104.7	117.0	43.68***
(SE)	(1.5)	(1.2)	
Phonology score (out of 30)	26.1	28.5	22.13***
(SE)	(0.4)	(0.3)	

$^{*}p < 0.05$; $^{**}p < 0.01$; $^{***}p < 0.001$.

Consistent with their diagnosis, dyslexics performed significantly more poorly than controls in standardized tests for literacy [Wide Range Achievement Test (WRAT-III), Reading and Spelling scales, Wilkinson, 1993] and phonological awareness (Phonological Assessment Battery (PhAB), Spoonerisms task, Fredrickson et al., 1997; Weschler Adult Intelligence Scale-Revised (WAIS-R) forward digit span subtest, Wechsler, 1981). Thus, despite the relatively high IQ of both groups (reflecting the fact that these were high-performing students at a world-class university), dyslexic participants still lagged behind their peers in their reading, spelling and phonological awareness skills. Both control and dyslexic participants also took part in other studies on rhythm perception and production (see also Leong and Goswami, 2014). Ethical approval for the study was obtained from the Cambridge Psychology Research Ethics Committee, and all participants were given a modest payment for taking part in the experiments.

MATERIALS

In line with our focus on rhythm, children's nursery rhymes were used as stimuli because these are a form of naturally-occurring, rhythmically-rich speech material, whose rhythm patterns (RPs) should be familiar to and easily identified by listeners. Four duplemeter nursery rhymes were used for the experiment, taking the first line of each nursery rhyme (8 syllables). The sentences fell into either of two RPs, as shown in **Table 2**. Two sentences had a "S-w" or trochaic pattern. These were "MA-ry MA-ry QUITE con-TRA-ry" and "SIM-ple SI-mon MET a PIE-man" (stressed syllables in CAPS). The other two sentences had a "w-S" or iambic pattern. These were "as I was GO-ing TO st IVES" and "the QUEEN of HEARTS she MADE some TARTS." We chose to use trochaic and iambic patterns because these are the dominant prosodic motifs found in children's nursery rhymes (Gueron, 1974), and were easily understood by our participants. A total of 4 sentences (2 per RP) were used to encourage participants to attend to the global "S-w" or "w-S" rhythm patterning that was common between the 2 exemplars of each pattern. Using two exemplars also prevented reliance on minor non-rhythmic variations (e.g., total stimulus length) to perform the task. We did not use more than 4 sentences as this would have unnecessarily increased the difficulty of the task (which was already high in difficulty). Each sentence was ~2 s in length (Mary: 2.01 s; Simon: 2.12 s; St Ives: 2.37 s; Queen: 2.31 s). The nursery rhymes were spoken by a female native speaker of British English who was articulating in time to a 4 Hz (syllable rate) metronome beat. The speaker was instructed to produce the RP of each nursery rhyme

Table 2 | List of nursery rhyme sentences and their rhythm pattern.

Rhythm pattern *(S, Strong; w, weak)*	Nursery rhyme sentence *(CAPS, Strong syllable)*
S w **S** w **S** w **S** w	"MA-ry MA-ry QUITE con-TRA-ry"
(trochaic)	"SIM-ple SI-mon MET a PIE-man"
w **S** w **S** w **S** w **S**	"as I was GO-ing TO st IVES"
(iambic)	"the QUEEN of HEARTS she MADE some TARTS"

as clearly as possible. Utterances were digitally recorded using a TASCAM digital recorder (44.1 kHz, 24-bit), and the metronome was not audible in the final recording.

RHYTHM PERCEPTION TASK

In each trial, participants heard one of four tone-vocoded nursery rhyme sentences. They were asked to indicate the target sentence (one of four) by selecting an appropriate response button. Participants were told to base their judgment on the *RP* of the stimulus. Given that the vocoded sentences had a clear rhythm but were unintelligible (see Section Signal Processing Steps for Tone Vocoding), we did not expect participants' sentence identification to exceed 50% in accuracy (i.e., we expected accurate discrimination *between* trochaic vs iambic sentences, but not *within* 2 trochaic or iambic sentences). All participants were first given 20 practice trials, during which they heard the four sentences as originally spoken, without any vocoding. This enabled participants to learn the RP of each sentence, and to become familiar with the response button mapping. Subsequently, participants performed the task with tone-vocoded stimuli only. The tone-vocoded stimuli retained the temporal pattern of each nursery rhyme sentence, but were completely unintelligible. Cartoon icons representing the four response options were displayed on the computer screen throughout the experiment to help to reduce the memory load of the task. Auditory stimuli were presented diotically using Sennheiser HD580 headphones at 70 dB SPL. The experimental task was programmed in Presentation and delivered using a Lenovo ThinkPad Edge laptop.

Signal processing steps for tone vocoding

AM bands were extracted from the amplitude envelope of the speech signal of each nursery rhyme sentence using two different methods. In the first method, the amplitude envelope was extracted using the Hilbert transform. This Hilbert envelope was then passed through a modulation filterbank (MFB) of band-pass filters, which effectively isolated speech AMs corresponding to the (1) "Stress" rate (0.8–2.3 Hz), (2) "Syllable" rate (2.3–7 Hz), and (3) "Sub-beat" (7–20 Hz) rate. Please see Stone and Moore (2003) for details of the spectral filterbank design, which was adapted to be used as a MFB here. It is possible that artificial modulations may be introduced into the stimuli by the MFB method, since band-pass filters can introduce modulations near the center-frequency of the filter, through "ringing." Therefore, a second AM-hierarchy extraction method was also used. This was Probabilistic Amplitude Demodulation (PAD; Turner and Sahani, 2011), and did not involve the Hilbert transform or filtering. Rather, the PAD method estimates the signal envelope using a model-based approach in which the signal is assumed to comprise the product of a positive slow envelope and a fast carrier. Bayesian statistical inference is used to invert the model, thereby identifying the envelope which best matches the data and the *a priori* assumptions (i.e., a positive-valued envelope whose mean is constant over time). This envelope extraction protocol can be run recursively at different timescales, yielding AMs at the same modulation rates as those derived from MFB filtering (Turner and Sahani, 2007; Turner, 2010). All participants heard both MFB-derived and PAD-derived vocoded stimuli in the same experiment. It was reasoned that if participants produced the same pattern of results with two methods of AM extraction that operate using very different sets of principles, the observed effects were likely to have arisen from real features in speech rather than filtering artifacts.

The MFB- and PAD-derived AMs were used to modulate a 500 Hz sine-tone carrier in a single-channel vocoder. A multi-channel vocoder was not used to ensure that the sentences would be completely unintelligible. As the dependent variable in the experiment was how well participants could identify each sentence on the basis of its AM RP, all other cues to sentence identity need to be removed. Therefore, the phonetic fine structure of the signal was intentionally discarded. In addition, the AMs derived from the amplitude envelope were used to modulate the sine-tone carrier, rather than being combined back with the fine structure of the signal. To create single-AM band stimuli (e.g., Stress only), the appropriate AM band was extracted and combined with the 500 Hz sine-tone carrier. A 30 ms-ramped pedestal at channel RMS power was added prior to combining with the carrier. To create double-AM band stimuli (e.g., Stress + Syllable), the two AM bands were first combined via addition (for MFB) or multiplication (for PAD) before combining with the carrier. All stimuli were equalized to 70 dB. These signal processing steps are illustrated in **Figure 2**.

The resulting tone-vocoded sentences had clear temporal patterns ranging from "Morse-code" to flutter, but were otherwise completely unintelligible (See **Audios 1–5** in Supplementary Material). **Figure 3** illustrates the different types of AM-vocoded stimuli used in the experiment, contrasting trochaic ("Mary Mary") and iambic ("the Queen of Hearts") sentences.

Design

As explained in Section Experimental Rationale and Hypotheses, five different AM bands or band combinations were used for vocoding. This generated 3 types of single AM band stimuli (Stress only; Syllable only; Sub-beat only) and 2 types of paired AM band stimuli (Stress + Syllable; Syllable + Sub-beat). For each AM combination, each of the 4 nursery rhyme sentences was presented 10 times (5 MFB and 5 PAD stimuli) in a fully randomized order, giving 40 trials per AM type and 200 trials in total for the entire experiment. Participants were scored in terms of their sentence identification accuracy for each AM type (Accuracy scores), and their ability to discriminate more generally between trochaic and iambic RPs (RP scores). We had previously found that control participants showed no difference in listening accuracy for MFB and PAD stimuli (Leong, 2012). In our preliminary analysis of the current data, we likewise found that there was no difference in performance for PAD as compared to MFB stimuli [$F_{(1, 44)} = 2.74$, $p = 0.11$]. Therefore, to simplify further analysis, the scores for the two types of stimuli in each condition were averaged into a single mean score for each participant.

RESULTS

SENTENCE IDENTIFICATION ACCURACY

Figure 4 shows the mean Accuracy scores achieved by the control and dyslexic groups for each AM type. To check for floor effects in performance (which could obscure group differences), we

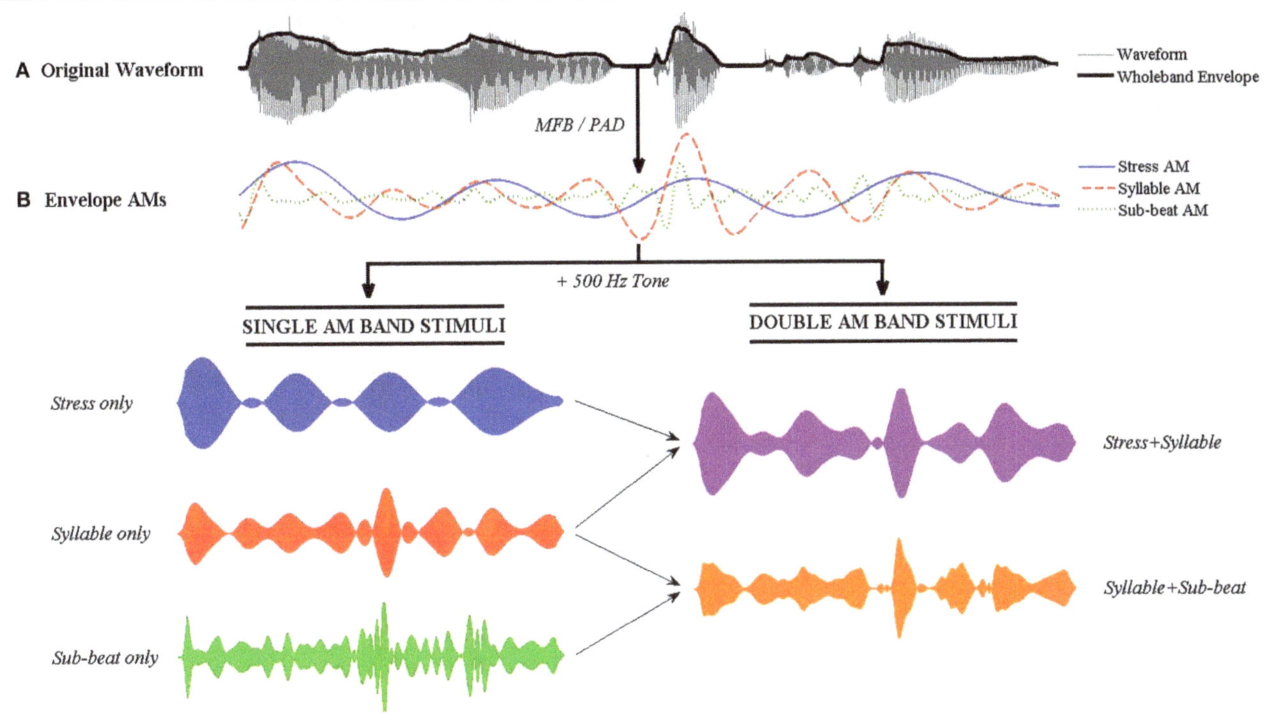

FIGURE 2 | Illustration of the signal processing steps involved in tone-vocoding for the nursery rhyme sentence "Mary Mary quite contrary." (A) The original speech signal with its wholeband amplitude envelope overlaid in bold. **(B)** The Stress AM, Syllable AM and Sub-beat AMs are extracted from the envelope using either the MFB or PAD method. Single and double AM band vocoded stimuli are then generated by combining the AMs with a 500 Hz sine tone. To generate single AM band stimuli (bottom left), each single AM band is multiplied individually with the sine tone. To generate double band AM stimuli (bottom right), the two AMs are first combined via addition (MFB) or multiplication (PAD) before multiplication with the sine tone. The resulting double band vocoded stimulus contains temporal patterning at two main rates (i.e., second-order modulation).

assessed whether participants' scores for each AM type were significantly above the level of chance (25%). Accordingly, separate one-sample t-tests were conducted for control and dyslexic groups against the test value of 0.25. As this necessitated 10 t-tests in total, Holm's sequential Bonferroni correction was applied to the p-value threshold for significance (Holm, 1979). Holm's sequential Bonferroni correction entails a smaller reduction in statistical power than the standard Bonferroni correction, and is a widely-used alternative for controlling for Type 1 familywise error (Rice, 1989; Perneger, 1998). In the Holm-Bonferroni method, the threshold for significance is computed as 0.05/(10-[rank of uncorrected p-value] +1). Therefore, for the smallest (rank 1) p-value, the Holm Bonferroni-corrected threshold for significance was $0.05/(10 - 1 + 1) = 0.005$, whereas for the largest (rank 10) p-value, the threshold for significance was $0.05/(10 - 10 + 1) = 0.05$. The results of the t-tests indicated that both controls and dyslexics performed significantly above chance for all 5 AM types. Accordingly, we investigated whether there were group differences across the 5 AM types.

Two repeated measures ANCOVA analyses were conducted. In the first analysis, we compared group performance for the 3 *single* AM bands (Stress only, Syllable only, Sub-beat only). Single AM band (3 levels) was entered into the ANCOVA as the within-subjects factor, and Group (2 levels) was entered as the between subjects factor. Age was entered as a covariate factor. The results of the first ANCOVA showed *no* significant main effect of Group [$F_{(1, 44)} = 0.14$, $p = 0.71$], and no interaction between single AM band and Group [$F_{(2, 88)} = 0.37$, $p = 0.69$]. This suggests that controls and dyslexics were performing equally well in their use of single AM-band information for rhythm perception.

In the second RM ANCOVA analysis, we investigated group differences in the ability to combine information across more than one AM band. The second ANCOVA entered double-AM band (2 levels, Stress + Syllable, Syllable + Sub-beat) as the within-subjects factor, and Group (2 levels) as the between subjects factor. Age was again entered as a covariate factor. This second ANCOVA showed a significant main effect of Group [$F_{(1, 44)} = 4.51$, $p < 0.05$], but the interaction between AM band and Group did not approach significance [$F_{(1, 44)} = 0.19$, $p = 0.66$]. Therefore, our dyslexic participants were worse at combining AM information across different rates, as they were significantly less accurate than control participants. For combined AM bands, the dyslexic participants were significantly poorer at combining the Syllable-rate AM with other AMs at the Stress rate or the Sub-beat rate.

RHYTHM PATTERN DISCRIMINATION

Next, we wanted to ascertain whether participants were able to use these speech AMs to discriminate between the two major

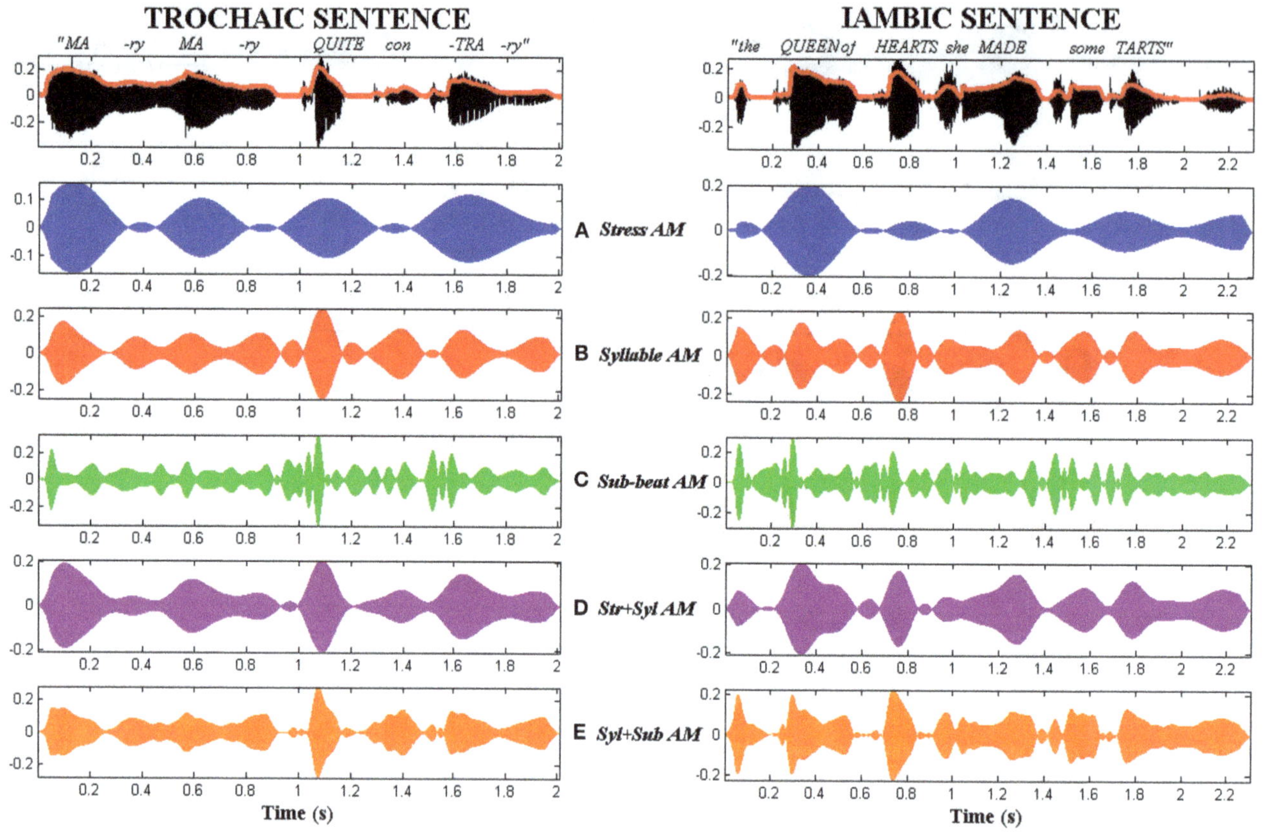

FIGURE 3 | Comparison of the 5 types of AM tone-vocoded stimuli produced for trochaic (S-w) and iambic (w-S) nursery rhyme sentences. Stimuli corresponding to the trochaic sentence "Mary Mary" are shown in the left column. Stimuli corresponding to the iambic sentence "the Queen of Hearts" are shown in the right column. Top row: Original acoustic waveform of each sentence in black, with whole-band amplitude envelope overlaid in red. Rows **(A–E)** Stress AM, Syllable AM, Sub-beat AM, Stress + Syllable AM and Syllable + Sub-beat AM stimuli respectively.

RPs that characterized the 4 nursery rhyme sentences [i.e., trochaic ("S-w") vs. iambic ("w-S")]. Accordingly, we re-scored participants responses according to whether they had correctly identified the *RP* of each sentence as trochaic or iambic, disregarding whether they had identified the actual sentence correctly (i.e., for the stimulus sentence "Mary Mary," responses of "Mary Mary" and "Simple Simon" were both scored as the correct RP, as both were trochaic responses). The resulting mean RP scores for iambic sentences (Ives, Queen) and trochaic sentences (Mary, Simon) are shown in **Figure 5**. To check for floor effects in performance (which could obscure group differences), we assessed whether participants' scores for each AM type were significantly above the level of chance (50%). Accordingly, separate one-sample *t*-tests were conducted for control and dyslexic groups against the test value of 0.5. As this necessitated 20 *t*-tests in total, Holm's sequential Bonferroni correction was applied to the *p*-value threshold for significance (Holm, 1979). For the smallest (rank 1) *p*-value, the Holm Bonferroni-corrected threshold for significance was $0.05/(20 - 1 + 1) = 0.0025$, whereas for the largest (rank 10) *p*-value, the threshold for significance was $0.05/(20 - 20 + 1) = 0.05$.

As shown in **Figure 5** (*), controls and dyslexics always performed significantly above chance when making a binary discrimination of the rhythm of trochaic (T) sentences (with the exception of controls in the Sub-beat AM condition). By contrast, for iambic (I) sentences, dyslexics *never* performed above chance in binary rhythm discrimination, whereas controls performed significantly above chance when listening to Stress-only, and Stress + Syllable AM types. Given the presence of clear floor effects for binary rhythm discrimination of iambic sentences, we were unfortunately unable to draw further conclusions regarding group differences for these sentence types (as both controls and dyslexics were performing at chance in many conditions). However, both groups had performed significantly above chance for trochaic sentences when listening to Stress only AMs, Syllable only AMs, Stress + Syllable AMs and Syllable + Sub-beat AMs. According, we performed repeated measures ANCOVAs on these RP scores for trochaic sentences only.

In the first ANCOVA analysis, we compared group performance for the 2 single AM bands only, taking single AM band (2 levels) as the within-subjects factor, Group (2 levels) as the between subjects factor, and Age as the covariate. Consistent with the previous Accuracy analysis, there was *no* significant main effect of Group [$F_{(1, 44)} = 0.16$, $p = 0.69$], and no interaction between single AM band and Group [$F_{(1, 44)} = 0.11$, $p = 0.75$]. This suggests that controls and dyslexics did not differ in their ability to use Stress only and Syllable only AM band information to make trochaic-iambic distinctions. We then analyzed double-AM band performance in a similar fashion. This time double-AM band (2 levels, Stress + Syllable, Syllable + Sub-beat) was the within-subjects factor, Group (2 levels) was the between subjects factor, and Age was the covariate. Unlike the Accuracy analysis, the ANCOVA showed no significant main effect of Group [$F_{(1, 44)} = 1.90, p = 0.17$]. There was also no interaction between double-AM band and Group [$F_{(1, 44)} = 0.17, p = 0.68$]. Hence dyslexic participants appeared to recognize trochaic RPs based on pairs of AM as well as controls.

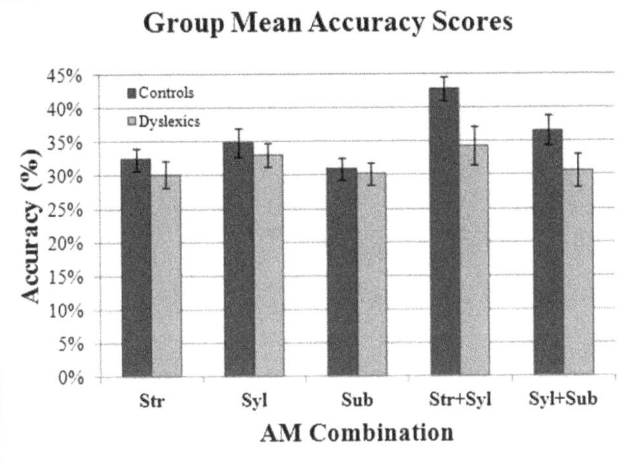

FIGURE 4 | Group mean Accuracy scores for each AM band and band combination. Error bars indicate standard error.

These results should be interpreted with caution, however. Firstly, only performance for trochaic sentences could be analyzed meaningfully (meaning that half the total dataset could not be analyzed). Secondly, the RP scores computed here reflect participants' rhythm discrimination *indirectly* rather than directly. The RP scores measure the *perceptual confusability* of sentences (i.e., how participants make guesses when they are unsure of the correct sentence identity). Perceptual confusability will depend in large part on the global RPs of the stimuli, but will also include other factors like total duration and perceptual grouping effects, as well as participants' own cognitive strategies. Nevertheless, the data show that perceptual confusability was maximal for trochaic sentences, for both groups.

CORRELATIONS BETWEEN AM PERCEPTION, PHONOLOGY, AND LITERACY

By hypothesis, a perceptual deficit in using AM patterns to discriminate rhythmic sentences should be related to both phonological awareness and reading skills in our participants. Accordingly, we investigated the relationship between participants' sentence identification Accuracy for each AM band or combination, and their performance on memory, reading and phonological tasks. **Table 3** shows the partial correlation matrix between accuracy of performance in the rhythm perception task (by AM type) and participants' memory, reading, and

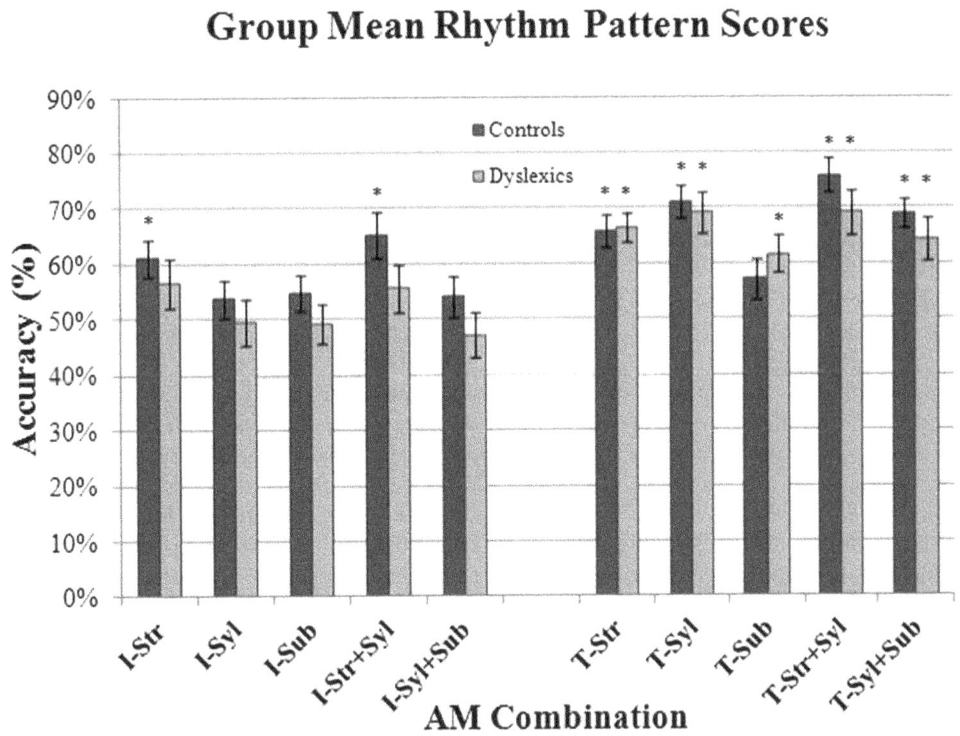

FIGURE 5 | Group mean Rhythm Pattern scores for each AM band and band combination, shown separately for iambic ("I": Ives & Queen) and trochaic ("T": Mary & Simon) sentences. Error bars indicate standard error. (*) AM bands where performance was above chance (50%) for each group.

Table 3 | Pearson's r partial correlation values between accuracy of performance in rhythm perception (by AM type), and general ability, literacy and phonology measures.

Partial correlations controlling for Age and IQ	AM Combination				
	Stress only	**Syllable only**	**Sub-beat only**	**Stress + Syllable**	**Syllable + Sub-beat**
AUDITORY STM					
All	0.05	0.11	0.13	0.35*	0.17
Con	−0.07	0.06	0.09	−0.09	−0.34
Dys	0.07	0.31	0.26	0.52*	0.55*
READING					
All	−0.14	0.02	0.21	0.13	0.21
Con	−0.07	0.13	$0.38^{\$}$	−0.21	0.09
Dys	−0.32	0.03	0.14	0.17	0.18
SPELLING					
All	−0.17	0.12	0.25^	0.17	0.32*
Con	−0.15	0.12	0.28	−0.09	0.11
Dys	−0.38	−0.06	0.48*	0.05	0.27
PHONOLOGY					
All	0.13	0.30*	0.18	0.40**	0.11
Con	0.04	0.27	0.22	−0.12	−0.16
Dys	0.17	$0.42^{\&}$	0.21	0.52*	0.07

For each cell, correlations over both groups are shown on the top left, correlations for controls only are shown on the middle right, and correlations for dyslexics only are shown on the bottom right. Age and IQ are controlled in all the correlations.
$^{*}p < 0.05$; $^{**}p < 0.01$; $^{\$}p = 0.07$; $^{\&}p = 0.074$; $^{\wedge}p = 0.096$.

phonological ability, with age and IQ controlled. Correlations were performed with both groups combined, as well as separately. As shown in **Table 3**, there were several significant relationships between AM performance, literacy and phonology. Taking the group as a whole, the conceptually important Stress + Syllable speech AMs were significantly related to phonological awareness ($r = 0.40$, $p < 0.01$), as well as to auditory short-term memory (digit span, $r = 0.35$, $p < 0.05$). Performance with the Syllable + Sub-beat level was also significantly associated with spelling performance, which was not predicted ($r = 0.32$, $p < 0.05$). When considering the dyslexic group alone, the table shows that dyslexics' phonological awareness was significantly related to their sensitivity to Stress + Syllable speech AMs ($r = 0.52$, $p < 0.01$), while the relationship between Syllable AM performance and phonological awareness approached significance ($r = 0.42$, $p = 0.074$). Further, spelling skills were significantly related to Sub-beat AM sensitivity ($r = 0.48$, $p < 0.05$). Dyslexics also showed a significant relationship between their auditory short-term memory skills and their performance in the two combined AM conditions ($r = 0.52$, $p < 0.05$ for Stress + Syllable; $r = 0.55$, $p < 0.05$ for Syllable + Sub-beat). This may indicate that dyslexics' ability to use multiple patterns of temporal information to recognize speech rhythm in our experimental paradigm was constrained by their lower short-term memory capacity in comparison to controls. When considered as a group, controls showed no significant relationships between performance in the AM RP recognition task, phonology and reading, although there was a trend toward a correlation between Sub-beat AM sensitivity and spelling ($r = 0.38$, $p = 0.07$). Overall, therefore, the partial correlations show that the perceptual deficit in using AM patterns to detect speech rhythm was related to phonological awareness for the dyslexic participants only.

DISCUSSION AND CONCLUSION

Here, we tested the hypothesis that perceptual difficulties in processing the AM patterns in speech that yield speech rhythm are associated with the development of impaired phonological representations for words by dyslexic individuals. The development of impaired phonological representations of speech is the cognitive hallmark of dyslexia across languages (Snowling, 2000; Ziegler and Goswami, 2005; Goswami, 2011). We tested the sensitivity of adults with dyslexia to AM patterning yielding speech rhythm for several different AM bands and band combinations below 20 Hz that are present within the amplitude envelope of speech. We found that dyslexic participants performed significantly more poorly than control adults when they were required to combine Syllable-rate AMs with AMs at other rates (Stress + Syllable or Syllable + Sub-beat).However, the dyslexic participants performed on par with controls when asked to utilize the temporal information at a single AM rate only (Stress only, Syllable only, or Sub-beat only). Accordingly, we conclude that dyslexics' difficulties with AM perception appear to occur across *more than one* speech timescale (particularly involving the Syllable rate). Moreover, as predicted by the temporal sampling framework, a perceptual deficit in utilizing AM patterns in speech is related to phonological development in dyslexia.

A deficit in Syllable-rate *combination* or *synchronization* with other rates would support the findings of Leong and Goswami (2014), in which the same group of adult dyslexics tested here showed differences in their *phase* of rhythmic entrainment at the Syllable rate in a rhythmic tapping task to nursery rhyme targets. A difference in Syllable *phase* of entrainment suggests that dyslexics have temporal differences in their processing of Syllable-rate information (e.g., they may perceive P-centers as occurring earlier in a speech sound as compared to controls). Here, participants with dyslexia were significantly poorer at recognizing the target nursery rhymes when they had to combine Syllable AM cues with prosodic stress AM cues (Stress + Syllable).

In fact, a circular-linear correlation analysis of the two datasets (Leong and Goswami, 2014 and the current study) revealed that there was a strong correlation between participants' Syllable AM phase of tapping in the entrainment task based on rhythmic tapping, and their sensitivity to Stress + Syllable AMs in the current task ($r = 0.55, p < 0.01$). An earlier Syllable AM phase of rhythmic tapping in Leong and Goswami (2014) was associated with poorer perception of Stress+Syllable AMs in the current study. No other AM band in the current study yielded significant correlations with tapping phase in the prior study. Others have argued that the perception and production of rhythm both rely on similar cognitive and neural mechanisms, such as the entrainment of neuronal oscillatory activity (Martin, 1972; Liberman and Mattingly, 1985; Kotz and Schwartze, 2010). In the current context, it is note-worthy that the common locus of dyslexic deficit across perception and production tasks involved the Syllable-rate of temporal processing.

Utilizing younger participants, Power et al. (2013) have shown in a rhythmic speech processing task that children with dyslexia also have a different preferred phase of entrainment in the *delta* band (2 Hz), both in response to auditory speech alone, and when speech information is audio-visual. The 'temporal misalignment' of both stress- and syllable-rate information in dyslexia found by Power et al. (2013) and the current study could explain why individuals with dyslexia develop phonological representations for words that are impaired (or specified differently) in comparison to those of unaffected individuals. If temporal processing of slower-rate information in speech is impaired, for example because oscillatory phase alignment is inaccurate, then this would affect the development of the entire mental lexicon of word forms, not simply of syllable-level and prosodic information. If syllable stress representation and syllabic parsing is different in dyslexia because of a perceptual deficit in utilizing AM patterns in speech, this would also affect phonetic-level information. Phonemes are perceived more accurately when they are in stressed syllables (Mehta and Cutler, 1988). Over the course of development, if dyslexic children consistently fail to capture rich, high-dimensional representations of the temporal patterns that occur on multiple timescales in speech (e.g., concurrently encoding Stress patterns, Syllable patterns and Phoneme patterns into an integrated representation of a word), this would yield the impoverished or atypical phonological representations that are developed by children with dyslexia across languages.

At first glance, our data appear to be inconsistent with the results of previous AM perception studies as summarized in the Introduction. These non-speech studies generally indicated that individuals with dyslexia had poorer AM perception at the 4 Hz rate (Syllable AM). Here, we find no differences in performance between controls and dyslexics when making rhythm judgments on the basis of the Syllable AM (4 Hz) only. However, it should be noted that the dependent variable being assessed in the current study is different from that of psychophysical AM studies. Whereas AM studies assess modulation detection *thresholds* based on just noticeable differences in modulation depth or rate (e.g., Lorenzi et al., 2000; Rocheron et al., 2002), here we assess nursery rhyme recognition using real-life speech AMs that contain strong (and likely supra-threshold) modulation patterns. As such, it is not surprising that no group differences were observed for our single AM rate stimuli. It is possible that significant group differences could have been observed at single AM rates if we had used sentences with weaker modulation patterns, such as whispered or mumbled speech. However, we *did* observe a significant difference in dyslexics' ability to *combine or integrate* speech modulation patterns across the Stress and Syllable rates, which is consistent with dyslexics' poorer speech perception performance in vocoder studies (e.g., Lorenzi et al., 2000; Johnson et al., 2011; Nittrouer and Lowenstein, 2013). This difference cannot be attributed to a general lack of attention or engagement by dyslexic participants, since they performed as well as controls with the single AM band stimuli. Rather, dyslexics appear to have a particular difficulty in making use of modulation information that is patterned at more than one timescale, here when Syllable-rate information has to be temporally synchronized with Stress-rate speech information or Sub-beat information. However, as we did not include paired AM combinations that did *not* involve the Syllable AM rate (e.g., Stress + Phoneme), we are not able to determine whether this difficulty is specific to Syllable AM combinations only, or whether it would also occur for other combinations of speech AMs.

It should also be observed that our participants found the rhythm judgment task very difficult. This high level of difficulty stemmed from the fact that the sentences were (deliberately) unintelligible, forcing our participants to rely solely on the acoustic modulations in the stimuli to perform rhythm judgments, without recourse to lexical factors. Consequently, accuracy scores for both controls and dyslexics (although significantly above chance) were relatively low (below 50%). In future studies, the issue of task difficulty may be ameliorated by using a tone-vocoder with more than 1 spectral channel (i.e., 3 or 4 channels), which would have the effect of increasing speech intelligibility. However, increasing the intelligibility of the stimuli would also introduce a new confound: participants would now be able to use their lexical knowledge to augment their perceptual judgments of speech rhythm. Nonetheless, this trade-off might produce stronger effects. Lexical "boot-strapping" effects could be reduced by using semantically unpredictable sentences (following Johnson et al., 2011).

According to the temporal sampling framework (Goswami, 2011), the combination impairment for Stress + Syllable rate AMs found here should affect speech perception even when listening to *clear (i.e., fully intelligible) speech,* which has strong modulation patterns that are above the threshold for detection. Interestingly, this was exactly what Lorenzi et al. (2000) found in their study. They reported that dyslexic children performed significantly more poorly than adults and control children even when listening to clear, unprocessed (not-vocoded) VCV syllables (these syllables will contain significant Syllable-rate modulation, but not Stress-rate modulation). This controversial result might possibly be explained by other factors like memory or attention, nonetheless data like these suggest that speech AM perception in dyslexia clearly requires more investigation. Current data suggest that individuals with dyslexia are less sensitive to small changes in modulation depth and rate, particularly around the syllable and stress rates in speech. Future studies should explore how dyslexics' difficulties with processing slow modulations affects their ability to integrate and synchronize slow-varying stress and syllable information with more quickly-varying phoneme-rate information in speech. These perceptual difficulties could be one source of the impaired or atypical phonological representations stored in the mental lexicon of word forms by dyslexic individuals.

Finally, we note that, given recent proposals by Poeppel and colleagues regarding neural oscillatory phase-locking to speech modulation patterns (e.g., Ghitza, 2011; Giraud and Poeppel, 2012), the perceptual difficulties that we observe here could be underpinned by impaired phase alignment and cross-frequency phase synchronization between different neuronal oscillatory rates. For example, dyslexics could have poorer neuronal oscillatory synchronization between theta oscillations (syllable rate) and delta (stress rate) or gamma (phoneme rate) oscillations in the cortex. Similarly, the neural interplay between theta (syllable rate) and alpha (8–13 Hz, similar to the sub-beat rate here) oscillations during speech comprehension might be atypical in dyslexia as well (Obleser and Weisz, 2012). To date, such *cross-frequency neural synchronization* has not been studied in dyslexia (although see Leong and Goswami, 2014, for an assessment of cross-frequency *AM* synchronization in dyslexics' speech). Such studies could be very informative in the quest to identify cross-linguistic perceptual and neural deficits underpinning cognitive markers such as impaired phonology in developmental dyslexia.

ACKNOWLEDGMENTS

This research was funded by a Harold Hyam Wingate Research Scholarship to Victoria Leong and by a Medical Research Council grant G0902375 to Usha Goswami.

REFERENCES

Allen, G. (1972). The location of rhythmic stress beats in English: an experimental study. *Lang. Speech* 15, 72–100.

Amitay, S., Ahissar, M., and Nelken, I. (2002). Auditory processing deficits in reading disabled adults. *J. Assoc. Res. Otolaryngol.* 3, 302–320. doi: 10.1007/s101620010093

Bradley, L., and Bryant, P. E. (1983). Categorising sounds and learning to read - a causal connection. *Nature* 301, 4190421. doi: 10.1038/301419a0

Cummins, F. (2003). Practice and performance in speech produced synchronously. *J. Phon.* 31, 139–148. doi: 10.1016/S0095-4470(02)00082-7

Cummins, F., and Port, R. (1998). Rhythmic constraints on stress timing in English. *J. Phon.* 26, 145–171. doi: 10.1006/jpho.1998.0070

Dauer, R. (1983). Stress-timing and syllable timing revisited. *J. Phon.* 11, 51–62.

de Bree, E., Wijnen, F., and Zonneveld, W. (2006). Word stress production in three-year-old children at risk of dyslexia. *J. Res. Read.* 29, 304–317. doi: 10.1111/j.1467-9817.2006.00310.x

Drullman, R. (2006). "The significance of temporal modulation frequencies for speech intelligibility," in *Listening to Speech: An Auditory Perspective*, eds S. Greenberg and W. A. Ainsworth (Mahwah, NJ: Lawrence Erlbaum Associates), 39–47.

Drullman, R., Festen, J. M., and Plomp, R. (1994a). Effect of temporal envelope smearing on speech reception. *J. Acoust. Soc. Am.* 95, 1053–1064. doi: 10.1121/1.408467

Drullman, R., Festen, J. M., and Plomp, R. (1994b). Effect of reducing slow temporal modulations on speech reception. *J. Acoust. Soc. Am.* 95, 2670–2680. doi: 10.1121/1.409836

Echols, C. H., Crowhurst, M. J., and Childers, J. B. (1997). The perception of rhythmic units in speech by infants and adults. *J. Mem. Lang.* 36, 202–225. doi: 10.1006/jmla.1996.2483

Fredrickson, N., Frith, U., and Reason, R. (1997). *Phonological Assessment Battery (Standardised Edn.)*. Windsor: NFER-Nelson.

Friederici, A., Friedrich, M., and Christophe, A. (2007). Brain responses in 4-month-old infants are already language-specific. *Curr. Biol.* 17, 1208–1211. doi: 10.1016/j.cub.2007.06.011

Ghitza, O. (2011). Linking speech perception and neurophysiology: speech decoding guided by cascaded oscillators locked to the input rhythm. *Front. Psychol.* 2:130. doi: 10.3389/fpsyg.2011.00130

Ghitza, O., and Greenberg, S. (2009). On the possible role of brain rhythms in speech perception: Intelligibility of time compressed speech with periodic and aperiodic insertions of silence. *Phonetica* 66, 113–126. doi: 10.1159/000208934

Giraud, A. L., and Poeppel, D. (2012). Cortical oscillations and speech processing: emerging computational principles and operations. *Nat. Neurosci.* 15, 511–517. doi: 10.1038/nn.3063

Gordon, J. W. (1987). The perceptual attack time of musical tones. *J. Acoust. Soc. Am.* 82, 88–105. doi: 10.1121/1.395441

Goswami, U. (2008). The development of reading across languages. *Ann. N.Y. Acad. Sci.* 1145, 1–12. doi: 10.1196/annals.1416.018

Goswami, U. (2011). A temporal sampling framework for developmental dyslexia. *Trends Cogn. Sci.* 15, 3–10. doi: 10.1016/j.tics.2010.10.001

Goswami, U., Fosker, T., Huss, M., Mead, N., and Szücs, D. (2011b). Rise time and formant transition duration in the discrimination of speech sounds: the ba-wa distinction in developmental dyslexia. *Dev. Sci.* 14, 34–43. doi: 10.1111/j.1467-7687.2010.00955.x

Goswami, U., Gerson, D., and Astruc, L. (2010). Amplitude envelope perception, phonology and prosodic sensitivity in children with developmental dyslexia. *Read. Writ.* 23, 995–1019. doi: 10.1007/s11145-009-9186-6

Goswami, U., and Leong, V. (2013). Speech rhythm and temporal structure: converging perspectives? *Lab. Phonol.* 4, 67–92. doi: 10.1515/lp-2013-0004

Goswami, U., Thomson, J., Richardson, U., Stainthorp, R., Hughes, D., Rosen, S., et al. (2002). Amplitude envelope onsets and developmental dyslexia: a new hypothesis. *Proc. Natl. Acad. Sci. U.S.A.* 99, 10911–10916. doi: 10.1073/pnas.122368599

Goswami, U., Wang, H.-L., Cruz, A., Fosker, T., Mead, N., and Huss, M. (2011a). Language-universal sensory deficits in developmental dyslexia: English, Spanish, and Chinese. *J. Cogn. Neurosci.* 23, 325–337. doi: 10.1162/jocn.2010.21453

Greenberg, S. (2006). "A multi-band framework for understanding spoken language," in *Understanding Speech: An Auditory Perspective*, eds S. Greenberg and W. Ainsworth (Mahweh, NJ: LEA), 411–434.

Greenberg, S., Carvey, H., Hitchcock, L., and Chang, S. (2003). Temporal properties of spontaneous speech - a syllable-centric perspective. *J. Phon.* 31, 465–485. doi: 10.1016/j.wocn.2003.09.005

Gueron, J. (1974). The meter of nursery rhymes: an application of the Halle-Keyser theory of meter. *Poetics* 12, 73–111. doi: 10.1016/0304-422X(74)90006-0

Hämäläinen, J. A., Leppänen, P. H. T., Eklund, K., Thomson, J., Richardson, U., Guttorm, T. K., et al. (2009). Common variance in amplitude envelope perception tasks and their impact on phoneme duration perception and reading and spelling in Finnish children with reading disabilities. *Appl. Psycholinguist.* 30, 511–530. doi: 10.1017/S0142716409090250

Hämäläinen, J. A., Rupp, A., Soltész, F., Szücs, D., and Goswami, U. (2012). Reduced phase locking to slow amplitude modulation in adults with dyslexia: an MEG study. *Neuroimage* 59, 2952–2961. doi: 10.1016/j.neuroimage.2011.09.075

Hämäläinen, J., Leppänen, P., Torppa, M., Müller, K., and Lyytinen, H. (2005). Detection of sound rise time by adults with dyslexia. *Brain Lang.* 94, 32–42. doi: 10.1016/j.bandl.2004.11.005

Hari, R., Sääskilahti, A., Helenius, P., and Uutela, K. (1999). Non–impaired auditory phase locking in dyslexic adults. *Neuroreport* 10, 2347–2348. doi: 10.1097/00001756-199908020-00023

Hirst, D. J. (2006). "Prosodic aspects of speech and language," in *Encyclopedia of Language and Linguistics, 2nd Edn.*, ed K. Brown (Oxford: Elsevier), 539–546.

Holliman, A. J., Wood, C., and Sheehy, K. (2010). The contribution of sensitivity to speech rhythm and non-speech rhythm to early reading development. *Educ. Psychol.* 30, 247–267. doi: 10.1080/01443410903560922

Holliman, A. J., Wood, C., and Sheehy, K. (2012). A cross-sectional study of prosodic sensitivity and reading difficulties. *J. Res. Read.* 35, 32–48. doi: 10.1111/j.1467-9817.2010.01459.x

Holm, S. (1979). A simple sequential rejective multiple test procedure. *Scand. J. Stat.* 6, 65–70.

Howell, P. (1984). "An acoustic determinant of perceived and produced anisochrony," in *Proceedings of the Tenth International Congress of Phonetic Sciences*, eds M. P. R. Van den Broecke and A. Cohen (Dordrecht: Foris).

Howell, P. (1988a). Prediction of P-center location from the distribution of energy in the amplitude envelope: I. *Percept. Psychophys.* 43, 90–93. doi: 10.3758/BF03208978

Howell, P. (1988b). Prediction of P-center location from the distribution of energy in the amplitude envelope: II. *Percept. Psychophys.* 43, 99. doi: 10.3758/BF03208980

Johnson, E. P., Pennington, B. F., Lowenstein, J. H., and Nittrouer, S. (2011). Sensitivity to structure in the speech signal by children with speech sound disorder and reading disability. *J. Commun. Disord.* 44, 294–314. doi: 10.1016/j.jcomdis.2011.01.001

Jusczyk, P. W., Cutler, A., and Redanz, N. (1993). Preference for the predominant stress patterns of English words. *Child Dev.* 64, 675–687. doi: 10.2307/1131210

Jusczyk, P. W., Houston, D., and Newsome, M. (1999). The beginnings of word segmentation in English-learning infants. *Cogn. Psychol.* 39, 159–207. doi: 10.1006/cogp.1999.0716

Kitzen, K. R. (2001). *Prosodic Sensitivity, Morphological Ability and Reading Ability in Young Adults With and Without Childhood Histories of Reading Difficulty.* Doctoral dissertation, University of Columbia. Dissertation Abstracts International, 62, 0460A.

Kotz, S. A., and Schwartze, M. (2010). Cortical speech processing unplugged: a timely subcortico-cortical framework. *Trends Cogn. Sci.* 14, 392–399. doi: 10.1016/j.tics.2010.06.005

Lakatos, P., Shah, A. S., Knuth, K. H., Ulbert, I., Karmos, G., and Schroeder, C. E. (2005). An oscillatory hierarchy controlling neuronal excitability and stimulus processing in the auditory cortex. *J. Neurophysiol.* 94, 1904–1911. doi: 10.1152/jn.00263.2005

Lehongre, K., Morillon, B., Giraud, A. L., and Ramus, F. (2013). Impaired auditory sampling in dyslexia: further evidence from combined fMRI and EEG. *Front. Hum. Neurosci.* 7:454. doi: 10.3389/fnhum.2013.00454

Lehongre, K., Ramus, F., Villiermet, N., Schwartz, D., and Giraud, A. L. (2011). Altered low-gamma sampling in auditory cortex accounts for the three main facets of dyslexia. *Neuron* 72, 1080–1090. doi: 10.1016/j.neuron.2011.11.002

Leong, V. (2012). *Prosodic Rhythm in the Speech Amplitude Envelope: Amplitude Modulation Phase Hierarchies (AMPHs) and AMPH Models.* Doctoral dissertation, University of Cambridge.

Leong, V., and Goswami, U. (2014). Assessment of rhythmic entrainment at multiple timescales in dyslexia: evidence for disruption to syllable timing. *Hear. Res.* 308, 141–161. doi: 10.1016/j.heares.2013.07.015

Leong, V., Hamalainen, J., Soltesz, F., and Goswami, U. (2011). Rise time perception and detection of syllable stress in adults with developmental dyslexia. *J. Mem. Lang.* 64, 59–73. doi: 10.1016/j.jml.2010.09.003

Liberman, A. M., and Mattingly, I. G. (1985). The motor theory of speech perception revised. *Cognition* 21, 1–36. doi: 10.1016/0010-0277(85) 90021-6

Lorenzi, C., Dumont, A., and Füllgrabe, C. (2000). Use of temporal envelope cues by children with developmental dyslexia. *J. Speech Lang. Hear. Res.* 43, 1367–1379. doi: 10.1044/jslhr.4306.1367

Martin, J. G. (1972). Rhythmic (hierarchical) versus serial structuring in speech and other behavior. *Psychol. Rev.* 79, 487–509. doi: 10.1037/h0033467

McAnally, K. I., and Stein, J. F. (1997). Scalp potentials evoked by amplitude-modulated tones in dyslexia. *J. Speech Lang. Hear. Res.* 40, 939–945.

Mehta, G., and Cutler, A. (1988). Detection of target phonemes in spontaneous and read speech. *Lang. Speech* 31, 135–156.

Menell, P., McAnally, K. I., and Stein, J. F. (1999). Psychophysical sensitivity and physiological response to amplitude modulation in adult dyslexic listeners. *J. Speech Lang. Hear. Res.* 42, 797–803.

Morton, J., Marcus, S. M., and Frankish, C. (1976). Perceptual centres (P-centres). *Psychol. Rev.* 83, 405–408. doi: 10.1037/0033-295X.83.5.405

Mundy, I. R., and Carroll, J. M. (2012). Speech prosody and developmental dyslexia: reduced phonological awareness in the context of intact phonological representations. *J. Cogn. Psychol.* 24, 560–581. doi: 10.1080/20445911.2012.662341

Nittrouer, S., and Lowenstein, J. H. (2013). Perceptual organization of speech signals by children with and without dyslexia. *Res. Dev. Disabil.* 34, 2304–2325. doi: 10.1016/j.ridd.2013.04.018

Obleser, J., Herrmann, J., and Henry, M. J. (2012). Neural oscillations in speech: don't be enslaved by the envelope. *Front. Hum. Neurosci.* 6:250. doi: 10.3389/fnhum.2012.00250

Obleser, J., and Weisz, N. (2012). Suppressed alpha oscillations predict intelligibility of speech and its acoustic details. *Cereb. Cortex* 22, 2466–2477. doi: 10.1093/cercor/bhr325

Perneger, T. V. (1998). What's wrong with Bonferroni adjustments. *Br. Med. J.* 316, 1236–1238. doi: 10.1136/bmj.316.7139.1236

Plomp, R. (1983). "Perception of speech as a modulated signal," *Proceedings of the 10th International Congress of Phonetic Sciences.* (Utrecht), 29–40.

Poelmans, H., Luts, H., Vandermosten, M., Boets, B., Ghesquière, P., and Wouters, J. (2011). Reduced sensitivity to slow-rate dynamic auditory information in children with dyslexia. *Res. Dev. Disabil.* 32, 2810–2819. doi: 10.1016/j.ridd.2011.05.025

Poelmans, H., Luts, H., Vandermosten, M., Boets, B., Ghesquière, P., and Wouters, J. (2012). Auditory steady state cortical responses indicate deviant phonemic-rate processing in adults with dyslexia. *Ear Hear.* 33, 134–143. doi: 10.1097/AUD.0b013e31822c26b9

Poeppel, D. (2003). The analysis of speech in different temporal integration windows: cerebral lateralization as 'asymmetric sampling in time'. *Speech Commun.* 41, 245–255. doi: 10.1016/S0167-6393(02)00107-3

Power, A. J., Mead, N., Barnes, L., and Goswami, U. (2012). Neural entrainment to rhythmically-presented auditory, visual and audio-visual speech in children. *Front. Psychol.* 3:216 doi: 10.3389/fpsyg.2012.00216

Power, A. J., Mead, N., Barnes, L., and Goswami, U. (2013). Neural entrainment to rhythmic speech in children with developmental dyslexia. *Front. Hum. Neurosci.* 7:777. doi: 10.3389/fnhum.2013.00777

Qin, M. K., and Oxenham, A. J. (2003). Effects of simulated cochlear implant processing on speech reception in fluctuating maskers. *J. Acoust. Soc. Am.* 114, 446–454. doi: 10.1121/1.1579009

Ragó, A., Honbolygó, F., Róna, Z., Beke, A., and Csépe, V. (2014). Effect of maturation on suprasegmental speech processing in full- and preterm infants: a mismatch negativity study. *Res. Dev. Disabil.* 35, 192–202. doi: 10.1016/j.ridd.2013.10.006

Rice, W. R. (1989). Analyzing tables of statistical tests. *Evolution* 43, 223–225. doi: 10.2307/2409177

Richardson, U., Thomson, J., Scott, S. K., and Goswami, U. (2004). Auditory processing skills and phonological representation in dyslexic children. *Dyslexia* 10, 215 233. doi: 10.1002/dys.276

Rocheron, I., Lorenzi, C., Füllgrabe, C., and Dumont, A. (2002). Temporal envelope perception in dyslexic children. *Neuroreport* 13, 1683–1687. doi: 10.1097/00001756-200209160-00023

Rosen, S. (1992). Temporal information in speech: acoustic, auditory and linguistic aspects. *Philos. Trans. R. Soc. Lond. B Biol. Sci.* 336, 367–373. doi: 10.1098/rstb.1992.0070

Schroeder, C. E., and Lakatos, P. (2009). Low-frequency neuronal oscillations as instruments of sensory selection. *Trends Neurosci.* 32, 9–18. doi: 10.1016/j.tins.2008.09.012

Scott, S. K. (1993). *P-Centres in Speech: An Acoustic Analysis.* Unpublished Ph.D. thesis, University College London.

Scott, S. K. (1998). The point of P-centres. *Psychol. Res.* 61, 4–11. doi: 10.1007/PL00008162

Shannon, R. V., Zeng, F.-G., Kamath, V., Wygonski, J., and Ekelid, M. (1995). Speech recognition with primarily temporal cues. *Science* 270, 303–304. doi: 10.1126/science.270.5234.303

Snowling, M. J. (1981). Phonemic deficits in developmental dyslexia. *Psychol. Res.* 43, 219–234. doi: 10.1007/BF00309831

Snowling, M. J. (2000). *Dyslexia, 2nd Edn.* Oxford: Blackwell Publishers.

Soltész, F., Szûcs, D., Leong, V., White, S., and Goswami, U. (2013). Differential entrainment of neuroelectric delta oscillations in developmental dyslexia. *PLoS ONE* 8:e76608. doi: 10.1371/journal.pone.0076608

Stefanics, G., Fosker, T., Huss, M., Mead, N., Szücs, D., and Goswami, U. (2011). Auditory sensory deficits in developmental dyslexia: a longitudinal ERP study. *Neuroimage* 57, 723–732. doi: 10.1016/j.neuroimage.2011.04.005

Stone, M. A., and Moore, B. C. J. (2003). Effect of the speed of a single-channel dynamic range compressor on intelligibility in a competing speech task. *J. Acoust. Soc. Am.* 114, 1023–1034. doi: 10.1121/1.1592160

Stuart, G. W., McAnally, K. I., McKay, A., Johnston, M., and Castles, A. (2006). A test of the magnocellular deficit theory of dyslexia in an adult sample. *Cogn. Neuropsychol.* 23, 1215–1229. doi: 10.1080/02643290600814624

Surányi, Z., Csépe, V., Richardson, U., Thomson, J. M., Honbolygó, F., and Goswami, U. (2009). Sensitivity to rhythmic parameters in dyslexic children: a comparison of Hungarian and English. *Read. Writ.* 22, 41–56. doi: 10.1007/s11145-007-9102-x

Tallal, P., and Piercy, M. (1974). Developmental aphasia: rate of auditory processing and selective impairment of consonant perception. *Neuropsychologia* 12, 83–93. doi: 10.1016/0028-3932(74)90030-X

Thomson, J., Fryer, B., Maltby, J., and Goswami, U. (2006). Auditory and motor rhythm awareness in adults with dyslexia. *J. Res. Read.* 29, 334–348. doi: 10.1111/j.1467-9817.2006.00312.x

Thomson, J. M., and Goswami, U. (2008). Rhythmic processing in children with developmental dyslexia: auditory and motor rhythms link to reading and spelling. *J. Physiol. Paris* 102, 120–129. doi: 10.1016/j.jphysparis.2008.03.007

Tierney, A., and Kraus, N. (2013). The ability to tap to a beat relates to cognitive, linguistic, and perceptual skills. *Brain Lang.* 124, 225–231. doi: 10.1016/j.bandl.2012.12.014

Tilsen, S., and Arvaniti, A. (2013). Speech rhythm analysis with decomposition of the amplitude envelope: characterizing rhythmic patterns within and across languages. *J. Acoust. Soc. Am.* 134, 628–639. doi: 10.1121/1.4807565

Tilsen, S., and Johnson, K. (2008). Low-frequency fourier analysis of speech rhythm. *J. Acoust. Soc. Am.* 124, EL34–EL39. doi: 10.1121/1.2947626

Treiman, R., and Zukowski, A. (1991). "Levels of phonological awareness," in *Phonological Processes in Literacy: a Tribute to Isabelle P. Liberman*, eds S. Brady and D. Shankweiler (Hillsdale, NJ: Erlbaum), 67–83.

Turner, R. E. (2010). *Statistical Models for Natural Sounds.* Doctoral dissertation, University College London. Available online at: http://www.gatsby.ucl.ac.uk/~turner/Publications/turner-2010.html

Turner, R. E., and Sahani, M. (2007). "Probabilistic amplitude demodulation," in *Proceedings of the 7th International Conference on Independent Component Analysis and Signal Separation*, 544–551. doi: 10.1007/978-3-540-74494-8_68

Turner, R. E., and Sahani, M. (2011). Demodulation as probabilistic inference. *IEEE Trans. Audio Speech Lang. Process.* 19, 2398–2411. doi: 10.1109/TASL.2011.2135852

Villing, R. (2010). *Hearing the Moment: Measures and Models of the Perceptual Centre.* Doctoral dissertation, National University of Ireland Maynooth. Available online at: http://eprints.nuim.ie/2284/1/Villing_2010_-_PhD_Thesis.pdf

Wechsler, D. (1981). *Manual for the Wechsler Adult Intelligence Scale-Revised.* New York, NY: The Psychological Corporation.

Wechsler, D. (1999). *Wechsler Abbreviated Scale of Intelligence.* San Antonio, TX: The Psychological Corporation.

Whalley, K., and Hansen, J. (2006). The role of prosodic sensitivity in children's reading development. *J. Res. Read.* 29, 288–303. doi: 10.1111/j.1467-9817.2006.00309.x

Wilkinson, G. S. (1993). *Wide Range Achievement Test 3.* Wilmington, DE: Wide Range.

Witton, C., Talcott, J. B., Hansen, P. C., Richardson, A. J., Griffiths, T. D., Rees, A., et al. (1998). Sensitivity to dynamic auditory and visual stimuli predicts nonword reading ability in both dyslexic and normal readers. *Curr. Biol.* 8, 791–797. doi: 10.1016/S0960-9822(98)70320-3

Wood, C., and Terrell, C. (1998). Pre-school phonological ability and subsequent literacy development. *Educ. Psychol.* 18, 253–274. doi: 10.1080/0144341980180301

Xu, L., Thompson, C. S., and Pfingst, B. E. (2005). Relative contributions of spectral and temporal cues for phoneme recognition. *J. Acoust. Soc. Am.* 117, 3255–3267. doi: 10.1121/1.1886405

Ziegler, J., and Goswami, U. (2005). Reading acquisition, developmental dyslexia, and skilled reading across languages: a psycholinguistic grain size theory. *Psychol. Bull.* 131, 3–29. doi: 10.1037/0033-2909.131.1.3

Zion Golumbic, E. M., Poeppel, D., and Schroeder, C. E. (2012). Temporal context in speech processing and attentional stream selection: A behavioral and neural perspective. *Brain Lang.* 122, 151–161. doi: 10.1016/j.bandl.2011.12.010

9

Preliteracy signatures of poor-reading abilities in resting-state EEG

Giuseppina Schiavone[1,2], Klaus Linkenkaer-Hansen[1]*, Natasha M. Maurits[3], Anna Plakas[3,4], Ben A. M. Maassen[5], Huibert D. Mansvelder[1], Aryan van der Leij[4] and Titia L. van Zuijen[4]

[1] *Department of Integrative Neurophysiology, Center for Neurogenomics and Cognitive Research, VU University Amsterdam, Amsterdam, Netherlands*
[2] *Body Area Network, imec/Holst Centre, Eindhoven, Netherlands*
[3] *Department of Neurology, University Medical Center Groningen, University of Groningen, Groningen, Netherlands*
[4] *Research Institute of Child Development and Education, University of Amsterdam, Amsterdam, Netherlands*
[5] *Center for Language and Cognition Groningen and University Medical Center Groningen, University of Groningen, Groningen, Netherlands*

***Correspondence:**
Klaus Linkenkaer-Hansen, Department of Integrative Neurophysiology, Center for Neurogenomics and Cognitive Research, VU University Amsterdam, Neuroscience Campus Amsterdam, De Boelelaan 1085, 1081 HV Amsterdam, Netherlands
e-mail: klaus.linkenkaer@cncr.vu.nl

The hereditary character of dyslexia suggests the presence of putative underlying neural anomalies already in preliterate age. Here, we investigated whether early neurophysiological correlates of future reading difficulties—a hallmark of dyslexia—could be identified in the resting-state EEG of preliterate children. The children in this study were recruited at birth and classified on the basis of parents' performance on reading tests to be at-risk of becoming poor readers ($n = 48$) or not ($n = 14$). Eyes-open rest EEG was measured at the age of 3 years, and the at-risk children were divided into fluent readers ($n = 24$) and non-fluent readers ($n = 24$) after reading assessment at their third grade of school. We found that fluent readers and non-fluent readers differed in normalized spectral amplitude. Non-fluent readers were characterized by lower amplitude in the delta-1 frequency band (0.5–2 Hz) and higher amplitude in the alpha-1 band (6–8 Hz) in multiple scalp regions compared to control and at-risk fluent readers. Interestingly, across groups these EEG biomarkers correlated with several behavioral test scores measured in the third grade. Specifically, the performance on reading fluency, phonological and orthographic tasks and rapid automatized naming task correlated positively with delta-1 and negatively with alpha-1. Together, our results suggest that combining family-risk status, neurophysiological testing and behavioral test scores in a longitudinal setting may help uncover physiological mechanisms implicated with neurodevelopmental disorders such as the predisposition to reading disabilities.

Keywords: precursors of reading disabilities, resting-state EEG, reading fluency, delta and alpha oscillations

INTRODUCTION

Dyslexia is a learning disorder that specifically impairs a child's technical reading ability. It affects about 5–10% of all children, with higher prevalence in families with one or more members having dyslexia (Lyon et al., 2003). Dyslexia cannot be explained by low intelligence, low-level vision, hearing impairments, or poor education, but phonological deficits and problems with rapid automatized naming are commonly observed reading-related deficits (Snowling et al., 2003; van Bergen et al., 2012). These reading impairments affect the ability to read fluently and are often a cause of frustration and distress for a child, producing severe social and psychological consequences in their lifespan (Vellutino and Scanlon, 1987; Humphrey and Mullins, 2004).

Several genes involved in early brain development have been suggested to cause susceptibility to dyslexia (Scerri and Schulte-Korne, 2010). Thus, even though dyslexia manifests in school years, underlying neural anomalies may already be present in the preliterate brain. This is supported by a number of longitudinal studies using auditory event-related potentials (Molfese, 2000; Guttorm et al., 2001; Maurer et al., 2003, 2009; Lyytinen et al., 2004; Van Zuijen et al., 2012, 2013) and visual event-related potentials (Regtvoort et al., 2006; Schulte-Korne and Bruder, 2010; Araujo et al., 2012) reporting differences in brain responses to reading-related stimuli (e.g., speech sounds or visual contrast) between familial risk and control groups, or between control children and children that later become poor readers.

In adults or school-aged children differences between dyslexics and typical readers have been reported in ongoing EEG activity. Comparing these two groups has pointed to higher delta and theta activity during phonological task (Rippon, 2000; Klimesch et al., 2001a; Spironelli et al., 2006; Penolazzi et al., 2008) and lower alpha and beta activity (Rumsey et al., 1989; Rippon, 2000; Klimesch et al., 2001b) during reading tasks in dyslexics. Several studies (Sklar et al., 1972; Colon et al., 1979; Ahn et al., 1980; Duffy et al., 1980; Pinkerton et al., 1989; Rumsey et al., 1989; Harmony et al., 1995; Clarke et al., 2002; Benasich et al., 2008; Gou et al., 2011; Babiloni et al., 2012) have also investigated EEG from the resting-state. However, differences in participant cohorts—ranging from preschool or school-age children, to adolescents or adults and varying degrees of language disability—and in EEG biomarker definitions has prevented a consensus about possible neuronal signatures of dyslexia.

Throughout development neuronal oscillations plays an important role in shaping the structural and functional neuronal connectivity that will support higher brain functions, such as language and cognition, later in life (Smit et al., 2011). Early impairments in resting-state EEG, reflecting underling neuronal activation, might prelude future developmental problems. In line with these considerations and previous findings, we test whether ongoing neuronal oscillations in preliterate children carry information about reading fluency later in life. We compared relative amplitude spectra of EEG measured at about 3 years of age in three groups of children: one control group of fluent readers and two at-risk groups of fluent and non-fluent readers. Reading fluency was assessed at third grade of school, when the children were about 9 years old. We identified two EEG biomarkers that correlated with reading performance and reading-related test scores collected in third grade.

MATERIALS AND METHODS

SUBJECTS AND SELECTION CRITERIA

The children that participated in this study are part of the Dutch Dyslexia Programme, a longitudinal research project. The study was approved by the medical ethics committee of the University of Nijmegen, the Netherlands. Informed consent was obtained from one of the parents of each child. Parents were recruited when expecting a baby. The children were first divided in control and at-risk groups, then the at-risk group was divided in fluent and non-fluent readers.

To assess whether the infants were at familial risk of becoming poor readers, the reading fluency of the parents was tested with a word reading task (Brus and Voeten, 1973) and a pseudoword reading task (Van den Bos et al., 1994). In addition, verbal reasoning was measured with the subtest Similarities of the Wechsler Adult Intelligence Scale (Wechsler, 1997; Dutch adaptation: Uterwijk, 2000). Children were included in the at-risk group when one of the parents scored (1) lower or at the 20th percentile on both reading tests, (2) lower or at the 10th percentile on one reading test and below the 50th percentile on the other reading test, (3) lower than the 15th percentile on one reading test and not higher than the 40th percentile on the other reading test, or (4) with a discrepancy of 60 percentiles or more between the verbal reasoning test and either of the two reading tests and the additional requirement that both reading scores were below the 50th percentile. The children were included in the control group when both parents scored at the 50th percentile or higher on both reading tests.

Reading in the children was assessed based on three measurements: at the beginning of second grade (2.4 months after starting second grade, SD 1.7 months; the children were 7 years and 6 months of age, SD 5.1 months) with two word-reading lists (1A and 1B from the 3-min test, Verhoeven, 1995), at the end of second grade (6.0 months after starting second grade, SD 0.9 month) with a word reading list (2A from the 3 min test, Verhoeven, 1995) and a pseudoword reading list (Van den Bos et al., 1994), and in the middle of third grade (3.5 months after starting third grade, SD 1.1 month) with a word reading list (Brus and Voeten, 1973) and a pseudoword reading list (Van den Bos et al., 1994). A child was classified as a "non-fluent reader" when it scored poor on two out of three measurements. A child was marked "poor" when it scored below or at the 10th percentile on one of the reading lists and below the 50th percentile on the other reading list, or below or at the 25th percentile on both reading lists. Two children, initially selected as part of the control group, scored as "non-fluent readers" and were excluded from the analysis. One child that was selected to be part of the at-risk group showed general cognitive delay and was omitted as well. This resulted in three groups: a control group of fluent readers (C, 14 children, 9 boys), a group of at-risk fluent readers (RF, 24 children, 16 boys) and a group of at-risk non-fluent readers (RNF, 24 children, 14 boys).

BEHAVIORAL EVALUATION

Children were submitted to a range of cognitive tests that were administered in the middle of third grade. Two subtests of the Wechsler Intelligence Scale for children (WISC-III, Wechsler, 1992; Dutch adaptation: Kort et al., 2002) were administered: the subtest Block Design measuring nonverbal visual-spatial skills and the subtest Vocabulary measuring expressive vocabulary. Two children from the at-risk fluent group and one child from the at-risk non-fluent group were absent during this evaluation; therefore, they were not included in the behavioral statistical analysis. Behavioral tests for assessing reading-related skills were the rapid automatized naming task (RAN, Van den Bos et al., 1994), a phoneme deletion task (Amsterdamse klankdeletietest, AKT, De Jong and Van der Leij, 2003) and an orthographic choice task (Horsley, 2005). RAN measures the speed of naming overlearned information. The child was requested to name 50 digits from a piece of paper. The naming time was measured and the score was then expressed in the number of digits a child could have named in a minute. The phoneme deletion task measures phonological awareness. The child was asked to repeat a pseudoword (e.g., "memslos"), and subsequently asked to leave out a specific phoneme (e.g., the sound "l"), and to pronounce the resulting word ("memsos"). The score is the number of correct items out of 27. The orthographic choice task measured orthographic knowledge. The child had to decide the correct spelling of a word presented together with two homophonic pseudowords (e.g., among "vurkeer, verkeer, verkir" the correct spelling is "verkeer"). The score was the number of correct answers out of 70 items that the child completed in 10 min.

EEG RECORDING

Neurophysiological data were collected at 35.1 months of age (SD 0.4 months). EEG was recorded from 64 channels (positioned according to the International 10–20 system; 500 Hz sampling rate; filtered at 0.01–100 Hz), including mastoid references and vertical and horizontal electrooculogram (SynAmps2 64 Channel Quik-Cap, Neuroscan). Three to five min eyes-open rest EEG were collected while the child was on the parent's lap; the child was awake and was encouraged to look at moving lines on a screen to keep it sitting as still as possible. To ensure objectively similar artifact rejection across the different cohorts, the recorded EEG was filtered and cleaned offline using FASTER, a Matlab toolbox for automatic EEG artifacts rejection (for details, see

Nolan et al., 2010). In brief, after filtering (0.4–30 Hz band-pass), FASTER segmented the signals into 1-s epochs, detected and interpolated noisy channels, removed contaminated epochs and ran Independent Components Analysis (ICA) for the identification and the rejections of ICs associated with EOG, EMG artifacts. Finally, the signals were re-referenced to the common average, i.e., the average of all remaining scalp electrodes. The mean number of interpolated channels was 2 (± 1 SD, standard deviation) and the mean distance between interpolated channels was in 86% of the cases greater than the distance between neighbor channels. Thus, the influence of the interpolation on the spatial density of scalp EEG was negligible. The duration of the artifact-free epochs in each recording was 1.9 ± 0.1 min (mean ± standard error).

SPECTRAL ANALYSIS OF EEG DATA

Artifact-free epochs were submitted to spectral analysis. Power spectral analysis was computed using Fast Fourier Transform (Welch technique, Hamming windowing function, with 4096 FFT points, resulting in frequency bins of width 0.1 Hz). We observed multiple peaks in the 6–12 Hz range in all subjects and, therefore, we calculated the individual alpha frequency using the gravity frequency peak definition $\left(\sum \frac{a(f) \times f}{\sum a(f)}\right.$, with a (f) denoting the power spectral density at frequency f, and $\sum()$ the sum computed over the frequency bins in the interval 6–12 Hz$\left.\right)$ (Klimesch, 1999). Mean gravity frequency peak across central electrodes (C1, Cz, C2, CP1, CPz, CP2) was obtained for each subject in each group (mean and standard error of mean for C: 8 ± 0.04 Hz; for RF: 8 ± 0.04 Hz; for RNF: 7.9 ± 0.07 Hz). No statistically significant differences were found between the groups [$F_{(2, 59)} = 1.17$; $p = 0.3$, ANOVA]; similarly, no differences for gender [$F_{(1, 60)} = 1.06$; $p = 0.3$, ANOVA] or for the interaction group × gender were found [$F_{(2, 56)} = 0.4$; $p = 0.7$, ANOVA]. Given these results we considered a common individual alpha frequency of 8 Hz (consistent with literature findings in this age range Stroganova et al., 1999; Marshall et al., 2002) and we defined the frequency bands accordingly (Klimesch, 1999; Babiloni et al., 2012): 0.5–2 Hz (delta-1), 2–4 Hz (delta-2), 4–6 Hz (theta), 6–8 Hz (alpha-1), 8–10 Hz (alpha-2), 10–13 Hz (alpha-3), 13–20 Hz (beta-1), 20–30 Hz (beta-2). The amplitude of EEG signals depends on several factors unrelated to neuro-electrical activity such as anatomical and physical properties of the brain and surrounding tissue (bone thickness, skull resistance and impedance). These parameters vary from one subject to another; however, their influence on the statistical analysis can be minimized by the use of relative amplitude spectra, because these factors equally affect all frequencies analyzed. Amplitude spectra for each electrode were computed as the square root of the power spectra. The relative amplitude spectra were obtained by normalizing as follows:

$$\frac{\langle P_{B_i} \rangle}{\sum_{i=1}^{n} \langle P_{B_i} \rangle}$$

where, $\langle \rangle$ indicates the average of the amplitude in a specific frequency band, P_{B_i}, across frequency bins, and $i = 1{:}n$, with $n = 8$, corresponds to the ith frequency band considered in the analysis. The relative amplitude in these eight frequency bands were computed with the NBT toolbox (www.nbtwiki.net) (Hardstone et al., 2012), and are referred to as "biomarkers" following the broad definition: "A characteristic that is objectively measured and evaluated as an indicator of normal biological processes, pathogenic processes, or pharmacological responses to a therapeutic intervention" (Frank and Hargreaves, 2003).

STATISTICAL ANALYSIS FOR BEHAVIORAL DATA

The behavioral tests of word and pseudoword reading, the nonverbal and verbal intelligence subtests, phoneme awareness test, orthographic knowledge test and the RAN tasks were evaluated by One-Way ANOVAs in order to determine differences among the three groups. Tukey's *post-hoc* test was used for *post-hoc* analysis with multiple comparison correction. For correlation analysis with EEG biomarkers, reading fluency performance scores were defined as a composite measure of performance in the two reading tasks measured at the middle of the third grade: word reading and pseudoword reading. Reading fluency performance scores were computed as the z-scores of the average z-scores of the performance in two reading tasks.

STATISTICAL ANALYSIS OF EEG DATA

Distributions of amplitude spectra in each group for each channel and frequency band were tested for normality with the Lilliefors test. For about 25% of the channels the null hypothesis of normal distribution was rejected ($p < 0.05$); for this reason non-parametric methods were used for the statistical analysis. Statistical analysis of differences between groups was performed with non-parametric One-Way ANOVA (Kruskal-Wallis test) with group (C, RF, RNF) as main factor for each electrode and frequency band. Wilcoxon rank-sum test for each channel was used for between-group comparison and to compare means across significant electrodes. As an alternative to multiple comparison correction, we performed binomial testing to validate the statistical significance of the results (Maris and Oostenveld, 2007; Montez et al., 2009; Nikulin et al., 2012); i.e., differences were only considered significant if at least 10 electrodes would reach a p-value below 0.05. The likelihood of having this many channels out of 64 reach a p-value below 0.05 by chance is less than 0.1% (cf., binomial distribution). No correction was applied across frequency bands.

CORRELATION ANALYSIS BETWEEN BEHAVIORAL AND NEUROPHYSIOLOGICAL DATA

The behavioral measures (the reading fluency scores, the scores on phonological awareness, orthographic knowledge, and RAN) that were all assessed in the middle of third grade were correlated with the mean amplitudes across significant channels of the most significant spectral bands using Spearman correlation. Correlation analysis was also performed for each channel as an alternative approach to identify brain regions with activity associated to later reading and reading-related skills.

RESULTS

BEHAVIORAL RESULTS

The three subject groups (control, C; at-risk fluent readers, RF; at-risk non-fluent readers, RNF) were assessed on a variety of reading and reading-related tests (see, **Table 1**).

Table 1 | Behavioral measures.

Measure	Control		Risk fluent		Risk non-fluent		*df*	*F*	*p*
	M	*SD*	*M*	*SD*	*M*	*SD*			
GRADE 2, EARLY									
RF words 1	64.7_a	14.9	58.8_a	16.1	25.0_b	8.5	(2,57)	51.1	0.001
RF words 2	56.2_a	21.3	47.0_a	18.7	14.3_b	6.4	(2,57)	37.9	0.001
GRADE 2, LATE									
RF words	77.5_a	13.6	61.2_b	15.9	25.2_c	9.4	(2,59)	81.5	0.001
RF pseudowords	43.3_a	13.9	33.6_b	11.0	15.5_c	5.5	(2,59)	38.2	0.001
GRADE 3, MIDDLE									
RF words	66.5_a	10.2	56.2_b	10.6	34.8_c	7.8	(2,55)	51.7	0.001
RF pseudowords	52.9_a	14.8	38.0_b	9.5	20.0_c	6.6	(2,55)	45.4	0.001
Phon. A.	16.5_a	1.6	15.6_a	2.4	11.6_b	3.8	(2,55)	16.2	0.001
RAN digits	113.6_a	21.5	109.8_a	18.5	95.8_b	12.0	(2,56)	5.8	0.005
Ortho. K.	57.1_a	8.8	55.3_a	6.9	35.4_b	6.7	(2,56)	51.5	0.001
Non-verbal IQ	40.6_a	13.3	45.9_a	10.7	42.3_a	11.3	(2,56)	1.0	0.360
Vocabulary	33.4_{ab}	5.7	34.5_b	3.7	30.3_a	6.1	(2,56)	3.8	0.027

Means in the same row that do not share subscript differ in Tukey's post-hoc test at $p < 0.05$. FR, reading fluency; Phon. A, phonological awareness; RAN, rapid automatized naming; Orhto.K, orthographic knowledge.

The RNF children scored lower than the two fluent reading groups for phonological awareness (RNF vs. RF, $p = 0.002$; RNF vs. C, $p = 0.001$), RAN digits (RNF vs. RF, $p = 0.022$; RNF vs. C, $p = 0.01$) and orthographic knowledge (RNF vs. RF, $p = 0.001$; RNF vs. C, $p = 0.001$) tasks. This confirms that non-fluent reading is accompanied by reading-related deficits in phonological awareness, rapid naming and orthographic knowledge (De Jong and Van der Leij, 2003; Vellutino et al., 2004).

The groups did not differ on the intelligence subtest of non-verbal IQ; however, the RNF readers scored lower than the RF readers in the vocabulary test ($p = 0.024$). This is a well-known effect and poor verbal abilities have been reported to be present already at preliteracy age in children later diagnosed with dyslexia studies (Snowling et al., 2003; van Bergen et al., 2013).

Performance on word and pseudoword reading fluency tests at the middle of the third grade differed between all groups with the control children performing best, followed by the at-risk fluent readers and the at-risk non-fluent readers (**Table 1**; for word reading: RNF vs. RF, $p = 0.001$; RNF vs. C, $p = 0.001$; RF vs. C, $p = 0.007$; and for pseudoword reading: RNF vs. RF, $p = 0.001$; RNF vs. C, $p = 0.001$; RF vs. C, $p = 0.001$). This indicates that the RNF children had subclinical reading deficits possibly as a result of a higher liability (van Bergen et al., 2012).

EEG CORRELATES OF FUTURE READING ABILITIES

To investigate the presence of differences in preliteracy measures of brain function between those children who would later become fluent readers and those that would become non-fluent readers, we analyzed eyes-open rest EEG recorded at about 3 years of age using classical spectral analysis (**Figure 1**, and Materials and Methods). We performed an ANOVA to compare relative amplitude in eight different frequency bands among the three groups and observed marked differences in the delta-1 and alpha-1 bands (**Figure 2**). Electrodes with a significant effect formed spatially connected clusters over frontal and centro-parietal scalp regions for the delta-1 band and over central and parieto-occipital regions for the alpha-1 band (see *p*-value topography maps in **Figure 2**, fourth column). For delta-1 we found 10 electrodes with a significant difference between groups at $p < 0.05$, whereas 18 electrodes reached this level for alpha-1. According to binomial testing, the probability of obtaining an equal or larger number of electrodes than 10 was negligibly small ($p <$ 1e−3; Materials and Methods). On the contrary, for the theta and alpha-2 bands the number of significant electrodes was too small to reject the null hypothesis of the binomial significance test. The ANOVA for delta-2 did not show a main group effect at any electrode. No effects were observed in the higher frequency bands of alpha-3, beta-1, or beta-2 (data not shown). We note that alpha-2 oscillations displayed peaks bilaterally over the sensorimotor regions for all groups as previously reported for this age (Marshall and Meltzoff, 2011), which suggests that the alpha-1 result is not the child equivalent of the sensorimotor mu rhythm.

To identify more specifically the group differences that gave rise to the significant effects in the overall group comparisons we performed rank-sum tests between groups for delta-1 and alpha-1 relative amplitude. The results indicated that the control group did not differ from the at-risk fluent group in either of the two frequency bands (**Figures 3A,B**, first row), whereas widespread differences were observed for the comparisons of the control and at-risk non-fluent groups as well as for at-risk fluent and the at-risk non-fluent groups. Relative delta-1 activity was low in at-risk non-fluent group compared to both the control and at-risk fluent group (**Figure 3A**, second and third row), whereas relative alpha-1 activity was higher in the at-risk non-fluent group compared to both control and at-risk fluent group (**Figure 3B**, second and third row). The number of electrodes with $p < 0.05$ in these comparisons varied between 7 and 33; the probability of obtaining an equal or larger number of electrodes for a binomial distribution was small ($p < 0.03$; Materials and Methods). Although one should be cautious in inferring the origin of the sources

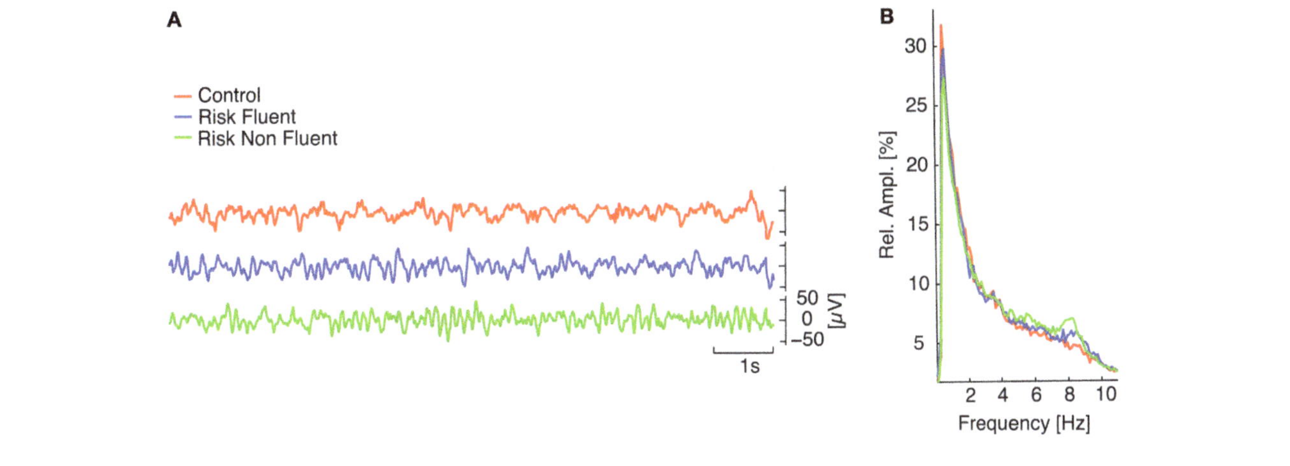

FIGURE 1 | EEG spectral analysis. (A) temporal evolution of 10 s of filtered signals (0.4–30 Hz) at the central electrode (Cz) for three children belonging to each of the different groups (red line refers to control; blue line to at-risk fluent readers; green line to at-risk non-fluent readers). **(B)** medians of relative amplitude spectra in Cz across each group.

giving rise to the scalp topographies shown in **Figure 3**, they could correspond to brain reading circuits identified in several neuroimaging studies to include parieto-temporal, occipito-temporal and inferior frontal lobes (Eckert et al., 2005; Richlan et al., 2009; Raschle et al., 2011). Together, these results indicate that children who became poor readers exhibited already at the age of three a peculiar resting-state EEG activity compared to both control and at-risk fluent groups.

CORRELATION BETWEEN EEG BIOMARKERS AND BEHAVIORAL MEASURES

Having identified relative amplitude of delta-1 and alpha-1 as putative biomarkers of future ability to read, we subsequently examined whether these EEG biomarkers could be related to performance in reading fluency and reading-related abilities (**Figure 4**, first row).

First, we computed the mean biomarker values of the delta-1 and alpha-1 across significant channels (see **Figure 2**, fifth column) and correlated these with the z-scores of the performance in the behavioral tests measured in the middle of the third grade. Within-group correlations did not reach statistical significance, which was expected given the restriction of range for the performance scores within groups. On the other hand, when considering all children together significant correlations were found between the EEG biomarkers and all the behavioral tests, i.e., Reading Fluency, Phonological Awareness, Orthographic Knowledge and RAN digits. Increasing performance on the different tasks correlated with increases in delta-1 amplitudes and decreases in alpha-1 amplitudes (correlation coefficients and p-values are reported in **Figure 4**, second row and third row). This result was to some extent expected given the group effects in the EEG and in the behavioral tests. Interestingly, however, when using the full range of correlations, scalp topographies revealed that also channels not showing a significant group difference were found to correlate with future performances (**Figure 5**).

Scalp topographies of correlations between the behavioral measures and the EEG biomarkers again suggested the involvement of multiple brain regions. In particular, delta-1's relative amplitude correlations with Reading Fluency, with Phonological Awareness and with RAN digits appeared both in frontal, central, and parieto-temporal regions. Similar regions showed correlations with Orthographic Knowledge and, interestingly, also occipito-parietal regions showed a robust positive correlation (**Figure 5**, first row) with Orthographic Knowledge. For alpha-1's relative amplitude significant correlations were stronger in central sites and correlations with performance on the orthographic task were also observed in the occipital region (**Figure 5**, second row). Noteworthy, correlations over occipital sites were more evident in the orthographic task where processing of visual information takes place. Additionally, the correlations we have found over frontal and parietal electrodes for the phonological task might be in agreement with previous studies associating phonological processing with activity in frontal lobes and parietal and temporal regions (Buchsbaum, 2001; Burton, 2009).

DISCUSSION

The present study aimed at investigating neurophysiological correlates of later emerging reading abilities in the preliterate brain. Uniquely to our study, having longitudinal data covering about 9 years of development, we showed that characteristic spectral pattern in the resting-state EEG activity of children at 3 years of age discriminate children that became poor readers from children that became fluent readers. The ability to read fluently develops gradually over time and through substantial practice but in dyslexics it is hampered by the presence of reading-related deficits in phonological processing, mapping phonemes to graphemes, and automatic word recognition. Our behavioral results confirm this effect in poor readers showing that at-risk non-fluent children scored lower than both at-risk fluent and control children in all reading-related tests (Phonological Awareness, Orthographical Knowledge and RAN). Our data on intelligence measures were in agreement with previous findings showing that dyslexics score slightly lower on verbal tasks despite having adequate reasoning

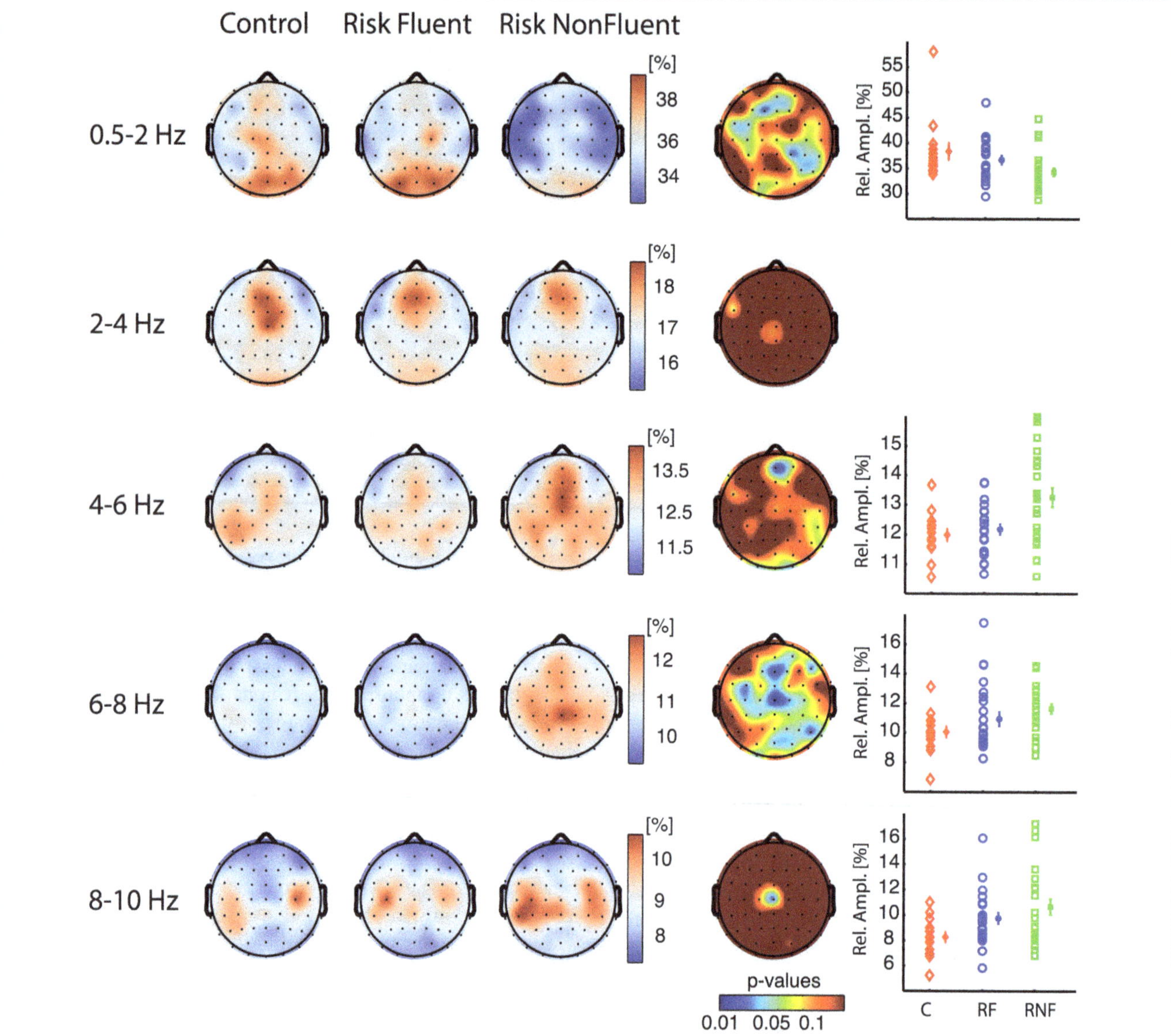

FIGURE 2 | Relative amplitude spectra in delta-1 (0.5–2 Hz) and alpha-1 (6–8 Hz) bands discriminate children becoming fluent from children becoming non-fluent readers. Grand-median topographies of delta-1, delta-2, theta, alpha-1, alpha-2 relative amplitude are shown for control (*first column*), at-risk fluent readers (*second column*), at-risk non-fluent readers (*third column*), together with ANOVA *p*-value topographies (*fourth column*). The fifth column contains plots of individual-subject values of mean relative amplitudes across significant electrodes ($p < 0.05$) for each group control (C, red diamonds), at-risk fluent readers (RF, blue circles), at-risk non-fluent readers (RNF, green squares); mean across subjects and standard error bars.

abilities compared to non-impaired readers (Snowling et al., 2003; van Bergen et al., 2013).

The comparison of EEG relative amplitude between the three groups of children, divided on the basis of their family-risk status and their reading fluency abilities, revealed several interesting findings. Our results show that two EEG biomarkers, delta-1 and alpha-1 relative amplitudes, emerged as putative preliterate discriminants of those children with a familiar risk of dyslexia who did become non-fluent readers. Non-fluent readers exhibited significantly lower levels of delta-1 activity and significantly higher alpha-1 activity compared to fluent readers (both control and at-risk fluent readers). Noteworthy, although the alpha-1 effect was prominent in central regions, we believe this does not reflect a sensorimotor mu rhythm deficit, because of the larger amplitude and clear bi-lateral topographic distribution of relative amplitude seen in alpha-2 band (Marshall and Meltzoff, 2011). Topographic distributions of the main group effect and of the correlations between the EEG biomarkers and behavioral data suggested the involvement of several scalp regions, which is in line with neuroimaging studies that have identified reading circuits both in parieto-temporal, occipito-temporal and inferior frontal lobes, albeit often with a left laterality (Eckert et al., 2005; Richlan et al., 2009; Raschle et al., 2011). Given that our statistical analysis was performed in sensor space, we are cautious with the interpretation

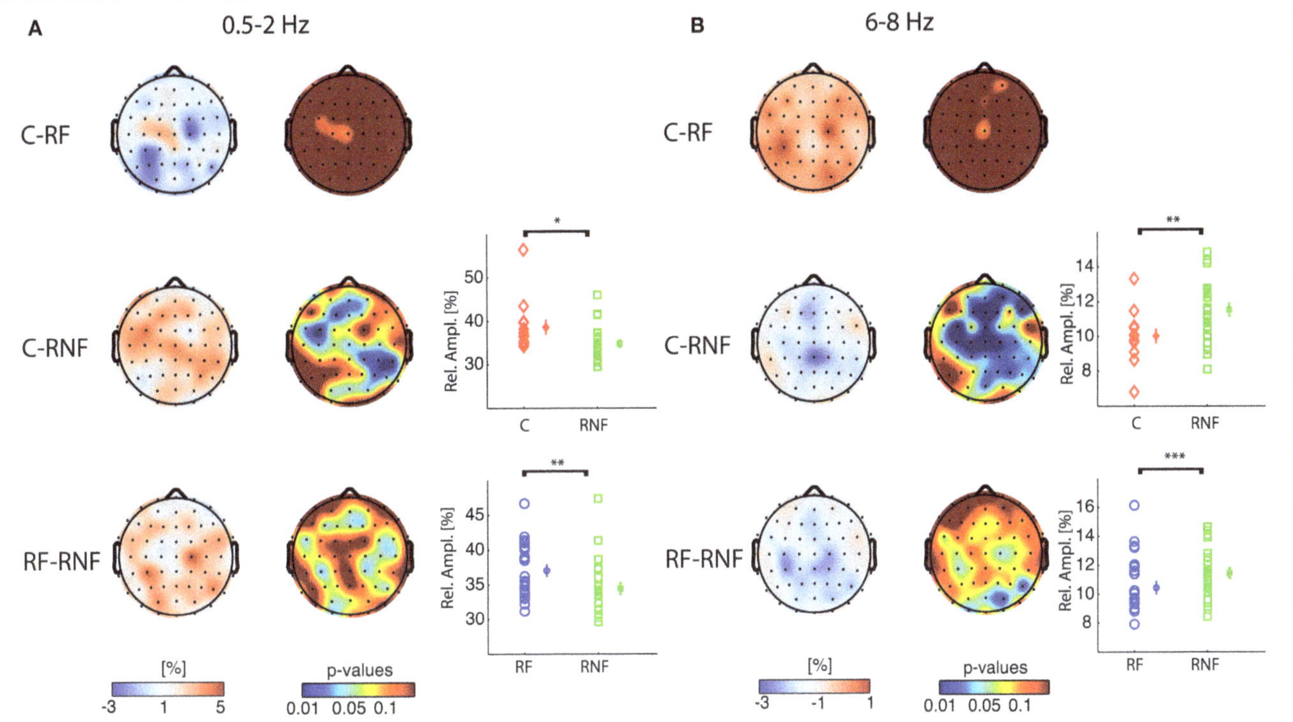

FIGURE 3 | At-risk non-fluent readers have altered delta-1 and alpha-1 compared to control and at-risk fluent readers. Pair wise group statistics (rank-sum tests) are displayed for relative amplitude for delta-1 **(A)** and alpha-1 **(B)**. In the first column: topographies of the difference of grand median values (cool-warm colormap) between controls and at-risk fluent readers (C-RF) in the first row, between controls and at-risk non-fluent readers (C-RNF) in the second row, between at-risk fluent readers and at-risk non-fluent readers (RF-RNF) in the third row. In the second column: p-value topographies for the three comparisons (jet colormap). In the third column: plots of individual-subject values of mean relative amplitudes across significant electrodes ($p < 0.05$) for each group control, mean across subjects and standard error bars (refer to **Figure 2** for explanation). The asterisks indicate significant differences obtained with rank-sum test, comparing the individual-subject average across significant electrodes between groups ($^{*}p = 0.005$; $^{**}p = 0.01$; $^{***}p = 0.03$).

of the source origin of the effects shown in **Figures 2, 3, 5**; however, we note that both delta-1 and alpha-1 relative amplitude exhibited strong correlations with Orthographic Knowledge in occipital areas, which have previously been associated with orthographic processing (Samuelsson, 2000). Differently, phonological processing is known to involve frontal areas (Burton, 2009), which could explain the prominent effects we have found in the frontal scalp regions, especially for the delta-1. These results might suggest a broader role of delta activity and a specificity of alpha-1 oscillations for visual processing, present even before the reading onset.

THE FUNCTION OF DELTA AND ALPHA OSCILLATIONS IN BRAIN MATURATION

It is well known that delta activity dominates the human EEG during early development and decreases over the course of normal development (John et al., 1980; Gasser et al., 1988; Harmony et al., 1990). Slow wave delta activity in development is believed to be important in pruning redundant cortical connections and supports brain maturation as reflected in the positive association between delta activity and gray matter volume (Whitford et al., 2007). If slow-wave delta activity is indeed a necessary mechanism for pruning and cortical development to take place, our finding of reduced delta-1 activity seem to be in agreement with the hypothesis of a cerebral maturation delay in 3-year old children that later on become poor readers. Later in life, delta waves remain dominant during slow-wave sleep; however, a relatively high delta activity in a wakeful state has been associated with pathological neuronal conditions (Spironelli and Angrilli, 2009; Babiloni et al., 2012) such as in adults with ADHD and dyslexia (Chabot et al., 2001; Penolazzi et al., 2008). Higher delta activity has also been observed in dyslexic school-age children (Spironelli et al., 2006; Penolazzi et al., 2008; Spironelli and Angrilli, 2010) and dyslexic young adults (Rippon, 2000), although these data were recorded during reading tasks. However, increased delta and theta activity in dyslexics or children with reading and writing disabilities have also been reported in resting-state EEG at the age of 9–18 years (Sklar et al., 1972; Colon et al., 1979; Pinkerton et al., 1989; Harmony et al., 1995). Thus, in line with the hypothesis of dysfunctional development (Spironelli et al., 2006, 2010, 2011; Penolazzi et al., 2008), it is plausible that failure to produce adequate delta at a young age is part of the mechanism causing a delay of cortical maturation, which in turn may be reflected in an increase of delta activity in at-risk non-fluent readers compared to fluent readers at school-age. To investigate this, future analyses will be done on resting-state EEG collected in the present cohort at the age of 11 years.

In the present study, we used relative amplitude measures to reduce the considerable genetic variance on oscillatory power (Linkenkaer-Hansen et al., 2007). Thus, it is plausible that our

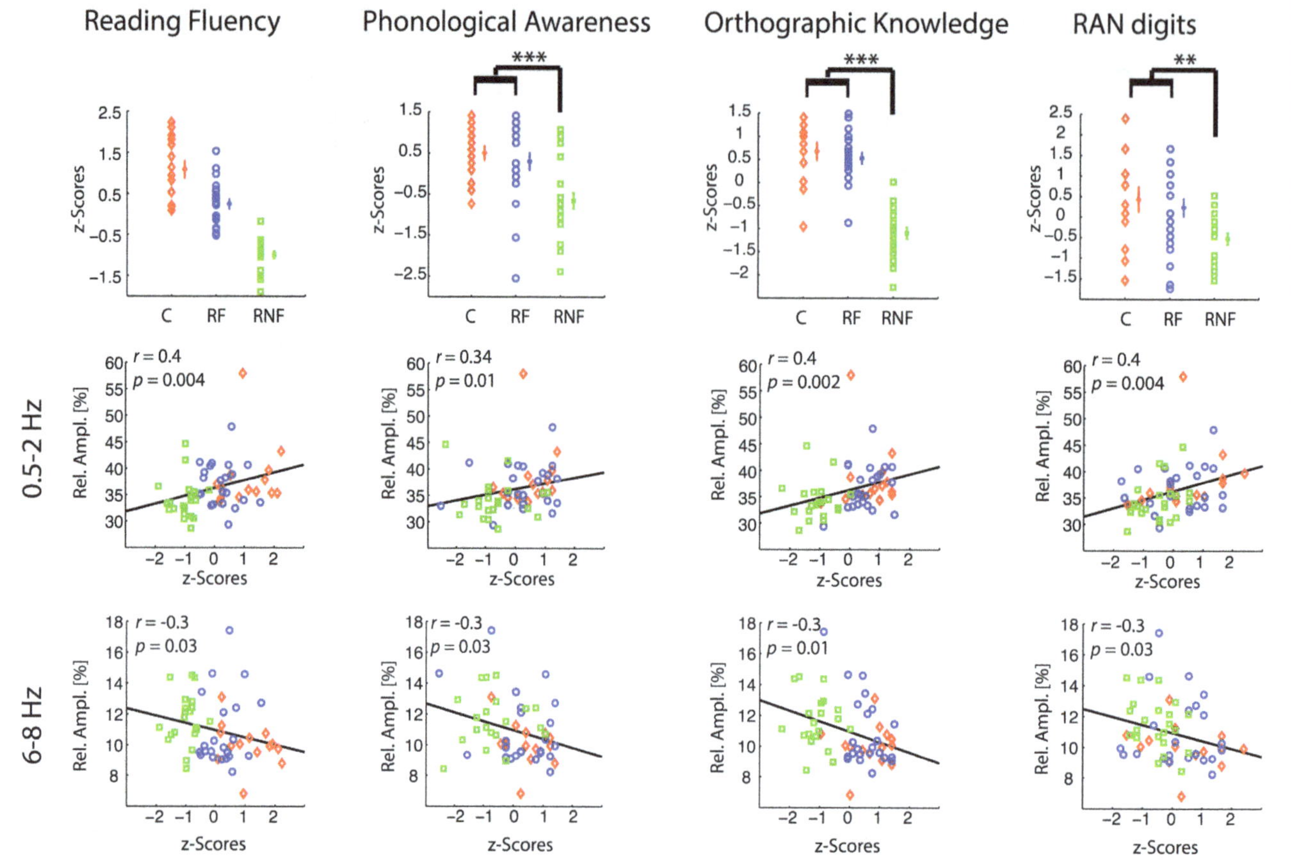

FIGURE 4 | Correlations between behavioral and neurophysiological measures. Each column refers to a specific behavioral task. Plots in the *first row* illustrate individual-subject z-scores, across subject means, and standard error bars for each group (control, C, small red diamonds; at-risk fluent readers, RF, blue circles; at-risk non-fluent readers, RNF, green squares). The asterisks indicate *p*-values of the statistics in **Table 1** (**$p = 0.005$; ***$p = 0.001$). For the reading fluency assessment (composite measure of performance scores in word reading and pseudoword reading tasks) in the top left plot, all the groups statistically differ ($p = 0.001$). The scatter plots in the remaining rows represent the correlations between individual-subject z-scores at each reading-related test and the individual-subject average across significant electrodes ($p < 0.05$) of relative amplitude in delta-1 (*second row*), and in alpha-1 (*third row*). Statistics is based on $n = 59$ children.

findings in the alpha-1 bands are to some extent related to those in the delta band. On the other hand, increases of lower alpha (spectral component just below the IAF) activity have been associated with difficulty in sustaining attention and inhibiting distracting environmental stimuli (Klimesch et al., 2001b). Thus, we cannot rule out that the children in our study differed in the level of attention paid to the moving lines, with the non-fluent reading group exhibiting low sustained attention, as reflected in higher alpha-1 amplitude compare to the other two groups.

COMPARISON WITH OTHER FAMILIAL RISK STUDIES

It is worth noting that our cohort resembles the cohort of the studies presented in Benasich et al. (2008) and Gou et al. (2011) where resting-state EEG of age-matched children (16, 24, and 36 months of age) with a family history of language-based learning impairment (LLI, FH+) and controls (FH−) were compared. Benasich et al. (2008) performed qualitative analysis among absolute power spectra in 9 frequency bins ranging from 5 to 50 Hz (excluding frequency components of the delta range) and across different scalp regions. They selected frontal and prefrontal regions and focused on two wide frequency ranges for their statistical analysis (5–30 Hz and 31–50 Hz, of which the latter was referred to as gamma). They reported lower frontal gamma power in FH+ compared to FH-, and found correlations of gamma power with attention, and expressive and receptive language skills measured at the same age. In a later study, using the same cohort of children, Gou et al. (2011) reported that resting frontal gamma power at 16, 24, and 36 months was associated with phonological memory and syntactical skill measured at the age of 4 and 5 years. Comparison with the present study are not possible for several reasons: (1) the definition of the family risk in our study is based on the parents' performance on reading tests, whereas in Benasich et al. (2008) it is associated to the presence of at least one sibling or parent diagnosed with LLI (75% were siblings Choudhury and Benasich, 2003); (2) none of the children in Gou et al. (2011) were themselves diagnosed with any language or learning disabilities, whereas our at-risk children were divided into groups that became fluent or non-fluent readers; (3) the EEG

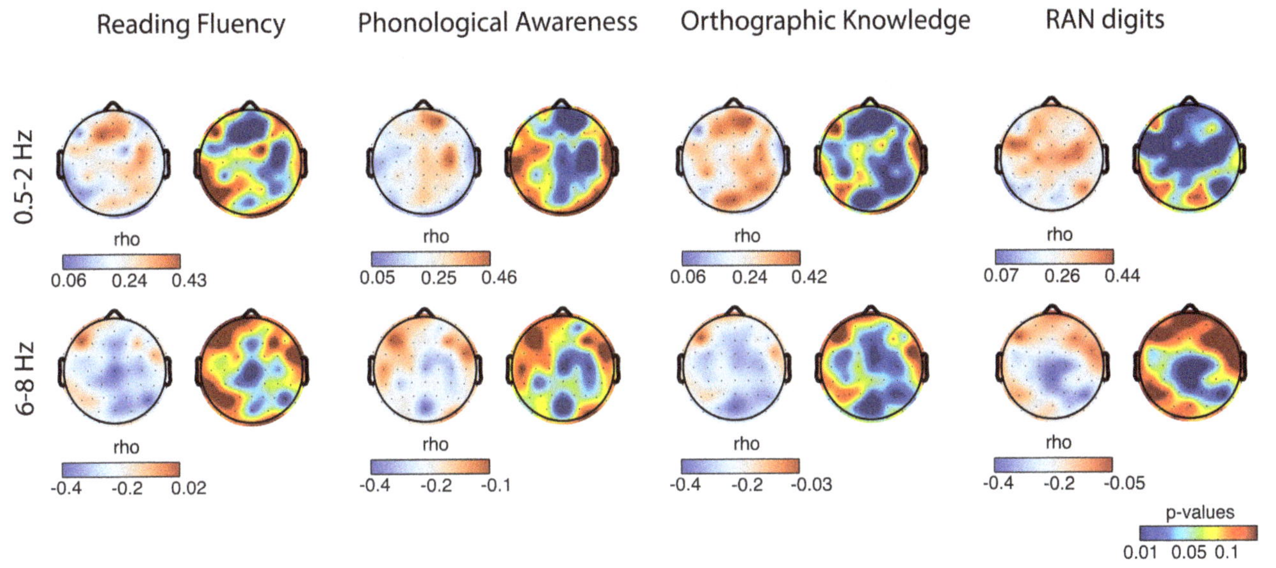

FIGURE 5 | Correlation topographies. For each behavioral task, correlations with delta-1 (*first row*) and alpha-1 (*second row*) relative amplitude of all the subjects are shown in the form of correlation coefficient (r) topographies (cool-warm color map) and *p*-value topographies (jet color map).

signal analysis performed in our study did not include frequency components higher than 30 Hz. Despite the differences in the cohort definition and in the EEG analysis, our results are congruent with the findings of Benasich et al. (2008) related to absence of statistical difference between control and at-risk fluent readers (comparable with FH+) for spectral amplitude lower than 30 Hz.

CONCLUSIONS

In conclusion, we showed that combining family-risk status assessment and resting-state EEG at preliterate age could provide preliminary indicators of future reading abilities. Specifically, our data suggest that delta and alpha oscillations are implicated with neurophysiological processes of importance for reading-related disabilities later in childhood. In particular, we confirm the role of delta activity as a physiological index of abnormal cerebral maturation. Further investigations are required to better understand the functional significance and the underlying mechanisms governing the dynamics of these oscillations in developmental dyslexia. For example, in this study we did not account for special training in addition to schooling that some poor-reading children have followed, partially influencing their performances in the reading-related tasks measured at the middle of the third grade. In this regard, future studies may investigate whether reading-intervention programs (Connor et al., 2007)affect the dynamics of the brain as reflected in the resting-state EEG.

ACKNOWLEDGMENTS

We thank the Netherlands Organization for Scientific Research (NWO) for funding the Dutch Dyslexia Programme (1997–2012) under project number 200-62-304. We also thank all children and their parents for their dedicated participation in this longitudinal research program.

REFERENCES

Ahn, H., Prichep, L., John, E. R., Baird, H., Trepetin, M., and Kaye, H. (1980). Developmental equations reflect brain dysfunctions. *Science* 210, 1259–1262. doi: 10.1126/science.7434027

Araujo, S., Bramao, I., Faisca, L., Petersson, K. M., and Reis, A. (2012). Electrophysiological correlates of impaired reading in dyslexic pre-adolescent children. *Brain Cogn.* 79, 79–88. doi: 10.1016/j.bandc.2012.02.010

Babiloni, C., Stella, G., Buffo, P., Vecchio, F., Onorati, P., Muratori, C., et al. (2012). Cortical sources of resting state EEG rhythms are abnormal in dyslexic children. *Clin. Neurophysiol.* 123, 2384–2391. doi: 10.1016/j.clinph.2012.05.002

Benasich, A. A., Gou, Z., Choudhury, N., and Harris, K. D. (2008). Early cognitive and language skills are linked to resting frontal gamma power across the first 3 years. *Behav. Brain Res.* 195, 215–222. doi: 10.1016/j.bbr.2008.08.049

Brus, B. T., and Voeten, M. J. M. (1973). *Een Minuut Test: Verantwoording En Handleiding (One Minute Test: Manual)*. Nijmegen: Berkhout.

Buchsbaum, B. (2001). Role of left posterior superior temporal gyrus in phonological processing for speech perception and production. *Cogn. Sci.* 25, 663–678. doi: 10.1207/s15516709cog2505_2

Burton, M. W. (2009). Understanding the role of the prefrontal cortex in phonological processing. *Clin. Linguist. Phon.* 23, 180–195. doi: 10.1080/02699200802394963

Chabot, R. J., di Michele, F., Prichep, L., and John, E. R. (2001). The clinical role of computerized EEG in the evaluation and treatment of learning and attention disorders in children and adolescents. *J. Neuropsychiatry Clin. Neurosci.* 13, 171–186. doi: 10.1176/appi.neuropsych.13.2.171

Choudhury, N., and Benasich, A. A. (2003). A family aggregation study: the influence of family history and other risk factors on language development. *J. Speech Lang. Hear. Res.* 46, 261. doi: 10.1044/1092-4388(2003/021)

Clarke, A. R., Barry, R. J., McCarthy, R., and Selikowitz, M. (2002). EEG analysis of children with attention-deficit/hyperactivity disorder and comorbid reading disabilities. *J. Learn. Disabil.* 35, 276–285. doi: 10.1177/002221940203500309

Colon, E. J., Notermans, S. L., De Weerd, J. P., and Kap, J. (1979). The discriminating role of EEG power spectra in dyslexic children. *J. Neurol.* 221, 257–262. doi: 10.1007/BF00314642

Connor, C. M., Morrison, F. J., Fishman, B. J., Schatschneider, C., and Underwood, P. (2007). Algorithm-guided individualized reading instruction. *Science* 315, 464–465. doi: 10.1126/science.1134513

De Jong, P. F., and Van der Leij, A. (2003). Developmental changes in the manifestation of a phonological deficit in dyslexic children learning to read a regular orthography. *J. Educ. Psychol.* 95, 22–40. doi: 10.1037/0022-0663.95.1.22

Duffy, F. H., Denckla, M. B., Bartels, P. H., and Sandini, G. (1980). Dyslexia: regional differences in brain electrical activity by topographic mapping. *Ann. Neurol.* 7, 412–420. doi: 10.1002/ana.410070505

Eckert, M. A., Leonard, C. M., Wilke, M., Eckert, M., Richards, T., Richards, A., et al. (2005). Anatomical signatures of dyslexia in children: unique information from manual and voxel based morphometry brain measures. *Cortex* 41, 304–315. doi: 10.1016/S0010-9452(08)70268-5

Frank, R., and Hargreaves, R. (2003). Clinical biomarkers in drug discovery and development. *Nat. Rev. Drug Discov.* 2, 566–580. doi: 10.1038/nrd1130

Gasser, T., Verleger, R., Bacher, P., and Sroka, L. (1988). Development of the EEG of school-age children and adolescents. I. Analysis of band power. *Electroencephalogr. Clin. Neurophysiol.* 69, 91–99. doi: 10.1016/0013-4694(88)90204-0

Gou, Z., Choudhury, N., and Benasich, A. A. (2011). Resting frontal gamma power at 16, 24 and 36 months predicts individual differences in language and cognition at 4 and 5 years. *Behav. Brain Res.* 220, 263–270. doi: 10.1016/j.bbr.2011.01.048

Guttorm, T. K., Leppanen, P. H., Richardson, U., and Lyytinen, H. (2001). Event-related potentials and consonant differentiation in newborns with familial risk for dyslexia. *J. Learn. Disabil.* 34, 534–544. doi: 10.1177/0022219401034 00606

Hardstone, R., Poil, S.-S., Schiavone, G., Jansen, R., Nikulin, V. V., Mansvelder, H. D., et al. (2012). Detrended fluctuation analysis: a scale-free view on neuronal oscillations. *Front. Physiol.* 3:450. doi: 10.3389/fphys.2012.00450

Harmony, T., Marosi, E., Becker, J., Rodríguez, M., Reyes, A., Fernández, T., et al. (1995). Longitudinal quantitative EEG study of children with different performances on a reading-writing test. *Electroencephalogr. Clin. Neurophysiol.* 95, 426–433. doi: 10.1016/0013-4694(95)00135-2

Harmony, T., Marosi, E., Díaz de León, A. E., Becker, J., and Fernández, T. (1990). Effect of sex, psychosocial disadvantages and biological risk factors on EEG maturation. *Electroencephalogr. Clin. Neurophysiol.*75, 482–491. doi: 10.1016/0013-4694(90)90135-7

Horsley, T. M. (2005). *Not all Dyslexics are Created Equal: Neurocognitive Evidence.* Thesis, Vrije Universiteit, Amsterdam.

Humphrey, N., and Mullins, P. M. (2004). Self-concept and self-esteem in developmental dys- lexia. *J. Res. Spec. Educ. Needs* 2, 1–13. doi: 10.1111/j.1471-3802.2002.00163.x

John, E. R., Alan, H., Prichep, L., Trepetin, M., Brown, D., and Kaye, H. (1980). Developmental equations for the EEG. *Science* 210, 1255–1258. doi: 10.1126/science.7434026

Klimesch, W. (1999). EEG alpha and theta oscillations reflect cognitive and memory performance: a review and analysis. *Brain Res. Rev.* 29, 169–195. doi: 10.1016/S0165-0173(98)00056-3

Klimesch, W., Doppelmayr, M., Wimmer, H., Gruber, W., Röhm, D., Schwaiger, J., et al. (2001b). Alpha and beta band power changes in normal and dyslexic children. *Clin. Neurophysiol.* 112, 1186–11895. doi: 10.1016/S1388-2457(01) 00543-0

Klimesch, W., Doppelmayr, M., Wimmer, H., Schwaiger, J., Röhm, D., Gruber, W., et al. (2001a). Theta band power changes in normal and dyslexic children. *Clin. Neurophysiol.* 112, 1174–1185. doi: 10.1016/S1388-2457(01) 00545-4

Kort, W., Compaan, E. L., Bleichrodt, N., Resing, W. C. M., Schittekatte, M., Bosmans, M., et al. (2002). *WISC-III NL. Handleiding.* London: The Psychological Corporation.

Linkenkaer-Hansen, K., Smit, D. J. A., Barkil, A., van Beijsterveldt, T. E. M., Brussaard, A. B., Boomsma, D. I., et al. (2007). Genetic contributions to long-range temporal correlations in ongoing oscillations. *J. Neurosci.* 27, 13882–13889. doi: 10.1523/JNEUROSCI.3083-07.2007

Lyon, G. R., Shaywitz, S. E., and Shaywitz, B. A. (2003). A definition of dyslexia. *Ann. Dyslexia* 53, 1–14. doi: 10.1007/s11881-003-0001-9

Lyytinen, H., Aro, M., Eklund, K., Erskine, J., Guttorm, T., Laakso, M. L., et al. (2004). The development of children at familial risk for dyslexia: birth to early school age. *Ann. Dyslexia* 54, 184–220. doi: 10.1007/s11881-004-0010-3

Maris, E., and Oostenveld, R. (2007). Nonparametric statistical testing of EEG-and MEG-data. *J. Neurosci. Methods* 164, 177–190. doi: 10.1016/j.jneumeth.2007.03.024

Marshall, P. J., Bar-Haim, Y., and Fox, N. A. (2002). Development of the EEG from 5 months to 4 years of age. *Clin. Neurophysiol.* 113, 1199–1208. doi: 10.1016/S1388-2457(02)00163-3

Marshall, P. J., and Meltzoff, A. N. (2011). Neural mirroring systems: exploring the EEG mu rhythm in human infancy. *Dev. Cogn. Neurosci.* 1, 110–123. doi: 10.1016/j.dcn.2010.09.001

Maurer, U., Bucher, K., Brem, S., Benz, R., Kranz, F., Schulz, E., et al. (2009). Neurophysiology in preschool improves behavioral prediction of reading ability throughout primary school. *Biol. Psychiatry* 66, 341–348. doi: 10.1016/j.biopsych.2009.02.031

Maurer, U., Bucher, K., Brem, S., and Brandeis, D. (2003). Altered responses to tone and phoneme mismatch in kindergartners at familial dyslexia risk. *Neuroreport* 14, 2245–2250. doi: 10.1097/00001756-200312020-00022

Molfese, D. L. (2000). Predicting dyslexia at 8 years of age using neonatal brain responses. *Brain Lang.* 72, 238–245. doi: 10.1006/brln.2000.2287

Montez, T., Poil, S.-S., Jones, B. F., Manshanden, I., Verbunt, J. P. A., Van Dijk, B. W., et al. (2009). Altered temporal correlations in parietal alpha and prefrontal theta oscillations in early-stage Alzheimer disease. *Proc. Natl. Acad. Sci. U.S.A.* 106, 1614–1619. doi: 10.1073/pnas.0811699106

Nikulin, V. V., Jönsson, E. G., and Brismar, T. (2012). Attenuation of long-range temporal correlations in the amplitude dynamics of alpha and beta neuronal oscillations in patients with schizophrenia. *Neuroimage* 61, 162–169. doi: 10.1016/j.neuroimage.2012.03.008

Nolan, H., Whelan, R., and Reilly, R. B. (2010). FASTER: fully automated statistical thresholding for EEG artifact rejection. *J. Neurosci. Methods* 192, 152–162. doi: 10.1016/j.jneumeth.2010.07.015

Penolazzi, B., Spironelli, C., and Angrilli, A. (2008). Delta EEG activity as a marker of dysfunctional linguistic processing in developmental dyslexia. *Psychophysiology* 45, 1025–1033. doi: 10.1111/j.1469-8986.2008.00709.x

Pinkerton, F., Watson, D. R., and McClelland, R. J. (1989). A neurophysiological study of children with reading, writing and spelling difficulties. *Dev. Med. Child Neurol.* 31, 569–581. doi: 10.1111/j.1469-8749.1989.tb04042.x

Raschle, N. M., Chang, M., and Gaab, N. (2011). Structural brain alterations associated with dyslexia predate reading onset. *Neuroimage* 57, 742–749. doi: 10.1016/j.neuroimage.2010.09.055

Regtvoort, A. G. F. M., van Leeuwen, T. H., Stoel, R. D., and van der Leij, A. (2006). Efficiency of visual information processing in children at-risk for dyslexia: habituation of single-trial ERPs. *Brain Lang.* 98, 319–331. doi: 10.1016/j.bandl.2006.06.006

Richlan, F., Kronbichler, M., and Wimmer, H. (2009). Functional abnormalities in the dyslexic brain: a quantitative meta-analysis of neuroimaging studies. *Hum. Brain Mapp.* 30, 3299–3308. doi: 10.1002/hbm.20752

Rippon, G. (2000). Trait and state EEG indices of information processing in developmental dyslexia. *Int. J. Psychophysiol.* 36, 251–265. doi: 10.1016/S0167-8760(00)00075-1

Rumsey, J. M., Coppola, R., Denckla, M. B., Hamburger, S. D., and Kruesi, M. J. (1989). EEG spectra in severely dyslexic men: rest and word and design recognition. *Electroencephalogr. Clin. Neurophysiol.* 73, 30–40. doi: 10.1016/0013-4694(89)90017-5

Samuelsson, S. (2000). Converging evidence for the role of occipital regions in orthographic processing: a case of developmental surface dyslexia. *Neuropsychologia* 38, 351–362. doi: 10.1016/S0028-3932(99)00096-2

Scerri, T. S., and Schulte-Korne, G. (2010). Genetics of developmental dyslexia. *Eur. Child Adolesc. Psychiatry* 19, 179–197. doi: 10.1007/s00787-009-0081-0

Schulte-Korne, G., and Bruder, J. (2010). Clinical neurophysiology of visual and auditory processing in dyslexia: a review. *Clin. Neurophysiol.* 121, 1794–1809. doi: 10.1016/j.clinph.2010.04.028

Sklar, B., Hanley, J., and Simmons, W. W. (1972). An EEG experiment aimed toward identifying dyslexic children. *Nature* 240, 414–416. doi: 10.1038/240414a0

Smit, D. J., de Geus, E. J. C., van de Nieuwenhuijzen, M. E., van Beijsterveldt, C. E. M., van Baal, G. C. M., Mansvelder, H. D., et al. (2011). Scale-free modulation of resting-state neuronal oscillations reflects prolonged brain maturation in humans. *J. Neurosci.* 31, 13128–13136. doi: 10.1523/JNEUROSCI.1678-11.2011

Snowling, M. J., Gallagher, A., and Frith, U. (2003). Family risk of dyslexia is continuous: individual differences in the precursors of reading skill. *Child Dev.* 74, 358–373. doi: 10.1111/1467-8624.7402003

Spironelli, C., and Angrilli, A. (2009). EEG delta band as a marker of brain damage in aphasic patients after recovery of language. *Neuropsychologia* 47, 988–994. doi: 10.1016/j.neuropsychologia.2008.10.019

Spironelli, C., and Angrilli, A. (2010). Developmental aspects of language lateralization in delta, theta, alpha and beta EEG bands. *Biol. Psychol.* 85, 258–267. doi: 10.1016/j.biopsycho.2010.07.011

Spironelli, C., Angrilli, A., Calogero, A., and Stegagno, L. (2011). Delta EEG band as a marker of left hypofrontality for language in schizophrenia patients. *Schizophr. Bull.* 37, 757–767. doi: 10.1093/schbul/sbp145

Spironelli, C., Penolazzi, B., Vio, C., and Angrilli, A. (2006). Inverted EEG theta lateralization in dyslexic children during phonological processing. *Neuropsychologia* 44, 2814–2821. doi: 10.1016/j.neuropsychologia.2006.06.009

Spironelli, C., Penolazzi, B., Vio, C., and Angrilli, A. (2010). Cortical reorganization in dyslexic children after phonological training: evidence from early evoked potentials. *Brain* 133, 3385–3395. doi: 10.1093/brain/awq199

Stroganova, T. A., Orekhova, E. V., and Posikera, I. N. (1999). EEG alpha rhythm in infants. *Clin. Neurophysiol.* 110, 997–1012. doi: 10.1016/S1388-2457(98)00009-1

Uterwijk, J. (2000). *WAIS-III. Nederlandstalige Bewerking. Technische Handleiding. David Wechsler.* Lisse: Swets Test Publishers.

van Bergen, E., de Jong, P. F., Maassen, B. A. M., Krikhaar, E., Plakas, A., and Van der Leij, A. (2013). IQ of four-year-olds who go on to develop dyslexia. *J. Learn. Disabil.* 47, 475–484. doi: 10.1177/0022219413479673

van Bergen, E., de Jong, P. F., Plakas, A., Maassen, B. A. M., and van der Leij, A. (2012). Child and parental literacy levels within families with a histroy of dyslexia. *J. Child Psychol. Psychiatry* 53, 28–36. doi: 10.1111/j.1469-7610.2011.02418.x

Van den Bos, K. P., lutje Spelberg, H. C., Scheepstra, A. J. M., and De Vries, J. R. (1994). *De Klepel, vorm A en B. Een Test Voor de Leesvaardigheid Van Pseudowoorden. Verantwoording, Handleiding, Diagnostiek en Behandeling.* Nijmegen: Berkhout. Test Materiaal.

Van Zuijen, T. L., Plakas, A., Maassen, B. A. M., Been, P., Maurits, N. M., Krikhaar, E., et al. (2012). Temporal auditory processing at 17 months of age is associated with preliterate language comprehension and later word reading fluency: an ERP study. *Neurosci. Lett.* 528, 31–35. doi: 10.1016/j.neulet.2012.08.058

Van Zuijen, T. L., Plakas, A., Maassen, B. A., Maurits, N. M., and Leij, A. (2013). Infant ERPs separate children at risk of dyslexia who become good readers from those who become poor readers. *Dev. Sci.* 16, 554–563. doi: 10.1111/desc.12049

Vellutino, F. R., Fletcher, J. M., Snowling, M. J., and Scanlon, D. M. (2004). Specific reading disability (dyslexia): what have we learned in the past four decades? *J. Child Psychol. Psychiatry* 45, 2–40. doi: 10.1046/j.0021-9630.2003.00305.x

Vellutino, F. R., and Scanlon, D. M. (1987). Phonological coding, phonological awareness, and reading ability: evidence from a longitudinal and experimental study. *Merrill Palmer Q.* 33, 321–363.

Verhoeven, L. (1995). *Drie-Minuten-Toets (DMT): Handleiding.* Arnhem: Cito.

Wechsler, D. (1997). *Wechsler Adult Intelligence Scale-Third Edition.* San Antonio, TX: The Psychological Corporation.

Wechsler, D. A. (1992). *Wechsler Intelligence Scale for Children-III.* San Antonio, TX: The Psychological Corporation.

Whitford, T. J., Rennie, C. J., Grieve, S. M., Clark, C. R., Gordon, E., and Williams, L. M. (2007). Brain maturation in adolescence: concurrent changes in neuroanatomy and neurophysiology. *Hum. Brain Mapp.* 28, 228–237. doi: 10.1002/hbm.20273

10

The eye-voice lead during oral reading in developmental dyslexia

Maria De Luca[1], Maria Pontillo[2], Silvia Primativo[1,2], Donatella Spinelli[1,3] and Pierluigi Zoccolotti[1,2]*

[1] Neuropsychology Unit, IRCCS Fondazione Santa Lucia, Rome, Italy
[2] Department of Psychology, Sapienza University of Rome, Rome, Italy
[3] Department of Human Movement Sciences and Health, University of Rome ≪Foro Italico≫, Rome, Italy

Correspondence:
Pierluigi Zoccolotti, Department of Psychology, Sapienza University of Rome, Via dei Marsi 78, 00176 Rome, Italy
e-mail: pierluigi.zoccolotti@uniroma1.it

In reading aloud, the eye typically leads over voice position. In the present study, eye movements and voice utterances were simultaneously recorded and tracked during the reading of a meaningful text to evaluate the eye-voice lead in 16 dyslexic and 16 same-age control readers. Dyslexic children were slower than control peers in reading texts. Their slowness was characterized by a great number of silent pauses and sounding-out behaviors and a small lengthening of word articulation times. Regarding eye movements, dyslexic readers made many more eye fixations (and generally smaller rightward saccades) than controls. Eye movements and voice (which were shifted in time because of the eye-voice lead) were synchronized in dyslexic readers as well as controls. As expected, the eye-voice lead was significantly smaller in dyslexic than control readers, confirming early observations by Buswell (1921) and Fairbanks (1937). The eye-voice lead was significantly correlated with several eye movements and voice parameters, particularly number of fixations and silent pauses. The difference in performance between dyslexic and control readers across several eye and voice parameters was expressed by a ratio of about 2. We propose that referring to proportional differences allows for a parsimonious interpretation of the reading deficit in terms of a single deficit in word decoding. The possible source of this deficit may call for visual or phonological mechanisms, including Goswami's temporal sampling framework.

Keywords: reading, eye movements, eye-voice lead, dyslexia, pronunciation time

INTRODUCTION

Reading aloud is a complex task that requires the synchronization of various subtasks or subcomponents which impinge on different ongoing fluxes of information. Thus, for reading to be effective orthographic stimuli have to be visually scanned, individual words have to be decoded and their corresponding entries in the phonological output lexicon have to be activated, a stream of utterances has to be produced and synchronized with the ongoing scanning of visual text and word meaning has to be decoded and maintained in short-term memory to place words in a context and reconstruct the sense of a sentence (or paragraph). By its very nature, scientific research tries to isolate different sub-tasks (using appropriate parameters), because complex behaviors are more difficult to study. This is also true in the study of reading and its disorders. For example, it is widely accepted that word level captures the difficulty of dyslexic children (Coltheart et al., 2001). Therefore, much research has aimed to examine single-word reading performance, often analysing the effects of psycholinguistic variables (such as word frequency or age of acquisition) by means of vocal reaction times (e.g., Ziegler et al., 2003) or lexical decision times (e.g., Martens and de Jong, 2006). As to the visual scanning of texts, research on eye movements has mainly examined the silent reading of lists of words or words embedded in simple sentences, and has avoided the complexities linked to the synchronization of voice outflow and limited the requests for text comprehension (Rayner, 2009).

The complexity of reading, with its multiple interacting subcomponents, represents an intriguing and challenging problem. In a recent study based on reading time measures (Zoccolotti et al., 2012), we contrasted the reading aloud of words presented singly or arranged in multiple arrays in control and dyslexic readers. Skilled readers showed a clear advantage with multiple over single items, indicating that they were able to process the subsequent visual stimulus while uttering the current target. By contrast, dyslexic readers did not show such an advantage and were actually slower in reading multiple than single items. We proposed that difficulty with arrays of words indicates a selective difficulty in integrating the multiple subcomponents of the reading task over and above the basic nuclear deficit in decoding words (Zoccolotti et al., 2012). Other studies (based on the Rapid Automatized Naming paradigm or RAN) also emphasized the particular difficulty of dyslexic children with the sequential nature of the naming task as opposed to the more artificial situation in which single items are presented one at a time and responded to (e.g., Georgiou et al., 2013; for a developmental analysis of this effect see also Protopapas et al., 2013). These observations raise interest in examining dyslexic readers' overall reading behavior, that is, from visual scanning to sentence utterance. Indeed, this might clarify two important aspects of developmental reading deficiencies.

First, the extent to which dyslexic readers are differentially impaired/spared in the different subcomponents that contribute to reading aloud could be evaluated. It could also be determined whether the requirement to integrate these multiple subcomponents causes, or at least contributes to, the reading difficulty. Some evidence concerning the second question has been cited above.

As to the first question, a large literature indicates that dyslexic readers have slower reaction times (RT) to visually presented words (and non-words) than control readers. This finding indicates that they have a basic deficit in decoding visually presented orthographic materials (e.g., Ziegler et al., 2003; Spinelli et al., 2005). By contrast, pronunciation time for words is much less affected (although it is not entirely normal), indicating a much weaker deficit in the production component (Davies et al., 2013; Martelli et al., 2013). Analysis of visual scanning generally indicates that dyslexic children show normal eye movement patterns with non-orthographic visual stimuli and have specific difficulty with orthographic materials in both irregular (e.g., Olson et al., 1983) and regular (e.g., Italian, the language studied here: De Luca et al., 1999) orthographies. There is growing evidence of difficulty also in the acoustic modality (i.e., dyslexia has been found to be associated with reduced perceptual sensitivity to amplitude envelope onset of sounds (e.g., Goswami et al., 2011; Leong et al., 2011). Within the temporal sampling framework (Goswami, 2011), the deficit in rise time sensitivity is associated with impaired low-frequency oscillatory mechanisms involved in parsing and perceiving syllables. Goswami (2011) noted that impairments in auditory entrainment are likely to have consequences for attention and also auditory–visual integration (are likely to affect attention and auditory-visual integration). Indeed, attentional deficits were also reported in dyslexic children (e.g., Hari and Renvall, 2001; Facoetti et al., 2010) and might contribute to the abnormal eye movement pattern shown in reading (see also Hawelka et al., 2010 for a link between word reading and eye movement control).

Even from this sketchy presentation, it is apparent that not all reading sub-components are equally impaired in dyslexic readers and that procedures which allow differentiating the level of involvement within the same general paradigm would be useful to fully describe the profile of reading slowness in these children.

In the present study, we moved in this direction by jointly examining the flow of eye movements and speech production in children with and without developmental dyslexia while they read aloud a short meaningful text. Interest in the inter-play between eye and voice during reading aloud was particularly keen in the first part of the last century (Buswell, 1920, 1921; Fairbanks, 1937; Tiffin and Fairbanks, 1937). These studies were aimed at separating peripheral and central phases of the reading process. By analysing reading errors in good and poor adult readers in relationship to eye movements, Fairbanks (1937) reported evidence that "*faulty eye movements cannot have caused the errors*" and concluded that "*the central processes in reading determine the nature of eye movements*" (Fairbanks, 1937). This position still has a large consensus today (see Rayner, 1998, 2009 for reviews).

Important observations in these studies concern the relationship between visual scanning and voice production during reading. Buswell (1921) effectively synthesized the characteristics of this phenomenon: "*A mature reader tends to maintain a comparatively wide average span between the eye and the voice, which at times may amount to the space occupied by seven or eight words. An immature reader, however, tends to keep the eye and voice very close together, in many cases not moving the eye from a word until the voice has pronounced it. Reading of this type becomes little more than a series of spoken words because there is no opportunity to anticipate the meaning in large units. An eye-voice span of considerable width is necessary in order that the reader may have an intelligent grasp of the material read, and that he may read it with good expression.*"

Fairbanks (1937) study of the eye-voice relationship was particularly thorough (although it has been rarely cited). He proposed that eye-voice lead (as compared to eye-voice span) was "*more descriptive of the eye-voice relation as it usually obtains*"; therefore, we will follow Fairbanks's terminology in the present work. Fairbanks (1937) examined the eye-voice lead in relationship to both spatial and linguistic parameters as well as the difficulty of words, defined by word frequency ("scarcity" in Fairbanks's terms) and the effect of stimulus length. The influence of these factors was clear in the pattern of eye movements as well as misreadings. Thus, "*in poor reading the influence of word scarcity is even greater*" than in superior readers, while "*word length has little effect upon good readers, but, to a degree at least, appears to be a measure of difficulty in inferior reading.*" Examining mispronunciations in a dynamic context, Fairbanks (1937) gave particular emphasis to multiple utterances, such as hesitations or repetitions with or without self-corrections. He noted that, when good readers repeated a word they did so after a misreading and made a self-correction. By contrast, poor readers often repeated correct words and nearly always failed to correct their errors.

Fairbanks (1937) observed that number of hesitations is also particularly important in discriminating good from poor readers even though they are difficult to measure as "*their determination is essentially qualitative*" and requires "*careful re-checking.*" Examining hesitations in association with eye movements, Fairbanks (1937) noted that "*one of the reasons for hesitation in poor reading is the necessity of regressing to words which give difficulty*" and "*...even though the determination of hesitations is a qualitative step, ... diagnosis of reading ability by means of describing oral reading should include this measure.*"

These observations are particularly revealing because, since the classical work of Marshall and Newcombe (1966, 1973), analysis of misreadings in dyslexia has focused on the cognitive interpretation of errors characterized by the production of a single, isolated response, while multiple utterances "*such as circumlocutions, self-corrections and multiple responses*" did not interest researchers in part because they "*do not occur with great frequency*" (Coltheart, 1980) and in part because they do not easily fit in the cognitive category framework. However, hesitations and repetitions are time-consuming and may be responsible for a large portion of the characteristic slowing reported for dyslexic readers in regular orthographies (Italian: Zoccolotti et al., 1999; German: Wimmer, 1993). Indeed, it has been observed that children learning regular orthographies rarely make "classical" substitution errors and more often produce a slow and fragmented approach to the target word (Bakker, 1992). Hendriks and Kolk (1997) referred to this as "*sounding out behaviour*" to mark reliance on phonologically recoding the target; this is referred to as a reading behavior (rather than error) because, by the end of the process, the child is often able to utter the target correctly. Recently, we confirmed that many of the mispronunciations of Italian children with dyslexia are due to sounding-out behavior, which discriminates them from skilled readers (Trenta et al., 2013). Although Fairbanks is not explicit in his description of hesitations, they seem to resemble the time-consuming errors described by Bakker (1992) or the sounding-out behavior posited by Hendriks and Kolk (1997).

Going back to the eye-voice-lead question, Fairbanks emphasized the role of linguistic factors (such as word scarcity) vs. spatial factors (such as stimulus position). Furthermore, *he* noted that "*since one of the most obvious effects of difficulty in poor oral reading is hesitation of the voice, it appears that this is the cause of increase in eye-voice lead*", and concluded that "*the amount of eye-voice lead is expressive of the combination of important factors involved in reading. It is a measure of the rate of recognition and assimilation.*" In the contrast between single and multiple word processing referred to above, we propose that a comparatively wide eye-voice lead should be taken as indication of the ability to integrate several sub-components of reading.

We have given particular space to the work of Fairbanks (1937) because it represents a very special case of a study in which an explicit attempt was made to cross-analyse the interplay between several sub-components of reading in both good and poor readers. After this pioneering period, interest in the vocal component of reading was seldom shown by eye movement research (for an exception see Morton, 1964), which relied almost completely on silent reading measures. Indeed, interest moved to perceptual or linguistic manipulations of written texts to determine the laws of eye movement control during reading, perceptual span and other topics related to cognitive processing during reading (for a review, see Rayner, 2009).

Consequently, research on eye-voice lead (or span) became rare. Some authors measured eye movements during oral reading by focusing on lexical processes and reading comprehension (Levin, 1979; Levy-Schoen, 1981). Inhoff et al. (2011) investigated the eye-voice span with the aim of refining models of eye movement control involved in reading aloud. Very recently, Pan et al. (2013) extended the study of the eye-voice lead to the multiple naming conditions typical of the RAN paradigm.

In the present study, we extended the early observations of Buswell (1921) and Fairbanks (1937) in measuring the eye-voice lead in Italian dyslexic readers and age-matched controls while they read aloud a meaningful text. By measuring eye movements and voice parameters together, we aimed to decompose the various reading sub-components to investigate which ones are more or less compromised in dyslexic readers. We also aimed to evaluate whether the integration of these multiple subcomponents contributes to generating the slowed reading that is found in children learning to read in regular orthographies (e.g., Wimmer, 1993; Zoccolotti et al., 1999). As a control condition, we also recorded eye movements during the silent reading of a text to evaluate the time advantage of silent over aloud reading.

As to eye movements, based on previous research in Italian children (De Luca et al., 1999, 2002) we expected to find problems associated with the number and duration of fixations. The distribution of fixation durations might be interesting in view of the temporal sampling framework (Goswami, 2011). Transposing Goswami's theory to the visual domain, we explored whether impaired low-frequency oscillatory mechanisms, which are important for mediating syllable perception, also have an effect at the visual level that is, on fixations in the same frequency range, with time durations of approximately 200 ms.

As to the vocal components, previous research indicates that articulation times are minimally affected in single word presentation in children with dyslexia (Davies et al., 2013; Martelli et al., 2013); however, no information is yet available on the articulation times of words immersed in a meaningful text, which was one of the aims of the present study. Finally, we also examined reading accuracy. In view of Fairbanks's (1937) observations, we focussed on sounding out behavior and pauses (which are time-consuming behaviors) in addition to classical substitution errors.

MATERIALS AND METHODS

PARTICIPANTS

Participants included 16 dyslexic readers and 16 chronological age-matched control readers. The school where participants were enrolled collected written informed consent provided by each student's family, as part of an agreement between the school and the Sapienza University of Rome. Groups were comparable for age, gender, and non-verbal IQ level (see **Table 1**). Each of the dyslexic readers scored at least 1.65 *SD* below the norm for either speed or accuracy on a standardized reading test (MT Reading test, Cornoldi and Colpo, 1995). In this test, the child reads a text

Table 1 | Summary statistics for the two groups of participants: mean age (in years, with range in square brackets); number of female and male participants; mean *z*-scores (and *SD* in parentheses) on Raven's Colored Matrices; mean reading times and mean number of errors on the MT Reading test; mean *z*-scores for reading time and accuracy on the same test.

	Dyslexic readers		Control readers		*p*-level
Age	11.9	[11.3–12.9]	11.6	[11.1–13.4]	n.s.
Males/females	9/7		10/6		n.s.
Raven test	−0.7	(0.6)	−0.3	(1.0)	n.s.
Reading time (s/syllable)	0.43	(0.14)	0.22	(0.02)	<0.001
Reading accuracy (number of errors)	22.5	(7.9)	4.7	(2.6)	<0.001
Reading time (*Z* score)	−2.3	(1.6)	0.2	(0.3)	<0.001
Reading accuracy (*Z* score)	−3.4	(1.8)	0.2	(0.5)	<0.001

Probability values for t-tests (except for gender, for which the Chi square test was used) comparisons between the two groups are reported ($p < 0.01$ values are considered significant after Bonferroni correction).

passage aloud with a 4-min time limit; reading time (s/syllable) and accuracy (number of errors, adjusted for the amount of text read) are scored (see **Table 1** for both raw and normalized values). Considering the reading speed raw data, the average reading time of the two groups was 0.22 (typically developing readers) and 0.43 s/syllable (children with dyslexia). This indicates slowing with a factor of 1.95 (below see further comments on this ratio). Non-verbal IQ level was assessed using Raven's Colored Progressive Matrices. All children scored well within the normal limits according to Italian norms (Pruneti et al., 1996). All participants had normal or corrected-to-normal visual acuity.

APPARATUS AND PROCEDURE

Eye movements from the dominant eye were recorded in binocular vision via an SR Research Ltd. Eye Link 1000 eye tracker (SR Research Ltd., Mississauga, Ontario, Canada) sampling at 1000 Hz, with spatial resolution of less than 0.04°. Head movements were avoided by using a headrest, but the chin was left free. The text was displayed on a 17″ CRT monitor at a viewing distance of approximately 57 cm. Screen resolution was 1024 × 768; refresh rate was 85 Hz. The ambient illumination level was kept constant across recordings by artificial lighting. A nine-point calibration procedure was run before the passage was shown. The calibration targets were presented randomly in different positions on the screen. Appearance of the text on the screen was triggered by fixation of a cross in the upper left position corresponding to the blank space adjacent to the initial letter of the passage.

Voice was digitally recorded by a system mounting a Shure microphone, a pre-amplifier, an E-MU sound card, and an ASIO driver, which was interfaced to the eye tracker by Eye Link Experiment Builder software.

Separately for each participant, eye movements and voice utterances were simultaneously recorded and stored in the same PC directory; the output consisted of two parallel recordings: an eye movement dataset and a sound file in wav format. Eye movements and audio recordings were synchronized by the eye-tracking device after eye-movement calibration. The voice-line recording onset and offset was automatically overlaid on the timeline of the eye movements recording output.

MATERIALS

Two text passages were used, one for reading aloud and one for silent reading; both were adapted from Aesop's fables and were appropriate for the age range of the observers. Each text subtended a visual angle of 22 × 13°, displayed at the center of the screen horizontally and at 5° from the top edge of the screen vertically. Passages were written in Times New Roman font (because it is similar to functional reading texts), with black letters on a white background. Average center-to-center letter distance subtended 0.4°. The two texts had the same number of lines (14) and were also matched for number of syllables and characters; finally, the content words of the two passages had comparable mean word frequency. The first line of both texts contained a filler sentence (ending with a full stop), which was not used in the analyses.

Only the three-line sentence, from the second to the fourth line of the text, for reading aloud was used for in-depth analyses of eye and voice parameters and will be described in detail. It contained 31 words (on average 10.3 words per line) and 173 letters (inter-word spaces included). Average word length was 4.6 letters. The mean log frequency of the words was 3.02 (range 0.7–4.9), according to a corpus of the Italian written language of 3,798,275 occurrences (CoLFIS; Bertinetto et al., 2005).

The order of the reading condition was randomized across participants. A cross was displayed in the upper-left quadrant of the screen (2° to the left of the first letter of the first text line) and served as the initial fixation target; the offset of the cross and the simultaneous onset of the display containing the passage was automatically triggered by the eye-tracking device when the participant steadily fixated the cross for at least 150 ms. Participants were asked to read each passage at their normal rate; in the reading aloud condition, the passage remained on the screen until the end of the last word uttered. To reliably assess the last fixation of silent reading, participants had to look at a two-figure number immediately after they finished reading, name the number aloud, and communicate that they had finished reading. The number subtended 0.25° and was displayed in the bottom right corner of the screen. To evaluate general comprehension, at the end of the reading participants were asked to answer questions; there was a yes/no question and an open question for each of the two text passages.

DATA ANALYSIS

Eye movements

Eye movement data were processed using the EyeLink Data Viewer software (SR Research Ltd., Mississauga, Ontario, Canada). Total viewing time (i.e., time needed to visually examine the text, from the beginning of the first fixation until the end of the last fixation) was computed for the whole passage (13 lines) for both oral and silent reading conditions. Only the above-mentioned three-line sentence of the reading aloud text was analyzed in detail: Besides total viewing time, total fixation time (i.e., the sum of all fixation durations), total number of fixations, mean fixation duration, forward saccade mean amplitude (in degrees of visual angle) and percentage of regressions were measured; fixation positions were mapped over the screenshot of the three-line sentence to determine which graphemes in the passage were fixated.

Audio tracks

Audio recordings were processed off-line using Audacity 2.0.2 software. The temporal onsets and offsets of utterances and the silent pauses were marked along the timeline interface of each audio file for the three-line sentence using a mixed criterion of visual inspection of the waveform image and listening to the audio track (the minimum duration for a pause to be reliably detected combining visual and audio information was 40 ms). In fluent readings, between-word pauses were rare; the final and initial phonemes of consecutive word utterances merged due to co-articulation.

Correct utterances, misreadings, and pauses between and within words were identified and labeled along the file timeline.

Total reading aloud time, total pronunciation time (i.e., the sum of utterances excluding pauses and including all kinds of misreadings), total duration of pauses (the sum of the durations of all silent pauses), mean duration of single silent pauses, number of silent pauses, and mean utterance duration for correctly read content words were scored (errors as well as sounding-out were excluded) for the three line sentence. Moreover, total reading aloud time was also computed for the whole text.

Accuracy was scored by considering the following categories of errors: sounding-out behavior (i.e., progressive approximation toward the correct utterance of the whole word made through sounding-out parts of the word; e.g., ['ta 'tavolo] instead of ['tavolo], "table"), word substitutions, word omissions or insertions and non-word production.

Eye-voice lead

The eye-voice lead was measured by detecting the within-word uttered phoneme for each fixation point in the first three lines of text. The lead was measured as the spatial distance, namely, number of letters, between the fixated grapheme and the simultaneously uttered phoneme. The single letter (grapheme) was chosen as the spatial unit (inter-word spaces counted as one letter). Each letter (and inter-word space) of the three-line sentence was progressively numbered from 1 to 173. Consistently, phoneme positions were progressively numbered along with the printed letters. Because of the transparency of the Italian writing system, there was a 1:1 correspondence between the number of graphemes and phonemes for 27 out of 31 words; three of the remaining four items had a number of phonemes equal to N–1 with respect to the corresponding printed word, and one had N–2 phonemes.

Then, each gaze position (i.e., fixation on a grapheme) was matched with the "voice position," that is, the phoneme uttered at the temporal onset of fixation. This was carried out by identifying the graphemes that were fixated on the eye movement output (see **Figure 1A**) and the phonemes that were simultaneously uttered (at each fixation onset) in the sound file output (see **Figure 1B**). For each of the fixation points, the corresponding grapheme position (number) was computed. Then, the phoneme uttered simultaneously with fixation onset (as determined by the time line of the recording) was "anchored" to the fixated grapheme (see red arrows in **Figure 1**) so that pairs of *grapheme position number* and *phoneme position number* were obtained for all fixations made during reading (N fixations = N pairs).

The eye-voice lead was measured at each fixation point as the difference between phoneme and grapheme positions in space (namely, difference between simultaneous phoneme and grapheme numbers). The individual eye-voice lead (across the three-line sentence) was measured in two ways: first, by averaging the difference values across the grapheme-phoneme pairs; second, by subtraction of the intercept values of the voice from the eye regression lines.

Statistical comparisons

Comparing groups with generally different performances by standard parametric analyses is problematic because groups may show systematic differences in variability (thus, violating the assumption of homogeneity of variance). However, it is generally believed that ANOVAs or Student *t*s are sufficiently robust comparisons for moderate violations of homogeneity. Therefore, *t*-tests for independent samples were run for all group comparisons and the Bonferroni correction was adopted for multiple comparisons.

To evaluate which variables contributed (and how much) to the impaired performance of the dyslexic children, standardized (i.e., Cohen's *d*) and unstandardized (i.e., ratio) effect sizes were computed. The first ones convey the size of an effect relative to the variability in the samples. Reference points for small, medium, and large effects are considered 0.20, 0.50, and 0.80, respectively. However, also unstandardized measures, such as ratios, are of particular interest because they allow comparing performances in proportional terms across conditions (and groups) showing very different variability. To this aim, the mean values of the dyslexic children were divided by the values of the control readers to obtain the ratios (except in the case of forward saccades amplitude, where the inverted ratio was calculated). In all cases, ratios greater than 1 indicate that dyslexic readers performed worse.

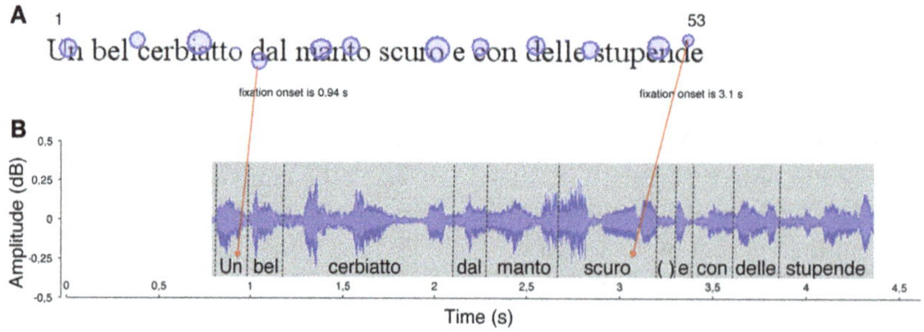

FIGURE 1 | An example of the method used to measure the eye-voice lead is reported for a typically developing reader. (A) In the spatial overlay of the eye movement pattern, the circles represent the localizations of eye fixations over the first line of the sentence. The size of the circles is proportional to fixation duration. The numbers 1 and 53 represent (for example) the first and last labels for letter position number in the line. The onset time of two fixations is indicated. **(B)** The waveform of reading aloud is shown as a function of time. The vertical dotted segments delimit the single word utterances, labeled along the timeline. Red arrows indicate the temporal correspondence between a fixation (the grapheme "d," of the word "dal," letter number 18) and the phoneme that was uttered at the time of fixation (the phoneme/u/, letter number 1). Each fixation (e.g., "d," of the word "stupende," number 52) was linked to the phoneme uttered at the moment of fixation onset (the phoneme /o/ of the word "scuro," number 32). The eye-voice lead was obtained by subtracting the phoneme position number from the grapheme position number for all of the grapheme-phoneme pairs (in the latter example: 52–32 = 20 letters).

Pearson correlations were run between eye-voice lead data and MT Reading Test, eye, and voice parameters for the whole group of children.

RESULTS

READING PERFORMANCE: VOICE DATA

The data based on the audio tracks are presented in **Table 2**. Total reading aloud time was significantly longer for dyslexic than control readers for both the three-line sentence and the total text (with similar ratios of about 2). Total pronunciation time (i.e., time excluding pauses) also distinguished the two groups, but with a lower ratio (1.4). For all these measures, *d* values greatly exceeded the reference for a large effect (0.80).

Utterance duration of single words (for content words correctly pronounced in the three-line sentence) was 119 ms slower in dyslexic with respect to control readers; notably, this effect was highly significant even though it indicated only a quantitatively modest 20% slowing (ratio = 1.2). When we restricted the computation to those words that were correctly pronounced by all children in the two groups, the difference was still present; thus, dyslexic readers needed 655 ms ($SD = 66$ ms) and control readers, 575 ms ($SD = 83$ ms); the 80 ms difference was highly significant ($t = 3.02$, $p < 0.01$) but again indicated a rather small effect (ratio = 1.1). Note that although the ratio was low, the standardized effect size for this measure was considerably higher and above the cut-off of 0.80 for a large effect size (see **Table 2**).

The children with dyslexia made many more pauses (ratio 4.5) and spent much more time in silence (with a 7.1 ratio for total duration of pauses) than control readers. Mean pause duration was slightly longer in dyslexic readers (this comparison just failed to be significant after Bonferroni correction). The frequency by duration of pauses distribution in the two groups is presented in **Figure 2**. The mode of the distribution was the 350–450 ms interval for control readers; the distribution was more complex for dyslexic readers, with two peaks at 40–150 ms and 450–550 ms (**Figure 2A**) and a third peak at very long intervals (**Figure 2B**; note the different interval scale).

Comments

When overall reading aloud time was considered, there was a remarkable group difference (90% or 1.9 ratio) in the time taken to read the three-line sentence. Notably, the same ratio was obtained in the MT Test reading time measure (1.9; based on data from **Table 1**). A very similar figure was reported by Martelli and co-workers who averaged six different studies (Martelli et al., 2013). Overall, a factor of 2.0 can be considered as a reference point to interpret reading time data as well as other reading parameters.

A quantitatively small (20% or 1.2 ratio), but highly significant, difference was present for pronunciation time of correctly read single words. Notably, all misreadings were excluded from these computations; therefore, the small lengthening in voice

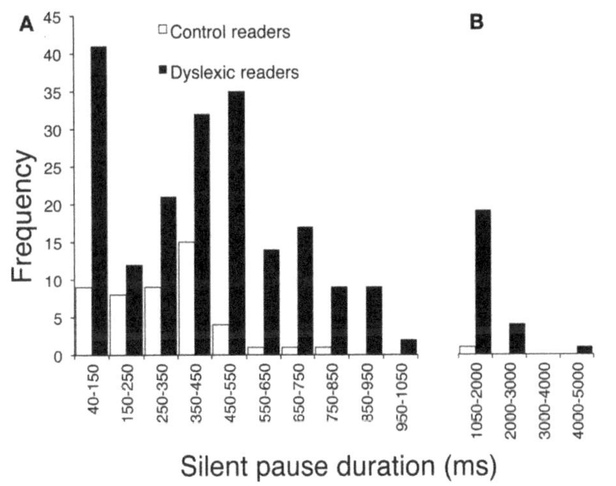

FIGURE 2 | Distribution of frequency for pause durations, separately for children with dyslexia and typically developing readers. (A) Intervals on the abscissa by 100 ms each (except for the first one, which ranges from 40 to 150 ms). **(B)** Intervals by 1000 ms each.

Table 2 | Group results for reading aloud data based on the audio tracks.

	Dyslexic readers		Control readers				
	Mean	***SD***	**Mean**	***SD***	***t***	**ratio**	***d***
Total reading aloud time	113.6	31.8	60.2	5.6	6.46	1.9	2.3
Total reading aloud time	22.1	7.4	11.4	1.5	5.67	1.9	2.0
Total pronunciation time	14.6	2.3	10.3	0.9	6.82	1.4	2.5
Mean single word utterance duration	0.608	0.054	0.489	0.046	6.76	1.2	2.4
Total duration of silent pauses	7.5	6.3	1.1	0.8	4.07	7.1	1.4
Mean duration of silent pauses	0.539	0.208	0.363	0.131	2.88*	1.5	1.0
Number of silent pauses	13.5	5.9	3.0	1.9	6.74	4.5	2.4

*The first row refers to the full passage (13 lines); the remaining rows to the three-line sentence. Time measures are reported in seconds. Total reading aloud time goes from the beginning of the first utterance to the last pronunciation (pauses and misreadings included). Total pronunciation time is the sum of the duration of all utterances (pauses excluded). The mean pronunciation time was computed for correctly uttered content words. Total duration of silent pauses is the sum of the durations of periods in which no utterance was made. Means and SDs are reported. T and probability values for statistical comparisons between groups ($p < 0.006$ is considered significant after Bonferroni correction) and ratios between the mean values of the two groups are also reported. All p's < 0.001, except * = 0.007.*

utterance must be taken as genuine. Furthermore, the difference remained when the computation was restricted to the words that were correctly articulated by all children, indicating that the effect on articulation times did not depend on differences in the actual words uttered. Interestingly, individual variability in utterance duration was very low and not different in the two groups of children. This is partially in keeping with the idea that execution times yield smaller individual differences than cognitive times; furthermore, execution times are assumed as a constant in models of decision processing (e.g., *difference engine model* by Myerson et al., 2003). Notably, a considerable difference was detected between unstandardized (ratio) and standardized effect sizes. Thus, the ratio indicated a very small group difference, whereas the standardized measure of effect size (due to the very low variability) indicated a very large group effect for this parameter ($d = 2.4$).

Finally, dyslexic children spent much more time in silent pauses than control readers. This effect was due to a large difference in the number of pauses and a smaller difference in terms of pause length. However, as shown in **Figure 2**, very long pauses were present only in the dyslexic readers. When total pronunciation time without pauses was considered, the ratio between the two groups was considerably smaller (1.40). Thus, frequent and long pauses represent an important characteristic of reading in dyslexia.

READING PERFORMANCE: ACCURACY AND COMPREHENSION

Table 3 reports the percentages of misreadings for the two groups of children. More than half of the inaccurate utterances in both groups indicated sounding-out behaviors. Notably, dyslexic children engaged in this behavior nearly in 10% of cases. They also made few word substitutions (4.4%) and rare omissions or insertions of words (0.8%); in a few instances, their productions resulted in non-words (0.8%). Controls engaged in a much smaller proportion of sounding-out behaviors and made fewer word substitutions and never omitted or inserted a word; furthermore, they never produced a non-word. Effect sizes (whether unstandardized or standardized) were all very large, particularly in the case of sounding-out behavior (i.e., dyslexic readers engaged in this behavior nearly six times more than control readers).

At the end of the reading task, both groups responded correctly to the open and closed questions: 15 out of 16 typically developing children responded well to the open question and 13 to the closed question. The figures were 14 (out of 16) and 15 in the case of dyslexic children. In silent reading, results were quite similar: 14 control readers responded well to the open question and 10 to the closed question. The figures were 14 (out of 16) and 12 in the case of dyslexic readers.

Comments

Misreadings mostly indicated a halting, but effective (i.e., eventually leading to correct pronunciation), approach to the target words (sounding-out behavior). This occurred much more often in dyslexic than control readers (i.e., almost six times more often). These data confirm the predominance of time-consuming errors recently reported in Italian dyslexic children (Trenta et al., 2013). Surprisingly, this ratio is quite similar to the one originally observed by Fairbanks (1937) in English-speaking children; in that study, poor readers made 5.6 more hesitations than good readers (i.e., 8.87 vs. 1.56%).

Word substitution errors also discriminated between the two groups but were relatively few in absolute terms, confirming previous observations in regular orthographies (Wimmer, 1993; Zoccolotti et al., 1999).

Finally, in agreement with previous data collected in silent reading conditions (De Luca et al., 1999), the slow and inaccurate reading of dyslexic children did not prevent adequate text comprehension.

EYE MOVEMENTS DURING READING

Representative eye movement patterns of children with mild and severe dyslexia are presented in **Figures 3B,C**, respectively; the high number of fixations is evident with respect to performance of a typically developing reader (**Figure 3A**).

Table 4 reports eye movement results for dyslexic and control readers.

The first part of the table reports total viewing time for the whole passage read aloud and that read silently. Both groups of children spent less time scanning the text when reading silently than when reading aloud (dyslexic readers: $t = 2.20$, $p < 0.01$; control readers: $t = 4.41$, $p < 0.001$). In absolute values, the

Table 3 | Group results for misreadings.

	Dyslexic readers		Control readers				
	Mean	*SD*	Mean	*SD*	*t*	ratio	*d*
Sounding-out behaviors (%)	9.5	4.8	1.6	2.0	5.90	5.9	2.15
Word substitutions (%)	4.4	3.7	1.2	2.3	2.95	3.7	1.04
Word omission or insertion (%)	0.8	1.4	0.0	0.0	–	–	–
Non-word production (%)	0.8	1.4	0.0	0.0	–	–	–
Total errors (%)	15.5	7.7	2.8	3.3	6.09	5.5	2.14

Both the percentage of total errors (last row) and the percentages for each category of misreadings (sounding-out behavior, word substitution, word omission or insertion, and non-word production) are presented. The percentages are calculated with respect to the total number of words in the three-line sentence. Means and SDs are reported. T-test comparisons between groups ($p < 0.017$ is considered significant after Bonferroni correction) and the ratios between values of the two groups are also reported. All p's at least < 0.01.

difference was greater in dyslexic children (22.3 s) than in control readers (10.5 s); however, the ratio between aloud and silent reading was quite similar in the two groups (dyslexic children = 1.24; control readers = 1.21). Also, the ratio between the two groups for viewing time was similar for reading aloud (1.9) and silent reading (1.8). Standardized effects were very large (over 2) and similar for aloud and silent reading.

The second part of **Table 4** reports eye movement results measured in greater depth for reading aloud the three-line sentence. Total viewing time data are consistent with those of the whole passage. Dyslexic readers showed a significantly higher number of fixations and a higher percentage of regressions and smaller forward saccade amplitude with respect to control readers. No significant difference was detected for fixation duration. The distribution of fixation durations for the two groups of children is presented in **Figure 4**: note that the two groups show a very similar number of short fixations (<100 ms), while the number of longer fixations is higher for dyslexic children and highest in the 175–225 ms time interval.

Ratios between the two groups were close to a factor of 2.0 for number of fixations and percentage of regressions and were lower for fixation duration and saccade amplitude. The *d* values were all above the critical value for a large effect, apart from mean fixation duration.

Comments

Both groups of children had longer viewing times when reading aloud than when reading silently. The group differences were quantitatively more marked in the former case but were proportionally constant across the two conditions, i.e., the children with

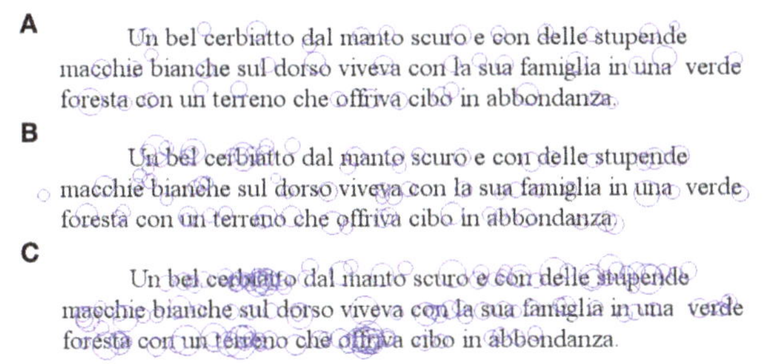

FIGURE 3 | Spatial overlay of the eye movement pattern during reading of the three-line sentence. Fixation points (circles) are indicated for a typically developing reader **(A)**, for a child with mild dyslexia **(B)** and a child with severe dyslexia **(C)**.

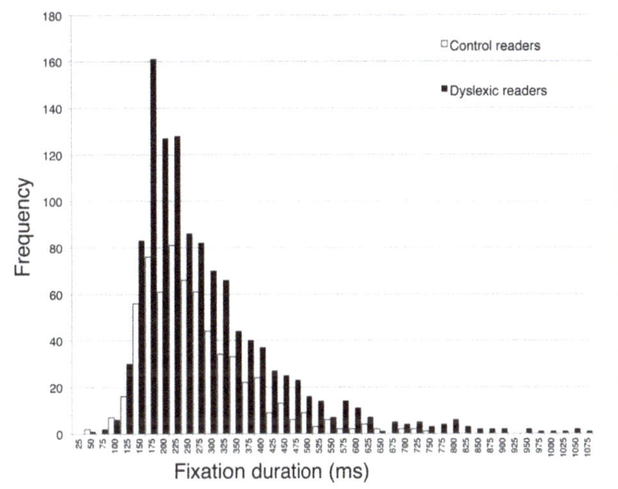

FIGURE 4 | Distribution of frequency for fixation duration, separately for dyslexic and control readers. Intervals on the abscissa by 25 ms each.

Table 4 | Group results for eye movement data.

	Dyslexic readers		Control readers				
	Mean	***SD***	**Mean**	***SD***	***t***	**ratio**	***d***
Total viewing time—aloud	114.1	32.0	60.5	5.5	6.60	1.9	2.3
Total viewing time—silent	91.8	25.1	50.0	7.8	6.34	1.8	2.2
Total viewing time	22.5	7.8	11.5	1.4	5.52	2.0	2.0
Total fixation time	20.7	7.3	10.4	1.2	5.52	2.0	2.0
Number of fixations	72.2	20.9	39.9	5.7	5.95	1.8	2.1
Mean fixation duration	0.29	0.04	0.263	0.026	1.86*	1.1	0.6
Forward saccades mean amplitude	1.68	0.30	2.02	0.24	3.50	1.2	1.2
Percentage of regressions	27.7	5.8	15.1	8.7	4.82	1.8	1.7

*The top part of the table refers to the full passage (13 lines) separately for aloud and silent reading, the bottom to the three-line sentence for reading aloud. Time is reported in seconds, saccade amplitude in degrees. Total viewing time indicates the time starting from the first fixation and ending with the last fixation. Total fixation time was the sum of all discrete fixation durations. Number of fixations includes all fixations (i.e., both first and second pass fixations). Mean fixation duration is the average of all discrete fixations that lasted more than 100 ms. Saccade amplitude is averaged across all rightward saccades, except for small corrective saccades occurring during the return sweeps. Means and SDs are reported. As for between- group comparisons, t-values are reported (p < 0.007 is considered significant after Bonferroni correction). The last column reports the ratio between the means of the two groups. The values of children with dyslexia were divided for the values of typically developing readers to obtain the ratios, except in the case of forward saccades amplitude, where the inverted ratio was calculated. In all cases, ratios greater than 1 indicate worse performance of children with dyslexia. All p's < 0.001, except * (n.s.).*

dyslexia were slower than typically developing readers by about a factor of 2 for reading aloud as well as for silent reading. In general, these data confirm well-known observations (e.g., Anderson and Swanson, 1937), but the authors focussed on absolute rather than proportional effects. This indicates a basic problem in analysing reading data. Whenever manipulations of the task (such as, here, reading aloud vs. silent reading) produce an increase in the time necessary to perform the task, group differences also increase; thus, absolute differences in performance change while proportional differences remain stable. Possible interpretations of this pattern of findings will be examined in the Discussion (see below).

As to the pattern of eye movements, children with dyslexia showed a slow and fragmented reading pattern characterized by many fixations, smaller forward saccade amplitude and a higher percentage of regressions with respect to typically developing readers. By contrast, there was a non-significant difference in mean fixation duration between the two groups. Using 200 ms as a standard temporal fixation threshold (Salthouse and Ellis, 1980), **Figure 4** shows that frequency of fixations around this temporal window was particularly high in dyslexic children. Ratios indicate that number of fixations and percentage of regressions were the parameters that distinguished most clearly between the two groups (with values close to the 2-ratio reference), whereas lower ratios emerged for fixation duration and saccade amplitude. Therefore, it seems that the main difference in eye movements between the two groups of children is related to number of movements rather than saccade amplitude or fixation duration.

EYE-VOICE LEAD

Figure 5 illustrates data for a control reader (left) and a child with mild dyslexia (right), respectively. A third example (**Figure 6**) reports data of a particularly severe case of dyslexia.

In the upper plots, the position numbers of the fixated grapheme/uttered phoneme pairs are plotted as a function of time for the three lines of text: filled circles refer to eye fixation data (referred to as "eye") and open triangles to the corresponding utterance data (referred to as "voice"). The ordinate axis reports the spatial position as number of letters. Note that eye data are always above voice data, indicating the leading of the eye.

Two regression lines are drawn separately for the fixation and utterance data; they allow computing the eye-voice lead independent of local variability at specific points of the text. Reading rate is marked by the slopes of the regression lines for both eye and voice data. Slopes are higher for the skilled reader (**Figure 5A**) than the child with mild dyslexia (**Figure 5B**) and the severe case of dyslexia (**Figure 6A**).

In all upper graphs, voice pauses can be detected where consecutive voice data points (triangles) align parallel to the abscissa. This is rare in skilled readers but clearer in dyslexic readers; one very long pause made by the child with severe dyslexia is highlighted in inset of **Figure 6C**. Note the multiple fixations (most of which followed rightward saccades) that characterized the scanning of the word "stupende" ("wonderful") by the child while he silently analyzed the text.

The eye-voice lead measured at each fixation point as the difference between phoneme and grapheme positions in space is

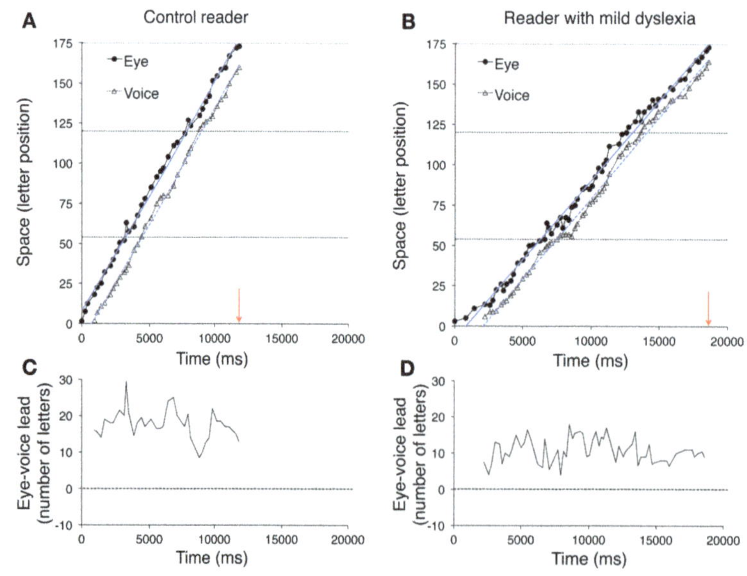

FIGURE 5 | The pairs of fixated grapheme/uttered phoneme positions are plotted as a function of time for a typically developing reader (A) and a child with mild dyslexia (B). The horizontal dashed lines represent the end of the first, second and third line of the sentence, from bottom to top, respectively. The arrows on the abscissa indicate the overall time necessary to read the three lines for each reader. Filled circles and open triangles represent fixations (i.e., eye position data) and utterances (i.e., voice position data), respectively. The ordinate reports the spatial position measured in number of letters (range: 1–173). The vertical space between simultaneous graphemes and phonemes expresses the eye-voice lead as a function of time. Eye and voice positions are fit by regression lines whose slopes indicate the reading rate, separately derived from eye movements and utterances. The intercepts on the ordinate axis (not visible in the figure because the negative part of the axes is not shown) may be used to compute the overall eye-voice lead. In plots **(C,D)**, the eye-voice lead is represented as a function of time as letter difference between pairs of simultaneous grapheme and phoneme positions.

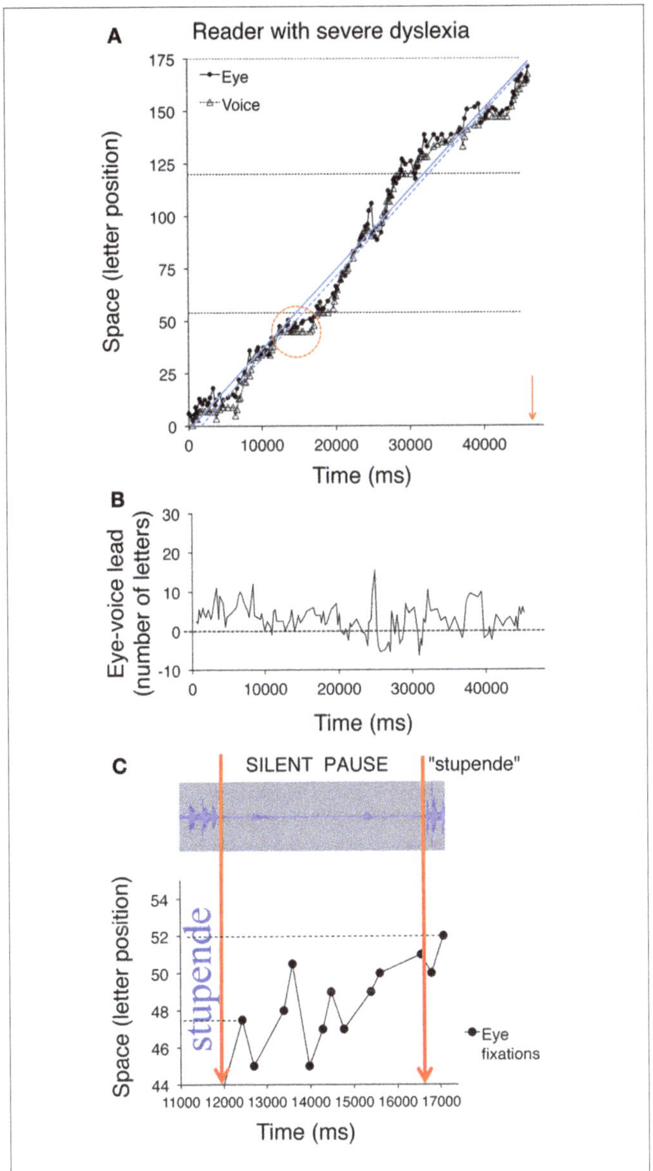

FIGURE 6 | Eye and voice data are presented for a child with severe dyslexia. Similar to **Figures 5A,B**, the pairs of fixated grapheme/uttered phoneme positions are plotted as a function of time in panel **(A)**. Note that the scale on the abscissa of panel **(A)** is twice that of **Figures 5A,B**, therefore the slope indicates a much slower reading rate than that of the child with mild dyslexia represented in **Figure 5B**. In panel **(B)** (as in **Figures 5C,D**) the eye-voice lead is represented as a function of time as letter difference between pairs of simultaneous grapheme and phoneme positions. The **(C)** inset (obtained by zooming on the marked area of plot **A**) represents a long silent pause made by the child, during which eye fixation scanning is characterized by eight rightward saccades and three regressions in the word "stupende" (English translation: "wonderful") before pronouncing it. The top part of the inset represents the spectral image of the audio track corresponding to the time interval represented in the bottom part, which corresponds to the pattern of fixations made on the word. Note that both the second and the fifth fixations (at letter position number 45) follow a regressive eye movement that brings the gaze to the inter-word blank space.

presented as a function of time in the lower graphs of **Figure 5** and the middle graph of **Figure 6**. Note that all values are positive, indicating that pronunciation of a word started after it had been visually inspected. Occasionally, however, in severe cases of dyslexia (including the one presented in **Figure 6**) there are also negative values. This occurred when the reader completed the utterance of a word while his gaze turned backward (second pass reading) to previously fixated portions of text.

Table 5 reports individual and group data for the slopes of eye movements and voice and the eye-voice lead. The eye slope was almost equal to the voice slope in all participants.

The mean eye-voice lead measured by averaging the differences between gaze and voice (as in **Figures 5C,D**, **6B**) was significantly smaller in dyslexic (7.9 letters) than in control (13.8 letters) readers. Computing the eye-voice lead based on the difference between the intercepts of the regression lines produced very similar results: the eye-voice lead was significantly smaller in dyslexic children (8.4 letters) than in control readers (14.0 letters). Note that intra-individual variability (as assessed by the averaged eye-voice position) was similar in the two groups.

Comments

For all individuals in both groups, the values of the slope of the regression lines separately fitting the eye data and the voice data were almost equal (thus, the lines are parallel in all cases). This indicates that, regardless of reading skill, eyes and voice proceeded in synchrony, with a pacing which, despite local variability at specific points of the text (such as in the case of pauses) was kept relatively constant across lines of text. The voice lead showed a ratio between dyslexic and control readers (i.e., 1.7) in line with other key parameters, such as total reading time.

In good readers, the eye and voice regression lines were well spaced (about 14 letters or 5.6° of visual angle on the screen); by contrast, the distance was short in dyslexic children (about 8 letters or 3.2°). Thus, in dyslexic readers, the spatial distance between the uttered phoneme and the fixated grapheme was closer (about half in terms of number of letters or degrees) than in skilled readers. Notably in dyslexic readers the overall processing time of the same three lines (i.e., 22.1 s) was about twice that of control readers (11.4 s). Thus, the time by space product was almost constant in the two groups.

EYE-VOICE LEAD: CORRELATION WITH EYE AND VOICE DATA

Correlations between eye-voice lead and eye and voice parameters as well as performance on the MT reading test are reported in **Table 6** for the whole group of children; after Bonferroni correction, correlations with $p < 0.003$ are considered significant. The eye-voice lead correlated highly with reading time and accuracy in the MT test. As for voice data, the eye-voice lead correlated highly with total reading aloud and total pronunciation time. Correlation with mean word utterance duration was also significant. Furthermore, eye-voice lead correlated highly with the number of pauses and their summed duration but only marginally with the mean duration of a single pause. As for eye data, correlation was high with viewing times, number of fixations, total fixation time and percentage of regressions, but was lower, and non-significant, with mean fixation duration and amplitude of rightward saccades.

Moreover, correlations were calculated considering silent reading of the whole text. The total viewing time for aloud reading was highly correlated with that for silent reading ($r = 0.85$,

Table 5 | Eye-voice lead: mean individual data and group results.

	Reading rate (letters/s)		Eye-voice lead (number of letters)		
	Eye slope	**Voice slope**	**Averaged eye-voice position differences**	***SD***	**Intercepts difference**
D1	10.0	10.0	10.7	3.4	11.2
D2	8.2	8.2	9.8	4.7	10.6
D3	9.1	9.1	9.6	4.6	10.2
D4	9.2	9.3	8.9	5.4	9.5
D5	10.3	9.9	11.2	4.7	9.0
D6	11.0	11.0	9.0	4.3	8.8
D7	8.4	8.4	8.0	4.2	8.6
D8	6.2	6.3	7.1	3.0	8.6
D9	10.4	10.4	8.1	5.1	8.3
D10	9.6	9.7	7.5	4.1	8.1
D11	11.6	11.7	6.9	3.6	7.8
D12	9.3	9.3	7.6	4.0	7.6
D13	6.3	6.5	7.1	4.2	9.1
D14	5.7	5.7	7.5	4.1	7.4
D15	6.7	6.7	4.9	2.8	5.1
D16	3.8	3.9	3.0	4.0	4.7
Dyslexic readers mean	**8.5**	**8.5**	**7.9**		**8.4**
SD	**2.2**	**2.1**	**2.1**		**1.7**
C1	17.9	18.4	16.5	4.8	19.3
C2	14.1	14.2	19.1	4.7	19.2
C3	14.4	14.5	17.7	4.0	18.4
C4	18.4	18.4	16.7	4.5	16.8
C5	18.0	17.9	16.9	4.2	16.4
C6	15.8	16.0	13.3	5.5	14.8
C7	18.2	18.1	15.2	5.5	14.4
C8	14.5	14.7	12.2	4.7	14.0
C9	16.5	16.2	15.4	4.5	13.8
C10	17.9	18.2	12.1	4.3	13.6
C11	15.4	15.5	11.3	5.5	12.3
C12	14.3	14.3	12.1	3.8	11.9
C13	13.1	12.8	13.0	3.5	11.6
C14	11.8	11.8	9.7	4.5	9.7
C15	12.6	12.5	9.7	4.1	9.3
C16	12.4	12.4	9.5	2.9	9.3
Control readers mean	**15.3**	**15.4**	**13.8**		**14.0**
SD	**2.3**	**2.3**	**3.1**		**3.3**
t	**8.68**	**8.65**	**6.36**		**6.02**
Control/Dyslexic readers ratio	**1.8**	**1.8**	**1.7**		**1.7**

*The first two columns report the reading rate (i.e., the number of letters read per second) as measured by eye and voice slopes, respectively. The mean eye-voice lead, reported in the third column, was obtained by averaging subtraction values of voice position data from eye position data (as in **Figures 5C,D, 6B**); in the fifth column the lead is reported as the difference between the intercepts of the eye and voice regression lines. T values for statistical comparisons ($p < 0.012$ is considered significant after Bonferroni correction) and ratios between the values of the two groups are also reported. All p's < 0.001.*

Table 6 | Pearson correlations between the eye-voice lead (based on averaged eye-voice position differences) and various parameters of functional reading (MT Reading test), reading aloud, and eye movement data.

		Total sample
MT Reading Test	Reading time	−0.76
	Accuracy	−0.77
Voice data	Total reading aloud time (whole passage)	−0.78
	Total reading aloud time	−0.77
	Total pronunciation time	−0.73
	Mean word utterance duration	−0.61
	Total duration of silent pauses	−0.70
	Mean duration of silent pauses	−0.50*
	Number of silent pauses	−0.83
Eye data	Total viewing time (whole passage)	−0.78
	Total viewing time	−0.76
	Total fixation time	−0.76
	Number of fixations	−0.76
	Mean fixation duration	−0.37°
	Forward saccades mean amplitude	0.40°
	Percentage of regressions	−0.69

*The values of the r coefficient are marked for $p < 0.003$, considered significant after Bonferroni correction. Voice and eye data refer to the first three lines of text unless otherwise specified. All p's < 0.003, except for * = 0.003 and ° (n.s.).*

$p < 0.001$). Finally, the eye-voice lead in reading aloud was highly correlated with the total viewing time in silent reading ($r = -0.75, p < 0.001$).

Comments

The pattern of correlation indicated a close relationship between eye-voice lead and several reading parameters associated with speed and accuracy. A large eye-voice lead was closely associated with faster and more accurate reading as well as fewer regressions and nearly absent silent pauses; conversely, a small eye-voice lead was associated with slower and more inaccurate reading, many pauses and regressions. Notably, it is the number of fixations, as well as pauses that carries this relationship, whereas the mean duration of fixations and pauses showed much weaker or non-significant relationships. Finally, utterance duration was also related to the eye-voice lead; this may indicate that, however, small, changes in utterance duration mark individual differences associated with the overall ability to integrate the various sub-components of reading behavior.

Due to limitations in sample sizes, correlations were examined in the whole sample of children. In view of the general differences in performance between the two groups, this might have been expected to inflate the size of the correlations. Examining the pattern of correlation within each of the groups of children yielded quantitatively very similar results; however, it still remains to be verified in larger samples of dyslexic and control readers whether the pattern of correlations found separately holds for these two groups.

DISCUSSION

In this study, we jointly measured several voice and eye movement parameters. Thus, the results allow us to make a comprehensive description of the reading profile of dyslexic and control readers. In reading texts, dyslexic children were slower than control peers. This slowness was expressed in a large number of silent pauses and sounding-out behaviors as well as slightly longer word articulation times. In scanning the text, their eyes were ahead of their voice, but much less so than in skilled readers, indicating that word processing and utterance production were much closer in time than in skilled readers. Errors such as word substitutions and non-word productions were few but considerably more than in control readers, whose accuracy was nearly flawless.

In comparing group differences across different parameters, standard statistical tests were not highly informative. Indeed, as expected, dyslexic children were different from control readers in nearly all parameters. A shortcoming of standard parametric analyses is that they do not easily cope with the over-additivity effect that is present in comparisons across groups, which vary for some general processing ability (Faust et al., 1999); namely, independent of their specific task characteristics, more difficult conditions tend to produce greater group differences. Indeed, previous research on dyslexia has underscored the tendency toward proportional differences between dyslexic and control readers across a large spectrum of conditions and tasks (e.g., Paizi et al., 2011). This has been interpreted as due to a multiplicative interaction between large basic differences in graphemic processing and condition difficulty (De Luca et al., 2010; Zoccolotti et al., 2008). Therefore, the possibility of comparing the reading subcomponents/parameters by using a dimensionless measure such as the ratio, which provides information on the proportional size of the effect, seems more interesting.

RATIOS IN THE COMPARISON OF GROUP PERFORMANCE

Across several eye movement and voice parameters, performance of dyslexic and control readers was expressed by a ratio of about 2. This was the case for total reading aloud time, total viewing time (whether aloud or silent) and number of fixations, as well as reading time on the MT test. Thus, we can consider a factor of 2.0 as a reference value to evaluate the size of group differences in reading parameters. The presence of consistent proportional differences across various different parameters is coherent with the literature, which indicates that dyslexic readers show a consistent deficit across very different stimulus materials (such as short vs. long words or words vs. non-words) when analyzed in ways that allow detecting global components in the data (e.g., Zoccolotti et al., 2008; Van den Broeck and Geudens, 2012).

Thus, within this perspective it is possible to consider unitarily group differences that, if expressed in terms of absolute scores, seem to be different in size. Consider the case of viewing time during silent or aloud reading. In keeping with Anderson and Anderson and Swanson's (1937) early observations, group differences were numerically greater in aloud than in silent reading; but the ratios for these two conditions were very similar, indicating that the increase in group differences can be parsimoniously explained as due to the greater difficulty in the aloud (than the silent) condition, without the need to refer to additional specific effects in the reading aloud condition. Furthermore, the 2-ratio approach allowed us to detect parameters that showed effects which were proportionally smaller or greater than this reference. In particular, pronunciation times showed only a 1.2 ratio or 20% prolongation; by contrast, number of pauses showed a much greater effect with a 4.5 ratio. Thus, the slow reading of dyslexic readers might be characterized as related more to an increase in the frequency of silent pauses and less (although significantly) to slowed articulation times. The data on pronunciation times also underscore the limits of using traditional standardized measures of effect size (such as Cohen's *d*). When *d* values were considered, group differences actually revealed a large group effect because of the very low inter-individual variability in pronunciation times. In this particular case, group differences in inter-individual variability were not merely due to differences in measurement reliability; rather, they reflect the well-known difference between cognitive and motor measures, with the former yielding much greater individual differences than the latter (e.g., Myerson et al., 2003).

However, some limits of the perspective based on ratio comparisons must also be underscored. Compared to models that make explicit predictions to test global components in the data (such as the *rate and amount model*, Faust et al., 1999; the *difference engine model*, Myerson et al., 2003; or the *state trace model*, Van den Broeck and Geudens, 2012), the use of ratios might be considered a rather rough measure for estimating the size of group differences in situations where group differences should be expected to increase multiplicatively due to the interaction of task difficulty and basic group differences in information processing. In particular, by teasing out different components of reaction time measures, models such as the difference engine model (Myerson et al., 2003) allow separating non-decisional from decisional components of the response. A similar outcome is reached with the diffusion model (e.g., Zeguers et al., 2011), which is based on very different assumptions. By contrast, referring to ratios does not allow distinguishing whether (and to what extent) group differences depend on decisional or non-decisional components of the response. At the same time, note that although the quoted models are considerably more powerful by themselves, they are typically used to deal with conditions that have several constraints and are usable only for rather specific predictions.[1] Overall, there

[1] For example, the rate and amount (Faust et al., 1999) as well as the difference engine (Myerson et al., 2003) model are suited to account for group differences in performance on timed tasks within a relatively short time range (ca. 0–3 s); further, they are based on rather strict linear relationships in the data and cannot deal with closed scale data (such as accuracy measures). Accordingly, although they are convenient for studying RTs, their extension to more natural task conditions, such as reading a meaningful text, is comparatively difficult. A model such as the state trace model (e.g., Van den Broeck and Geudens, 2012) does not have some of these limitations (particularly the requirement of linear predictions or the restriction to closed scales) but still applies best to selected experimental conditions; furthermore, by requiring an overlap in performance between the two groups, it is best suited for experiments with ad-hoc designs, which allow producing such an overlap. Similar considerations apply to the diffusion model. This has the advantage of dealing jointly with accuracy and time data but also requires ad-hoc designs and is difficult to extend to more natural situations, such as those in the present study. Note that in the particular case of reading accuracy may be very high in natural conditions at least in skilled readers, thus violating one requirement of the model.

are clear limitations in examining ratios compared to more formal approaches to modeling group data in cognitive tasks. At the same time, this approach does provide a general profile of the group differences across reading parameters, which would be impossible to tackle using the quoted models.

Some caution should be taken to avoid over-interpreting differences in ratios across conditions/parameters. In particular, we feel this applies to the conditions which greatly deviate from the pattern of variability expected in the case of an over-additivity effect, i.e., appreciably larger SDs for the impaired (dyslexic) group than the control group. For example, the present data indicated very large differences in accuracy between the two groups; namely, dyslexic readers made 5.5 more errors than control readers in reading the text (and, based on data in **Table 1**, a similar 4.8 ratio was present for errors in the case of the MT standard reading test). However, on the basis of these high ratios it seems far-fetched to consider that accuracy is more involved in the dyslexic deficit than speed. Indeed, skilled readers made an extremely small number of errors (or no errors), which is typical in transparent orthographies. We propose that this group difference can be explained in terms of a floor effect, i.e., several children did not actually make any substitution errors or engage in sounding-out behavior. This was clearly more frequent in the control group but spared performance in some parameters was present also in several dyslexic children. Accordingly, the large variability stems from the fact that only some of the children contributed to these measures, while some were flawless. Therefore, values for dyslexic children can easily override control's performance and generate very high ratios that cannot be directly compared with those based on time measures (where all individuals contribute some variability in generating the group average). Overall, it is difficult to directly compare accuracy with measures of eye movements or reading rate. However, in the accuracy measures, ratios may indicate that sounding-out behavior accounted for greater differences than word substitution errors. This finding is in keeping with previous observations in Italian children (Trenta et al., 2013) and indicates the tendency to phonologically recode words when a holistic approach to the target fails. In particular, Trenta et al. (2013) reported that sounding-out behavior was a significant predictor of dyslexic grouping in both text passages and word lists. Within the context of the present study, it is intriguing to observe that the "central" nature of sounding-out (called hesitations) was probably first understood by Fairbanks (1937), although he has not yet been credited for it. Interestingly, he noted that "*substantial positive inter-correlations between errors, hesitations, regressions ... were obtained, and the coefficients almost always were greater in poor reading ... Inclusion of hesitations as errors raised the correlation between errors and regressions, suggesting that even though the determination of hesitations is a qualitative step, more central errors were included.*"

EYE-VOICE LEAD

The present study aimed to investigate eye-voice lead. In the 1930s, this phenomenon was the center of attention of a group of studies on eye movements in reading. But when research began to focus on examining silent reading conditions, interest in the eye-voice lead reduced considerably.

The results of the present study confirm a clear difference in eye-voice lead in dyslexic and matched skilled readers. This finding, which was obtained with children who speak a language with regular orthography, is in keeping with the early observations of Buswell (1921) and Fairbanks (1937). At that time, this measure created a considerable technical challenge and investigations could be carried out only in selected laboratories. Contemporary standard eye movement equipment and appropriate audio software have simplified the recording of eye-voice lead; indeed, this measure can now be more easily included in experimental studies on eye movements in dyslexia.

Eye-voice lead is very sensitive to local influences (Fairbanks, 1937; Inhoff et al., 2011) and varies systematically along the line of text and as a function of psycholinguistic parameters of the stimuli, such as high vs. low frequency words. It also decreases when a reader needs to regress to a previous word. At the same time, the present results indicate that the systematic individual tendency can be detected by analyses that cut across these locally determined variations. Some individuals tend to move their eye scanning forward "without waiting" for the execution of voice output, whereas others are so slow in decoding written words that the voice output flow remains nearly simultaneous with decoding. In this sense, eye-voice lead probably represents the idiosyncratic reading style of an individual more than any other parameter. In this view, after years of reading experience the reader develops a systematic tendency to trade-off visual and vocal processing. Within the perspective of the present study, it is interesting that variations in eye-voice lead showed a ratio in the comparison between dyslexic and control readers in line with the reference 2-ratio (i.e., 1.7 for both types of obtained estimates). This indicates that eye-voice lead reflects the proportional differences between the two groups.

Interestingly, the pattern of correlation indicates a widespread relationship between eye-voice lead and critical parameters such as reading aloud time, number (and total duration) of pauses, total viewing time and percentage or regressions. Notably, a significant correlation was present also for utterance duration. Although variations in utterance durations were comparatively small, they contributed quantitatively to participants' setting-up style for integrating voice and eye parameters. Importantly, the eye-voice lead in aloud reading was also highly correlated with total viewing time in silent reading; indeed, the size of this correlation was indistinguishable from those described above. Since eye-voice lead and viewing time in silent reading were evaluated on a different text, this is in line with the idea that eye-voice lead represents a stable individual trait.

The idea that readers develop an idiosyncratic style of reading is in keeping with observations by Carver (1982, 1992). He proposed that through prolonged practice readers develop an optimal reading rate, which is best suited to comprehend the thoughts contained in sentences (which corresponds to ca. 300 words per minute in college students). Carver (1982) referred to this as a "rauding" rate to mark the continuity between reading and listening (or auding). Therefore, in this view the optimal reading rate is that used by an individual to optimize reading comprehension. In keeping with this idea, Carver (1982) observed lower comprehension efficiency when readers were forced to read at a faster or slower rate than their optimal one.

DECOMPOSING DYSLEXICS' READING SLOWNESS

One interesting question is how reading slowness in dyslexic readers expresses in the various sub-components of the reading task.

Dyslexic readers presented a much larger number of silent pauses than control readers. Indeed, in many cases the reading of skilled readers flowed continuously, with effective co-articulation of subsequent sounds regardless of whether or not they were part of the same word. It is clear that during silent pauses eye scanning is occurring through numerous fixations of the as yet unpronounced word, contributing to reading slowness by increasing the number of fixations. Furthermore, dyslexic children engaged much more often in other time- consuming behaviors such as resounding the stimulus target before uttering it correctly. Note that some lengthening was also detected in the articulation times of words pronounced without detectable hesitations or silent pauses.

Although the literature on reaction times to single-word presentation is immense, only a handful of studies have examined articulation times to singly presented words (Davies et al., 2013; Martelli et al., 2013). Both of the latter studies found that pronunciation times varied as a function of the lexicality and length of the stimulus (and also frequency in the case of Davies et al., 2013). These findings indicate that coding processes may indeed continue after response onset. Consistent results were also reported by Balota and Abrams (1995). These authors found that when the same arbitrary articulatory response was requested in a lexical decision task the duration of the utterance varied for stimuli of different word frequency. These findings, which indicate a spillover from the decoding phase of processing to the execution phase, point to a continuity between reaction and articulation times and speak against a clear-cut separation between cognitive and motor times. Notably, the effect of variables such as lexicality (Davies et al., 2013; Martelli et al., 2013) or frequency (Davies et al., 2013) on articulation times was very small in the case of singly presented targets; however, it was significant thanks to the extremely small variances present in the case of articulation times. For example, Martelli et al. (2013) found a delay of 6% (or a ratio of 1.06) between the articulation times of dyslexic and control readers across words and non-words. The effect was only 3% (or a ratio of 1.03) in the case of words and 9% (or a ratio of 1.09) in the case of non-words. Compared with these figures, the presence of a 24% delay (or ratio of 1.24) observed here in reading a meaningful text indicates an appreciable increase in the slowing in pronunciation in the case of multiple as opposed to single words (3%), even though the effect (24%) remains quantitatively small. In keeping with the idea that articulation times may indeed capture some of the variance connected with decoding and comprehension processes, it is interesting that they were correlated with a holistic parameter such as the eye-voice lead, that is, individuals with a smaller eye-voice lead showed longer articulation times than individuals with a larger eye-voice lead.

To the best of our knowledge, pronunciation times during reading a text passage have never been reported in dyslexic children; therefore, a comparison with other reading studies is impossible. However, the problem of comparing the predictive value of pauses vs. articulation times has received some attention in research on the RAN paradigm. Several studies have been based on the hypothesis that pause time is responsible for the well-known correlation between RAN tasks and reading speed (Neuhaus et al., 2001; Neuhaus and Swank, 2002; Georgiou et al., 2006). However, when pauses and articulation times were simultaneously recorded, both were highly correlated with reading speed and accuracy, at least for Greek and English observers (Georgiou et al., 2008). Indeed, Georgiou et al. (2008) proposed that the variance which is common to pause and articulation times is most correlated with reading.

Overall, these findings indicate that the slowing of dyslexic readers expresses through a variety of modifications in different parameters even though they occur within very different scales, i.e., producing large, evident differences as in the case of silent pauses (and number of fixations) or small, more difficult to detect, differences as in the case of articulation times.

TOWARD AN INTERPRETATION OF THE DEVELOPMENTAL READING DEFICIT

The present results are in keeping with the general idea that reading requires the efficiency of several cognitive processes, including fast and effective visual scanning, visual selective attention, fast retrieval of lexical entries, short-term memory, and executive functioning. The question is whether it is possible to have a unitary interpretation of the deficit of dyslexic children in dealing with the multiple components of reading or whether separate interpretations are necessary.

Several interpretations have focussed on the efficiency of each of these processes. For example, it has been proposed that dyslexic children show impaired visual scanning (e.g., Vidyasagar and Pammer, 1999). Others studies attributed deficient reading to a reduced visual-attention span (Prado et al., 2007) or to multisensory spatial attention deficits (Facoetti et al., 2010). And other authors have reported that dyslexic readers have low verbal short-term memory (e.g., Wagner and Torgesen, 1987). It has also been reported that developmental dyslexia is associated with poor executive functioning (e.g., Brosnan et al., 2002). This is just a brief list of the complex pattern of impairments which can putatively cause or contribute to causing developmental dyslexia. In this respect, it must be kept in mind that increasing evidence indicates that developmental disorders present a large spectrum of homotopic and heterotopic co-morbidities, which make causal interpretations problematic (for reviews see Pennington, 2006; Pennington and Bishop, 2009). Thus, we think that at least some of the quoted findings represent individual associations, not causal relationships.

An alternative, more parsimonious, interpretation is that dyslexic children have a single predominant deficit; but, given the interwoven nature of the reading task, this deficit spreads to affect all sub-components of reading behavior. Based on previous evidence, the most likely candidate for this nuclear deficit seems to be impaired word decoding. This deficit is very clear in experimentally isolated conditions (e.g., in vocal RTs to singly presented targets). When, in more natural conditions, the child has to couple this impaired decoding with the scanning of visual orthographic stimuli, holding the output phonological traces in memory up to utterance production etc., the impairment increases proportionally simply because of the difficulty in integrating a defective performance into a complex task. In this view, other impairments in relevant processes (such as visual scanning or short-term memory) may co-occur and exacerbate the reading pattern but they do not necessarily account for a severe and selective deficit in dealing with the multiple task requirements intrinsic in the reading task.

Nevertheless, even if one accepts this interpretation, the question is still open concerning the most likely mechanism at the base of the impairment in basic word decoding. Notably, the present results do not offer direct information on this point and only speculative interpretations can be presented. Based on a large body of literature, we feel that the two most likely candidates for this impairment are a deficit in visual or phonological processes. In the first class of mechanisms, one finds deficits in magnocellular functioning (Stein and Walsh, 1997) or visual crowding (Spinelli et al., 2002). For example, in visual crowding word recognition is possible only within an uncrowded window (Pelli et al., 2007), and differences in the size of this window account for the differential efficiency in the reading of dyslexic and control readers (Martelli et al., 2009). In the second class of mechanisms are hypotheses of continuity between acoustic deficits and phonological coding (Goswami et al., 2011). Both children and adults with developmental dyslexia have deficits in perceiving syllable stress in speech (Leong et al., 2011), and dyslexic children have difficulty in discriminating rise times of the speech signal for auditory presented syllables (Goswami et al., 2011). Poor sensitivity to the rhythmic structure of speech produces "*consequences for developing the high-quality phonological representations of spoken words necessary for the acquisition of literacy*" (Goswami, 2011). In particular, according to the temporal sampling framework, children with dyslexia have problems at the temporal integration window, which is typical of the syllable analysis, i.e., around 200 ms, not in the 20–50 ms range, which is typical of phonemes (Goswami, 2011). Although critical experiments on this model have been carried out in the acoustic modality (e.g., Goswami et al., 2011), we thought it would be interesting to compare the predictions of the model concerning the timing of information acquisition in the visual modality. To this aim, the most critical parameter seems to be the duration of individual fixations during reading. In the present study, the peak of fixation duration distribution (time window 175–225 ms) was comparable in young skilled and dyslexic readers; however, the frequency was higher in dyslexic children in the same temporal window than in other time windows, whereas the frequency of very short fixations was nearly comparable. Thus, it seems that there was a visual oversampling at a time window corresponding to the one that is critical for phonological syllable analysis. Based on these preliminary observations, it would be interesting to investigate the temporal sampling framework within the visual modality.

CONCLUSIONS

Overall, the results of the present study allow for a comprehensive description of the reading profile of dyslexic and control readers during the reading of a text, including several eye and voice parameters and accuracy measures. In this context, the eye-voice lead represents a key phenomenon that describes well the complexity of the reading task. Research on the eye-voice lead was at the center of attention in the early part of twentieth century, but then lost impetus; it seems that this measure (which is considerably easier to gather with modern equipment) might provide interesting information about reading efficiency.

Across several parameters, the difference in performance between dyslexic and control readers was expressed by a ratio of about 2. A much lower ratio was measured for pronunciation parameters, indicating that this subcomponent weighed less than other subcomponents in the overall reading time. Referring to proportional differences allows for a more parsimonious interpretation of the reading deficit; in particular, we propose that an impairment in word decoding is the key deficit and that it spreads in such a way as to produce severe difficulty in dealing with the multiple task requirements intrinsic to reading.

ACKNOWLEDGMENTS

This work was supported by grants from the Department of Health and Sapienza University.

REFERENCES

Anderson, I. H., and Swanson, D. E. (1937). Common factors in eye movements in silent and oral reading. *Psychol. Monogr.* 48, 61–69. doi: 10.1037/h0093393

Bakker, D. J. (1992). Neuropsychological classification and treatment of dyslexia. *J. Learn. Disabil.* 25, 102–109. doi: 10.1177/002221949202500203

Balota, D. A., and Abrams, R. A. (1995). Mental chronometry: beyond onset latencies in the lexical decision task. *J. Exp. Psychol. Learn. Mem. Cogn.* 21, 1289–1302. doi: 10.1037/0278-7393.21.5.1289

Bertinetto, P. M., Burani, C., Laudanna, A., Marconi, L., Ratti, D., Rolando, C., et al. (2005). *Corpus e Lessico di Frequenza dell'Italiano Scritto (CoLFIS).* Available online at: http://linguistica.sns.it/CoLFIS/Home.htm

Brosnan, M., Demetre, J., Hamill, S., Robson, K., Shepherd, H., and Cody, G. (2002). Executive functioning in adults and children with developmental dyslexia. *Neuropsychologia* 40, 2144–2155. doi: 10.1016/S0028-3932(02)00046-5

Buswell, G. T. (1920). "An experimental study of the eye-voice span in reading," in *Supplementary Educational Monographs*, eds W. S. Gray and M. W. Jernegan (Chicago, IL: University of Chicago), 1–104.

Buswell, G. T. (1921). The relationship between eye-perception and voice-response in reading. *J. Educ. Psychol.* 12, 217–227. doi: 10.1037/h0070548

Carver, R. P. (1982). Optimal rate of reading prose. *Read. Res. Quart.* 18, 56–88. doi: 10.2307/747538

Carver, R. P. (1992). Reading rate: theory, research, and practical implications. *J. Reading* 36, 84–95.

Coltheart, M. (1980). "The semantic error: types and theories." in *Deep Dyslexia*, eds M. Coltheart, K. Patterson, and J. C. Marshall (London: Routledge, Kegan Paul), 146–159.

Coltheart, M., Rastle, K., Perry, C., Langdon, R., and Ziegler, J. C. (2001). DRC: A dual route cascaded model of visual word recognition and reading aloud. *Psychol. Rev.* 108, 204–256. doi: 10.1037/0033-295X.108.1.204

Cornoldi, C., and Colpo, G. (1995). *Nuove Prove di Lettura MT per la Scuola Media Inferiore, Manuale.* Firenze: O. S. Organizzazioni Speciali.

Davies, R., Rodríguez-Ferreiro, J., Suárez, P., and Cuetos, F. (2013). Lexical and sublexical effects on accuracy, reaction time and response duration: impaired and typical word and pseudoword reading in a transparent orthography. *Read. Writ.* 26, 721–738. doi: 10.1007/s11145-012-9388-1

De Luca, M., Borrelli, M., Judica, A., Spinelli, D., and Zoccolotti, P. (2002). Reading words and pseudowords: an eye movement study of developmental dyslexia. *Brain Lang.* 80, 617–626. doi: 10.1006/brln.2001.2637

De Luca, M., Burani, C., Paizi, D., Spinelli, D., and Zoccolotti, P. (2010). Letter and letter-string processing in developmental dyslexia. *Cortex* 46, 1272–1283. doi: 10.1016/j.cortex.2009.06.007

De Luca, M., Di Pace, E., Judica, A., Spinelli, D., and Zoccolotti, P. (1999). Eye movement patterns in linguistic and non-linguistic tasks in developmental surface dyslexia. *Neuropsychologia* 37, 1407–1420. doi: 10.1016/S0028-3932(99)00038-X

Facoetti, A., Trussardi, A. N., Ruffino, M., Lorusso, M. L., Cattaneo, C., Galli, R., et al. (2010). Multisensory spatial attention deficits are predictive of phonological decoding skills in developmental dyslexia. *J. Cogn. Neurosci.* 22, 1011–1025. doi: 10.1162/jocn.2009.21232

Fairbanks, G. (1937). The relation between eye-movements and voice in the oral reading of good and poor silent readers. *Psychol. Monogr.* 48, 78–107. doi: 10.1037/h0093394

Faust, M. E., Balota, D. A., Spieler, D. H., and Ferraro, F. R. (1999). Individual differences in information processing rate and amount: implications for group differences in response latency. *Psychol. Bull.* 125, 777–799. doi: 10.1037/0033-2909.125.6.777

Georgiou, G. K., Parrila, R., Cui, Y., and Papadopoulos, T. C. (2013). Why is rapid automatized naming related to reading? *J. Exp. Child Psychol.* 115, 218–225. doi: 10.1016/j.jecp.2012.10.015

Georgiou, G. K., Parrila, R., and Kirby, J. (2006). Rapid naming speed components and early reading acquisition. *Sci. Stud. Read.*. 10, 199–220. doi: 10.1207/s1532799xssr1002_4

Georgiou, G. K., Parrila, R., and Liao, H. (2008). Rapid naming speed and reading across languages that vary in orthographic consistency. *Read. Writ.* 21, 885–903. doi: 10.1007/s11145-007-9096-4

Goswami, U. (2011). A temporal sampling framework for developmental dyslexia. *Trends Cogn. Sci.* 15, 3–10. doi: 10.1016/j.tics.2010.10.001

Goswami, U., Fosker, T., Huss, M., Mead, N., and Szücs, D. (2011). Rise time and formant transition duration in the discrimination of speech sounds: the Ba–Wa distinction in developmental dyslexia. *Dev. Sci.* 14, 34–43. doi: 10.1111/j.1467-7687.2010.00955.x

Hari, R., and Renvall, H. (2001). Impaired processing of rapid stimulus sequences in dyslexia. *Trends Cogn. Sci.* 5, 525–532. doi: 10.1016/S1364-6613(00)01801-5

Hawelka, S., Gagl, B., and Wimmer, H. (2010). A dual-route perspective on eye movements of dyslexic readers. *Cognition* 115, 367–379. doi: 10.1016/j.cognition.2009.11.004

Hendriks, A. W., and Kolk, H. H. J. (1997). Strategic control in developmental dyslexia. *Cogn. Neuropsychol.* 14, 321–366. doi: 10.1080/026432997381510

Inhoff, A. W., Solomon, M., Radach, R., and Seymour, B. A. (2011). Temporal dynamics of the eye-voice span and eye movement control during oral reading. *J. Cogn. Psychol.* 23, 543–558. doi: 10.1080/20445911.2011.546782

Leong, V., Hämäläinen, J., Soltész, F., and Goswami, U. (2011). Rise time perception and detection of syllable stress in adults with developmental dyslexia. *J. Mem. Lang.* 64, 59–73. doi: 10.1016/j.jml.2010.09.003

Levin, H. (1979). *The Eye-Voice Span.* Contributor A. Buckler-Addis, Cambridge, MA: The MIT Press.

Levy-Schoen, A. (1981). "Flexible and/or rigid control of oculomotor scanning behavior" in *Eye Movements: Cognition and Visual Perception,* ed D. F. Fisher, R. A. Monty, and J. W. Senders (Hillsdale, NJ: Erlbaum), 299–316.

Marshall, J. C., and Newcombe, F. (1966). Syntactic and semantic errors in paralexia. *Neuropsychologia* 4, 169–176. doi: 10.1016/0028-3932(66)90045-5

Marshall, J. C., and Newcombe, F. (1973). Patterns of paralexia: a psycholinguistic approach. *J. Psycholinguist. Res.* 2, 175–199. doi: 10.1007/BF01067101

Martelli, M., De Luca, M., Lami, L., Pizzoli, C., Pontillo, M., Spinelli, D., et al. (2013). Bridging the gap between different measures of the reading speed deficit in developmental dyslexia. *Exp. Brain Res.* doi: 10.1007/s00221-013-3735-6. [Epub ahead of print].

Martelli, M., Di Filippo, G., Spinelli, D., and Zoccolotti, P. (2009). Crowding, reading and developmental dyslexia. *J. Vis.* 9, 14.1–14.18. doi: 10.1167/9.414

Martens, V. E. G., and de Jong, P. F. (2006). The effect of word length on lexical decision in dyslexic and normal reading children. *Brain Lang.* 98, 140–149. doi: 10.1016/j.bandl.2006.04.003

Morton, J. (1964). The effects of context upon speed of reading, eye movements and eye-voice span, *Q. J. Exp. Psychol.* 16, 340–354. doi: 10.1080/17470216408416390

Myerson, J., Hale, S., Zheng, Y., Jenkins, L., and Widaman, K. F. (2003). The difference engine: a model of diversity in speeded cognition. *Psychon. Bull. Rev.* 10, 262–288. doi: 10.3758/BF03196491

Neuhaus, G., Foorman, B. R., Francis, D. J., and Carlson, C. D. (2001). Measures of information processing in rapid automatized naming (RAN) and their relation to reading. *J. Exp. Child Psychol.* 78, 359–373. doi: 10.1006/jecp.2000.2576

Neuhaus, G., and Swank, P. (2002). Understanding the relations between RAN letter subtest components and word reading in first-grade students. *J. Learn. Disabil.* 35, 158–174. doi: 10.1177/002221940203500206

Olson, R. K., Kliegl, R., and Davidson, B. J. (1983). Dyslexic and normal readers' eye movements. *J. Exp. Psychol. Human.* 9, 816–825. doi: 10.1037/0096-1523.9.5.816

Paizi, D., De Luca, M., Zoccolotti, P., and Burani, C. (2011). A comprehensive evaluation of lexical reading in Italian developmental dyslexics. *J. Res. Read.* 36, 323–329. doi: 10.1111/j.1467-9817.2011.01504.x

Pan, J., Yan, M., Laubrock, J., Shu, H., and Kliegl, R. (2013). Eye–voice span during rapid automatized naming of digits and dice in Chinese normal and dyslexic children. *Dev. Sci.* 16, 967–979. doi: 10.1111/desc.12075

Pelli, D. G., Tillman, K. A., Freeman, J., Su, M., Berger, T. D., and Majaj, N. J. (2007). Crowding and eccentricity determine reading rate. *J. Vis.* 7, 20.1–20.36. doi: 10.1167/7.2.20

Pennington, B. F. (2006). From single to multiple deficit models of developmental disorders *Cognition* 101, 385–413. doi: 10.1016/j.cognition.2006.04.008

Pennington, B. F., and Bishop, D. V. M. (2009). Relations among speech, language, and reading disorders. *Annu. Rev. Psychol.* 60, 283–306. doi: 10.1146/annurev.psych.60.110707.163548

Prado, C., Dubois, M., and Valdois, S. (2007). The eye movements of dyslexic children during reading and visual search: impact of the visual attention span. *Vis. Res.* 47, 2521–2530. doi: 10.1016/j.visres.2007.06.001

Protopapas, A., Altani, A., and Georgiou, G. K., (2013). Development of serial processing in reading and rapid naming. *J. Exp. Child Psychol.* 116, 914–929. doi: 10.1016/j.jecp.2013.08.004

Pruneti, C. A., Fenu, A., Freschi, G., Rota, S., Cocci, D., Marchionni, M., et al. (1996). Aggiornamento della standardizzazione italiana del test delle Matrici Progressive Colorate di Raven (CPM). *Boll. Psicol. Appl.* 217, 51–57.

Rayner, K. (1998). Eye movements in reading and information processing: 20 years of research. *Psychol. Bull.* 124, 372–422. doi: 10.1037/0033-2909.124.3.372

Rayner, K. (2009). Eye movements and attention in reading, scene perception, and visual search. *Q. J. Exp. Psychol.* 62, 1457–1506. doi: 10.1080/17470210902816461

Salthouse, T. A., and Ellis, C. L. (1980). Determinants of eye-fixation duration. *Am. J. Psychol.* 93, 207–234. doi: 10.2307/1422228

Spinelli, D., De Luca, M., Di Filippo, G., Mancini, M., Martelli, M., and Zoccolotti, P. (2005). Length effect in word naming latencies: role of reading experience and reading deficit. *Dev. Neuropsychol.* 27, 217–235. doi: 10.1207/s15326942dn2702_2

Spinelli, D., De Luca, M., Judica, A., and Zoccolotti, P. (2002). Crowding effects on word identification in developmental dyslexia. *Cortex* 38, 179–200. doi: 10.1016/S0010-9452(08)70649-X

Stein, J. F., and Walsh, V. (1997). To see but not to read: the magnocellular theory of dyslexia. *Trends Neurosci.* 20, 147–152. doi: 10.1016/S0166-2236(96)01005-3

Tiffin, J., and Fairbanks, G. (1937). An eye-voice camera for clinical and research studies. *Psychol. Monogr.* 48, 70–77.

Trenta, M., Benassi, M., Di Filippo, G., Pontillo, M., and Zoccolotti, P. (2013). Developmental dyslexia in a regular orthography: can the reading profile be reduced to strategic control? *Cogn. Neuropsychol.* 30, 147–171. doi: 10.1080/02643294.2013.814569

Van den Broeck, W., and Geudens, A. (2012). Old and new ways to study characteristics of reading disability: the case of the nonword-reading deficit. *Cogn. Psychol.* 65, 414–456. doi: 10.1016/j.cogpsych.2012.06.003

Vidyasagar, T. R., and Pammer, K. (1999). Impaired visual search in dyslexia relates to the role of the magnocellular pathway in attention. *Neuroreport* 10, 1283–1288. doi: 10.1097/00001756-199904260-00024

Wagner, R. K., and Torgesen, J. K. (1987). The nature of phonological processing and its causal role in the acquisition of reading skills. *Psychol. Bull.* 101, 192–212. doi: 10.1037/0033-2909.101.2.192

Wimmer, H. (1993). Characteristics of developmental dyslexia in a regular writing system. *Appl. Psychol.* 14, 1–33. doi: 10.1017/S0142716400010122

Zeguers, M. H., Snellings, P., Tijms, J., Weeda, W. D., Tamboer, P., Bexkens, A., et al. (2011). Specifying theories of developmental dyslexia: a diffusion model analysis of word recognition. *Dev. Sci.* 14, 1340–1354. doi: 10.1111/j.1467-7687.2011.01091.x

Ziegler, J. C., Perry, C., Ma-Wyatt, A., Ladner, D., and Schulte-Korne, G. (2003). Developmental dyslexia in different languages: Language-specific or universal? *J. Exp. Child Psychol.* 86, 169–193. doi: 10.1016/S0022-0965(03)00139-5

Zoccolotti, P., De Luca, M., Di Pace, E., Judica, A., Orlandi, M., and Spinelli, D. (1999). Markers of developmental surface dyslexia in a language (Italian) with high grapheme-phoneme correspondence. *Appl. Psychol.* 20, 191–216. doi: 10.1017/S0142716499002027

Zoccolotti, P., De Luca, M., Judica, A., and Spinelli, D. (2008). Isolating global and specific factors in developmental dyslexia: a study based on the rate and amount model (RAM). *Exp. Brain Res.* 186, 551–560. doi: 10.1007/s00221-007-1257-9

Zoccolotti, P., De Luca, M., Lami, L., Pizzoli, C., Pontillo, M., and Spinelli, D. (2012). Multiple stimulus presentation yields larger deficits in children with developmental dyslexia: a study with reading and RAN-type tasks. *Child Neuropsychol.* doi: 10.1080/09297049.2012.718325

11

Functional neuroanatomy of developmental dyslexia: the role of orthographic depth

Fabio Richlan*

Centre for Neurocognitive Research and Department of Psychology, University of Salzburg, Salzburg, Austria

Correspondence:
Fabio Richlan, Centre for Neurocognitive Research and Department of Psychology, University of Salzburg, Hellbrunnerstr. 34, 5020 Salzburg, Austria
e-mail: fabio.richlan@sbg.ac.at

Orthographic depth (OD) (i.e., the complexity, consistency, or transparency of grapheme-phoneme correspondences in written alphabetic language) plays an important role in the acquisition of reading skills. Correspondingly, developmental dyslexia is characterized by different behavioral manifestations across languages varying in OD. This review focuses on the question of whether these different behavioral manifestations are associated with different functional neuroanatomical manifestations. It provides a review and critique of cross-linguistic brain imaging studies of developmental dyslexia. In addition, it includes an analysis of state-of-the-art functional neuroanatomical models of developmental dyslexia together with orthography-specific predictions derived from these models. These predictions should be tested in future brain imaging studies of typical and atypical reading in order to refine the current neurobiological understanding of developmental dyslexia, especially with respect to orthography-specific and universal aspects.

Keywords: brain, developmental dyslexia, fMRI, language, neuroimaging, orthography, PET, reading

In this Review Article I will discuss current advances and future directions in the neurobiological understanding of developmental dyslexia. For this purpose, I will focus on brain imaging studies and will elaborate on the question of whether different behavioral manifestations of dyslexia across languages may be associated with different functional neuroanatomical manifestations. This question was not dealt with in previous review articles in the field (e.g., Pugh et al., 2000; Temple, 2002; McCandliss and Noble, 2003; Démonet et al., 2004; Heim and Keil, 2004; Sandak et al., 2004; Shaywitz and Shaywitz, 2005; Schlaggar and McCandliss, 2007). Of main interest will be whether orthographic depth (OD)—a well-known factor in reading acquisition—has an influence on the brain activation pattern during non-impaired and dyslexic reading. For this purpose, I will begin with a review of relevant studies, followed by a critique of some of these studies. Although the focus of the present paper is on OD in alphabetic writing systems, I will also cover cross-cultural studies comparing alphabetic with syllabic or logographic writing systems. This topic is of immediate interest as it can contribute to the understanding of universal and orthography-specific neurobiological manifestations of developmental dyslexia (Frost, 2012). Finally, I will put forward some model-based orthography-specific predictions of classical as well as newer functional neuroanatomical conceptions of developmental dyslexia, which may serve as blueprint for future hypothesis-driven brain imaging studies.

ORTHOGRAPHIC DEPTH AND READING ACQUISITION IN ALPHABETIC WRITING SYSTEMS

OD refers to the complexity, consistency, or transparency of grapheme-phoneme correspondences in written alphabetic language (Frost et al., 1987). A deep (or highly complex or inconsistent or opaque) orthography like English is characterized by multi-letter graphemes, context-dependent rules, and morphological effects resulting in a many-to-many mapping of graphemes to phonemes. In contrast, a shallow (or little complex or consistent or transparent) orthography like Finnish is characterized by consistent one-to-one mapping of graphemes to phonemes (Seymour et al., 2003).

OD has been identified as one of the most important environmental factors influencing learning to read (e.g., Seymour et al., 2003; Landerl et al., 2013). It has a direct effect on how easy or difficult it is for children to translate a new letter string into a phonological code by which phonological word forms can be accessed. The idea is that in deep orthographies phonology has to be retrieved from stored memory representations (i.e., from an internal lexicon), whereas in shallow orthographies phonology can be derived relatively easily and directly from print. The ability to translate letter strings into a phonological code is called phonological recoding and was labeled the *sine qua non* of reading acquisition. It provides the prerequisite for a self-teaching mechanism that enables a young reader to autonomously establish an orthographic lexicon (Share, 1995).

It has been shown numerous times that children exhibit different behavioral performance according to the language they are learning to read. The usual finding is a marked word and pseudoword reading accuracy advantage of children learning to read in a shallow orthography (e.g., Dutch, Finnish, German, Greek, Italian, Spanish) over children learning to read in a deep orthography (English). This pertains to non-impaired (e.g., Wimmer and Goswami, 1994; Cossu et al., 1995; Frith et al., 1998; Aro and

Wimmer, 2003; Seymour et al., 2003; Bergmann and Wimmer, 2008; Zoccolotti et al., 2009; Georgiou et al., 2012) as well as to impaired reading acquisition (i.e., developmental dyslexia) (e.g., Wimmer, 1993; Landerl et al., 1997; Landerl and Wimmer, 2000; Spinelli et al., 2005; Zoccolotti et al., 2005; Barca et al., 2006; Davies et al., 2007; Wimmer and Schurz, 2010).

Some accounts, however, emphasize the commonalities between reading in deep and shallow orthographies over their differences (e.g., Ziegler et al., 2003, 2010; Caravolas et al., 2012, 2013). For example, Ziegler et al. (2010) investigated whether the role of different cognitive predictors of reading development (phonological awareness (PA), rapid automatized naming (RAN), phonological short-term memory, vocabulary, and nonverbal IQ) varies with OD. They showed that, although its influence is weaker in shallow compared with deep orthographies, PA is a relatively universal predictor of reading performance in alphabetic languages. Likewise, developmental dyslexia was characterized by similar deficits (overall slow reading, increased difficulties with nonwords compared with words, and slow and effortful phonological decoding) in a shallow orthography (German) and a deep orthography (English) (Ziegler et al., 2003).

With respect to the developmental pattern of cognitive predictors, Vaessen et al. (2010) found a strong contribution of PA to reading fluency in beginning readers, followed by a gradual shift towards stronger contribution of RAN in more proficient readers. Importantly, this general developmental shift was not influenced by OD of the three studied languages (Hungarian, Dutch, Portuguese). The contribution of PA to reading fluency, however, was important for a longer period of time in deeper orthographies. Likewise, Moll et al. (2014) confirmed that PA and RAN both account for significant amounts of unique variance in literacy development across five orthographies (English, French, German, Hungarian, Finnish). In all studied languages, PA was the best predictor of reading accuracy and spelling, whereas RAN was the best predictor of reading speed. With respect to developmental dyslexia, Landerl et al. (2013) showed that both PA and RAN were strong concurrent predictors of reading problems. The influence of PA and RAN was larger in deeper orthographies, in which more participants were correctly classified as dyslexic. In sum, the results suggest that the same cognitive components underlie reading development in deep and shallow orthographies, but to a different degree that varies as a function of reading level.

One attempt to explain the differences in reading speed and reading accuracy across orthographies is psycholinguistic grain size theory (Ziegler and Goswami, 2005, 2006). This theory postulates that the behavioral differences can be attributed to differences in the size of the orthographic units on which phonological recoding is based. Specifically, readers in shallow orthographies can rely on small psycholinguistic grain size (i.e., single letters or letter clusters corresponding to single phonemes) because grapheme-phoneme correspondences are relatively consistent. In contrast, readers of deep orthographies additionally have to rely on larger psycholinguistic grain size (i.e., letter patterns corresponding to rimes, syllables, or even whole words), which are more consistent compared with the relatively inconsistent grapheme-phoneme correspondences. It was shown that especially the continuous switching between small unit recoding and large unit recoding strategies leads to the reading accuracy disadvantage in deep orthographies (Goswami et al., 2003). In addition, it is far more difficult for a beginning reader to remember the mapping from orthography to phonology based on the vast amount of letter pattern-rime/syllable correspondences compared with the limited number of grapheme-phoneme correspondences.

ORTHOGRAPHIC DEPTH AND BRAIN IMAGING IN ALPHABETIC WRITING SYSTEMS

Cross-linguistic brain imaging studies are extremely laborious and difficult to conduct. They require well-matched designs and samples and face many practical problems (e.g., availability and comparability of assessment tools, differences in the school system, socio-economic factors, matching of stimuli, data acquisition protocols, etc.). Therefore, it is not surprising that to date only few cross-linguistic brain imaging studies have been published. Another approach focuses on bilingual or biliterate participants and searches for the effect of OD on brain activation within participants. The findings from these two types of studies will be reviewed below. In addition, there are promising attempts to investigate the influence of OD by means of artificial language training studies (Mei et al., 2013; Taylor et al., 2014). These studies can potentially contribute to the understanding of language-related differences in reading development.

Motivated by findings on behavioral differences between readers in deep and shallow orthographies, Paulesu et al. (2000) conducted a seminal positron emission tomography (PET) study. They compared brain activation during word and nonword reading in Italian and English skilled adult readers. With a conjunction analysis, they identified a largely left-lateralized brain network showing common activation in both groups. Specifically, this network included left inferior frontal (IFG), precentral (PreG), fusiform (FFG), inferior (ITG) and middle temporal (MTG) regions as well as bilateral superior temporal gyri (STG).

In addition, orthography-specific effects were investigated in a direct comparison between Italian and English readers. In general, orthography-specific effects were reflected in quantitative rather than qualitative differences in brain activation. That is, the very same brain regions were active in both languages, but to a different degree and spatial extent. Specifically, the direct comparison identified the left posterior STG at the junction to the parietal cortex with higher activation in Italian readers and the left posterior ITG and anterior IFG with higher activation in English readers. The STG activation was interpreted as reflecting enhanced involvement of phonological processing, whereas the ITG and IFG activation was interpreted as reflecting enhanced involvement of the orthographic lexicon. The left IFG region was also associated with semantic processing. In sum, the results were taken as evidence for the shaping of the neurobiological systems for reading through specific properties (i.e., OD) of the written language.

In a follow-up study, Paulesu et al. (2001) investigated whether such language-related brain activation effects would also pertain to developmental dyslexia. They acquired PET scans from non-impaired and dyslexic university students from Italy, France, and the UK during the same activation tasks used in their earlier study.

The main finding was the identification of a large left hemisphere cluster comprising STG, MTG, and ITG as well as middle occipital gyri with higher activation in non-impaired readers compared with dyslexic readers, irrespective of orthography. Vice versa, no regions were identified with higher activation in dyslexic readers compared with non-impaired readers.

With respect to orthography-specific effects, Paulesu et al. (2001) could confirm their earlier findings on non-impaired reading. That is, they replicated the findings on the English non-impaired readers with the French non-impaired readers (which they classified as readers in a deep orthography). Crucially, however, no orthography-specific effects were found in the direct comparison of the dyslexic subsamples from the three languages varying in OD. Taken together with the fact that all of the dyslexic participants were selected based on a marked phonological deficit, the brain imaging results were interpreted as evidence for a universal neurocognitive basis of developmental dyslexia.

Subsequently, Silani et al. (2005) acquired structural magnetic resonance imaging (MRI) data in addition to the functional PET activation data of the Italian, French, and English participants of Paulesu et al. (2001). Their voxel-based morphometry (VBM) analysis sought to investigate the correspondence between regional dysfunctions (i.e., underactivation) and anatomical alterations (i.e., with respect to the cortical surface and underlying fibers) in developmental dyslexia. For gray matter density, consistent reduction in dyslexic readers across all three orthographies was identified in the left MTG (with consistent augmentation in an adjacent left posterior MTG region). For white matter density, consistent reduction in dyslexic readers across all three orthographies was identified underneath the left IFG, postcentral, and supramarginal cortices. Similar to the functional activation study, no orthography-specific effects of dyslexia were found.

A different approach to investigate orthography-specific effects in reading-related brain activation was recently put forward by Das et al. (2011). They studied mono- and biliterate English and Hindi adult readers during reading aloud English and Hindi words. Furthermore, the group of biliterate readers were divided into those who learnt to read both languages at the age of 5 (simultaneous biliterate readers) and those who learnt to read Hindi at the age of 5 and English at the age of 10 (sequential biliterate readers). Crucially, only biliterate adults who learnt to read both languages simultaneously at the age of 5 showed a similar activation pattern as monoliterates, that is, left ITG activation for English (deep orthography) and left inferior parietal lobule (IPL) activation for Hindi (shallow orthography). During English word reading, the sequential biliterates did not exhibit the left ITG activation found in simultaneous biliterates and English monoliterates. The divergence between simultaneous and sequential biliterate readers speaks for early orthography-specific functional tuning of reading networks in the brain that persists into adulthood. This unique fMRI study is particularly impressive because it shows orthography-specific effects within participants rather than between participants.

Similarly, Bar-Kochva and Breznitz (2012) used a within-subjects design to investigate the effect OD on brain activation during reading by means of event-related potentials (ERPs). They studied Hebrew speakers, which were familiar with two forms of script (pointed and unpointed) varying in OD. During a lexical decision task, the shallow pointed script evoked larger amplitudes around 165 ms over occipito-temporal (OT) electrodes, whereas the deep unpointed script evoked larger amplitudes around 340 ms over occipito-parietal electrodes. The same authors found these effects also in adult dyslexic readers, but with reduced and delayed amplitudes. These results were interpreted as a failure in dyslexic readers to fine-tune their reading strategies to the particular demands imposed by the deep and shallow orthographies (Bar-Kochva and Breznitz, 2014).

BRAIN IMAGING COMPARING ALPHABETIC WITH SYLLABIC OR LOGOGRAPHIC WRITING SYSTEMS

In addition to comparing written alphabetic languages with varying OD, there were attempts to compare brain activation of proficient readers in alphabetic writing systems with Chinese (logographic), Japanese Kana (syllabic), and Japanese Kanji (morpho-syllabic). In their coordinate-based meta-analysis, Bolger et al. (2005) found convergence of reading-related activation of all four writing systems in left STG, IFG, and OT regions. As expected, the activation patterns of the different writing systems also differed to some degree, mainly with respect to extension of clusters. Specifically, divergence was identified in a posterior aspect of the left STG (with higher activation for Western and Kana writing systems), in an anterior aspect of the left IFG (with higher activation for Chinese), and in the right OT cortex (again with higher activation for Chinese). The higher activation for the alphabetic and syllabic writing systems in the left posterior STG was interpreted as reflecting the mapping of written symbols to fine-grained speech sounds (phonemes and syllables)—in contrast to mapping to whole-word phonology in the case of Chinese and Kanji. The higher activation for Chinese (logographic) in the left anterior IFG was interpreted as reflecting synchronous processing of semantic and phonological information that is—due to the high number of homophones in Chinese—required for unambiguous identification of written symbols. Finally, the higher activation for Chinese in the right OT cortex was interpreted as reflecting global and low spatial frequency processing of the spatial arrangement of the written symbols. In line with these meta-analytic findings, a newer near-infrared spectroscopy (NIRS) study comparing English and Chinese readers during a homophone judgment task identified higher activation in the left STG in English readers and higher activation in the left middle frontal gyrus (MFG) in Chinese readers (Chen et al., 2008).

Another study with biliterate participants in Korean Hangul (phonographic) and Hanja (logographic) showed that the level of reading proficiency in the logographic orthography modulated the reading strategy and, correspondingly, the brain activation pattern during processing of the phonographic orthography (Jeon, 2012). Specifically, highly skilled readers, relying on the lexical route, activated anterior cingulate, MFG, and OT regions, whereas less skilled readers, relying on the sublexical route, activated IPL and IFG regions.

A developmental difference between English and Chinese readers was recently observed in an fMRI study using a word pair rhyme judgment task (Brennan et al., 2013). A network of left hemisphere regions (including STG, IPL, and IFG) showed an increase of activation in English adults compared with children but not in Chinese adults compared with children. This finding was taken as evidence for reorganization of the left hemisphere phonological network in readers of alphabetic but not in readers of logographic writing systems, possibly as a result from the differences in psycholinguistic grain size, with smaller units in English compared with Chinese.

First evidence for writing system-related brain activation abnormalities in developmental dyslexia was reported by Siok et al. (2004). They found marked underactivation of the left MFG in dyslexic compared with non-impaired Chinese children during homophone judgment and lexical decision. Further indication for a crucial influence of the writing system on the neurobiological manifestation of developmental dyslexia was provided in a follow-up study (Siok et al., 2008). Chinese dyslexic children not only exhibited functional underactivation of the left MFG in response to a rhyme judgment task but also showed reduced gray matter volume of this region compared with their age-matched non-impaired peers. Interestingly, the Chinese dyslexic readers did not exhibit the left posterior underactivation, which is distinctive of dyslexic readers in alphabetic writing systems. The unique engagement of the left MFG in Chinese non-impaired reading (and failure of engagement in dyslexia) was explained by the strong involvement of motor processes during learning to read Chinese. Children in primary school spend a lot of time copying newly learned characters and this likely involves recruitment of the left MFG just anterior to the motor cortex. It was shown that handwriting skills are the best predictor of reading ability, with both supported by long-term graphomotor memories of characters (Tan et al., 2005).

Although these data seem to challenge the universality of neurocognitive explanations of dyslexia, Ziegler (2006) argues that the phonological deficit theory still accounts for the problems of Chinese dyslexic readers. Instead of the mapping of graphemes onto phonemes, the phonological deficit of Chinese dyslexics lies in the association of complex graphomotor programs of logographs to whole-word phonology. That is, the universality of the phonological deficit is still valid, but its putative association with a left STG dysfunction is not. Another possibility is that the left MFG—as part of the central executive—subserves a coordination and integration function of orthographic, phonological, and semantic information, which is particularly important for Chinese reading (Perfetti et al., 2006).

In a direct cross-linguistic comparison, it was recently shown that the brain activation differences between dyslexic and non-impaired readers of Chinese and English are not that massive as previously thought. In a well-conceived fMRI study, Hu et al. (2010) found writing system-specific activation differences during a semantic word matching task between the two groups of non-impaired readers but not between the two groups of dyslexic readers. Specifically, Chinese non-impaired readers exhibited higher activation compared with English non-impaired readers in the left IFG sulcus and lower activation in left posterior superior temporal sulcus. Crucially, dyslexic readers of both languages showed reliable activation in these two regions, indicating the use of a similar reading strategy. The dyslexic readers shared, however, a common pattern of underactivation relative to non-impaired readers in the left MFG, left posterior MTG, left angular gyrus, and left OT sulcus. Thus, the functional neuroanatomical manifestation of dyslexia in English and Chinese is similar when a reading task with demands on semantic processing is used.

METHODOLOGICAL CONSIDERATIONS

Cross-linguistic brain imaging studies of developmental dyslexia have also been the target of serious criticism. For example, Hadzibeganovic et al. (2010) questioned the biological unity account of dyslexia because of both conceptual and methodological issues of some of the above mentioned studies. In particular, they focused their critique on the seminal studies by Paulesu et al. (2001) and Silani et al. (2005), which had the biggest impact on the field. The problems raised include (i) missing subtyping of dyslexia cases; (ii) differences in selection of participants across the three countries; and (iii) discounting of differences in cognitive demands for reading diverse orthographies.

Some of the points of criticism of Hadzibeganovic et al. (2010) are valid; however, I want to clarify the crucial aspects by providing some explanations for why the studies of the Paulesu group did not identify orthography-specific effects in the neurobiology of developmental dyslexia. First of all—and most importantly—Paulesu et al. (2001) and Silani et al. (2005) did not claim that all developmental dyslexics have the same brain abnormality. Rather, they showed that there is some shared component across the three alphabetic orthographies (Italian, French, English)—namely left posterior underactivation as well as reduced gray and white matter density. Although their finding of an absence of orthography-specific effects is suggestive of a complete overlap of brain abnormality patterns, the much more probable scenario—based on evidence from studies comparing different writing systems (e.g., Bolger et al., 2005; Hu et al., 2010)—is that there is some core dysfunction present in dyslexia in all writing systems with additional language-related variations and extensions. This means that there is a shared component (the core dysfunction), but with orthography-specific differences based on the particular properties of the language and the reader's experience. It is plausible to assume that the nature of orthography-specific differences is quantitatively rather than qualitatively. That is, that differential weighing of cognitive components is reflected mainly in the degree and spatial extent of activation clusters rather than in variation of anatomical location (Paulesu et al., 2000). There are several reasonable explanations for why the Paulesu et al. (2001) and Silani et al. (2005) studies did not identify these fine-grained language-related variations. These possibilities will be spelled out in detail below.

The logic behind Paulesu et al.'s search for orthography-specific effects in developmental dyslexia was not ideal. Paulesu et al. (2001) directly compared the activation patterns of the dyslexic readers across the three languages. It would be, however, more sensible to compare the abnormality patterns of the dyslexic readers (relative to the non-impaired readers) across the three languages. As an example, imagine the following situation (illustrated in **Figure 1A**): Italian but not English non-impaired readers show strong activation of the left STG. Both Italian and

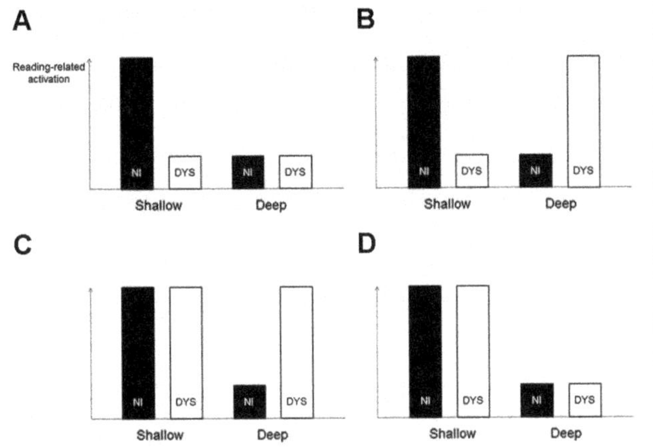

FIGURE 1 | Illustration of different activation patterns of non-impaired (NI) and dyslexic (DYS) readers. The strategy to compare abnormality patterns of dyslexic readers (relative to non-impaired readers) across languages would correctly identify the situations illustrated in sections **(A–C)** as showing an orthography-specific abnormality pattern and would correctly reject the situation illustrated in section **(D)**. In contrast, the actual strategy used by Paulesu et al. (2001) (i.e., comparing dyslexic activation directly across languages), would only correctly identify the situation illustrated in section **(B)**. It would fail to identify the situations illustrated in sections **(A)** and **(C)** and would incorrectly identify the situation illustrated in section **(D)**.

English dyslexic readers show weak activation of the left STG. In the case of the Italian dyslexics, let us assume that this weak activation is the result of a specific deficit of a cognitive process supported by this region, whereas in the case of the English dyslexics, it is simply the result of little requirement by the deep orthography of English to engage this very same process (hence only weak activation in non-impaired readers as well). A direct comparison of Italian versus English dyslexic readers—the strategy used by Paulesu et al. (2001)—would not identify this region with an orthography-specific deficit. In contrast, a comparison of the underactivation pattern (i.e., non-impaired > dyslexic) between Italian versus English would identify this region. The latter strategy is all the more sensible, given that there are known brain activation differences between Italian and English non-impaired readers (Paulesu et al., 2000), and dyslexia-related dysfunctions can be supposed to be associated with these very same regions.

Moreover, the strategy to search for orthography-specific differences in dyslexic under- or overactivation would yield reasonable results for the hypothetical situations illustrated in **Figures 1B–D**. Situation D deserves closer attention. Here, both non-impaired and dyslexic readers show a language-related effect, that is, higher reading-related activation in a shallow compared with a deep orthography. Crucially, however, there is no effect of dyslexia within a language. Therefore, this activation pattern should not be considered as showing an orthography-specific dyslexic abnormality pattern. Again, the proposed search strategy would yield a reasonable result because it would not identify a region with this activation pattern. With the knowledge from their previous study, that is, an orthography-specific effect in non-impaired readers (Paulesu et al., 2000), and the strategy to directly compare dyslexic readers across languages, it seems like Paulesu et al. (2001) searched for such a pattern of general language-related differences. This is, however, rather uninformative when it comes to orthography-specific dyslexic activation abnormality patterns.

A further possible explanation for why the Paulesu et al. (2001) and Silani et al. (2005) studies did not find orthography-specific dyslexic abnormalities relates to the small number of participants (six participants per group, per language, and per activation task) resulting in low statistical power (Button et al., 2013). In addition, as already suggested by Paulesu et al. (2001), the dyslexic readers may have used idiosyncratic and inter-individually heterogeneous reading strategies resulting in less consistent group-level brain activation. This would be in line with evidence for the engagement of inter-individually diverse neuronal networks for reading (Seghier et al., 2008; Kherif et al., 2009; Richardson et al., 2011). Finally, PET imaging (Paulesu et al., 2001) and the VBM method (Silani et al., 2005) are subject to inherent limitations such as low temporal and spatial resolution and reliance on block-designs (PET), and mis-registration of images, mis-classification of tissue, and a neuroanatomically unspecific measurement of local gray matter volume or density (e.g., Mechelli et al., 2005; Richlan et al., 2013b), which may obscure subtle and fine-grained orthography-specific differences.

PREDICTIONS DERIVED FROM FUNCTIONAL NEUROANATOMICAL MODELS

As argued above, it is not surprising that Paulesu et al. (2001) and Silani et al. (2005) did not find evidence for differences in the neurocognitive deficits between dyslexic readers in deep and shallow orthographies despite the documented orthography-specific effects in non-impaired readers (e.g., Paulesu et al., 2000; Das et al., 2011). As evident from the review of behavioral studies, the usual finding is that successful reading acquisition is based on the same cognitive components in deep and shallow orthographies. The general pattern of early contribution of PA and later contribution of RAN is independent of OD. What varies across languages is the degree to which these components contribute over time (Vaessen et al., 2010). In addition, it makes a difference whether reading accuracy or reading speed is assessed (Moll et al., 2014).

Functional neuroanatomical models of developmental dyslexia (e.g., Pugh et al., 2000; Richlan, 2012) provide a basis for testable hypotheses about different brain activation patterns in non-impaired and dyslexic readers between languages differing in OD. Although these models are not explicit in stating orthography-specific predictions, their architecture (e.g., which brain regions are engaged by certain cognitive processes) allows one to derive hypotheses about expected brain activation patterns. These model-based predictions will be described below. In line with the behavioral findings on the contribution of cognitive components to reading, activation of brain regions across orthographies is not a matter of all or none but rather a matter of degree. In addition, due to the usual spatial smoothness of functional brain imaging data, a higher level of brain activation can be expressed in larger spatial extent of activation clusters. Thus, the functional neuroanatomical models do not predict involvement of completely different brain regions across orthographies, but rather activation of the same brain regions to a different degree and extent (Pugh et al., 2005).

In addition to tuning of local brain activation it was put forward that the development of skilled reading relies on systems-level plasticity (i.e., on changes in the interactions between brain regions) (Schlaggar and McCandliss, 2007). The idea is that brain regions that are already partially active at the beginning of learning to read become better connected over time (both structurally and functionally), thus providing the basis for the development of skilled reading. This interactive specialization concept is incorporated in the predictions of the newer functional neuroanatomical model (Richlan, 2012). It relies on the many neuroimaging studies from the last years that investigated reading-related structural connectivity by means of diffusion tensor imaging (DTI; e.g., Ben-Shachar et al., 2007; Hoeft et al., 2011; Vandermosten et al., 2012; Boets et al., 2013; Thiebaut de Schotten et al., 2014) or functional and effective connectivity by means of both task-based and resting-state fMRI (e.g., Richardson et al., 2011; van der Mark et al., 2011; Koyama et al., 2013; Vogel et al., 2014; Schurz et al., 2014). In addition to this MRI-based research, valuable information on inter-regional functional coupling can be gained from the time course of activation of relevant brain regions via temporally precise techniques such as electroencephalography (EEG) and magnetoencephalography (MEG) (for a recent review see Carreiras et al., 2014).

THE CLASSICAL MODEL

Figure 2A illustrates the predictions for reading-related brain activation in non-impaired and dyslexic readers of deep and shallow orthographies based on the classical model by Pugh et al. (2000). This seminal model and its subsequent variations (e.g., McCandliss and Noble, 2003; Démonet et al., 2004; Sandak et al., 2004; Pugh et al., 2005) propose engagement of the left dorsal temporo-parietal (TP) cortex (including the posterior STG and the supramarginal and angular gyri of the IPL) during phonology-based reading processes (i.e., grapheme-phoneme conversion, phonological assembly) in non-impaired readers and a corresponding dysfunction (reflected in absent or reduced activation) in dyslexic readers. Consequently, for shallow orthographies, one would predict reading-related activation in non-impaired children and adults and underactivation in dyslexic readers. For deep orthographies, in contrast, one would expect activation only in non-impaired children or in tasks requiring phonology-based reading or explicit phonological analysis. The dyslexic readers, due to their proposed primary phonological TP deficit, would exhibit underactivation. In sum, the left dorsal TP system dominates at the beginning of learning to read in typically developing children, irrespective of orthography. Dyslexic readers, however, fail to properly activate this system.

Furthermore, the classical model proposes engagement of the left ventral OT cortex (including posterior ITG and FFG) during memory-based orthographic word recognition. In skilled readers, this system becomes the critical support for fast and efficient reading. In dyslexic readers, a secondary deficit of the left ventral OT system is assumed to follow from a primary deficit in left dorsal TP regions. The predictions for shallow orthographies are intermediate activation in non-impaired readers irrespective of reading age (unless explicit orthographic tasks require high engagement of this region) and little activation in dyslexic readers. For deep orthographies the predictions are strong activation in non-impaired adults and advanced children (that is, as soon as orthographic representations are built up) and underactivation in dyslexics. Therefore, the universal reading speed deficit of dyslexic readers across languages is thought to be reflected in underactivation of the left ventral OT cortex (Pugh, 2006).

Finally, the classical model includes a third anterior reading circuit, which is located in the left IFG. Its function is assumed to include (among others) speech-gestural articulatory recoding of print. According to the model and regardless of orthography, dyslexic readers should exhibit overactivation of this region and of additional right hemisphere posterior regions compared with non-impaired readers in order to compensate for their dysfunction in the two left posterior regions. This overactivation, however, is not present at the beginning of learning to read, but increases with age (Shaywitz et al., 2002).

THE NEW MODEL

LEFT INFERIOR PARIETAL LOBULE

Figure 2B illustrates the predictions for reading-related activation based on a newer model by Richlan (2012). The involved regions are largely the same (with some subtle anatomical variations) but the assumed functions in non-impaired reading and the associated dysfunctions in dyslexic reading are crucially different. Importantly, the model by Richlan (2012) divides the left TP circuit of Pugh et al. (2000) into a more dorsal IPL part adjacent to the intra-parietal sulcus and a more ventral STG part around the posterior sylvian fissure. The former was proposed to be engaged by more general attentional mechanisms, which are not exclusively related to reading (Shaywitz and Shaywitz, 2008). In the left dorsal IPL, as evidenced by meta-analysis, the typical finding is increased task-negative activation in dyslexic compared with non-impaired children during reading or reading-related processes (Richlan et al., 2011). That is, non-impaired readers show weak (de)activation relative to a low-level visual baseline, whereas dyslexic readers exhibit marked deactivation relative to baseline. This task-induced interruption of baseline activation was interpreted as reflecting greater mental effort during reading in dyslexic readers.

Note, however, that the left dorsal IPL can also be activated by non-impaired readers depending on the task and stimulus requirements. In this case, the typical finding is reduced task-positive activation in dyslexic readers (e.g., Cao et al., 2006; van der Mark et al., 2009; Richlan et al., 2010; Wimmer et al., 2010) and disrupted functional connectivity between the left dorsal IPL and the left ventral OT cortex (Cao et al., 2008; van der Mark et al., 2011). It is possible that the left dorsal IPL is involved in shifting attention from letter to letter within a string (e.g., Behrmann et al., 2004; Wager et al., 2004; Rosazza et al., 2009; Cabeza et al., 2012) and thus subserves serial decoding. This function is needed during reading based on

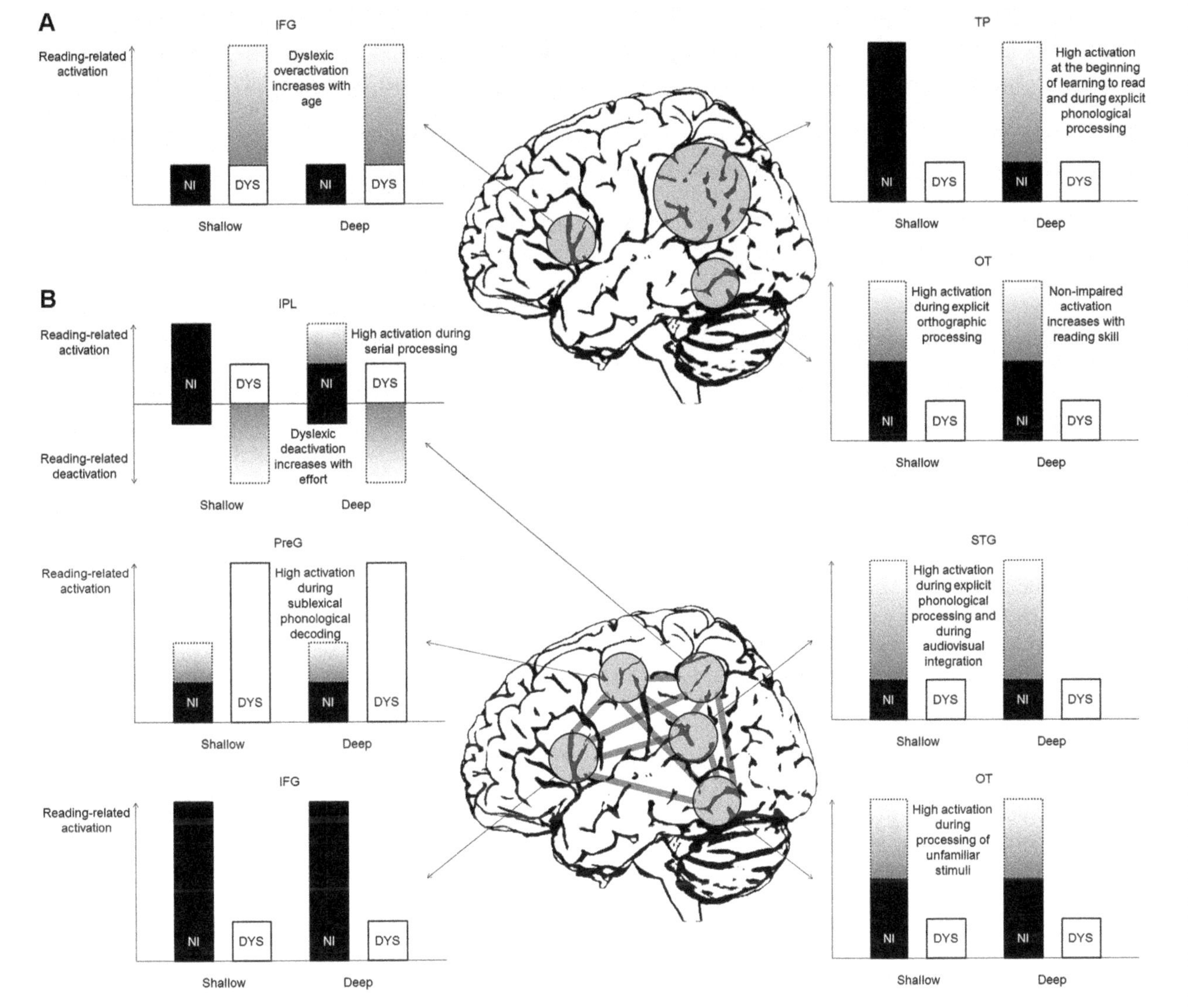

FIGURE 2 | Predictions for reading-related activation in non-impaired (NI) and dyslexic (DYS) readers in deep and shallow orthographies (A) based on the classical model by Pugh et al. (2000) and (B) based on the new model by Richlan (2012). Gray gradient bars represent activation that is only present under certain conditions (for detailed explanations see text). IFG = inferior frontal gyrus, IPL = inferior parietal lobule, OT = occipito-temporal cortex, PreG = precentral gyrus, STG = superior temporal gyrus, TP = temporo-parietal cortex.

grapheme-phoneme conversion but is irrelevant during reading based on whole-word representations. Accordingly, the left dorsal IPL was consistently identified with higher activation in response to pseudoword reading compared with word reading in a meta-analysis of 36 neuroimaging studies of typical readers (Taylor et al., 2013).

Assuming a functional role of the left dorsal IPL subserving serial decoding in non-impaired readers and a dysfunction in dyslexic readers, the prediction would be reduced dyslexic task-positive activation in shallow orthographies (with reliance on rule-based grapheme-phoneme conversion) or when serial processing is emphasized by task or stimulus demands (e.g., Cohen et al., 2008; Rosazza et al., 2009). In contrast, in deep orthographies (with reliance on memory-based word recognition) or when visual-orthographic whole-word processing is predominant, one would expect little engagement of the left dorsal IPL in non-impaired readers. Dyslexic readers, however, would exhibit increased task-negative activation (i.e., deactivation) in response to greater mental effort during reading, reflecting an interruption of the baseline activation of the left dorsal IPL (Richlan et al., 2011). Note that the orthography-specific predictions would be the same based on psycholinguistic grain size theory (Ziegler and Goswami, 2005, 2006). That is, non-impaired readers in shallow orthographies should rely more on the serial attention shifting mechanism in the left dorsal IPL compared with non-impaired readers in deep orthographies, due to the smaller size of the orthographic units. In order to distinguish whether dyslexic underactivation relative to non-impaired readers stems from differences in task-positive or task-negative activation, it is indispensable for future fMRI studies to include rest blocks (in the case of block-design fMRI) or appropriate interstimulus intervals and null-events (in the case of event-related fMRI).

With respect to neuroanatomy, it is important to note that the left dorsal IPL clusters found in the meta-analyses of dyslexic brain activation abnormalities (Richlan et al., 2009, 2011) correspond more to the supramarginal gyrus than to the angular gyrus. Among the functions discussed above, the former is thought to be involved in phonological processes, whereas the latter is thought to be involved in semantic processes (e.g., Vigneau et al., 2006; Binder et al., 2009; Cabeza et al., 2012; Carter and Huettel, 2013). This classical subdivision, however, might be too coarse (Seghier and Price, 2012). Recent evidence from studies on cytoarchitectonics (Caspers et al., 2006, 2008), receptor architectonics (Caspers et al., 2013), structural connectivity (Mars et al., 2011, 2012), and functional connectivity (Yeo et al., 2011; Bzdok et al., 2013) speaks for much more fine-grained parcellation of the parietal cortex into multiple subdivisions.

LEFT SUPERIOR TEMPORAL GYRUS

The second left TP region (left posterior STG adjacent to the sylvian fissure) is not assigned a key role in grapheme-phoneme conversion in the new model. This assumption stands in marked contrast to the classical model, in which this region is proposed to dominate at the beginning of learning to read. Consequently, in the new model it is not assumed that a primary deficit in the left STG leads to a secondary deficit in the left ventral OT cortex in dyslexic readers. Instead, the left perisylvian TP region seems to be involved when explicit fine-grained phonological analysis is required (e.g., Griffiths and Warren, 2002; Hickok et al., 2011; DeWitt and Rauschecker, 2012; Price, 2012) or when information from auditory linguistic inputs and visual linguistic inputs (i.e., speech sounds and letters) has to be integrated (e.g., van Atteveldt et al., 2004; Blau et al., 2010). Hence, activation of this region is predicted when the task involves unimodal auditory or bimodal audiovisual processing. For unimodal visual processing, engagement of this region is typically not reported, unless the task involves demanding phonological analysis. In a recent meta-analysis the left STG was not considered to be part of the reading network (Taylor et al., 2013).

There is emerging evidence that the neural correlates of multisensory letter-speech sound integration might be modulated by OD. Specifically, a study with English adult readers (Holloway et al., 2013) did not find congruency effects for letter-speech sound pairs in the STG as were previously reported in a similar study with Dutch adult readers (van Atteveldt et al., 2004). With respect to brain plasticity, it was shown that reading development has an influence on activation in the left STG regions associated with phonological processing, and that this influence is stronger in alphabetic compared with logographic writing systems (Brennan et al., 2013). In addition, a recent meta-analysis on structural brain abnormalities in dyslexia identified reduced gray matter volume in bilateral perisylvian TP regions, possibly reflecting reduced tuning of the phonological network as a result of reduced reading experience in dyslexics (Richlan et al., 2013b). Therefore, one may speculate that, opposite to the developmental assumption of the classical model, a primary left ventral OT dysfunction results in a secondary left STG dysfunction in dyslexia. The influence of OD within alphabetic writing systems on this developmental effect, however, is still a blank spot on the map.

LEFT VENTRAL OCCIPITO-TEMPORAL CORTEX

One may ask where in the brain, if not in the left perisylvian TP cortex, grapheme-phoneme conversion should be located in the new model. The idea is that the left ventral OT cortex is associated with both visual-orthographic whole-word processing and serial grapheme-phoneme conversion. Among others (e.g., Xu et al., 2001; Mechelli et al., 2003; Binder et al., 2005; Kronbichler et al., 2007, 2009; Bruno et al., 2008; Brem et al., 2010; Ludersdorfer et al., 2013), evidence comes from an fMRI study (Schurz et al., 2010), in which non-impaired German readers exhibited a length by lexicality interaction in the left ventral OT cortex (i.e., an increase of activation with increasing number of letters for pseudowords but not for words). German dyslexic readers exhibited overall lower activation and failed to show the modulation of activation by length of pseudowords (Richlan et al., 2010).

At least for German, other fMRI studies have also shown that dyslexic underactivation is more pronounced when orthographically unfamiliar stimuli (e.g., pseudowords or pseudohomophones) impose higher demands on phonological processing compared with orthographically familiar stimuli (words) (van der Mark et al., 2009; Wimmer et al., 2010). Future studies in other shallow orthographies (e.g., Dutch, Italian, or Spanish) are expected to yield similar results. Therefore, the prediction for shallow orthographies is intermediate activation for non-impaired readers with increasing activation when grapheme-phoneme conversion is required by task or stimulus demands (e.g., pseudowords). Dyslexic readers are expected to exhibit weak overall activation and failure to increase activation in response to unfamiliar stimuli.

Higher left ventral OT cortex activation for unfamiliar compared with familiar letter strings is a common finding also in the English-based literature and was interpreted as a reflection of sustained task-related top-down processing (Dehaene and Cohen, 2011). A different explanation was put forward by Price and Devlin (2011). In their interactive account, higher activation for unfamiliar compared with familiar letter strings in the left ventral OT cortex is explained by higher prediction error (i.e., the difference between bottom-up visual information and top-down predictions). The top-down predictions are generated automatically from prior experience in higher cortical levels that contribute to representing phonology, semantics, and actions. This view is in line with the role of the left ventral OT cortex in grapheme-phoneme conversion in the new model. In the Interactive Account, the left ventral OT underactivation exhibited by dyslexic readers is interpreted as failure to establish hierarchical connections and access top-down predictions. As top-down predictions from phonology and semantics play an important role in reading irrespective of OD, the left ventral OT activation pattern is expected to be similar in deep and shallow orthographies.

LEFT INFERIOR FRONTAL GYRUS

A further difference between the classical model (Pugh et al., 2000) and the new model (Richlan, 2012) refers to the left anterior reading component. In contrast to the classical model, the new model—supported by findings from meta-analyses (Richlan et al., 2009, 2011)—proposes a subdivision of the left anterior system into an IFG region and a dorsal precentral region. The former was consistently identified with dyslexic underactivation, whereas the latter was consistently identified with dyslexic overactivation.

The left IFG underactivation is thought to reflect the problem of dyslexic readers to access phonological output representations (Ramus and Szenkovits, 2008). This notion was recently supported by a study combining multivoxel pattern analysis, and functional and structural connectivity analysis (Boets et al., 2013). The main finding was reduced functional coupling in an auditory phoneme discrimination task and reduced white matter integrity as measured by DTI between left IFG and STG regions in dyslexic readers. In addition, the left IFG is assumed to have strong reciprocal connections and to interact with the left ventral OT cortex during non-impaired reading (e.g., Catani et al., 2005; Ben-Shachar et al., 2007; van der Mark et al., 2011; Vandermosten et al., 2012; Yeatman et al., 2013; Schurz et al., 2014).

Up to now, there are no indications of essential differences in dyslexic underactivation in shallow versus deep orthographies in the left IFG. Some accounts speak for engagement of the left IFG in grapheme-phoneme conversion (e.g., Jobard et al., 2003) or lexical access (e.g., Heim et al., 2013). There is, however, room for speculation because the IFG is a heterogeneous region, which is not only characterized by anatomical subdivisions based on neurotransmitter receptor architectonics (Amunts et al., 2010), but was associated with various different cognitive and emotional processes (e.g., Laird et al., 2011; Price, 2012; Richlan et al., 2013a).

LEFT DORSAL PRECENTRAL GYRUS

In line with the classical model, the left dorsal PreG was consistently identified with overactivation in dyslexic children and adults (Richlan et al., 2009, 2011). This overactivation is assumed to reflect compensatory reliance on articulatory processes during reading from an early age on. The left dorsal PreG is part of the sublexical phonological decoding route and typically identified with higher activation for pseudowords compared with words in non-impaired readers (Price, 2012; Taylor et al., 2013). Interestingly, in our study with dyslexic adolescents and young adults (Richlan et al., 2010), it was the only region which showed higher activation for pseudowords compared with words together with a length effect for pseudowords in dyslexic readers. With respect to OD, no differences are assumed in left dorsal PreG overactivation between dyslexic readers in deep and shallow orthographies, because of universal overreliance on articulatory processes.

FUNCTIONAL INTEGRATION/INTERACTIVE SPECIALIZATION

Following Schlaggar and McCandliss (2007), the new model incorporates the concept of interactive specialization, that is, the idea that the development of skilled reading relies on the functional integration of distributed brain regions. Changes through development are not only assumed to take place in local brain modules (reflected in tuning of regional activation patterns and structural cortical plasticity), but also on the systems-level (reflected in alterations in functional coupling and white matter connectivity between brain regions). As already mentioned in Section Predictions Derived from Functional Neuroanatomical Models, a number of studies investigated the functional and structural neuroanatomy of reading from this systems-level perspective.

A main focus was on connectivity of the left ventral OT cortex with other language-related brain regions. There is good evidence from studies with non-impaired readers (e.g., Koyama et al., 2011; Vogel et al., 2012), developmental dyslexic readers (e.g., Shaywitz et al., 2003; van der Mark et al., 2011), and acquired dyslexic readers (e.g., Epelbaum et al., 2008; Seghier et al., 2012; Woodhead et al., 2013), that integration of the left ventral OT cortex with frontal and parietal regions is vital for fast and efficient reading (Price and Devlin, 2011). In addition to functional integration, it was shown that skilled adult readers show functional segregation (i.e., decoupling) of the reading network with the typically task-negative default mode network (Koyama et al., 2011).

The connections between brain regions in **Figure 2B** should be taken as illustration of the interactive specialization framework. For reasons of simplicity, all possible connections between brain regions are drawn, but the assumption is not that all of the brain regions interact with each other in any given situation. Instead, the idea is that different parts of the overall network interact in flexible and temporal dynamic ways depending on the required cognitive processes for a given task or stimulus.

Based on the evidence available up to now, it is impossible to reliably predict differences in connectivity patterns between deep and shallow orthographies. Studies aimed at these differences, however, are likely to shed light on the functional neuroanatomical reflection of OD, despite potentially very subtle differences in local brain activation profiles. Therefore, I look forward to innovative future studies investigating the effect of OD within alphabetic writing systems and differences between alphabetic and other writing systems by means of structural, functional, and effective connectivity in task-based as well as resting-state fMRI.

SUMMARY AND CONCLUSION

To sum up, dyslexia-related differences between deep and shallow orthographies can be expected in a variety of left hemisphere brain regions, depending on task and stimulus demands and age of participants. The two models (Pugh et al., 2000; Richlan, 2012) differ in many respects as for how they predict the degree and extent of engagement in these regions. In addition, differences between deep and shallow orthographies are likely to be reflected in the dynamic interactions between brain regions.

Evidence from cross-linguistic brain imaging studies on developmental dyslexia is scarce. The different approaches of classical between-subjects designs, within-subjects designs (in the case of bilingual participants), and artificial orthography learning paradigms should be continued and expanded in the future. In addition, meta-analysis might provide a valuable tool to synthesize and compare a high number of original studies, which were conducted within a single language. A comparable strategy was already successfully applied in the investigation of child and adult studies of developmental dyslexia (Richlan et al., 2011).

The investigation of typical and atypical reading processes in different orthographies yields important implications for the neurobiological understanding of developmental dyslexia. The given variations in OD and the role of English as an "outlier" orthography (Share, 2008) should be considered as an opportunity to test the current neurocognitive models and to refine them. The present review article contributes to this endeavor by providing orthography-specific predictions derived from two distinct conceptions of the functional neuroanatomy of non-impaired and dyslexic reading. These predictions should be tested in future brain imaging studies of reading.

ACKNOWLEDGMENTS

I would like to thank Julia Sophia Crone, Benjamin Gagl, Stefan Hawelka, Florian Hutzler, Robin Litt, Anna Martin, Matthias Schurz, Sarah Schuster, Lorenzo Vignali, and Heinz Wimmer for their feedback during the preparation of this manuscript. This work was supported by the Austrian Science Fund (FWF P 23916-B18 and P 25799-B23).

REFERENCES

Amunts, K., Lenzen, M., Friederici, A. D., Schleicher, A., Morosan, P., Palomero-Gallagher, N., et al. (2010). Broca's region: novel organizational principles and multiple receptor mapping. *PLoS Biol.* 8:e1000489. doi: 10.1371/journal.pbio.1000489

Aro, M., and Wimmer, H. (2003). Learning to read: english in comparison to six more regular orthographies. *Appl. Psycholinguist.* 24, 621–635. doi: 10.1017/s0142716403000316

Barca, L., Burani, C., Di Filippo, G., and Zoccolotti, P. (2006). Italian developmental dyslexic and proficient readers: where are the differences? *Brain Lang.* 98, 347–351. doi: 10.1016/j.bandl.2006.05.001

Bar-Kochva, I., and Breznitz, Z. (2012). Does the reading of different orthographies produce distinct brain activity patterns? An ERP study. *PLoS One* 7:e36030. doi: 10.1371/journal.pone.0036030

Bar-Kochva, I., and Breznitz, Z. (2014). Reading proficiency and adaptability in orthographic processing: an examination of the effect of type of orthography read on brain activity in regular and dyslexic readers. *PLoS One* 9:e86016. doi: 10.1371/journal.pone.0086016

Behrmann, M., Geng, J. J., and Shomstein, S. (2004). Parietal cortex and attention. *Curr. Opin. Neurobiol.* 14, 212–217. doi: 10.1016/j.conb.2004.03.012

Ben-Shachar, M., Dougherty, R. F., and Wandell, B. A. (2007). White matter pathways in reading. *Curr. Opin. Neurobiol.* 17, 258–270. doi: 10.1016/j.conb.2007.03.006

Bergmann, J., and Wimmer, H. (2008). A dual-route perspective on poor reading in a regular orthography: evidence from phonological and orthographic lexical decisions. *Cogn. Neuropsychol.* 25, 653–676. doi: 10.1080/02643290802221404

Binder, J. R., Desai, R. H., Graves, W. W., and Conant, L. L. (2009). Where is the semantic system? A critical review and meta-analysis of 120 functional neuroimaging studies. *Cereb. Cortex* 19, 2767–2796. doi: 10.1093/cercor/bhp055

Binder, J. R., Medler, D. A., Desai, R., Conant, L. L., and Liebenthal, E. (2005). Some neurophysiological constraints on models of word naming. *Neuroimage* 27, 677–693. doi: 10.1016/j.neuroimage.2005.04.029

Blau, V., Reithler, J., van Atteveldt, N., Seitz, J., Gerretsen, P., Goebel, R., et al. (2010). Deviant processing of letters and speech sounds as proximate cause of reading failure: a functional magnetic resonance imaging study of dyslexic children. *Brain* 133, 868–879. doi: 10.1093/brain/awp308

Boets, B., Op de Beeck, H. P., Vandermosten, M., Scott, S. K., Gillebert, C. R., Mantini, D., et al. (2013). Intact but less accessible phonetic representations in adults with dyslexia. *Science* 342, 1251–1254. doi: 10.1126/science.1244333

Bolger, D. J., Perfetti, C. A., and Schneider, W. (2005). Cross-cultural effect on the brain revisited: universal structures plus writing system variation. *Hum. Brain Mapp.* 25, 92–104. doi: 10.1002/hbm.20124

Brem, S., Bach, S., Kucian, K., Guttorm, T. K., Martin, E., Lyytinen, H., et al. (2010). Brain sensitivity to print emerges when children learn letter-speech sound correspondences. *Proc. Natl. Acad. Sci. U S A* 107, 7939–7944. doi: 10.1073/pnas.0904402107

Brennan, C., Cao, F., Pedroarena-Leal, N., McNorgan, C., and Booth, J. R. (2013). Reading acquisition reorganizes the phonological awareness network only in alphabetic writing systems. *Hum. Brain Mapp.* 34, 3354–3368. doi: 10.1002/hbm.22147

Bruno, J. L., Zumberge, A., Manis, F. R., Lu, Z. L., and Goldman, J. G. (2008). Sensitivity to orthographic familiarity in the occipito-temporal region. *Neuroimage* 39, 1988–2001. doi: 10.1016/j.neuroimage.2007.10.044

Button, K. S., Ioannidis, J. P. A., Mokrysz, C., Nosek, B. A., Flint, J., Robinson, E. S. J., et al. (2013). Power failure: why small sample size undermines the reliability of neuroscience. *Nat. Rev. Neurosci.* 14, 365–376. doi: 10.1038/nrn3475

Bzdok, D., Langner, R., Schilbach, L., Jakobs, O., Roski, C., Caspers, S., et al. (2013). Characterization of the temporo-parietal junction by combining data-driven parcellation, complementary connectivity analyses and functional decoding. *Neuroimage* 81, 381–392. doi: 10.1016/j.neuroimage.2013.05.046

Cabeza, R., Ciaramelli, E., and Moscovitch, M. (2012). Cognitive contributions of the ventral parietal cortex: an integrative theoretical account. *Trends Cogn. Sci.* 16, 338–352. doi: 10.1016/j.tics.2012.04.008

Cao, F., Bitan, T., and Booth, J. R. (2008). Effective brain connectivity in children with reading difficulties during phonological processing. *Brain Lang.* 107, 91–101. doi: 10.1016/j.bandl.2007.12.009

Cao, F., Bitan, T., Chou, T.-L., Burman, D. D., and Booth, J. R. (2006). Deficient orthographic and phonological representations in children with dyslexia revealed by brain activation patterns. *J. Child Psychol. Psychiatry* 47, 1041–1050. doi: 10.1111/j.1469-7610.2006.01684.x

Caravolas, M., Lervåg, A., Defior, S., Seidlová Málková, G., and Hulme, C. (2013). Different patterns, but equivalent predictors, of growth in reading in consistent and inconsistent orthographies. *Psychol. Sci.* 24, 1398–1407. doi: 10.1177/0956797612473122

Caravolas, M., Lervåg, A., Mousikou, P., Efrim, C., Litavsky, M., Onochie-Quintanilla, E., et al. (2012). Common patterns of prediction of literacy development in different alphabetic orthographies. *Psychol. Sci.* 23, 678–686. doi: 10.1177/0956797611434536

Carreiras, M., Armstrong, B. C., Perea, M., and Frost, R. (2014). The what, when, where and how of visual word recognition. *Trends Cogn. Sci.* 18, 90–98. doi: 10.1016/j.tics.2013.11.005

Carter, R. M., and Huettel, S. A. (2013). A nexus model of the temporal-parietal junction. *Trends Cogn. Sci.* 17, 328–336. doi: 10.1016/j.tics.2013.05.007

Caspers, S., Eickhoff, S. B., Geyer, S., Scheperjans, F., Mohlberg, H., Zilles, K., et al. (2008). The human inferior parietal lobule in stereotaxic space. *Brain Struct. Funct.* 212, 481–495. doi: 10.1007/s00429-008-0195-z

Caspers, S., Geyer, S., Schleicher, A., Mohlberg, H., Amunts, K., and Zilles, K. (2006). The human inferior parietal cortex: cytoarchitectonic parcellation and interindividual variability. *Neuroimage* 33, 430–448. doi: 10.1016/j.neuroimage.2006.06.054

Caspers, S., Schleicher, A., Bacha-Trams, M., Palomero-Gallagher, N., Amunts, K., and Zilles, K. (2013). Organization of the human inferior parietal lobule based on receptor architectonics. *Cereb. Cortex* 23, 615–628. doi: 10.1093/cercor/bhs048

Catani, M., Jones, D. K., and ffytche, D. H. (2005). Perisylvian language networks of the human brain. *Ann. Neurol.* 57, 8–16. doi: 10.1002/ana.20319

Chen, H. C., Vaid, J., Bortfeld, H., and Boas, D. A. (2008). Optical imaging of phonological processing in two distinct orthographies. *Exp. Brain Res.* 184, 427–433. doi: 10.1007/s00221-007-1200-0

Cohen, L., Dehaene, S., Vinckier, F., Jobert, A., and Montavont, A. (2008). Reading normal and degraded words: contribution of the dorsal and ventral visual pathways. *Neuroimage* 40, 353–366. doi: 10.1016/j.neuroimage.2007.11.036

Cossu, G., Gugliotta, M., and Marshall, J. C. (1995). Acquisition of reading and written spelling in a transparent orthography: two non parallel processes? *Read. Writ.* 7, 9–22. doi: 10.1007/bf01026945

Das, T., Padakannaya, P., Pugh, K. R., and Singh, N. C. (2011). Neuroimaging reveals dual routes to reading in simultaneous proficient readers of two orthographies. *Neuroimage* 54, 1476–1487. doi: 10.1016/j.neuroimage.2010.09.022

Davies, R., Cuetos, F., and Glez-Seijas, R. M. (2007). Reading development and dyslexia in a transparent orthography: a survey of Spanish children. *Ann. Dyslexia* 57, 179–198. doi: 10.1007/s11881-007-0010-1

Dehaene, S., and Cohen, L. (2011). The unique role of the visual word form area in reading. *Trends Cogn. Sci.* 15, 254–262. doi: 10.1016/j.tics.2011.04.003

Démonet, J.-F., Taylor, M. J., and Chaix, Y. (2004). Developmental dyslexia. *Lancet* 363, 1451–1460. doi: 10.1016/S0140-6736(04)16106-0

DeWitt, I., and Rauschecker, J. P. (2012). Phoneme and word recognition in the auditory ventral stream. *Proc. Natl. Acad. Sci. U S A* 109, E505–E514. doi: 10.1073/pnas.1113427109

Epelbaum, S., Pinel, P., Gaillard, R., Delmaire, C., Perrin, M., Dupont, S., et al. (2008). Pure alexia as a disconnection syndrome: new diffusion imaging evidence for an old concept. *Cortex* 44, 962–974. doi: 10.1016/j.cortex.2008.05.003

Frith, U., Wimmer, H., and Landerl, K. (1998). Differences in phonological recoding in German- and English-speaking children. *Sci. Stud. Read.* 2, 31–54. doi: 10.1207/s1532799xssr0201_2

Frost, R. (2012). Towards a universal model of reading. *Behav. Brain Sci.* 35, 263–279. doi: 10.1017/s0140525x11001841

Frost, R., Katz, L., and Bentin, S. (1987). Strategies for visual word recognition and orthographical depth: a multilingual comparison. *J. Exp. Psychol. Hum. Percept. Perform.* 13, 104–115. doi: 10.1037//0096-1523.13.1.104

Georgiou, G. K., Torppa, M., Manolitsis, G., Lyytinen, H., and Parrila, R. (2012). Longitudinal predictors of reading and spelling across languages varying in orthographic consistency. *Read. Writ.* 25, 321–346. doi: 10.1007/s11145-010-9271-x

Goswami, U., Ziegler, J. C., Dalton, L., and Schneider, W. (2003). Nonword reading across orthographies: how flexible is the choice of reading units? *Appl. Psycholinguist.* 24, 235–247. doi: 10.1017/s0142716403000134

Griffiths, T. D., and Warren, J. D. (2002). The planum temporale as a computational hub. *Trends Neurosci.* 25, 348–353. doi: 10.1016/s0166-2236(02)02191-4

Hadzibeganovic, T., van den Noort, M., Bosch, P., Perc, M., van Kralingen, R., Mondt, K., et al. (2010). Cross-linguistic neuroimaging and dyslexia: a critical view. *Cortex* 46, 1312–1316. doi: 10.1016/j.cortex.2010.06.011

Heim, S., and Keil, A. (2004). Large-scale neural correlates of developmental dyslexia. *Eur. Child Adolesc. Psychiatry* 13, 125–140. doi: 10.1007/s00787-004-0361-7

Heim, S., Wehnelt, A., Grande, M., Huber, W., and Amunts, K. (2013). Effects of lexicality and word frequency on brain activation in dyslexic readers. *Brain Lang.* 125, 194–202. doi: 10.1016/j.bandl.2011.12.005

Hickok, G., Houde, J., and Rong, F. (2011). Sensorimotor integration in speech processing: computational basis and neural organization. *Neuron* 69, 407–422. doi: 10.1016/j.neuron.2011.01.019

Hoeft, F., McCandliss, B. D., Black, J. M., Gantman, A., Zakerani, N., Hulme, C., et al. (2011). Neural systems predicting long-term outcome in dyslexia. *Proc. Natl. Acad. Sci. U S A* 108, 361–366. doi: 10.1073/pnas.1008950108

Holloway, I. D., van Atteveldt, N., Blomert, L., and Ansari, D. (2013). Orthographic dependency in the neural correlates of reading: evidence from audiovisual integration in english readers. *Cereb. Cortex* doi: 10.1093/cercor/bht347. [Epub ahead of print].

Hu, W., Lee, H. L., Zhang, Q., Liu, T., Geng, L. B., Seghier, M. L., et al. (2010). Developmental dyslexia in Chinese and English populations: dissociating the effect of dyslexia from language differences. *Brain* 133, 1694–1706. doi: 10.1093/brain/awq106

Jeon, H. A. (2012). Effect of lexical proficiency on reading strategies used for shallow and deep orthographies. *Neuroreport* 23, 979–983. doi: 10.1097/wnr.0b013e32835a19ae

Jobard, G., Crivello, F., and Tzourio-Mazoyer, N. (2003). Evaluation of the dual route theory of reading: a metanalysis of 35 neuroimaging studies. *Neuroimage* 20, 693–712. doi: 10.1016/s1053-8119(03)00343-4

Kherif, F., Josse, G., Seghier, M. L., and Price, C. J. (2009). The main sources of intersubject variability in neuronal activation for reading aloud. *J. Cogn. Neurosci.* 21, 654–668. doi: 10.1162/jocn.2009.21084

Koyama, M. S., Di Martino, A., Kelly, C., Jutagir, D. R., Sunshine, J., Schwartz, S. J., et al. (2013). Cortical signatures of dyslexia and remediation: an intrinsic functional connectivity approach. *PLoS One* 8:e55454. doi: 10.1371/journal.pone.0055454

Koyama, M. S., Di Martino, A., Zuo, X. N., Kelly, C., Mennes, M., Jutagir, D. R., et al. (2011). Resting-state functional connectivity indexes reading competence in children and adults. *J. Neurosci.* 31, 8617–8624. doi: 10.1523/jneurosci.4865-10.2011

Kronbichler, M., Bergmann, J., Hutzler, F., Staffen, W., Mair, A., Ladurner, G., et al. (2007). Taxi vs. taksi: on orthographic word recognition in the left ventral occipitotemporal cortex. *J. Cogn. Neurosci.* 19, 1584–1594. doi: 10.1162/jocn.2007.19.10.1584

Kronbichler, M., Klackl, J., Richlan, F., Schurz, M., Staffen, W., Ladurner, G., et al. (2009). On the functional neuroanatomy of visual word processing: effects of case and letter deviance. *J. Cogn. Neurosci.* 21, 222–229. doi: 10.1162/jocn.2009.21002

Laird, A. R., Fox, P. M., Eickhoff, S. B., Turner, J. A., Ray, K. L., McKay, D. R., et al. (2011). Behavioral interpretations of intrinsic connectivity networks. *J. Cogn. Neurosci.* 23, 4022–4037. doi: 10.1162/jocn_a_00077

Landerl, K., Ramus, F., Moll, K., Lyytinen, H., Leppänen, P. H. T., Lohvansuu, K., et al. (2013). Predictors of developmental dyslexia in European orthographies with varying complexity. *J. Child Psychol. Psychiatry* 54, 686–694. doi: 10.1111/jcpp.12029

Landerl, K., and Wimmer, H. (2000). Deficits in phoneme segmentation are not the core problem of dyslexia: evidence from German and English children. *Appl. Psycholinguist.* 21, 243–262. doi: 10.1017/s0142716400002058

Landerl, K., Wimmer, H., and Frith, U. (1997). The impact of orthographic consistency on dyslexia: a German-English comparison. *Cognition* 63, 315–334. doi: 10.1016/s0010-0277(97)00005-x

Ludersdorfer, P., Schurz, M., Richlan, F., Kronbichler, M., and Wimmer, H. (2013). Opposite effects of visual and auditory word-likeness on activity in the visual word form area. *Front. Hum. Neurosci.* 7:491. doi: 10.3389/fnhum.2013.00491

Mars, R. B., Jbabdi, S., Sallet, J., O'Reilly, J. X., Croxson, P. L., Olivier, E., et al. (2011). Diffusion-weighted imaging tractography-based parcellation of the human parietal cortex and comparison with human and macaque resting-state functional connectivity. *J. Neurosci.* 31, 4087–4100. doi: 10.1523/JNEUROSCI.5102-10.2011

Mars, R. B., Sallet, J., Schüffelgen, U., Jbabdi, S., Toni, I., and Rushworth, M. F. (2012). Connectivity-based subdivisions of the human right "temporoparietal junction area": evidence for different areas participating in different cortical networks. *Cereb. Cortex* 22, 1894–1903. doi: 10.1093/cercor/bhr268

McCandliss, B. D., and Noble, K. G. (2003). The development of reading impairment: a cognitive neuroscience model. *Ment. Retard. Dev. Disabil. Res. Rev.* 9, 196–204. doi: 10.1002/mrdd.10080

Mechelli, A., Friston, K. J., Frackowiak, R. S., and Price, C. J. (2005). Structural covariance in the human cortex. *J. Neurosci.* 25, 8303–8310. doi: 10.1523/jneurosci.0357-05.2005

Mechelli, A., Gorno-Tempini, M. L., and Price, C. J. (2003). Neuroimaging studies of word and pseudoword reading: consistencies, inconsistencies and limitations. *J. Cogn. Neurosci.* 15, 260–271. doi: 10.1162/089892903321208196

Mei, L., Xue, G., Lu, Z. L., He, Q., Zhang, M., Xue, F., et al. (2013). Orthographic transparency modulates the functional asymmetry in the fusiform cortex: an artificial language training study. *Brain Lang.* 125, 165–172. doi: 10.1016/j.bandl.2012.01.006

Moll, K., Ramus, F., Bartling, J., Bruder, J., Kunze, S., Neuhoff, N., et al. (2014). Cognitive mechanisms underlying reading and spelling development in five European orthographies. *Learn. Instr.* 29, 65–77. doi: 10.1016/j.learninstruc.2013.09.003

Paulesu, E., Démonet, J.-F., Fazio, F., McCrory, E., Chanoine, V., Brunswick, N., et al. (2001). Dyslexia: cultural diversity and biological unity. *Science* 291, 2165–2167. doi: 10.1126/science.1057179

Paulesu, E., McCrory, E., Fazio, F., Menoncello, L., Brunswick, N., Cappa, S. F., et al. (2000). A cultural effect on brain function. *Nat. Neurosci.* 3, 91–96. doi: 10.1038/71163

Perfetti, C. A., Tan, L. H., and Siok, W. T. (2006). Brain-behavior relations in reading and dyslexia: implications of Chinese results. *Brain Lang.* 98, 344–346. doi: 10.1016/j.bandl.2006.04.010

Price, C. J. (2012). A review and synthesis of the first 20 years of PET and fMRI studies of heard speech, spoken language and reading. *Neuroimage* 62, 816–847. doi: 10.1016/j.neuroimage.2012.04.062

Price, C. J., and Devlin, J. T. (2011). The interactive account of ventral occipitotemporal contributions to reading. *Trends Cogn. Sci.* 15, 246–253. doi: 10.1016/j.tics.2011.04.001

Pugh, K. (2006). A neurocognitive overview of reading acquisition and dyslexia across languages. *Dev. Sci.* 9, 448–450. doi: 10.1111/j.1467-7687.2006.00528.x

Pugh, K. R., Mencl, W. E., Jenner, A. R., Katz, L., Frost, S. J., Lee, J. R., et al. (2000). Functional neuroimaging studies of reading and reading disability (developmental dyslexia). *Ment. Retard. Dev. Disabil. Rev.* 6, 207–213. doi: 10.1002/1098-2779(2000)6:3<207::aid-mrdd8>3.0.co;2-p

Pugh, K. R., Sandak, R., Frost, S. J., Moore, D., and Mencl, W. E. (2005). Examining reading development and reading disability in English language learners: potential contributions from functional neuroimaging. *Learn. Disabil. Res. Pract.* 20, 24–30. doi: 10.1111/j.1540-5826.2005.00117.x

Ramus, F., and Szenkovits, G. (2008). What phonological deficit? *Q. J. Exp. Psychol. (Hove)* 61, 129–141. doi: 10.1080/17470210701508822

Richardson, F. M., Seghier, M. L., Leff, A. P., Thomas, M. S. C., and Price, C. J. (2011). Multiple routes from occipital to temporal cortices during reading. *J. Neurosci.* 31, 8239–8247. doi: 10.1523/jneurosci.6519-10.2011

Richlan, F. (2012). Developmental dyslexia: dysfunction of a left hemisphere reading network. *Front. Hum. Neurosci.* 6:120. doi: 10.3389/fnhum.2012.00120

Richlan, F., Gagl, B., Hawelka, S., Braun, M., Schurz, M., Kronbichler, M., et al. (2013a). Fixation-related fMRI analysis in the domain of reading research: using self-paced eye movements as markers for hemodynamic brain responses during visual letter string processing. *Cereb. Cortex* doi: 10.1093/cercor/bht117. [Epub ahead of print].

Richlan, F., Kronbichler, M., and Wimmer, H. (2009). Functional abnormalities in the dyslexic brain: a quantitative meta-analysis of neuroimaging studies. *Hum. Brain Mapp.* 30, 3299–3308. doi: 10.1002/hbm.20752

Richlan, F., Kronbichler, M., and Wimmer, H. (2011). Meta-analyzing brain dysfunctions in dyslexic children and adults. *Neuroimage* 56, 1735–1742. doi: 10.1016/j.neuroimage.2011.02.040

Richlan, F., Kronbichler, M., and Wimmer, H. (2013b). Structural abnormalities in the dyslexic brain: a meta-analysis of voxel-based morphometry studies. *Hum. Brain Mapp.* 34, 3055–3065. doi: 10.1002/hbm.22127

Richlan, F., Sturm, D., Schurz, M., Kronbichler, M., Ladurner, G., and Wimmer, H. (2010). A common left occipito-temporal dysfunction in developmental dyslexia and acquired letter-by-letter reading? *PLoS One* 5:e12073. doi: 10.1371/journal.pone.0012073

Rosazza, C., Cai, Q., Minati, L., Paulignan, Y., and Nazir, T. A. (2009). Early involvement of dorsal and ventral pathways in visual word recognition: an ERP study. *Brain Res.* 1272, 32–44. doi: 10.1016/j.brainres.2009.03.033

Sandak, R., Mencl, W. E., Frost, S. J., and Pugh, K. R. (2004). The neurobiological basis of skilled and impaired reading: recent findings and new directions. *Sci. Stud. Read.* 8, 273–292. doi: 10.1207/s1532799xssr0803_6

Schlaggar, B. L., and McCandliss, B. D. (2007). Development of neural systems for reading: a cognitive neuroscience model. *Annu. Rev. Neurosci.* 30, 475–503. doi: 10.1146/annurev.neuro.28.061604.135645

Schurz, M., Kronbichler, M., Crone, J., Richlan, F., Klackl, J., and Wimmer, H. (2014). Top-down and bottom-up influences on the left ventral occipito-temporal cortex during visual word recognition: an analysis of effective connectivity. *Hum. Brain Mapp.* 35, 1668–1680. doi: 10.1002/hbm.22281

Schurz, M., Sturm, D., Richlan, F., Kronbichler, M., Ladurner, G., and Wimmer, H. (2010). A dual-route perspective on brain activation in response to visual words: evidence for a length by lexicality interaction in the visual word form area (VWFA). *Neuroimage* 49, 2649–2661. doi: 10.1016/j.neuroimage.2009.10.082

Seghier, M. L., and Price, C. J. (2012). Functional heterogeneity within the default network during semantic processing and speech production. *Front. Psychol.* 3:281. doi: 10.3389/fpsyg.2012.00281

Seghier, M. L., Lee, H. L., Schofield, T., Ellis, C. L., and Price, C. J. (2008). Inter-subject variability in the use of two different neuronal networks for reading aloud familiar words. *Neuroimage* 42, 1226–1236. doi: 10.1016/j.neuroimage.2008.05.029

Seghier, M. L., Neufeld, N. H., Zeidman, P., Leff, A. P., Mechelli, A., Nagendran, A., et al. (2012). Reading without the left ventral occipito-temporal cortex. *Neuropsychologia* 50, 3621–3635. doi: 10.1016/j.neuropsychologia.2012.09.030

Seymour, P. H. K., Aro, M., and Erskine, J. M. (2003). Foundation literacy acquisition in European orthographies. *Br. J. Psychol.* 94, 143–174. doi: 10.1348/000712603321661859

Share, D. L. (1995). Phonological recoding and self-teaching: sine qua non of reading acquisition. *Cognition* 55, 151–218; discussion 219–226. doi: 10.1016/0010-0277(94)00645-2

Share, D. L. (2008). On the anglocentricities of current reading research and practice: the perils of overreliance on an "outlier" orthography. *Psychol. Bull.* 134, 584–615. doi: 10.1037/0033-2909.134.4.584

Shaywitz, B. A., Shaywitz, S. E., Pugh, K. R., Mencl, W. E., Fulbright, R. K., Skudlarski, P., et al. (2002). Disruption of posterior brain systems for reading in children with developmental dyslexia. *Biol. Psychiatry* 52, 101–110. doi: 10.1016/s0006-3223(02)01365-3

Shaywitz, S. E., and Shaywitz, B. A. (2008). Paying attention to reading: the neurobiology of reading and dyslexia. *Dev. Psychopathol.* 20, 1329–1349. doi: 10.1017/s0954579408000631

Shaywitz, S. E., and Shaywitz, B. A. (2005). Dyslexia (specific reading disability). *Biol. Psychiatry* 57, 1301–1309. doi: 10.1016/j.biopsych.2005.01.043

Shaywitz, S. E., Shaywitz, B. A., Fulbright, R. K., Skudlarski, P., Mencl, W. E., Constable, R. T., et al. (2003). Neural systems for compensation and persistence: young adult outcome of childhood reading disability. *Biol. Psychiatry* 54, 25–33. doi: 10.1016/s0006-3223(02)01836-x

Silani, G., Frith, U., Demonet, J.-F., Fazio, F., Perani, D., Price, C. J., et al. (2005). Brain abnormalities underlying altered activation in dyslexia: a voxel based morphometry study. *Brain* 128, 2453–2461. doi: 10.1093/brain/awh579

Siok, W. T., Niu, Z., Jin, Z., Perfetti, C. A., and Tan, L. H. (2008). A structural-functional basis for dyslexia in the cortex of Chinese readers. *Proc. Natl. Acad. Sci. U S A* 105, 5561–5566. doi: 10.1073/pnas.0801750105

Siok, W. T., Perfetti, C. A., Jin, Z., and Tan, L. H. (2004). Biological abnormality of impaired reading is constrained by culture. *Nature* 431, 71–76. doi: 10.1038/nature02865

Spinelli, D., De Luca, M., Di Filippo, G., Mancini, M., Martelli, M., and Zoccolotti, P. (2005). Length effect in word naming in reading: role of reading experience and reading deficit in italian readers. *Dev. Neuropsychol.* 27, 217–235. doi: 10.1207/s15326942dn2702_2

Tan, L. H., Spinks, J. A., Eden, G. F., Perfetti, C. A., and Siok, W. T. (2005). Reading depends on writing, in Chinese. *Proc. Natl. Acad. Sci. U S A* 102, 8781–8785. doi: 10.1073/pnas.0503523102

Taylor, J. S., Rastle, K., and Davis, M. H. (2013). Can cognitive models explain brain activation during word and pseudoword reading? A meta-analysis of 36 neuroimaging studies. *Psychol. Bull.* 139, 766–791. doi: 10.1037/a0030266

Taylor, J. S., Rastle, K., and Davis, M. H. (2014). Distinct neural specializations for learning to read words and name objects. *J. Cogn. Neurosci.* doi: 10.1162/jocn_a_00614. [Epub ahead of print].

Temple, E. (2002). Brain mechanisms in normal and dyslexic readers. *Curr. Opin. Neurobiol.* 12, 178–183. doi: 10.1016/s0959-4388(02)00303-3

Thiebaut de Schotten, M., Cohen, L., Amemiya, E., Braga, L. W., and Dehaene, S. (2014). Learning to read improves the structure of the arcuate fasciculus. *Cereb. Cortex* 24, 989–995. doi: 10.1093/cercor/bhs383

Vaessen, A., Bertrand, D., Tóth, D., Csépe, V., Faísca, L., Reis, A., et al. (2010). Cognitive development of fluent word reading does not qualitatively differ between transparent and opaque orthographies. *J. Educ. Psychol.* 102, 827–842. doi: 10.1037/a0019465

van Atteveldt, N., Formisano, E., Goebel, R., and Blomert, L. (2004). Integration of letters and speech sounds in the human brain. *Neuron* 43, 271–282. doi: 10.1016/j.neuron.2004.06.025

van der Mark, S., Bucher, K., Maurer, U., Schulz, E., Brem, S., Buckelmüller, I., et al. (2009). Children with dyslexia lack multiple specializations along the visual word-form (VWF) system. *Neuroimage* 47, 1940–1949. doi: 10.1016/j.neuroimage.2009.05.021

van der Mark, S., Klaver, P., Bucher, K., Maurer, U., Schulz, E., Brem, S., et al. (2011). The left occipitotemporal system in reading: disruption of focal fMRI connectivity to left inferior frontal and inferior parietal language areas in children with dyslexia. *Neuroimage* 54, 2426–2436. doi: 10.1016/j.neuroimage.2010.10.002

Vandermosten, M., Boets, B., Wouters, J., and Ghesquière, P. (2012). A qualitative and quantitative review of diffusion tensor imaging studies in reading and dyslexia. *Neurosci. Biobehav. Rev.* 36, 1532–1552. doi: 10.1016/j.neubiorev.2012.04.002

Vigneau, M., Beaucousin, V., Hervé, P. Y., Duffau, H., Crivello, F., Houdé, O., et al. (2006). Meta-analyzing left hemisphere language areas: phonology, semantics and sentence processing. *Neuroimage* 30, 1414–1432. doi: 10.1016/j.neuroimage.2005.11.002

Vogel, A. C., Miezin, F. M., Petersen, S. E., and Schlaggar, B. L. (2012). The putative visual word form area is functionally connected to the dorsal attention network. *Cereb. Cortex* 22, 537–549. doi: 10.1093/cercor/bhr100

Vogel, A. C., Petersen, S. E., and Schlaggar, B. L. (2014). The VWFA: it's not just for words anymore. *Front. Hum. Neurosci.* 8:88. doi: 10.3389/fnhum.2014.00088

Wager, T. D., Jonides, J., and Reading, S. (2004). Neuroimaging studies of shifting attention: a meta-analysis. *Neuroimage* 22, 1679–1693. doi: 10.1016/j.neuroimage.2004.03.052

Wimmer, H. (1993). Characteristics of developmental dyslexia in a regular writing system. *Appl. Psycholinguist.* 14, 1–33. doi: 10.1017/s0142716400010122

Wimmer, H., and Goswami, U. (1994). The influence of orthographic consistency on reading development: word recognition in English and German children. *Cognition* 51, 91–103. doi: 10.1016/0010-0277(94)90010-8

Wimmer, H., and Schurz, M. (2010). Dyslexia in regular orthographies: manifestation and causation. *Dyslexia* 16, 283–299. doi: 10.1002/dys.411

Wimmer, H., Schurz, M., Sturm, D., Richlan, F., Klackl, J., Kronbichler, M., et al. (2010). A dual-route perspective on poor reading in a regular orthography: an fMRI study. *Cortex* 46, 1284–1298. doi: 10.1016/j.cortex.2010.06.004

Woodhead, Z. V., Penny, W., Barnes, G. R., Crewes, H., Wise, R. J., Price, C. J., et al. (2013). Reading therapy strengthens top-down connectivity in patients with pure alexia. *Brain* 136, 2579–2591. doi: 10.1093/brain/awt186

Xu, B., Grafman, J., Gaillard, W. D., Ishii, K., Vega-Bermudez, F., Pietrini, P., et al. (2001). Conjoint and extended neural networks for the computation of speech codes: the neural basis of selective impairment in reading words and pseudowords. *Cereb. Cortex* 11, 267–277. doi: 10.1093/cercor/11.3.267

Yeatman, J. D., Rauschecker, A. M., and Wandell, B. A. (2013). Anatomy of the visual word form area: adjacent cortical circuits and long-range white matter connections. *Brain Lang.* 125, 146–155. doi: 10.1016/j.bandl.2012.04.010

Yeo, B. T., Krienen, F. M., Sepulcre, J., Sabuncu, M. R., Lashkari, D., Hollinshead, M., et al. (2011). The organization of the human cerebral cortex estimated by intrinsic functional connectivity. *J. Neurophysiol.* 106, 1125–1165. doi: 10.1152/jn.00338.2011

Ziegler, J. C. (2006). Do differences in brain activation challenge universal theories of dyslexia? *Brain Lang.* 98, 341–343. doi: 10.1016/j.bandl.2005.05.002

Ziegler, J. C., and Goswami, U. (2005). Reading acquisition, developmental dyslexia and skilled reading across languages: a psycholinguistic grain size theory. *Psychol. Bull.* 131, 3–29. doi: 10.1037/0033-2909.131.1.3

Ziegler, J. C., and Goswami, U. (2006). Becoming literate in different languages: similar problems, different solutions. *Dev. Sci.* 9, 429–436. doi: 10.1111/j.1467-7687.2006.00509.x

Ziegler, J. C., Bertrand, D., Tóth, D., Csépe, V., Reis, A., Faísca, L., et al. (2010). Orthographic depth and its impact on universal predictors of reading: a cross-language investigation. *Psychol. Sci.* 21, 551–559. doi: 10.1177/0956797610363406

Ziegler, J. C., Perry, C., Ma-Wyatt, A., Ladner, D., and Schulte-Körne, G. (2003). Developmental dyslexia in different languages: language-specific or universal? *J. Exp. Child Psychol.* 86, 169–193. doi: 10.1016/s0022-0965(03)00139-5

Zoccolotti, P., De Luca, M., Di Filippo, G., Judica, A., and Martelli, M. (2009). Reading development in an orthographically regular language: effects of length, frequency, lexicality and global processing ability. *Read. Writ.* 22, 1053–1079. doi: 10.1007/s11145-008-9144-8

Zoccolotti, P., De Luca, M., Di Pace, E., Gasperini, F., Judica, A., and Spinelli, D. (2005). Word length effect in early reading and in developmental dyslexia. *Brain Lang.* 93, 369–373. doi: 10.1016/j.bandl.2004.10.010

12

The relationship of phonological ability, speech perception and auditory perception in adults with dyslexia

Jeremy M. Law[1]*, Maaike Vandermosten[1,2], Pol Ghesquiere[1] and Jan Wouters[2]

[1] *Faculty of Psychology and Educational Sciences, Parenting and Special Education Research Unit, KU Leuven, Leuven, Belgium*
[2] *Laboratory for Experimental ORL, Department of Neuroscience, KU Leuven, Leuven, Belgium*

Correspondence:
Jeremy M. Law, Faculty of Psychology and Educational Sciences, Parenting and Special Education Research Unit, KU Leuven, Leopold Vanderkelenstraat 32, PO Box 3765, 3000 Leuven, Belgium
e-mail: jeremy.law@ppw.kuleuven.be

This study investigated whether auditory, speech perception, and phonological skills are tightly interrelated or independently contributing to reading. We assessed each of these three skills in 36 adults with a past diagnosis of dyslexia and 54 matched normal reading adults. Phonological skills were tested by the typical threefold tasks, i.e., rapid automatic naming, verbal short-term memory and phonological awareness. Dynamic auditory processing skills were assessed by means of a frequency modulation (FM) and an amplitude rise time (RT); an intensity discrimination task (ID) was included as a non-dynamic control task. Speech perception was assessed by means of sentences and words-in-noise tasks. Group analyses revealed significant group differences in auditory tasks (i.e., RT and ID) and in phonological processing measures, yet no differences were found for speech perception. In addition, performance on RT discrimination correlated with reading but this relation was mediated by phonological processing and not by speech-in-noise. Finally, inspection of the individual scores revealed that the dyslexic readers showed an increased proportion of deviant subjects on the slow-dynamic auditory and phonological tasks, yet each individual dyslexic reader does not display a clear pattern of deficiencies across the processing skills. Although our results support phonological and slow-rate dynamic auditory deficits which relate to literacy, they suggest that at the individual level, problems in reading and writing cannot be explained by the cascading auditory theory. Instead, dyslexic adults seem to vary considerably in the extent to which each of the auditory and phonological factors are expressed and interact with environmental and higher-order cognitive influences.

Keywords: dyslexia, literacy, phonological processing, speech perception, auditory processing, amplitude rise time, frequency modulation

INTRODUCTION

Dyslexia is a neurological condition affecting 5–10% of the population. This specific learning disability impacts an individual's ability in learning to read and write despite adequate intelligence, education, and remediation (Vellutino et al., 2004). It has been well established in the literature that the major causes of the expressed literacy problems lay within a deficit in the phonological domain, specifically in the quality and accuracy of phonological representations (Snowling, 2000). In this paper the auditory temporal processing deficit theory of dyslexia, and its cascading effects on speech and phonological processing will be examined. To this end, measures of slow-rate modulation, and speech perception will be assessed along with phonological and literacy measures in a population of university level dyslexic and non-dyslexic adult readers.

A vital part in the development of phonological representations is the awareness of how speech sounds correspond to a written symbol. Findings of the past few decades have begun to suggest the existence of an underlying deficit in low-level auditory temporal processing within the dyslexic population (Farmer and Klein, 1995; Habib, 2000; Boets et al., 2006). Thus, if dyslexic readers perceive speech or related auditory cues inaccurately, the mapping of speech sounds onto their corresponding symbols will be problematic.

Beginning with Tallal's (1980) study of temporal order judgment of children with specific language impairments, research has explored the idea that the primary deficit of dyslexics could lay in deviant auditory processing skills. Early research related the interpretation of "temporal processing" restrictively to rapid succession or short durational cues (e.g., Tallal, 1980). However, recent studies have demonstrated that the deficits observed in dyslexic readers are not merely limited to the processing of short, rapidly presented stimuli, but also to slow-rate dynamic acoustic stimuli such as frequency modulations (FMs) and sound rise time discrimination (RT). Such a deficit has been theorized to produce a cascade ultimately disrupting an individual's reading and spelling abilities. If an individual were to be affected by poor auditory processing of slow-rate modulations (between 2 and 20 Hz), it would be expected that speech perception would ultimately be affected, since the identification of phonemes and syllables depends on changes in the amplitude that occur respectively around 50 ms (i.e., 20 Hz) to 500 ms (i.e., 2 Hz). Such speech perception difficulties could impact the segmentation of aspects of the speech signal into smaller elements, thus hampering the development of phonological representations and ultimately disrupting the creation of accurate mapping schemes between speech sound and corresponding graphemes (Poelmans et al., 2011). Ultimately, these poor phoneme-grapheme representations will be expressed as poor coding and decoding abilities impacting word reading and spelling.

Slow-rate auditory modulations can be assessed by two different tasks, FM and rise time (RT) detection task. FM detection assesses the individual's ability to detect frequency fluctuations in a carrier frequency at a certain modulation rate. Such FMs could be said to represent the fine structure found within the envelopes of the speech waveform (Rosen, 1992). Research on FM detection of dyslexics and controls have found significant group differences, where dyslexics have been shown to have a reduced sensitivity compared to controls, thus demonstrating FM task's ability to differentiate between adult, school aged, and pre-reading dyslexics from normal readers (Witton et al., 1998, 2002; Ramus et al., 2003; Boets et al., 2007). Yet, of the 12 papers examining FM perception in a review study by Hämäläinen et al. (2013), three of the studies were not able to replicate these group differences (Halliday and Bishop, 2006; Stoodley et al., 2006; White et al., 2006).

In addition to findings of group differences, a study by Witton et al. (1998) found phonological decoding skills of both dyslexics and controls to be significantly correlated with FM sensitivity of 2 and 40 Hz. The review paper by Hämäläinen et al. (2013) noted 8 separate studies that reported correlations between FM detection thresholds and reading and/or spelling skills. Yet, 3 studies were unable to replicate these results (Van Ingelghem et al., 2005; Heath et al., 2006; Dawes et al., 2009).

An alternative measure of auditory processing that taps into aspects of slow-rate dynamic processing mechanisms and that has been indicated to be a sensitive measure in discriminating between populations of dyslexic and normal readers is rise time discrimination (RT). Rise time, in comparison with FM tasks, measures the larger grain size of the speech waveform, which focuses specifically on the speech envelope (Rosen, 1992). Specifically, the RT task accesses an individual's ability to detect subtle differences in the rate of change of an amplitude envelope. The perceptions of such cues are utilized in the segmentation of the speech signal into its base parts, such as syllables or onsets and rhymes, which is necessary for speech perception (Goswami et al., 2010). Detection of such cues has been shown to be significantly associated with reading, writing and phonological skills in an adult population (Hämäläinen et al., 2005). Goswami et al. (2002) demonstrated that 25% of unique variance in reading and spelling in children could be predicted by individual differences in rise time sensitivity, with IQ and age being controlled for. Findings demonstrating RT's relation to reading have also remained consistent across different orthographies (Goswami et al., 2011). When comparing persons with dyslexia to typical readers, child studies have demonstrated consistent group differences in RT perception across various measurement techniques (for a review see Hämäläinen et al., 2013; note the exception of Hämäläinen et al., 2009). On the other hand, adult studies have not been so clear. Despite some adult studies showing significant poorer performance on RT tasks in adults with dyslexia (Hämäläinen et al., 2005; Thomson et al., 2006; Corriveau et al., 2007), findings vary between the different measurement techniques employed (see Thomson et al., 2006; Pasquini et al., 2007). Traditionally, pure tone carrier signals are modulated in RT-tasks, but this lacks important frequencies of real speech. Hence, they do not activate a broader frequency region in the auditory system compared to speech weighted noise signals. In an effort to mimic the demand of real speech within the RT detection measure, Poelmans et al. (2011) utilized a single ramp rise time discrimination task that consists of a speech-weighted noise with a linear amplitude rise time. They showed that the application of a speech weighted noise signal resulted in reliable performance in children and did not produce any ceiling or floor effects, which differed from pilot studies of pure tone carrier signals.

However, not all auditory processing aspects seem to be impaired in dyslexic readers. In contrast to slow-rate dynamic auditory processing (RT, FM), intensity discrimination (ID) does not display group differences between typical and dyslexic readers (for a review see Hämäläinen et al., 2013). This suggests that related task demands, attention and cognitive aspects are not the driving factor of the observed auditory problems since they are equal across RT, FM, and ID tasks. In addition, as the RT measure includes changes of intensity over time, the lack of group differences on the ID tasks suggests that a poorer performance on the RT-task is not a reflection of difficulties in ID ability but rather of the changes in intensity.

An understanding of slow-rate dynamic modulations such as RT and FM is important due to their prevalence in the speech signal, appearing at various grain sizes of phonological information ranging from intonation, onset and rhyme to the phoneme. If an individual has a deficit in processing these modulations, it is believed that it would be expressed in their ability to perceive speech.

Most often speech sound processing of dyslexics is assessed through the use of a categorical perception measure. Studies utilizing categorical perception tasks have demonstrated that subjects with dyslexia possess a reduced capacity for perception and categorization of phonemes (for a review see Vandermosten et al., 2010, 2011). However, results from such tasks are often restricted to a subset of the dyslexic population sampled (Manis et al., 1997; Adlard and Hazan, 1998) or to a specific speech condition or task (Maassen et al., 2001; Blomert and Mitterer, 2004). Typically, categorical perception tasks utilize optimal listening conditions. Such conditions allow for compensation of specific deficits in phoneme identification (Manis et al., 1997; Assmann and Summerfield, 2004; Ziegler et al., 2009). Although speech-in-noise tasks are influenced by higher-order cognitive processes such as lexical and phonotactic knowledge, they provide a more ecological and natural measure of speech sound processing than categorical perception. By presenting speech stimuli in the presence of a masking noise, a participant's ability to identify and comprehend real speech sounds under varying noise-masking scenarios is assessed. The ability to identify speech-in-noise requires the individual to separate out the background noise from the target speech signal. This isolation allows for the individual to produce precise representations of the rapidly evolving spectral information. It has been shown that, although all listeners demonstrate some reduced capacity for perception under noisy background conditions, dyslexic children (Snowling et al., 1986; Wible et al., 2002; Bradlow et al., 2003; Ziegler et al., 2005, 2009; Boets et al., 2011) and dyslexic adults (Dole et al., 2012) exhibit pronounced difficulty with this task while often not demonstrating any impairment of speech perception in silent conditions (Brady et al., 1983; Bradlow et al., 2003). Yet, Hazan et al. (2009) were not able to replicate these findings in an adult population.

Although studies have demonstrated deficits independently in the slow-rate dynamic processing and speech-in-noise perception in individuals with dyslexia, only two studies have assessed both of these measures of signal processing in the same population (Boets et al., 2011; Poelmans et al., 2011). Boets et al. retrospectively explored this relationship in a population of preschool children who later developed dyslexia and showed that these children were already impaired in slow-rate FM sensitivity and speech perception prior to reading instruction. These pre-reading measures were also found to relate to each other and uniquely predicted later growth in reading. A more recent study by Poelmans et al. (2011), which followed up the same students of Boets, in 6th-grade children showed no clear evidence supporting relations between slow-rate dynamic auditory processing and speech perception itself. Given that this correlation was present at an earlier age (Boets et al., 2011), this might suggest that the link between auditory and speech perception skills is disappearing through development. However, more validation in adult participants is needed.

Although studies such as that of Boets and colleagues have found support for the auditory temporal processing deficit theory of dyslexia, the theory is not without its controversy. Criticism has arisen from the heterogeneity of the found deficits. It has been suggested that differences between group means are a reflection of a small number of poor performing dyslexic subjects. Ramus et al. (2003) examined an adult population and noted that auditory deficits were limited to only 39% of the subjects with dyslexia and that auditory processing had only a weak correlation with phonology and reading. Other criticisms have suggested that general difficulties with task completion might underlie the poor performance of subjects with dyslexia in psychophysical studies and lead researchers to misinterpret non-sensory difficulties as sensory ones (Stuart et al., 2001; Roach et al., 2004).

Our study will investigate the different levels of processing skills (i.e., auditory, speech-in-noise perception, and phonological processing) in one and the same sample of dyslexic and normal reading adults. So far, such an integrative approach has not been applied to adults, despite being vital to understand the interrelations between auditory processing, speech perception, phonological processing, and reading (problems). Furthermore, in contrast to previous studies, our study will not only investigate the interrelation between these skills and compare performance between groups, but we will also examine the individual level deviance scores.

Given that dyslexia is a disability measured and defined as deviant performance, research should reflect this by demonstrating a substantial number of individuals whose performance significantly differs from normal performance (Ramus et al., 2003; Heath et al., 2006; Ziegler et al., 2008; Hazan et al., 2009). As noted in Hazan et al. (2009) group comparisons could potentially mask significant individual differences or highlight differences which may not essentially be deviant, hence it is not sufficient in dyslexia research to merely demonstrate significant group differences without investigating the individual deviance scores. In addition, according to the auditory deficit theory, dyslexic readers should show consistent deficiencies across each level of processing, otherwise phonological impairments are presumably not secondary to speech and lower-level auditory problems.

Given that performance in adults is more prone to compensational mechanisms, the slow-rate dynamic tasks (FM and RT) will be assessed together with a control measure for attention and task complexity (ID). Although the inclusion of such well-matched control task helps in distinguishing effects of task demands from true effects, so far no study has included them as a control within all levels of statistical analyses. A few studies have included a control variable for attention and task related demands in group matching (Hämäläinen et al., 2005; Thomson et al., 2006; Pasquini et al., 2007), yet this does not prevent individual variation in groups exhibiting a significant role in relationships between psychophysical, phonological, and literacy measures.

In sum, this study will address three main questions: (i) Do adults with dyslexia demonstrate deficits in auditory processing, speech perception, and phonological abilities at the group level and at the individual level? (ii) Does a close relationship exist between the auditory processing, speech perception, and phonological skills or do they rather contribute independently to reading skills? (iii) Based on individual deviance analyses, do the same participants display deviant scores across the three skills (i.e., auditory processing, speech perception, and phonological processing)?

To achieve this, auditory processing skills will be assessed by two slow-rate modulation tasks, i.e., RT and FM, and by a control task, i.e., ID. Speech perception will be assessed by a word and sentences in noise task. Lastly, phonological processing will be accessed through the classical threefold of phonological awareness (PA), verbal short-term memory (VSTM), and rapid automatic naming (RAN) tasks.

MATERIALS AND METHODS

PARTICIPANTS

A total number of 90 undergraduate students were recruited for this study, 54 (36 female and 18 male) non-dyslexic and 36 (26 female and 10 male) participants with dyslexia. In order to participate, the dyslexic students needed to have a diagnosis completed by a registered and qualified clinical psychologist in secondary school or earlier and had to be registered at the office of Student Development & Services. The fact that the adults with dyslexia were selected from a university population, a higher level of reading achievement is expected than in a general sample of individuals of the same age, due to the selectivity of universities. This is reflected in some dyslexic student's normal reading and spelling scores as seen in **Table 1**. Based on their higher than expected literacy scores these participants may be considered as "compensated" dyslexics. Research has shown that strengths in cognitive abilities, such as the use of contextual cues

Table 1 | Participant characteristics.

Measure	NR		DYS		*t*	*p*
	M	*SD*	*M*	*SD*		
Age (years)	22.0	3.0	21.8	4.8	0.227	1
Non-Verbal IQ (APM)	112.7	9.9	107.0	20.7	1.777	0.158
LITERACY						
Word-reading[a] (SS) (WRAT-III)	106.1	5.8	91.7	10.1	8.575	<0.002
Spelling[a] (SS) (WRAT-III)	107.6	6.6	90.8	8.8	10.305	<0.002
Literacy (z-score)	−0.1	1.1	−3.3	1.7	11.396	<0.001

All p-values are Bonferroni adjusted for multiple comparisons. APM, Raven advanced progressive matrices; WRAT-III, Wide Range Achievement Test III.
[a]Scores are standardized (M = 100, SD = 15).

(Frith and Snowling, 1983; Nation and Snowling, 1998), semantic knowledge (Snowling et al., 2000), visual memory (Campbell and Butterworth, 1985), and morphological knowledge (Elbro and Arnbak, 1996) help this group of individuals with dyslexia to minimize the expression of their reading difficulties.

The non-dyslexic population were comprised of students who have no documentation or history of reading difficulty and whose word reading scores did not fall in the bottom 5% of the WRAT norms (Wilkinson, 1993). Recruitment of the dyslexic population for the study was made through the University's Student Services, while the control population was gathered based on class announcements and posters placed throughout each campus.

All participants were at least 18 years of age and attended one of three universities in Ontario, Canada. All participants were native English speakers without a history of brain damage, language problems, psychiatric symptoms or visual problems which could not be corrected for by a corrective lens. Additionally all participants had adequate audiometric pure-tone hearing thresholds for the test ear (i.e., 25 dB HL or less on 0.25–8.0 kHz) and adequate non-verbal IQ defined by a standard score greater than 85 on Raven's advanced progressive matrices. **Table 1** shows participant characteristics for the two groups. Groups did not differ in age, gender, and non-verbal IQ.

TASKS

Literacy

Literacy was assessed by the WRAT-III reading and spelling subtests (Wilkinson, 1993). The reading subtest required the subject to read aloud a list of 42 words. The subject received a single point for each correctly pronounced word to a maximum score of 42. The spelling subtest required the subject to accurately spell a series of dictated words. The words were presented orally by the test administrator preceding and following a sentence containing the target word. The test was scored by giving one point for each correctly spelled word to a maximum score of 40 points.

Phonological skills

Each domain of one's phonological skills, as represented in Wagner and Torgesen (1987), was individually tested.

Phonological awareness (PA) was assessed through the use of the Spoonerism subtest from the Phonological Assessment Battery (PhAB) (Frederickson et al., 1997). Spoonerism tasks have been demonstrated to be able to significantly differentiate between an adult dyslexic population and control groups (Ramus et al., 2003). This test of PA targeted onset-rhyme awareness and requires phoneme manipulation and deletion. This task involved two parts. The first required the participant to replace the first sound of a word with a new sound (e.g., cot with a /g/ gives "got"). In part two, word pairs were orally presented to the participant; in turn they were requested to transpose the onset of the sounds of the two words. For example, "plane crash" will become "crane plash" or "King John" becomes "Jing Kon." Rate scores, measured in number of correct items per second, were calculated as the total correct responses divided by the total time to complete the task. Due to ceiling level being reached within the control group accuracy was not separately evaluated.

Verbal short-term memory was assessed by The Number Repetition (digit span forward) subtest from The Clinical Evaluation of Language Fundamentals 4th edition (CELF-4) (Semel et al., 2003). Digit span forward required the immediate serial recall of an orally presented series of digits. List length was incrementally increased from two to nine digits and presented orally at a rate of one digit per second. The test score was calculated as the total number of correctly recalled lists with a maximum score of 16.

Verbal short-term memory was also assessed by the non-word recall subtest from the Working Memory Test Battery (WMTB) (Pickering and Gathercole, 2001). For this task sequences of single syllable non-sense words were presented orally to the participants. Each participant was requested to repeat the sequence in the correct order. The list length was incrementally increased, from one to six words in length. Six trials were available for presentation at each list length. The task was discontinued when three errors were made in a given list length. The test score was calculated as the total number of correctly recalled lists with a maximum score of 36.

Rapid Automatic Naming (RAN) was assessed through two naming tasks. A color-naming test adapted from Boets et al. (2006) was selected. Five colors (black, yellow, red, green, and blue) were presented in 5 rows containing 10 color stimuli each. In addition, the object-naming subtest from The Phonological Assessment Battery (PhAB) (Frederickson et al., 1997) was used. Five line drawings of common objects (desk, ball, door, hat, box) were presented in 5 rows each containing 10 items. For both tasks participants were instructed to name aloud each of the objects or colors as quickly and as accurately as possible. A score of the number of symbols named per second was calculated.

Auditory processing and speech perception experimental setup

All tasks were conducted on campus and were administered individually in a private room, with minimal background noise and distraction. All auditory and speech perception tasks were performed on a Dell Latitude D510 and controlled by APEX software (Laneau et al., 2005; Francart et al., 2008). Speech perception and auditory processing stimuli were presented through Sennheiser HDA 200 headphones to the right ear. Auditory processing procedure and tasks were adapted from those used and described by Poelmans et al. (2011).

Auditory processing tasks

All auditory processing task thresholds were estimated by means of a one-up, two-down adaptive staircase procedure which is designed to target a threshold corresponding to 70.7% correct responses (Levitt, 1971). Tasks were presented within a three-alternative forced-choice, "odd-one-out" paradigm. In each trial three stimuli were presented requiring the participant to determine which sound differed from the others. An inter-stimulus interval of 350 ms was used. All tasks were terminated after ten reversals. Thresholds were the arithmetic mean of the last 4 reversals. Each participant completed two threshold runs of each task.

FM-detection task required participants to detect a 2 Hz sinusoidal FM of a 1 kHz carrier tone with varying modulation depth. The reference stimulus was a pure tone of 1 kHz. Modulation depth decreased by a factor of 1.2 from 100 to 11 Hz. At this point modulation depth decreases by a step size of 1 Hz. The length of both the reference and the target stimulus was 1000 ms including 50 ms cosine-gated onset and offset. The detection threshold was defined as the minimum depth of frequency deviation (in Hz) required to detect the modulation.

Sound rise time discrimination sensitivity consisted of a speech weighted noise with linear amplitude rise times. Rise times varied logarithmically between 15 and 500 ms in 41 steps. The total duration of the stimulus was fixed to 800 ms, including a linear fall time of 75 ms. The stimulus of 15 ms rise time was used as the reference stimulus for each trial. Discrimination thresholds were defined as the minimal difference in the rise time required discriminating between the reference and target stimulus.

Intensity discrimination task was identical to the FM and RT discrimination task in its presentation and procedure. Stimuli, of an 800 ms duration, consisting of a speech-weighted noise and a linear rise time and fall time of 75 ms were used. The stimulus of 70 dB SPL was utilized as a reference stimulus for each trial. Intensity was varied linearly between 70 and 80 dB SPL in 40 steps of 0.25 dB SPL each. Discrimination thresholds were defined as the minimal intensity difference (in dB SPL) required to discriminate between the reference and the target stimulus.

Speech-in-noise perception

Speech-in-noise intelligibility was assessed for both words and sentences. During testing, the speech level was varied while the background noise level was fixed at 70 dB SPL. To assess the association of RT and FM discrimination in speech perception, two speech-in-noise tasks were administered. The first dealing with words-in-noise which would require less reliance on rise time processing and more on FM and the second which included sentences in noise which would rely more heavily on RT discrimination to accurately decompose and segment the sentence into finer grained elements for processing.

Words-in-noise perception was assessed with The Computer Aided Speech Perception Assessment (CASPA) developed by Boothroyd (2006) (for application see McCreery et al., 2010). A random selection of 3 lists of 10 CVC words were presented orally by a female speaker against a competing speech weighted noise at varying signal-to-noise ratios (SNR) (−5, −10, and −13 dB). Each list contained a single occurrence of the same set of 30 phonemes (20 consonants and 10 vowels). A practice list of 0 dB SNR was first administered to the participant. Participants were instructed to repeat each target word after presentation; if the participant was unable to repeat the target word correctly they were instructed to repeat every perceived phoneme. The percentage of correctly perceived phonemes was calculated for each SNR. The Speech Reception Threshold (SRT) was calculated for each participant through fitting to the data a logistic function relating the percentage of correct responses to SNR level (for a similar approach see Poelmans et al., 2011).

Speech-in-noise intelligibility of sentences was assessed using stimuli adapted from The Hearing in Noise Test (HINT) (Nilsson et al., 1994). Speech material consisted of English sentences spoken by a male speaker. The HINT stimuli consisted of a 70 dB long-term average speech spectrum masking noise and 12 equivalent 20-sentence lists. Two lists were administered after one practice list was presented. Lists were randomly selected from the 12 available. In the HINT adaptive procedure, beginning at 58 dB, the presentation level of all sentences were adjusted by 2 dB steps. Speech-in-noise intelligibility thresholds for each participant were calculated by averaging the last 6 SNR. Final values for each measure were inverted by multiplying by a factor of −1 to obtain a positive correlation matrix and for the creation of *z*-scores.

STATISTICAL ANALYSES

All data were checked with Shapiro-Wilk's test for normality. The assumption of homogeneity of variance was assessed by Levene's Test for Equality of Variances.

Individual deviance analyses of composite scores

A two-step process, as in Ramus et al. (2003) (also see Boets et al., 2006, 2007; Reid et al., 2007; Hazan et al., 2009), was used to create *z*-scores for each variable and to examine group differences in the proportion of deviant subjects on literacy tasks, phonological tasks, speech-in-noise perception, and dynamic auditory perception. As done in Ramus et al. (2003) a control mean and standard deviation were calculated for each measured variable based on the scores of the normal reading sample. However, any subject of the NR sample scoring below the set threshold of −1.65 *SD* (bottom 5% of the population) was removed to compute the final control mean and *SD*. This extra step was a means to prevent any inattentive or distracted control from exaggerating the normal range of performance. *Z*-scores for all subjects were then recalculated based on this new final control mean and *SD*. Individual deviance was calculated from these *z*-scores and defined as any subject falling below the −1.65 *SD* threshold. For the purposes of this paper the term deviancy score is referring only to those scores falling below this threshold. We do not imply any answer to the delay/deficit discussion concerning dyslexia. In acknowledgment of the possible exaggeration of the dyslexics' deficits by such a two-step method, the more strict threshold of −1.65 *SD* was chosen.

The resulting Z-scores were used to create composite scores. For each participant a literacy score was calculated by averaging the z-scores of the WRAT reading and spelling subtests (Literacy); a phonological awareness (PA) score was calculated as the z-score of the Spoonerism task, The two RAN z-scores were averaged into one overall RAN score (RAN). Digit span and non-word recall tasks were averaged to create a verbal short-term memory score (VSTM). Due to the lack of strength in the correlations found within the auditory processing and within speech perception measures no composite scores were created for these groups of variables.

Multiple comparison corrections

In order to avoid the possibility of making a false positive conclusion in group comparisons all reported p-values for t-tests and ANOVAs were adjusted using a Bonferroni correction, which entailed the multiplication of the given p-value by the total number of comparisons per question to a maximum Bonferroni adjusted p-value of 1. If the adjusted p-value remains less than the original alpha of 0.05 then the null hypothesis was rejected.

RESULTS

PERFORMANCE OF DYSLEXIC vs. NORMAL READING ADULTS

Literacy

Literacy results are presented in **Table 1**. There was a statistically significant difference in the mean scores of reading and spelling between groups, with the dyslexic group preforming significantly poorer, $t_{(50.283)} = 8.575$; $p < 0.005$, and $t_{(60.675)} = 10.305$, $p < 0.005$.

Phonological skills

Each domain of one's phonological skills, as represented in Wagner and Torgesen (1987), was tested. Phonological awareness (PA) was tested by the spoonerism task of the PhAB, verbal short-term memory (VSTM) by digit span and non-word recall and RAN by object and color naming. Test scores are presented in **Table 2**.

Independent sample t-tests were run to determine differences between groups in measures on phonological skills. Scores of the non-word recall and Spoonerism tasks were not found to be normally distributed. In order to approach a normal distribution they were transformed by a square root transformation. Adults with dyslexia were found to perform significantly poorer then controls on all measures.

Speech perception and auditory processing

In order to approach a normal distribution for more variables, the best score on the FM measure was transformed by a logarithmic transformation after the scores had been reversed, while the best score on the ID measure was transformed by the use of a square root transformation after the scores had been reversed, and the RT scores were transformed using a square root transformation (Field, 2009).

Since the aim of this research is to evaluate threshold estimations as an indicator of a subject's sensory capability, the two threshold trials were not averaged and instead the best score of each test was selected (for a similar approach see Boets et al., 2006). Threshold means and standard deviations of all auditory measures for each group can be found in **Table 3**.

Results demonstrated that dyslexic readers scored significantly poorer on measures of RT discrimination and ID, but not on FM-detection nor on the two tasks for speech-in-noise perception. Given the unexpected findings of a group difference in ID, ID was introduced as a control variable in order to determine whether a significant group difference on RT was due to general cognitive demands related to task design or intensity-related processes rather than dynamic-related processes. This confirmed the group difference for RT discrimination, $F_{(1, 87)} = 9.492$, $p = 0.012$, partial $\eta^2 = 0.098$, while FM remained insignificant, $F_{(1, 87)} = 0.643$, $p = 1$ (p-values are Bonferroni adjusted for multiple comparisons).

RELATIONS BETWEEN LITERACY, PHONOLOGICAL, AND AUDITORY SKILLS

To assess the relations between subjects' literacy skills, phonological abilities and auditory processing skills, Pearson's correlation coefficients were calculated between the subjects' scores on measures of literacy, phonology, slow-rate dynamic auditory processing and speech-in-noise perception (lower left portion of **Table 4**). Phonological awareness was related to all measures of literacy, verbal short term memory and RAN, as well as RT and ID. Although FM was only found to relate to RT and ID, RT significantly correlated with measures of reading, spelling and measures of PA (spoonerisms and both RAN tasks).

Table 2 | Phonological abilities: descriptive statistics and t- and p-values from independent t-tests.

Measure	NR		DYS		t	p
	M	SD	M	SD		
Spoonerism (correct/s)	0.23	0.08	0.10	0.04	9.042	<0.005
Digit span	12.32	1.87	10.78	2.00	3.712	<0.005
Non-word recall	20.09	2.25	17.61	2.62	4.795	<0.005
RAN (color)	2.01	0.33	1.72	0.31	4.262	<0.005
RAN (object)	1.77	0.24	1.50	0.25	5.059	<0.005

All p-values are Bonferroni adjusted for multiple comparisons.

Table 3 | Auditory and speech-in-noise measures: descriptive statistics and t and p-values from independent t-tests.

Measure	NR		DYS		t	p
	M	SD	M	SD		
FM (Hz)	3.82	1.38	4.58	2.38	−1.922	0.174
RT (ms)	73.07	47.41	117.22	65.94	−3.695	0.003
ID (dB)	1.04	0.54	1.46	0.76	−3.100	0.009
HINT (SRT in dB)	−3.03	0.93	−3.11	0.91	−0.373	1
CASPA (SRT in dB)	−11.06	0.92	−11.01	1.02	0.243	1

All p-values are Bonferroni adjusted for multiple comparisons.

Table 4 | Correlations among measures for auditory processing, speech perception, phonology and literacy skills, with (upper part) and without (lower part) controlling for group.

Measure	1	2	3	4	5	6	7	8	9	10	11	12
1. Spell	–	0.366***	0.093	0.316**	0.385***	0.137	0.207(*)	0.065	0.061	−0.030	−0.123	0.033
2. Read	0.675***	–	0.227*	0.239*	0.323**	0.055	0.001	−0.073	0.146	0.064	−0.041	−0.010
3. DS	0.329***	0.404***	–	0.511***	0.301**	0.138	0.191	0.166	0.150	−0.128	0.117	0.147
4. NWR	0.521**	0.466***	0.591***	–	0.413***	0.170	0.194	0.071	−0.002	−0.042	0.106	0.275*
5. PA	0.700***	0.642***	0.457**	0.582***	–	298**	0.388***	−0.075	0.031	−0.221*	−0.028	0.224*
6. RANob	0.431***	0.356**	0.288**	0.349**	0.518***	–	0.722***	−0.255*	−0.014	−0.206	0.018	−0.042
7. RANcol	0.430***	0.280*	0.314**	0.346**	0.542***	0.775***	–	−0.175	0.081	−0.281**	−0.033	121
8. RT	−0.220*	−0.304**	0.005	−0.115	−0.314**	−0.382***	−0.301**	–	0.124	0.135	−0.108	−0.183
9. FM	−0.093	−0.042	0.057	−0.101	−0.132	−0.109	−0.015	0.211*	–	0.350**	−0.023	−0.033
10. ID	−0.241***	−0.173	−0.229*	−0.182	−0.375***	−0.321***	−0.249*	0.249*	0.402***	–	−0.047	−0.196
11. HINT	−0.112	−0.057	0.094	0.076	−0.047	−0.003	−0.046	−0.085	−0.015	−0.032	–	0.219*
12. CASPA	−0.024	−0.035	0.119	0.225*	0.132	−0.059	0.090	−0.165	−0.043	−0.181	0.220*	–

Read, WRAT reading; Spell, WRAT spelling; DS, Digit Span; NWR, non-word recall; PA, Spoonerism; RANob, RAN object naming; RANcol, RAN color naming.
$^{*}p < 0.05$; $^{**}p < 0.01$; $^{***}p < 0.001$; $^{(*)}$Approaching significance of 0.05.

Since the correlational analyses showed that reading and spelling correlate with both PA and RT, the independent contribution of each was assessed through a multiple regression analyses with both RT and PA for predicting reading and spelling (see **Table 5**). Analyses showed that RT offers no unique influence to both literacy measure above that offered through PA.

The addition of ID in the model to control for attention mechanisms produced the same pattern of results for reading, $F_{(3,\,85)} = 21.512$, $p < 0.001$, $R^2 = 0.432$, and spelling, $F_{(3,\,85)} = 27.258$, $p < 0.001$, $R^2 = 0.490$, as well as the addition of age and IQ with ID, $F_{(5,\,83)} = 13.802$, $p < 0.001$, $R^2 = 0.454$, and $F_{(5,\,83)} = 17.591$, $p < 0.001$, $R^2 = 0.514$.

Yet further investigation of RT's relationship with literacy within the dyslexic and the normal reading population did not reveal the same relationships present above. More specifically, the addition of group as a control measure to the regression model produced a larger significant contribution of PA, and none of RT, to reading, $F_{(6,\,82)} = 16.683$, $p < 0.001$, $R^2 = 0.550$ and spelling, $F_{(6,\,82)} = 23.392$, $p < 0.001$, $R^2 = 0.631$. In a similar vein, the other significant relationships that RT had across the entire population (lower left portion of **Table 4**) disappeared when controlling for group, with the exception of RAN object (upper right portion of **Table 4**).

Table 5 | Stepwise regressions showing the unique variance in the word reading, and spelling accounted for by PA and RT (R^2 change and standardized Beta).

Step	Word reading		Spelling	
	R^2 change	β	R^2 change	β
1. PA	0.412***	0.935	0.490***	0.983
2. RT	0.012	−0.171	0.000	−0.030

$^{***}p < 0.001$.

INDIVIDUAL DEVIANCE ANALYSES

Individual differences

The examination of performance at the individual level in both the NR and DYS group allows for a better understanding of the proportion of individuals within each group showing poor performance on each measured variable, even when group differences are not found. Such analyses will also allow determining if any individual subject had consistent deviant performance across all levels of processing, or whether deviant performance is a more random occurrence indicating the involvement of influences different from an auditory perceptual deficit (Heath et al., 2006).

Individual performance of the *z*-scores of RT, FM, ID, CASPA, HINT, PA, RAN, and VSTM were analyzed. A deviancy threshold of −1.65 was used. Thus, any *z*-score falling below this threshold would be considered as deviant performance as described by Ramus et al. (2003) and subsequently used by Boets et al. (2006, 2007), Reid et al. (2007), and Hazan et al. (2009).

The number and proportion of deviant subject per group on each of the variables are presented in **Table 6**. All measures, with the exception of CASPA, HINT, ID, and FM, demonstrated a significantly higher portion of deviant subjects in the DYS group when compared with the NR group.

An evaluation of subjects with at least one score deviating more than 1.65 *SD* for the various auditory, speech and phonological measures, demonstrated that deficits appeared inconsistent, with some subjects deviating only on one task, while others on two or three tasks. Due to the observation of a high percentage of deviancy found on measures of RT (58%) and PA (72%) within the dyslexic group, an exploration of the interrelation between deficiencies in these different skills were made. ID was included to address any questions of influence of task related demands and/or attention. **Figure 1** shows the calculated number of subjects showing isolated vs. overlapping deficits. Results show that 28% of the dyslexic subjects possess a deficit in only PA (30% when controlled for ID), while 14% dyslexic subjects were found to only have a RT deficit (19% when controlled for

Table 6 | Individual deviancy analysis for each variable.

Measure	DYS		NR		χ^2	*p*
	n	%	*n*	%		
Literacy	31	86	0	0	70.932	<0.001
PA	26	72	1	2	50.184	<0.001
RAN	11	31	3	6	10.277	0.001
VSTM	19	53	2	4	29.079	<0.001
RT	21	58	12	22	12.129	<0.001
FM	11	31	8	15	3.213	0.073
ID	9	25	8	15	1.463	0.227
HINT	1	3	1	2	0.085	0.643
CASPA	5	14	9	17	0.127	0.722

Where cells have expected count less than 5, the Fisher's Exact test p-values are reported.

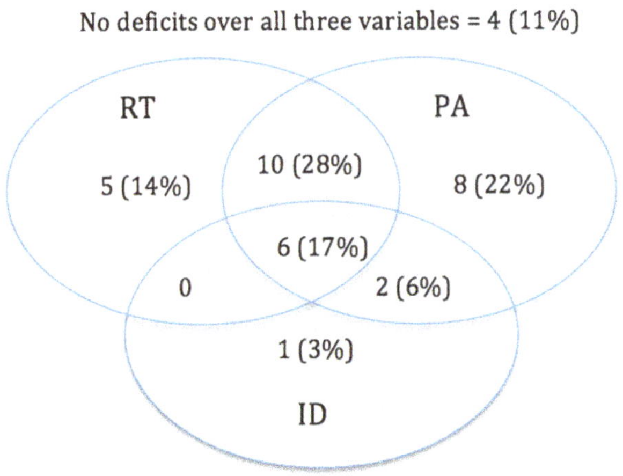

FIGURE 1 | Distribution of RT, PA, and ID deficits in the total sample of 36 dyslexic adult participants. Measured in absolute numbers and percentages of impaired subjects.

ID). Dyslexic adults possessing an overlap in deficits were found to represent nearly half of the dyslexic subjects, 44% (37% when controlled for ID). Although a large percentage of overlap is present, the proportion of shared PA and RT deficit does not exceed the expected proportions represented within the whole dyslexic group. Investigation of the normal reading individuals revealed no overlap between deviancy of RT and PA, yet this might be due to a low number of deviant subjects.

DISCUSSION

It has been well established in the literature that dyslexic readers struggle with a phonological processing deficit and that such skills are related to literacy development and achievement (Snowling, 2000). Yet debate surrounds the question of whether this phonological processing impairment stems from a more primary deficit, such as a deficit in processing of speech sounds or due to a reduced sensitivity to slow-rate dynamic auditory information. This current study was set out to investigate speech perception and slow-rate dynamic auditory processing, in the form of RT and FM detection, in relation to phonological processing and literacy measures in dyslexic and normal reading adults.

SLOW-RATE AUDITORY PROCESSING DEFICIT

In line with the auditory temporal processing deficit theory of dyslexia, we had expected our auditory measures of RT and FM to differentiate between dyslexic and non-dyslexic students but not our non-temporal auditory ID task.

With regard to the slow-rate auditory processing tasks, group analyses revealed significant differences between adults with dyslexia and normal readers in RT while the uncorrected *p*-value was found to be approaching significance in FM. The lack of a significant group difference for the FM measure was unexpected, since the majority of studies in dyslexic adults have demonstrated clear group differences (Witton et al., 1998, 2002; Ramus et al., 2003; Heath et al., 2006). With regard to RT, our results are in line with the bulk of previous studies demonstrating a lower performance in dyslexic children (e.g., Goswami et al., 2002; Fraser et al., 2010; Poelmans et al., 2011) and adults (e.g., Hämäläinen et al., 2005; Thomson et al., 2006; Pasquini et al., 2007), suggesting a RT-deficit across development and languages.

Plausible hypotheses to explain the unexpected finding of not finding a group difference for FM in the presence of a RT-deficit may be (1) low sensitivity of the behavioral measures used, (2) the influence of task demands and attention difficulties, or (3) specific characteristics of the auditory stimuli being used.

Stoodley et al. (2006) suggested that in a population, such as the one included in this study, psychophysical measures may not be sensitive enough to detect subtle auditory processing impairments due to possible compensation. They found dyslexic adults to be unimpaired in psychophysical FM discrimination tasks, yet group differences were found when electrophysiological recordings were used. In doing so, Stoodley and colleagues demonstrated that the inability to detect low level auditory processing deficits in some groups of high functioning dyslexics can be attributed to the task sensitivity and the level of compensation achieved by the individual. The lack of group differences for FM discrimination for our adult population differed from behavioral studies in pre-schoolers (Boets et al., 2007) and children (Poelmans et al., 2011), which employed similar methodologies and stimuli. Yet findings on the RT measures were found to be significant, which would not have been expected if Stoodley's theory of compensation influences is consistent across all psychophysical tasks, unless RT tasks offer greater sensitivity.

Criticism regarding the influence of task demand and complexity of psychophysical tasks (see Roach et al., 2004) could explain the inconsistency of these results and the unexpected group differences on the ID task. Of the 16 studies reviewed by Hämäläinen et al. (2013) that included a measure of ID, only two found a significant group difference between individuals with dyslexia and normal readers. In the only adult study which found a group difference in ID (Thomson et al., 2006), the authors attributed their findings to the task difficulty of their ID measure. Such findings of unexpected differences may support Roach et al.'s (2004) claim that poor performance and findings of group differences on psychophysical tasks are likely to be a function of attention and general task performance. In order to control for such task demand differences, ID was included in the statistical analyses as a control measure for all levels of analyses. After controlling for ID, group differences on RT remained present, indicating that this difference is rooted in processing stimuli-related properties differently rather than in attention differences.

Since our results do not clearly support the two explanations above, it is more likely that the pattern of results can be explained by a very specific deficit in slow-rate dynamic auditory processing. FM and RT tasks differ in how the auditory information is represented in the speech signal. As discussed by Rosen (1992), FM represents the fine structure of the speech waveform, while RT represents amplitude aspects of the speech envelope. The distinct pattern of results between RT and FM suggests that in adult dyslexics, the primary auditory dysfunction is more likely to be found in the perception of slow-rate dynamic auditory cues related to the speech envelope, as measured by RT, and not in the fine-structure, as measured by FM. Such findings reinforce previous studies in both child and adult populations (Goswami et al., 2002; Thomson et al., 2006; Fraser et al., 2010; Poelmans et al., 2011).

In sum, our results do not support a general deficit in slow-rate auditory processing of adult with dyslexia, yet, a subgroup of the adult dyslexic population may possess a more specific slow-rate dynamic processing deficit specific to the envelopes of the speech waveform.

SPEECH-IN-NOISE PERCEPTION DEFICIT IN INDIVIDUALS WITH DYSLEXIA

Slow-rate dynamic auditory cues are found in abundance in speech. It is believed that a deficit in the processing of these auditory cues, such as RT and FM, would ultimately lead to a disruption in speech perception.

Unlike the results of auditory processing, this present study was not able to demonstrate any evidence to support the continuation of the speech-processing deficit observed in youth (Snowling et al., 1986; Wible et al., 2002; Bradlow et al., 2003; Boets et al., 2007; Ziegler et al., 2005, 2009) into adulthood, suggesting developmental or task related influences. Although our speech masking stimuli were in line with previous studies with children, it may not have offered sufficient difficulty for use in an adult or a highly compensated population (Pennington et al., 1990). According to a recently published study by Dole et al. (2012), a stationary speech weighted background noise, as used in the present study, is less effective in differentiating between dyslexic and normal reading adults than modulated noises and background speech masks. Under the masking conditions of background speech or modulated noise an individual must rely on temporal dips in the masking noise to extract signals of the target speech signal (Howard-Jones and Rosen, 1993). It is thought that individuals with dyslexia may have difficulty perceiving these temporal dips, which is in line with our results of a RT deficit. Future studies should take into account Dole's findings to further assess the potential cascade of the RT difficulties observed in some dyslexics.

SLOW-RATE AUDITORY PROCESSING AND SPEECH PERCEPTION RELATIONSHIP

Our findings showed significantly poorer performance in adult dyslexic readers on the RT task assessing slow-rate dynamic auditory processing, which relates to amplitude aspects of the speech envelope. If an indirect path of an RT deficit through speech perception existed, we would have expected to find a correlation with the sentence in noise measure that required a greater reliance on larger grain segmentation of the sentence stimuli. However, examination of the relationships between these variables could not clearly support this hypothesis. Yet, once controlled for group, CASPA was found to relate to phonological skills.

As discussed earlier, the use of stationary noise in our speech perception tasks may have limited our ability to find relationships with RT, which might be more closely related to speech perception in modulated noise. An alternative interpretation is that slow-rate auditory processing independently relates to reading related measures and not via speech perception measures. However, such a situation remains unlikely considering the prevalence of slow-rate dynamic auditory cues in the speech signal. Therefore one would expect to find a relationship between these two variables. Finally, Poelmans et al. (2011) offered an alternative explanation, stating that the lack of relationship could be a consequence of the fact that the developmental link between these variables diminishes over time and is no longer evident in later years.

Due to the lack of evidence found to support the relationship of auditory deficits and speech perception in adults, our results do not support the theoretical cascade effect of the auditory deficit through speech perception to one's phonological representations.

SLOW-RATE DYNAMIC AUDITORY PROCESSING, PHONOLOGICAL PROCESSING, AND LITERACY

No significant correlations were found with FM nor with speech perception tasks. On the other hand, RT was found to correlate with measures of reading, spelling, phonological awareness and RAN, similar to findings of Thomson et al. (2006). Taking the regression analyses into account, it appears that any relationship between RT and reading is mediated through phonological processing and not speech-in-noise. These findings were similar to that of Pasquini et al. (2007). As discussed by Hämäläinen et al. (2005) it is highly improbable that the lower level skills of RT discrimination could be influenced by an individual's poor phonological awareness. Therefore, it is reasonable to assume that either this relationship reflects the same underlying perceptual deficit, or the ability to detect rapid changes in the speech envelope has a causal role in the development of PA. Although once controlled for group these relationships could no longer be supported, indicating that RT is not a good predictor of reading abilities in dyslexic or in normal readers. Yet, it is worth noting that a different pattern of findings might have emerged if a more direct assessment of decoding was employed, such as non-word reading measure (Hämäläinen et al., 2005).

Although the correlational analyses across all participants suggest interrelations between PA and RT, this finding should be nuanced at the individual level. When the prevalence and overlap of deviant performance on PA and RT was evaluated at the individual level, nearly half (45%) of the dyslexic population was found to possess a deficit in both, while 28 and 14% of the dyslexic population was found to have an isolated deficit in PA or RT, respectively (30 and 19% when controlled for ID). Despite co-occurrence in a large subsample of dyslexics, independence is suggested because the overlap between these variables is in proportion to what would be expected based on the frequency of each deficit in the total dyslexic group (i.e., 72% for a PA-deficit and 53% for a RT-deficit). Complemented with the lack of relationships once group was controlled for, it appears that phonological deficits seem not to be necessarily secondary to auditory problems since both deficits do not co-occur in every dyslexic subject. To increase our understanding, a longitudinal pre-reading study will be needed to assess the prevalence of the double deficit in RT and PA at earlier stages of reading development. In addition, training studies could help in verifying how one skill influences the other.

Given that in our adult study a large proportion of reading (problems) still remains unexplained, a multifactorial approach should be explored to fully identify the mechanisms underlying dyslexia. By investigating alternative cognitive factors, such as orthographic or morphological processing (Bekebrede et al., 2009), perceptual factors (Stein, 2001) and biological explanations (Nicolson et al., 2001), the variance and comorbid symptoms associated with the dyslexic population can be better understood.

LIMITATIONS AND IMPLICATIONS

A limitation of this study was the sole inclusion of university students with dyslexia. It is reasonable to assume that by mere virtue of the fact that these young adults have reached university level education, varying levels of compensation are present in this specific group. Research has shown that the presence of relatively stronger cognitive abilities in some children with dyslexia allows for the minimization of parts of their phonological deficit later in life, allowing for the attainment of normal reading ability (Shaywitz et al., 2003). For example, a reliance or a strength in the use of contextual cues (Frith and Snowling, 1983; Nation and Snowling, 1998), semantic knowledge (Snowling et al., 2000), visual memory (Campbell and Butterworth, 1985), and morphological knowledge (Elbro and Arnbak, 1996) had been shown to aid in a dyslexic's ability to minimize the impact of the deficit in the expressed reading abilities. Stoodley et al. (2006) had also noted similar top down compensation processes influencing results of slow-rate dynamic auditory processing tasks (for a description of possible top down compensation processes see Pichora-Fuller, 2008). Therefore, percentages of observed deviant performance on slow-rate dynamic auditory processing tasks and phonological awareness measures could be underrepresented within our sample. Such potential levels of compensation limit our ability to extrapolate any findings to the general adult dyslexic population and could have potentially limited our ability in establishing clear group differences or correlations between variables. Having said this, our results do have implications in typifying the characteristics of dyslexic adults in higher education and broadening our understanding of how compensation may be expressed. This is especially relevant since accommodations are offered based on valid diagnosis given to them. Although the RT task sensitivity is lower than the phonological tasks' sensitivity, our result did demonstrate its potential to be included as an additional screening measure, for it was able to characterize a proportion of dyslexic adults not identified by a PA measure alone. Our data showed that purely relying on a PA tasks will result in missing a small subsample of dyslexics (in our study 14%).

A second implication is that a control task should be included. Our findings show the possible overestimation of the number of dyslexics when attention and task related demands are not accounted for. To avoid overestimation, future research should apply such a control task as presented in this paper, when designing a psychophysical testing battery and screening tools. Therefore, future development and study of this measure is still needed.

CONCLUSION

In summary, our results suggest that the lower sensitivity to RT cues that was observed in dyslexic children is still observable in adulthood, while FM deficits are not. Hence, our results suggest that a general slow-rate dynamic auditory processing deficit may not be present within an adult dyslexic population, but may be confined to speech envelope cues rather than to fine structure. RT's influence on literacy outcomes was not direct and was found to be mediated through phonological processing (this relationship was lost once controlled for group). Unlike studies in younger children (Boets et al., 2006), the existence of speech-in-noise perception deficits and its mediating role in auditory processing and reading-related measures was not observed. Further research is needed in this area with attention to the selection of speech-in-noise masking stimuli and the sampling of a more diverse adult population, which does not primarily contain a university sample.

Although findings of a deficit in RT and its correlation with phonological skills are significant when examined across the entire population, many dyslexic subjects with a severe deficit in one of these skills were often found unimpaired in the other skills. At best, conclusions regarding the primary deficit of dyslexia being a slow-rate dynamic auditory processing deficit should be restricted to the processing of RT cues and can only be generalized to a subgroup of adults with dyslexia. Such a lack of consistency could implicate the necessity of a multifactorial model of dyslexia.

ACKNOWLEDGMENTS

We would like to acknowledge the help and support of Hanne Poelmans and Sophie Vanvooren in the calibration and setup of the auditory processing and speech perception instruments and task. We are also grateful to Mike Walker for his help in participant recruitment and the arrangement of testing facilities. This research has been financed by the research fund of the KU Leuven (grants dBOF/12/014 and OT/12/044). Funding was also provided by the Science Foundation Flanders (grant G.0920.12).

REFERENCES

Adlard, A., and Hazan, V. (1998). Speech perception in children with specific reading difficulties (dyslexia). *Q. J. Exp. Psychol.* 51, 153–177. doi: 10.1080/713755750

Assmann, P., and Summerfield, Q. (2004). "The perception of speech under adverse conditions," in *Speech Processing in The Auditory System*, eds S. Greenberg, W. A. Ainsworth, A. N. Popper, and R. R. Fry (New York, NY: Springer), 231–308.

Bekebrede, J. I., van der Leij, A., and Share, D. L. (2009). Dutch dyslexic adolescents: phonological-core variable-orthographic differences. *Read. Writ.* 22, 133–165. doi: 10.1007/s11145-007-9105-7

Blomert, L., and Mitterer, H. (2004). The fragile nature of the speech-perception deficit in dyslexia: natural vs. synthetic speech. *Brain Lang.* 89, 21–26. doi: 10.1016/S0093-934X(03)00305-5

Boets, B., Vandermosten, M., Poelmans, H., Luts, H., Wouters, J., and Ghesquiere, P. (2011). Preschool impairments in auditory processing and speech perception uniquely predict future reading problems. *Res. Dev. Disabil.* 32, 560–570. doi: 10.1016/j.ridd.2010.12.020

Boets, B., Wouters, J., van Wieringen, A., and Ghesquiere, P. (2006). Auditory temporal information processing in preschool children at family risk for dyslexia: relations with phonological abilities and developing literacy skills. *Brain Lang.* 97, 64–79. doi: 10.1016/j.bandl.2005.07.026

Boets, B., Wouters, J., van Wieringen, A., and Ghesquiere, P. (2007). Auditory processing, speech perception and phonological ability in preschool children at high-risk for dyslexia: a longitudinal study of the auditory temporal processing theory. *Neuropsychologia* 45, 1608–1620. doi: 10.1016/j.neuropsychologia.2007.01.009

Boothroyd, A. (2006). *CASPA 5.0. Software.* San Diego, CA: A Boothroyd.

Bradlow, A. R., Kraus, N., and Hayes, E. (2003). Speaking clearly for children with learning disabilities: sentence perception in noise. *J. Speech Lang. Hear. Res.* 46, 80–97. doi: 10.1044/1092-4388(2003/007)

Brady, S., Shankweiler, D., and Mann, V. (1983). Speech perception and memory coding in relation to reading ability. *J. Exp. Child Psychol.* 35, 345–367. doi: 10.1016/0022-0965(83)90087-5

Campbell, R., and Butterworth, B. (1985). Phonological dyslexia and dysgraphia in a highly literate subject: a developmental case with associated deficits of phonemic processing and awareness. *Q. J. Exp. Psychol.* 37, 435–475.

Corriveau, K., Pasquini, E., and Goswami, U. (2007). Basic auditory processing skills and specific language impairment: a new look at an old hypothesis. *J. Speech Lang. Hear. Res.* 50, 647–666. doi: 10.1044/1092-4388(2007/046)

Dawes, P., Sirimanna, T., Burton, M., Vanniasegaram, I., Tweedy, F., and Bishop, D. V. M. (2009). Temporal auditory and visual motion processing of children diagnosed with auditory processing disorder and dyslexia. *Ear Hear.* 30, 675–686. doi: 10.1097/AUD.0b013e3181b34cc5

Dole, M., Hoen, M., and Meunier, F. (2012). Speech-in-noise perception deficit in adults with dyslexia: effects of background type and listening configuration. *Neuropsychologia* 50, 1543–1552. doi: 10.1016/j.neuropsychologia.2012.03.007

Elbro, C., and Arnbak, E. (1996). The role of morpheme recognition and morphological awareness in dyslexia. *Ann. Dyslexia* 46, 209–240. doi: 10.1007/BF02648177

Farmer, M. E., and Klein, R. M. (1995). The evidence for a temporal processing deficit linked to dyslexia: a review. *Psychon. Bull. Rev.* 2, 460–493. doi: 10.3758/BF03210983

Field, A. P. (2009). *Discovering Statistics Using SPSS: and Sex and Drugs and Rock 'n' Roll, 3rd Edn.* London: Sage.

Francart, T., van Wieringen, A., and Wouters, J. (2008). APEX 3: a multi-purpose test platform for auditory psychophysical experiments. *J. Neurosci. Methods* 172, 283–293. doi: 10.1016/j.jneumeth.2008.04.020

Fraser, J., Goswami, U., and Conti-Ramsden, G. (2010). Dyslexia and specific language impairment: the role of phonology and auditory processing. *Sci. Stud. Read.* 14, 8–29. doi: 10.1080/10888430903242068

Frederickson, N., Frith, U., and Reason, R. (1997). *Phonological Assessment Battery (Manual and Test Materials).* Windsor: NFER-Nelson.

Frith, U., and Snowling, M. (1983). Reading for meaning and reading for sound in autistic and dyslexic children. *Br. J. Dev. Psychol.* 1, 329–342. doi: 10.1111/j.2044-835X.1983.tb00906.x

Goswami, U., Fosker, T., Huss, M., Mead, N., and Szucs, D. (2011). Rise time and formant transition duration in the discrimination of speech sounds: the Ba-Wa distinction in developmental dyslexia. *Dev. Sci.* 14, 34–43. doi: 10.1111/j.1467-7687.2010.00955.x

Goswami, U., Gerson, D., and Astruc, L. (2010). Amplitude envelope perception, phonology and prosodic sensitivity in children with developmental dyslexia. *Read. Writ.* 23, 995–1019. doi: 10.1007/s11145-009-9186-6

Goswami, U., Thomson, J., Richardson, U., Stainthorp, R., Hughes, D., Rosen, S., et al. (2002). Amplitude envelope onsets and developmental dyslexia: a new hypothesis. *Proc. Natl. Acad. Sci. U.S.A.* 99, 10911–10916. doi: 10.1073/pnas.122368599

Habib, M. (2000). The neurological basis of developmental dyslexia. *Brain* 123, 2373–2399. doi: 10.1093/brain/123.12.2373

Halliday, L. F., and Bishop, D. V. M. (2006). Auditory frequency discrimination in children with dyslexia. *J. Res. Read.* 29, 213–228. doi: 10.1111/j.1467-9817.2006.00286.x

Hämäläinen, J., Leppänen, P. H. T., Torppa, M., Muller, K., and Lyytinen, H. (2005). Detection of sound rise time by adults with dyslexia. *Brain Lang.* 94, 32–42. doi: 10.1016/j.bandl.2004.11.005

Hämäläinen, J. A., Leppänen, P. H. T., Eklund, K., Thomson, J., Richardson, U., Guttorm, T. K., et al. (2009). Common variance in amplitude envelope perception tasks and their impact on phoneme duration perception and reading and spelling in Finnish children with reading disabilities. *Appl. Psycholinguist.* 30, 511–530. doi: 10.1017/S014271640 9090250

Hämäläinen, J. A., Salminen, H. K., and Leppanen, P. (2013). Basic auditory processing deficits in dyslexia: systematic review of the behavioral and event-related potential/field evidence. *J. Learn. Disabil.* 46, 413–427. doi: 10.1177/0022219411436213

Hazan, V., Messaoud-Galusi, S., Rosen, S., Nouwens, S., and Shakespeare, B. (2009). Speech perception abilities of adults with dyslexia: is there any evidence for a true deficit? *J. Speech Lang. Hear. Res.* 52, 1510–1529. doi: 10.1044/1092-4388(2009/08-0220)

Heath, S. M., Bishop, D. V. M., Hogben, J. H., and Roach, N. W. (2006). Psychophysical indices of perceptual functioning in dyslexia: a psychometric analysis. *Cogn. Neuropsychol.* 23, 905–929. doi: 10.1080/02643290500538398

Howard-Jones, P. A., and Rosen, S. (1993). The perception of speech in fluctuating noise. *Acustica* 78, 258–272.

Laneau, J., Boets, B., Moonen, M., van Wieringen, A., and Wouters, J. (2005). A flexible auditory research platform using acoustic or electric stimuli for adults and young children. *J. Neurosci. Methods* 142, 131–136. doi: 10.1016/j.jneumeth.2004.08.015

Levitt, H. (1971). Transformed up-down methods in psychoacoustics. *J. Acoust. Soc. Am.* 49, 467–477. doi: 10.1121/1.1912375

Maassen, B., Groenen, P., Crul, T., Assman-Hulsmans, C., and Gabreëls, F. (2001). Identification and discrimination of voicing and place of articulation in developmental dyslexia. *Clin. Linguist. Phon.* 15, 319–339. doi: 10.1080/02699200010026102

Manis, F. R., McBride-Chang, C., Seidenberg, M. S., Keating, P., Doi, L. M., Munson, B., et al. (1997). Are speech perception deficits associated with developmental dyslexia? *J. Exp. Child Psychol.* 66, 211–235. doi: 10.1006/jecp.1997.2383

McCreery, R., Ito, R., Spratford, M., Lewis, D., Hoover, B., and Stelmachowicz, P. G. (2010). Performance-intensity functions for normal-hearing adults and children using computer-aided speech perception assessment. *Ear Hear.* 31, 95–101. doi: 10.1097/AUD.0b013e3181bc7702

Nation, K., and Snowling, M. (1998). Individual differences in contextual facilitation evidence from dyslexia and poor reading comprehension. *Child Dev.* 69, 996–1011. doi: 10.1111/j.1467-8624.1998.tb06157.x

Nicolson, R. I., Fawcett, A. J., and Dean, P. (2001). Developmental dyslexia: the cerebellar deficit hypothesis. *Trends Neurosci.* 24, 508–511. doi: 10.1016/S0166-2236(00)01896-8

Nilsson, M., Soli, S. D., and Sullivan, J. A. (1994). Development of the hearing in noise test for the measurement of speech reception thresholds in quiet and in noise. *J. Acoust. Soc. Am.* 95, 1085–1099. doi: 10.1121/1.408469

Pasquini, E. S., Corriveau, K. H., and Goswami, U. (2007). Auditory processing of amplitude envelope rise time in adults diagnosed with developmental dyslexia. *Sci. Stud. Read.* 11, 259–286. doi: 10.1080/10888430701344280

Pennington, B. F., Van Orden, G. C., Smith, S. D., Green, P. A., and Haith, M. M. (1990). Phonological processing skills and deficits in adult dyslexics. *Child Dev.* 61, 1753–1778. doi: 10.2307/1130836

Pichora-Fuller, M. K. (2008). Use of supportive context by younger and older adult listeners: balancing bottom-up and top-down information processing. *Int. J. Audiol.* 47, 72–82. doi: 10.1080/14992020802307404

Pickering, S. J., and Gathercole, S. E. (2001). *Working Memory Battery for Children.* Bristol: University of Bristol.

Poelmans, H., Luts, H., Vandermosten, M., Boets, B., Ghesquiere, P., and Wouters, J. (2011). Reduced sensitivity to slow-rate dynamic auditory information in children with dyslexia. *Res. Dev. Disabil.* 32, 2810–2819. doi: 10.1016/j.ridd.2011.05.025

Ramus, F., Rosen, S., Dakin, S. C., Day, B. L., Castellote, J. M., White, S., et al. (2003). Theories of developmental dyslexia: insights from a multiple case study of dyslexic adults. *Brain* 126, 841–865. doi: 10.1093/brain/awg076

Reid, A. A., Szczerbinski, M., Iskierka-Kasperek, E., and Hansen, P. (2007). Cognitive profiles of adult developmental dyslexics: theoretical implications. *Dyslexia* 13, 1–24. doi: 10.1002/dys.321

Roach, N. W., Edwards, V. T., and Hogben, J. H. (2004). The tale is in the tail: an alternative hypothesis for psychophysical performance variability in dyslexia. *Perception* 33, 817–830. doi: 10.1068/p5207

Rosen, S. (1992). Temporal information in speech: acoustic, auditory and linguistic aspects. *Philos. Trans. R. Soc. Lond. B Biol. Sci.* 336, 367–373. doi: 10.1098/rstb.1992.0070

Semel, E., Wiig, E. H., and Secord, W. A. (2003). *Clinical Evaluation of Language Fundamentals (CELF—4th Edn.)*. San Antonio, TX: Harcourt Assessment.

Shaywitz, S. E., Shaywitz, B. A., Fulbright, R. K., Skudlarski, P., Mencl, E. W., Todd, R., et al. (2003). Neural systems for compensation and persistence: young adult outcome of childhood reading disability. *Biol. Psychiatry* 54, 25–33. doi: 10.1016/S0006-3223(02)01836-X

Snowling, M., Bishop, D., and Stothard, S. (2000). Is preschool language impairment a risk factor for dyslexia in adolescence. *J. Child Psychol. Psychiatry* 41, 587–600. doi: 10.1111/1469-7610.00651

Snowling, M., Goulandris, N., Bowlby, M., and Howell, P. (1986). Segmentation and speech perception in relation to reading skill: a developmental analysis. *J. Exp. Child Psychol.* 41, 489–507. doi: 10.1016/0022-0965(86)90006-8

Snowling, M. J. (2000). *Dyslexia*. Oxford: Blackwell.

Stein, J. (2001). The magnocellular theory of developmental dyslexia. *Dyslexia* 7, 12–36. doi: 10.1002/dys.186

Stoodley, C. J., Hill, P. R., Stein, J. F., and Bishop, D. V. M. (2006). Auditory event-related potentials differ in dyslexics even when auditory psychophysical performance is normal. *Brain Res.* 1121, 190–199. doi: 10.1016/j.brainres.2006.08.095

Stuart, G. W., McAnally, K. I., and Castles, A. (2001). Can contrast sensitivity functions in dyslexia be explained by inattention rather than a magnocellular deficit? *Vision Res.* 41, 3205–3211. doi: 10.1016/S0042-6989(01)00176-6

Tallal, P. (1980). Auditory temporal perception, phonics and reading disabilities in children. *Brain Lang.* 9, 182–198. doi: 10.1016/0093-934X(80)90139-X

Thomson, J. M., Fryer, B., Maltby, J., and Goswami, U. (2006). Auditory and motor rhythm awareness in adults with dyslexia. *J. Res. Read.* 29, 334–348. doi: 10.1111/j.1467-9817.2006.00312.x

Vandermosten, M., Boets, B., Luts, H., Poelmans, N., Wouters, J., and Ghesquière, P. (2011). Impairments in speech and nonspeech sound categorization in children with dyslexia are driven by temporal processing difficulties. *Res. Dev. Disabil.* 32, 593–603. doi: 10.1016/j.ridd.2010.12.015

Vandermosten, M., Boets, B., Luts, H., Poelmans, H., Golestani, N., Wouters, J., et al. (2010). Adults with dyslexia are impaired in categorizing speech and nonspeech sounds on the basis of temporal cues. *Proc. Natl. Acad. Sci. U.S.A.* 107, 10389–10394. doi: 10.1073/pnas.0912858107

Van Ingelghem, M., Boets, B., van Wieringen, A., Onghena, P., Ghesquiere, P., Vandenbussche, E., et al. (2005). "An auditory temporal processing deficit in children with dyslexia?" in *Children With Learning Disabilities: A Challenge to Teaching and Instruction* eds P. Ghesquiere and A. J. J. M. Ruijssenaars (Leuven: University Press), 47–63.

Vellutino, F. R., Fletcher, J. M., Snowling, M. J., and Scanlon, D. M. (2004). Specific reading disability (dyslexia): what have we learned in the past four decades? *J. Child Psychol. Psychiatry* 45, 2–40. doi: 10.1046/j.0021-9630.2003.00305.x

Wagner, R. K., and Torgesen, J. K. (1987). The nature of phonological processing and its causal role in the acquisition of reading skills. *Psychol. Bull.* 101, 192–212. doi: 10.1037/0033-2909.101.2.192

White, S., Milne, E., Rosen, S., Hansen, P., Swettenham, J., Frith, U., et al. (2006). The role of sensorimotor impairments in dyslexia: a multiple case study of dyslexic children. *Dev. Sci.* 9, 237–255. doi: 10.1111/j.1467-7687.2006.00483.x

Wible, B., Nicol, T. G., and Kraus, N. (2002). Abnormal neural encoding of repeated speech stimuli in noise in children with learning problems. *Clin. Neurophysiol.* 113, 485–494. doi: 10.1016/S1388-2457(02)00017-2

Wilkinson, G. (1993). *Wide Range Achievement Test – 3rd Edn. (Wrat-3)*. Wilmington, DE: Wide Range Inc.

Witton, C., Stein, J. F., Stoodley, C. J., Rosner, B. S., and Talcott, J. B. (2002). Separate influences of acoustic AM and FM sensitivity on the phonological decoding skills of impaired and normal readers. *J. Cogn. Neurosci.* 14, 866–874. doi: 10.1162/089892902760191090

Witton, C., Talcott, J. B., Hansen, P. C., Richardson, A. J., Griffiths, T. D., Rees, A., et al. (1998). Sensitivity to dynamic auditory and visual stimuli predicts nonword reading ability in both dyslexic and normal readers. *Curr. Biol.* 8, 791–797. doi: 10.1016/S0960-9822(98)70320-3

Ziegler, J. C., Castel, C., Pech-Georgel, C., George, F., Alario, F. X., and Perry, C. (2008). Developmental dyslexia and the dual route model of reading: simulating individual differences and subtypes. *Cognition* 107, 151–178. doi: 10.1016/j.cognition.2007.09.004

Ziegler, J. C., Pech-Georgel, C., George, F., Alario, F. X., and Lorenzi, C. (2005). Deficits in speech perception predict language learning impairment. *Proc. Natl. Acad. Sci. U.S.A.* 102, 14110–14115. doi: 10.1073/pnas.0504446102

Ziegler, J. C., Pech-Georgel, C., George, F., and Lorenzi, C. (2009). Speech perception in noise in dyslexia. *Dev. Sci.* 12, 732–745. doi: 10.1111/j.1467-7687.2009.00817.x

13

Magnocellular-dorsal pathway and sub-lexical route in developmental dyslexia

Simone Gori[1,2] *, Paolo Cecchini[3], Anna Bigoni[3], Massimo Molteni[2] and Andrea Facoetti[1,2]

[1] Developmental and Cognitive Neuroscience Laboratory, Dipartimento di Psicologia Generale, Università degli Studi di Padova, Padova, Italy
[2] Developmental Neuropsychology Unit, Istituto Scientifico "E. Medea" di Bosisio Parini, Lecco, Italy
[3] Ophthalmological Unit, Istituto Scientifico "E. Medea" di San Vito al Tagliamento, Pordenone, Italy

Correspondence:
Simone Gori, Developmental and Cognitive Neuroscience Laboratory, Dipartimento di Psicologia Generale, Università degli Studi di Padova, Via Venezia, 8 35131 Padova, Italy
e-mail: simone.gori@unipd.it

Although developmental dyslexia (DD) is frequently associate with a phonological deficit, the underlying neurobiological cause remains undetermined. Recently, a new model, called "temporal sampling framework" (TSF), provided an innovative prospect in the DD study. TSF suggests that deficits in syllabic perception at a specific temporal frequencies are the critical basis for the poor reading performance in DD. This approach was presented as a possible neurobiological substrate of the phonological deficit of DD but the TSF can also easily be applied to the visual modality deficits. The deficit in the magnocellular-dorsal (M-D) pathway - often found in individuals with DD - fits well with a temporal oscillatory deficit specifically related to this visual pathway. This study investigated the visual M-D and parvocellular-ventral (P-V) pathways in dyslexic and in chronological age and IQ-matched normally reading children by measuring temporal (frequency doubling illusion) and static stimuli sensitivity, respectively. A specific deficit in M-D temporal oscillation was found. Importantly, the M-D deficit was selectively shown in poor phonological decoders. M-D deficit appears to be frequent because 75% of poor pseudo-word readers were at least 1 SD below the mean of the controls. Finally, a replication study by using a new group of poor phonological decoders and reading level controls suggested a crucial role of M-D deficit in DD. These results showed that a M-D deficit might impair the sub-lexical mechanisms that are critical for reading development. The possible link between these findings and TSF is discussed.

Keywords: transient system, reading acquisition, phonological decoding, reading disability, visual disorder, dorsal stream

INTRODUCTION

Developmental dyslexia (DD) is often defined as a deficit in reading acquisition despite normal intelligence and access to conventional instruction (American Psychiatric Association [APA], 1994). According to the dual-route model (see Perry et al., 2007 for a review), written words can be processed either by the sub-lexical route or by the lexical route. The sub-lexical route is based on grapheme-to-phoneme correspondences and allows reading of unfamiliar words and pseudo-words. The lexical route is based on lexical unit correspondences and is crucial to read familiar and irregular words only. Both acquired and developmental disorders of reading have been generally discussed within this psycholinguistic framework (e.g., Castles and Coltheart, 1993). Phonological dyslexics show great difficulty in reading unfamiliar words and pseudo-words compared to known words, and this is thought to arise from damage to the sub-lexical route. In contrast, surface dyslexia is characterized by impaired reading of irregular words, and this is thought to arise from a damaged lexical route (e.g., Castles and Coltheart, 1993), potentially linked to an under-stimulation of the visual word recognition system resulting from low experience with literacy.

However, in shallow orthographies such as Italian, spelling-sound irregularity is limited to the supra-segmental level (i.e., to stress assignment). Thus, in Italian dyslexic children the increased weight of sub-lexical processing does not permit precise measurement of the efficiency of the lexical-route (see also Ruffino et al., 2014). It is crucial to note that — regardless of spelling-sound regularity – for a beginner reader all words are at first pseudo-words because the lexical-orthographic representations still have to be developed. Accordingly, most longitudinal studies have shown that beginner readers primarily use the sub-lexical route (see Sprenger-Charolles et al., 2003 for a review).

Phonological decoding, which is typically measured by examining children's pseudo-word reading performance, is one of the most critical skills for successful reading acquisition (e.g., Share, 1995). Interestingly, Ziegler et al. (2003) showed that dyslexics with regular (German-speaking children) and irregular (English-speaking children) spelling-to-sound correspondences present an extremely slow and serial phonological decoding mechanism. Thus, in learning to read it is of utmost importance to acquire an accurate and fluent use of the sub-lexical route (e.g., Goswami, 2000; see Vellutino et al., 2004 for a review).

Although there are a number of theories attempting to account for DD, two main views received major support. The first approach proposes that DD arises from deficits in systems that are specifically linguistic in nature. In particular, the phonological deficit theory suggests that DD arises from deficits in phonological processing (e.g., Snowling, 2000). In contrast, many authors suggest that deficits in underlying non-linguistic sensory mechanisms are the real core abnormality in DD (e.g., Stein and Walsh, 1997; Vidyasagar and Pammer, 2010 for visual deficits; Wright et al., 2000; Tallal, 2004 for auditory deficits). This theory, known as the temporal processing hypothesis is the multi-sensory (i.e., visual and auditory) version of the magnocellular dorsal (M-D) theory of DD, suggesting that children with DD have specific deficits in processing rapidly presented or brief sensory stimuli in either the visual or auditory modalities (see Farmer and Klein, 1995; Hari and Renvall, 2001 for reviews). Chiefly, the M-D temporal hypothesis explicitly claims that phonological decoding deficits in dyslexics could arise from impairments in sensory processing of visual and auditory dynamic-stimuli (e.g., Facoetti et al., 2010a,b). The well known M-D theory of DD is often referred specifically to the visual modality, and it is a comprehensive, albeit controversial account (e.g., Amitay et al., 2002; Sperling et al., 2005; Olulade et al., 2013). This theory stems from the observation that some reading disabled children are impaired in the specific visual M-D pathway (see Stein and Walsh, 1997; Boden and Giaschi, 2007; Vidyasagar and Pammer, 2010 for reviews). The M-D pathway originates in the ganglion cells of the retina, passes through the M-layer of the lateral geniculate nucleus (LGN), and finally reaches the occipital and parietal cortices (Maunsell and Newsome, 1987). The M-D stream is considered blind to colors, and responds optimally to contrast differences, low spatial frequencies, and to high temporal frequencies and motion (Livingstone and Hubel, 1987). The M-D stream seems to be impaired in individuals with DD, whereas the other major parallel pathway of the visual system, the parvocellular-ventral (P-V) stream, is intact (see Stein and Walsh, 1997; Boden and Giaschi, 2007; Vidyasagar and Pammer, 2010 for reviews). The P-V pathway is characterized by both lower temporal resolution and superior sensitivity to high spatial frequencies, and it is also sensitive to color changes (Livingstone and Hubel, 1987). Several studies showed the specificity of the M-D pathway deficit in individuals with DD in comparison to P-V processing in the normal range, suggesting the crucial role of the M-D pathway as the dominant visual stream for text reading (e.g., Lovegrove et al., 1986; Chouake et al., 2012). Dyslexics are less sensitive than typically reading controls to luminance patterns and motion displays with high temporal and low spatial frequencies (e.g., Eden et al., 1996), visual features that are primarily associated with the M-D pathway, but they perform normally on tasks primarily associated with the P-V pathway, such as those involving color and form (Merigan and Maunsell, 1993).

Most of the evidence for the visual M-D deficit theory has derived from studies of coherent dot motion perception (see Stein, 2001 for a review), which taps the cortical portion of the M-D pathway.

However, the coherent dot motion deficit is rarely found in all individuals in a dyslexic sample (e.g., Talcott et al., 2013). Children or adult poor readers may be specifically impaired in motion perception only in the presence of high external noise, but not in the presence of low external noise or when the signal is clearly defined (Sperling et al., 2006), weakening the strongest evidence for the more dorsal portion of the M-D pathway deficit in DD. In addition, pure M-D deficits have rarely been documented in dyslexic subjects (e.g., Amitay et al., 2002; Sperling et al., 2005). Disabled readers show impaired performance in non-M-D tasks requiring fine frequency discrimination, and the stimuli used in those tasks were neither modulated in time nor briefly presented (e.g., Amitay et al., 2002). Dyslexic children had difficulties detecting both gratings with high temporal frequency and low spatial frequency (i.e., M-D stimuli) and gratings with low temporal frequency and high spatial frequency (i.e., P-V stimuli) when the grating were embedded in external noise (Sperling et al., 2005). Nevertheless, these results did not falsify the evidence obtained from a large population of studies demonstrating significant and replicable differences between dyslexic and control groups and longitudinal studies in the coherent motion perception task (e.g., Cornelissen et al., 1995; Talcott et al., 2000, 2002, 2013; Boets et al., 2011). In addition, it has been reported that up to 75% of dyslexic individuals show visual temporal processing deficits (Lovegrove et al., 1986). Important literature supports the transient subsystem deficit hypothesis in DD which suggests a dissociation in sensitivity between low spatial, high temporal versus high spatial, low temporal grating stimuli (e.g., Martin and Lovegrove, 1987; Keen and Lovegrove, 2000). These grating stimuli tap into the receptive field characteristics of the M system at a retino-cortical level providing the most relevant support for the lower portion of the M-D theory deficit. Moreover, a post mortem study, in a small sample, showed that in the brain of individuals with DD the M neurons of the LGN were noticeably smaller than those found in normal readers' brains, while the P neurons did not differ (Livingstone et al., 1991).

It should be noted that the M-D pathway terminates mainly in the posterior parietal cortex (Mishkin and Ungerleider, 1982; Merigan and Maunsell, 1993), which is the cortical region controlling selective attention in humans (Facoetti and Molteni, 2000; see Corbetta and Shulman, 2002, 2011 for reviews). Thus, a weakened or abnormal M-D input to the dorsal-stream could result in a spatial and temporal attention deficit in dyslexic children and adults (e.g., Brannan and Williams, 1987; Williams et al., 1987; Valdois et al., 1995; Cestnick and Coltheart, 1999; Hari et al., 1999, 2001; Vidyasagar and Pammer, 1999; Facoetti et al., 2000, 2001, 2005, 2006, 2008, 2010a,b; Iles et al., 2000; Buchholz and McKone, 2004; Bosse et al., 2007; Buchholz and Aimola Davies, 2007; Roach and Hogben, 2007; Ruffino et al., 2010; see Vidyasagar, 1999; Hari and Renvall, 2001; Boden and Giaschi, 2007; Vidyasagar and Pammer, 2010; Gori and Facoetti, 2014 for reviews) and specifically in dyslexics, a more severe poor pseudo-word reading ability in comparison to word reading skills (Buchholz and McKone, 2004; Facoetti et al., 2006, 2010a; Roach and Hogben, 2007; Jones et al., 2008; Ruffino et al., 2010, 2014). Children with autism spectrum disorder have shown attentional zooming-out and dorsal pathway disorders (e.g., Ronconi et al., 2012, 2013a,b, 2014), the visual attentional deficit is now recognized as a core feature of DD (Franceschini et al., 2012, 2013; Zorzi et al., 2012; see Gori and Facoetti, 2014 for a review). The sub-lexical route is crucial for reading pseudo-words or new words during reading acquisition in all alphabetic languages, and it specifically requires serial attentional graphemic parsing (Facoetti et al., 2010a).

Recently, a new model, labeled "temporal sampling framework" (TSF), was proposed by Goswami (2011) providing a new, different and, intriguing prospect in the DD study. TSF integrates the data on the auditory processing deficit with the findings on neural oscillatory mechanisms related to the temporal sampling of speech. In short, the innovative proposal by Goswami (2011) suggests that deficits in syllabic perception at relatively low temporal frequencies (inside of the range of the delta/theta, i.e., <10 Hz) are the critical basis for the reading disability in DD (Power et al., 2013). This hypothesis is supported by the findings that show the role of neuronal oscillations in speech perception (Luo and Poeppel, 2007). Although this approach was presented as a possible neurophysiological substrate of the phonological deficit of DD the TSF it is not only limited to that but also, can easily be applied to all the stages of processing within the visual system (Vidyasagar, 2013). TSF also has the potential to integrate several low level deficits already associated with DD (Vidyasagar, 2013; Pammer, 2014). As suggested by Vidyasagar (2013) the D-stream deficit could also be integrated in the TSF theory because the TSF fits well in describing the attentional feedback within the D-stream. What is expected is a deficit in neural oscillation at higher temporal frequency than in the auditory modality because the M-D visual stream process relatively high temporal frequency (Vidyasagar, 2013).

Assuming that the M-D pathway deficit is the neurobiological basis of visual selective attention disorders in DD, we predict that the M-D deficit should be found mainly in poor phonological decoders. Therefore, the aim of the present study was to investigate the efficiency of the visual M-D pathway inside the TSF approach in dyslexic and typically reading children (age- and reading-matched) using the frequency doubling (FD) illusion. The FD illusion is a visual illusion that was first described by Kelly (1966). Measuring a visual illusion, even if it sounds counter-intuitive, can be done in a very accurate way (e.g., Gori et al., 2006, 2008, 2010a, 2011; Yazdanbakhsh and Gori, 2008; Giora and Gori, 2010; Gori and Spillmann, 2010; Ito, 2012). The FD illusion appears to be dependent on the spatial and temporal frequency of a flickering grating. When a grating with a spatial frequency of 0.1–4 c/deg is flickering faster than 15 Hz, the viewer perceives a grating with double the physical spatial frequency. The FD was later explained by Kelly (1981) in terms of the full wave rectification carried out by the visual system. Such rectification is found in M(y)-cells of the primate retina (Benardete et al., 1992) and LGN (Kaplan and Shapley, 1982; Marrocco et al., 1982). It is therefore suggested, that responses from the M(y)-cells underlie perception of the FD illusion (see Maddess et al., 1992 for a detailed discussion regarding the relationship between M(y)-cells and frequency doubling). A previous study (Pammer and Wheatley, 2001) showed that individuals with DD are less sensitive to the FD illusion than normal readers, supporting a low-level deficit in the M-D pathway. Kevan and Pammer (2008) demonstrated that children at risk of DD already show a higher threshold for the FD illusion even at the pre-reading stage. Importantly, the threshold for the FD illusion at the pre-reading stage predicts future reading skills (Kevan and Pammer, 2009). The FD illusion is, therefore, a consolidated M-D index which taps the lower portion of the M-D pathway and can be difficultly described in terms of signal-to-noise exclusion (e.g., Sperling et al., 2005, 2006; Olulade et al., 2013). Interestingly, the FD illusion was never previously tested in children with DD in shallow languages as Italian. More importantly, the FD illusion is a temporal stimulus that fit well with the opportunity to measure the M-D pathway functionality inside the context of the TSF. What is expected, indeed, is that if a neural oscillation deficit is present also in the visual system of children with DD and specifically in their M-D stream (Vidyasagar, 2013), the children with DD will need more contrast to perceive the flickering stimulus at the same oscillation frequency in comparison with the chronological-age control group.

In addition, we studied the efficiency of the P-V pathway in the same children to rule out the alternative explanation that perceptual processing is generally inefficient in dyslexic children (e.g., because of poor perceptual noise exclusion). The task employed was High-Pass Resolution (HPR) perimetry which measures the detection threshold for fixed ring-shaped stimuli of different sizes. HPR perimetry is commonly adopted for selective analysis of the lower portion of the P-V pathway.

A crucial aim of this study was to investigate if a specific subgroup of children with DD, i.e., poor phonological decoders, were affected by the M-D deficit. In the Experiment 1 we selected a poor phonological decoder subgroup and we compared them with the chronological-age control group. In the Experiment 2 we collected a new poor phonological decoder group in order to carry out a replication study. Stringently, we contrast the new group with a reading-level (RL) control group. The RL children (see Goswami, 2003) were never included in previous studies using FD illusion. The inclusion of the RL group is particularly important to address the issue of the causal link between FD illusion perception and poor phonological decoding.

EXPERIMENT 1

METHODS

Participants

Seventeen dyslexic children (mean age 11 years, SD = 2), were selected from a sample of children referred to the Neuropsychiatric Unit of the scientific Hospital "E. Medea" of San Vito al Tagliamento, Pordenone, Italy, because of specific reading disability. These children had been diagnosed as dyslexic based on standard criteria (American Psychiatric Association [APA], 1994). Their performance reading aloud had to be two standard deviations below the norm in one reading subtest or 1 standard deviation below the norm in at least two reading subtests according to the Italian age-standardized tests (Sartori et al., 1995). The ability to read aloud was measured using a clinical standardized Italian test composed of 112 words (separated into four lists; word reading task, Sartori et al., 1995) and phonological decoding ability was measured using three standardized clinical lists of 48 Italian pseudo-words (pseudo-word Reading task, Sartori et al., 1995). Finally, reading fluency and errors in age-standardized prose passages from Italian clinical tests were used to measure ecological-context reading (Sartori et al., 1995).

The children with DD were selected on the basis of:

(1) a full-scale IQ greater than, or equal to, 85, as measured by the Wechsler intelligence scale for children-revised (WISC-R; Wechsler, 1986);

(2) normal or corrected-to-normal vision and hearing;
(3) absence of neurological and/or psychiatric disorders;
(4) absence of specific language impairments (American Psychiatric Association [APA], 1994); and
(5) absence of attention deficit disorders with or without hyperactivity (ADHD and ADD; American Psychiatric Association [APA], 1994). Several recent studies have shown that sustained attention deficits are significant covariates in group studies using dyslexics and controls pointing out the relevance of this exclusion criterion (e.g., Rochelle et al., 2009).

The children with DD were divided into two subgroups (i.e., poor and non-impaired phonological decoders) according to their performance on the pseudo-word reading test (Sartori et al., 1995). Children were considered poor phonological decoders (PPD, $n = 12$ dyslexic children) if their performance, in terms of mean between accuracy and speed of pseudo-word reading, was below two standard deviation from the norm. The remaining children were assigned to the non-impaired phonological decoders subgroup (NPD, $n = 5$ dyslexic children). Note that pseudo-word reading efficiency is the most appropriate measure of phonological decoding skills. A performance well below the normative data implies that the child is a poor phonological decoder (e.g., Facoetti et al., 2006, 2010a; Ruffino et al., 2010, 2014). In dyslexic children with a regular spelling-to-sound correspondence, like Italian, it is practically impossible to apply the classical English sub-typing (i.e., phonological and surface DD; e.g., Castles and Coltheart, 1993; Talcott et al., 2013) because the English language presents an higher number of irregular words. Importantly, the two dyslexic groups did not differ in word reading [$t_{(14)} = 0.68$, $p > 0.05$] nor in text reading [$t_{(14)} = -0.01$, $p > 0.05$] abilities, excluding that our PPDs were simply more severely impaired dyslexic children.

Twenty four chronological, age- and IQ-matched typically reading children (mean age 10 years, SD = 2) were randomly selected from the same primary school. They were of average or above average intelligence on three WISC-R (Wechsler, 1986) sub-tests (i.e., Block Design and Comprehension).

All participants' parents gave informed consent.

Table 1 shows the mean and SD of age, Block Design, Comprehension and text reading tests for the control and dyslexic groups. Controls and dyslexics were comparable to chronological age and IQ. In contrast, controls and dyslexics were significantly different on accuracy and speed of word and text reading. In **Table 2** we showed that PPD and NPD groups differed only for the pseudo-word reading mean (accuracy and speed).

All participants underwent a complete ophthalmological evaluation, consisting of "Early Treatment Diabetic Retinopathy Study" (ETDRS) chart (standardized eye charts and visual acuity test), orthoptic examination, anterior segment slit lamp examination, cycloplegic refraction, and indirect ophthalmoscopy.

Apparatus and stimuli

Frequency doubling perimetry. The FD perimetry relies on the frequency doubling illusion described in the Introduction. The settings resembled the ones adopted, in a previous study, by Pammer and Wheatley (2001). A low spatial frequency grating displayed in counter-phase flicker mode at a high temporal frequency is perceived as if it had twice its actual spatial frequency. The Humphrey Matrix perimeter was the presentation tool used with the program threshold set to 30-2. The threshold is expressed as contrast attenuation in decibels (dB) and it is calculated by a staircase algorithm built into the Humphrey Matrix perimeter tool. Thresholds ranged from 0 to 38 db. The stimulus was presented at 69 locations in the 30 central degrees of the visual field. The background luminance was 100 cd/m^2. The pattern consisted of a sinusoidal grating presented at different contrast levels, arranged in $5° \times 5°$ square stimuli, and a circular macular stimulus of 2.5° radius. The spatial frequency of the bar target was 0.50 cy/deg, the counter-phase flickered at 18 Hz and was presented for 300 ms. The FD provides selective stimulation of the M-retinal ganglion cells and M LGN neurons. Due to the design of the target, no P-cell activity should be stimulated. Visual fields with 20% or less false positive or false negative responses, and 30% or less fixation errors were considered acceptable.

High-pass resolution (ophthimus) perimetry. The Ophthimus system HPR perimetry uses ring-shaped stimuli, consisting of dark borders and a lighter core. Fourteen different sized targets are available (ranged from 1.26 to 17.64 dB). The target contrast was held constant while the size varied in steps of 1.26 dB. The background luminance was 20 cd/m^2. The luminance of the ring borders was 15 cd/m^2 and the luminance of the ring core was 25 cd/m^2. The target was "high-pass spatial frequency filtered". The participants either detected and resolved it, or it was invisible to them. The perimeter assesses resolution thresholds as the smallest stimulus

Table 1 | Mean (M) and standard deviation (SD) of age, Comprehension, Block Design sub-test (WISC-R; Wechsler, 1986), text reading errors and speed in the control and dyslexic groups.

	Controls ($N = 24$)		Dyslexics ($N = 17$)		Comparison	
	M	SD	*M*	SD	*T*(39)	*P*
Age (months)	124	21	128	27	−0.46	0.65
Comprehension (standard score)	10.9	2.3	12	2.6	−1.49	0.14
Block design (standard score)	13.8	2.2	12.5	2.9	1.71	0.09
Text reading errors (number) (*Z*-score)	2.1, 0.54	2.5, 0.56	10.7, −1.05	6.7, 1.19	−5.78, −5.66	<0.001, <0.001
Text reading speed (s) (*Z*-score)	33, 0.31	20.7, 0.48	82, −2.58	49.9, 1.5	−4.31, −8.81	<0.001, <0.001

Table 2 | Mean (M) and standard deviation (SD) of Comprehension, Block Design sub-test (WISC-R; Wechsler, 1986), text reading mean (errors and speed), word reading mean (errors and speed), pseudo-word reading mean (errors and speed) in the two dyslexic subgroups: the poor phonological decoders (PPD) and the non-impaired phonological decoders (NPD) groups.

	PPD ($N = 12$)		NPD ($N = 5$)		Comparison	
	M	SD	*M*	SD	*T*(15)	*P*
Comprehension (standard score)	12.5	2.58	11	2.45	1.11	0.28
Block design (standard score)	12.67	2.64	12	2.67	0.42	0.68
Text reading mean (*Z*-score)	−1.66	0.85	−2.15	1.02	−1.02	0.33
Word reading mean (*Z*-score)	−4.03	1.95	−3.33	1.86	0.68	0.51
Pseudoword reading mean (*Z*-score)	−3.26	1.09	−0.92	0.67	4.39	<0.001

size seen in the 50 locations over the central 30° of the visual field. The blindspot is not mapped. The high-pass spatial frequency filter allows for selective analysis of the P-cells of the retina and probably of the LGN. Due to the software characteristics, fixation errors were not tested for the HPR perimetry.

Procedures

All participants performed the FD and the HPR perimetry in random order, beginning with one of the two eyes. On another day, they performed the two visual field tests again, beginning with the other eye, in order to avoid fatigue and any learning effects. The children were verbally instructed on how to perform the two tests and were given the opportunity to practice. Two pauses were given throughout each test, and a 5-min pause was permitted between testing of the first and second eye.

Each child was seated comfortably with their face against the eyepiece. For the FD testing the child was given a description of the display, and instructed to press the response button each time she/he saw a pattern against the homogeneous background. For the HPR task each child had to report whenever they saw a circle in any tested position of the visual field.

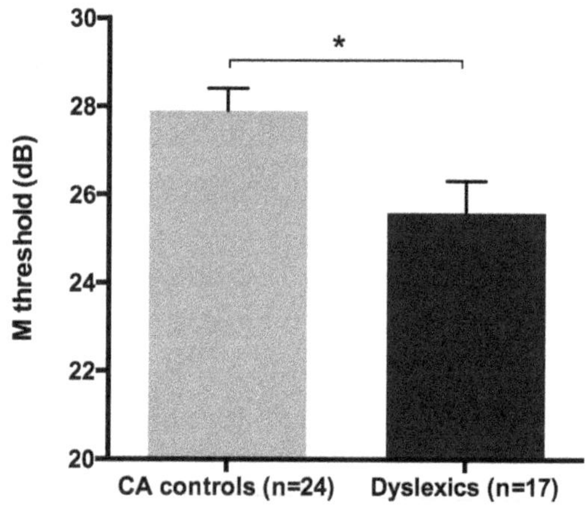

FIGURE 1 | The difference between the chronological age- and IQ-matched (CA) controls and dyslexic children in the FD task measuring the M-D pathway functionality (i.e., M threshold) in the Experiment 1. $^*p < 0.05$.

RESULTS

FD results

All groups and subgroups were normally distributed as showed by a non-significant Shapiro-Wilk test of normality (all *ps* > .05). The mean FD thresholds (averaged for all positions and the two eyes) for the children with DD ($n = 17$) differed significantly [*t*-test: $t_{(39)} = 2.697$, $p < 0.05$] in comparison to the normal reader age- and IQ-matched controls ($n = 24$), showing that the dyslexic group was less sensitive to the FD illusion at 18 Hz of temporal frequency of (see the **Figure 1** and the plot of the individual data in **Figure 6A**). An univariate ANCOVA (omnibus test) was run in which the independent variable was group (chronological age- and IQ-matched controls, PPDs and NPDs) and the dependent variable was the mean FD threshold, co-varied for the participant's age [$F_{(3,37)} = 11.999$, $p < 0.05$, $\eta_p^2 = 0.493$; see **Figure 2** and the plot of the individual data in **Figure 6A**]. A planned comparison (univariate ANCOVA) was then run where the independent variable was group (chronological age- and IQ-matched controls vs. PPDs) and the dependent variable was the mean FD threshold, co-varied for the participants' ages [$F_{(2,33)} = 15.139$, $p < 0.05$, $\eta_p^2 = 0.478$]. Finally another planned comparison (univariate ANCOVA), where the independent variable was the group (age- and IQ-matched controls vs. NPDs) and the dependent variable was the mean FD threshold, co-varied for the participants' ages [$F_{(1,26)} = 1.899$, $p > 0.05$, $\eta_p^2 = 0.068$]. In summary, only the PPDs were significantly worse than the controls in their mean FD threshold.

Although PPD children showed a significantly worse performance in the FD task at the group level, in comparison with the controls, it is important to establish how reliable is this abnormal pattern at the individual level. In the PPD group, 75% of them were at least 1 SD below the mean of the controls (**Figure 3**).

Based on these results indicating a specific relationship between M-D pathway and the spelling to sound translation process we concentrate our Experiment 2 only on the PPDs.

HPR results

All groups and subgroups were normally distributed as showed by a non-significant Shapiro-Wilk test of normality (all *ps* > 0.05). The mean HPR thresholds (averaged for all positions and the two

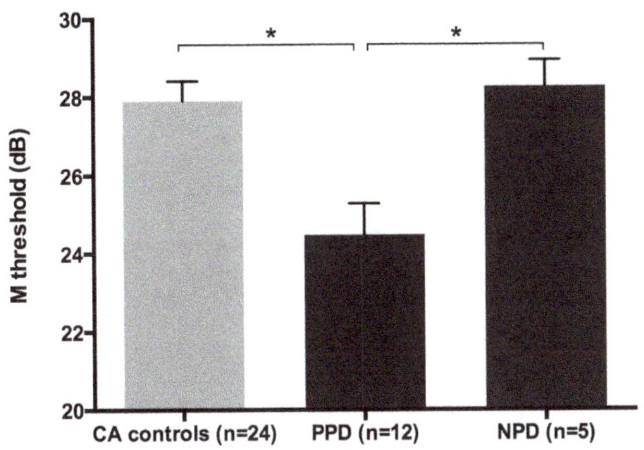

FIGURE 2 | The difference between chronological-age and IQ matched (CA) controls and the subtypes of children with DD (i.e., poor phonological decoders, hereafter PPD and non-impaired phonological decoders, hereafter NPD) in the FD task (Experiment 1). $^*p < 0.05$.

eyes) for the children with DD ($n = 17$) and the normal reader age- and IQ-matched controls ($n = 24$) did not differ significantly [t-test: $t_{(39)} = 0.432$, $p > 0.05$] showing that the dyslexic and normal reader groups were similar in their P-V pathway performance (see **Figure 4** and the plot of the individual data in **Figure 6B**).

The relationship between M-D functioning and reading text ability

Partial correlation between M-D pathway functioning (indexed by FD threshold) and the text reading efficiency (the mean between speed and errors z-scores) in the entire sample ($n = 40$; a child with DD score is missing), controlling for chronological age, IQ (block design and similarities), and the P-V functioning, was significant ($r = 0.43$, $p < 0.01$).

To determine the predictive relationships between M-D pathway functioning and ecological reading skills in a more stringent way, we computed a three-step fixed-entry multiple regression analysis in which the dependent variable was text reading efficiency. To control for the effects of chronological age, verbal and nonverbal IQ, and P-V pathway functioning, the predictors entered at the three steps were as follows: (1) age, block design and similarities, (2) P-V pathway threshold, and (3) M-D pathway threshold. The ANOVA regression model was significant [$F_{(5,34)} = 2805$, $p < 0.05$] explaining the 29% of the text reading quote of variance. Only the M-D pathway measure, entered last, accounted for a significant quote of unique variance in text reading efficiency (r^2 change $= 0.16$, $p < 0.01$).

EXPERIMENT 2

METHODS

Participants

In a replication study, we selected a new sample of 8 PPDs (mean age 11 years, SD = 2) and a RL matched control group (10 younger children well matched to the dyslexics for reading ability and IQ, mean age 7 years, SD = 1). In order to find an RL group in Italian speaking language population, it is necessary to search for younger children than would be use in countries with deeper orthographic-to-phonological mapping than in Italian. All the inclusion criteria were the same for the Experiment 1. For details of the new two groups check **Table 3**. All participants' parents gave informed consent.

Apparatus and stimuli

Frequency doubling perimetry. The procedure was exactly the same for the Experiment 1. The HPR perimetry task was not performed because the results were not be discriminative in the Experiment 1.

RESULTS

The mean FD thresholds (averaged for all positions and the two eyes) for PPDs ($n = 8$) and the typical readers IQ- and RL matched

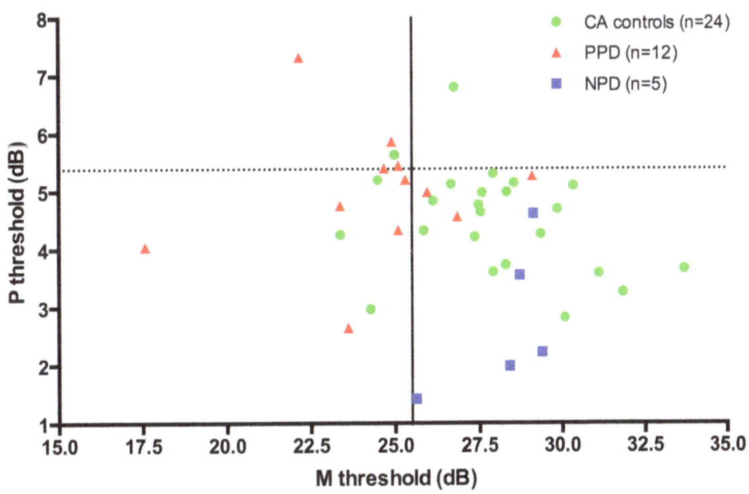

FIGURE 3 | The scatter-plot shows that at individual level the 75% of the PPDs (the red triangle) are at least 1 SD under the mean of the CA controls (the green circle) in the FD task (Experiment 1).

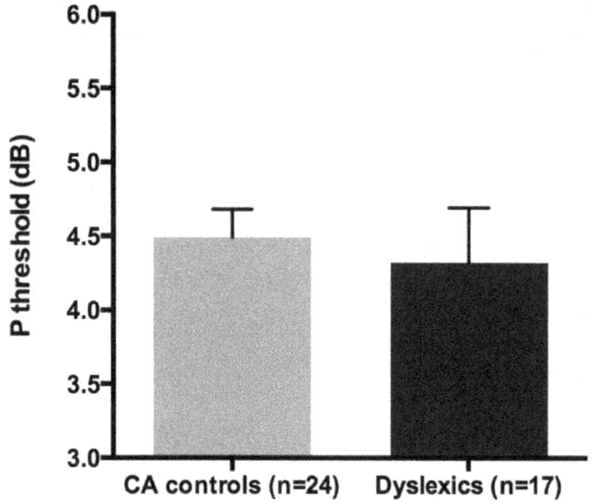

FIGURE 4 | No difference was found between age and IQ matched (CA) controls and the children with DD in the HPR task measuring the P-V pathway functionality (i.e., P threshold) in the Experiment 1.

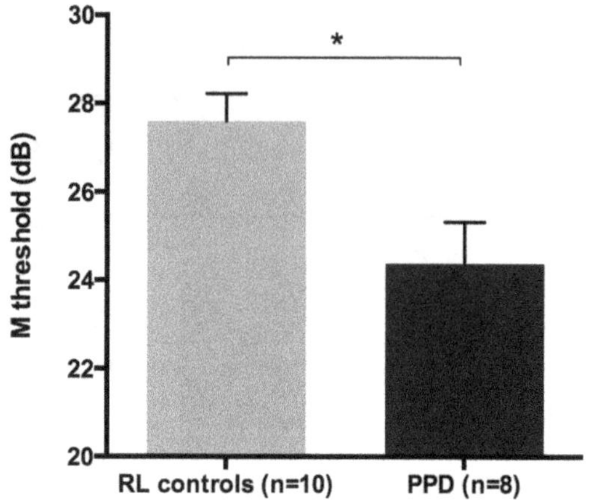

FIGURE 5 | The difference between the new sample of PPDs and reading-level and IQ-matched (RL) controls in the FD task (Experiment 2). $*p < 0.05$.

controls ($n = 10$) differed significantly [t-test: $t_{(16)} = 2.962$, $p < 0.05$] showing that the PPDs were less sensitive to the FD illusion at 18 Hz of temporal frequency even compared to younger normal readers with the same reading abilities (see **Figure 5** and the plot of the individual data in **Figure 6A**). The two control groups (CA and RL) did not differ in the FD illusion threshold ($p > 0.05$). It is not surprising that age did not affect that task because the M-D pathway should be completely operative much before the age of 7 years (e.g., Gori et al., in press).

Although the study was designed as two independent experiments the PPDs of the Experiment 1 and 2 were very similar in age and they did not differ in other relevant variables. Additionally, we found it could be of interest to merge the two groups of PPDs and contrast them with the CA and the RL controls. We applied an univariate ANOVA with the FD threshold as the independent variable and groups (PPD, $n = 25$, CA, $n = 24$ and RL, $n = 10$) as the between subjects factor. The Group main effect was significant [$F_{(2,56)} = 7.33$; $p < 0.05$] and PPD group differed from CA and from RL (Bonferroni multiple comparison with $ps < 0.05$). This result confirmed the results obtained separately in Experiment 1 and 2.

DISCUSSION

These results provide strong support for an M-D deficit in DD that has its origins at the sub-cortical level of the pathway (i.e., at the LGN). Notably, this deficit characterized only a subgroup of dyslexics, namely the poor phonological decoders.

The absence of differences in the P-V task between groups emphasizes the selectivity of the visual deficit that seems to be associated with the reading disability in the sub-lexical route. It is therefore impossible to attribute the difference found in the FD task to poor testing endurance, as the children with DD performed as well as the typically reading children on the HPR task. The absence of a difference between the two groups in the P-V task cannot be attributed to a ceiling or a floor effect that could mask a poor performance of children with DD as shown by the individual data shown in **Figure 6B**. The graph shows that the data of both groups were not clustered on the limits of the stimulation range. Consequently, even if the M-D and the P-V task could be different in difficulty, both tasks should have enough sensitivity to show a possible difference between groups.

Moreover, the poor phonological decoders with DD not only demonstrated less sensitivity to the FD illusion compared to the typical reading age- and IQ-matched group (supporting Pammer and Wheatley, 2001), but also to a reading-level and IQ-matched

Table 3 | Mean (M) and standard deviation (SD) of chronological age, Block Design sub-test (WISC-R; Wechsler, 1986), phonological decoding speed and errors in the reading-level (RL) controls and poor phonological decoders (PPD) of the Experiment 2.

	RL controls ($N = 10$)		PPD ($N = 8$)		Comparison	
	M	SD	*M*	SD	*T*(16)	*P*
Block design (standard score)	11.5	1.43	11	1.51	0.72	0.48
Chronological age (months)	91.5	5.4	126.2	8.67	10.41	0.001
Pseudo-word reading speed (s)	54.5	14.96	64.12	25.38	1.01	0.33
Pseudo-word reading errors (errors)	7.3	2.54	7.9	2.74	0.46	0.65

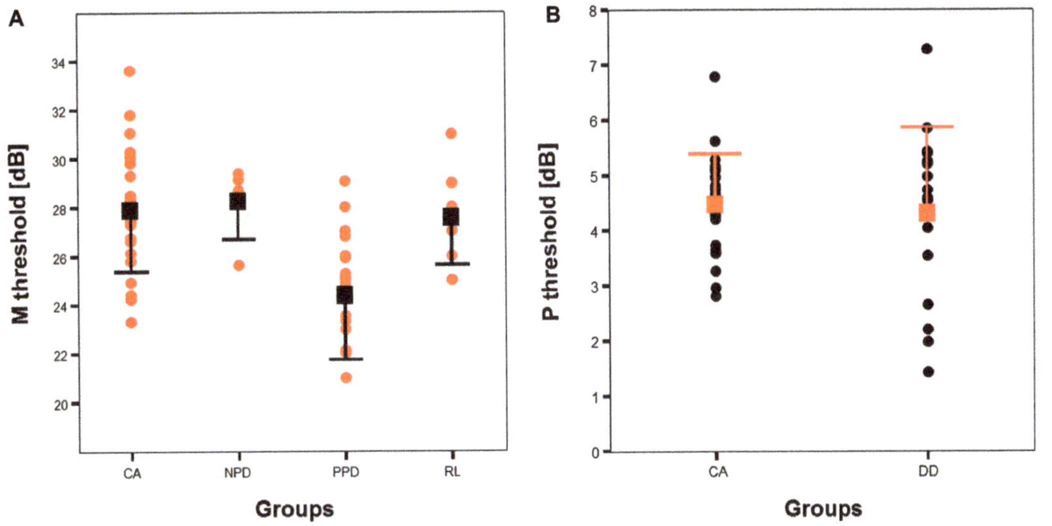

FIGURE 6 | (A) The scatter-plot of the individual data showing the difference between the children without DD (i.e., CA and RL controls) and the subtypes of children with DD (NPD and PPD) in the FD task measuring the M-D pathway functionality (Experiment 1 and 2). The findings did not change running the ANCOVA without the outliers. Error bars represent one standard deviation of the mean. **(B)** The plot of the individual data showing the difference between the children without (i.e., CA controls) and with DD in the HPR task (Experiment 1). Error bars represent one standard deviation of the mean.

control group. The latter result excludes that the M-D deficit is simply an effect of DD.

This is the first study to show that the M-D deficit in children with DD is present also when compared with younger children with the same reading performance, challenging the idea that the M-D deficit is a simple effect of reading deprivation and not a cause, as recently suggested by Olulade et al. (2013). Importantly, the results obtained in the between-group analyses cannot be attributed to the presence of a few (and perhaps peculiar) dyslexic children in the PPD group but were fully confirmed by the analyses at the level of individual cases. M-D deficits were present in a large part of the PPDs (75%) in comparison to CA. Moreover, none of the NPDs presents a deficit in the FD task. Thus, the FD task allowed us to accurately discriminate between poor phonological decoders and CA controls. Regardless of whether children in the NPD group constitute a specific subtype in shallow orthographies (e.g., Wimmer, 1993) or they have partly compensated for their reading deficit, M-D pathway functioning seems to play an important role in phonological decoding. In general, the results from the current study provide evidence for an M-D stream involvement in DD characterized by poor phonological decoding (the most frequent pattern even in Italian individuals with DD; see Facoetti et al., 2006). This conclusion was supported by the finding that individual differences in the M-D pathway were predictive of reading performance even after controlling for age, IQ, and P-V pathway functioning. The FD task allowed us to show an M-D deficit that seems to be in the lower portion of this visual stream (the subcortical component and/or the primary visual cortex) and that cannot be interpreted as a signal-to-noise exclusion deficit (which could be consider the weak point of the coherent dot motion task) or as an effect of reading level (as clearly highlighted by the difference with the RL group). The present results could be interpreted inside the framework of the TSF (Goswami, 2011). A multi-sensory (auditory and visual) temporal sampling disorder of neural oscillations could include the M-D deficit theory as one of several possible causes of DD. While an auditory deficit in low temporal frequency is observed in DD (e.g., Goswami, 2011; Power et al., 2013), in the visual modality a higher temporal frequency processing seems to be damaged in children with DD which is in agreement with the Vidyasagar (2013) prediction of a temporal oscillation deficit in the M-D pathway. However, the spatial and temporal sampling of the orthographic information could also be considered as a proxy deficit for auditory modality deficits in phonological decoding (e.g., Vidyasagar and Pammer, 2010). Moreover, as recently suggested (Vidyasagar, 2013; Pammer, 2014) the TSF seems to be very appropriate to model not only for the auditory deficits of DD but also the visual deficits that appear to be common in DD. Our results, based on temporal illusion sensitivity seem to be the first experimental test of the TSF in visual modality. The fact that children with DD need more contrast to see the FD pattern at 18 hz of temporal frequency, in comparison with both control groups supports the hypothesis of a neural oscillation deficit in the M-D pathway of children with DD. This neural oscillation defict seems to be selective for the M-D stream as theorized by Vidyasagar (2013).

Further research is now necessary to better understand the role of the cortical component of the M-D pathway in DD. In order to pursue that goal a sensitivity task employing specific motion illusions (i.e., Gori and Hamburger, 2006; Gori et al., 2006, 2010b, 2011; Gori and Yazdanbakhsh, 2008; Yazdanbakhsh and Gori, 2008, 2011; Hamburger, 2012) could be devised given the fact that this kind of illusory motion is processed by

V5/MT (Ruzzoli et al., 2011). Potential differences in this task could not be related to a general perceptual noise exclusion deficit.

In conclusion, sensitivity to the FD illusion could provide a simple and powerful diagnostic tool for the evaluation and identification of the risk of DD, even at the pre-reading stage (Kevan and Pammer, 2008, 2009) and the results obtained with the RL group strongly point in the direction of a causal role of a neural oscillatory deficit in the M-D pathway of individuals with DD.

ACKNOWLEDGMENT

We would like to thank Luca Ronconi and Julia R. Duggan for their helpful comment on the manuscript.

REFERENCES

American Psychiatric Association (APA). (1994). *Task Force on DSM-IV. Diagnostic and Statistical Manual of Mental Disorders.* Washington, DC: American Psychiatric Press, 886.

Amitay, S., Ben-Yehudah, G., Banai, K., and Ahissar, M. (2002). Disabled readers suffer from visual and auditory impairments but not from a specific magnocellular deficit. *Brain* 125, 2272–2285. doi: 10.1093/brain/awf231

Benardete, E. A., Kaplan, E., and Knight, B. W. (1992). Contrast gain control in the primate retina: P cells are not X-like, some M cells are. *Vis. Neurosci.* 8, 483–486. doi: 10.1017/S0952523800004995

Boden, C., and Giaschi, D. (2007). M-stream deficits and reading-related visual processes in developmental dyslexia. *Psychol. Bull.* 133, 346–366. doi: 10.1037/0033-2909.133.2.346

Boets, B., Vandermosten, M., Cornelissen, P., Wouters, J., and Ghesquière, P. (2011). Coherent motion sensitivity and reading development: changing relations in the transition from pre-reading to reading stage. *Child Dev.* 82, 854–869. doi: 10.1111/j.1467-8624.2010.01527.x

Bosse, M., Tainturier, M. J., and Valdois, S. (2007). Developmental dyslexia: the visual attention span deficit hypothesis. *Cognition* 104, 198–230. doi: 10.1016/j.cognition.2006.05.009

Brannan, J. R., and Williams, M. C. (1987). Allocation of visual attention in good and poor readers. *Percept. Psychophys.* 41, 23–28. doi: 10.3758/BF03208209

Buchholz, J., and Aimola Davies, A. (2007). Attentional blink deficits observed in dyslexia depend on task demands. *Vision Res.* 47, 1292–1302. doi: 10.1016/j.visres.2006.11.028

Buchholz, J., and McKone, E. (2004). Adults with dyslexia show deficits on spatial frequency doubling and visual attention tasks. *Dyslexia* 10, 24–43. doi: 10.1002/dys.263

Castles, A., and Coltheart, M. (1993). Varieties of developmental dyslexia. *Cognition* 47, 149–180. doi: 10.1016/0010-0277(93)90003-E

Cestnick, L., and Coltheart, M. (1999). The relationship between language-processing and visual-processing deficits in developmental dyslexia. *Cognition* 71, 231–255. doi: 10.1016/S0010-0277(99)00023-2

Chouake, T., Levy, T., Javitt, D. C., and Lavidor, M. (2012). Magnocellular training improves visual word recognition. *Front. Hum. Neurosci.* 10:6–14. doi: 10.3389/fnhum.2012.00014

Corbetta, M., and Shulman, G. L. (2002). Control of goal-directed and stimulus-driven attention in the brain. *Nat. Rev. Neurosci.* 3, 201–215. doi: 10.1038/nrn755

Corbetta, M., and Shulman, G. L. (2011). Spatial neglect and attention networks. *Annu. Rev. Neurosci.* 34, 569–599. doi: 10.1146/annurev-neuro-061010-113731

Cornelissen, P., Richardson, A., Mason, A., Fowler, S., and Stein, J. (1995). Contrast sensitivity and coherent motion detection measured at photopic luminance levels in dyslexics and controls. *Vision Res.* 35, 1483–1494. doi: 10.1016/0042-6989(95)98728-R

Eden, G. F., VanMeter, J. W., Rumsey, J. M., Maisog, J. M., Woods, R. P., and Zeffiro, T. A. (1996). Abnormal processing of visual motion in dyslexia revealed by functional brain imaging. *Nature* 382, 66–69. doi: 10.1038/382066a0

Facoetti, A., Lorusso, M. L., Cattaneo, C., Galli, R., and Molteni, M. (2005). Visual and auditory attentional capture are both sluggish in children with developmental dyslexia. *Acta Neurobiol. Exp.* 65, 61–72.

Facoetti, A., and Molteni, M. (2000). Is attentional focusing an inhibitory process at distractor location? *Brain Res. Cogn. Brain Res.* 1–2, 185–188. doi: 10.1016/S0926-6410(00)00031-8

Facoetti, A., Paganoni, P., Turatto, M., Marzola, V., and Mascetti, G. G. (2000). Visual-spatial attention in developmental dyslexia. *Cortex* 36,109–123. doi: 10.1016/S0010-9452(08)70840-2

Facoetti, A., Ruffino, M., Peru, A., Paganoni, P., and Chelazzi, L. (2008). Sluggish engagement and disengagement of non-spatial attention in dyslexic children. *Cortex* 44, 1221–1233. doi: 10.1016/j.cortex.2007.10.007

Facoetti, A., Trussardi, A. N., Ruffino, M., Lorusso, M. L., Cattaneo, C., Galli, R., et al. (2010a). Multisensory spatial attention deficits are predictive of phonological decoding skills in developmental dyslexia. *J. Cogn. Neurosci.* 22, 1011–1025. doi: 10.1162/jocn.2009.21232

Facoetti, A., Corradi, N., Ruffino, M., Gori, S., and Zorzi, M. (2010b). Visual spatial attention and speech segmentation are both impaired in preschoolers at familial risk for developmental dyslexia. *Dyslexia* 16, 226–239. doi: 10.1002/dys.413

Facoetti, A., Turatto, M., Lorusso, M. L., and Mascetti, G. G. (2001). Orienting of visual attention in dyslexia: evidence for asymmetric hemispheric control of attention. *Exp. Brain Res.* 138, 46–53. doi: 10.1007/s002210100700

Facoetti, A., Zorzi, M., Cestnick, L., Lorusso, M. L., Molteni, M., Paganoni, P., et al. (2006). The relationship between visuo-spatial attention and non-word reading in developmental dyslexia. *Cogn. Neuropsychol.* 23, 841–855. doi: 10.1080/02643290500483090

Farmer, M. E., and Klein, R. M. (1995). The evidence for a temporal processing deficit linked to dyslexia: a review. *Psychon. Bull. Rev.* 2, 460–493. doi: 10.3758/BF03210983

Franceschini, S., Gori, S., Ruffino, M., Pedrolli, K., and Facoetti, A. (2012). A causal link between visual spatial attention and reading acquisition. *Curr. Biol.* 22, 814–819. doi: 10.1016/j.cub.2012.03.013

Franceschini, S., Gori, S., Ruffino, M., Viola, S., Molteni, M., and Facoetti, A. (2013). Action video games make dyslexic children read better. *Curr. Biol.* 23, 462–466. doi: 10.1016/j.cub.2013.01.044

Giora, E., and Gori, S. (2010). The perceptual expansion of a filled area depends on textural characteristics. *Vision Res.* 50, 2466–2475. doi: 10.1016/j.visres.2010.08.033

Gori, S., and Facoetti, A. (2014). Perceptual learning as a possible new approach for remediation and prevention of developmental dyslexia. *Vision Res.* 99, 78–87. doi: 10.1016/j.visres.2013.11.011

Gori, S., Giora, E., and Agostini, T. (2010a). Measuring the Breathing Light Illusion by means of induced simultaneous contrast. *Perception* 39, 5–12. doi: 10.1068/p6489

Gori, S., Giora, E., and Stubbs, D. A. (2010b). Perceptual compromise between apparent and veridical motion indices: the unchained-dots illusion. *Perception* 39, 863–866. doi: 10.1068/p6678

Gori, S., Giora, E., and Pedersini, R. (2008). Perceptual multistability in figure-ground segregation using motion stimuli. *Acta Psychol.* 129, 399–409. doi: 10.1016/j.actpsy.2008.09.004

Gori, S., Giora, E., Yazdanbakhsh, A., and Mingolla, E. (2011). A new motion illusion based on competition between two kinds of motion processing units: the accordion grating. *Neural Netw.* 24, 1082–1092. doi: 10.1016/j.neunet.2011.06.017

Gori, S., and Hamburger, K. (2006). A new motion illusion: the rotating-tilted-lines illusion. *Perception* 35, 853–857. doi: 10.1068/p5531

Gori, S., Hamburger, K., and Spillmann, L. (2006). Reversal of apparent rotation in the Enigma-figure with and without motion adaptation and the effect of T-junctions. *Vision Res.* 46, 3267–3273. doi: 10.1016/j.visres.2006.03.009

Gori, S., Mascheretti, S., Giora, E., Ronconi, L., Ruffino, M., Quadrelli, E., et al. (in press). The DCDC2 intron 2 deletion impairs illusory motion perception unveiling the selective role of magnocellular-dorsal stream in reading (dis)ability. *Cereb. Cortex.*

Gori, S., and Spillmann, L. (2010). Detection vs. grouping thresholds for elements differing in spacing, size and luminance. An alternative approach towards the psychophysics of Gestalten. *Vision Res.* 50, 1194–1202. doi: 10.1016/j.visres.2010.03.022

Gori, S., and Yazdanbakhsh, A. (2008). The riddle of the rotating-tilted-lines illusion. *Perception* 37, 631–635. doi: 10.1068/p5770

Goswami, U. (2000). Phonological representations, reading development and dyslexia: towards a cross-linguistic theoretical framework. *Dyslexia* 6, 133–151. doi: 10.1002/(SICI)1099-0909(200004/06)6:2<133::AID-DYS160>3.0.CO;2-A

Goswami, U. (2003). Why theories about developmental dyslexia require developmental designs. *Trends Cogn. Sci.* 7, 534–540. doi: 10.1016/j.tics.2003.10.003

Goswami, U. (2011). A temporal sampling framework for developmental dyslexia. *Trends Cogn. Sci.* 15, 3–10. doi: 10.1016/j.tics.2010.10.001

Hamburger, K. (2012). Still motion? Motion illusions and luminance contrast. *Perception* 41, 113–116. doi: 10.1068/p7005

Hari, R., and Renvall, H. (2001). Impaired processing of rapid stimulus sequences in dyslexia. *Trends Cogn. Sci.* 5, 525–532. doi: 10.1016/S1364-6613(00)01801-5

Hari, R., Renvall, H., and Tanskanen, T. (2001). Left minineglect in dyslexic adults. *Brain* 124, 1373–1380. doi: 10.1093/brain/124.7.1373

Hari, R., Valta, M., and Uutela, K. (1999). Prolonged attentional dwell time in dyslexic adults. *Neurosci. Lett.* 271, 202–204. doi: 10.1016/S0304-3940(99)00547-9

Iles, J., Walsh, V., and Richardson, A. (2000). Visual search performance in dyslexia. *Dyslexia* 6, 163–177. doi: 10.1002/1099-0909(200007/09)6:3<163::AID-DYS150>3.0.CO;2-U

Ito, H. (2012). Illusory object motion in the centre of a radial pattern: the pursuit–pursuing illusion. *Iperception* 3, 59–87. doi: 10.1068/i0430

Jones, M. W., Branigan, H. P., and Kelly, M. L. (2008). Visual deficits in developmental dyslexia: relationships between non-linguistic visual tasks and their contribution to components of reading. *Dyslexia* 14, 95–115. doi: 10.1002/dys.345

Kaplan, E., and Shapley, R. (1982). X and Y cells in the lateral geniculate nucleus of macaque monkeys. *J. Physiol. (Lond.)* 330, 125–143.

Keen A. G., and Lovegrove W. J. (2000).Transient deficit hypothesis and dyslexia: examination of whole-parts relationship, retinal sensitivity, and spatial and temporal frequencies. *Vision Res.* 40, 705–715. doi: 10.1016/S0042-6989(99)00208-4

Kelly, D. (1966). Frequency doubling in visual responses. *JOSA* 56, 1628–1632. doi: 10.1364/JOSA.56.001628

Kelly, D. (1981). Nonlinear visual responses to flickering sinusoidal gratings. *JOSA* 71, 1051–1055. doi: 10.1364/JOSA.71.001051

Kevan, A., and Pammer, K. (2008). Visual deficits in pre-readers at familial risk for dyslexia. *Vision Res.* 48, 2835–2839. doi: 10.1016/j.visres.2008.09.022

Kevan, A., and Pammer, K. (2009). Predicting early reading skills from pre-reading measures of dorsal stream functioning. *Neuropsychologia* 47, 3174–3181. doi: 10.1016/j.neuropsychologia.2009.07.016

Livingstone, M. S., and Hubel, D. H. (1987). Psychophysical evidence for separate channels for the perception of form, color, movement, and depth. *J. Neurosci.* 7, 3416–3468.

Livingstone, M. S., Rosen, G. D., Drislane, F. W., and Galaburda, A. M. (1991). Physiological and anatomical evidence for a magnocellular defect in developmental dyslexia. *Proc. Natl. Acad. Sci. U.S.A.* 88, 7943–7947. doi: 10.1073/pnas.88.18.7943

Lovegrove, W., Martin, F., and Slaghuis, W. (1986). A theoretical and experimental case for a visual deficit in specific reading disability. *Cogn. Neuropsychol.* 3, 225–267. doi: 10.1080/02643298608252677

Luo, H., and Poeppel, D. (2007). Phase patterns of neuronal responses reliably discriminate speech in human auditory cortex. *Neuron* 54, 1001–1010. doi: 10.1016/j.neuron.2007.06.004

Maddess, T., Hemmi, J. M., and James, A. C. (1992). Evidence for spatial aliasing effects in the Y-like cells of the magnocellular visual pathway. *Vision Res.* 38, 1843–1859. doi: 10.1016/S0042-6989(97)00344-1

Marrocco, R. T., McClurkin J. W., and Young R. A. (1982). Spatial summation and conduction latency classification of cells of the lateral geniculate nucleus of macaques. *J. Neurosci.* 2, 1275–1291.

Martin, F., and Lovegrove, W. (1987). Flicker contrast sensitivity in normal and specifically disabled readers. *Perception* 16, 215–221. doi: 10.1068/p160215

Maunsell, J. H. R., and Newsome, W. T. (1987). Visual processing in monkey extrastriate cortex. *Annu. Rev. Neurosci.* 10, 363–401. doi: 10.1146/annurev.ne.10.030187.002051

Merigan, W. H., and Maunsell, J. H. (1993). How parallel are the primate visual pathways? *Annu. Rev. Neurosci.* 16, 369–402. doi: 10.1146/annurev.ne.16.030193.002101

Mishkin, M., and Ungerleider, L. G. (1982). Contribution of striate inputs to the visuospatial functions of parieto-preoccipital cortex in monkeys. *Behav. Brain Res.* 6, 57–77. doi: 10.1016/0166-4328(82)90081-X

Olulade, O. A., Napoliello, E. M., and Eden, G. F. (2013). Abnormal visual motion processing is not a cause of dyslexia. *Neuron* 79, 1–11. doi: 10.1016/j.neuron.2013.05.002

Pammer, K. (2014). Temporal sampling in vision and the implication in dyslexia. *Front. Hum. Neurosci.* 7:1–18. doi: 10.3389/fnhum.2013.00933

Pammer, K., and Wheatley, C. (2001). Isolating the M (y)-cell response in dyslexia using the spatial frequency doubling illusion. *Vision Res.* 41, 2139–2147. doi: 10.1016/S0042-6989(01)00092-X

Perry, C., Ziegler, J. C., and Zorzi, M. (2007). Nested incremental modeling in the development of computational theories: the CDP model of reading aloud. *Psychol. Rev.* 114, 273–315. doi: 10.1037/0033-295X.114.2.273

Power, A. J., Mead, N., Barnes, L., and Goswami U. (2013). Neural entrainment to rhythmic speech in children with developmental dyslexia. *Front. Hum. Neurosci.* 7:777. doi: 10.3389/fnhum.2013.00777

Roach, N. W., and Hogben, J. H. (2007). Impaired filtering of behaviourally irrelevant visual information in dyslexia. *Brain* 130, 771–785. doi: 10.1093/brain/awl353

Rochelle, K. S., Witton, C., and Talcott, J. B. (2009). Symptoms of hyperactivity and inattention can mediate deficits of postural stability in developmental dyslexia. *Exp. Brain Res.* 192, 627–633. doi: 10.1007/s00221-008-1568-5

Ronconi, L., Basso, D., Gori, S., and Facoetti, A. (2014). TMS on right frontal eye fields induces an inflexible focus of attention. *Cereb. Cortex* 24, 396–402. doi: 10.1093/cercor/bhs319

Ronconi, L., Gori, S., Ruffino, M., Franceschini, S., Urbani, B., Molteni, M., et al. (2012). Decreased coherent motion discrimination in autism spectrum disorder: the role of attentional zoom-out deficit. *PLoS ONE* 7:e49019. doi: 10.1371/journal.pone.0049019

Ronconi, L., Gori, S., Ruffino, M., Molteni, M., and Facoetti, A. (2013a). Zoom-out attentional impairment in children with autism spectrum disorder. *Cortex* 49, 1025–1033. doi: 10.1016/j.cortex.2012.03.005

Ronconi, L., Gori, S., Giora, E., Ruffino, M., Molteni, M., and Facoetti, A. (2013b). Deeper attentional masking by lateral objects in children with autism. *Brain Cogn.* 82, 213–218. doi: 10.1016/j.bandc.2013.04.006

Ruffino, M., Gori, S., Boccardi D., Molteni, M., and Facoetti, A. (2014). Spatial and temporal attention are both sluggish in poor phonological decoders with developmental dyslexia. *Front. Hum. Neurosci.* 8:1–13. doi: 10.3389/fnhum.2014.00331

Ruffino, M., Trussardi, A. N., Gori, S., Finzi, A., Giovagnoli, S., Menghini, D., et al. (2010). Attentional engagement deficits in dyslexic children. *Neuropsychologia* 8, 3793–3801. doi: 10.1016/j.neuropsychologia.2010.09.002

Ruzzoli, M., Gori, S., Pavan, A., Pirulli, C., Marzi, C. A., and Miniussi, C. (2011). The neural basis of the Enigma illusion: a transcranial magnetic stimulation study. *Neuropsychologia* 49, 3648–3655. doi: 10.1016/j.neuropsychologia.2011.09.020

Sartori, G., Job, R., and Tressoldi, P. E. (1995). *Batteria per la Valutazione Della Dislessia e Della Disortografia Evolutiva.* Firenze: Organizzazioni Speciali.

Share, D. L. (1995). Phonological recoding and self-teaching: sine qua non of reading acquisition. *Cognition* 55, 151–218. doi: 10.1016/0010-0277(94)00645-2

Snowling M. (2000). *Dyslexia.* Oxford: Blackwell.

Sperling, A. J., Lu, Z., Manis, F. R., and Seidenberg, M. S. (2005). Deficits in perceptual noise exclusion in developmental dyslexia. *Nat. Neurosci.* 8, 862–863. doi: 10.1038/nn1474

Sperling, A. J., Lu, Z. L., Manis, F. R., and Seidenberg, M. S. (2006). Motion-perception deficits and reading impairment: it's the noise, not the motion. *Psychol. Sci.* 17, 1047–1053. doi: 10.1111/j.1467-9280.2006.01825.x

Sprenger-Charolles, L., Siegel, L. S., Béchennec, D., and Serniclaes, W. (2003). Development of phonological and orthographic processing in reading aloud, in silent reading, and in spelling: a four-year longitudinal study. *J. Exp. Child Psychol.* 84, 194–217. doi: 10.1016/S0022-0965(03)00024-9

Stein, J. (2001). The magnocellular theory of developmental dyslexia. *Dyslexia* 7, 12–36. doi: 10.1002/dys.186

Stein, J., and Walsh, V. (1997). To see but not to read; the magnocellular theory of dyslexia. *Trends Neurosci.* 20, 147–152. doi: 10.1016/S0166-2236(96)01005-3

Talcott, J. B., Witton, C., Hebb, G. S., Stoodley, C. J., Westwood, E. A., France, S. J., et al. (2002). On the relationship between dynamic visual and auditory processing and literacy skills; results from a large primary-school study. *Dyslexia* 8, 204–225. doi: 10.1002/dys.224

Talcott, J. B., Witton, C., McLean, M. F., Hansen, P. C., Rees, A., Green, G. G., et al. (2000). Dynamic sensory sensitivity and children's word decoding skills. *Proc. Natl. Acad. Sci. U.S.A.* 97, 2952–2957. doi: 10.1073/pnas.040546597

Talcott, J. B., Witton, C., and Stein, J. F. (2013). Probing the neurocognitive trajectories of children's reading skills. *Neuropsychologia* 51, 472–481. doi: 10.1016/j.neuropsychologia.2012.11.016

Tallal, P. (2004). Improving language and literacy is a matter of time. *Nat. Rev. Neurosci.* 5, 721–728. doi: 10.1038/nrn1499

Valdois, S., Gérard, C., Vanault, P., and Dugas, M. (1995). Peripheral developmental dyslexia: a visual attentional account? *Cogn. Neuropsychol.* 12, 31–67. doi: 10.1080/02643299508251991

Vellutino, F. R., Fletcher, J. M., Snowling, M. J., and Scanlon, D. M. (2004). Specific reading disability (dyslexia): what have we learned in the past four decades? *J. Child Psychol. Psychiatry* 45, 2–40. doi: 10.1046/j.0021-9630.2003.00305.x

Vidyasagar, T. R. (1999). A neuronal model of attentional spotlight: parietal guiding the temporal. *Brain Res. Rev.* 30, 66–76. doi: 10.1016/S0165-0173(99)00005-3

Vidyasagar, T. R. (2013). Reading in to neuronal oscillations in the visual system: implications for developmental dyslexia. *Front. Hum. Neurosci.* 7:811. doi: 10.3389/fnhum.2013.00811

Vidyasagar, T. R., and Pammer, K. (1999). Impaired visual search in dyslexia relates to the role of the magnocellular pathway in attention. *Neuroreport* 10, 1283–1287. doi: 10.1097/00001756-199904260-00024

Vidyasagar, T. R., and Pammer, K. (2010). Dyslexia: a deficit in visuo-spatial attention, not in phonological processing. *Trends Cogn. Sci.* 14, 57–63. doi: 10.1016/j.tics.2009.12.003

Wechsler, D. (1986). *WISC-R: Scala di Intelligenza Wechsler per Bambini Riveduta.* Firenze: Organizazioni Speciali.

Williams, M., Brannan, J., and Lartigue, E. (1987). Visual search in good and poor readers. *Clin. Vis. Sci.* 1, 367–371.

Wimmer, H. (1993). Characteristics of developmental dyslexia in a regular writing system. *Appl. Psycholinguist.* 14, 1–33. doi: 10.1017/S0142716400010122

Wright, B. A., Bowen, R. W., and Zecker, S. G. (2000). Nonlinguistic perceptual deficits associated with reading and language disorders. *Curr. Opin. Neurobiol.* 10, 482–486. doi: 10.1016/S0959-4388(00)00119-7

Yazdanbakhsh, A., and Gori, S. (2008). A new psychophysical estimation of the receptive field size. *Neurosci. Lett.* 438, 246–251. doi: 10.1016/j.neulet.2008.04.040

Yazdanbakhsh, A., and Gori, S. (2011). Mathematical analysis of the accordion grating illusion: a differential geometry approach to introduce the 3D aperture problem. *Neural Netw.* 24, 1093–1101. doi: 10.1016/j.neunet.2011.06.016

Ziegler, J. C., Perry, C., Ma-Wyatt, A., Ladner, D., and Schulte-Körne, G. (2003). Developmental dyslexia in different languages: language-specific or universal? *J. Exp. Child Psychol.* 86, 169–193. doi: 10.1016/S0022-0965(03)00139-5

Zorzi, M., Barbiero, C., Facoetti, A., Lonciari, I., Carrozzi, M., Montico, M., et al. (2012). Extra-large letter spacing improves reading in dyslexia. *Proc. Natl. Acad. Sci. U.S.A.* 109, 11455–11459. doi: 10.1073/pnas.1205566109

14

Neuroimaging correlates of handwriting quality as children learn to read and write

Paul Gimenez[1], Nicolle Bugescu[1,2], Jessica M. Black[3], Roeland Hancock[1], Kenneth Pugh[4], Masanori Nagamine[1,5], Emily Kutner[1,2], Paul Mazaika[6], Robert Hendren[1], Bruce D. McCandliss[7] and Fumiko Hoeft[1,4,6,8]*

[1] Division of Child and Adolescent Psychiatry, Department of Psychiatry, UCSF, San Francisco, CA, USA
[2] Department of Psychology, Pacific Graduate School of Psychology, Palo Alto University, Palo Alto, CA, USA
[3] Graduate School of Social Work, Boston College, Chestnut Hill, MA, USA
[4] Haskins Laboratories, Yale University, New Haven, CT, USA
[5] Division of Behavioral Sciences, National Defense Medical College Research Institute, Tokorozawa, Saitama, Japan
[6] Department of Psychiatry and Behavioral Sciences, Center for Interdisciplinary Brain Sciences Research, Stanford University School of Medicine, Stanford, CA, USA
[7] Department of Psychology and Human Development, Vanderbilt University, Nashville, TN, USA
[8] Department of Neuropsychiatry, Keio University School of Medicine, Shinjuku-ku, Tokyo, Japan

Correspondence:
Fumiko Hoeft, Division of Child and Adolescent Psychiatry, Department of Psychiatry, University of California, 401 Parnassus Ave. Box 0984-F, San Francisco, CA 94143, USA
e-mail: fumiko.hoeft@ucsf.edu

Reading and writing are related but separable processes that are crucial skills to possess in modern society. The neurobiological basis of reading acquisition and development, which critically depends on phonological processing, and to a lesser degree, beginning writing as it relates to letter perception, are increasingly being understood. Yet direct relationships between writing and reading development, in particular, with phonological processing is not well understood. The main goal of the current preliminary study was to examine individual differences in neurofunctional and neuroanatomical patterns associated with handwriting in beginning writers/readers. In 46 5–6 year-old beginning readers/writers, ratings of handwriting quality, were rank-ordered from best to worst and correlated with brain activation patterns during a phonological task using functional MRI, and with regional gray matter volume from structural T1 MRI. Results showed that better handwriting was associated negatively with activation and positively with gray matter volume in an overlapping region of the pars triangularis of right inferior frontal gyrus. This region, in particular in the left hemisphere in adults and more bilaterally in young children, is known to be important for decoding, phonological processing, and subvocal rehearsal. We interpret the dissociation in the directionality of the association in functional activation and morphometric properties in the right inferior frontal gyrus in terms of neural efficiency, and suggest future studies that interrogate the relationship between the neural mechanisms underlying reading and writing development.

Keywords: phonological processing, voxel-based morphometry, functional MRI, inferior frontal gyrus pars triangularis, writing, reading

INTRODUCTION

Writing by hand occupies 30–60% of a child's school day (Stewart, 1992; Simner, 1998; Feder and Majnemer, 2007; Sassoon, 2007) and correlates with self-esteem and future academic success. Children with deficient handwriting (10–30% of children; Karlsdottir and Stefansson, 2002) take longer to complete writing tasks such as homework, which can increase the difficulty of schoolwork and result in oppositional attitudes toward writing assignments that can generate problems both at school and at home (Racine et al., 2008). Crucially, handwriting performance also shares links with other language related skills. Of particular relevance, there are important associations between reading and learning to write. Studies have shown that learning to write can improve letter perception (Longcamp et al., 2005), pseudoletter learning (Richards et al., 2011), and word reading (e.g., Berninger et al., 2004, 2006a; James and Engelhardt, 2012). Correspondingly, children with learning disabilities such as developmental dyslexia, a specific reading impairment that is believed to have phonological deficits at its core, often display writing difficulties (O'Hare and Khalid, 2002).

With the increasing integration of computers into the education system, the implied implications of reduced handwriting practice have strengthened the interest of scientific investigators. Recent neuroimaging studies have concluded that while free-form handwriting practice clearly supports reading acquisition, typing (Longcamp et al., 2005) and even tracing (James and Engelhardt, 2012) do not. Impressively, James and Engelhardt (2012) showed that preliterate children recruit well established reading related brain regions, such as the fusiform gyrus, posterior parietal cortex, and the inferior frontal gyrus, during letter processing exclusively after handwriting practice compared to typing or tracing. The emerging consensus is that the motor experience of manually creating letterforms helps children discriminate the essential properties of each letter, which leads to more accurate representations bolstering both skilled letter recognition and later reading fluency. Therefore, understanding the underlying neurological mechanisms that support handwriting development is important not only for its independent relevance to educational achievement, but also for its supportive role in successful acquisition of other language skills such as reading.

The neurological basis underlying handwriting is not well understood but converging evidence points to key regions including: (a) the fusiform gyrus, which has apparent selectivity to letter (James and Gauthier, 2006) and word stimuli (Cohen et al., 2000; Cohen and Dehaene, 2004) over other visual stimuli and may provide a perceptual component for deriving "word-form" representations that facilitate grapheme writing (Dehaene et al., 2005; James, 2010); (b) the superior parietal lobule (SPL), a region important for carrying out actions in space (Goodale and Milner, 2005) that is thought to be involved in both visuospatial and visuomotor processing (Petrides and Pandya, 1984; Morecraft et al., 2004; Segal and Petrides, 2012), and the execution of writing sequences (Otsuki et al., 1999); (c) the inferior frontal gyrus (IFG), implicated for its involvement in phonological processes (Eckert et al., 2003) and its associations with encoding letterforms and words (Grafton et al., 1997; Berninger and Winn, 2006b; Longcamp et al., 2008); and (d) Exner's area, thought to be the interface of orthographic or graphemic representations and the complex movement sequences necessary for generating letters and words (Anderson et al., 1990; Lubrano et al., 2004; Roux et al., 2009) and may also be involved in retrieving letter shapes from memory (James and Gauthier, 2006).

While advances have been made, a complete understanding of the brain's writing system remains elusive. The inherent complexities involved in the task of writing, coupled with the excessive variability of its definition in the existing literature, make it challenging to delineate the extent of neuronal specialization specific to handwriting from other inter-related aspects, such as spelling. In a recent neuroimaging metaanalysis of writing in adults, however, authors dissociated linguistic input and motoric aspects of writing and identified IFG for processing linguistic input as it relates to writing, and left superior frontal sulcus/middle frontal gyrus (Exner's), left superior parietal lobule, and the right cerebellum as "writing-specific" regions (Planton et al., 2013). Another study has shown that the brain differentially recruits specialized regions based on a multiplicity of letter representations (e.g., motoric similarities "B" vs. "P," visual similarities "A" vs. "R," abstract similarities "A" vs. "a") (Rothlein and Rapp, 2014). What is lacking is detailed examination of the emergence of "neural specialization" during the period when writing skills develop and the brain basis of the underlying process (except see work by Karen James cited in this paper). Further, more investigations of association between the brain basis of writing and other processes of written language such as reading is greatly needed. Findings from such studies may not only offer important insights to improve research methodology and educational instruction, but may also contribute to a fuller understanding of the development of written language processing in the human brain.

The present study sought to focus on the neural correlates of *handwriting quality* in children at the beginning of formal handwriting instruction. Operationally, handwriting quality refers to the legibility, form, slant, spacing, and general appearance of letters and words. Handwriting researchers have generally agreed on the relevance of these key features (Freeman, 1959; Kaminsky and Powers, 1981; Graham, 1982; Ziviani and Elkins, 1984; Graham and Weintraub, 1996). Given that handwriting exposure in preliterate children has been associated with reading related processes such as letter perception and related brain activation (James and Engelhardt, 2012), it is plausible to consider that especially during early stages of development, handwriting also share links with phonological processing a skill that for decades has been casually linked to reading acquisition (Castles and Coltheart, 2004; Byrne et al., 2008). Therefore, we sought to investigate the unproven idea that handwriting and reading may rely on a common neuroanatomical mechanism at an early developmental stage of reading/writing. We therefore hypothesized handwriting quality will be associated with neuroanatomical patterns in one or more of the following: (a) IFG if phonological decoding coding is relevant to handwriting quality, (b) Exner's area if successful integration of orthography and motor programs are relevant to handwriting quality, (c) SPL if sequential motor movements and/or kinesthetic modulation are relevant to handwriting quality, and/or (d) fusiform gyrus if visual letter or word recognition is relevant to handwriting skill. Then, in order to investigate the direct relationship of handwriting and reading abilities, in particular of phonological processing, we associated handwriting quality with brain activation during a task aimed at engaging the brain's phonological processing circuit. If handwriting is associated with the development of reading, and phonological processing plays a causal and reciprocal relationship with reading acquisition, we hypothesized that brain activation patterns associated with phonological processing, may also be associated with handwriting skills in these emergent readers / writers.

MATERIALS AND METHODS

Our data come from a study focused on examining brain activation during phonological processing and the relationship between reading-related behavioral measures. While the original study was not focused on the brain basis of handwriting, and hence the behavioral measures and fMRI tasks were not necessarily optimized for the purpose of the current study, yet these data provided an opportunity to investigate whether neuroanatomical patterns and brain activation during phonological processing are associated with handwriting in beginning readers and writers.

PARTICIPANTS

A total of 51 (29 boys, 22 girls) healthy, native English-speaking 5- and 6-year-old children (aged 5.59 ± 0.42) toward the beginning of formal schooling participated in this study. Standard behavioral assessments of the children, along with MRI data were collected. We later excluded five left-handed children, leaving 46 remaining right-handed children to be included in all analyses unless there was missing data or excessive movement motion or severe scanner artifacts (fMRI analyses, $N = 41$). While we did not exclude children based on attention deficit hyperactivity disorder (ADHD) for example, the children in this study did not have any parental report of formal diagnosis of neurological or psychiatric disorders besides specific learning disabilities; they were not on medication and had no contraindications to MRI. Behavioral Assessment System for Children −2 (Reynolds and Kamphaus, 2006) showed that all children were within typical range.

To help prepare participants for imaging, parents received a packet of informational material, including a CD of common scanner sounds and a DVD of a child going into the scanner. Parents were instructed to review these supplemental materials with their children to familiarize and desensitize participants to the scanner environment. In addition, children participated in a guided MRI simulation at the center where they practiced lying still in the bore and underwent training to minimize motion related artifacts. Participants with excessive, uncorrectable motion were eliminated from the study.

The Stanford University Panel on Human Subjects in Medical Research and the University of California, San Francisco Human Research Protection Program approved the study and informed consent and assent were obtained from parents/guardians and participants, respectively.

BEHAVIORAL MEASURES

We administered a standard battery of neuropsychological assessments, which included the Woodcock-Johnson III (WJ-III) Spelling (Woodcock et al., 2001), an untimed real-word spelling test, in order to assess spelling accuracy and handwriting quality (see below); the Beery Visual-Motor Integration (BVMI; Beery and Beery, 2004), where children copied and traced a series of moderately complex geometric figures; and the Oromotor Sequences subtest from the Developmental Neuropsychological Assessment (NEPSY-II; Korkman et al., 2007) to assess oral-motor praxis, or the ability to sequence oral-motor movements without articulation difficulty, without visual demands. Additionally, the Home Literacy Inventory (Marvin and Ogden, 2002) was used to investigate the differences in the exposure and practice of reading activities at home.

HANDWRITING QUALITY

In order ensure participants were unaware that their handwriting was under investigation, handwriting samples were drawn from the WJ-III Spelling subtest were used as a basis for assessing and defining handwriting skills. Two blinded investigators, who were trained to score handwriting quality holistically based on letterform, slant, spacing and general appearance irrespective of spelling errors and speed, each rank-ordered (1 = poor handwriting, 51 = best handwriting) participants' writing sample from best to worst three times. Since spelling inaccuracies can inadvertently bias rankings, writing samples included both letters and small words. Intraclass correlation coefficients were calculated to examine intra-rater reliability (Cronbach's alpha = 0.994 for rater 1; 0.989 for rater 2), and inter-rater reliability (Cronbach's alpha = 0.980) was calculated after the three sets of scores were averaged across raters. The final ranking used was based on the mean of each investigator's scores.

VISUOMOTOR (COPYING) SKILLS

A subset of test items (items 17–19) from the BMVI task was selected by the investigators to evaluate visuomotor skills; these items were developmentally appropriate, yet were also sufficiently difficult. Specifically, these were the most difficult items (non-letter objects) that all participants were able to complete. According to the manual, the validity and reliability of the task are sufficient for the age of our participants (Beery, 1997). Following the same rank-ordering procedures as for handwriting quality, two blind investigators rated participants' reproductions, which were based on copying geometric shapes (1 = poor reproduction, 51 = best reproduction). Intraclass correlation coefficients were calculated to examine intra-rater reliability (Cronbach's alpha = 0.993 for rater 1; 0.974 for rater 2) and inter-rater reliability (Cronbach's alpha = 0.969) was calculated after the three sets of scores were averaged across raters. The final ranking used was based on the mean of each investigator's scores.

FUNCTIONAL MRI TASKS

Three tasks measuring a range of cognitive abilities were used to investigate neurological associations to handwriting. The first was a phonological processing task in which participants were asked to determine if the first sound of the names of two pictures of common objects matched (**Figure 1A**). This task was adapted from a sound-matching subtask of the Comprehensive Test of Phonological Processing (Wagner et al., 1999) and is well established as reliable in phonological processing investigation (e.g., Katzir et al., 2005). The second task was a non-verbalizable visual-symbol matching task in which participants were presented with unfamiliar Japanese hiragana (no participants knew that they were letters from another language). Visually similar hiraganas (e.g., あ vs. め) were presented to try to maximize difficulty (**Figure 1B**). This task was used to at least partially account for visual input and motor response often associated with fMRI tasks that requires processing of letters and explicit motor responses (Henson et al., 2000). Finally, the third task was a color-matching task in which participants were asked to determine whether two colors matched (**Figure 1C**). The pair of stimuli were of the same hue but of different lightness with close value optimized in a pilot study to avoid using names of the colors to perform the task and to maximize difficulty. Although there is no assumed relationship between color-matching and handwriting, this task was included as another task to help account for some of the confounds, such as the color dissimilarities in the stimuli used in the phonological task and the decision making nature of all three tasks. These latter two tasks were only obtained in a portion of the children ($N = 18$). We therefore performed a secondary analysis of the phonological fMRI task matched to include only those participants that also completed the visual-symbol matching and color matching control tasks when comparing between tasks. The results of the phonological fMRI task were unchanged regardless of the sample-size and were specific to the phonological task.

All three tasks utilized the same procedure. Each required participants to determine whether two visually presented stimuli matched for either the first syllables of the names of pictures, visual symbols or color. Stimuli were presented simultaneously in one condition (without enabling working memory, WM−)

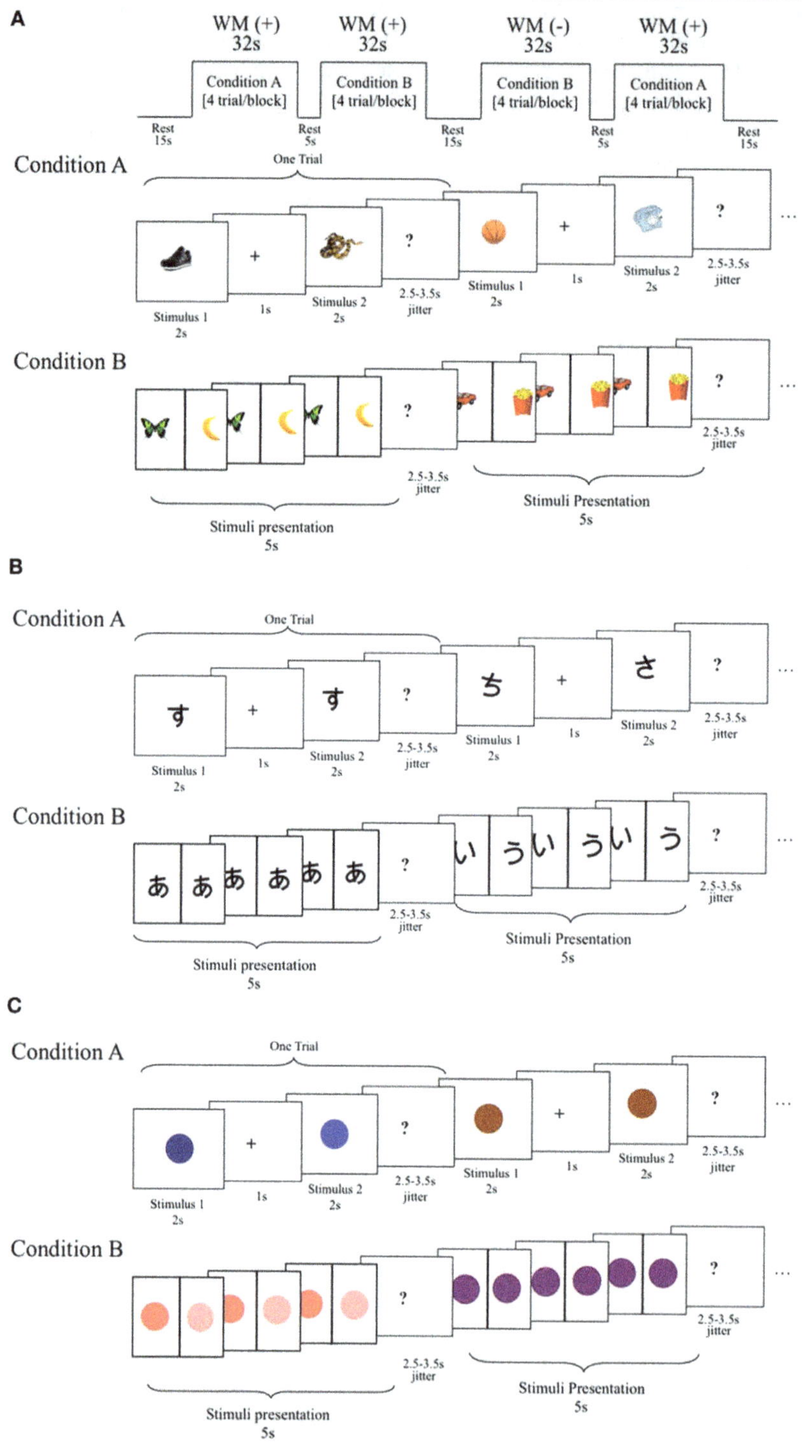

FIGURE 1 | Schematic diagram of the functional magnetic resonance imaging (fMRI) tasks. (A) Phonological processing fMRI task. In this block design fMRI task, participants were asked to determine whether the name of the pictured stimuli begin with matching sounds. Condition A: required working memory (WM+), stimulus presented one after another for 2 s each with 1 s intervals (must be retained across a delay). Condition B: no working memory required (WM−), stimuli presented side-by-side for 5 s. Conditioned collapsed for the purposes of this study. **(B)** A visual-symbol matching block design fMRI task. Design was the same as phonological task except that Japanese hiragana symbols were presented instead of pictured objects, and participants were asked to determine whether these unrecognized symbols matched. Note: working memory was pertinent to the parent study, but it was not crucial to this study, and for the purposes of this study WM+ and WM− conditions were collapsed into one condition. **(C)** A color discrimination block design fMRI task. Design was the same as the other tasks except that colors were presented instead of pictured objects or symbols, and participants were asked to determine whether these colors were the same. Note: working memory was pertinent to the parent study, but it was not crucial to this study, and for the purposes of this study WM+ and WM− conditions were collapsed into one condition.

and after a small delay (enabling working memory, WM+) (**Figures 1A–C**). In this study, we report results collapsing the two conditions. The exploration of the role of working memory in reading and writing may answer important theoretical questions and should be examined in future studies. This is not however, explored further in the current study because of the non-significant difference between conditions, which may have been due to a number of factors such as the short interstimulus interval. Rest was used as the control condition because our preliminary study showed difficulty of children performing a phonological task (sound matching of first syllable) alternating with a control condition (such as visual shape matching). We therefore opted to use the two other visual fMRI tasks to show specificity of the effects to the sound-matching task. Participants completed two runs of each task. Each of the two runs began with a 6 s countdown and a 2 s rest period. In the WM− condition, stimuli were presented side-by-side continuously for 3.5 s (followed by a 2.5–3.5 s jitter with a mean average of 3 s), whereas the WM+ condition displayed stimuli at the center one at a time for 2 s each with a jitter of 2.5–3.5 s (mean average 3 s) between stimuli (paired stimuli were also followed by a 2.5–3.5 s jitter with an mean average of 3 s). There were 5 trials per block. The 4 task blocks in each run were 32 s in duration and the order of the condition was varied from Run1 (WM−→WM+→WM+→WM−) and Run2 (WM+→ WM−→ WM−→WM+), with a 5, 15, and 5 s intervals between blocks. Participants ($N = 41$) completed 2 runs, with each run being 170 s in length (174 s total with the first 4 s of the scans in each run being discarded to establish equilibrium in MR signal). All stimuli were presented against a plain, white background and participants responded with their right finger if the stimuli matched and with their left finger if they did not match. Since participants may think of different words than intended for the pictured stimuli used in the phonological task, *post-hoc* testing asking names of each picture was performed for each child to verify whether there were discrepancies between potentially ambiguous images that may have alternative, yet still correct, pronunciations. This was necessary to ensure accurate task performance calculation tailored for each subject. Due to the young age of participants, data were used if their task accuracy total was greater than chance. Overall accuracy as well as reaction times for all correctly answered trials are shown in **Table 1**.

STRUCTURAL AND FUNCTIONAL MRI DATA ACQUISITION

Imaging was conducted at the Lucas Center for Imaging at the Stanford University School of Medicine. Imaging data was acquired using GE Healthcare 3.0 Tesla 750 scanner and an 8-channel phased array head coil (GE Healthcare, Waukesha, WI). Images acquired included an axial-oblique 3D T1-weighted sequence (fast spoiled gradient recalled echo [FSPGR] pulse sequence, inversion recovery preparation pulse [TI] = 400 ms; repetition time [TR] = 8.5 ms; echo-time [TE] = 3.4 ms; flip angle = 15°; Receiver bandwidth ± 32 kHz; slice thickness = 1.2 mm; 0.86 × 0.86 mm in-plane resolution; 128 slices; number of excitations = 1; field-of-view [FOV] = 22 cm; acquisition matrix = 256×192). The total scan time was 4:54.

Functional MRI (fMRI) data were acquired using an axial 2D GRE Spiral In/Out (SPRLIO; Glover and Law, 2001) pulse sequence ($TR = 2000$ ms; $TE = 30$ ms; flip angle = 80°; Receiver bandwidth +125 kHz; slice thickness = 4.0 mm; number of slices = 31, descending; 3.44 × 3.44 mm in-plane resolution; number of temporal frames = 85; FOV = 22 cm). The total duration of each task was 5:12.

REGIONS OF INTERESTS (ROIs)

Bilateral regions-of-interest (ROIs) used in this study were: (a) pars triangularis and pars opercularis of the IFG (IFGtri and IFGop, respectively) based on previous studies of language development, literacy, and handwriting in IFG (Longcamp et al., 2003, 2008), (b) Exner's region based on its role in generating graphemic-motor commands (Exner, 1881; Ritaccio et al., 1992; Roux et al., 2010; Planton et al., 2013), (c) SPL based on its involvement with complex motor sequences that contribute to the accuracy of written expression (Alexander et al., 1992; Sakurai et al., 2007), and (d) fusiform gyrus based on its role in letter (James and Gauthier, 2006) and word processing (Cohen et al., 2000). Automated Anatomical Labeling (AAL) (Tzourio-Mazoyer et al., 2002) in the WFU PickAtlas toolbox (Maldjian et al., 2003) was used to generate ROIs (a), (c), and (d). Exner's area ROI (b) was selected based on a neuroimaging study (Matsuo et al., 2003) as a region of the left precentral gyrus (PreCG, BA 6), adjacent to BA 9 and BA 44 (Talairach coordinates [TAL]: −46, 3, 27). A sphere with a diameter of 10 mm centered around these coordinates was used as the Exner's area ROI.

PREPROCESSING OF fMRI IMAGES

Processing of fMRI data was performed with statistical parametric mapping software (SPM8; Wellcome Department of Cognitive Neurology, London, UK) in the MATLAB computing environment (The MathWorks, Natick, MA). After image reconstruction, each participant's data were slice time corrected, realigned to a reference volume and corrected for motion and artifacts using both SPM and in-house tools (http://www.nitrc.org/projects/art_repair/). Data were spatially normalized to Montreal Neurological Institute (MNI) space using normalization parameters obtained from the children's segmented gray matter images of high resolution T1 MRI normalized to standard template and applied to the mean functional image. Resultant images were resampled to 2 × 2× 2 mm voxels in MNI stereotaxic space. Spatial smoothing was done with an 8-mm isotropic Gaussian kernel. Each participant's data were high pass filtered at 128 s, and analyzed using a fixed effects model examining task; rest was not modeled and was included as implicit baseline. Five of the 46 participant's data were not included (final $N = 41$) because of excessive motion (criteria: relative motion <1.0 mm), at or below chance task performance (criteria: accuracy ≤50%), and/or scanner artifact ($N = 5$).

STATISTICAL ANALYSES OF fMRI DATA: MAIN ANALYSES OF INTEREST

Statistical analysis was performed first using a fixed effects analysis for each participant modeling each condition. Task vs. rest contrasts were used for further group analysis for the purposes of this study as stated in the Functional MRI Tasks section above. Using random effects analysis, a one sample t-test was performed to examine brain regions that were active during the phonological

Table 1 | Demographics and correlations.

Measure	Association with handwriting quality					
	Mean (*SD*)	*t, r,* or *p*	*p*-value			
Age	5.59 (0.42)	$r = 0.27$	0.075			
Gender	26 boys / 20 girls	$t = 2.64$	0.012*			
Handedness (all right)	82.27(19.81)	$r = 0.17$	0.26			
Mother's education (years)	17.02 (2.07)	$P = -0.12$	0.42			
	Raw scores			**Standard/scaled scores**		
	Mean (*SD*)	*r*	*p*–value	Mean (*SD*)	*r*	*p*–value
Handwriting quality[a]	0 (1)	1	0.00**	NA	NA	NA
Phonological fMRI (accuracy)	72.01% (12.66)	−0.137	0.447	NA	NA	NA
Phonological fMRI (reaction time)	2601.78 ms (511.56)	−0.115	0.462	NA	NA	NA
FSIQ[b] WJIII BIA[c]	NA	NA	NA	119.24 (2.07)	−0.17	0.27
PPVT[d]	119.57 (14.11)	0.016	0.92	122.00 (9.21)	0.20	0.18
WRMT[e] letter identification	31.48 (7.96)	0.13	0.39	111.87 (10.95)	0.20	0.18
WRMT word identification	15.26 (19.38)	0.11	0.46	119.41 (31.84)	0.090	0.55
CTOPP[f] phonological awareness	NA	NA	NA	112.54 (14.78)	0.040	0.79
CTOPP elision	6.59 (4.44)	−0.099	0.51	12.00 (2.87)	−0.099	0.51
CTOPP blending	8.45 (3.43)	−0.13	0.38	12.48 (2.04)	−0.154	0.31
CTOPP phonological memory	NA	NA	NA	106.28 (11,75)	0.090	0.21
RAN[g] object	1.76 (1.40)	0.097	0.52	101.93 (15.41)	0.030	0.84
RAN color	0.39 (1.02)	0.079	0.60	99.43 (15.53)	−0.050	0.75
Visuomotor (BVMI[h] rank)	0 (1)	0.45	0.0020**	NA	NA	NA
WJIII spelling	14.48 (3.55)	0.36	0.013*	112.04 (12.13)	0.18	0.24
BVMI right	16.43 (2.75)	0.38	0.010**	108.39 (14.53)	0.25	0.092
NEPSY[i] oromotor	38.5 (10.40)	−0.0050	0.96	3.00 (0.84)	0.090	0.56
Home literacy inventory	8.62 (3.47)	0.036	0.815	NA	NA	NA
TGMV[j]	710.95 (63.24)	−0.14	0.36	NA	NA	NA
TWMV[k]	455.7 (43.97)	−0.17	0.27	NA	NA	NA

*$p < 0.05$ level (2-tailed).

**$p < 0.01$ level (2-tailed).

[a] *Writing samples derived from Woodcock-Johnson III Spelling (subtest from Test of Cognitive Abilities).*

[b] *Full Scale Intelligence Quotient.*

[c] *Brief Intellectual Ability.*

[d] *Peabody Picture Vocabulary Test.*

[e] *Woodcock Reading Mastery Tests.*

[f] *Comprehensive Test of Phonological Processing (Phonological Awareness = Elison + Blending).*

[g] *Rapid Automatized Naming.*

[h] *Beery-Buktenica Developmental Test of Visual-Motor integration.*

[i] *Developmental Neuropsychological Assessment.*

[j] *Total Gray Matter Volume.*

[k] *Total While Matter Volume.*

fMRI task [$p = 0.05$ family-wise error (FWE) corrected, at the whole brain level].

Next, simple correlation analysis was performed between brain activation during the fMRI tasks and handwriting skills in the ROIs using a statistical threshold of $p = 0.05$ family-wise error (FWE) corrected for height using small volume correction. We also examined voxel-by-voxel associations in the whole brain at a more lenient threshold of $p = 0.001$ uncorrected for height to examine whether there are any clusters outside the ROIs that showed significant effects at this more lenient threshold.

STATISTICAL ANALYSES OF fMRI DATA: CONTROL ANALYSES

Control analyses were performed in several ways. First, analyses examining associations between handwriting quality and brain activation during the phonological task regressing out the non-handwriting motor and writing abilities such as visuomotor skills (rank order of BVMI), oromotor skills (NEPSY-II oromotor subtest), and spelling (WJ-III spelling subtest), as well as correlated demographic variables [age (there was a trend for significant effects of older age correlating with better handwriting), gender (males had significantly poorer handwriting than females)] were performed. Second, ROI based regression analyses between brain activation during the phonological task and these aforementioned non-handwriting motor and writing abilities were performed. Statistical threshold was set similarly to the main analysis at $p = 0.05$ FWE corrected for the ROIs (and $p = 0.001$ uncorrected for the whole brain to examine whether there are any clusters outside the ROIs that showed significant effects at this more lenient threshold). Third, whole-brain and ROI analyses were performed correlating brain activation during the supplemental visual-symbol matching and color matching tasks and handwriting skills (rank order of WJ-III spelling writing samples). Since we only had data from these tasks in half of the participants, in order to show that the significant effect in the meta-phonological task and not the supplementary tasks was not due to power issues, we went back and repeated the main correlation analysis (between brain activation during the meta-phonological processing task and handwriting skills) using a smaller sample with data from both the meta-phonological and supplementary tasks.

PREPROCESSING AND STATISTICAL ANALYSIS OF T1 STRUCTURAL MR IMAGES

Voxel-based morphometry (VBM) analysis of T1-weighted MRIs was performed using Statistical Parametric Mapping, version 8, (SPM8) (http://www.fil.ion.ucl.ac.uk/spm). After alignment to AC-PC axis, T1-weighted images were bias-corrected and segmented to gray matter, white matter, and cerebrospinal fluid, using SPM8 default tissue probability maps and "New Segment" tool, which also included an affine regularization to warp images to the included International Consortium for Brain Mapping (ICBM) template, producing rigidly aligned tissue class images. Inter-subject registration was achieved with Diffeomorphic Anatomical Registration Through Exponentiated Lie Algebra (DARTEL), using default settings. Jacobian-scaled ("modulated"), warped tissue class images were created with DARTEL's "Normalize to MNI Space" tool, which spatially normalized images to MNI space, converted voxel sizes to $1.5 \times 1.5 \times 1.5\,\text{mm}^3$ to match the DARTEL template, and smoothed images with a standard Gaussian filter of full-width at half-maximum (FWHM) equal to 8 mm. For each participant, segmentation and normalization accuracy were manually inspected. 41 of 46 participants were included in this analysis due to usability issues caused either by artifacts or excessive motion. Statistical analyses were performed similarly to fMRI analyses using the same statistical thresholds but additionally controlling for total gray matter volume. Finally, associations between regional gray matter volume and brain activation were performed where the spatial location at least partially overlapped. The reported Talairach coordinates were converted from MNI space using the mni2tal function (http://www.mrc-cbu.cam.ac.uk/Imaging/Common/mnispace.shtml). Talairach Daemon (Research Imaging Center, University of Texas Health Science Center; Lancaster et al., 1997, 2000) and the atlas by Talairach and Tournoux (1988) were initially used to identify Brodmann Areas. The final anatomic locations are reported according to their anatomic location overlaid on the custom template.

RESULTS

BEHAVIORAL RESULTS

Table 1 shows demographic and behavioral characteristics as well as associations between these measures and handwriting quality. Age, handedness, and maternal education, often used as a proxy for environment, did not yield any significant associations with handwriting performance (all p's > 0.05). However, as one might expect based on the fact that the handwriting measure was ranked-ordered and not standardized, even though the range of ages in these children were narrow (5–6 years of age), age showed a trend for significant positive association with handwriting [$r_{(44)} = 0.27$; $p = 0.075$], and gender effects were found [$t_{(44)} = 2.64$, $p = 0.012$] with boys demonstrating significantly weaker handwriting performance as compared to girls. Further, while handwriting performance was not significantly correlated with spelling standard scores [**Table 1**, $r_{(44)} = 0.18, p = 0.24$], spelling raw scores were significantly related [$r_{(44)} = 0.36$, $p = 0.013$]. (Since the ranking of handwriting quality was not a standardized measure, this was expected). Visuomotor skill ratings (see above for definition) were also significantly correlated with BVMI standard scores, which is expected since visuomotor integration skill was the construct being evaluated [$r_{(44)} = 0.658, p < 0.001$]. We also found, as anticipated, that rater's ranking of handwriting and visuomotor skills were associated with one another [$r_{(44)} = 0.45$, $p = 0.002$].

fMRI RESULTS

First we examined brain regions that showed significant activation during the reading-related phonological processing task in all participants. We found that these emerging readers elicited significant activation at $p = 0.05$ corrected in bilateral (left > right) IFG, left superior, middle frontal gyrus and PreCG, left inferior parietal lobule and bilateral occipito-temporal region (**Figure 2**, **Table 2**). It is important to note that the behavioral profiles of participants included in this study are not representative of a normal population (see **Table 1**), so the results presented here are not yet generalizable.

Phonological activity was negatively associated with better handwriting quality in the right IFG within Broca's Area/Brodmann Area 45 / pars triangularis [TAL: $X = 44$, $Y = 24$, $Z = 15$; peak $T = 3.74$; $p = 0.033$ corrected; mean cluster $r_{(39)} = -0.43$; **Figure 3A**]. Even when performing whole-brain analysis at a lenient threshold of $p = 0.001$ uncorrected, a cluster in the right IFGtri was the only region that showed a significant effect (TAL: $X = 40$, $Y = 27$, $Z = 17$; peak $T = 3.77$; $p < 0.001$ uncorrected). Exner's area (TAL: $X = 48$, $Y = 7$, $Z = 22$), although non-significant, also showed a distinctive trend in the same direction ($p = 0.054$ corrected). Given Exner's well-documented involvement in handwriting, this trend was included in **Figure 3**). No significant positive correlations were observed either at $p = 0.05$ corrected or $p = 0.001$ uncorrected. Activity in the right IFGtri cluster during the phonological task was also negatively correlated with CTOPP phonological memory composite scores ($r = -0.31$, $p = 0.049$) and memory for digits subtest ($r = -0.37$, $p = 0.017$).

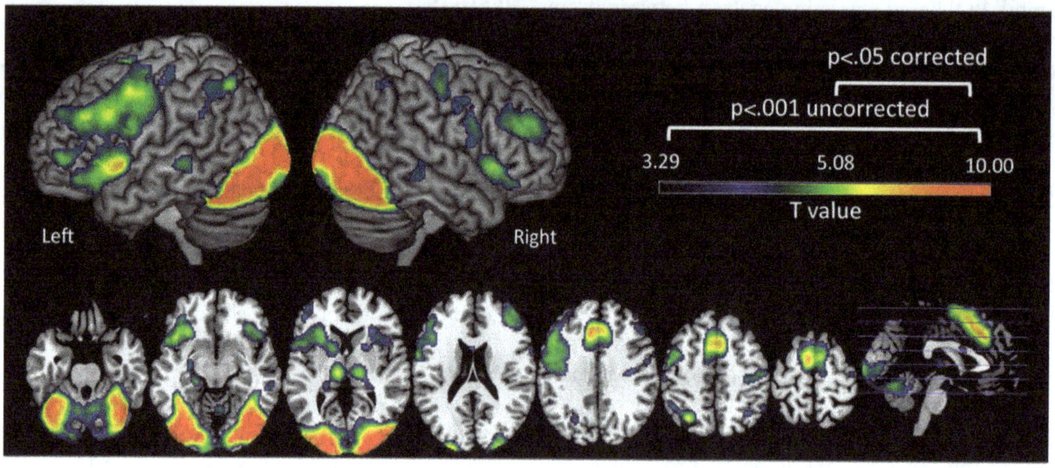

FIGURE 2 | Brain activation during the phonological processing fMRI task. Clusters in warm colors indicate those significant at $p < 0.05$ family wise error (FWE) corrected. Those significant at $p < 0.001$ uncorrected, cluster extent = 10 are also included to show the extent of these clusters at a more lenient threshold. Note: Left Hemisphere is shown on left side.

Table 2 | Regional brain coordinates.

Brain region	Brodmann area (BA)	TAL coordinates			T values (peak)	P value (FWE)	Cluster size (voxels)
		x	y	z			
Right fusiform, inferior, middle occipital gyri	18, 19	42	−78	−3	15.35	<0.001	11557
		38	−66	−8	15.31	<0.001	
		26	−93	10	13.6	<0.001	
Left medial frontal, right cingulate gyri	9, 6, 32	−8	27	30	7.92	<0.001	2125
		−8	1	59	7.74	<0.001	
		6	21	39	7.44	<0.001	
Left inferior frontal, superior temporal gyri, lentiform nucleus (Putamen)	47, 22	−28	21	−3	7.71	<0.001	798
		−46	11	−4	7.53	<0.001	
		−18	10	1	5.43	0.020	
Left parahippocampal gyrus	27	−20	−29	−2	6.77	0.001	88
Left superior parietal lobule	7	−30	−58	47	6.34	0.002	60
Left middle frontal gyrus	6, 9, 46	−46	6	42	6.21	0.002	424
		−50	19	27	5.96	0.005	
		−48	36	24	5.94	0.005	
Left thalamus		−10	−17	5	6.15	0.003	114
Right inferior frontal gyrus	47	32	27	−3	6.13	0.003	163
Right thalamus (ventral posterior lateral nucleus)		16	−17	6	5.67	0.011	39
Right thalamus		22	−27	0	5.4	0.022	7
Right middle frontal gyrus	10	40	40	18	5.24	0.033	8
Right culmen		4	−65	−10	5.24	0.034	8
Left precentral gyrus	6	−63	3	20	5.2	0.037	3
Right declive		6	−55	−14	5.19	0.039	6
Left inferior frontal gyrus	10	−44	47	−2	5.16	0.041	2
Left declive		−10	−59	−16	5.13	0.044	1
Right middle frontal gyrus	10	44	48	20	5.12	0.046	2
Left precentral gyrus	6	−46	−2	30	5.09	0.049	1

Control analyses were performed in three ways. First, the negative correlation in the right IFGtri remained significant using whole-brain regression analysis of the phonological fMRI task even after regressing out variables that correlated with handwriting quality as well as other motor and writing skills such as age, gender, visuomotor skill (rank ordered BVMI responses), oromotor skills, BVMI (dominant/right hand) raw scores, and WJ-III Spelling raw scores ($r = -0.369$, $p = 0.029$).

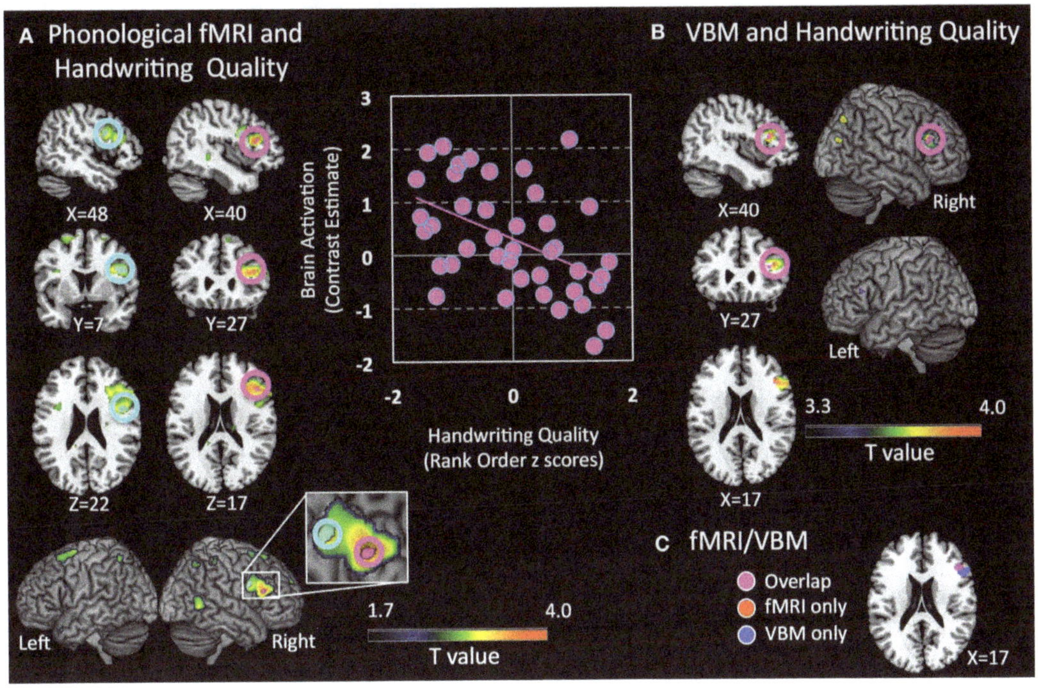

FIGURE 3 | Brain regions associated with handwriting quality. **(A)** Clusters that show negative association with brain activation during a phonological processing fMRI task are shown. Pink circles indicate a cluster that is significant at $p = 0.05$ corrected (right inferior frontal gyrus pars triangularis, IFGtri), and cyan circles indicate a cluster that shows a trend $p = 0.054$ corrected (right Exner's area). Clusters indicate voxels significant at a lenient threshold of $p = 0.05$ uncorrected to show greater extent of activation. XYZ coordinates are in Talairach coordinates. Panel on the right shows a scatter plot representation of the cluster that shows significant negative association at $p = 0.05$ corrected (pink cluster). Brain activation is defined as contrast estimates, which are based on combined beta estimates of the phonological condition vs. rest. **(B)** Clusters that show positive association with regional gray matter volume are shown. Pink circles indicate clusters that are significant at $p = 0.05$ corrected in the right IFGtri. Clusters indicate all voxels significant at $p = 0.001$ uncorrected, cluster extent = 10 as reference to show the extent of these clusters at a more lenient threshold. A small cluster in the left IFGtri is observed at this threshold. XYZ coordinates are in Talairach coordinates. **(C)** Voxels that show overlap in fMRI activation from **(A)** and VBM gray matter volume from **(B)** in the right inferior frontal region. Note: Left Hemisphere is shown on left side.

Second, control analyses were then performed using ROI-based (IFGtri and IFGop from AAL) and whole-brain regression between activation during phonological processing and motor and writing skills other than handwriting skills. Correlations between right IFG activation and unstandardized visuomotor skills (see Methods for definition) (peak $T = 2.51$; $p = 0.19$ corrected; $p = 0.008$ uncorrected; **Figure 4**), oromotor skills (peak $T = 3.03$; $p = 0.071$ corrected; $p = 0.002$ uncorrected) and spelling (peak $T = 0.42$; $p = 0.85$ corrected; $p = 0.29$ uncorrected) were not significant, controlling for age (either by regressing age out or by using normed scores).

Third, no significant positive or negative correlation was observed with handwriting quality and brain activation during either the visual-symbol matching or color matching tasks, demonstrating that the association is likely to be specific to the phonological processing task. Since we only had data from half the sample for both the visual-symbol and color matching tasks (in what we called Cohort 1), we repeated the main correlation analysis between brain activation during phonological processing and handwriting skills using the participants included in this control analysis and still found significant results in the right IFGtri ($r = -0.49$, $p = 0.024$).

VBM RESULTS

We specifically examined whether there were structural correlates of the functional finding by evaluating whether there were significant associations with the right IFG regional gray matter volume and handwriting quality controlling for total gray matter volume. We found a significant *positive* correlation between handwriting quality and regional gray matter volume in the right IFGtri, spatially overlapping with the fMRI results (TAL: $X = 40$, $Y = 27$, $Z = 17$; peak $T = 3.66$; $p = 0.027$ corrected; **Figures 3B,C**). The association was however, positive and in the opposite direction to the fMRI findings. Even when the whole-brain was examined rather than the a priori hypothesized ROIs, four clusters in right IFGtri—middle frontal gyrus, left IFGtri, right middle temporal gyrus, and right postcentral gyrus—intraparietal sulcus (inferior/superior parietal lobule) were the only regions that showed a significant effect at a lenient threshold of $p = 0.001$. There were no brain regions that showed significant negative association with gray matter volumes or significant positive or negative association with white matter. The positive correlation in the right IFGtri remained significant using even after regressing out variables that correlated with handwriting skills such as age, gender, visuomotor skill (rank ordered BVMI responses), BVMI (dominant/right hand) raw scores, and WJ-III Spelling raw

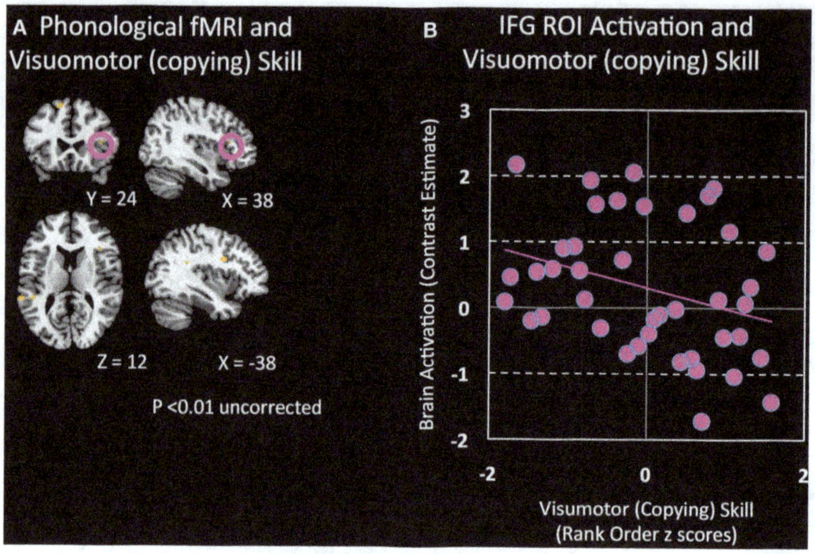

FIGURE 4 | Brain regions associated with visuomotor (copying) skill. **(A)** Clusters that show a negative association ($p = 0.01$ uncorrected) between visuomotor (copying) skill and brain activation during a phonological processing fMRI task are shown. **(B)** Non-significant correlation between visuomotor (copying) skill and activation in the right IFG during phonological processing.

scores ($r = 0.536$, $p = 0.001$). Further, regional gray matter volume significantly correlated with functional activation from the main analysis ($r = -0.323$, $p = 0.043$).

DISCUSSION

We have presented results examining beginning writers/readers' association between handwriting quality and brain activation. Our preliminary results showed that poorer handwriting quality was associated with stronger activation of the right IFGtri when children judged whether a pair of pictures starts with the same sound. Furthermore, these results overlapped spatially with reduced regional gray matter volume in the right IFGtri in children with less proficient handwriting. Brain activation during supplementary fMRI tasks, where children judged visual similarities between pairs of unfamiliar symbols and discriminated between colors, were not associated with handwriting quality. Regional gray matter volume associations were also significantly correlated with the functional associations specific to the right IFG during the phonological task. These findings show the significance of IFG in handwriting quality in beginning writers, demonstrating that increased activation in the right IFGtri during a task likely related to the phonological processes involved in reading is associated with reduced handwriting quality, which in turn showed structural brain correlates. While our control condition was rest in our phonological fMRI task because of the young age of our participants (see Methods—Functional MRI Tasks above), we believe the task taps at least partially into phonological processing. This is because other studies using comparable tasks as well as our own study have successfully shown phonological processing related reading networks to be active during the task (see Methods). Additionally, we have included two supplementary tasks to show that the findings were at least not due to more non-specific aspects of the task such as visual perception, judgment and motoric responses. The results of this study show that the neuroanatomical properties and phonologically related neurofunctional properties of the IFG may be essential in the development of complex motor skills required in handwriting.

The IFG is a heterogeneous region with many functions. Existing literature on the IFG suggests its involvement in an exhaustive list of language abilities, including: syntactic processing (Embick et al., 2000), accessing orthographic long-term memories in the form of stored motor plans (Hillis et al., 2002; Rapp and Dufor, 2011), coordinating orthographic lexical selection and retrieval (Purcell et al., 2011), verbal working memory (Paulesu et al., 1993), letter perception and letter transcription (James and Gauthier, 2006), activation during speech generation (Liotti et al., 1994), grasping and manipulating objects (Rizzolatti et al., 1988), silent naming of manipulable objects (Grafton et al., 1997), observation of manipulable objects (Grafton et al., 1997), and when handwriting novel letterforms (Longcamp et al., 2008). Regarding its purported function in relation to writing, a recent meta-analysis of handwriting studies (Planton et al., 2013) found evidence for IFG involvement in writing, and in particular when contrasted against a control motor task (e.g., vocalization), but not for contrasts that controlled for linguistic input processing. This supports the role of the IFG in processing linguistic input during writing rather than motoric output (Planton et al., 2013). In our study, we additionally show that handwriting quality correlated not only with IFG volume, but also with activation during a task that was at least partially related to phonological processing. This suggests that at the beginning stage of reading and writing, there is a tight coupling between IFG—albeit right lateralized—and handwriting, possibly via phonological processing. It is interesting to note that handwriting quality also correlated with a behavioral measure of phonological encoding (spelling). We interpret our predominant results on the right hemisphere (left hemisphere involvement was present but only at subthreshold) in terms of neuronal efficiency, which we discuss below.

Although there is evidence for IFG involvement in a variety of tasks, its robust associations with phonological processing and lexical retrieval are likely the most relevant with respect to reading. Many aspects of language processing show leftward functional asymmetry in the IFG in most adults (Price, 2010). Although children show some indication of frontal left hemisphere asymmetry, the degree of asymmetry increases into adulthood (Holland et al., 2001; Szaflarski et al., 2006). Increased left functional asymmetry for language production has been linked to increased vocabulary and non-word reading scores in children (Groen et al., 2012) and more bilateral or right hemisphere IFG activations found in disabled populations, such as reading impaired dyslexics (Calvert et al., 2000; Pugh et al., 2001; Hoeft et al., 2011). Larger activation extents in the IFG have also been reported in children during linguistic tasks (Gaillard et al., 2000; Hoeft et al., 2011). This suggests a developmental reorganization and refinement of frontal language circuits through young adulthood. Our finding of a negative correlation between children's handwriting performance and right IFG activation is consistent with a common maturational process affecting handwriting and phonological processing. Children with high activation in the right IFG during phonological processing may be developmentally delayed with respect to adult-like patterns of functional asymmetry for language processing and consequently be delayed in the development of handwriting performance, either via a direct link between phonological skills and handwriting or a more general, domain independent delay. However, the specificity of our findings argues against a general delay.

An alternative account, which does not assume functional homology between the left and right IFG, is that improved handwriting is associated with increased computational efficiency or neural coding—and hence reduced BOLD signal increase—in the right IFG for reading-related functions. This phenomenon, known as neural efficiency, posits that brighter individuals use their brains more efficiently and is often used to explain the inverse relationship between brain activation and task performance (Haier et al., 1988). A recent study by Holland et al. (2011) has shown that greater recruitment of the IFG is associated with slower naming (reduced proficiency) during a picture-naming task. Further, decrease in right IFG activation during an orthographic processing task has been shown with orthographic training, a process known to contribute uniquely to handwriting, spelling, and composition (Richards et al., 2006a). Training-induced reduction in right IFG activation has also been shown to correlate with improved phonological decoding (Richards et al., 2006b). The positive association between handwriting performance and gray matter volume may be compatible with this interpretation. Morphometric studies have found that increased regional gray matter volume may result in less energy consumption when that area is employed (Haier et al., 2004), and it is generally accepted that increased volume denotes increased cognitive capacity. This interpretation is further supported by the negative correlation between behavioral measures of phonological memory and right IFG activation during the phonological task. In our study, while both age and gender showed associations to handwriting quality (see **Table 1**), our findings persisted even when these factors were regressed out. Moreover, there were no significant correlations with environmental measures (e.g., Home Literacy Inventory) used as proxies to control for differential exposure to reading/writing materials. Thus, there is some indication that observed differences are not related to age or environmental differences, but instead to differences in maturational development of language related processes or neural efficiency.

Recent studies of handwriting in children have found differences in activation within the fusiform gyrus (Longcamp et al., 2008; Richards et al., 2009a,b), an area known as critical for orthographic processing and implicated both in letter and word perception, critical components for both reading development and handwriting acquisition (James and Engelhardt, 2012). Other studies note the importance of Exner's area and the SPL. Exner's area has been implicated for its role in bridging the gap between orthography and the motor programs necessary for handwriting (Roux et al., 2010; Planton et al., 2013), and the emerging consensus regarding the SPL posits that this region is involved in the abstract representation, sequential selection, and production of letter shapes (Rapp and Dufor, 2011; Planton et al., 2013; Rothlein and Rapp, 2014). We did not demonstrate a significant association between handwriting quality and neuroanatomical structure or activation in ROIs other than the IFG, such as Exner's area, fusiform gyrus and the SPL. The absence of significant results in Exner's area (though there was a trend for significance also on the right hemisphere) and the SPL may be explained by the fact that most studies that have reported these regions have used adult participants. Research has shown that in adults specific neural substrates respectively correspond to differing letter representations (Rothlein and Rapp, 2014), but this cerebral organization is likely very different in early development. It may be that the phonological processing subserved by the IFG becomes less necessary for writing as language skills become more automatic. Once this occurs, regions such as Exner's and SPL, important in the motoric and visuo-spatial component become more involved (regions thought to be specialized for fluent, automatic handwriting). It may also be the case that significant effects may have been observed in these regions if a different fMRI task was used that emphasize more motoric and visuo-spatial components, though this will not explain the lack of associations neuroanatomically. Another probable explanation is that the inverse correlation with activation in the IFG may correspond with the emergence of neural circuits in posterior writing areas in better readers. It is possible that this was not detected in our study due to the small, age-limited sample. In which case, the IFG activation may relate not to letter formation, but rather to its well-established role in motor planning and executive function. Further, while the activation observed in our study is assumed to be essential for the phonological task, some studies have shown that activation does not necessarily correspond to what is necessary for the particular tasks being administered (Rothlein and Rapp, 2014). Future studies will need to dissociate these possibilities.

The lack of association between handwriting quality and activation and neuroanatomical patterns in fusiform gyrus is more difficult to explain, especially as significant association with handwriting and reading (letter perception) was found in beginning writers / readers. While again, this requires further investigation (as described in limitations), it is possible that the lack of significant findings in the fusiform gyrus is related to the nature of the phonological task we used, as our task requires no orthographic processing, and hence no interaction was found with handwriting quality in the fusiform gyrus. Thus, it is very likely that if we included another fMRI task related to letter perception or orthographic processing as in James and Engelhardt (2012), we would have seen associations with handwriting in the fusiform gyrus (and SPL) also even though this will not account for the lack of neuroanatomical findings in this region.

Our study provides insights into why some children with dyslexia have been found to have poorer handwriting as well (Berninger et al., 2008). Previous literature has indicated children with dyslexia taught both word decoding and handwriting showed improvement in reading as well as orthographic decoding (Berninger et al., 2008; Berninger and Richards, 2011). It has also been shown in adults with pure alexia that reading performance can be improved through handwriting practice (Seki et al., 1995; Bartolomeo et al., 2002). Recently, a related study on the relationship between handwriting experience and neurological development in beginning readers showed that those with more experience printing and tracing activated the IFG during letter perception more than children with experience typing or copying (James and Engelhardt, 2012). Accepting past literature showing the IFG as important for linking features together to construct an organized whole, these researchers proposed that the IFG may be important for motor planning, control and execution. At a minimum, our study is distinguished from James and Engelhardt in that rather than investigating letter perception, our tasks did not include stimuli related to written languages (e.g., letters and words) and still found significant associations. Further, we find neuroanatomical evidence of associations between IFG and writing. Our findings hence provide novel findings adding to the important role of the process of writing in reading development.

FUTURE DIRECTIONS AND LIMITATIONS

Future studies investigating handwriting quality and development may assess the role of maturation, lateralization and neural efficiency related to handwriting by following children longitudinally, and by examining lower level visual and motor processing, spelling and writing compositions. Attention also plays a role in successful handwriting (McCutchen, 1996) and while we did incentivize and encourage attention, future studies may examine better ways to control or account for attention.

There are several limitations to our study that will need to be addressed in future research. First, our phonological processing task where children judged whether the initial sounds of the names of pictures matched did not have a well-matched control condition such as a picture matching condition. Although we included supplementary fMRI tasks we had available (e.g., visual matching and color matching tasks), these may have been inadequate to serve as control tasks. This determination was based on our preliminary study in young children (see Methods—Functional MRI Tasks for details). Second, while unrealistic to keep children in kindergarten in the scanner for long periods of time, future studies may include fMRI tasks specifically related to writing, orthographic, visual and motor processing in addition to phonological processing to examine task induced differences in activation patterns as it relates to handwriting. Third, while qualitative/holistic approaches remain the most common way to assess handwriting quality (Wagner et al., 2011), there is need to find more quantitative methods, such as using computer algorithms to interpret handwriting quality and errors. Fourth, the working memory condition during fMRI was not significantly different from the non-working memory condition, and hence we were unable to address the issue of working memory in writing. Fifth, the participants included in this study were gifted compared to normative populations with standardized behavioral profiles well above average (see **Table 1**), potentially reducing the extent to which our results are generalizable. Finally, we compared a copying task (BVMI) to a spelling task (WJ-III), and there were differences in task requirements, such as encoding differences, and letters vs. symbols, as well as other potential differences such as verbal short-term memory and visual long-term memory (remembering shapes of letters); these should be dissociated in future studies. Despite these limitations, our study is an important step in identifying the neural substrates of handwriting quality in beginning writers.

CONCLUSIONS

In the current study, we provide evidence of direct neural links between handwriting quality, a skill that has been strongly associated with higher level writing skills and reading, and neural processing underlying phonological processing, which is thought to be causally related to reading acquisition. In contrast to studies focused on neurologically impaired individuals (e.g., Benson, 1979; Exner, 1881; Kaplan and Goodglass, 1981), we took a dimensional approach to investigate handwriting and have provided preliminary but novel evidence that the IFG may be a key link between phonological processing and handwriting quality during early phases of language development. The findings in the current study indicate that during early development of reading and writing skills, successful handwriting quality, measured by one's ability to shape and form letters coherently, relies on the right IFG, and that this efficiency corresponds to successful phonological processing.

ACKNOWLEDGMENTS

This study was supported by grants from the National Institute of Child Health and Human Development (K23HD054720), Child Health Research Program (CHRP), Lucile Packard Foundation for Children's Health (LPFCH), Spectrum Child Health, Clinical and Translational Science Award, and the Dyslexia Foundation (TDF)'s Extraordinary Brain Series to FH. We thank Anne Sawyer and Gary Glover for assistance with MRI data collection.

REFERENCES

Alexander, M. P., Fischer, R. S., and Friedman, R. (1992). Lesion localization in apractic agraphia. *Arch. Neurol.* 49, 246–251. doi: 10.1001/archneur.1992.00530270060019

Anderson, S. W., Damasio, A. R., and Damasio, H. (1990). Troubled letters but not numbers. Domain specific cognitive impairments following focal damage in frontal cortex. *Brain* 113(Pt. 3), 749–766.

Bartolomeo, P., Bachoud-Lévi, A. C., Chokron, S., and Degos, J.-D. (2002). Visually- and motor-based knowledge of letters: evidence from a pure alexic patient. *Neuropsychologia* 40, 1363–1371. doi: 10.1016/S0028-3932(01)00209-3

Beery, K. E. (1997). *The Beery-Buktenica VMI: Developmental Test of Visual-Motor Integration with Supplemental Developmental Tests of Visual Perception and Motor Coordination: Administration, Scoring, and Teaching Manual.* Parsippany, NJ: Modern Curriculum Press.

Beery, K. E., and Beery, N. A. (2004). *The Beery-Buktenica Developmental Test of Visual-Motor Integration with Supplemental Developmental Tests of Visual Motor Integration and Motor Coordination and Stepping Stones Age Norms From Birth to Age Six: Administration, Scoring and Teaching Manual, 5th Edn.* Minneapolis, MN: NCS Pearson, Inc.

Benson, D. F. (1979). *Aphasia, Alexia, and Agraphia.* New York, NY: Churchill Livingstone.

Berninger, V. W., Dunn, A., Lin, S. C., and Shimada, S. (2004). School evolotion: scientist-practioner educators creating optimal learning environments for all students. *J. Learn Disabil.* 37, 500–508. doi: 10.1177/00222194040370060401

Berninger, V. W., Nielsen, K. H., Abbott, R. D., Wijsman, E., and Raskind, W. (2008). Writing problems in developmental dyslexia: under-recognized and under-treated. *J. Sch. Psychol.* 46, 1–21. doi: 10.1016/j.jsp.2006.11.008

Berninger, V. W., and Richards, T. (2011). Inter-relationships among behavioral markers, genes, brain and treatment in dyslexia and dysgraphia. *Future Neurol.* 5, 591–617. doi: 10.2217/fnl.10.22

Berninger, V. W., Rutberg, J. E., Abbott, R. D., Garcia, N., Anderson-Youngstrom, M., Brooks, A., et al. (2006a). Tier 1 and Tier 2 early interventions for handwriting and composing. *J. Sch. Psychol.* 44, 3–30. doi: 10.1016/j.jsp.2005.12.003

Berninger, V. W., and Winn, W. (2006b). "Implications of advancements in brain research and technology for writing development, writing instruction, and educational evolution," in *Handbook of Writing Research,* eds C. MacArthur, S. Graham, and J. Fitzgerald (New York, NY: Guilford Press), 96–114.

Byrne, B., Coventry, W. L., Olson, R. K., Hulslander, J., Wadsworth, S., DeFries, J. C., et al. (2008). A behaviour-genetic analysis of orthographic learning, spelling and decoding. *J. Res. Read.* 31, 8–21. doi: 10.1111/j.1467-9817.2007.00358.x

Calvert, G. A., Brammer, M. J., Morris, R. G., Williams, S. C., King, N., and Matthews, P. M. (2000). Using fMRI to study recovery from acquired dysphasia. *Brain Lang.* 71, 391–399. doi: 10.1006/brln.1999.2272

Castles, A., and Coltheart, M. (2004). Is there a causal link from phonological awareness to success in learning to read? *Cognition* 91, 77–111. doi: 10.1016/S0010-0277(03)00164-1

Cohen, L., and Dehaene, S. (2004). Specialization within the ventral stream: the case for the visual word form area. *Neuroimage* 22, 466–476. doi: 10.1016/j.neuroimage.2003.12.049

Cohen, L., Dehaene, S., Naccache, L., Lehéricy, S., Dehaene-Lambertz, G., Hénaff, M. A., et al. (2000). The visual word form area: spatial and temporal characterization of an initial stage of reading in normal subjects and posterior split-brain patients. *Brain* 123(Pt. 2), 291–307. doi: 10.1093/brain/123.2.291

Dehaene, S., Cohen, L., Sigman, M., and Vinckier, F. (2005). The neural code for written words: a proposal. *Trends Cogn. Sci.* 9, 335–341. doi: 10.1016/j.tics.2005.05.004

Eckert, M. A., Leonard, C. M., Richards, T. L., Aylward, E. H., Thomson, J., and Berninger, V. W. (2003). Anatomical correlates of dyslexia: frontal and cerebellar findings. *Brain* 126(Pt. 2), 482–494. doi: 10.1093/brain/awg026

Embick, D., Marantz, A., Miyashita, Y., O'Neil, W., and Sakai, K. L. (2000). A syntactic specialization for Broca's area. *Proc. Natl. Acad. Sci. U.S.A.* 97, 6150–6154. doi: 10.1073/pnas.100098897

Exner, S. (1881). *Untersuchungen über die Localisation der Functionen in der Grosshirnrinde des Menschen.* Vienna: Wilhelm Braumüller.

Feder, K. P., and Majnemer, A. (2007). Handwriting development, competency, and intervention. *Dev. Med. Child Neurol.* 49, 312–317. doi: 10.1111/j.1469-8749.2007.00312.x

Freeman, F. N. (1959). A new handwriting scale. *Elementary Sch. J.* 59, 218–221. doi: 10.1086/459718

Gaillard, W. D., Hertz-Pannier, L., Mott, S. H., Barnett, A. S., LeBihan, D., and Theodore, W. H. (2000). Function anatomy of cognitive development: fMRI of verbal fluency in children and adults. *Neurology* 54, 180–185. doi: 10.1212/WNL.54.1.180

Glover, G. H., and Law, C. S. (2001). Spiral-in/out BOLD fMRI for increased SNR and reduced susceptibility artifacts. *Magn. Reson. Med.* 46, 515–522. doi: 10.1002/mrm.1222

Goodale, M., and Milner, D. (2005). *Sight Unseen.* Oxford: Oxford University Press.

Grafton, S. T., Fadiga, L., Arbib, M. A., and Rizzolatti, G. (1997). Premotor cortex activation during observation and naming of familiar tools. *Neuroimage* 6, 231–236. doi: 10.1006/nimg.1997.0293

Graham, S. (1982). Measurement of handwriting skills: a critical review. *Diagnostique* 8, 32–42.

Graham, S., and Weintraub, N. (1996). A review of handwriting research: progress and prospects from 1980 to 1994. *Educ. Psychol. Rev.* 8, 8–87. doi: 10.1007/BF01761831

Groen, M. A., Whitehouse, A. J. O., Badcock, N. A., and Bishop, D. V. M. (2012). Does cerebral lateralization develop? A study using functional transcranial Doppler ultrasound assessing lateralization for language production and visuospatial memory. *Brain Behav.* 2, 256–269. doi: 10.1002/brb3.56

Haier, R. J., Jung, R. E., Yeo, R. A., Head, K., and Alkire, M. T. (2004). Structural brain variation and general intelligence. *Neuroimage* 23, 425–433. doi: 10.1016/j.neuroimage.2004.04.025

Haier, R. J., Siegel, K. H., Nuechterlein, E., Hazlett, J. C., Wu, J. C., Paek J., et al. (1988). Cortical glucose metabolic rate correlates of abstract reasoning and attention studied with positron emission tomography. *Intelligence* 12, 199–217. doi: 10.1016/0160-2896(88)90016-5

Henson, R. N. A., Burgess, N., and Frith, C. D. (2000). Recoding, storage, rehearsal and grouping in verbal short-term memory: an fMRI study. *Neuropsychologia* 38, 426–440. doi: 10.1016/S0028-3932(99)00098-6

Hillis, A. E., Kane, A., Tuffiash, E., Beauchamp, N. J., Barker, P. B., Jacobs, M. A., et al. (2002). Neural substrates of the cognitive processes underlying spelling: evidence from MR diffusion and perfusion imaging. *Aphasiology* 16, 425–438. doi: 10.1080/02687030244000248

Hoeft, F., McCandliss, B. D., Black, J. M., Gantman, A., Zakerani, N., Hulme, C., et al. (2011). Neural systems predicting long-term outcome in dyslexia. *Proc. Natl. Acad. Sci. U.S.A.* 108, 361–366. doi: 10.1073/pnas.1008950108

Holland, R., Leff P., Josephs, O., Galea, J. M. M., Desikan, M., Price, C., et al. (2011). Speech facilitation by left inferior frontal cortex stimulation. *Curr. Biol.* 21, 1403–1407. doi: 10.1016/j.cub.2011.07.021

Holland, S. K., Plante, E., Byars, A. W., Strawsburg, R. H., Schmithorst, V. J., and Ball, W. S. (2001). Normal fMRI brain activation patterns in children performing a verb generation task. *Neuroimage* 14, 837–843. doi: 10.1006/nimg.2001.0875

James, K. H. (2010). Sensori-motor experience leads to changes in visual processing in the developing brain. *Dev. Sci.* 13, 279–288. doi: 10.1111/j.1467-7687.2009.00883.x

James, K. H., and Engelhardt, L. (2012). The effects of handwriting experience on functional brain development in pre-literate children. *Trends Neurosci. Educ.* 1, 32–42. doi: 10.1016/j.tine.2012.08.001

James, K. H., and Gauthier, I. (2006). Letter processing automatically recruits a sensory-motor brain network. *Neuropsychologia* 44, 2937–2949. doi: 10.1016/j.neuropsychologia.2006.06.026

Kaminsky, S., and Powers, R. (1981). Remediation of handwriting difficulties, a practical approach. *Acad. Ther.* 17, 19–25.

Kaplan, E., and Goodglass, H. (1981). "Aphasia-related disorders," in *Acquired Aphasia, 3rd Edn.,* ed M. T. Sarno (San Diego, CA: Academic Press), 309–333.

Karlsdottir, R., and Stefansson, T. (2002). Problems in developing functional handwriting. *Percept. Mot. Skills* 94, 623–662. doi: 10.2466/pms.2002.94.2.623

Katzir, T., Misra M., and Poldrack A. (2005). Imaging phonology without print: assessing the neural correlates of phonemic awareness using fMRI. *Neuroimage* 27, 106–115. doi: 10.1016/j.neuroimage.2005.04.013

Korkman, M., Kirk, U., and Kemp, S. I. (2007). *NEPSY II, 2nd Edn.* San Antonio, TX: PsychCorp/Pearson Clinical Assessment.

Lancaster, J. L., Rainey, L. H., Summerlin, J. L., Freitas, C. S., Fox, P. T., Evans, A. C., et al. (1997). Automated labeling of the human brain: a preliminary report on the development and evaluation of a forward-transform method. *Hum. Brain Mapp.* 5, 238–242. doi: 10.1002/(SICI)1097-0193(1997)5:4<238::AID-HBM6>3.0.CO;2-4

Lancaster, J. L., Woldorff, M. G., Parsons, L. M., Liotti, M., Freitas, C. S., Rainey, L., et al. (2000). Automated Talairach Atlas labels for functional brain mapping. *Hum. Brain Mapp.* 10, 120–131. doi: 10.1002/1097-0193(200007)10:3<120::AID-HBM30>3.0.CO;2-8

Liotti, M., Gay, C. T., and Fox, P. T. (1994). Functional imaging and language: evidence from positron emission tomography. *J. Clin. Neurophysiol.* 11, 175–190.

Longcamp, M., Anton, J.-L., Roth, M., and Velay, J.-L. (2003). Visual presentation of single letters activates a premotor area involved in writing. *Neuroimage* 19, 1492–1500. doi: 10.1016/S1053-8119(03)00088-0

Longcamp, M., Boucard, C., Gilhodes, J.-C., Anton, J.-L., Roth, M., Nazarian, B., et al. (2008). Learning through hand- or typewriting influences visual recognition of new graphic shapes: behavioral and functional imaging evidence. *J. Cogn. Neurosci.* 20, 802–815. doi: 10.1162/jocn.2008.20504

Longcamp, M., Zerbato-Poudou, M.-T., and Velay, J.-L. (2005). The influence of writing practice on letter recognition in preschool children: a comparison between handwriting and typing. *Acta Psychol.* 119, 67–79. doi: 10.1016/j.actpsy.2004.10.019

Lubrano, V., Roux, F.-E., and Démonet, J.-F. (2004). Writing-specific sites in frontal areas: a cortical stimulation study. *J. Neurosurg.* 101, 787–798. doi: 10.3171/jns.2004.101.5.0787

Maldjian, J. A., Laurienti, P. J., Kraft, R. A., and Burdette, J. H. (2003). An automated method for neuroanatomic and cytoarchitectonic atlas-based interrogation of fMRI data sets. *Neuroimage* 19, 1233–1239. doi: 10.1016/S1053-8119(03)00169-1

Marvin, C., and Ogden, N. (2002). A home literacy inventory: assessing you children's contexts for emergent literacy. *Except. Young Child.* 5, 2–10. doi: 10.1177/109625060200500201

Matsuo, K., Kato, C., Sumiyoshi, C., Toma, K., Duy Thuy, D. H., Moriya, T., et al. (2003). Discrimination of Exner's area and the frontal eye field in humans–functional magnetic resonance imaging during language and saccade tasks. *Neurosci. Lett.* 340, 13–16. doi: 10.1016/S0304-3940(03)00050-8

McCutchen, D. (1996). A capacity theory of writing: working memory in composition. *Educ. Psychol. Rev.* 8, 299–325. doi: 10.1007/BF01464076

Morecraft, R. J., Cipolloni, P. B., Stilwell-Morecraft, K. S., Gedney, M. T., and Pandya, D. N. (2004). Cytoarchitecture and cortical connections of the posterior cingulate and adjacent somatosensory fields in the rhesus monkey. *J. Comp. Neurol.* 469, 37–69. doi: 10.1002/cne.10980

O'Hare, A., and Khalid, S. (2002). The association of abnormal cerebellar function in children with developmental coordination disorder and reading difficulties. *Dyslexia* 8, 234–248. doi: 10.1002/dys.230

Otsuki, M., Soma, Y., Arai, T., Otsuka, A., and Tsuji, S. (1999). Pure apraxic agraphia with abnormal writing stroke sequences: report of a Japanese patient with a left superior parietal haemorrhage. *J. Neurol. Neurosurg. Psychiatr.* 66, 233–237. doi: 10.1136/jnnp.66.2.233

Paulesu, E., Frith, C., and Frackowiak, R. (1993). The neural correlates of the verbal component of work- ing memory. *Nature* 362, 342–345. doi: 10.1038/362342a0

Petrides, M., and Pandya, D. N. (1984). Projections to the frontal cortex from the posterior parietal region in the rhesus monkey. *J. Comp. Neurol.* 228, 105–116. doi: 10.1002/cne.902280110

Planton, S., Jucla, M., Roux F-E., and Demonet, J.-F. (2013). The "handwriting brain": a meta-analysis of neuroimaging studies of motor versus orthographic processes. *Cortex* 49, 2772–2787. doi: 10.1016/j.cortex.2013.05.011

Price, C. J. (2010). The anatomy of language: a review of 100 fMRI studies published in 2009. *Ann. N. Y. Acad. Sci.* 1191, 62–88. doi: 10.1111/j.1749-6632.2010.05444.x

Pugh, K. R., Mencl, W. E., Jenner, A. R., Katz, L., Frost, S. J., Lee, J. R., et al. (2001). Neurobiological studies of reading and reading disability. *J. Commun. Disord.* 34, 479–492. doi: 10.1016/S0021-9924(01)00060-0

Purcell, J. J., Turkeltaub, P. E., Eden, G. F., and Rapp, B. (2011). Examining the central and peripheral processes of written word production through meta-analysis. *Front. Psychol.* 2:239. doi: 10.3389/fpsyg.2011.00239

Racine, M. B., Majnemer, A., Shevell, M., and Snider, L. (2008). Handwriting performance in children with attention deficit hyperactivity disorder (ADHD). *J. Child Neurol.* 23, 399–406. doi: 10.1177/0883073807309244

Rapp, B., and Dufor, O. (2011). The neurotopography of written word production: an fMRI investigation of the distribution of sensitivity to length and frequency. *J. Cogn. Neurosci.* 23, 4067–4081. doi: 10.1162/jocn_a_00109

Reynolds, C. R., and Kamphaus, R. W. (2006). *Behavior Assessment System for Children – Second Edition (BASC-2), Self-Report of Personality Interview Edition (SRP-I).* Circle Pines, MN: American Guidance Service.

Richards, T. L., Aylward, E., Berninger, V. W., Field, K., Parsons, A., Richards, A., et al. (2006a). Individual fMRI activation in orthographic mapping and morpheme mapping after orthographic or morphological spelling treatment in child dyxlexics. *J. Neurolinguistics* 22, 58–86. doi: 10.1016/j.jneuroling.2005.07.003

Richards, T. L., Aylward, E., Raskind, W., Abbott, R., Field, K., Parsons, A., et al. (2006b). Converging evidence for triple word form theory in dyslexia. Special Issue on Brain Imaging. *Dev. Neuropsychol.* 30, 547–589. doi: 10.1207/s15326942dn3001_3

Richards, T. L., Berninger, V. W., and Fayol, M. (2009a). "The writing brain of normal child writers and children with writing disabilities: generating ideas and transcribing them through the orthographic loop," in *Writing: A Mosaic of Perspectives and Views,* eds E. Grigorenko, E. Mambrino, and D. Preiss (New York, NY: Psychology Press), 85–105.

Richards, T. L., Berninger, V. W., and Fayol, M. (2009b). fMRI activation differences between 11-year-old good and poor spellers' access in working memory to temporary and long-term orthographic representations. *J. Neurolinguistics* 22, 327–353. doi: 10.1016/j.jneuroling.2008.11.002

Richards, T. L., Berninger, V. W., Stock, P., Altemeier, L., Trivedi, P., and Maravilla, K. R. (2011). Differences between good and poor child writers on fMRI contrasts for writing newly taught and highly practiced letter forms. *Read. Writ.* 24, 493–516. doi: 10.1007/s11145-009-9217-3

Ritaccio, A. L., Hickling, E. J., and Ramani, V. (1992). The role of dominant premotor cortex and grapheme to phoneme transformation in reading epilepsy. A neuroanatomic, neurophysiologic, and neuropsychological study. *Arch. Neurol.* 49, 933–939. doi: 10.1001/archneur.1992.00530330055016

Rizzolatti, G., Camarda, R., Fogassi, L., Gentilucci, M., Luppino, G., and Matelli, M. (1988). Functional organization of inferior area 6 in the macaque monkey. II. Area F5 and the control of distal movements. *Exp. Brain Res. Experimentelle Hirnforschung. Expérimentation cérébrale* 71, 491–507. doi: 10.1007/BF00248742

Rothlein, D., and Rapp, B. (2014). The similarity structure of distributed neural responses reveals the multiple representations of letters. *NeuroImage* 89, 331–344. doi: 10.1016/j.neuroimage.2013.11.054

Roux, F.-E., Draper, L., Köpke, B., and Démonet, J.-F. (2010). Who actually read Exner? Returning to the source of the frontal "writing centre" hypothesis. *Cortex* 46, 1204–1210. doi: 10.1016/j.cortex.2010.03.001

Roux, F.-E., Dufor, O., Giussani, C., Wamain, Y., Draper, L., Longcamp, M., et al. (2009). The graphemic/motor frontal area Exner's area revisited. *Ann. Neurol.* 66, 537–545. doi: 10.1002/ana.21804

Sakurai, Y., Onuma, Y., Nakazawa, G., Ugawa, Y., Momose, T., Tsuji, S., et al. (2007). Parietal dysgraphia: characterization of abnormal writing stroke sequences, character formation and character recall. *Behav. Neurol.* 18, 99–114. doi: 10.1155/2007/906417

Sassoon, R. (2007). *Handwriting of the Twentieth Century.* Bristol: Intellect Books.

Segal, E., and Petrides, M. (2012). The anterior superior parietal lobule and its interactions with language and motor areas during writing. *Eur. J. Neurosci.* 35, 309–322. doi: 10.1111/j.1460-9568.2011.07937.x

Seki, K., Yajima, M., and Sugishita, M. (1995). The efficacy of kinesthetic reading treatment for pure alexia. *Neuropsychologia* 33, 595–609. doi: 10.1016/0028-3932(94)00138-F

Simner, M. L. (1998). An empirically derived basis for using geometric-form copy tasks to identify kindergarten children at risk for early school failure. *Can. J. Sch. Psychol.* 13, 61–76. doi: 10.1177/082957359801300206

Stewart, S. (1992). "Development of written language proficiency: methods for teaching text structure," in *Communication Skills and Classroom Success,* ed C. S. Simon (Eau Claire, WI: Thinking Publications), 419–432.

Szaflarski, J. P., Holland, S. K., Schmithorst, V. J., and Byars, A. W. (2006), fMRI study of language lateralization in children and adults. *Hum. Brain Mapp.* 27, 202–212. doi: 10.1002/hbm.20177

Talairach J., and Tournoux P. (1988). *Co-planar Stereotaxic Atlas of the Human Brain.* New York, NY: Thieme.

Tzourio-Mazoyer, N., Landeau, B., Papathanassiou, D., Crivello, F., Etard, O., Delcroix, N., et al. (2002). Automated anatomical labeling of activations in SPM using a macroscopic anatomical parcellation of the MNI MRI single-subject brain. *Neuroimage* 15, 273–289. doi: 10.1006/nimg.2001.0978

Wagner, R. K., Puranik, C. S., Foorman, B., Foster, E., Wilson, L. G., Tschinkel, E., et al. (2011). Modeling the development of written language. *Read. Writ.* 24, 203–220. doi: 10.1007/s11145-010-9266-7

Wagner, R. K., Torgesen, J. K., and Rashotte, C. A. (1999). *Comprehensive Test of Phonological Processing (CTOPP).* Austin, TX: Pro-Ed.

Woodcock, W., Kevin, S., Mather, M., and Mather, N. (2001). *Woodcock-Johnson Tests of Achievement (WJ III).* Itasca, IL: Riverside Publishing.

Ziviani, J., and Elkins, J. (1984). An evaluation of handwriting performance. *Educ. Rev.* 36, 249–261. doi: 10.1080/0013191840360304

15

Order short-term memory is not impaired in dyslexia and does not affect orthographic learning

Eva Staels and Wim Van den Broeck*

Department of Clinical and Lifespan Psychology, Faculty of Psychology and Educational Sciences, Vrije Universiteit Brussel, Brussels, Belgium

***Correspondence:**
Wim Van den Broeck, Faculty of Psychology and Educational Sciences, Vrije Universiteit Brussel, Pleinlaan 2, 1050 Brussel, Belgium
e-mail: willem.van.den.broeck@vub.ac.be

This article reports two studies that investigate short-term memory (STM) deficits in dyslexic children and explores the relationship between STM and reading acquisition. In the first experiment, 36 dyslexic children and 61 control children performed an item STM task and a serial order STM task. The results of this experiment show that dyslexic children do not suffer from a specific serial order STM deficit. In addition, the results demonstrate that phonological processing skills are as closely related to both item STM and serial order STM. However, non-verbal intelligence was more strongly involved in serial order STM than in item STM. In the second experiment, the same two STM tasks were administered and reading acquisition was assessed by measuring orthographic learning in a group of 188 children. The results of this study show that orthographic learning is exclusively related to item STM and not to order STM. It is concluded that serial order STM is not the right place to look for a causal explanation of reading disability, nor for differences in word reading acquisition.

Keywords: dyslexia, short-term memory, serial order, reading acquisition, orthographic learning, phonological processing

INTRODUCTION

Developmental dyslexia is commonly defined as a disability characterized by low reading achievement and deficiencies in learning to spell and write (Snowling, 2012). Since the beginning of the research into dyslexia, a number of causal hypotheses have been formulated. The most dominant theory attributes the specific problems associated with dyslexia to a phonological processing deficit (for reviews, see Stanovich and Siegel, 1994; Vellutino et al., 2004; Ziegler and Goswami, 2005). However, based on the observations that dyslexic persons often show impairments on a wider variety of cognitive tasks, some researchers believe that the underlying cause of dyslexia should be situated in a more general process. Recently several new causal hypotheses have been formulated. Ahissar and co-authors proposed the anchoring-deficit hypothesis (Ahissar et al., 2006) which suggests that dyslexics have a general difficulty in automatic extraction of stimulus regularities from auditory inputs. Also recently formulated is the visual attention span hypothesis which proposes that difficulties in processing visual elements simultaneously is at least one cause of dyslexia (Bosse et al., 2007), and according to the visual crowding hypothesis, dyslexics are impaired in recognizing a target due to the presence of neighboring objects in the peripheral visual field (Spinelli et al., 2002). Again another hypothesis has been put forward that attributes the problems of dyslexics to a deficit in the perceptual experience of rhythmic timing (Goswami et al., 2002). All these hypotheses about the underlying deficit in dyslexia have mainly been investigated in one research group. On the one hand, this proliferation of causal theories is an exciting and positive feature of contemporary dyslexia research, but on the other hand there is also a dire need for critical replication studies. One of the most recent causal hypotheses of dyslexia attributes the specific problems of dyslexics to a general problem with learning serial order information, or at least to an additional serial learning problem. As learning to read words can be understood as the acquisition of grapheme and phoneme sequences, these researchers suggest that people with dyslexia have a specific deficit in serial order learning. This idea has been investigated by two groups of researchers. First, there is a group of researchers who consider that dyslexics experience difficulties with the consolidation or transfer of serial order information, initially stored in short-term memory (STM), into a stable long-term memory trace. Szmalec et al. (2011) reported empirical evidence for this hypothesis by showing a deficient Hebb repetition effect in dyslexic individuals, even for non-verbal modalities. However, these results could not be confirmed in a recent replication of this study including some methodological improvements (Staels and Van den Broeck, in press). As the results of this replication study show that dyslexics do not suffer from a specific deficit in the consolidation of serial order information in long-term memory, we may wonder whether the problem with storing serial order information is actually not situated in long-term memory but rather in STM. This idea has already been investigated by Martinez Perez and co-authors (Martinez Perez et al., 2012b, 2013) and will also be the main research question of the current study. We will first discuss recent studies and the underlying theoretical assumptions regarding STM deficits in dyslexia. Afterwards, we will also focus on the relationship between STM and reading development.

Martinez Perez and co-authors (Martinez Perez et al., 2012b, 2013) investigated whether the verbal STM deficits often reported in dyslexia can be explained exclusively by the poor phonological processing abilities that characterize dyslexia or whether dyslexics in fact suffer from an additional deficit at the level of serial order STM. Previously, verbal STM deficits in dyslexia had been mainly investigated using tasks that confounded item and serial order information recall (Kramer et al., 2000; Tijms, 2004). Hence, it was not clear whether the poor performance of dyslexic children on these tasks is due to a specific deficit in item STM, order STM, or both. Some recent STM models (Henson, 1998; Brown et al., 1999; Burgess and Hitch, 1999; Gupta, 2003) suggested that verbal item information is stored via temporary activation of phonological and lexo-semantic representations in the language network. Hence, storage of item information would depend directly on the quality of phonological representations in long-term memory and it would only be logical that this is impaired in dyslexia. On the other hand, storage of serial order information would occur via a language-independent system and should therefore be less sensitive to verbal long-term memory representations. Martinez Perez et al. (2012b) argued that if dyslexics would not only show impairments in item STM but would also show impairments in serial order STM, this deficit could not be explained by exclusively referring to poor phonological processing abilities but would be the result of a specific deficit of serial order STM. To investigate this hypothesis they used the distinction between STM for item information and STM for serial order information. In their first seminal study (Martinez Perez et al., 2012b), they administered two tasks designed to maximize either serial order or item retention abilities in a group of dyslexic children, a chronological age-matched group and a reading-level matched group. To assess item retention capacity a non-word delayed repetition task was constructed. In every trial a non-word was presented auditorily to the participants. Participants had to repeat the non-word after a period of time during which they had to perform a distractor task. To assess serial order retention capacity a serial order reconstruction task was administered. For this task in every trial participants had to remember sequences of two to seven real words that were also presented auditorily. Afterwards they were instructed to arrange pictures of these real words in the exact same order as they were presented. The researchers observed that children with dyslexia showed not only impairments on STM for item information but also on STM for serial order information. They concluded that the impairment on STM for serial order information was the most severe since the dyslexic group showed significantly lower performance on the serial order STM task relative to both the age-matched and the reading-level matched control groups, whereas the item STM impairment was only apparent relative to the chronological age-matched control group. In a second study, Martinez Perez et al. (2013) conducted a similar study as the one described previously, but this time they selected a group of adult dyslexics and a chronological age-matched control group without any reading problems. After observing item and serial order STM deficits in the dyslexic group in their first experiment by using the same tasks as in their first study, in a second and third experiment they assessed item and serial order STM retention capacities within the same STM task trying to make a more direct comparison. Additionally, in the third experiment they attempted to equate task sensitivity (difficulty) of item and serial order memory assessments. Again, the authors reported item and serial order STM deficits in the dyslexic group and most importantly they observed that the deficit was stronger at the level of order retention capacities.

As Martinez Perez and co-authors suggest that dyslexia is characterized by a specific deficit in serial order STM, they argue that this impairment in serial order retention capacity could have a negative effect on reading acquisition because learning to read new words can be understood as the acquisition of grapheme and phoneme sequences (Martinez Perez et al., 2012a). In a number of recent studies these researchers have explored the relation among item STM, order STM and language development. They observed that serial order STM capacity is a critical determinant of (oral) vocabulary knowledge and acquisition relative to item STM (Majerus et al., 2006a,b, 2008a,b; Leclercq and Majerus, 2010). Therefore, they argue that serial order STM capacity not only depends on a language-independent system but also appears to be important for the acquisition of new phonological representations (Martinez Perez et al., 2012a). In a recent longitudinal study, Martinez Perez et al. (2012a) investigated if this idea could also be extended to the acquisition of reading and, more precisely, to the acquisition of decoding processes. They investigated the relationship between item STM, order STM and reading development by administering an item and a serial order STM task at the age of kindergarten, and reading decoding ability was assessed 1 year later using a non-word reading task. They reported that serial order STM but not item STM predicted independent variance in reading decoding abilities. Based on the results of this study, the authors argue for a causal role of order STM capacity in reading acquisition.

The current study consists of two experiments. The first experiment will investigate STM deficits in dyslexic children by conceptually replicating the study of Martinez Perez et al. (2012b). However, the method they used will be modified as we believe that some adjustments can improve our study. The second goal of this study is to investigate the relationship between STM and reading acquisition. As STM for order information seems to play a specific role in reading decoding acquisition, order STM capacity could also be important for the acquisition of new long-term orthographic representations as Martinez Perez et al. (2012b) suggest. For that reason, in our second experiment we will use Share's (1995, 1999) self-teaching paradigm to assess reading acquisition. More information about the purpose and the theoretical background of the second experiment will be given in the introduction of Experiment 2. We will first continue by discussing our concerns about a number of methodological issues we encountered in recent studies. Afterwards, we present the methodological improvements we will introduce in our study to address these issues.

First of all we are concerned about the use of a reading-level match (RLM) design. Although this design is still used in some recent studies, it was formally proven that this method often entails methodological problems as it typically confounds diagnostic status with age (cf. Van den Broeck et al., 2010; Van den Broeck and Geudens, 2012; but see Zhou et al., 2014, for a notable exception in which a retrospective RLM-design is used comparing groups when they are at the same age).

In the RLM design of the Martinez Perez study, individuals with reading disabilities were matched with younger typical readers on a measure of reading ability (a text reading test). After this match both groups were compared on the two STM tasks and the researchers concluded that the dyslexic group had a specific deficit for serial order STM. However, Van den Broeck and Geudens (2012) have shown that a RLM design is likely to create processing deficit findings that may in fact be the result of the age differences between groups. One plausible scenario is that the group of older dyslexic readers reached the same reading score in the text reading test as the younger typical readers because they could rely on better word specific knowledge simply because they are older (for evidence see Van den Broeck et al., 2010). The younger normal readers on the other hand probably depended more on their decoding ability in order to reach the same performance level as the older dyslexic readers on the text reading task. This reasoning implies that the RLM matching procedure created an imbalance in decoding ability between both groups. As decoding ability is plausibly associated with the ability to remember order information, it is possible that the younger control group of normal readers only performed better on the serial order STM task as a result of the created imbalance by the design. To be sure that impaired serial-order learning in STM is a genuine characteristic of reading disability, a more direct comparison between typical and disabled readers of the same age is required.

Another methodological problem that occurs in many studies is the fact that researchers rely on the presence of a statistical interaction as evidence for a group related difference. In both studies of Martinez Perez et al. (2012b, 2013), they interpret their results in terms of an interaction effect between task (item memory vs. serial order memory) and group (dyslexic vs. age control group or RL control group). Although this interaction effect was not tested statistically they took the fact that the dyslexic group only showed a significantly lower performance than the reading-level matched control group on the serial order but not on the item STM task, as an indication that the serial order STM deficit was the most severe. The problem with this kind of interpretation is that researchers are usually unaware of the precise form of the relationship between the observed measures and the underlying constructs (Dunn and James, 2003). Therefore, it has been argued that relying on the presence of a statistical interaction as evidence for a qualitative group-related difference is not without problems (Loftus, 1985; Loftus et al., 1987, 2004). Even non-ordinal interaction effects can be made to disappear or reverse by applying a suitable monotonic non-linear transformation to the dependent variable (Bogartz, 1976; Loftus, 1978). This scale-dependency problem is still exacerbated in research where non-experimental variables such as age or pathology are involved because in such situations it is likely that an unspecific general factor influences performance (Kliegl et al., 1994). In the study of Martinez Perez et al. (2012b) one can easily imagine that an overall STM deficit could influence both STM tasks in an unequal manner (for an example of the effects of a general factor, see Van den Broeck and Geudens, 2012, p. 425). As a consequence, an observed interaction effect would be fictitious. This scale-dependency problem also arises when floor or ceiling effects occur in the data (Loftus, 1985).

A last methodological concern in the studies of Martinez Perez et al. (2012b, 2013) is the fact that they did not match their dyslexic and control groups on attentional functioning. Although the authors mention attentional functioning as a potential confounding factor, they refute this possibility by arguing that the order STM task was attentionally not more demanding than the item STM task because error rates were larger in the item STM task than in the order STM task. Furthermore, they convey that dyslexic participants with associated attentional impairment were excluded from the study and therefore they find it unlikely that attentional difficulties could explain the serial order STM impairment in the dyslexic group. However, as the comorbidity of developmental dyslexia and attention deficit disorders (ADHD) is a well-known fact (Araujo, 2012; Boada et al., 2012), and the serial order STM task is very demanding on sustained and focused attention, a serial order STM effect is not necessarily the result of a deficit in serial order retention, but may be attributed to the differential impact of comorbid attention problems on the two memory tasks (see also Wimmer's critique on the automatization deficit hypothesis, Wimmer et al., 1999). For this reason, any research aiming to compare a dyslexic group with a control group on cognitive processing should always make sure that both groups are matched on, or at least controlled for, attentional functioning.

As a result of these three major concerns we will adjust the method used by Martinez Perez et al. (2012b, 2013). To investigate whether dyslexics do suffer from a specific serial order learning deficit in STM it is crucial to make a direct comparison of serial order STM retention capacity when item STM retention capacity is equated between the dyslexic group and a control group of the same age. Indeed, a specific problem in serial order retention can only be proven by directly comparing dyslexic and typical individuals who score equally on the item retention task. When there is considerable overlap between the item retention scores of both groups, state trace analysis (STA) used as an equivalence method is an excellent technique to perform this comparison (see Van den Broeck and Geudens, 2012). In general, STA as a matching technique could be effectively adopted whenever a group showing a particular disorder has to be matched with a typical group, in order to test for a hypothesized specific deficit.

MATERIALS AND METHODS

EXPERIMENT 1

In Experiment 1 we investigated item and serial order STM capacities in a group of dyslexic and a group of control children matched on IQ and age.

Method

Participants. A total of 97 children of fourth and fifth grade participated in this study. Thirty-six children had an official diagnosis of dyslexia (20 boys and 16 girls) and 61 were IQ-matched control children without any reading problems (29 boys and 32 girls). Dyslexic participants were either diagnosed by an individual speech therapist or by a specialized center. The diagnoses were all based on three criteria which are used by the Stichting Dyslexie Nederland (2008) (Foundation Dyslexia Netherlands): (1) reading and/or spelling abilities are significantly below the level of performance expected for their age, that is below percentile 10; (2) resistance to instruction despite effective teaching; (3) impairment cannot be explained by extraneous factors, such as sensory deficits. For further validation two norm-referenced Dutch word reading tests that are diagnostic for dyslexia were administered. The first test is the One Minute Test (OMT; Brus and Voeten, 1973), a word reading test in which participants are instructed to read aloud as many words correctly as possible within 1 min. The test consists of 116 real words (nouns, verbs, adjectives, etc.). These words are ordered from lower to higher reading difficulty degree. The second test is the Klepel (Van den Bos et al., 1994), a non-word reading test in which participants are instructed to read aloud as many non-words correctly as possible within 2 min. This test consists of 116 non-words of increasing difficulty. For both reading tests the raw score is the number of words read correctly. In addition to the reading tests, we administered several phonological processing tasks to characterize reading-related skills of both groups. These tests consisted of a phonological awareness task, a phonemic discrimination task and a rapid automatized color and digit naming task (Van den Bos and lutje Spelberg, 2007).

To match the dyslexic and the control groups on IQ, a short-form IQ measure was used including a verbal comprehension subtest (Vocabulary) and a perceptual reasoning subtest (Block design) of the Wechsler Intelligence Scale for Children III (Dutch version) (Wechsler et al., 2005). We also included the Dutch ADHD questionnaire (AVL) (Scholte and Van der Ploeg, 2005) to examine attentional functioning. The questionnaire results in two partial scores: a measure of attentional functioning and a measure of impulsiveness and hyperactivity. As we were only interested in attentional functioning, we only used the partial score on attentional functioning. The questionnaire was completed by the teacher of the participant. **Table 1** shows that the experimental group and the control group only differed on the two measures that are diagnostic for dyslexia and on two of the phonological processing tasks. The dyslexic group also showed higher scores on the attentional functioning questionnaire but this difference just missed statistical significance.

All children attended regular elementary schools, located in Flanders (Dutch-speaking part of Belgium). Most children were from indigenous families (60%) and children from foreign origins were mainly of Moroccan descent. All children were checked and had sufficient command of the Dutch language to be able to study the Dutch curriculum. Two test assistants were instructed to perform this study.

Experimental design and procedure. Testing took place on an individual basis in a quiet classroom at the participant's school. The experimental procedure consisted of two test phases. Each test phase lasted approximately 40 min. All tasks were administered in a fixed order to ensure that the test situation was the same for every participant. During the first session the Block design subtest of the WISC, the OMT, the Klepel, the Serial order STM task and the phonological awareness task were administered. During the second session the Vocabulary subtest of the WISC, the item information STM task, the phonemic discrimination task and the rapid automatized color and digit tasks were administered. All computerized experiments were programmed and presented on a laptop computer using Microsoft Office PowerPoint (2007).

Table 1 | Characteristics of the dyslexic and control groups (means and standard deviations).

	Controls ($N = 61$)	Dyslexics ($N = 36$)	Group difference
Age (years)	10.53 (0.75)	10.75 (0.78)	$p = 0.192$
Word reading test (OMT) (raw score)	**59.44 (9.26)**	**46.06 (10.22)**	$p = 0.000$
Non-word reading test (Klepel) (raw score)	**66.33 (12.44)**	**43.78 (12.29)**	$p = 0.000$
WISC-III block design (standard score)	8.89 (3.15)	8.75 (3.02)	$p = 0.836$
WISC-III vocabulary (standard score)	8.52 (3.16)	8.11 (2.97)	$p = 0.526$
AVL teacher (ADHD questionnaire) (raw score)	6.36 (6.50)	9.28 (7.18)	$p = 0.054$
Phonemic discrimination (raw score)	**95.68 (3.47)**	**91.08 (5.73)**	$p = 0.000$
Phonological awareness (raw score)	**19.37 (3.55)**	**16.31 (4.80)**	$p = 0.002$
Rapid automatized color naming (raw score)	42.11 (9.96)	46.07 (11.00)	$p = 0.072$
Rapid automatized digit naming (raw score)	25.27 (4.12)	26.45 (5.14)	$p = 0.218$

Values in bold are statistically significant at $p = 0.05$.

Materials

Phonological processing tasks.

Phonemic discrimination task. Phoneme discrimination abilities were measured using a minimal pair discrimination task. One hundred pairs of nonsense CCV or CCCV syllables were constructed. Fifty pairs of syllables were identical (e.g., sta-sta), 25 pairs differed in one phonetic feature (e.g., dra-pra) and 25 pairs contained a phoneme transposition (e.g., spo-pso). Stimuli were digitally recorded by a female speaker and presented auditorily through headphones. Immediately after presenting a syllable pair, participants were asked to indicate whether both nonsense syllables were identical. The score was the total number of correct answers. Unidimensionality was tested by fitting a one-factor model on categorical data with MPlus 7.11 (Muthén and Muthén, 1998-2012). This model fitted the data well (chi square = 3809.11, $df = 3827$, $p = 0.585$; CFI = 1.00, RMSEA = 0.000). Cronbach's alpha was 0.795, indicating good reliability of the test scores.

Phonological awareness task. Phonological awareness abilities were assessed using a position analysis task. For this task, a list of 24 non-words was constructed as stimuli. Every non-word consisted of two syllables and had a length of six or seven letters. Stimuli were digitally recorded by a female speaker and presented auditorily through headphones. Immediately after presenting a non-word participants were asked to repeat the sound that came immediately before or after a target phoneme in the non-word indicated by the experimenter. Half of the items involved identifying the sound before and half after a target phoneme (e.g., which sound comes before "r" in "pristak"?; which sounds comes after "f" in "dreflo"?). The score was the total number of correct answers. A one-factor model fitted the data (chi square = 278.94, $df = 252, p = 0.117$; CFI = 0.943, RMSEA = 0.034). Cronbach's alpha was 0.837, indicating good reliability of the test scores.

Rapid automatized naming. To assess the speed of lexical access, we used two tasks from the CB and WL test (Van den Bos and lutje Spelberg, 2007), automatic color naming and automatic digit naming. The color naming task involved five colors (black, yellow, red, green, and blue), each presented 10 times. The digit naming task involved five digits (2, 4, 8, 5, 9), each presented 10 times. Each test card contained 50 items of the five colors/digits in random order presented in five columns. In both tasks participants were asked to name the colors/digits as quickly as possible. The score was the time participants needed to name all colors/digits irrespective of response accuracy. Reliability estimates offered by the authors of the test are very good (split half reliability for colors is 0.88 for 4the grade and 0.93 for 5th grade; for digits 0.80 for 4the grade and 0.89 for 5th grade).

Short-term memory tasks.

Item short-term memory task. As a measure of STM for item information we used a similar task as the delayed item repetition task of Martinez Perez et al. (2012b) and Leclercq and Majerus (2010). A list of 30 CVC non-words was constructed as stimuli (see Appendix A). To maximize the phonological processing demands of this task, stimuli were new and diphone frequency and phonological neighborhood were significantly lower relative to a representative sample of word stimuli. Stimuli were digitally recorded by a female speaker and presented auditorily through headphones to the participant. Each non-word was presented separately. Immediately after the presentation of an item, participants were asked to repeat the non-word to confirm that they had correctly perceived the item. After repeating the item, participants had to count in steps of 2 during 6 s. Afterwards participants were asked to repeat the item again. No feedback was given to the participants. The score was the number of correctly repeated items. A one-factor model fitted the data (chi square = 422.18, $df = 405$, $p = 0.268$; CFI = 0.931, RMSEA = 0.021). Cronbach's alpha was 0.783, indicating good reliability of the test scores.

The task was presented to the child as a game (Leclercq and Majerus, 2010):

> You are on an adventure in a castle. The castle has many doors which you have to open. In order to do so, you have to remember a password. You will hear the password through the headphones. The password is a word from a magic language you don't know. Pay close attention to the word and repeat the word out loud. Immediately afterwards start to count out loud by steps of two (0, 2, 4, 6, 8,...) until I say stop and ask you to repeat the password again. Okay?

Serial order short-term memory task. As a measure of STM for serial order information we used a similar serial order reconstruction task as Martinez Perez et al. (2012b) and Leclercq and Majerus (2010). Seven names of highly familiar animals (kat, hond, vis, beer, aap, leeuw, kip [cat, dog, fish, bear, monkey, lion, chicken]) were chosen to form lists with lengths ranging from two to seven items. All items were monosyllabic words and every item could only appear once in one trial. The trials were presented by increasing list length, with four trials for each length. The trials were digitally recorded by a female speaker and presented auditorily through headphones to the participant. At the end of each trial, participants received cards of the mentioned animals in random order and were asked to rearrange them in the same order as they were presented. In this task, retention requirements for serial order information were maximized by offering the participant only the cards which contained the pictures that represented the animals that were named in that trial and retention requirements for item information were minimized by using stimuli that were highly frequent and well known in advance. All participants completed all trials and sequence lengths. Since items within a series are correlated, a one-factor model with correlated errors for items belonging to the same series was fitted to the data (chi square = 796.89, $df = 700$, $p = 0.006$; CFI = 0.956, RMSEA = 0.038). Cronbach's alpha was 0.874. However, with correlated errors this index may underestimate or overestimate reliability (Raykov, 1998, 2001). A more conservative estimate is given by the Spearman-Brown coefficient, which was 0.702, indicating at least reasonable reliability of the test scores.

The experimenter presented the task as follows (Leclercq and Majerus, 2010):

> Every year, animals from all over the world gather to have a huge race. This year, seven animals are participating: a cat, a dog, a chicken, a lion, a fish, a bear, and a monkey [the experimenter shows the cards of the corresponding animals]. Several races take place. Sometimes only two animals are participating. Sometimes there are three, four, or five animals. At other times, there are big races with six or seven animals. Through the headphones, you will hear someone announce the animal's order of arrival at the finish line, from the first to the last animal. Immediately after I give you the cards with the animals, you have to put the pictures of the animals on the podium in their order of arrival. The animal arriving first has to be put on the highest step and the last one on the lowest step. Okay?

Results

First we analyze our data exactly as Martinez Perez et al. (2012b) did in their study. Afterwards we will address the methodological issues we mentioned before. For the item STM task we determined the proportion of items correctly repeated as the dependent variable (**Figure 1**). The mean proportion of items correctly repeated was significantly higher in the control group (67%) than in the dyslexic group (53%), $t_{(95)} = 4.192, p = 0.000$. For the serial order STM task we determined the proportion of correctly placed items by pooling over all trials as the dependent variable (**Figure 2**). The mean proportion of items correctly placed over all trials was significantly higher in the control group (71%) than in the dyslexic group (64%), $t_{(95)} = 3.200, p = 0.002$.

We also analyzed performance on the serial order STM task as a function of serial position to obtain a qualitative view of the serial order retention process. As we noticed that all participants

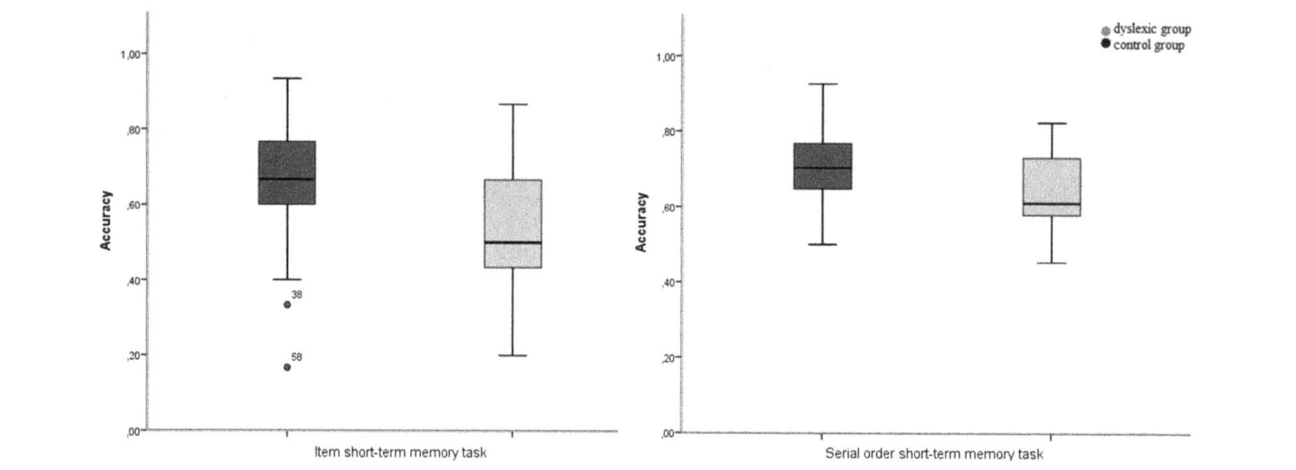

FIGURE 1 | Boxplot of performance on the item and serial order short-term memory tasks as a function of group (proportion correct).

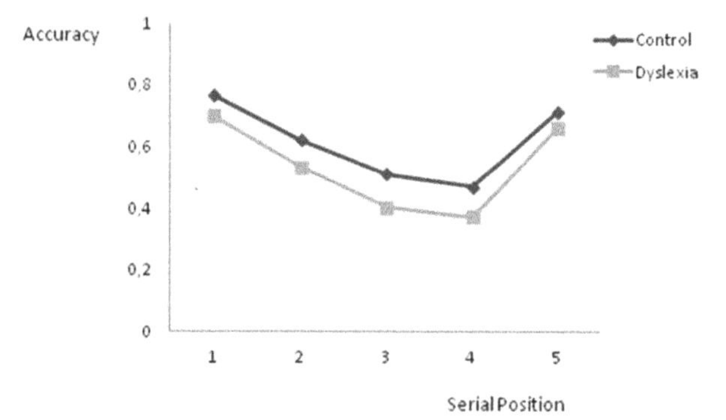

FIGURE 2 | Proportion of correct responses on the serial order short-term memory task as a function of group and serial position.

obtained a maximum score on all trials of with length of 2, 3, and 4, we restricted our analyses to list lengths of 5–7 to avoid floor effects. To increase the sensitivity of the analysis we combined serial positions 4 and 5 of list length 6 and serial positions 3 and 4 as well as 5 and 6 of list length 7. This means that we used the scores on the five positions of list length 5, and for list length 6 five scores were assembled (score on items in position 1, score on items in position 2, score on items in position 3, mean score on items in positions 4 and 5 and score on items in position 6) and for list length 7 also five scores were constructed (total score on items in position 1, total score on items in position 2, mean score on items in positions 3 and 4, mean score on items in positions 5 and 6 and score on items in position 7). Consequently, scores on five serial positions were entered into the analysis. **Figure 2** shows the proportion of correct responses as a function of group and serial position. A repeated measurements ANOVA revealed significant main effects of group, $F_{(1,\ 95)} = 8.610$, $p = 0.004$, and serial position, $F_{(4,\ 92)} = 176.532$, $p = 0.000$. No group by serial position interaction effect was found, $F_{(4,\ 92)} = 1.372$, $p = 0.250$.

In order to verify whether reading disability affected one STM task after statistically controlling for the other memory task, we conducted analyses of covariance (ANCOVA). By entering a covariate into an ANOVA the covariance of this variable with the other independent variable(s) is removed before the influence on the dependent variable is determined. For the item STM task the effect of group remained significant when the performance on the serial order STM task was entered as a covariate, $F_{(1,\ 94)} = 8.587$, $p = 0.004$. This means that even if the reading groups are statistically equated on the performance on the serial order STM task, the effect of group on the item STM task still remains significant. This result was in line with the results of Martinez Perez et al. (2012b). However, in contrast with their results, for the serial order STM task the effect of group disappeared when the performance on the item STM task was entered as a covariate, $F_{(1,\ 94)} = 1.906$, $p = 0.171$. This implies that the difference between the dyslexic and control group on the serial order STM task is no longer statistically significant when differences on the item STM task are taken into account. This result demonstrates that the item STM task and the serial order STM task do not measure entirely independent processes.

Martinez Perez et al. (2012b) also predicted that item STM but not order STM should be related to phonological processing measures. In order to investigate their prediction, we performed a set of correlation analyses. We only report the correlations observed in the total group (virtually the same results were observed for the dyslexic and control groups when analyzed separately). The results of these analyses not only reveal significant correlations between item STM and both phonological tasks (phonemic discrimination and phonological awareness), but also between serial order STM and the phonological tasks (see **Table 2**). In fact, the latter were even somewhat larger. No significant correlations were observed between item STM or serial order STM and rapid automatized naming tasks. In contrast to the results of Martinez Perez et al. (2012b), our data show clearly that both item STM and serial order STM are related to phonological processing measures. Remarkably, serial order STM was significantly related

Table 2 | Correlations and partial correlations controlling for age (between brackets) between short-term memory tasks, phonological processing tasks, reading tests and IQ-subtests for all participants ($N = 97$).

	Item short-term memory		Serial order short-term memory	
Phonemic discrimination	**0.390 (0.397)**	$p = 0.000$	**0.443 (0.461)**	$p = 0.000$
Phonological awareness	**0.466 (0.474)**	$p = 0.000$	**0.546 (0.561)**	$p = 0.000$
Rapid automatized color naming	−0.061 (−0.042)	$p = 0.553$	−0.161 (− 0.087)	$p = 0.116$
Rapid automatized digit naming	−0.115 (−0.116)	$p = 0.262$	−0.094 (− 0.113)	$p = 0.358$
Word reading test (OMT) (raw score)	**0.473 (0.476)**	$p = 0.000$	**0.400 (0.426)**	$p = 0.000$
Non-word reading test (Klepel) (raw score)	**0.448 (0.461)**	$p = 0.000$	**0.359 (0.387)**	$p = 0.000$
WISC-III block design (standard score)	0.063 (0.061)	$p = 0.540$	**0.387 (0.357)**	$p = 0.000$
WISC-III vocabulary (standard score)	0.150 (0.165)	$p = 0.144$	**0.236 (0.228)**	$p = 0.020$

Values in bold are statistically significant at $p = 0.05$.

Table 3 | Characteristics of the dyslexic and control groups after matching on attentional functioning (means and standard deviations).

	Controls ($N = 41$)	Dyslexics ($N = 36$)	Group difference
Age (years)	10.63 (0.76)	10.75 (0.78)	$p = 0.530$
Word reading test (OMT) (raw score)	**59.34 (9.82)**	**46.06 (10.22)**	$p = 0.000$
Non-word reading test (Klepel) (raw score)	**66.32 (12.51)**	**43.78 (12.29)**	$p = 0.000$
WISC-III block design (standard score)	8.68 (3.09)	8.75 (3.02)	$p = 0.924$
WISC-III vocabulary (standard score)	8.37 (2.95)	8.11 (2.97)	$p = 0.707$
AVL teacher (ADHD questionnaire)	9.22 (6.14)	9.28 (7.18)	$p = 0.970$
Phonemic discrimination	**95.35 (2.65)**	**91.08 (5.73)**	$p = 0.000$
Phonological awareness	**18.83 (3.85)**	**16.31 (4.80)**	$p = 0.013$
Rapid automatized color naming	42.91 (11.26)	46.07 (11.00)	$p = 0.217$
Rapid automatized digit naming	25.34 (4.62)	26.45 (5.14)	$p = 0.325$

Values in bold are statistically significant at $p = 0.05$.

to both IQ-subtests, especially with block design, whereas item STM was not.

State trace analysis

We now analyze our data using STA as an improved matching design. In the analysis we present here, another methodological improvement is introduced. The dyslexic group and the control group were not only matched on intellectual functioning but on attentional functioning as well. By discarding 20 control subjects and no dyslexic subject from the initial sample, we obtained similar distributions for both groups on the attention questionnaire. As **Table 3** indicates, after this additional matching, the newly formed groups of dyslexic children and control children only differed on the two measures that are diagnostic for dyslexia and on the two measures of phonological processing.

Using STA, serial order STM performance can be compared directly between the two groups at each level of item STM performance. Compared to the traditional method of interpreting interaction effects by comparing group differences across tasks, STA is more sensitive to detect a specific serial order STM deficit because by matching dyslexic and control subjects on item STM performance, both groups are equated on STM processing without involving the crucial serial order information. After inspecting that both groups show substantial overlap on the item STM performance, serial order STM is regressed on performance on item STM separately for the dyslexic group and the control group. It is tested whether a single line is suitable to explain the data (the null model not including reading group) or whether two different lines (one for dyslexic children and one for control children) are needed to describe the relation between serial order STM performance and item STM performance (the full model). If a single line would fit the data, this would imply that the relation between serial order STM performance and item STM performance is not affected by dyslexia. If, on the other hand, two lines would fit our data better, and the one for dyslexic children would be situated lower than the one for control children, this would be direct evidence for a specific serial order STM deficit in dyslexic children[1].

In this analysis, for each participant item and serial order scores were averaged and then plotted against each other (see **Figure 3**). Then, we tested in a hierarchical regression analysis whether group contributed significantly to serial order STM after including item STM performance in the regression equation. This analysis showed that adding group as a predictor doesn't significantly improve fit [R^2 null model = 0.271 R^2 full model = 0.285; $\Delta R^2 = 0.014$; F change$_{(1, 74)} = 1.488$; $p = 0.226$].

Hence, the null hypothesis—that the state trace curves for the typical and for the disabled readers do not differ—could not be rejected. This means that if there was no difference between the curves of the two groups (if H0 is true) in reality, the probability of finding a difference as large as or even larger than in our sample is 0.23. As STA entails that the null hypothesis is in fact a substantive hypothesis, this number does not seem really convincing. Note that a non-significant result due to a lack of power must not be confused with support for the null hypothesis. What

[1]Although STA as a matching design is conceptually very similar to the idea of controlling for item STM capacity in an ANCOVA, ANCOVA or hierarchical linear regression analysis are only a few data-analytical techniques that can be used to apply the broader concepts of STA (see Prince et al., 2012).

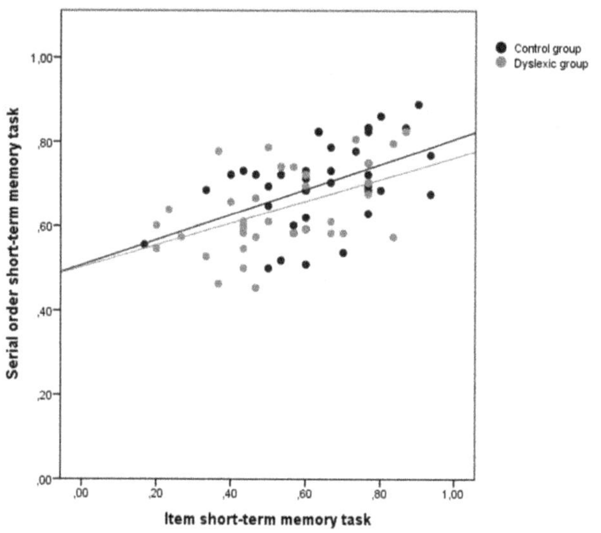

FIGURE 3 | State trace analysis with performance on the item STM task on the x-axis and performance on the serial order STM task on the y-axis (proportions correct).

we really want to know is the probability that the null hypothesis or the alternative hypothesis is true given the observed data (the inverse probability). To this end, a Bayesian analysis was performed in which the probability of the null model was compared to the probability of the full model given the data and given the assumption that no model was preferred above the other. For this comparison Bayesian Information Criteria (BIC) were calculated for both models. The BIC has been proposed by Raftery (1996) as an index to assess the overall fit of a model and allows a comparison of models (see also Long, 1997). Given that BIC assesses whether the model fits the data sufficiently well to justify the number of parameters that are used, the model with the lowest BIC is the best fitting, yet parsimonious model. The BIC-values indicated that the null model fitted the data best (BICnull = −144.88 and BICfull = −142.13). Based on the difference between these BIC-values the "Bayesian factor" could be calculated (Kass and Raftery, 1995). The Bayesian factor is equal to the posterior odds in favor of the most likely hypothesis. The posterior odds of the null model (MN) relative to the full model (MF) equal:

$$\frac{\text{Pr}\,(M_N/\text{Observed Data})}{\text{Pr}\,(M_F/\text{Observed Data})}$$

The Bayesian factor favoring the null model was 2.75. According to the criteria proposed by Kass and Raftery (1995), the data provided "positive" evidence for the null hypothesis.

EXPERIMENT 2

The results of a longitudinal study of Martinez Perez et al. (2012a) indicate that order STM abilities in kindergarten predict later reading decoding abilities. They make the stimulating suggestion that besides this specific contribution of order STM in reading decoding processes, order STM capacity might also be important for the acquisition of orthographic representations of new written words in long-term memory, and hence could be a major factor in reading development. Therefore, in this second experiment we will focus on the prediction of a differential role of item STM and serial order STM capacity in the orthographic learning of primary school readers over the entire range of reading ability. Additionally, we test the hypothesis that serial order STM would be impaired in a group of relatively poorer readers.

Item STM and order STM abilities were measured using the same tasks as used in Experiment 1. We also administered the same phonological awareness task as used in Experiment 1 to investigate whether item STM and serial order STM are related to phonological processing abilities. To assess reading and spelling ability, two word reading tests and a spelling test were administered. In addition, orthographic learning was assessed using Share's (1999) self-teaching paradigm. According to the self-teaching hypothesis (Share, 1995, 1999, 2004) children are able to acquire orthographic representations independently from an external teacher. Orthographic learning, the process through which orthographic representations are formed, consists of two independent processes. First, an unfamiliar written word is phonologically recoded into its spoken form by using known grapheme-phoneme associations. If this step succeeds, the phonological code of the word will be mapped onto its orthographic counterpart, establishing word-specific knowledge of the spelling of the new word. The self-teaching hypothesis was supported in a number of studies using an experimental paradigm adapted from Reitsma (1983). In these studies, target words were presented several (four or six) times in a natural text (Share, 1999). These targets were pseudowords representing a fictitious place, animal or fruit. Every pseudoword (e.g., yait) had an alternative homophone spelling (e.g., yate) and in each case only one spelling, the target spelling, was presented to the participant. Each participant was asked to read aloud the stories and to answer some questions about the content of the stories afterwards to ensure that they understood the text. Following Reitsma's (1983) procedure, orthographic learning was assessed 3 days after text reading using three types of measures: an orthographic choice task, a naming task and a spelling task. For the first measure, orthographic choice, children were asked to select the correct spelling of the target among the two homophone spelling alternatives. Secondly, children were instructed to read a list of words appearing on a computer screen as quickly and accurately as possible. The list of words contained all targets and their homophone spellings. Finally, the last test of orthographic learning required children to reproduce the target spelling in writing. The general outcome of studies based on this paradigm was that 3 days after independently reading the stories aloud, target spellings were recognized more often, named faster and spelled more accurately than their alternate homophone spellings. Relatively few successful identifications of an unfamiliar word appeared to be sufficient to acquire orthographic representations for young children (Hogaboam and Perfetti, 1978; Reitsma, 1983; Manis, 1985) and also for poor readers Staels and Van den Broeck (2013). Although most evidence for the self-teaching hypothesis is based on oral reading, recent studies have shown the appearance of orthographic learning in silent reading as well (Bowey and Muller,

2005; Bowey and Miller, 2007; de Jong and Share, 2007; de Jong et al., 2009). These findings provide important support for orthographic learning occurring in independent daily reading.

Method

Participants. One hundred and eighty eight third (38), fourth (93), and fifth (57) grade children participated in this study (96 boys, 92 girls). All children of entire classes were selected to participate in this study. Their age ranged from 7 years 11 months to 11 years 10 months, with a mean age of 9 years 6 months. All children attended regular elementary schools, located in several regions in Flanders and in urban and rural areas. Most children were from indigenous families (73%) and for 83% of the children their home language was Dutch. All children were checked and had sufficient command of the Dutch language to be able to study the Dutch curriculum. Four test assistants were instructed to perform this study.

Experimental design and procedure. The experimental procedure consisted of two phases. In the first test session a spelling test, based on the PI-dictee (Geelhoed and Reitsma, 1999) was administered for the entire class group. Afterwards the reading phase of Share's (1999) self-teaching paradigm was carried out. All students in the class were instructed to read all eight stories once in silence. They were encouraged to read the texts very attentively as they were warned that immediately after each text, two questions would be posed about the content of the stories to check text comprehension. All students were given enough time to read the texts and answer the questions at their own pace. This session lasted approximately 30 min. The second test phase took place on an individual basis in a quiet classroom at the participant's school. Two Dutch reading tests (OMT; Brus and Voeten, 1973 and the Klepel; Van den Bos et al., 1994), two measures of orthographic learning (orthographic choice task and orthographic spelling task), two STM tasks (serial order STM task and item STM task), the phonological awareness task and the Vocabulary subtest of the WISC-III (Dutch version) (Wechsler et al., 2005) were administered. All tasks were run in the indicated fixed order, except for the order of the two orthographic learning tasks which was counterbalanced across participants. All computerized experiments were programmed and presented on a laptop computer using Microsoft Office PowerPoint (2007).

We also included the Dutch ADHD questionnaire (AVL) (Scholte and Van der Ploeg, 2005) to examine attentional functioning in our experimental procedure. As we were only interested in attentional functioning, we only used the partial score on attentional functioning of the questionnaire. The questionnaire was completed by the teacher of the participant.

Materials

Spelling task. A spelling task was constructed based on the Dutch spelling test PI-dictee (Geelhoed and Reitsma, 1999). As children of the third, fourth and fifth grade participated in this study fifteen words were selected varying in difficulty. Five words to assess spelling in every grade were chosen from the PI-dictee. For every word a sentence in which the word occurs was read aloud by the test assistant. The word the participants had to write down was repeated afterwards. The score was the total number of correctly written words. A one-dimensional model fitted the data well (chi square $= 97.73$, $df = 90$, $p = 0.271$; CFI $= 0.993$, RMSEA $=$ 0.021). Cronbach's alpha was 0.827, indicating good reliability of the test scores.

Phonological awareness task. The same phonological awareness task as in Experiment 1 was used. A one-factor model fitted the data not quite well (chi square $= 303.49$, $df = 252$, $p = 0.0145$; CFI $= 0.929$, RMSEA $= 0.033$). After inspection of the modification indices, a two-factor model was fitted with all items requiring to give the phoneme(s) before the target phoneme loading in one factor, and all items requiring to give the phoneme(s) after the target phoneme loading in another factor (chi square $= 256.70$, $df = 251$, $p = 0.389$; CFI $= 0.992$, RMSEA $= 0.011$). Because the correlation of both factors was quite high ($r = 0.672$) and because both factors showed very similar correlations with all other tests, we decided to treat this test as measuring one concept. Cronbach's alpha was 0.835, indicating good reliability of the test scores.

Short-term memory tasks.

Item short-term memory task. The same item STM task as in Experiment 1 was used. Although a one-factor model with all items included fitted the data reasonably well, inspection of the factor loadings revealed that one item "pob" did not load significantly in this factor. Probably the reason for this is the fact that this item is phonetically not a non-word in Dutch. After removing this item in a one-factor model a nice fit was obtained (chi square $= 380.38$, $df = 377$, $p = 0.442$; CFI $=$ 0.995, RMSEA $= 0.007$). Cronbach's alpha was 0.803, indicating good reliability of the test scores.

Serial order short-term memory task. The same serial order STM task as in Experiment 1 was used. Since items within a series are correlated, a one-factor model with correlated errors for items belonging to the same series was fitted to the data (chi square $= 802.84$, $df = 700$, $p = 0.004$; CFI $= 0.955$, RMSEA $= 0.028$). Cronbach's alpha was 0.90. However, with correlated errors this index may underestimate or overestimate reliability (Raykov, 1998, 2001). A more conservative estimate is given by the Spearman-Brown coefficient, which was 0.639, indicating at least reasonable reliability of the test scores.

Self-teaching phase. The self-teaching phase of this study is based on Share's (1999) self-teaching paradigm. Eight short Dutch texts, similar to Share's (1999) stories, were composed for this study. All texts were adjusted to the overall reading level of the participants and ranged in length from 65 to 148 words (mean length 94). Targets were eight novel letter strings (pseudowords) representing a fictitious animal or person. Each target included two phonemes that could be represented by two alternate graphemes. These alternate letters occurred at various positions across target strings. The eight designed target quadruplets had a length of one or two syllables and ranged from five to seven letters. Four versions of each story were created, each employing one of the four homophone spellings of the following target quadruplets: Bleip/Blijp/Bleib/Blijb; Traug/Trauch/Troug/Trouch; Drouft/Droufd/Drauft/Draufd; Reilt/Reild/Rijlt/Rijld; Weipsik/Wijpsik/Weipzik/

Wijpzik; plijmap/pleimap/plijmab/plijmab; Kauwand/Kouwand/Kauwant/Kouwant; Hichtop/Higtop/Hichtob/Higtob. Each target appeared six times in one of the eight texts and once in one of the two comprehension questions. Texts were presented separately on A4 paper.

Orthographic learning tasks. Orthographic learning was assessed 1–7 days after the self-teaching phase with an orthographic choice task and a spelling task (Share, 1999).

Orthographic choice task. Participants were first asked a question to recall the target word (e.g., "Do you remember the name of the monkey who wanted to move to the zoo in the story?"). Each participant was then shown the four alternatives of the target word. The examiner presented a sheet of paper to the participant with the four alternate spellings of the target words written next to each other. The words were written in a random order. Participants were asked to choose the spelling of the pseudoword they had read in the story. The score on this task was the total number of items correctly chosen with a maximum score of eight.

Spelling task. Participants were asked to spell the target spelling of the animal or person they had read about in the story. If the participant could not recall the name of the target, the name was provided by the examiner. The score was the sum of the number of target graphemes written correctly within all pseudowords. This means that for every target word a score of 0, 1, or 2 was given with a maximum score of 16 on the entire task.

Results

Item and serial order STM. For the item STM task we determined the proportion of items correctly repeated. The mean proportion of items correctly repeated was 72%. For the serial order STM task the proportion of correctly placed items was determined by pooling over all trials. The mean proportion of items correctly placed over all trials was 73%. As in our first experiment, we performed an analysis on performance as a function of serial position to obtain a qualitative view of the serial order retention process. Again, we restricted our analyses to list lengths 5–7 and we combined serial positions 4 and 5 of list length 6 and serial positions 3 and 4 as well as 5 and 6 of list length 7. Consequently, five serial positions were entered into the analysis (see **Figure 4**).

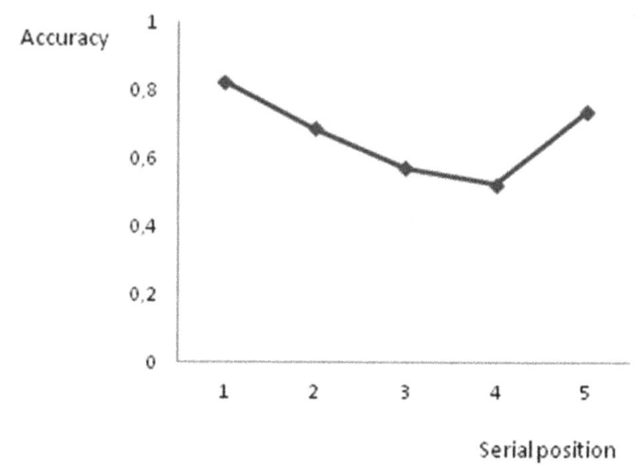

FIGURE 4 | Proportion of correct responses on the serial order short-term memory task as a function of serial position.

Orthographic learning. Because we used a silent reading procedure, it was not possible to determine the proportion of correctly decoded pseudowords. On the comprehension questions the mean proportion of correct answers was 93%, indicating that these questions were simple, yet effective to check whether the children read the texts carefully.

The dichotomous categorical (success/failure) data from the orthographic choice tasks were tested using a one-tailed t-test for the divergence of the predetermined chance-level proportion of 25%. We determined a chance level of 25% for the orthographic choice task because participants were forced to choose one of the four presented homophone foils. A random pick would therefore yield a score of 25%. For the orthographic spelling task participants were asked to write down the target pseudoword. As the pseudoword was provided auditorily by the experimenter, participants had a chance of 50% to write each of the two homophone graphemes that occurred in the pseudoword correctly. Hence, they had a chance of 25% to write both homophone graphemes correctly in every pseudoword. The overall proportion of correct choices on the orthographic choice task was 0.43 (SD = 0.20), which was significantly larger than the chance level proportion correct of 0.25, $t_{(186)} = 12.374$, $SE = 0.015$, $p = 0.000$, one-tailed. The proportion of correctly spelled target graphemes in the spelling task was 0.64 ($SD = 0.15$), which was also significantly larger than the proportion correct of 0.25, $t_{(186)} = 34.704$, $SE = 0.011$, $p = 0.000$, one-tailed. Summarized, these results demonstrate that target spellings were recognized more often and correctly spelled more often than chance level.

To investigate the relationship between STM and reading acquisition we performed a number of correlation analyses. **Table 4** shows that of the two orthographic learning measures only the orthographic choice task is related to item STM capacity. Serial order STM is clearly not related to orthographic learning. We even found a small but significant negative effect of serial order STM on the orthographic spelling task after controlling for item STM (beta = –0.168, $t = -2.17$, $p = 0.031$). **Table 4** also reveals significant correlations between both STM tasks and the phonological awareness task. The correlation between the phonological awareness task and serial order STM is almost as high as the correlation between phonological awareness and item STM.

Item and serial order STM in relatively poor readers and typical readers. We divided the group of participants in two groups based on their reading level. To define these groups, the mean of the standard scores of the two Dutch reading tests (OMT; Brus and Voeten, 1973 and the Klepel; Van den Bos et al., 1994) was taken. Participants who scored one standard deviation below this mean were assigned to the group of poor readers. All other participants were assigned to the group of typical readers. **Table 5** shows that the two groups differ on the two reading tests, on the attention

Table 4 | Correlations and partial correlations controlling for age (between brackets) between short-term memory tasks, orthographic learning tasks, spelling and reading tasks, vocabulary knowledge, and phonological awareness task for all participants ($N = 188$).

(Raw scores)	Item STM		Serial order STM	
Orthographic choice task	**0.160 (0.153)**	$p = 0.028$	−0.010 (−0.011)	$p = 0.887$
Orthographic spelling task	0.065 (0.055)	$p = 0.378$	−0.129 (−0.132)	$p = 0.079$
Phonological awareness	**0.477 (0.462)**	$p = 0.000$	**0.440 (0.444)**	$p = 0.000$
Spelling task	**0.337 (0.312)**	$p = 0.000$	**0.203 (0.213)**	$p = 0.005$
WISC-III vocabulary	**0.231 (0.198)**	$p = 0.000$	**0.282 (0.304)**	$p = 0.000$
Word reading test (OMT)	**0.434 (0.408)**	$p = 0.000$	**0.206 (0.206)**	$p = 0.004$
Non-word reading test (Klepel)	**0.356 (0.329)**	$p = 0.000$	0.101 (0.095)	$p = 0.167$

Values in bold are statistically significant at p = 0.05.

Table 5 | Characteristics of the group of poor readers and the group of typical readers (means and standard deviations).

	Typical readers ($n = 158$)	Poor readers ($n = 30$)	Group difference
Age (years)	9.44 (0.85)	9.71 (0.98)	$p = 0.127$
Word reading test (OMT) (raw score)	**59.92 (11.73)**	**36.70 (8.85)**	$p = 0.000$
Non-word reading test (Klepel) (raw score)	**62.94 (15.61)**	**32.23 (10.41)**	$p = 0.000$
WISC-III vocabulary (standard score)	10.68 (2.87)	9.90 (2.54)	$p = 0.168$
AVL teacher (ADHD questionnaire) (raw score)	**3.50 (4.73)** ($N = 156$)	**7.00 (5.96)** ($N = 30$)	$p = 0.000$
Phonological awareness	**20.97 (3.38)**	**17.53 (5.08)**	$p = 0.000$
Spelling task	**9.04 (3.26)**	**5.97 (2.68)**	$p = 0.000$
Orthographich choice task	3.50 (1.63)	3.10 (1.32)	$p = 0.218$
Orthographic spelling task	10.32 (2.49)	9.83 (2.30)	$p = 0.321$

Values in bold are statistically significant at p = 0.05.

questionnaire, on the phonological awareness task, the spelling task and on both STM tasks.

The mean proportion of items correctly repeated in the item STM task was significantly higher in the typical readers group (75%) than in the poor readers group (58%), $t_{(186)} = -5.371$, $p = 0.000$. For the serial order STM task, the mean proportion of items correctly placed over all trials was significantly higher in the typical readers group (74%) than in the poor readers group (69%), $t_{(186)} = -2.541, p = 0.012$.

In order to verify whether reading ability affected one STM task after statistically controlling for the other memory task, we conducted analyses of covariance (ANCOVA). For the item STM task as the dependent variable, the effect of group remained significant when the performance on the serial order STM task was entered as a covariate, $F_{(1,\ 185)} = 22.339, p = 0.000$. In contrast, for the serial order STM task as the dependent variable, the effect of group disappeared when the performance on the item STM task was entered as a covariate, $F_{(1,\ 185)} = 0.728, p = 0.395$. These results are similar to the results of our first experiment and demonstrate that the item STM task and the serial order STM task do not measure entirely independent processes. More specifically, when differences on the item STM task are taken into account, serial order STM differences between the reading groups disappear.

Table 6 | Characteristics of the group of poor readers and the group of typical readers after matching on attentional functioning (means and standard deviations).

	Normal readers ($N = 67$)	Poor readers ($N = 30$)	Group difference
Age (years)	9.36 (0.90)	9.71 (0.98)	$p = 0.085$
Word reading test (OMT) (raw score)	**56.64 (10.89)**	**36.70 (8.85)**	$p = 0.000$
Non-word reading test (Klepel) (raw score)	**60.58 (15.29)**	**32.23 (10.41)**	$p = 0.000$
WISC-III vocabulary (standard score)	9.70 (3.12)	9.90 (2.54)	$p = 0.761$
AVL teacher (ADHD questionnaire) (raw score)	7.05 (4.70)	7.00 (5.96)	$p = 0.968$
Phonological awareness	**20.96 (3.90)**	**17.53 (5.08)**	$p = 0.000$
Spelling task	**8.21 (3.21)**	**5.97 (2.68)**	$p = 0.001$
Orthographich choice task	3.18 (1.57)	3.10 (1.32	$p = 0.821$
Orthographic spelling task	9.85 (2.73)	9.83 (2.30)	$p = 968$

Values in bold are statistically significant at p = 0.05.

To directly compare serial order STM performance in both groups for each level of item STM performance, we analyze our data again using STA. First, the poor readers group and the typical readers group were not only matched on intellectual functioning but on attentional functioning as well. By discarding 91 normal readers and no poor readers from the initial sample, we obtained similar distributions for both groups on the attention questionnaire. As **Table 6** shows, after this additional matching, the newly formed groups of poor readers and typical readers differed on the two measures that are diagnostic for dyslexia, on the phonological awareness task and on the spelling task.

After inspecting that both groups show substantial overlap on the item STM performance, serial order STM is regressed on performance on item STM separately for the poor reading group and the typical reading group. In this analysis, for each participant item and serial order scores were averaged and then plotted

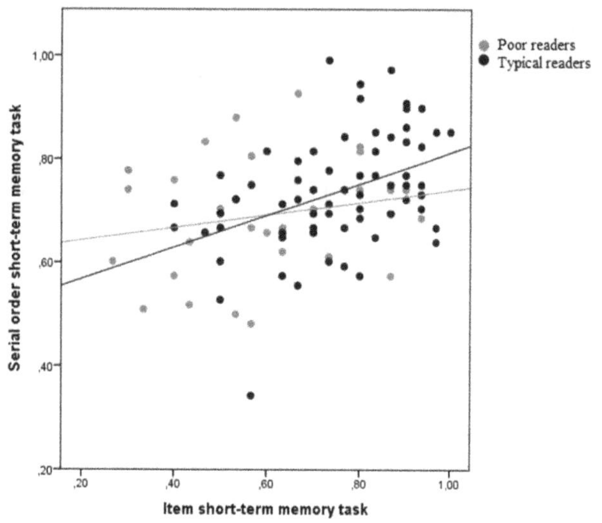

FIGURE 5 | State trace analysis with performance on the item STM task on the x-axis and performance on the serial order STM task on the y-axis (proportions correct).

against each other (see **Figure 5**). Then, we tested in a hierarchical regression analysis whether group contributed significantly to serial order STM after including item STM performance in the regression equation. This analysis showed that adding group as a predictor doesn't significantly improve fit [R^2 null model = 0.146 R^2 full model = 0.147; $\Delta R^2 = 0.001$; F change $_{(1, 94)} = 0.104$; $p = 0.747$]. Hence, the null hypothesis—that the state trace curves for the typical and for the disabled readers do not differ—could not be rejected. A Bayesian analysis was performed in which the probability of the null model was compared to the probability of the full model given the data and given the assumption that no model was preferred above the other. The BIC-values indicated that the null model fitted the data best (BICnull = 759.57 and BICfull = 764.04). Based on the difference between these BIC-values the "Bayesian factor" could be calculated (Kass and Raftery, 1995). The Bayesian factor favoring the null model was 4.47. According to the criteria proposed by Kass and Raftery (1995), the data provided "positive" evidence for the null hypothesis.

DISCUSSION

The main aim of Experiment 1 was to try to replicate the specific serial order STM deficit in dyslexic readers as reported by Martinez Perez and co-authors (Martinez Perez et al., 2012b, 2013). As our results showed, we were unable to detect a specific deficit in serial order STM capacity in dyslexic children. However, a potential limitation of this experiment is that many participants were in fact bilingual. Although all children were proficient in Dutch, as they typically attended Flemish (Dutch speaking) schools from first grade on, it is possible that the reading problems of the bilingual dyslexic children were partly affected by their bilingual status. To examine this potential confound of language background, the interaction effect of diagnostic category with language spoken at home (coded 1 for Dutch speaking children and 0 for all other children) was tested. This effect was not significant ($p = 0.33$) implying that the effect of being dyslexic or not on serial order STM performance was not different for bilingual children and monolingual Dutch speaking children. Moreover, when only the Dutch speaking children were included in the hierarchical regression analysis (13 dyslexic and 13 control), the group factor (being dyslexic or not) did not contribute significantly after controlling for item STM ($p = 0.14$). Likewise, in Experiment 2 no specific serial order STM deficit was detected in poor readers. Given that both experiments were designed with more power (larger samples sizes) than those of Martinez Perez et al. and with a direct comparison between item and serial order STM performance, using STA, we can be confident to conclude that the impairments in STM often reported in dyslexia are not due to a specific impairment in the retention of serial order information. Although it would be difficult to speculate on why the results of Martinez Perez and co-authors (Martinez Perez et al., 2012b, 2013) did show such a dyslexic deficit and our experiments did not, it seems that the use of STA enabled a more direct comparison of serial order STM performance after equating item STM performance between groups. The lack in their studies of a more stringent match on attentional functioning does not seem to be an important factor as the conclusions of our own studies were not different when we analyzed the entire original group of participants without matching on attention (not reported). Probably the match on item STM performance which is inherent in STA is already sufficient to match the groups on attentional functioning. The apparent instability of a serial order STM deficit in dyslexic individuals is also evident from two recent studies. Hachmann et al. (2014) found evidence for such a deficit in dyslexic adults whereas Binamé and Poncelet (2014) reported an item STM deficit in adult poor spellers as well as a serial order STM deficit. Based on the data of these authors we found that the serial order STM deficit disappeared after controlling for item STM performances[2]. Moreover, these authors could not find a deficient Hebb repetition effect in their sample of poor spellers. Everything being taken into account, would a serial order STM deficit in dyslexics be a robust phenomenon, one would have expected a more consistent pattern of results.

A second important conclusion that follows from both reported experiments is that the measurement of serial order STM is at least as strongly related to phonological processing as is the measurement of item STM. What do these results tell us about theories assuming the separability of both STM components, and about the role of phonology as a basis of reading (dis)ability? First, when the serial order STM task bears a phonological component (names of animals), even if the phonological demands are minimized, the relationship with phonological abilities proves to be at least as strong as is the case for item STM. This implies that the assumed disconnection between item and serial order STM processes does not coincide with the phonology/non-phonology distinction. On the other hand, our results are in agreement with the idea of Martinez-Perez and co-authors that both STM processes are partly independent. As the correlations between item STM performance and serial order STM performance are far below the reliability estimates of both tasks ($r = 0.50$ in Experiment 1

[2]We thank the authors for kindly providing their data for further analysis.

and $r = 0.34$ in Experiment 2), it is clear that serial order STM scores contain some unique variance that is not accounted for by item STM scores. There is both behavioral and neurological evidence that item information and sequence information are coded distinctly in STM. The recall of verbal item information is shown to be affected by psycholinguistic properties such as word frequency and semantic content, while recall of the order of the items is not (e.g., Saint-Aubin and Poirier, 1999; Nairne and Kelley, 2004). Moreover, neuroimaging studies have shown that the retention of item memory during STM-tasks is associated with activation of phonological and semantic processing areas in the bilateral temporal lobes, whereas non-linguistic brain areas in the right intraparietal sulcus are activated when processing order information in STM (Majerus et al., 2006b, 2008a, 2010). Quite interestingly, in Experiment 1 we found that serial order STM and not item STM shows a substantial correlation with block design of the WISC-III ($r = 0.38$ vs. $r = 0.06$). Martinez Perez et al. (2012a) reported a similar result ($r = 0.48$ vs. $r = 0.28$) for a group of Kindergarten children. Taken together, the evidence seems to indicate that the partial independence of both STM processes is not attributable to a difference in phonological involvement, but is a result of the influence of non-verbal intelligence processes in serial order STM. Apparently, reconstructing the serial order of a number of elements is aided by active higher order restructuring of the material, possibly involving a visuospatial component mediated by the right intraparietal sulcus (Van Dijck et al., 2013; for a review see Majerus, 2009). Theoretically, we think that item STM could be considered as a necessary condition for serial order STM, but not as a sufficient condition, since it needs an additional non-verbal intelligence component. To conclude this issue, serial order STM, as it is involved with higher-order intelligent processes, seems not to be the right place to look for an explanation of a deficiency in the acquisition of the "modular" word reading process (Stanovich, 1988, 1990).

Our finding of an equal contribution of phonological processes in both STM tasks could be interpreted as support for the phonological deficit hypothesis of dyslexia as it indicates that verbal STM deficits (for item or order information) often reported in dyslexia can be explained by the poor phonological processing abilities that characterize dyslexia. However, our findings do not prove that serial order STM *per se* is phonological in nature. It remains to be seen in further empirical research whether the relationship between serial order STM and phonological abilities has to be attributed to serial order processing as such, or to the phonological nature of the stimulus material. As we adopted the serial order STM task from the study of Martinez Perez et al. (2013) we used the same phonological stimuli as they did. Although this task minimizes phonological demands, it would be worthwhile to investigate the role of phonological processes in serial order STM by using a task with non-phonological stimuli. In a study on Hebb learning (Staels and Van den Broeck, in press), we observed a substantial correlation between serial order learning of abstract visual forms that could not be verbalized with pseudoword reading and real word reading. Although this finding is suggestive for a role of serial order learning *per se* in reading ability, further research has to determine whether this relationship persists if item STM for visual abstract forms is tested. We suggest using a design in which item vs. serial order STM tasks, and phonological vs. non-phonological item material are bifactorially manipulated.

The main purpose of Experiment 2 was to investigate which STM process, item memory or serial order memory, is most closely related to orthographic learning, the process by which a beginning reader stores the orthographic details of specific words. As the ability to decode unfamiliar written words into their spoken equivalent is the central means by which orthographic representations are acquired, Martinez Perez et al. (2012a) suggested that STM for serial order information could also be important for the acquisition of orthographic representations. Again the results were unambiguous. Only item STM was significantly related to orthographic learning, and only in the most sensitive test of orthographic learning, i.e., orthographic choice (see Staels and Van den Broeck, 2013). Serial-order STM capacity, on the contrary, did not show any positive relationship at all with orthographic learning. Congruent with these findings is the robust observation in both experiments that word reading ability is more strongly related to item STM than to serial order STM. Again, more research is needed to find out whether the nature of the stimulus material (phonological or not) influences this relationship.

It is important to note that in Experiment 2 we tested a novel prediction made by Martinez Perez et al. (2012a) concerning the role of serial order STM in orthographic learning, but no attempt was made to replicate their longitudinal study. Hence, our differing conclusions about the role of serial order STM may stem from the fact that we measured orthographic learning and serial order STM concurrently in already literate children, while Martinez Perez et al. (2012a) measured serial order STM in kindergarten and followed up the children for their reading ability at the end of first grade. Although there is ample evidence that (serial) phonological recoding constitutes the first step in orthographic learning (Share, 1995, 2008), it is possible that the role of serial order STM in orthographic learning is less pronounced in literate children than in beginning readers, because with increasing reading ability orthographic learning may depend more on already existing orthographic structures. However, the results of the two studies are probably more in accordance than at first sight appears. In the study of Martinez Perez et al. (2012a) serial order STM was not a stronger unique predictor of later non-word reading after controlling for item STM than item STM was after controlling for serial order STM (equal beta's). Only after additionally controlling for phonological awareness, serial order STM predicted somewhat more unique variance in non-word reading than item STM did, although the difference in the beta's (0.31 vs. 0.22) was not statistically tested and the proportion of explained unique variance (8%) was rather small. Clearly, more convincing empirical evidence is needed to sustain the hypothesis that serial order STM plays a substantial role in explaining reading (dis)ability.

REFERENCES

Ahissar, M., Lubin, Y., Putter-Katz, H., and Banai, K. (2006). Dyslexia and the failure to form a perceptual anchor. *Nat. Neurosci.* 9, 1558–1564. doi: 10.1038/nn1800

Araujo, A. P. (2012). Attention deficit hyperactivity disorder and dyslexia: a history of overlap. *Arq. Neuro Psiquiatr.* 70, 83–84. doi: 10.1590/S0004-282X2012000200001

Binamé, F., and Poncelet, M. (2014). "Orthographic learning skills and retention of order information in memory among adult good and poor spellers," in *Poster Presented at the 21th Conference of the Society for the Scientific Study of Reading* (Santa Fé, NM).

Boada, R., Willcutt, E. G., and Pennington, B. F. (2012). Understanding the comorbidity between dyslexia and attention-deficit/hyperactivity disorder. *Top. Lang. Disord.* 32, 264–284. doi: 10.1097/TLD.0b013e31826203ac

Bogartz, R. S. (1976). On the meaning of statistical interactions. *J. Exp. Child Psychol.* 22, 178–183. doi: 10.1016/0022-0965(76)90099-0

Bosse, M. L., Tainturier, M. J., and Valdois, S. (2007). Developmental dyslexia: the visual attention span deficit hypothesis. *Cognition* 104, 198–230. doi: 10.1016/j.cognition.2006.05.009

Bowey, J. A., and Miller, R. (2007). Correlates of orthographic learning in third-grade children's silent reading. *J. Res. Read.* 30, 115–128. doi: 10.1111/j.1467-9817.2007.00335.x

Bowey, J. A., and Muller, D. (2005). Phonological recoding and rapid orthographic learning in third-graders' silent reading: a critical test of the self-teaching hypothesis. *J. Exp. Child Psychol.* 92, 203–219. doi: 10.1016/j.jecp.2005.06.005

Brown, G., Vousden, J., McCormack, T., and Hulme, C. (1999). The development of memory for serial order: a temporal-contextual distinctiveness model. *Int. J. Psychol.* 34, 389–402. doi: 10.1080/002075999399747

Brus, B. T., and Voeten, M. J. M. (1973). *Eén-Minuut-Test. [One Minute Test].* Nijmegen: Berkhout.

Burgess, N., and Hitch, G. (1999). Memory for serial order: a network model of the phonological loop and its timing. *Psychol. Rev.* 106, 551–581. doi: 10.1037/0033-295X.106.3.551

de Jong, P. F., Bitter, D. J. L., van Setten, M., and Marinus, E. (2009). Does phonological recoding occur during silent reading and is it necessary for orthographic learning? *J. Exp. Child Psychol.* 104, 267–282. doi: 10.1016/j.jecp.2009.06.002

de Jong, P. F., and Share, D. L. (2007). Orthographic learning during oral and silent reading. *Sci. Stud. Read.* 11, 55–71. doi: 10.1207/s1532799xssr1101_4

Dunn, J. C., and James, R. N. (2003). Signed difference analysis: theory and application. *J. Math. Psychol.* 47, 389–416. doi: 10.1016/S0022-2496(03)00049-X

Geelhoed, J., and Reitsma, P. (1999). *PI-dictee.* Duivendrecht: Swets and Zeitlinger.

Goswami, U., Thomson, J., Richardson, U., Stainthorp, R., Hughes, D., Rosen, S., et al. (2002). Amplitude envelope onsets and developmental dyslexia: a new hypothesis. *Proc. Natl. Acad. Sci. U.S.A.* 99, 10911–10916. doi: 10.1073/pnas.122368599

Gupta, P. (2003). Examining the relationship between word learning, nonword repetition, and immediate serial recall in adults. *Q. J. Exp. Psychol. A* 56A, 1213–1236. doi: 10.1080/02724980343000071

Hachmann, W. M., Bogaerts, L., Szmalec, A., Woumans, E., Duyck, W., and Job, R. (2014). Short-term memory for order but not for item information is impaired in developmental dyslexia. *Ann. Dyslexia* 64, 121–136. doi: 10.1007/s11881-013-0089-5

Henson, R. (1998). Short-term memory for serial order: the start-end model. *Cogn. Psychol.* 36, 73–137. doi: 10.1006/cogp.1998.0685

Hogaboam, T. W., and Perfetti, C. A. (1978). Reading skill and the role of verbal experience in decoding. *J. Educ. Psychol.* 70, 717–729. doi: 10.1037/0022-0663.70.5.717

Kass, R. E., and Raftery, A. E. (1995). Bayes factors. *J. Am. Stat. Assoc.* 90, 773–795. doi: 10.1080/01621459.1995.10476572

Kliegl, R., Mayr, U., and Krampe, R. T. (1994). Time-accuracy functions for determining process and person differences: an application to cognitive aging. *Cogn. Psychol.* 26, 134–164. doi: 10.1006/cogp.1994.1005

Kramer, J. H., Knee, K., and Delis, D. C. (2000). Verbal memory impairments in dyslexia. *Arch. Clin. Neuropsychol.* 15, 83–93. doi: 10.1093/arclin/15.1.83

Leclercq, A.-L., and Majerus, S. (2010). Serial-order short-term memory predicts vocabulary development: evidence from a longitudinal study. *Dev. Psychol.* 46, 417–427. doi: 10.1037/a0018540

Loftus, G. R. (1978). On interpretation of interactions. *Mem. Cognit.* 6, 312–319. doi: 10.3758/BF03197461

Loftus, G. R. (1985). Evaluating forgetting curves. *J. Exp. Psychol. Learn. Mem. Cogn.* 11, 396–405. doi: 10.1037/0278-7393.11.2.397

Loftus, G. R., Oberg, M. A., and Dillon, A. M. (2004). Linear theory, dimensional theory, and the face-inversion effect. *Psychol. Rev.* 111, 835–863. doi: 10.1037/0033-295X.111.4.835

Loftus, G. R., Truax, P. E., and Nelson, W. W. (1987). "Age-related differences in visual information processing: qualitative or quantitative?" in *Cognitive Functioning and Social Structure Over the Life Course*, eds C. Schooler and K. W. Schaie (Norwood, NJ: Ablex), 59–77.

Long, J. S. (1997). *Regression Models for Categorical and Limited Dependent Variables.* Thousand Oaks, CA: Sage Publications, Inc.

Majerus, S. (2009). "Verbal short-term memory and temporary activation of language representations: the importance of distinguishing item and order information," in *Interactions Between Short-Term and Long-Term Memory in the Verbal Domain*, eds A. Thorn and M. Page (Hove, UK: Psychology Press), 244–276.

Majerus, S., Belayachi, S., De Smedt, B., Leclercq, A. L., Martinez, T., Schmidt, C., et al. (2008a). Neural networks for short-term memory for order differentiate high and low proficiency bilinguals. *Neuroimage* 42, 1698–1713. doi: 10.1016/j.neuroimage.2008.06.003

Majerus, S., D'Argembeau, A., Martinez Perez, T., Belayachi, S., Van der Linden, M., Collette, F., et al. (2010). The commonality of neural networks for verbal and visual short-term memory. *J. Cogn. Neurosci.* 22, 2570–2593. doi: 10.1162/jocn.2009.21378

Majerus, S., Poncelet, M., Greffe, C., and Van der Linden, M. (2006a). Relations between vocabulary development and verbal short-term memory: the relative importance of short-term memory for serial order and item information. *J. Exp. Child Psychol.* 93, 95–119. doi: 10.1016/j.jecp.2005.07.005

Majerus, S., Poncelet, M., Van der Linden, M., Albouy, G., Salmon, E., Sterpenich, V., et al. (2006b). The left intraparietal sulcus and verbal short-term memory: focus of attention or serial order? *Neuroimage* 32,880–891. doi: 10.1016/j.neuroimage.2006.03.048

Majerus, S., Poncelet, M., Van der Linden, M., and Weekes, B. (2008b). Lexical learning in bilingual adults: the relative importance of short-term memory for serial order and phonological knowledge. *Cognition* 107, 395–419. doi: 10.1016/j.cognition.2007.10.003

Manis, F. R. (1985). Acquisition of word identification skills in normal and disabled readers. *J. Educ. Psychol.* 77, 78–90. doi: 10.1037/0022-0663.77.1.78

Martinez Perez, T., Majerus, S., and Poncelet, M. (2012a). The contribution of short-term memory for serial order to early reading acquisition: evidence from a longitudinal study. *J. Exp. Child Psychol.* 111, 708–723. doi: 10.1016/j.jecp.2011.11.007

Martinez Perez, T., Majerus, S., and Poncelet, M. (2013). Impaired short-term memory for order in adults with dyslexia. *Res. Dev. Disabil.* 34, 2011–2223. doi: 10.1016/j.ridd.2013.04.005

Martinez Perez, T., Majerus, S., Mahot, A., and Poncelet, M. (2012b). Evidence for a specific impairment of serial order short-term memory in dyslexic children. *Dyslexia* 18, 94–109. doi: 10.1002/dys.1438

Microsoft Office PowerPoint 2007©. (2007). *Microsoft Corporation. Redmond, WA.*

Muthén, L. K., and Muthén, B. O. (1998-2012). *Mplus User's Guide, 7th Edn.* Los Angeles, CA: Muthén and Muthén.

Nairne, J. S., and Kelley, M. R. (2004). Separating item and order information through process dissociation. *J. Mem. Lang.* 50, 113–133. doi: 10.1016/j.jml.2003.09.005

Prince, M., Brown, S., and Heathcote, A. (2012). The design and analysis of state-trace experiments. *Psychol. Methods* 17, 78–99. doi: 10.1037/a0025809

Raftery, A. E. (1996). "Bayesian model selection in social research," in *Sociological Methodology*, Vol. 25, ed P. V. Marsden (Oxford: Basil Blackwell), 111–163.

Raykov, T. (1998). Cronbachs alpha and reliability of composite with interrelated nonhomogenous items. *Appl. Psychol. Meas.* 22, 375–385. doi: 10.1177/014662169802200407

Raykov, T. (2001). Bias of coefficient alpha for congeneric measures with correlated errors. *Appl. Psychol. Meas.* 25, 69–76. doi: 10.1177/01466216010251005

Reitsma, P. (1983). Word-specific knowledge in beginning reading. *J. Res. Read.* 6, 41–56. doi: 10.1111/j.1467-9817.1983.tb00237.x

Saint-Aubin, J., and Poirier, M. (1999). Semantic similarity and immediate serial recall: is there a detrimental effect on order information? *Q. J. Exp. Psychol. A* 52, 367–394. doi: 10.1080/713755814

Scholte, E. M., and Van der Ploeg, J. D. (2005). *AVL-vragenlijst.* Houten: Bohn Stafleu Van Loghum.

Share, D. L. (1995). Phonological recoding and self-teaching: sine qua non of reading acquisition. *Cognition* 55, 151–218. doi: 10.1016/0010-0277(94)00645-2

Share, D. L. (1999). Phonological recoding and orthographic learning: a direct test of the self-teaching hypothesis. *J. Exp. Child Psychol.* 72, 95–129. doi: 10.1006/jecp.1998.2481

Share, D. L. (2004). Orthographic learning at a glance: on the time course and developmental onset of self-teaching. *J. Exp. Child Psychol.* 87, 267–298. doi: 10.1016/j.jecp.2004.01.001

Share, D. L. (2008). On the anglocentricities of current reading research and practice: the perils of overreliance on an "outlier" orthography. *Psychol. Bull.* 134, 584–615. doi: 10.1037/0033-2909.134.4.584

Snowling, M. J. (2012). Changing concepts of dyslexia: nature, treatment and comorbidity. *J. Child Psychol. Psychiatry* 53, e1–e3. doi: 10.1111/j.1469-7610.2009.02197.x

Spinelli, D., De Luca, M., Judica, A., and Zoccolotti, P. (2002). Crowding effects on word identification in developmental dyslexia. *Cortex* 38, 179–200. doi: 10.1016/S0010-9452(08)70649-X

Staels, E., and Van den Broeck, W. (2013). Orthographic learning and the role of text-to-speech software in dutch disabled readers. *J. Learn. Disabil.* doi: 10.1177/0022219413487407. [Epub ahead of print].

Staels, E., and Van den Broeck, W. (in press). No solid empirical evidence for the SOLID (serial order learning impairment) hypothesis of dyslexia. *J. Exp. Psychol. Learn. Mem. Cogn.*

Stanovich, K. E. (1988). The right and wrong places to look for the cognitive locus of reading disability. *Ann. Dyslexia* 38, 154–177. doi: 10.1007/BF02648254

Stanovich, K. E. (1990). Concepts in developmental theories of reading skill: cognitive resources, automaticity, and modularity. *Dev. Rev.* 10, 72–100. doi: 10.1016/0273-2297(90)90005-O

Stanovich, K. E., and Siegel, L. S. (1994). Phenotypic performance profile of children with reading disabilities: a regression-based test of the phonological-core variable-difference model. *J. Educ. Psychol.* 86, 24–53. doi: 10.1037/0022-0663.86.1.24

Szmalec, A., Loncke, M., Page, M. P., and Duyck, W. (2011). Order or disorder? Impaired Hebb learning in dyslexia. *J. Exp. Psychol. Learn. Mem. Cogn.* 37, 1270–1279. doi: 10.1037/a0023820

Tijms, J. (2004). Verbal memory and phonological processing in dyslexia. *J. Res. Read.* 27, 300–310. doi: 10.1111/j.1467-9817.2004.00233.x

Van den Bos, K. P., and lutje Spelberg, H. C. (2007). *Continu Benoemen and Woorden Lezen. Een test voor het diagnosticeren van taal- en leesstoornissen.* Handleiding; Amsterdam: Boom Testuitgevers.

Van den Bos, K. P., lutje Spelberg, H. C., Scheepsma, A. J. M., and de Vries, J. R. (1994). *De Klepel. Vorm A en B. Een test voor de leesvaardigheid van pseudowoorden. Verantwoording Handleiding Diagnostiek en be- handeling [The Klepel. Forms A and B. A test for readability of pseu- dowords. Justification manual diagnostics and treatment].* Nijmegen: Berkhout.

Van den Broeck, W., and Geudens, A. (2012). Old and new ways to study characteristics of reading disabilty: the case of the nonword-reading deficit. *Cogn. Psychol.* 65, 414–456. doi: 10.1016/j.cogpsych.2012.06.003

Van den Broeck, W., Geudens, A., and Van den Bos, K. P. (2010). The nonword-reading deficit of disabled readers: a developmental interpretation. *Dev. Psychol.* 46, 717–734. doi: 10.1037/a0019038

Van Dijck, J.-P., Abrahamse, E. L., Majerus, S., and Fias, W. (2013). Spatial attention interacts with serial order retrieval in verbal working memory. *Psychol. Sci.* 24, 1854–1859. doi: 10.1177/0956797613479610.

Vellutino, F. R., Fletcher, J. M., Snowling, M. J., and Scanlon, D. M. (2004). Specific reading disability dyslexia): what have we learned in the past four decades. *J. Child Psychol. Psychiatry* 45, 2–40. doi: 10.146/j.0021-9630.2003.00305.x

Wechsler, D., Nederlandstalige bewerking: Kort, W., Schittekatte, M., Bosmans, M., Compaan, E. L., Dekker, P. H., et al. (2005). *Wechsler Intelligence Scale for Children, 3rd Edn. (WISC-III-NL).* Amsterdam: Pearson Assessment and Information B.V.

Wimmer, H., Mayringer, H., and Raberger, T. (1999). Reading and balancing: evidence against the automatization deficit explanation of developmental dyslexia. *J. Learn. Disabil.* 32, 473–478. doi: 10.1177/002221949903200513

Zhou, Y., McBride-Chang, C., Bui-Yan Law, A., Li, T., Cho-Yi Cheung, A., Wong, A., et al. (2014). Development of reading-related skills in chinese and english among hong kong chinese children with and without dyslexia. *J. Exp. Child Psychol.* 122, 75–91. doi: 10.1016/j.jecp.2013.12.003

Ziegler, J. C., and Goswami, U. C. (2005). Reading acquisition, developmental dyslexia and skilled reading across languages: a psycholinguistic grain size theory. *Psychol. Bull.* 131, 3–29. doi: 10.1037/0033-2909.131.1.3

16

Physiologic discrimination of stop consonants relates to phonological skills in pre-readers: a biomarker for subsequent reading ability?†

***Travis White-Schwoch*[1,2] *and Nina Kraus*[1,2,3,4,5] ***

[1] *Auditory Neuroscience Laboratory, Northwestern University, Evanston, IL, USA*
[2] *Department of Communication Sciences, Northwestern University, Evanston, IL, USA*
[3] *Institute for Neuroscience, Northwestern University, Evanston, IL, USA*
[4] *Department of Neurobiology and Physiology, Northwestern University, Evanston, IL, USA*
[5] *Department of Otolaryngology, Northwestern University, Chicago, IL, USA*

Correspondence:
Nina Kraus, Auditory Neuroscience Laboratory, Northwestern University, 2240 Campus Drive, Evanston 60208, IL, USA
e-mail: nkraus@northwestern.edu

†***Submitted for:*** *"Oscillatory "Temporal Sampling" and Developmental Dyslexia: Towards an Overarching Theoretical Framework" (Eds. Usha Goswami, Andrea Facoetti, Marie Lallier & Alan Power).*

Reading development builds upon the accurate representation of the phonological structure of spoken language. This representation and its neural foundations have been studied extensively with respect to reading due to pervasive performance deficits on basic phonological tasks observed in children with dyslexia. The subcortical auditory system – a site of intersection for sensory and cognitive input – is exquisitely tuned to code fine timing differences between phonemes, and so likely plays a foundational role in the development of phonological processing and, eventually, reading. This temporal coding of speech varies systematically with reading ability in school age children. Little is known, however, about subcortical speech representation in pre-school age children. We measured auditory brainstem responses to the stop consonants [ba] and [ga] in a cohort of 4-year-old children and assessed their phonological skills. In a typical auditory system, brainstem responses to [ba] and [ga] are out of phase (i.e., differ in time) due to formant frequency differences in the consonant-vowel transitions of the stimuli. We found that children who performed worst on the phonological awareness task insufficiently code this difference, revealing a physiologic link between early phonological skills and the neural representation of speech. We discuss this finding in light of existing theories of the role of the auditory system in developmental dyslexia, and argue for a systems-level perspective for understanding the importance of precise temporal coding for learning to read.

Keywords: reading, dyslexia, temporal sampling, phase locking, brainstem, phonological awareness, temporal coding

INTRODUCTION

Learning to read scaffolds on the development of more basic language skills. One such primitive is phonological awareness, the knowledge that spoken language is made up of smaller units such as syllables and phonemes (Sandak et al., 2004; Kovelman et al., 2012; Pugh et al., 2013). Phonological processing has been an area of keen interest in the study of reading for years due to the observation of pervasive performance deficits in dyslexics on basic phonological tasks (Swan and Goswami, 1997; Pugh et al., 2013; Ramus et al., 2013). Theories of developmental dyslexia, and theories of reading more generally, must therefore account for the biological mechanisms supporting phonological processing and related language skills.

Developmental dyslexia affects approximately 5–10% of children and is characterized by a failure to develop effective reading skills despite typical intelligence and adequate support from parents, teachers, and caregivers (Démonet et al., 2004). As a group, children (and adults) with dyslexia have a constellation of deficits in auditory processing. There are, for example, extensive performance gaps between dyslexic and typically developing children on a variety of basic auditory tasks (Wright et al., 1997; Goswami et al., 2002; Ahissar et al., 2006). Children with dyslexia have difficulty coding rapidly changing frequency content in speech such as formant transitions in consonant–vowel syllables (Tallal and Piercy, 1975; Tallal, 1980). Dyslexics also have difficulty tracking amplitude envelope modulations in speech, such as in syllable onsets (Goswami et al., 2002, 2011). However, it remains unknown whether these deficits are each observed within an individual or if there are variable manifestations of developmental dyslexia.

Neurophysiologic deficits associated with dyslexia include increased variability in neural firing as observed in auditory midbrain in humans (Hornickel and Kraus, 2013) and cortex in a rat model of dyslexia (Centanni et al., 2013), in addition to decreased auditory cortical phase-locking to the acoustic envelope (Abrams et al., 2009; Lehongre et al., 2011). Our own group has identified a number of deficits in speech coding throughout the central auditory system that are linked to poor reading (Kraus et al., 1996; Wible et al., 2005; Abrams et al., 2009; Banai et al., 2009; Chandrasekaran et al., 2009; Hornickel and Kraus, 2013).

In light of the wide variety of auditory deficits identified in dyslexics, a plethora of theories as to the disorder's biological origin have emerged, each of which has tried to identify a "core deficit." Although these theories are not necessarily mutually exclusive, there is little accord in the literature (cf. Livingstone et al., 1991; Wright et al., 2000; Stein, 2001; Ahissar, 2007; Vidyasagar and Pammer, 2010; Goswami, 2011; Lallier et al., 2013). Many theories have centered on a core deficit in phonological processing and, consequently, a number of neurophysiologic investigations have characterized the biology underlying this skill and deficits thereof. Neuroimaging studies have identified diminished activity in left-lateralized language networks in dyslexic children performing phonological tasks (Kovelman et al., 2012; Pugh et al., 2013). Lehongre et al. (2011) used magnetoencephalography to measure neural entrainment to amplitude modulated noise bursts, and found that dyslexics had poorer phase-locking in the "low gamma" range (~30 Hz), correlating with poor performance on phonological tasks. Finally, the discrimination of stop consonants in auditory midbrain is linked to reading ability in school age children (Hornickel et al., 2009).

While these studies (in addition to many others) have offered insight into the pathophysiology underlying phonological and/or reading deficits, they are complicated by the reciprocal relationship between phonological processing and reading. For although phonological awareness likely bootstraps reading development, the first years of reading themselves influence phonological awareness (Castles and Coltheart, 2004). Therefore, here, we assessed the relationship between phonological awareness and neurophysiologic discrimination of stop consonants in a group of typically developing 4-year-old children. We hypothesized that early phonological awareness is linked to the precision of physiologic speech sound discrimination. To test this hypothesis, we measured neural responses to a pair of speech stimuli previously shown to vary systematically with phonological processing in school-age children (Hornickel et al., 2009). By assessing physiologic processing of speech in pre-school age children we hope to gain insight into the developmental trajectory of reading development. Moreover, we may identify a potential biomarker to predict subsequent reading ability.

MATERIALS AND METHODS

SUBJECTS

Four-year-old children ($N = 26$, 14 female) were recruited from the Chicago area to participate in a developmental study at Northwestern University. No child had a history of a neurologic or otologic condition, second language experience, or a diagnosis of autism spectrum disorder. Four children had immediate family histories of dyslexia (parent or sibling). All children passed a brief screening of peripheral auditory function (normal tympanometry and distortion product otoacoustic emissions at least 6 dB above the noise floor for octaves from 1–8 kHz). Additionally, all children had normal click-evoked auditory brainstem responses (Wave V latency < 6.0 ms, measured by a 100 μs click presented at 80 dB SPL to the right ear at 31.25 Hz).

Although we consider these children too young to have attained fully developed reading skills, and so refer to them as "pre-readers," we note that many of them may have begun some explicit instruction. We did not formally evaluate their reading skills and acknowledge this as a limitation. Nevertheless, we suggest that our cohort represents children who have either not yet begun to learn to read, or are only in the first stages, and so offers novel insight into the relationship between phonological processing and auditory-neurophysiologic responses to speech early in life.

Parents provided informed consent for their children to participate in the study, and the subjects provided verbal assent. The Institutional Review Board of Northwestern University approved all procedures and children were paid $10/hr for their participation.

BEHAVIORAL MEASURE – PHONOLOGICAL AWARENESS

Phonological awareness was measured with the Clinical Evaluation of Language Fundamentals Preschool, 2nd edn., phonological awareness subtest (CELF 2; Wiig et al., 2004). The test evaluates a child's knowledge of the sound structure of the English language and measures a child's ability to manipulate sound through: compound word and syllable blending, sentence and syllable segmentation, and rhyme awareness and production. Raw scores are computed and were used for analysis. The maximum score is 24, and higher scores correspond to better performance. All children met the age-appropriate "criterion" cutoff, indicating that they are within the range of typically developing children. Therefore our data represent a cohort of children with developmentally appropriate performance on the phonological awareness test but with a large range of variability.

NEUROPHYSIOLOGY: STIMULI

Auditory brainstem responses were elicited in response to the stop consonants [ba] and [ga]. Both consonant–vowel (CV) syllables were 170 ms stimuli that have been described previously (Hornickel et al., 2009). Briefly, both begin with a 5 ms stop burst and have a 50 ms transition from the consonant to the vowel. The vowel is sustained for 120 ms. Both stimuli have a flat fundamental frequency ($F_0 = 100$ Hz) and during the 50 ms transition the first three formant frequencies shift. The [ba] and [ga] differ only in the F_2 onset frequency ($F_{2OF[ba]} = 900$ Hz; $F_{2OF[ga]} = 2480$ Hz) but are identical in F_2 frequency for the vowel portion ($F_{2VOWEL} = 1240$ Hz; see **Figure 1**). The remaining formants are identical ($F_1 = 400$–720 Hz; $F_3 = 2580$–2500 Hz) with F_{4-6} steady through the 170 ms stimuli ($F_4 = 3300$ Hz, $F_5 = 3750$ Hz, $F_6 = 4900$ Hz). Stimuli were presented monaurally to the right ear at 80.4 dB SPL through electromagnetically shielded insert earphones (ER-3, Etymotic Research, Elk Grove Village, IL, USA). Stimulus presentation was controlled by E-Prime 2.0 (Psychology Software Tools, Inc., Sharpsburg, PA, USA) and stimuli were presented in alternating polarity with an 81 ms interstimulus interval. 4200 sweeps of each stimulus were presented, and the presentation order was randomized for each subject.

NEUROPHYSIOLOGY: RECORDING AND DATA PROCESSING

Brainstem responses were collected using a BioSEMI Active2 recording system with ABR module. Active electrodes were placed at Cz and each ear with CMS/DRL placed on the forehead, one-half centimeter on either side of Fpz. Only ipsilateral (Cz-A2) responses are used in analysis. Responses were digitized at

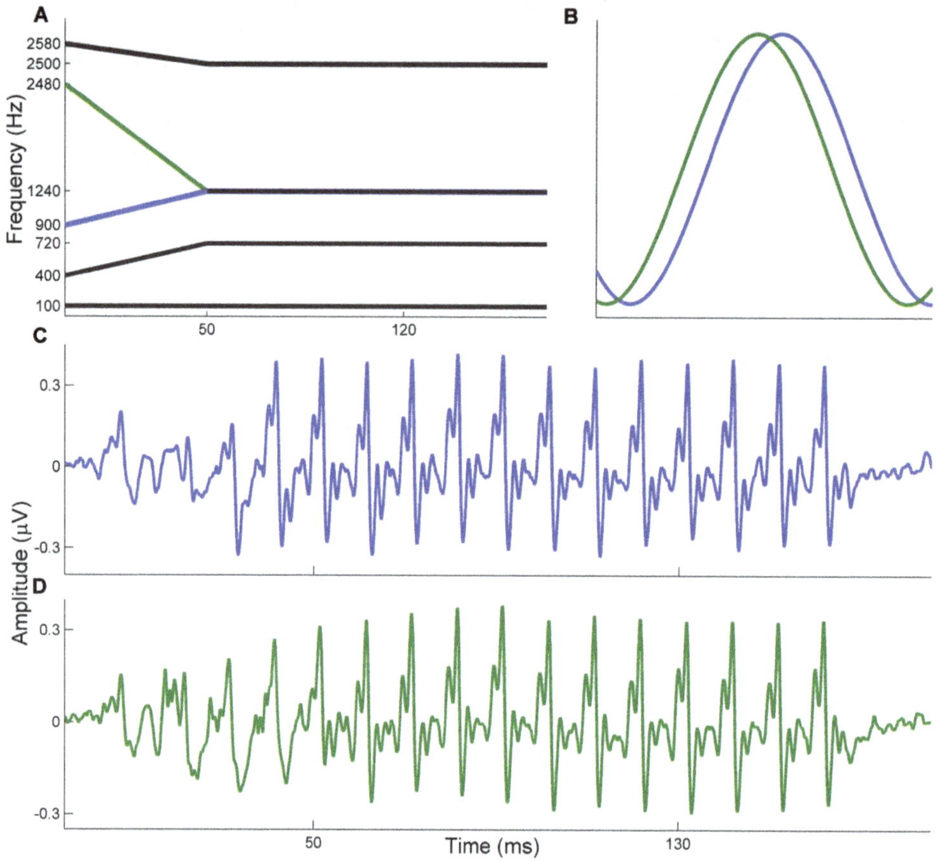

FIGURE 1 | (A) Schematic illustrating formant information for the [ba] and [ga] stimuli. The F_0, F_1, and F_3 are identical. The stimuli differ in F_2 onset frequencies with [ba] (blue) ascending and [ga] (green) descending to stabilize for the vowel portion. **(B)** Schematic illustrating the expected phase relationship between brainstem responses to the [ba] and [ga]. Since the [ga] (green) has a higher F_2 onset frequency it is expected that brainstem responses to [ga] phase lead those to [ba]. **(C,D)** Grand average waveforms are displayed for the [ba] (top, blue) and [ga] (bottom, green).

16.384 kHz and collected with online filters from 100–3000 Hz (20 dB/decade roll-off) in the BioSEMI ActiABR and recorded into LabView 2.0 (National Instruments, Austin, TX, USA). Since speech-evoked brainstem responses are ideally filtered with a high-pass of 70 Hz (Skoe and Kraus, 2010), in MATLAB responses were offline amplified in the frequency domain with an inverse power ramp, 20 dB per decade for 3 decades below 100 Hz (i.e., from 0.1 to 100 Hz, then flat from 0.1 Hz down to DC). Next, a bandpass filter (70–2000 Hz, Butterworth filter, 12 dB/octave roll-off) was applied to frequency-amplified responses. Responses were epoched from −40–213 ms (stimulus onset at 0 ms) and baseline corrected. Artifact rejection was set at ± 35 μVs. Final responses comprised 2000 artifact-free sweeps of each polarity, and responses from alternating polarities were added to emphasize the envelope-following brainstem response while minimizing the influence of stimulus artifact and cochlear microphonic (Campbell et al., 2012).

NEUROPHYSIOLOGY DATA ANALYSIS: PHASE DISTINCTION BETWEEN RESPONSES

Due to the tonotopicity of the ascending auditory system, stimuli that differ in frequency elicit brainstem responses which are out of phase (Gorga et al., 1988). Therefore, it is expected that responses to [ba] and [ga] begin out of phase from each other (during the transition portion) and are phase-aligned during the vowel, when the stimuli are acoustically identical. In this regard, the relative phases of the two responses are used as proxies for the relative timing of the responses at each frequency. A schematic illustrating this expected relationship is presented in **Figure 1**.

The phase relationship between responses to [ba] and [ga] was measured using custom routines in MATLAB (Skoe et al., in press). Responses were divided into overlapping 20 ms windows from −40–170 ms (1 ms separating each adjacent window) and ramped with a 20 ms Hanning window. The cross-power spectral density function (cspd) was applied between brainstem responses, and power estimates were converted to phase angles to index alignment of the two signals. A larger phase angle (in radians) indicates that the responses are farther out of phase and, therefore, that there is a larger timing lag between responses at a given frequency. A three dimensional "cross-phaseogram" figure is constructed illustrating time (ms, x-axis), frequency (Hz, y-axis), and phase angle (radians, colorbar). During the transition region positive phase angles indicate better neural consonant distinction, as this indicates that

[ga] phase-leads [ba], the expected relationship since [ga] has a higher F_{2OF}.

SUBJECT GROUPS

Scores on the CELF formed a normal distribution with a mean score of 18.96 (SD, 3.80; Kolmogorov–Smirnov $D(26) = 0.146$, $p = 0.160$). Children were grouped based on their performance on the CELF with a median split defining the top phonological awareness "Top PA" (CELF > 19, $N = 14$, 6 female) and bottom phonological awareness "Bottom PA" (CELF < 19, $N = 12$, 6 female) groups. Five subjects in the Top PA performed at ceiling on the test (scores of 24). Each group included two children with a family history of dyslexia. Groups did not differ in distribution of males and females ($\chi^2 = 0.154$, $p = 0.70$) nor on non-verbal intelligence (matrix reasoning subtest, Wechsler Preschool and Primary Scale of Intelligence, Revised; Wechsler, 1989; $p = 0.35$). As expected, the groups did statistically differ in performance on the CELF, $t(24) = 9.11$, $p < .001$, Cohen's $d = 3.56$. Summary statistics for the two groups are presented in **Table 1**.

RESULTS

SUMMARY OF RESULTS

Group average cross-phaseograms are presented in **Figure 2**. The Top phonological awareness group (Top PA) evinces a large phase distinction corresponding in time to the transitions in the stimuli, which occurs in the responses from approximately 300–700 Hz (indicated by a large orange–red swatch) and a more moderate phase shift from approximately 750–1000 Hz. Conversely, relatively small phase distinctions were observed in the bottom group (Bottom PA) suggesting that the frequency difference between the stimuli was not strongly represented in these children. Phase distinctions for individual subjects are presented in **Figure 3**, along with group means. No phase distinctions were observed in the response region corresponding to the steady state vowel in either group, as is expected since the stimuli are acoustically identical in the vowel portions.

PHASE DISTINCTIONS IN THE CONSONANT-VOWEL TRANSITION, 300-700 Hz

Mean phase angle distinctions were calculated for the lower frequency region (15–55 ms × 300–700 Hz). This was the primary

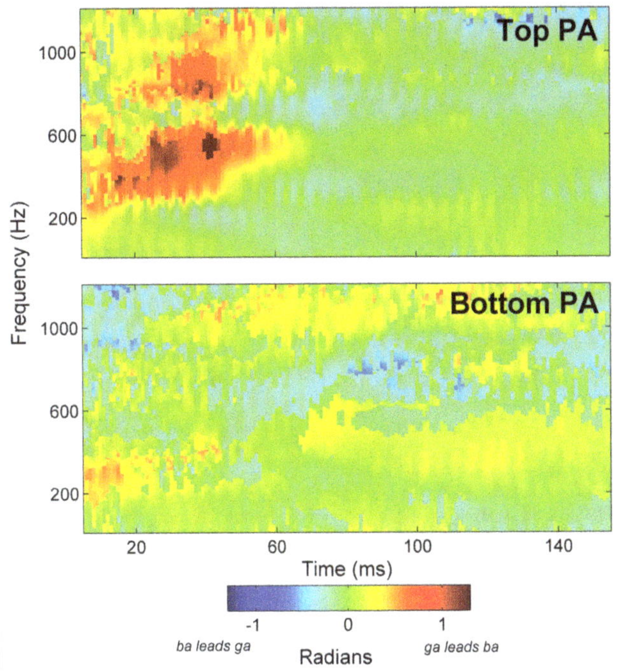

FIGURE 2 | Group average cross-phaseograms are presented for the Top phonological awareness (PA) and Bottom PA groups. The Top PA more strongly codes the difference between the [ba] and [ga] stimuli, as indicated by the large red–orange swatches in response to the CV transition.

region of interest, since it corresponds best to previous reports (Skoe et al., in press; Parbery-Clark et al., 2012). In the Top PA there was a larger mean phase distinction than in the Bottom PA group, $t(24) = 2.61$, $p = .015$, Cohen's $d = 1.07$. See **Table 2** for descriptive statistics. Since there was a slightly skewed distribution in the Top PA group, this comparison was repeated, and confirmed, with the non-parametric Mann–Whitney U test ($p = 0.015$).

Individual phase distinctions for each group are presented in **Figure 3**. The majority of subjects in the Top PA group had positive phase distinctions whereas most subjects in the Bottom PA group had either very small phase distinctions or distinctions in the opposite of the expected direction (i.e., responses to [ba] phase lead those to [ga]). It is also noteworthy that the magnitude of the largest phase distinctions in the Top PA group exceeds those observed in the Bottom PA group.

Finally, a trending correlation between CELF score and phase distinction was observed (Spearman's $\rho(26) = 0.38$, $p = .056$) with higher scores on the CELF corresponding to larger phase distinction. We suspect that with a larger subject group, and relatively fewer subjects at ceiling on the CELF, this relationship would be stronger.

Table 1 | Demographics for the top and bottom phonological awareness groups are summarized.

	Top PA ($N = 14$)	Bottom PA ($N = 12$)
Males	6	6
Family history of dyslexia	2	2
CELF cutoff	≥ 20	≤ 18
CELF (raw score)	22.0 (1.7)	15.4 (2.0)
Non-verbal IQ (percentile)	70.8 (24.6)	79.4 (19.9)

Groups are matched on all criteria except CELF score. The number of males and number of subjects in each group with a family history of dyslexia are reported. Means (with SDs) are reported for the CELF and for the non-verbal IQ test (Matrix Reasoning sub-test of the WPPSI)

PHASE DISTINCTIONS IN THE CONSONANT-VOWEL TRANSITION, 750-1000 Hz

To further explore group differences, and to ensure that there were no phase distinctions in response to the vowel, additional analyses were pursued. The first analysis focused on the higher frequency phase distinction (25–55 ms × 750–1000 Hz). As indicated in

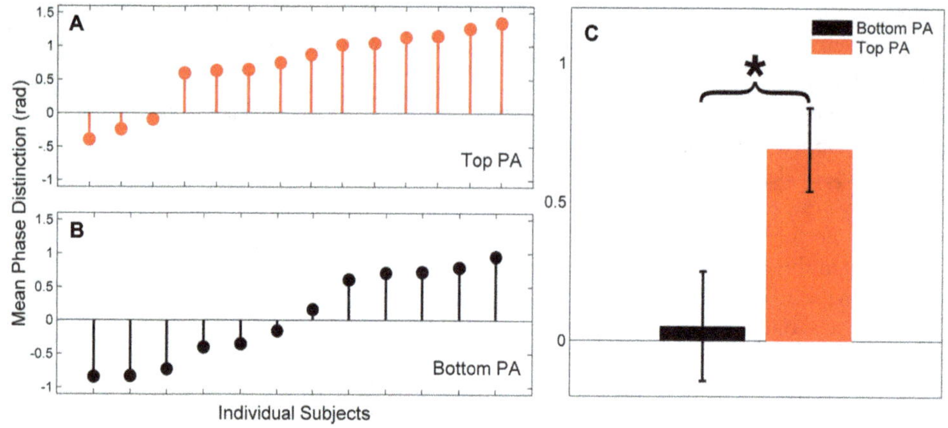

FIGURE 3 | (A,B) Phase distinctions for individual subjects (15–55 ms × 300–600 Hz) are presented for the Top PA (Panel A, red) and Bottom PA (Panel B, black) groups. **(C)** Group means are presented. Error bars, ± 1 SEM; $*p < 0.05$.

Table 2 | Mean phase distinctions for the two frequency ranges are reported for each group (in rad, with SDs).

		Top PA	Bottom PA
300–700 Hz	Transition	0.690 (0.56)	0.053 (0.69)
	Vowel	−0.041 (0.16)	0.084 (0.56)
750–1000 Hz	Transition	0.551 (0.50)	0.074 (0.74)
	Vowel	−0.075 (0.34)	−0.144 (0.29)

Figure 2, the Top PA group had a larger mean phase distinction than the Bottom PA group, $t(24) = 2.00$, $p = 0.06$, Cohen's $d = 0.82$.

PHASE DISTINCTIONS IN THE VOWEL REGION

Since the [ba] and [ga] stimuli are identical in the steady state vowel portions no phase distinction is expected in this region. This is reflected in **Figure 2** where green indicates a phase difference of about 0 rad. To confirm this statistically, mean phase angles were calculated for the same frequency regions as in the transition from 60 to 155 ms. There were no group differences in phase distinction for the lower frequency region (300–700 Hz; $t(24) = 0.81$, $p = 0.427$) or higher frequency region (750–1000 Hz, $t(24) = 0.55$, $p = 0.589$).

DISCUSSION

We assessed the physiologic discrimination of stop consonants in a group of 4-year-old children and reveal a link between this discrimination and phonological awareness. Children with higher phonological awareness had superior neural discrimination of the stop consonants [ba] and [ga], as inferred by far-field electrophysiology. Conversely, children who performed worse on the phonological awareness test, on average, did not robustly distinguish these speech sounds. This relationship has previously been observed in school age children, with neural speech discrimination varying in concert with phonological awareness (Hornickel et al., 2009). By demonstrating this relationship in pre-school children too young to have attained full reading competence we can begin to trace the developmental trajectory of the primitives necessary for complex language-based tasks such as reading. However, we do not know if these children with weak consonant differentiation will soon develop a strong neural differentiation and end up as normal readers, or if they will face challenges as they learn to read. The latter possibility would suggest that these children are at risk for a reading disorder. Regardless, this relationship highlights the role of central auditory processing in developing language skills, and complements phonological deficit theories of reading.

One interpretation of the current results is that they reflect different levels of maturation. The auditory system undergoes rapid developmental plasticity through the first several years of life, and this is reflected in subcortical (Johnson et al., 2008; Skoe et al., in press) and cortical evoked potentials (Choudhury and Benasich, 2011). Individual differences in this rate of maturation may explain the variability in the [ba]-[ga] phase distinction. We do not think this vitiates the link between subcortical auditory function and phonological processing, however. After all, slower maturation of the neural processes important for phonological development may set certain children at a disadvantage when they begin learning to read. Nevertheless, the functional developmental consequences of this maturation for reading (dis)ability remain to be seen.

TEMPORAL SAMPLING: A SYSTEM-WIDE PERSPECTIVE

Goswami (2011) has proposed a theoretical framework to understand developmental dyslexia, the "temporal sampling framework" (TSF). Under TSF, the core deficit in dyslexia is phonological and is due to impaired oscillatory phase locking for low frequency temporal coding in auditory cortex. An attractive feature of TSF is that it resolves many apparent discrepancies between competing theories of developmental dyslexia. Support for TSF may be found in a large series of psychophysical and neurophysiologic investigations (Witton et al., 1998; Goswami et al., 2002, 2011; Serniclaes et al., 2004; Noordenbos et al., 2012, 2013; Leong and Goswami, 2013; Power et al., 2013).

Although TSF predicts deficient slow cortical phase locking in dyslexia (at rates < 30 Hz; Goswami, 2011), our demonstration of a link between high frequency phase locking in the subcortical auditory system and phonological processing may also be consistent with TSF. While TSF predicts superior *cortical* phase locking at fast rates for dyslexics, and here we report a deficit for high frequency temporal coding in auditory midbrain, we advocate for a systems-level perspective with different "optimal" rates of phase locking as a function of the physiology of the site of interest along the auditory pathway. We see this as compatible with TSF because our view is that the auditory system is best thought of as an integrated circuit that interacts dynamically with cognitive, reward, and other sensory systems (Kraus and Nicol, in press; Kraus and Chandrasekaran, 2010; Bajo and King, 2012; Anderson et al., 2013). The subcortical evoked response we analyzed in the current paper (and others from our group) is generated predominantly by inferior colliculus (IC; for review see Chandrasekaran and Kraus, 2010). Most IC neurons phase lock in the range of 100–1000 Hz (Liu et al., 2006) which is 10-fold the range of the impaired theta and delta oscillatory phase locking in auditory cortex observed in dyslexia (Goswami, 2011). Optimal phonological coding may rely on the interaction of rapid temporal sampling in IC with relatively slow sampling in auditory cortex. Indeed, Abrams et al. (2006) reported that subcortical timing was linked to the temporal integrity of auditory cortical speech coding. Wible et al. (2005) reported correlated subcortical and cortical neural synchrony in representing speech, both of which were diminished in children with language-based learning problems.

That said, relatively little is known about the temporal coding of low frequency information in IC (i.e., < 30 Hz), which may in fact be deficient in dyslexics. Recordings from cat IC do demonstrate phase locking as low as 10 Hz (Langner and Schreiner, 1988), however, the lower limits of phase locking in human IC, and more broadly the oscillatory dynamics of IC, remain an avenue for future research. Temporal coding at multiple rates may occur in parallel through the auditory pathway; evidence from a guinea pig model suggests that a paralemniscal thalamocortical pathway relays slow temporal information to auditory cortex in parallel with fast temporal information relayed through a lemniscal pathway (Abrams et al., 2011). Therefore, a full elucidation of the relationship between auditory phase locking and reading ability on a system-wide level will likely have to accommodate simultaneous temporal coding at multiple rates.

Further support for this integrated view of system-wide temporal coding comes from the rhythm perception literature, which has connected poor reading with an impaired ability to entrain to an external beat and impoverished perception of musical meter (Thomson et al., 2006; Huss et al., 2011; Tierney and Kraus, 2013b). This rhythmic entrainment seems to rely on auditory cortical phase locking (Power et al., 2012). However, the ability to entrain to an external beat is also linked to rapid *subcortical* phase locking and neural synchrony (Tierney and Kraus, 2013a), again suggesting that phase locking across multiple temporal rates may support perceptual skills linked to reading, if not phonological processing itself. An overarching theoretical framework for reading, then, may have to include relatively rapid subcortical phase locking as a key component that interacts with slower cortical oscillatory sampling. Both rapid and slow sampling likely rely on the synchronous firing of neurons in the auditory system, which supports precise representation of transient sounds (McGinley et al., 2012), 0.1 ms precision timing (Anderson et al., 2012), and speech discrimination (Engineer et al., 2008). And once again, dyslexia has been linked to deficits in neural synchrony as observed in humans (Hornickel and Kraus, 2013) and a rat model (Centanni et al., 2013).

This view would be also consistent with the Rapid Auditory Processing theory of developmental dyslexia (RAP; Tallal, 1980; Benasich and Tallal, 2002). Decreased sensitivity to rapidly changing phonological features could drive the impoverished distinction between speech sounds. Previous work has demonstrated that lengthening formant transitions in speech can improve the *cortical* discrimination of speech sounds (Bradlow et al., 1999; Steinschneider and Fishman, 2011), but it is unknown what effect this has on *subcortical* discrimination. Finally, we note that these our findings would be broadly consistent with the view that there are general, non-linguistic sensory deficits in dyslexia (Wright et al., 1997; Stein, 2001; Ahissar et al., 2006). Future work, therefore, should consider the interactions of acoustics, phonemics, and behavioral relevance in subcortical temporal processing.

A BIOMARKER FOR SUBSEQUENT READING ABILITY?

Although it is important to develop and refine empirically based theories of reading, it is also important to develop methods to identify children at risk for reading disorders. Previous neurophysiologic studies have identified cortical predictors of dyslexia, such as slower right hemisphere polarity shifts in evoked responses to speech (Guttorm et al., 2005; for review, see Leppänen et al., 2012). The structural integrity and volume of left articulate fasciculus is diminished in young children with poor phonological awareness (Saygin et al., 2013). Performance on speech perception tasks is also predictive (Benasich and Tallal, 2002), in addition to oscillatory dynamics in the infant brain (Gou et al., 2011). While the current analysis is not longitudinal, the techniques employed here may one day be useful for predicting future reading ability, either independently or as a complement to existing techniques. In fact, the children in the current study will be tracked over the next several years in hopes of identifying early predictors of subsequent reading ability. We note that the CELF phonological awareness test combines many subskills under the phonological awareness construct (Wiig et al., 2004); it is unknown if group differences are driven primarily by one or two of these subskills, and future investigation is warranted to look specifically at which aspects of phonological awareness are linked to auditory system development.

There are a number of attractive features of the "cross-phaseogram" as a potential biomarker. For one, it is a fast and objective automated procedure. Moreover, as we illustrate here, this measure relates to individual differences in language-based skills. Subcortical evoked responses to speech are relatively easy to obtain and meaningful in individuals (Skoe and Kraus, 2010). From a practical standpoint, responses may be elicited when a child is sleeping or watching a video, thereby eliminating the need for subject compliance in task-related physiologic measurements. And by following the children in this study longitudinally, we may be able to explore individual differences in neurophysiology that distinguish between individual presentations of dyslexia.

DYSLEXIA, TREATMENT, AND THE SEARCH FOR A CORE DEFICIT

A number of short-term interventions have been employed to improve phonological abilities and reading skills, and these offer further insight into the biological foundations of reading. Some of these studies have focused on perceptual deficits related to poor phonological processing (Tallal et al., 1996; Temple et al., 2003). Other interventions have been broader, such as assistive listening devices that improve classroom signal-to-noise ratios by directing attention to meaningful sound – and in fact also improve neural synchrony in response to speech (Hornickel et al., 2012). Non-speech training such as playing action video games, which improve attentional abilities (Green and Bavelier, 2012), can also improve reading skills (Franceschini et al., 2013), suggesting a role for non-auditory mechanisms in reading development and/or remediation.

Music training, which engenders a host of auditory perceptual and cognitive benefits, may also hold promise. Since precise temporal coding of sound supports fundamental reading skills, and this coding is strengthened by musical experience, it stands to reason that music training may promote the development of reading-related skills (Tierney and Kraus, 2013c). In fact, music experience has been directly linked to improved phonological skills and reading (Moreno et al., 2009; Besson et al., 2011), in addition to physiologic discrimination of speech sounds, as presented in the current study (Parbery-Clark et al., 2012; Strait et al., 2013). Given the established link between rhythm skills and phonological abilities, the rhythmic components of music training may be especially important for developing language-based skills. In fact, Bhide et al. (2013) reported that a comprehensive rhythm training regimen improves phonological skills.

To understand the biological bases of reading, and develop strategies that engender reading skills and remediate dyslexia, it is important to identify which skills to target. In this regard, the quest for the core deficit is important. That said, this search may at times cloud the principal problem, namely, that certain children have tremendous difficulty learning to read. Moreover, the possibility remains that no single deficit accounts for every child who has difficulty reading. Our view is that even without a full understanding of the pathophysiology of dyslexia it is important to identify children at risk as early as possible. Here we have identified a neural correlate of early phonological awareness in pre-school age children. Due to the importance of precise phonological representations for reading this correlate may indicate a biological bottleneck certain children face when they begin to learn to read.

AUTHOR CONTRIBUTIONS

Travis White-Schwoch and Nina Kraus designed the study; Travis White-Schwoch oversaw data collection and analyzed the data; Travis White-Schwoch and Nina Kraus wrote the paper.

ACKNOWLEDGMENTS

We thank members of the Auditory Neuroscience Laboratory for their assistance with data collection, especially Dana L. Strait for contributions to study development. We also thank Trent Nicol, Jane Hornickel, Adam Tierney, Karen Chan Barrett, and Samira Anderson for their input on earlier drafts of the manuscript. Supported by NIH R01HD069414 and the Knowles Hearing Center.

REFERENCES

Abrams, D. A., Nicol, T., Zecker, S. G., and Kraus, N. (2006). Auditory brainstem timing predicts cerebral asymmetry for speech. *J. Neurosci.* 26, 11131–11137. doi: 10.1523/JNEUROSCI.2744-06.2006

Abrams, D. A., Nicol, T., Zecker, S., and Kraus, N. (2009). Abnormal cortical processing of the syllable rate of speech in poor readers. *J. Neurosci.* 29, 7686–7693. doi: 10.1523/JNEUROSCI.5242-08.2009

Abrams, D. A., Nicol, T., Zecker, S., and Kraus, N. (2011). A possible role for a paralemniscal auditory pathway in the coding of slow temporal information. *Hear. Res.* 272, 125–134. doi: 10.1016/j.heares.2010.10.009

Ahissar, M. (2007). Dyslexia and the anchoring-deficit hypothesis. *Trends Cogn. Sci.* 11, 458–465. doi: 10.1016/j.tics.2007.08.015

Ahissar, M., Lubin, Y., Putter-Katz, H., and Banai, K. (2006). Dyslexia and the failure to form a perceptual anchor. *Nat. Neurosci.* 9, 1558–1564. doi: 10.1038/nn1800

Anderson, S., Parbery-Clark, A., White-Schwoch, T., and Kraus, N. (2012). Aging affects neural precision of speech encoding. *J. Neurosci.* 32, 14156–14164. doi: 10.1523/JNEUROSCI.2176-12.2012

Anderson, S., White-Schwoch, T., Parbery-Clark, A., and Kraus, N. (2013). A dynamic auditory-cognitive system supports speech-in-noise perception in older adults. *Hear. Res.* 300, 18–32. doi: 10.1016/j.heares.2013.03.006

Bajo, V. M., and King, A. J. (2012). Cortical modulation of auditory processing in the midbrain. *Front. Neural Circuits* 6:114. doi: 10.3389/fncir.2012.00114

Banai, K., Hornickel, J., Skoe, E., Nicol, T., Zecker, S., and Kraus, N. (2009). Reading and subcortical auditory function. *Cereb. Cortex* 19, 2699–2707. doi: 10.1093/cercor/bhp024

Benasich, A. A., and Tallal, P. (2002). Infant discrimination of rapid auditory cues predicts later language impairment. *Behav. Brain Res.* 136, 31–49. doi: 10.1016/S0166-4328(02)00098-0

Besson, M., Chobert, J., and Marie, C. (2011). Transfer of training between music and speech: common processing, attention, and memory. *Front. Psychol.* 2:94. doi: 10.3389/fpsyg.2011.00094

Bhide, A., Power, A., and Goswami, U. (2013). A hythmic musical intervention for poor readers: a comparison of efficacy with a letter-based intervention. *Mind Brain Educ.* 7, 113–123. doi: 10.1111/mbe.12016

Bradlow, A. R., Kraus, N., Nicol, T. G., McGee, T. J., Cunningham, J., Zecker, S. G., et al. (1999). Effects of lengthened formant transition duration on discrimination and neural representation of synthetic CV syllables by normal and learning-disabled children. *J. Acoust. Soc. Am.* 106, 2086. doi: 10.1121/1.427953

Campbell, T., Kerlin, J. R., Bishop, C. W., and Miller, L. M. (2012). Methods to eliminate stimulus transduction artifact from insert earphones during electroencephalography. *Ear Hear.* 33, 144. doi: 10.1097/AUD.0b013e3182280353

Castles, A., and Coltheart, M. (2004). Is there a causal link from phonological awareness to success in learning to read? *Cognition* 91, 77–111. doi: 10.1016/S0010-0277(03)00164-1

Centanni, T., Booker, A., Sloan, A., Chen, F., Maher, B., Carraway, R., et al. (2013). Knockdown of the dyslexia-associated gene kiaa0319 impairs temporal responses to speech stimuli in rat primary auditory cortex. *Cereb. Cortex* doi: 10.1093/cercor/bht028 [Epub ahead of print].

Chandrasekaran, B., Hornickel, J., Skoe, E., Nicol, T., and Kraus, N. (2009). Context-dependent encoding in the human auditory brainstem relates to hearing speech in noise: implications for developmental dyslexia. *Neuron* 64, 311–319. doi: 10.1016/j.neuron.2009.10.006

Chandrasekaran, B., and Kraus, N. (2010). The scalp-recorded brainstem response to speech: neural origins and plasticity. *Psychophysiology* 47, 236–246. doi: 10.1111/j.1469-8986.2009.00928.x

Choudhury, N., and Benasich, A. A. (2011). Maturation of auditory evoked potentials from 6 to 48 months: prediction to 3 and 4 year language and cognitive abilities. *Clin. Neurophysiol.* 122, 320–338. doi: 10.1016/j.clinph.2010.05.035

Démonet, J.-F., Taylor, M. J., and Chaix, Y. (2004). Developmental dyslexia. *Lancet* 363, 1451–1460. doi: 10.1016/S0140-6736(04)16106-0

Engineer, C. T., Perez, C. A., Chen, Y. T. H., Carraway, R. S., Reed, A. C., Shetake, J. A., et al. (2008). Cortical activity patterns predict speech discrimination ability. *Nat. Neurosci.* 11, 603–608. doi: 10.1038/nn.2109

Franceschini, S., Gori, S., Ruffino, M., Viola, S., Molteni, M., and Facoetti, A. (2013). Action video games make dyslexic children read better. *Curr. Biol.* 23, 462–466. doi: 10.1016/j.cub.2013.01.044

Gorga, M. P., Kaminski, J. R., Beauchaine, K. A., and Jesteadt, W. (1988). Auditory brainstem responses to tone bursts in normally hearing subjects. *J. Speech Hear. Res.* 31, 87–97.

Goswami, U. (2011). A temporal sampling framework for developmental dyslexia. *Trends Cogn. Sci.* 15, 3–10. doi: 10.1016/j.tics.2010.10.001

Goswami, U., Fosker, T., Huss, M., Mead, N., and Szûcs, D. (2011). Rise time and formant transition duration in the discrimination of speech sounds: the Ba–Wa distinction in developmental dyslexia. *Dev. Sci.* 14, 34–43. doi: 10.1111/j.1467-7687.2010.00955.x

Goswami, U., Thomson, J., Richardson, U., Stainthorp, R., Hughes, D., Rosen, S., et al. (2002). Amplitude envelope onsets and developmental dyslexia: a new hypothesis. *Proc. Natl. Acad. Sci. U.S.A.* 99, 10911–10916. doi: 10.1073/pnas.122368599

Gou, Z., Choudhury, N., and Benasich, A. A. (2011). Resting frontal gamma power at 16, 24 and 36 months predicts individual differences in language and cognition at 4 and 5 years. *Behav. Brain Res.* 220, 263–270. doi: 10.1016/j.bbr.2011.01.048

Green, C., and Bavelier, D. (2012). Learning, attentional control, and action video games. *Curr. Biol.* 22, R197–R206. doi: 10.1016/j.cub.2012.02.012

Guttorm, T. K., Leppänen, P. H., Poikkeus, A. -M., Eklund, K. M., Lyytinen, P., and Lyytinen, H. (2005). Brain event-related potentials (ERPs) measured at birth predict later language development in children with and without familial risk for dyslexia. *Cortex* 41, 291–303. doi: 10.1016/S0010-9452(08)70267-3

Hornickel, J., and Kraus, N. (2013). Unstable representation of sound: a biological marker of dyslexia. *J. Neurosci.* 33, 3500–3504. doi: 10.1523/JNEUROSCI.4205-12.2013

Hornickel, J., Skoe, E., Nicol, T., Zecker, S., and Kraus, N. (2009). Subcortical differentiation of stop consonants relates to reading and speech-in-noise perception. *Proc. Natl. Acad. Sci. U.S.A.* 106, 13022–13027. doi: 10.1073/pnas.0901123106

Hornickel, J., Zecker, S. G., Bradlow, A. R., and Kraus, N. (2012). Assistive listening devices drive neuroplasticity in children with dyslexia. *Proc. Natl. Acad. Sci. U.S.A.* 109, 16731–16736. doi: 10.1073/pnas.1206628109

Huss, M., Verney, J. P., Fosker, T., Mead, N., and Goswami, U. (2011). Music, rhythm, rise time perception and developmental dyslexia: perception of musical meter predicts reading and phonology. *Cortex* 47, 674–689. doi: 10.1016/j.cortex.2010.07.010

Johnson, K. L., Nicol, T., Zecker, S. G., and Kraus, N. (2008). Developmental plasticity in the human auditory brainstem. *J. Neurosci.* 28, 4000–4007. doi: 10.1523/JNEUROSCI.0012-08.2008

Kovelman, I., Norton, E. S., Christodoulou, J. A., Gaab, N., Lieberman, D. A., Triantafyllou, C., et al. (2012). Brain basis of phonological awareness for spoken language in children and its disruption in dyslexia. *Cereb. Cortex* 22, 754–764. doi: 10.1093/cercor/bhr094

Kraus, N., and Chandrasekaran, B. (2010). Music training for the development of auditory skills. *Nat. Rev. Neurosci.* 11, 599–605. doi: 10.1038/nrn2882

Kraus, N., McGee, T. J., Carrell, T. D., Zecker, S. G., Nicol, T. G., and Koch, D. B. (1996). Auditory neurophysiologic responses and discrimination deficits in children with learning problems. *Science* 273, 971–973. doi: 10.1126/science.273.5277.971

Kraus, N., and Nicol, T. (in press). "The cognitive auditory system," in *Springer Handbook of Auditory Research*, eds R. Fay and A. Popper (New York: Springer).

Lallier, M., Donnadieu, S., and Valdois, S. (2013). Developmental dyslexia: exploring how much phonological and visual attention span disorders are linked to simultaneous auditory processing deficits. *Ann. Dyslexia* 63, 97–116. doi: 10.1007/s11881-012-0074-4

Langner, G., and Schreiner, C. E. (1988). Periodicity coding in the inferior colliculus of the cat. I. Neuronal mechanisms. *J. Neurophysiol.* 60, 1799–1822.

Lehongre, K., Ramus, F., Villiermet, N., Schwartz, D., and Giraud, A.-L. (2011). Altered low-gamma sampling in auditory cortex accounts for the three main facets of dyslexia. *Neuron* 72, 1080–1090. doi: 10.1016/j.neuron.2011.11.002

Leong, V., and Goswami, U. (2013). Assessment of rhythmic entrainment at multiple timescales in dyslexia: evidence for disruption to syllable timing. *Hear. Res.* doi: 10.1016/j.heares.2013.07.015 [Epub ahead of print].

Leppänen, P., Hämäläinen, J., Guttorm, T., Eklund, K., Salminen, H., Tanskanen, A., et al. (2012). Infant brain responses associated with reading-related skills before school and at school age. *Neurophysiol. Clin. Neurophysiol.* 42, 35–41. doi: 10.1016/j.neucli.2011.08.005

Liu, L.-F., Palmer, A. R., and Wallace, M. N. (2006). Phase-locked responses to pure tones in the inferior colliculus. *J. Neurophysiol.* 95, 1926–1935. doi: 10.1152/jn.00497.2005

Livingstone, M. S., Rosen, G. D., Drislane, F. W., and Galaburda, A. M. (1991). Physiological and anatomical evidence for a magnocellular defect in developmental dyslexia. *Proc. Natl. Acad. Sci. U.S.A.* 88, 7943–7947. doi: 10.1073/pnas.88.18.7943

McGinley, M. J., Liberman, M. C., Bal, R., and Oertel, D. (2012). Generating synchrony from the asynchronous: compensation for cochlear traveling wave delays by the dendrites of individual brainstem neurons. *J. Neurosci.* 32, 9301–9311. doi: 10.1523/JNEUROSCI.0272-12.2012

Moreno, S., Marques, C., Santos, A., Santos, M., Besson, M., and Castro, S.L. (2009). Musical training influences linguistic abilities in 8-year-old children: more evidence for brain plasticity. *Cereb. Cortex* 19, 712–723. doi: 10.1093/cercor/bhn120

Noordenbos, M.W., Segers, E., Serniclaes, W., Mitterer, H., and Verhoeven, L. (2012). Neural evidence of allophonic perception in children at risk for dyslexia. *Neuropsychologia* 50, 2010–2017. doi: 10.1016/j.neuropsychologia.2012.04.026

Noordenbos, M. W., Segers, E., Serniclaes, W., and Verhoeven, L. (2013). Neural evidence of the allophonic mode of speech perception in adults with dyslexia. *Clin. Neurophysiol.* 124, 1151–1162 doi: 10.1016/j.clinph.2012.12.044

Parbery-Clark, A., Tierney, A., Strait, D. L., and Kraus, N. (2012). Musicians have fine-tuned neural distinction of speech syllables. *Neuroscience* 219, 111–119. doi: 10.1016/j.neuroscience.2012.05.042

Power, A. J., Mead, N., Barnes, L., and Goswami, U. (2012). Neural entrainment to rhythmically presented auditory, visual, and audio-visual speech in children. *Front. Psychol.* 3:216. doi: 10.3389/fpsyg.2012.00216

Power, A. J., Mead, N., Barnes, L., and Goswami, U. (2013). Neural entrainment to rhythmic speech in children with developmental dyslexia. *Front. Hum. Neurosci.* 7:777. doi: 10.3389/fnhum.2013.00777

Pugh, K. R., Landi, N., Preston, J. L., Mencl, W. E., Austin, A. C., Sibley, D., et al. (2013). The relationship between phonological and auditory processing and brain organization in beginning readers. *Brain Lang.* 125, 173–183. doi: 10.1016/j.bandl.2012.04.004

Ramus, F., Marshall, C. R., Rosen, S., and van der Lely, H. K. (2013). Phonological deficits in specific language impairment and developmental dyslexia: towards a multidimensional model. *Brain* 136, 630–645. doi: 10.1093/brain/aws356

Sandak, R., Mencl, W. E., Frost, S. J., and Pugh, K. R. (2004). The neurobiological basis of skilled and impaired reading: Recent findings and new directions. *Sci. Stud. Read.* 8, 273–292. doi: 10.1207/s1532799xssr0803_6

Saygin, Z. M., Norton, E. S., Osher, D. E., Beach, S. D., Cyr, A. B., Ozernov-Palchik, O., et al. (2013). Tracking the roots of reading ability: white matter volume and integrity correlate with phonological awareness in prereading and early-reading kindergarten children. *J. Neurosci.* 33, 13251–13258. doi: 10.1523/JNEUROSCI.4383-12.2013

Serniclaes, W., Heghe, S. V., Mousty, P., Carré, R., and Sprenger-Charolles, L. (2004). Allophonic mode of speech perception in dyslexia. *J. Exp. Child Psychol.* 87, 336–361. doi: 10.1016/j.jecp.2004.02.001

Skoe, E., and Kraus, N. (2010). Auditory brain stem response to complex sounds: a tutorial. *Ear Hear* 31, 302–324. doi: 10.1097/AUD.0b013e3181cdb272

Skoe, E., Krizman, J., Anderson, S., and Kraus, N. (in press). Stability and plasticity of auditory brainstem function across the lifespan. *Cereb. Cortex.*

Skoe, E., Nicol, T., and Kraus, N. (2011). Cross-phaseogram: objective neural index of speech sound differentiation. *J. Neurosci. Methods* 196, 308–317. doi: 10.1016/j.jneumeth.2011.01.020

Stein, J. (2001). The magnocellular theory of developmental dyslexia. *Dyslexia* 7, 12–36. doi: 10.1002/dys.186

Steinschneider, M., and Fishman, Y. I. (2011). Enhanced physiologic discriminability of stop consonants with prolonged formant transitions in awake monkeys based on the tonotopic organization of primary auditory cortex. *Hear. Res.* 271, 103–114. doi: 10.1016/j.heares.2010.04.008

Strait, D. L., O'Connell, S., Parbery-Clark, A., and Kraus, N. (2013). Musicians' enhanced neural differentiation of speech sounds arises early in life: developmental evidence from ages three to thirty. *Cereb. Cortex* doi: 10.1093/cercor/bht103 [Epub ahead of print].

Swan, D., and Goswami, U. (1997). Phonological awareness deficits in developmental dyslexia and the phonological representations hypothesis. *J. Exp. Child Psychol.* 66, 18–41. doi: 10.1006/jecp.1997.2375

Tallal, P. (1980). Auditory temporal perception, phonics, and reading disabilities in children. *Brain Lang.* 9, 182–198. doi: 10.1016/0093-934X(80)90139-X

Tallal, P., Miller, S. L., Bedi, G., Byma, G., Wang, X., Nagarajan, S. S., et al. (1996). Language comprehension in language-learning impaired children improved with acoustically modified speech. *Science* 271, 81–84. doi: 10.1126/science.271.5245.81

Tallal, P., and Piercy, M. (1975). Developmental aphasia: the perception of brief vowels and extended stop consonants. *Neuropsychologia* 13, 69–74. doi: 10.1016/0028-3932(75)90049-4

Temple, E., Deutsch, G. K., Poldrack, R. A., Miller, S. L., Tallal, P., Merzenich, M. M., et al. (2003). Neural deficits in children with dyslexia ameliorated by behavioral remediation: evidence from functional MRI. *Proc. Natl. Acad. Sci. U.S.A.* 100, 2860–2865. doi: 10.1073/pnas.0030098100

Thomson, J. M., Fryer, B., Maltby, J., and Goswami, U. (2006). Auditory and motor rhythm awareness in adults with dyslexia. *J. Res. Read.* 29, 334–348. doi: 10.1111/j.1467-9817.2006.00312.x

Tierney, A. T., and Kraus, N. (2013a). The ability to move to a beat is linked to the consistency of neural responses to sound. *J. Neurosci.* 33, 14981–14988. doi: 10.1523/JNEUROSCI.0612-13.2013

Tierney, A. T., and Kraus, N. (2013b). The ability to tap to a beat relates to cognitive, linguistic, and perceptual skills. *Brain Lang.* 124, 225–231. doi: 10.1016/j.bandl.2012.12.014

Tierney, A. T., and Kraus, N. (2013c). "Music training for the development of reading skills," in *Applying Brain Plasticity to Advance and Recover Human Ability Progress in Brain Research*, eds M. M. Merzenich, M. Nahum, and T. van Vleet (London: Elsevier).

Vidyasagar, T. R., and Pammer, K. (2010). Dyslexia: a deficit in visuo-spatial attention, not in phonological processing. *Trends Cogn. Sci.* 14, 57–63. doi: 10.1016/j.tics.2009.12.003

Wechsler, D. (1989). *WPPSI-R: Wechsler Preschool and Primary Scale of Intelligence.* San Diego: Psychological Corporation Harcourt Brace Jovanovich.

Wible, B., Nicol, T., and Kraus, N. (2005). Correlation between brainstem and cortical auditory processes in normal and language-impaired children. *Brain* 128, 417–423. doi: 10.1093/brain/awh367

Wiig, E. H., Secord, W., and Semel, E. M. (2004). *CELF Preschool 2: Clinical Evaluation of Language Fundamentals Preschool.* Toronto: Pearson/PsychCorp.

Witton, C., Talcott, J., Hansen, P., Richardson, A., Griffiths, T., Rees, A., et al. (1998). Sensitivity to dynamic auditory and visual stimuli predicts nonword reading ability in both dyslexic and normal readers. *Curr. Biol.* 8, 791–797. doi: 10.1016/S0960-9822(98)70320-3

Wright, B. A., Bowen, R. W., and Zecker, S. G. (2000). Nonlinguistic perceptual deficits associated with reading and language disorders. *Curr. Opin. Neurobiol.* 10, 482–486. doi: 10.1016/S0959-4388(00)00119-7

Wright, B. A., Lombardino, L. J., King, W. M., Puranik, C. S., Leonard, C. M., and Merzenich, M. M. (1997). Deficits in auditory temporal and spectral resolution in language-impaired children. *Nature* 387, 176–178. doi: 10.1038/387176a0

17

The effect of morphology on spelling and reading accuracy: a study on Italian children

Paola Angelelli[1]*, Chiara Valeria Marinelli[2] and Cristina Burani[3,4]

[1] Department of History, Society and Human Studies, University of Salento, Lecce, Italy
[2] Istituto di Ricovero e Cura a Carattere Scientifico (IRCCS) Santa Lucia, Rome, Italy
[3] Istituto di Scienze e Tecnologie della Cognizione, Consiglio Nazionale delle Ricerche, Rome, Italy
[4] Department of Life Sciences, University of Trieste, Trieste, Italy

***Correspondence:**
Paola Angelelli, Department of History, Society and Human Studies, University of Salento, 45/47 Stampacchia Street, 73100 Lecce, Italy
e-mail: paola.angelelli@unisalento.it

In opaque orthographies knowledge of morphological information helps in achieving reading and spelling accuracy. In transparent orthographies with regular print-to-sound correspondences, such as Italian, the mappings of orthography onto phonology and phonology onto orthography are in principle sufficient to read and spell most words. The present study aimed to investigate the role of morphology in the reading and spelling accuracy of Italian children as a function of school experience to determine whether morphological facilitation was present in children learning a transparent orthography. The reading and spelling performances of 15 third-grade and 15 fifth-grade typically developing children were analyzed. Children read aloud and spelled both low-frequency words and pseudowords. Low-frequency words were manipulated for the presence of morphological structure (morphemic words vs. non-derived words). Morphemic words could also vary for the frequency (high vs. low) of roots and suffixes. Pseudo-words were made up of either a real root and a real derivational suffix in a combination that does not exist in the Italian language or had no morphological constituents. Results showed that, in Italian, morphological information is a useful resource for both reading and spelling. Typically developing children benefitted from the presence of morphological structure when they read and spelled pseudowords; however, in processing low-frequency words, morphology facilitated reading but not spelling. These findings are discussed in terms of morpho-lexical access and successful cooperation between lexical and sublexical processes in reading and spelling.

Keywords: morphology, spelling, orthography, typically developing readers/spellers, transparent orthographies

INTRODUCTION

Analysis of the corpora and databases of several languages revealed that about 60% of less familiar words are either derived by affixation or compounds (see, e.g., Nagy and Anderson, 1984; Thornton et al., 1997, for American English and Italian, respectively). Thus, a large proportion of the unfamiliar words read and spelled by children in primary school are likely to be morphologically complex (Nagy and Anderson, 1984). In the last few decades it has been frequently shown that familiarity with morphemic patterns helps children to reasonably guess the meanings of unfamiliar words and is a powerful tool in vocabulary acquisition (see, e.g., Bertram et al., 2000). Morphology also provides reading strategies for correctly decoding and spelling unfamiliar words (Verhoeven and Perfetti, 2003, 2011). Knowledge of word morphology develops early in children, confirming that morphological structure is one of the main organizing principles of the mental lexicon. Morphological awareness improves with age and in each subsequent grade is more predictive of both reading and spelling achievement in children exposed to different orthographies (e.g., Mann and Singson, 2003; Berninger et al., 2010; Casalis et al., 2011). Morphological awareness usually predicts unique variance in addition to phonological awareness and has different degrees of association with word recognition (and spelling) in different scripts (McBride-Chang et al., 2003, 2005). Knowledge of derived words, in particular, may contribute to both reading and spelling achievement in older children, such as 6th graders (see, e.g., for Dutch, Rispens et al., 2008). Overall, access to morphemic constituents of words fosters reading and spelling performance in the course of literacy acquisition in several languages that vary for morphological richness and orthographic transparency (Verhoeven and Perfetti, 2011).

The effect of morphology on reading in Italian has received a good deal of attention in the last decade. A series of studies demonstrated that morpheme-based reading is available and efficient in Italian developing readers. In Italian, morphology has been found to have a main effect on reading fluency. Both typically developing Italian children ranging from 2nd to 7th grade and children with dyslexia read aloud pseudowords made up of a root and a derivational suffix (e.g., *donn-ista*, "woman-ist") faster than pseudowords that did not include morphemes (e.g., *dennosto*, Burani et al., 2002, 2008; Traficante et al., 2011). Analogously, words with a morphological structure (e.g., *cass-iere*, "cashier") were read faster than simple words (e.g., *cammello*, "camel") of the same length and frequency. Morphological facilitation of word reading speed was found in the youngest readers (2nd graders) and in children with dyslexia, but it was limited to low-frequency words in older skilled children (Burani et al., 2008; Marcolini et al., 2011; see also, for a review, Burani, 2010). The facilitation induced by morphology on the reading performance of less skilled readers may reflect access to lexical reading units (morphemes) that are shorter than the whole word when this reading unit is too long and complex for the reader. Morphemes (specifically roots and suffixes) can be efficient reading units because they have an intermediate grain size between single letters—which entail extremely slow and analytical sublexical processing—and the word—which for beginning readers and children with dyslexia is usually too large a unit to be processed as a whole. By contrast, for skilled readers who master lexical reading of familiar word units, recourse to morphemic units is beneficial only for low frequency words. In this case, morphemes (roots and affixes) usually have a higher frequency than the word in which they occur. Therefore, access to morphemes may facilitate lexical reading for a low-frequency word that otherwise would probably not be represented as a whole in the mental lexicon.

Italian has a transparent orthography and knowledge of morphology is not necessary for assigning the correct pronunciation to print or for correct spelling. This is different from opaque orthographies, such as English, Danish and French, in which word spelling is to some degree morphologically governed and knowledge of morphemes may help to assign the correct pronunciation or to make the appropriate choice between graphemic alternatives for spelling a word (see, e.g., Seymour, 1997; Verhoeven and Perfetti, 2003; Pacton and Deacon, 2008 and see below for examples). As a consequence, in Italian the impact of morphological structure on reading accuracy is weaker than that on reading speed. However, the presence of morphemes in a stimulus positively affected reading accuracy in the case of novel (pseudo-) words (Burani et al., 2002, 2008; Traficante et al., 2011), but not in the case of words, irrespective of word frequency or reading skill (Burani et al., 2008; Marcolini et al., 2011).

As to word spelling, the effect of morphological structure in opaque orthographies has been studied in relation to the existence of two different spelling procedures, one based on phonology-to-orthography conversion rules (Patterson, 1986; Tainturier and Rapp, 2000) and the other relying on access to word-specific memories in the orthographic lexicon (e.g., Barry, 1994). Within this framework, morphosyntax has been considered a third source of information for spelling. In opaque orthographies, morphological information may contribute to spelling accuracy in several ways. For example, in English the use of morphological information allows: (1) choosing between several possible spellings of a given sound (e.g., the vowel /e/ in *health* can be spelled correctly if one knows the spelling of its root, *heal*); (2) spelling certain words for which phonology is misleading (the past tense of regular verbs ends in *–ed* although their pronunciation can be /d/, /t/ and /Id/); and (3) spelling cases that are morphologically distinct although phonologically identical, as in the case of the apostrophe (*boys*, *boy's* and *boys'* sound the same but are spelled differently based on their morphological structure). Especially in the latter case, morphosyntactic information is necessary to to spell correctly because the use of markers cannot be retrieved from memory but depends on the syntactic context in which they occur. Evidence of the useful role of morphology in spelling mainly regards English and French. Many studies highlighted that children learning to spell in these two languages use various sources of morphosyntactic information to spell correctly (for a review see Pacton and Deacon, 2008). However, there is no agreement about the timing (early vs. late) of children's use of morphological information.

In a longitudinal study, Nunes et al. (1997) examined the appreciation of morphological conventions such as those required for the correct spelling of regular past tense verbs in 6- to 9-year-old English children. The authors used a dictation task with regular past tense verbs (ending in *–ed* as in *called* and *dressed*), irregular past tense verbs (endings spelled phonetically as in *found* and *felt*), and non-verbs ending with /d/ and /t/ (such as in *bird* and *soft*). Four developmental stages were identified: in the first stage children wrote /d/ and /t/ endings phonetically, irrespective of stimulus type; then, they generalized the *–ed* ending to grammatically inappropriate words, as in spelling the adjective (e.g., *sofed* for *soft*). Later these generalizations applied to grammatically appropriate words (verbs) but incorrectly to irregular verbs (e.g., *keeped* for *kept*), and finally they were properly confined to regular past tense verbs. The authors concluded that children grasp the morphological principles of spelling only at late stages of literacy.

Other studies (e.g., Treiman et al., 1994; Kemp, 2006) found that very young children (5–8 years old) were able to use the principle of root consistency, although not to its full extent. Kemp (2006) examined whether young children used their knowledge of the spelling of base words to spell inflected and derived forms. The author examined how children spelled the /z/ sound in one- and two-morpheme words. In the case of two-morpheme words, the different alternatives to represent the word-medial /z/ sound (e.g., *S, Z, ZZ*) can be determined by knowledge of the base form spelling. The author found that 5- to 9-year-olds were more accurate in representing the medial /z/ sound of words derived from base forms (e.g., *noisy* from *noise*) with respect to one-morpheme control words (e.g., *busy*). These findings support the view that English-speaking children identify and represent links of meaning between words relatively early and that morphological information is a resource used also by relatively young learners. Similar conclusions come from studies in French-speaking children. Sénéchal (2000) found that children even in the first year of formal schooling spelled words that have morphologically related words better than words that do not. More recently, in a study in 8-year-old children Pacton et al. (2013) found that a facilitation due to morphological relatedness was present also when they learned to spell new words.

In transparent orthographies with consistent phoneme-to-grapheme correspondences, such as Spanish, Finnish and Italian, the mapping of phonology onto orthography is in principle sufficient to spell most words correctly. However, there is evidence that morphological knowledge may have a role in spelling also in transparent orthographies. One piece of evidence comes from the study of Defior et al. (2008) in Spanish first- to third-grade children, in which the recourse to morphological information in spelling was investigated by capitalizing on one of the few conditions of non-transparency in oral-to-written mapping. In Andalusia, the region where the experiment was conducted, the final /s/ of words is not pronounced. Since the final /s/ marks plurals and the second person singular of verbs, its presence in the children's spellings was considered an index of their adequate use of morphosyntactic knowledge. The study included two morphological conditions (high- and low-frequency plural nouns and second person verbs), and a lexical control condition (high- and low-frequency singular nouns ending in /s/, e.g., *martes* "Tuesday"). Results showed that although Spanish spelling relies mainly on phonology, morphological information is also a spelling resource: with low-frequency words, children's spelling accuracy on verbs and plural nouns (items with morphologically motivated /s/ endings) was greater than that on control words with a final /s/ (not morphologically motivated). However, the results also showed that the children did not use morphology systematically: in high-frequency words, they used fewer /s/ endings in plural nouns than in uninflected control words.

To our knowledge, no study on Italian has investigated the role of morphology in spelling. However, a recent study in first- to eighth-grade Italian typically developing readers (Notarnicola et al., 2012) reported several findings of interest in this respect: (*i*) in agreement with the hypothesis that reliance on the different procedures depends on the degree of regularity of an orthography (for reviews, see Sprenger-Charolles, 2003; Caravolas, 2004), in Italian main reliance on the sublexical phoneme-to-grapheme spelling procedure was found in all grades; (*ii*) data also showed very early reliance on the lexical procedure, with a lexicality effect (regular words spelled better than pseudowords) and an early positive influence of a lexical-semantic variable, such as word age-of-acquisition, on ambiguous word spelling found in first graders; and (*iii*) data generally supported the view of an interaction between lexical and sublexical spelling processes in Italian children. Results showed a pattern of correlations that was generally consistent with the view that spelling regular words benefits from the cooperation of both spelling procedures, with sublexical processing assisting accuracy in spelling lexical items.

In the cited study on Italian, no morphologically complex words were used. Consequently, the impact of morphology on spelling could not be estimated. However, it can be conjectured that, similarly to what happens in reading long unfamiliar stimuli, access to morphemes might help Italian children recognize lexical chunks of information and use them for (morpho-) lexical spelling, thus bypassing the use of single phoneme-to-grapheme correspondences. Thus, the spelling of long and complex words might benefit from the possibility of segmenting the phoneme-grapheme array into units, such as morphemes, that are meaningful and more coherent than single phonemes or syllables. Some support to the view that morphemes may provide an efficient principle for stimulus segmentation comes from an interesting study by Lehtonen and Bryant (2005) on Finnish, a richly inflected language with highly transparent orthography. The authors used two-morpheme words in which target clusters of letters (the sequences LL and SS) appeared in different morphemes of the words, either in the root (unbound morpheme) or in the inflection for case. In Finnish, case inflections are a more prominent part of morphology than derivation, because they occur in nouns, adjectives, pronouns and numerals. The authors tested children at two different times during the first year of school and found that by the end of the year they began to spell target clusters better in case inflections than in word roots, which suggested emerging sensitivity to the morphological structure of words in spelling. Similar results were found for pseudowords: letter clusters occurring in endings corresponding to case inflections were spelled with greater accuracy than those occurring in pseudo-roots, suggesting that case-like endings prompted morphological parsing during spelling. According to the authors, the facilitation arises because the children's mental lexicon is organized in morphemes and case inflections are solidly acquired and represented in the mental lexicon due to the high frequency with which they occur. This in turn helps the subsequent parsing of words into their constituent morphemes, favoring the oral-to-written transcription process.

In the present study we investigated the effects of morphology on both reading and spelling accuracy of pseudowords and words in typically developing children in different grades, i.e., in third and fifth grade. For both reading and spelling, we expected that pseudowords made up of familiar morphemes (roots and derivational suffixes) would be read and spelled better than matched pseudowords that did not include any morphemic constituent. The expected findings would confirm those already obtained for reading (see Burani et al., 2002, 2008; Traficante et al., 2011) and would extend them to spelling. As to words, in preceding studies on Italian no evidence was found of an effect of morphological structure on reading accuracy. However, preceding studies on word reading either involved words of medium frequency (Burani et al., 2008), or, when low-frequency words were investigated, readers were in 6th–7th grade. Thus, we still do not know whether the presence of familiar morphemes in a low-frequency word favors reading (and spelling) accuracy in children as young as 3rd and 5th graders who might not yet possess a lexical representation for low-frequency words. In the present study, children's reading and spelling performance on low-frequency morphologically complex words was compared to their performance on words with no derivational structure. In order to better qualify the effect of morphology, two types of morphologically complex words were investigated: words made-up of high-frequency morphemes (root and suffix) and words with low-frequency morphemes. Some studies have found that English-speaking children in 3rd to 6th grades read aloud derived words with a high frequency base more accurately than derived words with a low frequency base matched for surface frequency

(Mann and Singson, 2003; Carlisle and Stone, 2005; Deacon et al., 2011). The new experimental contrasts adopted here, in which both types of morphologically complex words (i.e., including either high-frequency or low-frequency morphemes) were compared to words that did not include morphemes, allowed us to investigate an issue that has never been studied in Italian children. Higher accuracy was expected for morphological words including high-frequency morphemes as compared to words including low-frequency roots and suffixes and words not decomposable into morphemes. The advantage for words including high-frequency morphemes was expected to hold for both 3rd and 5th graders.

Administration of the same pseudowords and words for both reading and spelling allowed us to directly compare the children's performance on both tasks. Overall, we expected that morphological knowledge would enhance not only reading but also spelling performance in Italian by facilitating the parsing process of the stimulus by retrieving lexical units smaller than the whole stimulus. Similarly to what has been observed for morpheme-based reading, morphological facilitation in spelling was expected to be evident for pseudowords, irrespective of the children's reading ability. For low-frequency words, we expected that only those made up of high-frequency morphemes would result in a morphological benefit in spelling, with no substantial differences between children in different grades.

MATERIALS AND METHOD

PARTICIPANTS

Participants were selected during screening activities, as part of a research agreement between the University of Bari and a local public primary school. The study was conducted according to the principles of the Helsinki Declaration and was approved by the school authority (Teaching body). Parents were informed of the screening activities and had to approve their child's participation. All data concerning individual performances were analyzed strictly for research purposes.

Participants were typically developing readers and spellers selected according to the following criteria: *(i)* normal reading speed and accuracy on a standard reading test (MT reading test, Cornoldi and Colpo, 1998; see paragraph Reading Assessment), *(ii)* normal spelling performance on a standard spelling test (DDO Test for the Diagnosis of Developmental Dysgraphia, Angelelli et al., 2008; see paragraph Spelling Assessment); and *(iii)* normal performance on a nonverbal general intelligence test (Raven's Colored Progressive Matrices, CPM; i.e., above the 10th percentile for age range according to normative Italian data by Pruneti et al., 1996). Participants included 15 children in 3rd grade (7F, 8M; mean age = 8.65 year, sd = 0.27) and 15 children in 5th grade (7F, 8M; mean age = 10.34 year, sd = 0.38), matched one-to-one for gender and performance on Raven's CPM intelligence test (*z* scores; $F_{(1,29)} = 0.00$, ns).

Data pertaining to the 3rd and 5th grade children's performance on Raven's CPM, the MT reading tasks (speed and errors) and the spelling test are summarized in **Table 1**. As reported in the Table, 5th grade children, compared to 3rd grade children, performed better in terms of reading speed and reduced error rates in reading as well as in all spelling subsets. Both groups of children performed close to normative data (*z* scores about zero) for Raven's CPM (3rd grade children: $z = -0.38$; 5th grade children: $z = -0.40$), reading speed (3rd grade children: $z = -0.22$; 5th grade children: $z = -0.43$), reading accuracy (3rd grade children: $z = 0.28$; 5th grade children: $z = -0.44$) and for the total spelling task (3rd grade children: $z = -0.32$; 5th grade children: $z = 0.07$), indicating only marginal deviations from the same-age normative sample.

READING ASSESSMENT

Reading level was assessed using a standard reading achievement test (i.e., the MT Reading test, Cornoldi and Colpo, 1998). Participants read aloud a meaningful text passage within a 4-min time limit; speed (time in seconds per number of syllables read) and accuracy (number of errors, adjusted for the amount of text read) were computed. Stimulus materials and related reference norms varied depending on school grade. Raw scores were converted to *z* scores according to standard reference data. Normative data for third and fifth graders were based on 285 and 305 children, respectively (Cornoldi and Colpo, 1998).

SPELLING ASSESSMENT

The participants' spelling abilities were tested with a standard *spelling to dictation test* (DDO test, Angelelli et al., 2008), which consisted of four sections:

Section A: regular words with full one-sound-to-one-letter correspondence ($N = 70$).

Section B: regular words requiring the application of context-sensitive sound-to-spelling rules ($N = 10$). In Italian, context-sensitive rules are required when the orthographic transcription of a phoneme depends on the following letter. For example, the phoneme /k/ is spelled C, when followed by a consonant (e.g., in *clima* (/klima/ "climate") or by A, O, U (e.g., in *casa* /kaza/ "home"; *cono* /kono/ "cone"; and *cubo* /kubo/ "cube") and CH when followed by E or I (e.g., in *chilo*/kilo/ "kilogram").

Section C: ambiguous words (words with two or more possible transcriptions along the phonology-to-orthography conversion routine; (e.g., words containing the syllables /tʃe/, /ʃe/ and /dʒe/, which may or may not require an I (e.g., /ʃentsa/ "science" is spelled *scienza* and not *scenza*, while /ʃena/ "scene" is spelled *scena* and not *sciena*) ($N = 55$).

Section D: pseudowords with one-sound-to-one-letter correspondence ($N = 25$).

Words with one-sound-to-one-letter correspondence and pseudowords were controlled for orthographic complexity (i.e., number of consonant clusters, double consonants) and length.

Normative data are available for first- to eighth-grade children (Angelelli et al., 2008). Reference data for third and fifth graders are based on 95 and 105 children, respectively. Raw scores were converted to *z* scores.

EXPERIMENTAL LISTS

Different sets of low-frequency words and pseudowords were created.

Words: Three sets of 15 low-frequency words (Istituto di Linguistica Computazionale, CNR, unpublished) were used. Words in the first set (e.g., bruttezza, "ugliness") consisted of a root

Table 1 | Mean (and SD) of 3rd and 5th grade children on the intelligence test (Raven's Colored Progressive Matrices), the MT Reading test (Cornoldi and Colpo, 1998), and the writing task (Angelelli et al., 2008).

	3rd grade children		5th grade children	
	Mean	**SD**	**Mean**	**SD**
Raven' CPM accuracy (*n* = 36)	24.20	3.76	28.47	4.14
MT reading speed	38.98	9.54	26.06	4.51
MT reading errors	6.30	2.66	3.20	1.62
Regular words 1:1 spelling accuracy (*n* = 70)	22.93	2.55	24.87	0.35
Context-sensitive words spelling accuracy (*n* = 10)	68.53	1.06	69.40	0.83
Ambiguous words spelling accuracy (*n* = 55)	9.60	0.83	9.87	0.35
Pseudoword spelling accuracy (*n* = 25)	45.40	4.21	50.40	3.38
Total spelling accuracy (*n* = 160)	146.47	6.40	154.53	3.76

Note: Regular words 1:1 = words with one-sound-to-one-letter correspondence; context-sensitive words = words requiring the application of context-sensitive sound-to-spelling rules; ambiguous words = words with unpredictable transcription along the phonology-to-orthography conversion routine.

(brutt- "ugly") and a derivational suffix (-ezza, "ness"), which were both of high frequency (HD). Words in the second set (*e.g.*, agrumeto, "citrus grove") consisted of a root (agrum-, "citrus plant") and a derivational suffix (-eto, indicating a place where trees or flowers grow), which were both of low frequency (LD). The third set of words included simple non-derived words (ND) (e.g., aragosta, "lobster"). The three sets of words were matched for word frequency and did not differ for relevant psycholinguistic variables such as length (number of letters), consonant clusters, geminate letters, number of contextual rules and bigram frequency (all *ps* > 0.05). As expected, the first and the second set were different for root frequency ($F_{(1,28)} = 17.73$, $p < 0.001$) and suffix frequency ($F_{(1,28)} = 15.79$, $p < 0.001$). All words (with frequency values) are reported in Appendix A.

Pseudowords: Two sets of 16 pseudowords of three to four syllables (length range: 8–10 letters) were generated: pseudowords in the first set were morphologically complex (root + suffix) and consisted of a root and a derivational suffix (R^+S^+) in a combination that does not exist in the Italian language (e.g., lampadista, constituted by the bound root lampad-, meaning "lamp" and the suffix –ista, "-ist"). Pseudowords in the second set (non-root + non-suffix) were made up of orthographic sequences that did not correspond to any existing Italian root or suffix (R^-S^-) (*e.g.*, livonosto). Analogously to the ND words, the pseudowords in the latter set had no morphological structure. The two sets of morphemic and non-morphemic pseudowords were matched for number of contextual rules, consonant clusters, geminate letters, length (in letters) and bigram frequency (all *Fs* < 1). The two sets of pseudowords were also matched for the frequency of the final orthographic sequence, which corresponded either to a real suffix in the R^+S^+ set or a non-suffix in the R^-S^- set. All pseudowords with frequency values of constituent parts are reported in Appendix B.

We added 43 filler stimuli to the list, that is, 15 non-morphologically complex words and 18 pseudowords; half were morphologically complex and half were simple. A total of 110 stimuli were presented to each child for dictation; half were words and half were pseudowords, half were morphologically complex and half were simple. This list of words and pseudowords was intended to favor lexical reading without explicitly inducing morphological decomposition.

PROCEDURE

For the reading condition words and pseudowords were randomized and presented in three blocks of either 36 or 37 items each, using different random orders. Stimuli were displayed at the center of the computer screen; they were printed in black lower case (Arial font, 24 pt). Each trial consisted of the following sequence: a fixation point for 500 ms; a blank stimulus for 250 ms; the stimulus, which remained visible until the onset of pronunciation. Participants read each stimulus aloud as accurately as possible. Mispronunciation errors were recorded and noted by two experimenters, who verified their annotations at the end of the experimental sections. The experimental sections were preceded by a training block of 10 stimuli, that is, five words and five pseudowords.

For the spelling condition, words and pseudowords were randomized and administered in a spelling-to-dictation task. The examiner read each item aloud in a neutral tone without emphasizing the presence of possible orthographic difficulties. To ensure that the children had correctly perceived the items, the examiner asked them to repeat each one before they wrote it down in capital letters. No feedback was provided on the correctness of the written response. Pauses were allowed if requested. Spontaneous corrections were accepted.

The reading and spelling tests were administered with an interval of about 20 days between them (were administered about 20 days apart). The order of the tasks was balanced in the experimental sample: half of the children performed the reading task first and then the spelling test, and the other half performed the tasks in reverse order; children were randomly assigned to the first or second sub-group. They were tested individually in a quiet room at their school.

DATA ANALYSIS

Reading and spelling accuracy were analyzed with Logistic Mixed Effect Models (Guo and Zhao, 2000; Quené and van den Bergh, 2008) by means of SPSS 22.0 statistics software.

Logistic Mixed Effect Models were used to control for the presence of a floor effect as well as for item and participant variability. In this analysis the dependent variable was accuracy on each item of each participant in each experimental condition/sample; thus, the number of observations was very high.

Data on words and pseudowords were analyzed separately. In both analyses, *Task* (reading vs. spelling), *Grade* (3rd vs. 5th grade) and *Morphology* were entered as fixed factors, and *Items* and *Participants* were entered as Random factors. Note that in the case of words the effect of *Morphology* refers to words made up of high-frequency roots and high-frequency derivational suffixes [HD], low-frequency roots and low-frequency derivational suffixes [LD] and non-derived words [ND]; in the case of pseudowords, *Morphology* refers to pseudowords made up of real roots and derivational suffixes [R^+S^+] and pseudowords, including orthographic sequences that did not correspond to any existing Italian root or suffix [R^-S^-]. Interactions were explored by means of pairwise *post-hoc* tests.

Although comparisons between word sets for word frequency were non-significant (see paragraph Experimental Lists), words in the LL condition showed some rather unbalanced word frequencies relative to the other two sets. Therefore, to ensure that the results obtained were not a by-product of some word frequency differences between sets, a second analysis was performed in which word frequency was entered as a covariate.

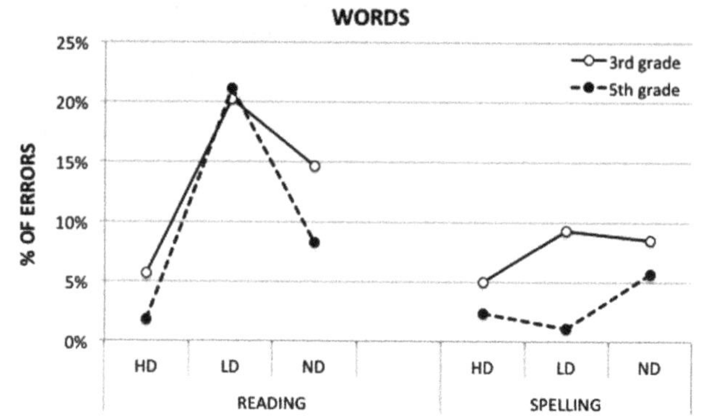

FIGURE 1 | Reading and spelling performance (percentage of errors) on words with high-frequency roots and suffixes (HD), low-frequency roots and suffixes (LD) and non-derived words by typically developing 3rd and 5th grade children.

RESULTS

Words

The Logistic Mixed Effect Model showed a significant effect of *Task* ($F_{(1,2732)} = 20.64$, $p < 0.0001$), *Grade* ($F_{(1,2732)} = 11.80$, $p < 0.001$) and *Morphology* ($F_{(1,2732)} = 4.47$, $p < 0.01$), with a higher error rate in reading with respect to spelling (9.3% vs. 4.3%, respectively), in 3rd compared to 5th grade children (9.5% vs. 4.2%), and in ND and LD words with respect to HD words (8.8% and 8.5% vs. 3.3%, respectively). The *Morphology* × *Task* interaction ($F_{(1,2732)} = 10.76$, $p < 0.0001$) was significant, showing an effect of morphology in reading ($p < 0.0001$) but not in spelling. Exploration of means revealed that HD words were read significantly better than LD and ND words ($p < 0.001$ and $p < 0.01$, respectively) and that LD words were read worse than ND words ($p < 0.05$). Furthermore, *post-hoc* analysis showed that the HD condition led to comparable error percentages in reading and spelling, but the LD and ND words had a significantly higher error rate in reading than in spelling (for LD, difference between reading and spelling = 17.5%, $p < 0.0001$; for ND, difference between reading and spelling = 4.2%, $p < 0.05$).

The *Task* × *Morphology* × *Grade* interaction ($F_{(1,2732)} = 5.57$, $p < 0.01$) was significant. **Figure 1** shows how morphology modulates reading and spelling performance for words in 3rd and 5th grade children. **Table 2** reports mean error percentages (and standard errors values) as a function of task and stimulus type. The effect of morphology was significant in reading for both 3rd and 5th graders ($p < 0.01$ and $p < 0.0001$, respectively), but not in spelling (either for 3rd or 5th graders). Exploration of means showed that in reading both 3rd and 5th grade children performed more incorrectly on LD than HD words (difference = 14.6%, and 19.3% in 3rd and 5th grade, respectively, at least $p < 0.01$); and on ND compared to HD words (difference = 9.0% and 6.5%, in 3rd and 5th grade, respectively, at least $p < 0.05$); only 5th graders showed a difference also between LD and ND (difference = 12.8%, $p < 0.05$), indicating that the LD condition was the most difficult one. In spelling, both groups had very low and comparable percentages of errors on HD and LD words; the only significant effect was in 5th graders, who spelled ND words less correctly than morphologically complex stimuli (ND vs. LD diff. = 4.5%, $p < 0.05$). Finally, progressing from 3rd to 5th grade, errors decreased for HD words ($p < 0.05$) and ND words ($p = 0.06$) in reading and for LD words ($p < 0.01$) in spelling. A comparison between reading and spelling performances showed significantly lower accuracy in reading than in spelling only for the LD condition in both 3rd and 5th graders ($p < 0.01$ and $p < 0.0001$, respectively).

The random effects of *Items* ($Z = 3.52$; $p < 0.0001$) and *Participants* ($Z = 2.15$; $p < 0.05$) were significant.

When word frequency was added as a covariate in the analysis it approached significance ($F_{(1,2.732)} = 3.45$, $p = 0.06$). However, the effects of *Task* ($F_{(1,2732)} = 20.64$, $p < 0.0001$), *Grade* ($F_{(1,2732)} = 11.80$, $p < 0.001$), *Morphology* ($F_{(1,2732)} = 4.47$, $p < 0.05$), as well as the second level interaction *Task* × *Morphology* × *Grade* ($F_{(1,2732)} = 5.57$, $p < 0.01$) remained unchanged.

Pseudowords

Figure 2 shows the effect of morphology on the reading and spelling accuracy performance of 3rd and 5th grade children on pseudowords. **Table 3** reports mean error percentages (and standard error values) as a function of task and stimulus type. The analyses indicated significant effects of *Task* ($F_{(1,1944)} = 35.71$, $p < 0.0001$), *Grade* ($F_{(1,1944)} = 14.94$, $p < 0.0001$) and *Morphology* ($F_{(1,1944)} = 16.66$, $p < 0.0001$). Exploration of the main effects showed higher error rates in reading (15.9%) than in spelling (3.1%) in 3rd graders compared to 5th graders (12.6% vs. 4.6%,

The data that emerged from the present study have clear empirical implications. The facilitatory effect of morphology in reading and in spelling new words could be used to enrich standard teaching methods and rehabilitation strategies in the case of learning disabilities. Regarding reading, in our study only accuracy was considered. However, previous reports showed that morphology enhanced reading fluency (see Burani, 2010, for a review) in Italian children with dyslexia who are characterized by a prevalent deficit of reading speed (Zoccolotti et al., 1999). In the present study we found small but reliable effects in the spelling of regular stimuli of 3rd and 5th grade children. Studies in larger populations are needed to confirm the present data. However, considering that the transcription of regular stimuli is optimized very early in Italian (see Notarnicola et al., 2012), larger facilitatory effects might be found in younger learners. Furthermore, considering that some errors on ambiguous words are still present in 8th grade typically developing children and that a selective impairment of ambiguous word transcription characterizes the writing deficit of Italian children with learning disabilities (Angelelli et al., 2004, 2010), we believe that recourse to morphology is particularly helpful in situations of spelling ambiguity (e.g., knowledge of the spelling of SCIENZA "science" may facilitate the spelling of SCIENZIATO "scientist", FANTASCIENZA "science fiction", etc.). In this sense the introduction of morphemes in teaching materials and an emphasis on morphemic strategies could be particularly useful in the early phases of literacy acquisition as well as in children with learning disabilities (see, e.g., Elbro and Arnbak, 1996; Traficante, 2012). Explicit training using morphological strategies might induce children to identify patterns of letters that are consistent among several words and foster the processing of units that are larger than single phonemes/graphemes. However, future research is needed to further explore the possible benefits of morphological training, especially in transparent orthographies.

Overall the present study extends the role of morphology from reading to the spelling of newly encountered stimuli in a language with transparent orthography (Italian) and highlights the possible role of morphological knowledge in promoting literacy acquisition.

REFERENCES

Angelelli, P., Judica, A., Spinelli, D., Zoccolotti, P., and Luzzatti, C. (2004). Characteristic of writing disorders in Italian dyslexic children. *Cogn. Behav. Neurol.* 17, 18–31. doi: 10.1097/00146965-200403000-00003

Angelelli, P., Notarnicola, A., Costabile, D., Marinelli, C. V., Judica, A., Zoccolotti, P., et al. (2008). *DDO- Diagnosi dei Disturbi Ortografici in Età Evolutiva [Diagnosis of Orthographic Deficits in Childhood]*. Trento: Erickson.

Angelelli, P., Notarnicola, A., Judica, A., Zoccolotti, P., and Luzzatti, C. (2010). Spelling impairment in Italian dyslexic children: phenomenological changes in primary school. *Cortex* 46, 1299–1311. doi: 10.1016/j.cortex.2010.06.015

Barry, C. (1994). "Spelling routes (or roots or rutes)," in *Handbook of Spelling: Theory, Process and Intervention*, eds G. D. A. Brown and N. C. Ellis (Chichester: John Wiley), 27–49.

Berninger, V. W., Abbott, R. D., Nagy, W., and Carlisle, J. (2010). Growth in phonological, orthographic and morphological awareness in grades 1 to 6. *J. Psycholinguist Res.* 39, 141–163. doi: 10.1007/s10936-009-9130-6

Bertram, R., Laine, M., and Virkkala, M. M. (2000). The role of derivational morphology in vocabulary acquisition: get by with a little help from my morpheme friends. *Scand. J. Psychol.* 41, 287–296. doi: 10.1111/1467-9450.00201

Burani, C. (2010). Word morphology enhances reading fluency in children with developmental dyslexia. *Lang. Lang.* 9, 177–198. doi: 10.1418/33326

Burani, C., Marcolini, S., De Luca, M., and Zoccolotti, P. (2008). Morpheme-based reading aloud: evidence from dyslexic and skilled Italian readers. *Cognition* 108, 243–262. doi: 10.1016/j.cognition.2007.12.010

Burani, C., Marcolini, S., and Stella, G. (2002). How early does morpho-lexical reading develop in readers of a shallow orthography? *Brain Lang.* 81, 568–586. doi: 10.1006/brln.2001.2548

Caravolas, M. (2004). Spelling development in alphabetic writing systems: a cross-linguistic perspective. *Eur. Psychol.* 9, 3–14. doi: 10.1027/1016-9040.9.1.3

Carlisle, J. F., and Stone, C. A. (2005). Exploring the role of morphemes in word reading. *Read. Res. Q.* 40, 428–449. doi: 10.1598/rrq.40.4.3

Casalis, S., Deacon, S. H., and Pacton, S. (2011). How specific is the connection between morphological awareness and spelling? A study of French children. *Appl. Psycholinguist.* 32, 499–511. doi: 10.1017/s014271641100018x

Chua, S. M., and Liow, S. J. R. (2014). The locus of word frequency effects in skilled spelling-to-dictation. *Q. J. Exp. Psychol. (Hove)* 67, 1720–1741. doi: 10.1080/17470218.2013.868915

Cornoldi, C., and Colpo, G. (1998). *Prove di Lettura MT. Guida all'uso [The MT Reading Test: User Manual]*. Firenze, IT: Organizzazioni Speciali.

Deacon, S. H., Whalen, R., and Kirby, J. R. (2011). Do children see the danger in dangerous? Grade 4, 6 and 8 children's reading of morphologically complex words. *Appl. Psycholinguist.* 32, 467–481. doi: 10.1017/s0142716411000166

Defior, S., Alegría, J., Titos, R., and Martos, F. (2008). Using morphology when spelling in a shallow orthographic system: the case of Spanish. *Cogn. Dev.* 23, 204–215. doi: 10.1016/j.cogdev.2007.01.003

Elbro, C., and Arnbak, E. (1996). The role of morpheme recognition and morphological awareness in dyslexia. *Ann. Dyslexia* 46, 209–240. doi: 10.1007/bf02648177

Guo, G., and Zhao, H. X. (2000). Multilevel modeling for binary data. *Annu. Rev. Sociol.* 26, 441–462. doi: 10.1146/annurev.soc.26.1.441

Kemp, N. (2006). Children's spelling of base, inflected and derived words: links with morphological awareness. *Read. Writ.* 19, 737–765. doi: 10.1007/s11145-006-9001-6

Lehtonen, A., and Bryant, P. (2005). Active players or just passive bystanders? The role of morphemes in spelling development in a transparent orthography. *Appl. Psycholinguist.* 26, 137–155. doi: 10.1017/s0142716405050113

Mann, V., and Singson, M. (2003). "Linking morphological knowledge to English decoding ability: large effects of little suffixes," in *Reading Complex Words: Cross-Language Studies*, eds E. Assink and D. Sandra (New York: Kluwer Academic/Plenum Publishers), 1–25.

Marcolini, S., Traficante, D., Zoccolotti, P., and Burani, C. (2011). Word frequency modulates morpheme-based reading in poor and skilled Italian readers. *Appl. Psycholinguist.* 32, 513–532. doi: 10.1017/s0142716411000191

Marinelli, C. V., Angelelli, P., Notarnicola, A., and Luzzatti, C. (2009). Do Italian dyslexic children use the lexical reading route efficiently? An orthographic judgment task. *Read. Writ.* 22, 333–351. doi: 10.1007/s11145-008-9118-x

McBride-Chang, C., Cho, J.-R., Liu, H., Wagner, R. K., Shu, H., Zhou, A., et al. (2005). Changing models across cultures: associations of phonological awareness and morphological structure awareness with vocabulary and word recognition in second graders from Beijing, Hong Kong, Korea and the United States. *J. Exp. Child Psychol.* 92, 140–160. doi: 10.1016/j.jecp.2005.03.009

McBride-Chang, C., Shu, H., Zhou, A., Wat, C., and Wagner, R. K. (2003). Morphological awareness uniquely predicts young children's Chinese character recognition. *J. Educ. Psychol.* 95, 743–751. doi: 10.1037/0022-0663.95.4.743

Nagy, W. E., and Anderson, R. C. (1984). How many words are there in printed school English? *Read. Res. Q.* 19, 304–330. doi: 10.2307/747823

Notarnicola, A., Angelelli, P., Judica, A., and Zoccolotti, P. (2012). The development of spelling skills in a shallow orthography: the case of the Italian language. *Read. Writ.* 25, 1171–1194. doi: 10.1007/s11145-011-9312-0

Nunes, T., Bryant, P., and Bindman, M. (1997). Morphological spelling strategies: development stages and processes. *Dev. Psychol.* 33, 637–649. doi: 10.1037//0012-1649.33.4.637

Pacton, S., and Deacon, S. H. (2008). The timing and mechanisms of children's use of morphological information in spelling: a review of evidence from English and French. *Cogn. Dev.* 23, 339–359. doi: 10.1016/j.cogdev.2007.09.004

Pacton, S., Foulin, J. N., Casalis, S., and Treiman, R. (2013). Children benefit from morphological relatedness when they learn to spell new words. *Front. Psychol.* 4:696. doi: 10.3389/fpsyg.2013.00696

Patterson, K. E. (1986). Lexical but nonsemantic spelling. *Cogn. Neuropsychol.* 3, 341–367. doi: 10.1080/02643298608253363

Pruneti, C. A., Fenu, A., Freschi, G., Rota, S., Cocci, D., Marchionni, M., et al. (1996). Aggiornamento alla standardizzazione italiana del test delle Matrici Progressive Colorate di Raven (CPM). [Update of the Italian standardization of Raven's coloured progressive matrices]. *Boll. Psicol. Appl.* 217, 51–57.

Quené, H., and van den Bergh, H. (2008). Examples of mixed-effects modeling with crossed random effects and with binomial data. *J. Mem. Lang.* 59, 413–425. doi: 10.1016/j.jml.2008.02.002

Rispens, J. E., McBride-Chang, C., and Reitsma, P. (2008). Morphological awareness and early and advanced word recognition and spelling in Dutch. *Read. Writ.* 21, 587–607. doi: 10.1007/s11145-007-9077-7

Schreuder, R., and Baayen, R. H. (1995). "Modeling morphological processing," in *Morphological Aspects of Language Processing*, eds L. B. Feldman (Hillsdale, N.J.: Erlbaum), 131–154.

Sénéchal, M. (2000). Morphological effects in children's spelling of French words. *Can. J. Exp. Psychol.* 54, 76–86. doi: 10.1037/h0087331

Seymour, P. H. K. (1997). "Foundations of orthographic development," in *Learning to Spell*, eds C. Perfetti, L. Rieben and M. Fayol (Hillsdale, N.J.: Erlbaum), 319–337.

Sprenger-Charolles, L. (2003). "Reading acquisition: cross linguistic data," in *Handbook of Children's Literacy*, eds T. Nunes and P. Bryant (Dordrecht: Kluwer Academic Publishers), 43–65.

Tainturier, M. J., and Rapp, B. (2000). "The spelling process," in *What Deficits Reveal about the Human Mind: A Handbook of Cognitive Neuropsychology*, ed B. Rapp (Philadelphia, PA: Psychology Press), 263–289.

Thornton, A. M., Iacobini, C., and Burani, C. (1997). *BDVBD Una Base di Dati Sul Vocabolario di Base Della Lingua Italiana [BDVDB: A Database for the Italian Basic Dictionary]*. Roma: Bulzoni.

Traficante, D. (2012). From graphemes to morphemes: an alternative way to improve skills in children with dyslexia. *J. Res. Speech* 2, 163–185.

Traficante, D., and Burani, C. (2003). "Visual processing of Italian verbs and adjectives: the role of inflectional family size," in *Morphological Structure in Language Processing*, eds H. R. Baayen and R. Schreuder (Berlin: Mouton de Gruyter), 45–64.

Traficante, D., Marcolini, S., Luci, A., Zoccolotti, P., and Burani, C. (2011). How do roots and suffixes influence reading of pseudowords: a study of Italian children with and without dyslexia. *Lang. Cogn. Process.* 26, 777–793. doi: 10.1080/01690965.2010.496553

Treiman, R., Cassar, M., and Zukowski, A. (1994). What type of linguistic information do children use in spelling? The case of flaps. *Child Dev.* 65, 1318–1337. doi: 10.2307/1131501

Verhoeven, L., and Perfetti, C. (2003). Introduction to this special issue: the role of morphology in learning to read. *Sci. Stud. Read.* 7, 209–217. doi: 10.1207/s1532799xssr0703_1

Verhoeven, L., and Perfetti, C. A. (2011). Morphological processing in reading acquisition: a cross-linguistic perspective. *Appl. Psycholinguist.* 32, 457–466. doi: 10.1017/s0142716411000154

Zoccolotti, P., De Luca, M., Di Pace, E., Judica, A., Orlandi, M., and Spinelli, D. (1999). Markers of developmental surface dyslexia in a language (Italian) with high grapheme-phoneme correspondence. *Appl. Psycholinguist.* 20, 191–216. doi: 10.1017/s0142716499002027

18

The locus of impairment in English developmental letter position dyslexia

Yvette Kezilas[1]*, Saskia Kohnen[1], Meredith McKague[2] and Anne Castles[1]

[1] *Department of Cognitive Science, ARC Centre of Excellence in Cognition and its Disorders, Macquarie University, Sydney, NSW, Australia*
[2] *Melbourne School of Psychological Science, The University of Melbourne, Melbourne, VIC, Australia*

****Correspondence:***
Yvette Kezilas, Department of Cognitive Science, ARC Centre of Excellence in Cognitive and its Disorders, Macquarie University, Australian Hearing Hub, Level 3, 16 University Avenue, NSW 2109, Australia
e-mail: yvette.kezilas@mq.edu.au

Many children with reading difficulties display phonological deficits and struggle to acquire non-lexical reading skills. However, not all children with reading difficulties have these problems, such as children with selective letter position dyslexia (LPD), who make excessive migration errors (such as reading *slime* as "smile"). Previous research has explored three possible loci for the deficit – the phonological output buffer, the orthographic input lexicon, and the orthographic-visual analysis stage of reading. While there is compelling evidence against a phonological output buffer and orthographic input lexicon deficit account of English LPD, the evidence in support of an orthographic-visual analysis deficit is currently limited. In this multiple single-case study with three English-speaking children with developmental LPD, we aimed to both replicate and extend previous findings regarding the locus of impairment in English LPD. First, we ruled out a phonological output buffer and an orthographic input lexicon deficit by administering tasks that directly assess phonological processing and lexical guessing. We then went on to directly assess whether or not children with LPD have an orthographic-visual analysis deficit by modifying two tasks that have previously been used to localize processing at this level: a same-different decision task and a non-word reading task. The results from these tasks indicate that LPD is most likely caused by a deficit specific to the coding of letter positions at the orthographic-visual analysis stage of reading. These findings provide further evidence for the heterogeneity of dyslexia and its underlying causes.

Keywords: phonological output deficit, orthographic input lexicon deficit, orthographic-visual analysis deficit, migration errors, substitution errors, developmental dyslexia

INTRODUCTION

The last three decades have seen an emphasis on the role that impaired phonological processing plays in developmental dyslexia. Various researchers have posited that at the core of dyslexia lies an impairment in the ability to represent, store, and retrieve speech sounds (Stanovich, 1988; Snowling, 1998, 2001; Ramus, 2003). This phonological deficit is proposed to be linked to the difficulty children with dyslexia experience in learning the mappings between letters and speech sounds, which is often remediated using phonics training (see Castles et al., 2009; McArthur et al., 2012). The phonological deficit account of dyslexia is supported by a multitude of correlational, longitudinal, and training studies that have found developmental dyslexia to typically be associated with poor phonological awareness (e.g., Høien et al., 1989), slow lexical retrieval skills (e.g., Denckla and Rudel, 1976), and poor verbal short-term memory (e.g., Mann et al., 1980; Mann and Liberman, 1984).

However, not all children with dyslexia have a phonological impairment. For example, children with surface dyslexia appear to have no difficulties with mapping letters onto speech sounds, as is evidenced by their ability to read non-words as proficiently as their peers (e.g., Castles and Coltheart, 1993; Broom and Doctor, 1995; Castles and Coltheart, 1996; Temple, 1997). Instead, surface dyslexics have been thought to have problems with orthographic processing, resulting in excessive reading errors where an irregular word is sounded out incorrectly using common letter-sound rules (e.g., *yacht* is read as if it rhymed with *matched*). The existence of cases of developmental dyslexia where phonological processing appears intact suggests that while some dyslexias may be attributed to an impairment in phonological processing, other dyslexias are not. Here, we provide further evidence for the heterogeneity of dyslexia and its underlying causes by furthering the investigation of the locus of impairment in English-speaking children with developmental letter position dyslexia (LPD).

The hallmark symptom of LPD is an elevated tendency to make "migration errors," where the order of letters within migratable words (more commonly known as anagrams) is confused, resulting in the misreading of a word as its migration partner (e.g., *slime* is read as "smile"). While migration errors are frequently made by beginning readers (Kohnen and Castles, 2013), English children with LPD have been found to make up to four times the number of migration errors made by their peers (Kohnen et al., 2012). Children with LPD have particularly high migration error rates when reading words where the transposition of letters in the middle of a word can lead to another word (e.g., *slime–smile, diary–dairy*). Intriguingly, cases of selective LPD have been documented, where all other reading processes appear intact (Friedmann and Rahamim, 2007; Kohnen et al., 2012). Children with selective LPD read as accurately and as fluently as their peers – except when they are asked to read migratable words.

There are four studies that have investigated the locus of impairment in developmental LPD – two in Hebrew (Friedmann and Rahamim, 2007; Friedmann et al., 2010a), one in Arabic (Friedmann and Haddad-Hanna, 2012), and most recently one in English (Kohnen et al., 2012). All four studies have used the cognitive model of reading aloud illustrated in **Figure 1** to identify the locus of impairment in LPD. Following this model, when a word is encountered in print, its visual properties undergo orthographic-visual analysis. This stage involves identifying the word's letters, coding the position of the letters within the word, and binding the letters to the word. Following these initial computations, the word is processed via three routes: (1) the lexical route (orthographic input lexicon to phonological output lexicon), (2) the lexical-semantic route (orthographic input lexicon to phonological output lexicon via the semantic system), and (3) the non-lexical route (grapheme–phoneme conversion). Typically, the lexical and lexical-semantic routes successfully process all words within a reader's orthographic input lexicon (storage for familiar words) but fail to process non-words. In contrast, the non-lexical route successfully sounds out non-words and words that follow typical letter to sound rules ("regular words" such as *surf*, *blame*, and *hand*), but fails to provide accurate pronunciation for irregular words (such as *yacht*, *come*, and *friend*). According to the model, after the written input has progressed through these routes, the phonemes that make up the word are assembled and held active in the phonological output buffer until a verbal response is made.

Using this model, previous research has proposed three possible loci for the migration errors seen in LPD (Friedmann and Rahamim, 2007; Kohnen et al., 2012). First, the migration errors may occur at the phonological output buffer as the phonological code is being prepared for pronunciation. Strong evidence against this hypothesis comes from the observation that children with LPD perform within the average range on standardized tests that draw heavily on the phonological output buffer (e.g., phonological awareness and verbal short-term memory assessments; Friedmann and Rahamim, 2007; Kohnen et al., 2012). Furthermore, Kohnen et al. (2012) reported that the majority of the migration errors made by their sample of English LPDs could not be attributed to the swapping of phonemes in the output buffer. For example, the swapping of the phonemes in *cloud* (/k/ /l/ /aw/ /d/) does not create the migration error "could" (/k/ /ʊ/ /d/; Kohnen et al., 2012). Rather, the deficit causing this error must occur before the graphemes in the word have been converted into their appropriate phonemes.

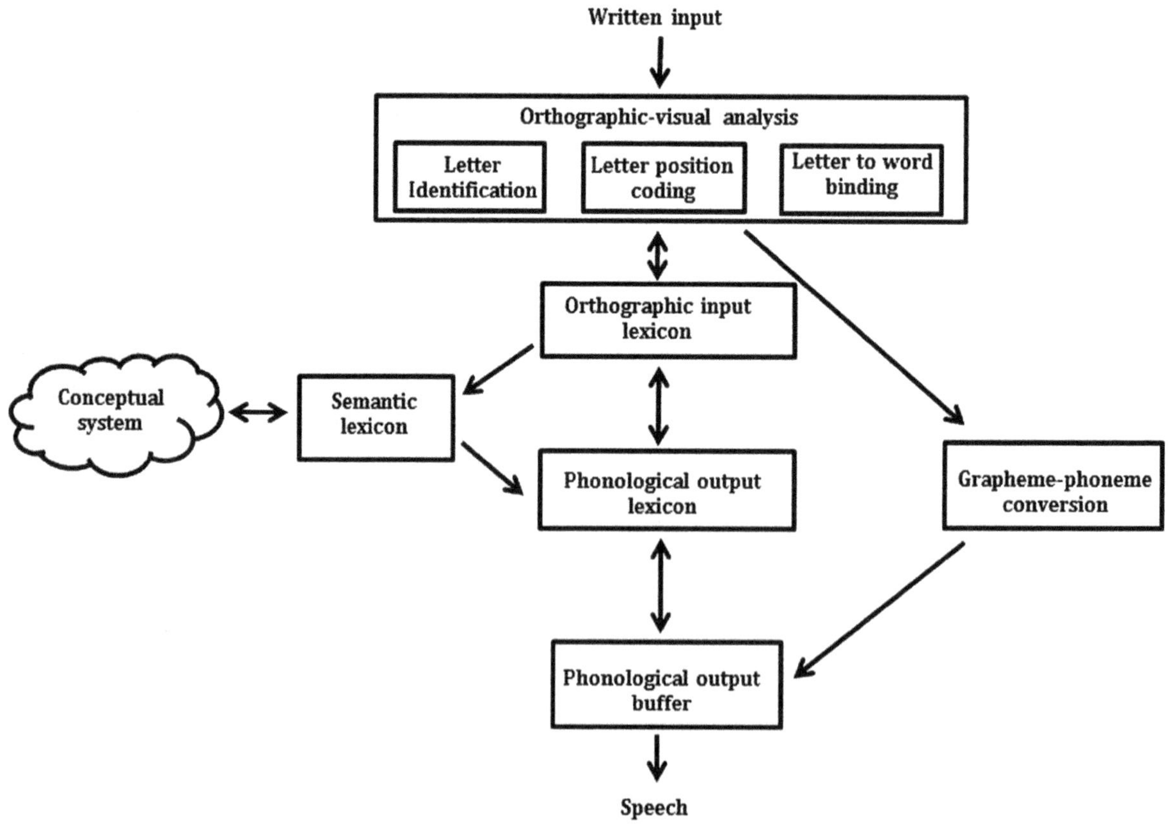

FIGURE 1 | A cognitive model of reading aloud (e.g., Friedmann and Rahamim, 2007; Kohnen et al., 2012) detailing the three reading routes: (1) the lexical route (orthographic input lexicon to phonological output lexicon), (2) the lexical-semantic route (orthographic input lexicon to phonological output lexicon via the semantic system), and (3) the non-lexical route (grapheme–phoneme conversion). Double-headed arrows indicate feed-forward and -backward activation.

Second, migration errors may occur due to an orthographic input lexicon deficit. On this account, LPDs are proposed to have fewer lexical entries in their orthographic input lexicon (i.e., have a smaller sight-word vocabulary) than is typical for their age. When the lexical entry matching a target word cannot be found in the lexicon, a lexical guessing strategy is adopted resulting in an error that is visually similar to the target word. This possibility is unlikely however, as LPDs have been found to read non-migratable, irregular words (e.g., *yacht*) as proficiently as their peers, indicating that their orthographic input lexicon is intact (Friedmann and Rahamim, 2007; Kohnen et al., 2012). Furthermore, if the migration errors made by LPDs are the result of lexical guessing, they should also make other lexical similarity errors, such as substitution errors (e.g., reading *slime* as "slide"). This is not the case – their reading errors appear to be selective to the transposition of letters within words (Friedmann and Rahamim, 2007; Kohnen et al., 2012).

The third and final possibility following **Figure 1** is that LPD is caused by a deficit specific to the coding of letter positions within words at the orthographic-visual analysis stage of reading. Of the three possible deficits (phonological output buffer, orthographic input lexicon, and orthographic-visual analysis), an orthographic-visual analysis deficit currently provides the most parsimonious explanation for the available data. Two pieces of evidence suggest that LPD is caused by an orthographic-visual analysis deficit. First, in Hebrew, LPDs have been found to make excessive migration errors on a same-different decision task (e.g., responding "same" to *slime-smile*; Friedmann and Rahamim, 2007; Friedmann et al., 2010a). Two of the three cases of English LPD reported by Kohnen et al. (2012) also showed this effect. Because the same-different decision task is thought to tap prelexical processing (see Besner et al., 1984; Kinoshita and Norris, 2009), LPDs' poor performance on this task has been taken as evidence for an orthographic-visual analysis deficit (Kohnen et al., 2012). Second, in Hebrew, LPDs have been found to make more word responses to migratable items (e.g., reading *slime* as "smile," and *forg* as "frog") as well as non-word responses (e.g., reading *pilf* as "plif"), indicating that the cognitive mechanism that is defective in LPD is common to both lexical and non-lexical routes (Friedmann and Rahamim, 2007). There are two components of the model that are common to both routes: orthographic-visual analysis and the phonological output buffer. As previously outlined, there is strong evidence refuting a phonological output buffer deficit account of LPD. Therefore, the finding that LPDs in Hebrew make more word and non-word responses to migratable items has been taken as evidence for an orthographic-visual analysis deficit, which then has knock on effects to both lexical and non-lexical reading.

There are, however, two pieces of data that appear inconsistent with an orthographic-visual analysis deficit account of English LPD. First, one of the three LPD cases reported by Kohnen et al. (2012) did not make excessive migration errors on a same-different decision task. As the same-different decision task should reveal an orthographic-visual analysis deficit, this finding may suggest that the migration errors made by this case (identified as EL) are not caused by this deficit. Second, while the LPDs in Kohnen et al.'s (2012) study made more word responses to migratable items (e.g., reading *slime* as "smile," and *forg* as "frog") than controls, they did not make more non-word migration responses than controls (e.g., reading *pilf* as "plif"). This finding proves problematic for an orthographic-visual analysis deficit account of English LPD, as a deficit at the initial, orthographic-visual analysis stage of reading should produce migration errors in both lexical and non-lexical reading. The aim of the present study was to follow up on these two unexpected findings to clarify the locus of impairment in English LPD.

One plausible reason why EL did not make excessive migration errors on the same-different decision task is that he was adopting a strategy during the task whereby he compared each letter across the two words. In Kohnen et al.'s (2012) task, participants were presented with two words side by side, and were given as much time as they needed to make their response. As Kohnen et al. (2012) have suggested, these task conditions give participants the opportunity to compare each letter across the two words, rather than comparing the two words to one another as is intended by the task. If attention is focused on each individual letter, each letter's position is no longer processed in relation to the position of the other letters within the word. This means that letter positions will less likely be confused, and migration errors will less likely be made.

Additionally, there are two plausible reasons why the LPDs in Kohnen et al.'s (2012) study may not have made excessive non-word migration responses, where the order of letters in a non-word stimulus is confused, resulting in a non-word response (e.g., reading *pilf* as "plif"). First, while letters in familiar words are thought to be processed in parallel via the lexical routes, letters in non-words are thought to be processed serially via the non-lexical route (Rastle and Coltheart, 1998; Friedmann and Rahamim, 2007). The serial processes that underpin non-word reading might therefore reduce the likelihood that an LPD will make non-word migration errors (Friedmann and Rahamim, 2007; Kohnen et al., 2012). Second, research in both Hebrew and English has shown that there are specific variables that influence whether or not LPDs make word migration errors. For example, LPDs are most likely to make a word migration error when a low-frequency word can migrate into a higher frequency word via the transposition of two adjacent, internal letters [e.g., reading *trail* (frequency = 18) as "trial" (frequency = 58)]. It is plausible, therefore, to hypothesize that there is also a set of variables that influence whether a non-word migration error will be made, and that variation across item sets on such variables might account for differences in results.

THE PRESENT STUDY

The aim of this multiple single-case study with three English-speaking LPDs was to replicate and extend previous research regarding the locus of impairment in LPD.

First, we aimed to replicate previous findings suggesting that LPD is not caused by a phonological output buffer deficit. We then sought to replicate the finding that the migration errors seen in LPD are not the result of lexical guessing due to an orthographic input lexicon deficit.

Following this, we aimed to address two findings that appear to be inconsistent with an orthographic-visual analysis deficit account of LPD. The first inconsistent finding is that EL, one of Kohnen et al.'s (2012) LPDs, did not make more migration errors on a same-different decision task than controls. The second finding that appears at odds with this account is that all three LPDs in Kohnen et al.'s (2012) study did not make more non-word migration responses (e.g., reading *pilf* as "plif") than controls. The present study therefore aimed to extend Kohnen et al.'s (2012) study by modifying the same-different decision task and the non-word reading task in an attempt to clarify the locus of impairment. Specifically, we extended Kohnen et al.'s (2012) work by (1) administering a sequential presentation variant of the same-different decision task, (2) including a consonant–string condition in the same-different decision task, and (3) manipulating the bigram frequency of the non-words presented in the reading aloud task.

A sequential variant of the same-different decision task was administered to eliminate a possible letter-by-letter matching strategy. That is, rather than presenting the words side by side, where a direct comparison between each word's letters can be made, we presented items one after the other. Under sequential presentation, we expected all three LPDs in the present study to be significantly poorer than controls at detecting when two migratable words are different. To provide a further test of the orthographic-visual analysis deficit account of LPD, we included a consonant–string condition in the task. If LPD is due to a letter position coding deficit at the orthographic-visual analysis stage of reading, then LPDs should be poorer than controls at identifying when two migratable items are different from one another, regardless of the lexicality of the items.

In the present study, we also manipulated the bigram frequency of the non-words in the reading aloud task. One plausible reason why Kohnen et al.'s (2012) LPDs did not make more non-word migration errors than controls when reading aloud non-words (e.g., reading *pilf* as "plif") is that there may be various factors that influence whether or not a non-word migration error will be made. Previous research has shown that the written frequency of a word's migration counterpart, relative to the item itself, influences whether or not a migration error will be made. For example, Friedmann and Gvion (2001) found that the most common migration error made by LPDs was the reading of a non-word (which by definition has a written frequency of 0) as a word (e.g., *coisun* read as "cousin"). The next most common migration error was the reading of a word as its higher frequency counterpart [e.g., *trail* (frequency = 18) read as "trial" (frequency = 58)]. Following these findings, it is plausible to hypothesize that the bigram frequency of the non-word migration counterpart, relative to the bigram frequency of the non-word itself, will influence whether or not a non-word migration error will be made. Our exploratory hypothesis was therefore that LPDs would be more likely to migrate a low bigram frequency non-word into its higher bigram frequency non-word counterpart [e.g., reading *plif* (BF = 180) as "pilf" (BF = 1251)].

MATERIALS AND METHODS

Ethics approval for this project was granted by Macquarie University Human Research Ethics Committee. Participants and their parents gave verbal and written consent to their involvement in the study.

PARTICIPANTS

Participants in this study were three children: LM, EL, and LL. LM, was a 9-year 8-month-old girl in her second semester of grade 4 when we first met her and was homeschooled by her mother[1]. EL was a participant in Kohnen et al.'s (2012) study and was recruited for the present study when he was 9 years 8 months old and about to commence grade 5 at a mainstream school. Our third participant, LL, was an 11-year 9-month-old girl who had commenced grade 7 at a mainstream school two weeks before we met her.

All three children were initially referred to us because their parents were concerned about their spelling ability. Their reading skills were reported by their parents to be within the average range for their age. Both LM and LL's hearing and vision were reported as normal. EL had long-sightedness and astigmatism, which were corrected for with glasses. He had also been diagnosed with pendular nystagmus (involuntary repetitive rhythmic movement of eyes from side to side). All three children had no diagnoses of developmental delay or difficulties [e.g., AD(H)D, SLI].

Each LPD's performance on the standardized tests used to assess for a phonological output buffer deficit was compared to the test's age-appropriate normative data. Each LPD's performance on the experimental tasks was compared to a control group of average readers without LPD. We recruited two different grade-matched control groups. Six grade 4 controls were used as a control group for LM and EL (*M* age = 10 years 1 month, SD age = 2 months). Two grade 6 controls and three grade 7 controls were used as a control group for LL (*M* age = 12 years 3 months, SD age = 7 months).

PROCEDURE

Participants were tested over multiple testing sessions at Macquarie University. Testing sessions went for between 90–150 min in length including breaks. All relevant property statistics for the experimental tasks were derived from N-Watch (Davis, 2005). All experimental reading aloud tasks and the visual lexical decision task were administered using flash cards. Unless otherwise specified, Crawford and Garthwaite's (2002) *t*-test was used to compare each LPD's task performance to controls, and Fisher's exact was used to compare each LPD's performance on one condition to another condition.

RESULTS

TESTS DETERMINING ELIGIBILITY

LM, EL and LL were identified as having LPD based on their scores on the Letter Position Test (LetPos: Kohnen et al., 2014). The LetPos is a reading aloud test consisting of 60 anagram words (30 anagram pairs, e.g., *slime – smile*), presented over two pages. There are three types of errors that can be made on this test: "migration errors" (reading a word as its migration partner, e.g., reading *slime* as "smile"), "word errors" (reading a word as any word other than its migration partner, e.g., reading *slime* as "slide"), and "other

[1]Homeschooling for LM followed a strict and regulated curriculum matched to mainstream education. The work completed by home-schooled students has to be documented and monitored regularly.

errors" (reading a word as a non-word, e.g., reading *slime* as "slome"). The normative data for the LetPos was collected in the final term of the school year. LPDs were selected on the basis that their LetPos performance was more than one standard deviation below the mean for "migration errors," and within one standard deviation of the mean for "word errors" and "other errors," when compared to the grade-appropriate normative data.

LPD participants were also selected to have no obvious reading problems, other than the reading of migratable words. Specifically, they were selected only if they had normal irregular word and non-word reading, as assessed by the Castles and Coltheart Reading Test (CC2: Castles et al., 2009). Both LM and EL were within the average range for their age (an *z*-score between −1 and +1) on both the irregular word and non-word reading components of the test. While LL was within the average range on the irregular word component of the CC2, she was below average on the non-word reading component of the test[2]. She was included in the study, however, because her non-word reading errors appeared to stem from an underlying problem with reading letters in their correct order. For example, LL made non-word migration errors such as reading *borp* as "brop." When these migration errors were removed from her score, her non-word reading was within the average range.

Control participants were selected to be average on the irregular word and non-word reading subtests of the CC2 and to be within one standard deviation of the mean on each component (migration, word and other errors) of the LetPos.

ASSESSING THE PHONOLOGICAL OUTPUT BUFFER

A phonological output deficit should manifest itself in poor performance on tasks that require phoneme production and/or manipulation. To investigate whether LPD is caused by a phonological output buffer deficit, LM, EL and LL were assessed on phonological awareness, speed of lexical retrieval and verbal short-term and working memory. If their migration errors are caused by a phonological output buffer deficit, they should be below average on these tasks compared to age-appropriate normative data.

Phonological awareness was assessed using the Segmenting Non-words and Phoneme Reversals subtests of the Comprehensive Test of Phonological Processing (CTOPP, Wagner et al., 1999). In the Segmenting Non-words subtest children are given a series of non-words, which they are asked to repeat, and then say one sound at a time (e.g., "dray, d – r – ay"). In the Phoneme Reversal subtest children are asked to first repeat a non-word, and then to reverse the sounds to make it sound like a real word (e.g., "nus, sun").

Speed of lexical retrieval was assessed using the Rapid Naming subtests of the CTOPP. LPDs were assessed on their ability to rapidly name letters, digits, objects and colors, which were each assessed separately. In these subtests, LPDs were asked to name 36 items presented on a single page as quickly as they could.

The Repetition of Nonsense Words subtest of the NEPSY (Korkman et al., 1998) and the Digit Span subtest of the Weschsler Intelligence Scale for Children Fourth Edition (WISC-IV; Wechsler, 2003) were used to assess verbal short-term and working memory. In the Repetition of Nonsense Words subtest, children are asked to repeat non-words (e.g., *bu-lɛks-tɪs*). The Digit Span subtest has two components – Forward Digit Span, and Backwards Digit Span. In the Forward Digit Span children are asked to repeat strings of digits in the same order as they heard them, and in the Backwards Digit Span subtest children have to repeat strings of digits in reverse order.

Table 1 shows that all LPD participants were within (or even above) the average range (*z*-score between −1 and +1) on all nine measures of phonological processing. In addition LM, EL, and LL were asked to orally repeat the words after the experimenter for which they had previously made a migration error on in a reading aloud task. Each LPD performed this task without making a single migration error.

[2]Note that there are currently no normative data published for children who are LL's age (11 years 9 months). LL's performance on the CC2, as well as that of her control group, was therefore compared to the normative data of children between the ages 11 years and 11 years 5 months.

Table 1 | *Z* scores on standardized tests used to assess for a phonological output deficit (average range is between −1 and +1).

		LM	EL	LL
Phonological awareness	Segmenting nonwords (CTOPP)	0.33	1.67	1.67
	Phoneme reversals (CTOPP)	0.33	0.67	−0.67
Lexical retrieval	Rapid naming (CTOPP)			
	Digits	1.33	0.33	−0.67
	Letters	1.00	0.67	−1.00
	Colors	1.00	0.33	−1.00
	Objects	1.33	−0.67	−0.33
Verbal memory	Digit span (WISC-IV)			
	Forward	1.00	0.33	1.00
	Backward	0.00	−0.33	0.67
	Repetition of nonsense words (NEPSY)	1.00	1.00	0.33

Taken together, these findings indicate that the migration errors made by the three LPDs in the present study cannot be attributed to a phonological output buffer deficit.

ASSESSING THE ORTHOGRAPHIC INPUT LEXICON

To investigate whether LM, EL and LL have an orthographic input lexicon deficit we administered a reading aloud non-migratable, irregular words task. Irregular words were used to ensure that access to the orthographic input lexicon was obligatory for a correct response to be made. If LPDs have an orthographic input lexicon deficit, they should be poorer at this task than controls.

To explicitly test whether their excessive migration errors are the result of lexical guessing, we administered two tasks: a reading aloud migratable and substitution words task, and a visual lexical decision task. If LPDs' migration errors are the result of lexical guessing, they should make more substitution errors than controls on a reading aloud task (e.g., reading *track* as "trick"), as well as more substitution errors on a visual lexical decision task (e.g., accepting *esho* (derived from *echo*) as a word).

Reading non-migratable, irregular words

Participants were asked to read aloud 87 non-migratable words which were selected to contain at least one letter-sound rule that was atypical (e.g., pearl, cousin) according to Regcelex (Baayen et al., 1995), a program used to compute the rule based pronunciation of a letter-string (Coltheart et al., 2001). Because we were interested in each LPD's lexical reading skills, errors that appeared to stem from a difficulty in ordering letters in words (e.g., reading *chalk* as "chlak") were removed from the error analysis. Both LM and EL made 12.64% errors on this task, which was not significantly different from their control group, who made 9.58% errors (SD = 2.48%; $t = 1.14$, $p = 0.15$ one-tailed). LL made 6.90% errors on this task, which was not significantly different from her control group who made 8.28% errors (SD = 2.36%; $t = 0.53$, $p = 0.31$ one-tailed).

Eighteen of the 87 experimental words were items that had already been administered in the irregular word reading component of the CC2. We therefore conducted an additional analysis including irregular words that were not part of the CC2 ($N = 69$). All three LPD's made as many errors as controls in this additional analysis (all $p > 0.15$ one-tailed).

This finding suggests that LM, EL and LL have as many entries in their orthographic input lexicon as controls, and that they have no difficulty in accessing these entries.

Reading aloud migratable and substitution words

Participants read aloud 58 migratable words, which were created from 29 word pairs that were different via the transposition of two internal letters (e.g., *slime-smile*). Migratable words were intermixed with 30 substitution words created from 15 pairs of words that were different via the substitution of a single internal letter (e.g., *track-trick*). Substitution words were matched as closely as possible to migratable words on length (migratable: $M = 5.07$, SD = 0.53; substitution: $M = 5.07$, SD = 0.69), relative written frequency between a word and its partner (migratable: $M = 27.51$, SD = 36.83; substitution: $M = 36.61$, SD = 36.62), and the number of substitution neighbors (migration: $M = 4.86$, SD = 3.48; substitution: $M = 4.90$, SD = 3.18). The item pairs were presented over separate tasks such that participants did not read a word and its partner in the same task. These words were intermixed with 122 words, which were not used to address the research questions in the present study.

Three error types were analyzed: (1) migration errors, where a migratable word was read as its partner, (2) substitution errors, where a substitution word was read as its partner, and (3) "*N*" errors, which included substitution errors (e.g., reading *slime* as "slide"), addition errors (reading *slime* as "slimes"), and deletion errors (reading *slime* as "slim") made on all migratable and substitution words. Incorrect reading responses that were potentially due to sounding the word out rather than one of these three error types (e.g., reading *bread* as "breed") were not included in the analysis.

The results are outlined in **Table 2**. All three LPDs made more migration errors than controls (LM: $t = 21.95$, $p < 0.001$ one-tailed; EL: $t = 9.49$; $p < 0.001$ one-tailed; LL: $t = 4.81$, $p < 0.01$ one-tailed). Because there was no variance in the number of substitution errors made by controls, a Fisher's exact test was used (instead of Crawford's *t*-tests) to compare LPDs' performance to their respective control groups. All three LPDs made as many substitution errors as controls (all $p > 0.5$ one-tailed). Both LM and EL made as many *N* errors as controls (both $t = 1.11$, $p = 0.16$ one-tailed). Because there was no variance in the number of *N* errors made by LL's control group, a Fisher's exact test was used instead of Crawford's *t*-test, which indicated that she made as many *N* errors on the task as controls ($z = 0.71$, $p = 0.24$ one-tailed).

The finding that LM, EL and LL's reading errors were selective to the migration of letters within words suggests that their LPD cannot be attributed to lexical guessing.

Table 2 | Percentage of errors on reading aloud words in the migration and substitution conditions.

	LM	EL	LM and EL controls	LL	LL controls
Migration errors	27.59***	15.52***	6.32 (0.89)	12.07**	2.07 (1.89)
Substitution errors	3.33	0.00	0.00 (0.00)	0.00	0.00 (0.00)
N errors	2.27	2.27	0.95 (1.12)	2.27	0.00 (0.00)

Numbers in parentheses denote standard deviation of the mean for control groups.
***p < 0.01, ***p < 0.001 compared to control group.*

Visual lexical decision

A visual lexical decision task was also administered to determine whether migration errors made by LPDs were the result of lexical guessing. Forty non-migratable words formed the word condition in this task. Three non-word conditions were created by modifying the word items – a migratable non-word condition (*coisun* (derived from *cousin*); $N = 16$), a single-substitution non-word condition (*eamly* (derived from *early*), $N = 12$), and a double-substitution non-word condition (*provare* (derived from *private*); $N = 12$). Single and double substitution items were included because both have previously been used in research as a comparison condition for migratable items (e.g. Perea and Lupker, 2004; Perea and Fraga, 2006; Beyersmann et al., 2011, 2012, 2013).

Items in the migratable non-word condition were matched as closely as possible to items in the single- and double-substitution condition on bigram frequency (migration condition: $M = 719.04$, SD = 415.91; single-substitution condition: $M = 578.54$, SD = 336.08; double-substitution condition: $M = 713.68$, SD = 553.36), and the written frequency of the words that they were derived from (migratable $M = 87.56$, SD = 125.20; single-substitution: $M = 96.89$, SD = 116.29; double-substitution: $M = 72.64$, SD = 112.39). Words and non-words were intermixed with 112 additional items, which were not used to address the research questions in the present study. Items were presented over two separate tasks, such that a non-word and the word it was derived from were not presented in the same task.

So that we could be relatively certain that a "word" response to a non-word was due to the participant misreading the non-word as the word it was derived from, non-words in the migration condition and the double-substitution condition did not have a single substitution neighbor. Furthermore, the non-words in the single substitution condition did not have a single substitution neighbor other than the word that they were derived from. To further ensure that participants' "word" responses were due to their misreading of the non-word as its word partner, we removed non-words derived from words that participants did not know. We determined whether or not a participant knew a word based on their performance on the "word" condition of the visual lexical decision task, and their reading aloud of these words. If a participant could not read aloud the word *and* did not recognize the word in the visual lexical decision task, the word was defined as unknown, and hence its non-word counterpart was removed from their individual analysis. This comprised 5.00% of LM's data, 2.50% of EL's data, and 2.92% (SD = 3.68%) of their control group's data. For LL, 2.50% of her data was removed, and 1.00% (SD = 2.24%) of her control group's data was removed.

The results are outlined in **Table 3**. All three LPDs accepted more migratable non-words as words than controls (LM: $t = 3.59$, $p = 0.01$ one-tailed; EL: $t = 2.59$, $p = 0.02$ one-tailed; LL: $t = 2.90$, $p = 0.02$ one-tailed). Both EL and LL accepted as many single and double substitution non-words as words as controls (both $t < 1.12$, $p > 0.16$ one-tailed). LM, however, accepted more single and double substitution non-words as words than controls (single: $t = 2.51$, $p = 0.03$ one-tailed; double: $t = 4.54$, $p = 0.003$ one-tailed).

The finding that EL and LL's excessive errors on the visual lexical decision task were selective to the migration condition suggests that their migration errors are not the result of lexical guessing. In contrast, LM's excessive errors on the task were not selective to the migration condition – she also made more substitution errors on the task than controls. This finding suggests that a lexical guessing strategy may have been the cause of LM's migration errors on the visual lexical decision task.

ASSESSING THE ORTHOGRAPHIC-VISUAL ANALYSIS STAGE OF READING

To investigate whether LPD is caused by an orthographic-visual analysis deficit, we administered a sequential same-different decision task and a reading aloud non-words task. If LPD is caused by an orthographic-visual analysis deficit, LPDs should make more migration errors than controls on tasks that tap prelexical processing (e.g., same-different decision) since orthographic-visual analysis is a prelexical process. Furthermore, if their migration errors are caused by an orthographic-visual analysis deficit, LPDs should make more migration errors than controls during lexical and non-lexical reading.

Sequential same-different decision

The sequential same-different decision task consisted of 139 word pairs and 139 consonant–string pairs[3], which were four or five letters in length. Half of the items were the same (e.g., *beard–beard*; *bfgsk–bfgsk*), and half were different (*beard–bread*; *bfgsk–bfsgk*). Half of the items in the different condition were different via the transposition of internal letters (e.g., *trial–trail*), and half were different via the substitution of a single letter (e.g., *chuck–check*). Items were included in both the same and the different condition (i.e., participants made responses to both *trial–trail* and *trial–trial*). Six versions of the task were created and presented over two sessions, such that participants only saw one version of the item (either in the same *or* in the different condition) in a single session. These 280 items were intermixed with an additional 280 items (half same, half different), which were not used to address the research questions in the present study.

Same-different decision trials were presented using DMDX software (Forster and Forster, 2003). A schematic of a single trial is outlined in **Figure 2**. The first item was both backwards masked and presented in a different case to the second item to ensure that participants could not match the items based on low-level perceptual overlap. Participants were instructed to press a button with their right hand if they thought the two items were the same, and to press a button with their left hand if they thought the two items were different. Participants were given eight practice trials before commencing the task. No performance-based feedback was given to participants at any stage during the task.

As LPDs have been found to have intact letter identification skills (Friedmann and Rahamim, 2007; Kohnen et al., 2012), the

[3]The task was designed to have 140 word pairs and 140 consonant–string pairs. However, one word pair in the same migration condition (e.g., *slime–slime*) and one consonant–string pair in the different migration condition (e.g., *dktlp–dltkp*) were removed from the analysis as they were not presented correctly.

Table 3 | Percentage of migration errors, single-substitution (sub) errors and double-substitution (sub) errors on the visual lexical decision task.

	LM	EL	LM and EL controls	LL	LL controls
Migration errors	64.29*	53.33*	24.89 (10.16)	43.75*	12.58 (9.82)
Single-sub errors	33.33*	8.33	6.94 (9.74)	8.33	3.33 (4.56)
Double-sub errors	25.00**	8.33	2.90 (4.51)	0.00	3.33 (7.45)

Numbers in parentheses denote standard deviation of the mean for control groups.
$^{*}p < 0.05$, $^{**}p < 0.01$ compared to control group.

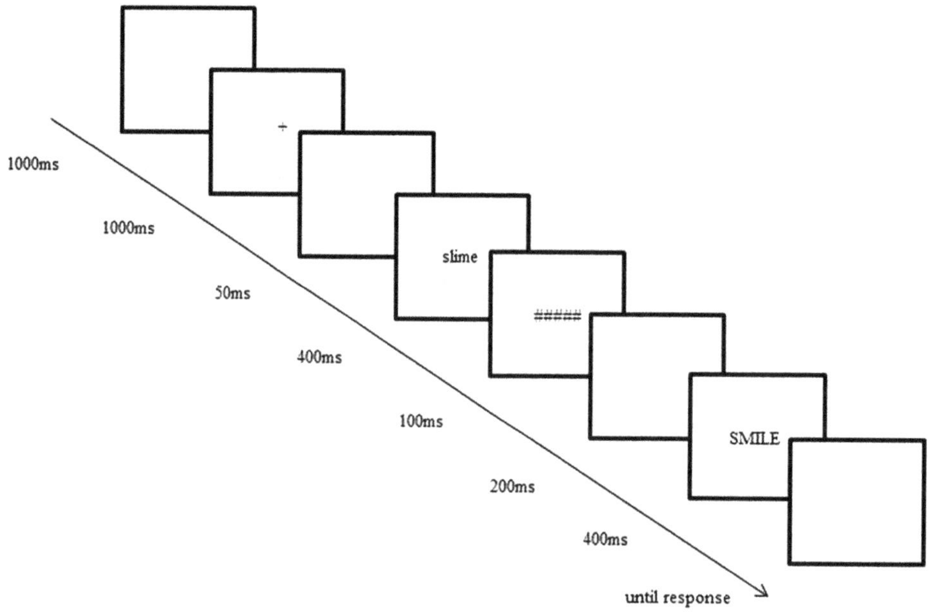

FIGURE 2 | Schematic of a single same-different decision trial.

substitution condition was used as an indication of baseline performance on the task. If LPD is due to an orthographic-visual analysis deficit, LPDs should be poorer than controls at detecting a difference between two migratable items (e.g., *slime–smile*), relative to the baseline condition (e.g., *tiger–timer*).

Table 4 displays participants' accuracy on the different conditions (i.e., their ability to detect that two items are different). Participants' d' scores based on their hits (correctly responding "different" to two different items e.g., *slime–smile*) and false alarms (incorrectly responding "different" to two same items e.g., *slime–slime*) on the migration and substitution condition are also included in **Table 4**.

All statistical analyses for the task were based on participants' accuracy on the different migration condition relative to their accuracy on the different substitution condition, using the Revised Standardized Difference Test (RSDT: Crawford and Garthwaite, 2005). All three LPDs were significantly poorer than controls at detecting that two migratable words were different relative to the substitution condition, however this only reached significance for EL and LL (EL: $t = 4.68$, $p = 0.003$ one-tailed; LL: $t = 2.82$, $p = 0.02$ one-tailed; LM: $t = 1.74$, $p = 0.07$). All three LPDs were not significantly poorer than controls at detecting that two migratable consonant strings were different, relative to the substitution condition (all $t < 1.10$, $p > 0.16$).

The finding that all three LPDs were no poorer than controls at detecting a difference between two migratable consonant–strings seems inconsistent with an orthographic-visual analysis deficit account of LPD. If LPD is caused by an orthographic-visual analysis deficit, then LM, EL and LL should be poorer than controls at detecting a difference between two migratable items, regardless of their lexicality.

However, this result may have been due to participants not having enough time to process the entire consonant–string. Letters in words are thought to be processed in parallel as a single unit of information. In contrast, there is no higher-order representation for consonant strings, and therefore each letter needs to be processed serially as its own unit of information. The limited stimulus presentation time in the task (400 ms) may have therefore meant that children only had enough time to process the beginning letters of the items in the consonant–string condition. If only the beginning letters are processed, then a correct response to many of the items in the different migration condition would require intact letter identification skills, but not necessarily intact letter position coding skills. For example, if participants

Table 4 | Percentage accuracy for the different migration (mig) and substitution (sub) conditions on the same-different decision task, and *d′* scores.

		LM		EL		LM and EL controls		LL		LL controls	
		Accuracy	*d′*	Accuracy	*d′*	Accuracy	*d′*	Accuracy	*d′*	Accuracy	*d′*
Words	Mig	40.00	1.22	54.29	1.00	89.52 (6.68)	3.03 (0.68)	71.43	1.83	94.29 (5.35)	3.69 (0.59)
	Sub	80.00	3.01	100.00	3.35	93.81 (2.81)	3.25 (0.45)	91.43	2.60	96.00 (8.94)	3.85 (0.99)
Consonants	Mig	41.18	1.08	67.65	0.34	65.69 (8.86)	0.73 (0.53)	85.29	0.61	74.71 (25.01)	1.66 (1.08)
	Sub	22.86	0.43	80.00	0.78	60.00 (15.65)	1.16 (0.45)	65.71	0.29	73.71 (15.31)	1.68 (0.78)
Non-words	Mig	58.33	1.67	54.17	0.96	88.54 (9.85)	3.24 (0.77)	66.67	1.35	88.33 (11.56)	2.83 (0.99)
	Sub	70.83	1.99	100.00	2.92	96.88 (6.25)	3.85 (0.78)	87.50	2.02	95.83 (5.10)	3.22 (0.75)

Numbers in parentheses denote standard deviation of the mean for control groups.

are presented with the consonant–string pair *stlkd-skltd*, but they only have enough time to process the first three letters of the consonant string, *stl-skl*, participants need only detect that the letter identities *t* and *k* are different from one another to make a correct response. If participants were only processing the beginning letters of the consonant–string pairs, then the finding that LPDs did not make more errors on the migration condition is not surprising, as LPDs have been found to have intact letter identification abilities (Friedmann and Rahamim, 2007; Kohnen et al., 2012).

One way to investigate whether or not participants had enough time to process all letters in the consonant–string condition is to see whether there is a position effect. If participants did not have enough time to process the entire consonant–string, we should find that they are better at detecting a difference between two consonant strings if the letters are different at the beginning of the pair, than if the letters are different at the end of the pair.

In a *post hoc* analysis, we explored whether there was merit in this alternative hypothesis. Items that differed via the substitution of a single letter in the first internal position of the word (e.g., *nkdcg-njdcg*) were classified as having a "beginning difference," and items that differed via the substitution of a single letter in the final internal position of the word (e.g., *fkmzd-fkmtd*) were classified as having an "end difference." The substitution condition rather than the migration condition was used because many of the different migratable items had both a beginning and end difference (e.g., *xtkjd-xjktd*).

All participants were combined to form one group for this item analysis. We used a Wilcoxon matched pairs test to compare the proportion correct on the two groups of items. Participants identified significantly more beginning differences (74.60%) in the consonant–string condition than end differences (58.574%; $z = 2.51$, $p = 0.006$ one-tailed). In contrast, participants identified as many beginning differences (93.57%) in the word condition as end differences (94.76%; $z = 0.51$, $p = 0.304$ one-tailed).

Following this finding, we decided to administer a same-different decision task with orthographically legal non-words (e.g., *scirm-scrim*). While the letters in legal non-words are not thought to be processed in parallel like words, the letters can be mapped onto a higher-order representation. For example, the consecutive letters *i* and *r* in the non-word *scirm* can be mapped onto the digraph *ir*. That is, the letters in legal non-words can be "chunked" (*s*, *c*, *ir* and *m*) and, for this reason, are likely to be processed faster than consonant–strings which cannot be chunked.

The non-word same-different decision task consisted of 96 non-word pairs. Forty-eight of the pairs were in the same condition, and 48 were in the different condition. Half of the items in the different condition were different via the transposition of two internal letters (e.g., *scirm-scrim*), and half were different via the substitution of a single letter (e.g., *froy-floy*). The same condition consisted of 48 non-word pairs. In contrast to the word and consonant string same-different decision task, non-words in the same condition were a new set of items, not derived from the items in the different condition (i.e., participants did not see *scirm-scrim* and *scirm-scirm*). Non-words were presented to participants during a single task, and under the same presentation conditions as described for the words and consonant–strings task.

By the time we assessed LM and EL on this task they were in the second semester of grade 5. Therefore, we compared their performance on this task to a new control group of 4 children in their second semester of grade 5.

Table 4 displays participants' accuracy on the different conditions. Participants' *d′* scores based on their hits (correctly responding "different" to two different items e.g., *scirm-scirm*) and false alarms (incorrectly responding "different" to two same items e.g., *garp-garp*) on each condition are also included in **Table 4.** False alarms were calculated from participants' performance on all 48 items in the same condition.

EL was significantly poorer than controls at detecting when two migratable non-words were different relative to the substitution condition (EL: $t = 4.47$, $p = 0.01$ one-tailed). LM and LL, however, did not show this effect (both $t < 1.64$, $p > 0.10$). We assessed for a position effect in the same way as we did for the consonant–string and word items. Participants correctly identified as many beginning differences (95.14%) as end differences (91.67%; $z = 0.54$, $p = 0.30$ one-tailed), indicating that they had enough time to process the entire letter string.

The finding that all three LPDs made more word migration errors than controls on a sequential same-different decision task is consistent with an orthographic-visual analysis deficit account of LPD, as is the finding that EL made more non-word migration errors on the task. The finding that LM and LL did not make more non-word migration errors on the sequential same-different decision task is, however, inconsistent with an orthographic-visual analysis deficit and will be followed up in the discussion.

Reading aloud non-words. Non-words were created from 25 non-word pairs which were migratable via the transposition of two internal adjacent letters (e.g., *torm–trom*). Pairs were selected to have a significant difference in bigram frequency between the two non-words (lower bigram frequency counterpart: $M = 789.56$ SD $= 594.36$; higher bigram frequency counterpart: $M = 1389.80$, SD $= 841.41$). Non-words were selected to match their migration partner as closely as possible on substitution N (lower bigram frequency counterpart: $M = 2.44$, SD $= 2.38$; higher bigram frequency counterpart: $M = 3.00$, SD $= 2.65$). Non-words were randomized and intermixed with 25 additional monosyllabic non-words that were not used to answer the research questions in this paper. Three versions of the task were created such that participants did not see a non-word and its migration partner in the same task. Participants were told that all items were nonwords before commencing the task.

The results from the nonword reading task are presented in **Table 5**. Both LM and LL made significantly more non-word migration errors on the task than controls (LM: $t = 6.46$, $p < 0.001$ one-tailed; LL: $t = 2.96$, $p = 0.02$ one-tailed) and made as many non-migration related errors as controls (LM: $t = 0.04$, $p = 0.48$ one-tailed; LL: $t = 1.82$, $p = 0.07$ one-tailed). EL did not make more nonword migration errors than controls ($t = 0.18$, $p = 0.43$ one-tailed) and made more non-migration related errors than controls ($t = 2.95$, $p = 0.02$ one-tailed).

Following the finding that EL showed the opposite effect to that displayed by LM and LL (i.e., as many migration errors as controls, but more non-migration related errors than controls), we decided to inspect EL's non-word reading data more closely. We found that 23% of ELs non-migration errors were what we have termed, "over-sequential" errors. An "over-sequential" error was defined as an error that appeared likely to have occurred as a result of sounding out each letter in the non-word in isolation, and then blending these sounds together to form a spoken response. For example, EL read *kerm* as /k /ɛ/ /r/ /m/. That is, instead of reading the letters *e* and *r* together to correctly form the sound /ər/, he sounded out these two letters separately. For two of these errors, EL first misread the non-word as its migration partner, and then self-corrected with an over-sequential error. Furthermore, for all but one of EL's over-sequential errors, EL demonstrated that he knew the sound associated with the multi-letter grapheme he over-sequentialized by correctly producing it on at least two other items within the list. EL's control group did not make a single "over-sequential" error on this task. This finding suggests that EL's limited migration errors on this task (compared to the other LPDs in the study) may have been the result of him sounding out each letter in isolation of the other letters within the word.

The findings from the reading aloud non-words task suggest that LPD is most likely caused by an orthographic-visual analysis deficit. However, there appears to be variation in task performance among the three LPDs in the present study.

Table 5 | Percentage of migration errors (mig error) and non-migration related errors (non-mig error) on reading aloud non-words.

	LM	EL	LM and EL controls	LL	LL controls
Mig error	40***	6	5.00 (5.02)	16*	4.40 (3.58)
Non-mig error	12	36*	12.33 (7.42)	20	7.20 (6.42)

Numbers in parentheses denote standard deviation of the mean for control groups.
**p < 0.05, ***p < 0.001 compared to control group.*

Item variables influencing non-word migration errors. In the present study, we also explored the possibility that there may be specific item variables that influence whether or not LPDs will make non-word migration errors. Specifically, we explored whether the bigram frequency of the non-word migration counterpart relative to the bigram frequency of the non-word itself, influenced whether or not a non-word migration error will be made.

We investigated the influence of bigram frequency on non-word reading by analyzing the migration errors made by LM and LL. Specifically, we compared the number of migration errors made on the lower bigram frequency partner ($N = 25$) to the number of migration errors made on the higher bigram frequency partner ($N = 25$). The other participants' results (EL and both control groups) were not investigated in this additional analysis as they made very few migration errors on the task. Both LM and LL read as many non-words as their higher bigram frequency migration partner (LM: 40%, LL: 8%) as they did non-words as their lower bigram frequency partner (LM: 40%; LL: 24%; both Fisher's exact $p > 0.12$ one-tailed).

While bigram frequency was not found to mediate migration errors on this task, a *post hoc* analysis revealed that LM and LL's migration errors were influenced by the complexity of the graphemes that made up each non-word. LM and LL were more likely to migrate a two-letter grapheme into two single-letter graphemes (e.g., reading *kerm* as "krem") than to migrate two single-letter graphemes into a two-letter grapheme (e.g., reading *krem* as "kerm"). Both LM and LL were found to migrate significantly more two-letter graphemes into single letter graphemes (LM: 66.67%, LL: 33.33%) than two single-letter graphemes into a two letter grapheme (LM: 11.11%, LL: 0%, both Fisher's exact $p < 0.02$ two-tailed).

An examination of the order of item presentation was conducted to investigate whether the errors where a two-letter grapheme migrated into two single-letter graphemes were due to participants being primed by the two single-letter graphemes. That is, we examined whether participants saw the two single letter graphemes (e.g., *frempt*) prior to making an error where they migrated a two-letter grapheme into these two-single letters (e.g., reading *kerm* as *krem*). Of the 18 errors made by LM and LL where a two-letter grapheme was migrated into two single letters (e.g., where *k<u>er</u>m* was read as "k<u>re</u>m"), only three errors were made directly after having seen a non-word that comprised the same two single letters (e.g., *f<u>re</u>mpt*).

DISCUSSION

This study investigated the locus of impairment in three English-speaking children with developmental LPD. Previous research has used a cognitive model of reading aloud to identify three alternative processing components that may be the cause of LPD: the phonological output buffer, the orthographic input lexicon, and orthographic-visual analysis. First, we aimed to replicate previous findings that have ruled out a phonological output buffer deficit and an orthographic input lexicon deficit account of LPD. We then went on to extend previous findings that suggest LPD is caused by an orthographic-visual analysis deficit.

ASSESSING THE PHONOLOGICAL OUTPUT BUFFER

It is plausible to assume that the excessive migration errors made by LPDs are due to the phonemes in the phonological output buffer being swapped around before the word is pronounced. Together with previous studies, our findings strongly refute this hypothesis (Friedmann and Rahamim, 2007; Kohnen et al., 2012; see also Collis et al., 2013). All three LPDs in the present study were either within or above the average range on various standardized tests that draw heavily on a functioning phonological output buffer to be completed successfully. Furthermore, LPDs were asked to repeat a subset of the migratable words that they had previously made a migration error on in a reading aloud task. Each LPD performed this task without making a single migration error, indicating that their reading aloud errors were not caused by an inability to produce the word's phonemes in the correct order.

In recent years, various researchers have suggested that underlying dyslexia is a phonological processing deficit (Stanovich, 1988; Snowling, 1998, 2001; Ramus, 2003). The findings from the present study indicate that, while some children with reading difficulties have phonological processing difficulties, other children's reading difficulties are likely to reflect an alternative processing deficit. For example, surface dyslexia is most likely caused by an orthographic processing deficit (e.g., Castles and Coltheart, 1993, 1996; Broom and Doctor, 1995; Temple, 1997), attentional dyslexia is most likely caused by a letter-to-word binding deficit (Rayner et al., 1989; Friedmann et al., 2010b), and LPD is most likely caused by a letter position coding deficit (for more discussion of heterogeneity within developmental dyslexia, see Castles et al., 2010; Zoccolotti and Friedmann, 2010; McArthur et al., 2013).

ASSESSING THE ORTHOGRAPHIC INPUT LEXICON

It is also plausible to assume that the migration errors made by LM, EL and LL are the result of lexical guessing due to an impoverished orthographic input lexicon. The finding that all three LPDs read aloud non-migratable irregular words as well as controls indicates that this is not the case. Furthermore, EL and LL made more migration errors than controls during a reading aloud task and a visual lexical decision task but did not make more substitution and *N* errors than controls. These findings indicate that EL and LL's errors on these tasks were specific to the migration of letters within the word and were therefore not due to lexical guessing.

In contrast to EL and LL, LM made more migration errors than controls on the visual lexical decision task *and* more substitution errors on the task. This finding suggests that perhaps LM's tendency to make excessive migration errors is the result of lexical guessing. While this finding does not fall in line with our predictions, we believe that LM's lexical guessing was confined to this task, and that her broader tendency to make more migration errors than her peers cannot be attributed to a lexical guessing strategy. If LM's excessive migration errors are the result of lexical guessing, then she should have been found to make more errors that are visually similar to the target word when reading aloud (e.g., reading *slime* as "slide" or "slim") than controls. This was not the case. Like EL and LL, LM made more migration errors than controls when reading aloud, but the same amount of substitution and *N* errors.

ASSESSING THE ORTHOGRAPHIC-VISUAL ANALYSIS STAGE OF READING

The first aim of the present study was to replicate the finding that LPD cannot be attributed to a phonological output buffer deficit or an orthographic input lexicon deficit. Our findings converge with previous research that has ruled out these two possible loci as the source of migration errors seen in LPD (Friedmann and Rahamim, 2007; Kohnen et al., 2012). Having addressed our first aim, we now turn to a discussion of our second aim: to extend the investigation of a possible orthographic-visual analysis deficit account of LPD.

The present study extended Kohnen et al.'s (2012) study in three ways: (1) administering a sequential same-different decision task, (2) administering consonant–strings and orthographically legal non-words in the sequential same-different decision task, and (3) manipulating bigram frequency in a non-word reading task. We hoped that making these changes would provide us with tasks that were more sensitive to an orthographic-visual analysis deficit, and hence enable us to draw stronger conclusions regarding the locus of impairment in English LPD.

In the present study, we administered a sequential same-different decision task to ensure that participants would be unable to adopt a strategy whereby they compare each letter in the pair to one another. We found that EL and LL made significantly more word migration errors on the task than controls. LM also showed this trend, however it did not reach significance. One key difference between the present study and Kohnen et al.'s (2012) study was EL's performance on the same-different decision task. While EL did not make more migration errors on Kohnen et al.'s (2012) simultaneous same-different decision task, he made significantly more migration errors on a sequential variant of the task in the present study. One interpretation of this finding is that EL was adopting a letter-by-letter matching strategy during Kohnen et al.'s (2012) simultaneous same-different decision task. When he was unable to adopt this strategy during the present study, due to the sequential presentation of words, he made significantly more migration errors than controls.

An alternative interpretation of EL's excessive migration errors on the same-different matching task in the present study is that a sequential variant of the task encourages participants to convert the word into a phonological form due to the limited presentation time of the items. It might therefore be that EL made excessive migration errors on the sequential task because he compared the words in each pair based on phonological form, whereas in Kohnen et al.'s (2012) simultaneous task, words were compared based on their orthographic form. We believe this alternative hypothesis to be unlikely for two reasons. Firstly, a wealth of research has shown that responses made on a same-different decision task are based on prelexical orthographic representations rather than phonological representations (e.g., Besner et al., 1984; Kinoshita and Norris, 2009). Secondly, EL was found to be within (or above) the average range on tests that assess phonological processing. It is therefore highly unlikely that EL's excessive migration errors on the sequential same-different decision task could be reflecting a difficulty in comparing phonological forms.

A consonant–string condition in the same-different decision task was included in the present study under the assumption that a letter position coding deficit should manifest itself in responses to all letter-strings, regardless of lexicality. Contrary to our prediction, LPDs did not make more migration errors than controls on the consonant–string condition. We believe that this finding was due to the different mechanisms underlying the processing of letters in words and in consonant–strings. While letters in words are thought to be processed in parallel as a single unit, each letter in a consonant–string needs to be processed serially as a single unit. This means that letters in consonant–strings are likely to take longer to process than letters in words. The *post hoc* finding that participants were significantly better at identifying a difference between two consonant strings when the difference occurred toward the beginning of the consonant pair (*f**k**tzm-f**l**tzm*) than when the difference occurred toward the end of the consonant pair (*fkt**z**m-fkt**l**m*) suggests that 400ms was not enough time for participants to process the entire consonant–string. For this reason, we believe that participants' performance on the consonant–string condition cannot be taken as evidence for or against an orthographic-visual analysis deficit account of LPD.

Following this finding, we conducted a sequential same-different decision task with orthographically legal non-words. We found that while EL made significantly more migration errors than controls on this task, LM and LL did not. The finding that EL made more word *and* non-word migration errors on a same-different decision task strongly suggests that EL's excessive migration errors are caused by an orthographic-visual analysis deficit. In contrast, the finding that LM and LL made more migration errors on the word condition, but not on the non-word condition is not predicted by an orthographic-visual analysis deficit account of LPD. Rather, LM and LL should have been found to make more migration errors on a sequential same-different decision task, regardless of the lexicality of the items. However, LM and LL's data are still most consistent overall with an orthographic-visual analysis deficit. Further investigations may need to focus on the interaction between lexicality effects and orthographic-visual analysis deficits in LPD.

We also administered a non-word reading task in the present study. If LPD is caused by an orthographic-visual analysis deficit, we should find that LPDs not only make more word migration errors (e.g., reading *slime* as "smile") than controls, but also more non-word migration errors (e.g., reading *pilf* as "plif"), as a deficit at the orthographic-visual analysis stage of reading should impede both lexical and non-lexical reading. In the present study, we found that LM and LL made more non-word migration errors (e.g., reading *pilf* as "plif") than controls. This finding is in contrast with Kohnen et al.'s (2012) finding that all three LPDs made as many non-word migration errors as controls. Interestingly, the one LPD in the present study who did not make excessive non-word migration errors (EL) was one of the three LPDs in Kohnen et al.'s (2012) study who did not make excesive non-word migration errors when reading aloud. This finding is consistent with research in Hebrew that has found that while some LPDs make non-word migration errors, others do not (Friedmann and Rahamim, 2007). EL's over-sequential errors (where each letter was sounded out in isolation and then blended together to form a response) in the present study suggest that individual differences in strategy use might be one predictor of whether or not LPDs will make non-word migration errors.

Contrary to our exploratory hypothesis, we found non-word bigram frequency to have no influence over whether or not a migration error was made. That is, LM and LL were no more likely to read a non-word as its higher bigram frequency partner than they were to read a non-word as its lower bigram frequency partner. The majority of migration errors made by LPDs occur when two adjacent letters in the middle of a word can migrate to form a new word. Considering it is the internal letters of the non-word that are most prone to migration, it is perhaps not surprising that the bigram frequency of the entire letter-string (external letters included) did not influence whether or not a migration error occurred. Instead, it may be other factors specific to the letters that are most susceptible to migration that influence whether or not a migration error will be made.

This suggestion was supported by the *post hoc* finding that the complexity of the non-word's internal grapheme/s influenced whether or not a migration error was made. We found that LM and LL were more likely to swap the letters in a two-letter grapheme around to form two single-letter graphemes, than to swap two single letters around to form a two-letter grapheme (i.e., *k**er**m* was read as "k**re**m" more than *k**re**m* read as "k**er**m")[4]. One plausible explanation for this finding is that children are likely to be introduced to the sounds that the letters of the alphabet make (single-letter graphemes) before they are introduced to the sounds that two letters of the alphabet make together (two-letter graphemes). What this finding might therefore reflect is an age of acquisition effect. When the non-lexical route is provided with ambiguous letter position information, the default may be to resort to the letter-sounds that were first learnt. Future studies may seek to further our *post hoc* finding by directly testing the hypothesis that some graphemes may be more susceptible to migration than others.

---

[4]Note that following this finding we also analysed the influence of internal bigram frequency on migration errors using Solso and Juel's (1980) bigram frequency count database. That is, we analyzed whether or not LM and LL were more likely to migrate the lower frequency bigram *li* in the non-word *p**li**m* into the higher frequency bigram *il* (resulting in the misreading of the non-word as "p**il**m"). We found no influence of internal bigram frequency on LM and LL's migration errors.

CONCLUSION

The aim of this multiple single case study was to both replicate and extend previous findings regarding the locus of impairment in English LPD. Our findings converge with previous research by strongly suggesting that LPD cannot be attributed to a phonological output buffer or orthographic input lexicon deficit. Rather, our results suggest that LPD is most likely caused by a deficit specific to the coding of letter position at the orthographic-visual analysis stage of reading.

In line with previous studies, however, there was some variability in performance amongst the three children on the tasks designed to explicitly assess for an orthographic-visual analysis deficit. One thing that is becoming increasingly clear as research on LPD progresses is that localizing the source of the migration errors seen in LPD is no easy feat. While identifying what *does not cause* migration errors (i.e., a phonological output or orthographic input lexicon deficit) is relatively straightforward, identifying what *causes* migration errors is not as clear-cut. The findings from the present study suggest that variations in the manifestation of an orthographic-visual analysis deficit may be, at least in part, due to individual differences in strategy use. Therefore, to maximize the potential of localizing the deficit underpinning LPD, future research needs to ensure that the tasks used either eliminate or greatly reduce the opportunity for compensatory strategies to be adopted.

Finally, the finding that the three children in the present study were found to have great difficulty in reading migratable words, in the absence of any other obvious reading or spoken language difficulty, attests to the heterogeneity of dyslexia and its underlying causes. Our findings strongly suggest that not all children with reading difficulties have an impairment in phonological processing. Rather, our findings join a growing body of research in advocating the need to map this heterogeneity in developmental dyslexia, and to develop diagnostic tools that assess the variety of its underlying causes.

ACKNOWLEDGMENTS

The authors thank LM, EL and LL, and their families for their participation in this study. They also thank Kristina Barisic, Danielle Colenbrander, and Erin Banales for their help with recruiting control participants for the study. They also thank Professor John Crawford for his advice regarding statistical analyses. This study was supported by a Macquarie University Research Excellence Scholarship (MQRES) to the first and an Australian Research Council Discovery Project grant (DP110103822) to the second author.

REFERENCES

Baayen, R. H., Piepenbrock, R., and Gulikers, L. (1995). *The CELEX Lexical Database (CD-ROM)*. Philadelphia, PA: Linguistic Data Consortium.

Besner, D., Coltheart, M., and Davelaar, E. (1984). Basic processes in reading: computation of abstract letter identities. *Can. J. Psychol.* 38, 126–134. doi: 10.1037/h0080785

Beyersmann, A. E., Duñabeitia, J. A., Carreiras, M., Coltheart, M., and Castles, A. (2013). Early morphological decomposition of suffixed words: masked priming evidence with transposed-letter nonword primes. *Appl. Psycholinguist.* 34, 869–892. doi: 10.1017/S0142716412000057

Beyersmann, A. E., Castles, A., and Coltheart, M. (2011). Early morphological decomposition during visual word recognition: evidence from masked transposed-letter priming. *Psychon. Bull. Rev.* 18, 937–942. doi: 10.3758/s13423-011-0120-y

Beyersmann, A. E., Coltheart, M., and Castles, A. (2012). Parallel processing of whole-words and morphemes in visual word recognition. *Q. J. Exp. Psychol.* 65, 1306–1326. doi: 10.1080/17470218.2012.656661

Broom, Y. M., and Doctor, E. A. (1995). Developmental surface dyslexia: a case study of the efficacy of a remediation programme. *Cogn. Neuropsychol.* 12, 69–110. doi: 10.1080/02643299508251992

Castles, A., and Coltheart, M. (1993). Varieties of developmental dyslexia. *Cognition* 47, 149–180. doi: 10.1016/0010-0277(93)90003-E

Castles, A., and Coltheart, M. (1996). Cognitive correlates of developmental surface dyslexia: a single case study. *Cogn. Neuropsychol.* 13, 25–50. doi: 10.1080/026432996382051

Castles, A., Coltheart, M., Larsen, L., Jones, K., Saunders, S., and McArthur, G. (2009). Assessing the basic components of reading: a revision of the Castles and Coltheart test with new norms. *Aust. J. Learn. Difficult.* 14, 67–88. doi: 10.1080/19404150902783435

Castles, A., Coltheart, M., Wilson, K., Valpied J., and Wedgwood, J. (2009). The genesis of reading ability: what helps children learn letter-sound correspondences? *J. Exp. Child Psychol.* 104, 68–88. doi: 10.1016/j.jecp.2008.12.003

Castles, A., McLean, G. M. T., and McArthur, G. (2010). Dyslexia (neuropsychological). *Wiley Interdiscip. Rev. Cogn. Sci.* 1, 426–432. doi: 10.1002/wcs.16

Collis, N. L., Kohnen, S., and Kinoshita, S. (2013). The role of visual spatial attention in adult developmental dyslexia. *Q. J. Exp. Psychol.* 66, 245–260. doi: 10.1080/17470218.2012.705305

Coltheart, M., Rastle, K., Perry, C., Langdon, R., and Ziegler, J. (2001). DRC: a dual route cascaded model of visual word recognition and reading aloud. *Psychol. Rev.* 108, 204–256. doi: 10.1037/0033-295X.108.1.204

Crawford, J. R., and Garthwaite, P. H. (2002). Investigation of the single case in neuropsychology: confidence limits on the abnormality of test scores and test score differences. *Neuropsychologia* 40, 1196–1208. doi: 10.1016/S0028-3932(01)00224-X

Crawford, J. R., and Garthwaite, P. H. (2005). Testing for suspected impairments and dissociations in single case studies in neuropsychology: evaluation of alternatives using Monte Carlo simulations and revised tests for dissociations. *Neuropsychology* 19, 318–331. doi: 10.1037/0894-4105.19.3.318

Davis, C. J. (2005). N-Watch: a program for deriving neighbourhood size and other psycholinguistic statistics. *Behav. Res. Methods* 37, 65–70. doi: 10.3758/BF03206399

Denckla, M. B., and Rudel, R. G. (1976). Rapid "automatized" naming (R.A.N): dyslexia differentiated from other learning disabilities. *Neuropsychologia* 14, 471–479. doi: 10.1016/0028-3932(76)90075-0

Forster, K. I., and Forster, J. C. (2003). DMDX: a windows display program with millisecond accuracy. *Behav. Res. Methods Instrum. Comput.* 35, 116–124. doi: 10.3758/BF03195503

Friedmann, N., and Gvion, A. (2001). Letter position dyslexia. *Cogn. Neuropsychol.* 18, 673–696. doi: 10.1080/02643290143000051

Friedmann, N., and Haddad-Hanna, M. (2012). Letter position dyslexia in Arabic: from form to position. *Behav. Neuropsychol.* 25, 193–203. doi: 10.3233/BEN-2012-119004

Friedmann, N., Dotan, D., and Rahamim, E. (2010a). Is the visual analyzer orthographic-specific? Reading words and numbers in letter position dyslexia. *Cortex* 46, 982–1004. doi: 10.1016/j.cortex.2009.08.007

Friedmann, N., Kerbel, N., and Shvimer, L. (2010b). Developmental attentional dyslexia. *Cortex* 46, 1216–1237. doi: 10.1016/j.cortex.2010.06.012

Friedmann, N., and Rahamim, E. (2007). Developmental letter position dyslexia. *J. Neuropsychol.* 1, 201–236. doi: 10.1348/174866407X204227

Høien, T., Lundberg, I., Larsen, J. P., and Tønnessen, F. E. (1989). Profiles of reading related skills in dyslexic families. *Read. Writ.* 1, 381–392. doi: 10.1007/BF00386268

Kinoshita, S., and Norris, D. (2009). Transposed-letter priming of prelexical orthographic representations. *J. Exp. Psychol. Learn.* 35, 1–18. doi: 10.1037/a0014277

Kohnen, S., and Castles, A. (2013). Pirates at parties: letter position processing in developing readers. *J. Exp. Child Psychol.* 115, 91–107. doi: 10.1016/j.jecp.2012.08.011

Kohnen, S., Marinus, E., Friedmann, N., Anandakumar, T., Castles, A., Nickels, L., et al. (2014). *The Letter Position Test (LetPos)*. Available at: www.motif.org.au

Kohnen, S., Nickels, L., Castles, A., Friedmann, N., and McArthur, G. (2012). When 'slime' becomes 'smile': developmental letter position dyslexia in English. *Neuropsychologia* 50, 3681–3692. doi: 10.1016/j.neuropsychologia.2012.07.016

Korkman, M., Kirk, U., and Kemp, S. (1998). *A Developmental Neuropsychological Assessment (NEPSY)*. San Antonio, TX: The Psychological Corporation.

Mann, V. A., and Liberman, I. Y. (1984). Phonological awareness and verbal short-term memory. *J. Learn. Disabil.* 17, 592–599. doi: 10.1177/00222194840 1701005

Mann, V. A., Liberman, I. Y., and Shankweiler, D. (1980). Children's memory for sentences and word strings in relation to reading ability. *Mem. Cogn.* 8, 329–335. doi: 10.3758/BF03198272

McArthur, G., Eve, P. M., Jones, K., Banales, E., Kohnen, S., Anandakumar, T., et al. (2012). Phonics training for English speaking poor readers. *Cochrane Database. Syst. Rev.* 12, 1–104. doi: 10.1002/14651858.CD009115.pub2

McArthur, G., Kohnen, S., Larsen, L., Jones, K., Anandakumar, T., Banales, E., et al. (2013). Getting to grips with the heterogeneity of developmental dyslexia. *Cogn. Neuropsychol.* 30, 1–24. doi: 10.1080/02643294.2013.784192

Perea, M., and Fraga, I. (2006). Transposed-letter and laterality effects in lexical decision. *Brain Lang.* 97, 102–109. doi: 10.1016/j.bandl.2005.08.004

Perea, M. L., and Lupker, S. J. (2004). Can CANISO activate CASINO? Transposed-letter similarity effects with nonadjacent letter positions. *J. Mem. Lang.* 51, 231–246. doi: 10.1016/j.jml.2004.05.005

Ramus, F. (2003). Developmental dyslexia: specific phonological deficit or general sensorimotor dysfunction? *Curr. Opin. Neurobiol.* 13, 212–218. doi: 10.1016/S0959-4388(03)00035-7

Rastle, K., and Coltheart, M. (1998). Whammies and double whammies: the effect of length on nonword reading. *Psychon. Bull. Rev.* 5, 277–282. doi: 10.3758/BF03212951

Rayner, K., Murphy, L. A., Henderson, J. M., and Pollatsek, A. (1989). Selective attentional dyslexia. *Cogn. Neuropsychol.* 6, 357–378. doi: 10.1080/02643298908253288

Snowling, M. (1998). Dyslexia as a phonological deficit: evidence and implications. *Child Adolesc. Mental Health* 3, 4–11. doi: 10.1111/1475-3588.00201

Snowling, M. (2001). From language to reading and dyslexia. *Dyslexia* 7, 37–46. doi: 10.1002/dys.185

Solso, R. L., and Juel, C. L. (1980). Instrumentation and techniques: positional frequency and versatility of bigrams for two- through nine-letter English words. *Behav. Res. Methods Instrument.* 12, 297–343. doi: 10.3758/BF03201669

Stanovich, K. E. (1988). Explaining the differences between dyslexia and the garden-variety poor reader. The phonological-core variable-difference model. *J. Learn. Disabil.* 21, 590–604. doi: 10.1177/002221948802101003

Temple, C. (1997). *Developmental Cognitive Neuropsychology.* Hove: Psychology Press.

Wagner, R., Torgesen, J., and Rashotte, C. (1999). *Comprehensive Test of Phonological Processing (CTOPP).* Austin, TX: PRO-ED.

Wechsler, D. (2003). *Wechsler Intelligence Scale for Children-Fourth Edition (WISC-IV).* San Antonio, TX: The Psychological Corporation.

Zoccolotti, P., and Friedmann, N. (2010). From dyslexia to dyslexias, from dysgraphia to dysgraphias, from a cause to causes: a look at current research on developmental dyslexia and dysgraphia. *Cortex* 46, 1211–1215. doi: 10.1016/j.cortex.2010.09.003

19

Developmental dyslexia: dysfunction of a left hemisphere reading network

Fabio Richlan*

Department of Psychology, Center for Neurocognitive Research, University of Salzburg, Salzburg, Austria

***Correspondence:**
Fabio Richlan, Department of Psychology, Center for Neurocognitive Research, University of Salzburg, Hellbrunnerstr. 34, 5020 Salzburg, Austria.
e-mail: fabio.richlan@sbg.ac.at

This mini-review summarizes and integrates findings from recent meta-analyses and original neuroimaging studies on functional brain abnormalities in dyslexic readers. Surprisingly, there is little empirical support for the standard neuroanatomical model of developmental dyslexia, which localizes the primary phonological decoding deficit in left temporo-parietal (TP) regions. Rather, recent evidence points to a dysfunction of a left hemisphere reading network, which includes occipito-temporal (OT), inferior frontal, and inferior parietal regions.

Keywords: brain, developmental dyslexia, fMRI, meta-analysis, neuroimaging, reading

INTRODUCTION

Developmental dyslexia is defined as a specific disorder of reading development. It is characterized by an unexpected impairment in the acquisition of reading skills despite normal intelligence, motivation, and adequate schooling (Ferrer et al., 2010). According to the diagnostic criteria of DSM-IV (American Psychiatric Association, 2000) and ICD-10 (World Health Organization, 2007), performance in reading accuracy and/or fluency, reading comprehension, and/or spelling is substantially below the performance expected from the person's chronological age, intelligence, education, and sensory acuity. In addition, the difficulties significantly interfere with academic achievement or activities in everyday life that require reading skills. In a substantial number of cases, delayed development of oral language skills in early childhood is the first sign of dyslexia. Problems with vocabulary and grammatical structures are often comorbid with reading difficulties and frequently persist into adulthood.

With respect to neurocognitive explanations, a number of competing hypotheses exist but the dominant explanation posits a phonological deficit as proximal cause (e.g., Snowling, 2000; Shaywitz and Shaywitz, 2005; Vellutino and Fletcher, 2005). This deficit is assumed to affect the emergence of phoneme awareness at the beginning of learning to read, which in turn has a negative effect on the acquisition of self-reliant phonological word reading based on serial grapheme-phoneme coding. The phonological decoding difficulty is assumed to secondarily compromise the build-up of the orthographic lexicon, which is required for fast automatic word recognition and correct spelling. Support for this account was provided by the specific difficulty of dyslexic readers to come up with correct readings of pseudowords. However, this difficulty with pseudowords was typically found in English-based studies and does not generalize to more regular orthographies like German (e.g., Landerl et al., 1997; Ziegler et al., 2001). Accordingly, this version of the phonological deficit explanation is difficult to apply to regular orthographies. Wimmer (1993) proposed that, in regular orthographies, the phonological deficit becomes manifest as a speed impairment in the access to both lexical and sublexical phonology. In a similar way, Wolf and Bowers (1999) modified the phonological deficit explanation by positing an additional visual-verbal speed deficit. Their double deficit explanation was backed up by the finding that performance on tasks requiring rapid naming of pictured objects before learning to read predicted later reading skills.

The classical phonological deficit explanation served as a framework for the functional neuroanatomical study of developmental dyslexia. Narrative reviews of the existing research culminated in a standard model positing three left hemisphere regions with abnormal function in dyslexic readers (Pugh et al., 2000; McCandliss and Noble, 2003; Démonet et al., 2004; Sandak et al., 2004; Shaywitz and Shaywitz, 2005; Schlaggar and McCandliss, 2007). The primary phonological word decoding difficulty is seen as resulting from a dysfunction of a left dorsal temporo-parietal (TP) region, including the posterior aspect of the superior temporal gyrus and adjacent parietal regions. The secondary difficulty with fast word recognition—based on stored orthographic word representations—is seen as resulting from a dysfunction of a left ventral occipito-temporal (OT) region including lateral extrastriate, fusiform, and inferior temporal regions. A third abnormality—presumably reflecting compensatory reliance on effortful articulatory processes—is overactivation of the left inferior frontal gyrus (IFG).

RECENT INSIGHTS FROM FUNCTIONAL NEUROIMAGING

This mini-review provides an evaluation of the standard model. It is based on recent meta-analyses and original functional magnetic resonance imaging (fMRI) studies on brain activation abnormalities in dyslexic readers. The main benefit of the meta-analytic approach is that it reveals consistent effects across studies in an unbiased and objective way. Therefore, it may lead to findings that were overlooked in the original studies and in the narrative reviews because they did not seem to be interesting for theoretical reasons. Certainly, synthesizing over heterogeneous studies also entails potential pitfalls. One such problem is the averaging across different languages. However, despite different behavioral manifestations, there is considerable agreement that the neuronal fingerprint of developmental dyslexia is quite common across different languages (Paulesu et al., 2001; Hu et al., 2010). In addition, the meta-analytic results by definition should only show those regions, which are consistently under or overactivated in dyslexic readers in most of the studies. Therefore, the results may be viewed as the lowest common denominator of the original studies. For a discussion of further limitations of the present meta-analyses see Richlan et al. (2011).

Our first attempt to evaluate the standard neuroanatomical model used quantitative, coordinate-based meta-analysis of 17 published functional neuroimaging studies (Richlan et al., 2009). The results lent support to the central role of left hemisphere TP and OT dysfunctions. Specifically, convergent dyslexic underactivation across studies was found in the left inferior parietal lobule (IPL), superior temporal, middle temporal, inferior temporal, and fusiform regions. A novel finding was underactivation in a left IFG region associated with access to lexical and sublexical phonological representations. Dyslexic overactivation was found in the primary motor cortex and in the anterior insula, presumably reflecting compensatory reliance on articulatory-based phonological processes. The meta-analysis included original studies from quite different age levels, which is problematic in relation to the developmental assumption of the standard model. To recapitulate, this model posits an early dysfunction of the left TP region resulting in an additional secondary dysfunction of the left OT region. Therefore, one would expect to find dominance of left TP underactivation in children with dyslexia and both left TP and left OT underactivation in adults with dyslexia.

A second meta-analysis (Richlan et al., 2011) investigated this expectation by dividing the original studies into nine studies with dyslexic children (age means: 9–11 years) and nine studies with dyslexic adults (age means: 18–30 years). Contrary to expectation, left TP underactivation was present in the adult studies but not in the child studies. There was dyslexic underactivation in bilateral IPL regions in the meta-analysis of the child studies but this underactivation was localized superior to the typical TP regions. With respect to left OT dysfunction, widespread underactivation was found for the adult dyslexic readers. In contrast, for dyslexic children left OT underactivation was limited to an anterior portion of the left ventral OT cortex. This finding is in agreement with the notion of an important role of the left OT region in skilled, efficient reading (e.g., Shaywitz et al., 2007). The finding of left OT underactivation in children is compatible with recent evidence in favor of early left OT engagement in normal reading development (Brem et al., 2010), and early failure of such engagement in dyslexia (Maurer et al., 2007; Bach et al., 2012; Raschle et al., 2012). In summary, the findings of the second meta-analysis raised serious doubts on the validity of the standard model. Specifically, there was no support for the critical developmental assumption that the primary and early emerging dysfunction resides in the left TP cortex. Rather, the findings suggest that an early small left OT dysfunction becomes increasingly extended and is later accompanied by a left TP dysfunction.

Further doubts on the critical role of the left TP region in phonological decoding came from an fMRI study with German adolescent and adult dyslexic readers (Wimmer et al., 2010). The participants were visually presented with phonologically and orthographically familiar words (e.g., *Taxi*), phonologically familiar but orthographically unfamiliar pseudohomophones (e.g., *Taksi*), and phonologically and orthographically unfamiliar pseudowords (e.g., *Tazi*). The task required phonological lexical decisions (i.e., *Does it sound like an existing word?*). From the standard model one would expect dyslexic readers to exhibit underactivation of the left OT cortex in response to familiar words and underactivation of the left TP cortex in response to unfamiliar pseudowords. However, the non-impaired readers exhibited generally little activation in response to pseudohomophones and pseudowords in left TP regions. These unfamiliar letter strings led to marked activation in left hemisphere OT, IFG, and IPL regions. Importantly, the left IPL activation may not be subsumed under the left TP reading circuit because it was localized quite far from the proposed core regions of phonological reading processes in left posterior superior temporal regions. In response to unfamiliar letter strings, dyslexic readers exhibited underactivation in all three major components of the non-impaired activation pattern (left OT, left IFG, left IPL). Dyslexic overactivation was identified in early visual occipital regions, reflecting prolonged visual processing, as well as in a network of premotor/motor and subcortical regions, presumably reflecting increased reliance on silent articulatory processes.

A follow-up study by Richlan et al. (2010) provided further evidence for dyslexic underactivation in left OT, IFG, and IPL regions. The primary novel feature was the introduction of a new experimental manipulation: stimulus length, with short items consisting of 3–5 letters and long items consisting of 6–10 letters. The manipulation of item length for pseudowords was of specific importance as it allowed the localization of brain regions engaged by serial phonological decoding. If indeed the left hemisphere network of OT, IFG, and IPL regions is engaged by reading of both familiar and unfamiliar letter strings, then non-impaired readers should exhibit a length effect for pseudowords but not for words, and dyslexic readers may again exhibit reduced engagement of the non-impaired reading network. The results confirmed these expectations. In response to both familiar and unfamiliar letter strings, non-impaired readers showed activation in the left hemisphere network of OT, IFG, and IPL regions. Furthermore, activation in the left OT and in the left IFG, but not in the left IPL, was specifically sensitive to the length of pseudowords. Apart from the more superior localization of the left IPL cluster, this feature adds evidence against the summarization of this brain region under the phonological left TP reading circuit. As hypothesized, dyslexic readers exhibited marked underactivation in response to pseudowords in left OT, left IFG, and left IPL regions. They also failed to show the increase in activation in response to the length of pseudowords shown by the non-impaired readers. Similar to the previous fMRI study, the dyslexic readers exhibited overactivation in left premotor, subcortical, and cerebellar regions, presumably engaged by slow and effortful articulatory-based reading. Consistent with this interpretation was the finding of a marked length effect for pseudowords in the left premotor region of dyslexic readers.

EVIDENCE FOR A LEFT TEMPORO-PARIETAL DYSFUNCTION?

To recapitulate, the first meta-analysis (Richlan et al., 2009) found evidence for dyslexic underactivation in left TP regions. The second meta-analysis (Richlan et al., 2011), with a separation of child and adult studies, modified this pattern by finding left TP underactivation only for adults but not for children. As pointed out, the latter finding stands in contrast to the central developmental assumption of the standard neuroanatomical model. This model assumes an early occurring primary left TP dysfunction. However, despite this missing support for the developmental assumption, the two meta-analyses—at least for the adult studies—support the standard model by speaking for an important role of core left TP regions for non-impaired reading processes, and a dysfunction of these regions for dyslexic reading processes.

Surprisingly, the findings from the two fMRI studies with young adult German readers question this conclusion. For core components of the left TP reading circuit (posterior superior temporal regions), the non-impaired readers in this study exhibited generally little activation and consequently there could be no reduced activation for the dyslexic readers. The absence of reliable activation observed for non-impaired readers is specifically remarkable as the standard model localizes serial phonological decoding in left TP regions, and the in-scanner tasks presented unfamiliar letter strings in the context of a phonological lexical decision task. As expected from serial phonological decoding of pseudowords, the non-impaired readers of Richlan et al. (2010) exhibited a marked length effect for pseudowords (but not for words) in a left IFG region and a left OT region. Meanwhile, dyslexic readers exhibited a similar specific length effect in left premotor regions. Thus, there were specific regions apparently engaged by serial decoding, but the left TP cortex was not among these regions. However, both of the original studies identified a left IPL region with reading-related activation exhibited by non-impaired readers, and reduced activation exhibited by dyslexic readers. In some formulations of the standard model (e.g., Pugh et al., 2000; Sandak et al., 2004) the left IPL is subsumed under the left TP circuit. However, some aspects differ from the assumption of the standard model that the left TP circuit is mainly engaged by serial phonological decoding: the non-impaired readers of Richlan et al. (2010) did not exhibit a length effect for pseudowords on left IPL activation. Therefore, the reduced left IPL activation of dyslexic readers—different from the standard model—cannot be interpreted as reflecting a dysfunction with respect to the demands of serial phonological decoding. An alternative account of the function of the left IPL was formulated by Shaywitz and Shaywitz (2008), who linked the left IPL to general attentional mechanisms, which may interact with reading processes. Evidence for this interpretation is only beginning to emerge and certainly more studies on the role of the left IPL during reading are required. Interestingly, a recent meta-analysis of fMRI studies with healthy children found that reading, numerical processing, and tasks posing demands on executive functions led to activation of a similar left IPL region (Houdé et al., 2010).

DYSFUNCTION OF A LEFT HEMISPHERE READING NETWORK

Convergence between the findings of the original studies and the meta-analyses exists with respect to underactivation in a left hemisphere reading network consisting of OT, IFG, and IPL regions. The identification of left IFG underactivation in the two meta-analyses (Richlan et al., 2009, 2011) was a novel finding and stood in contrast to overactivation in a close-by left precentral region. This finding was of particular importance, as in dominant formulations of the standard neuroanatomical model (e.g., Pugh et al., 2000) it is assumed that a reading circuit in anterior frontal language regions exhibits overactivation in dyslexic readers in order to compensate for the dysfunction in posterior language regions. Obviously, the meta-analytic findings speak for a marked distinction within left frontal regions; that is, between a left IFG region and a left precentral region, with dyslexic underactivation in the former and dyslexic overactivation in the latter. The findings from the two fMRI studies (Richlan et al., 2010; Wimmer et al., 2010) provided further evidence for such a distinction. Both studies identified dyslexic underactivation in the left IFG and dyslexic overactivation in left precentral/motor regions. The former is presumably engaged by access to lexical and sublexical phonological representations, and the latter presumably by silent articulatory reading processes. In a series of studies, Heim and colleagues showed that cytoarchitectonic subdivisions of the left IFG differently contribute to lexical access (area 44) and lexical selection (area 45) (Heim et al., 2005, 2009a,b). Dyslexic children (Grande et al., 2011) and adults (Heim et al., 2012) were recently shown to exhibit functional abnormalities in both of these left IFG subdivisions.

For non-impaired readers, reading-related activation of the left IFG was accompanied by activation in left OT and left IPL regions. All three components of this reading network were found to be underactivated in dyslexic readers. Additional findings of the two fMRI studies were that non-impaired readers exhibited very similar activation patterns in the left OT and the left IFG, with marked increases of activation from familiar to unfamiliar letter strings (Wimmer et al., 2010) and from short to long pseudowords (Richlan et al., 2010). The similarity of activation patterns speaks for a striking functional connectivity between left OT and left IFG regions. The modulation of activation in response to reading demands in non-impaired readers was missing in dyslexic readers. This finding is in line with evidence from studies of functional and effective connectivity which reported coupling of left OT and left IFG regions in non-impaired readers and disruption in dyslexic readers (Shaywitz et al., 2003; Cao et al., 2008; van der Mark et al., 2011).

Based on these findings, a model of the impaired left hemisphere reading network in developmental dyslexia including OT,

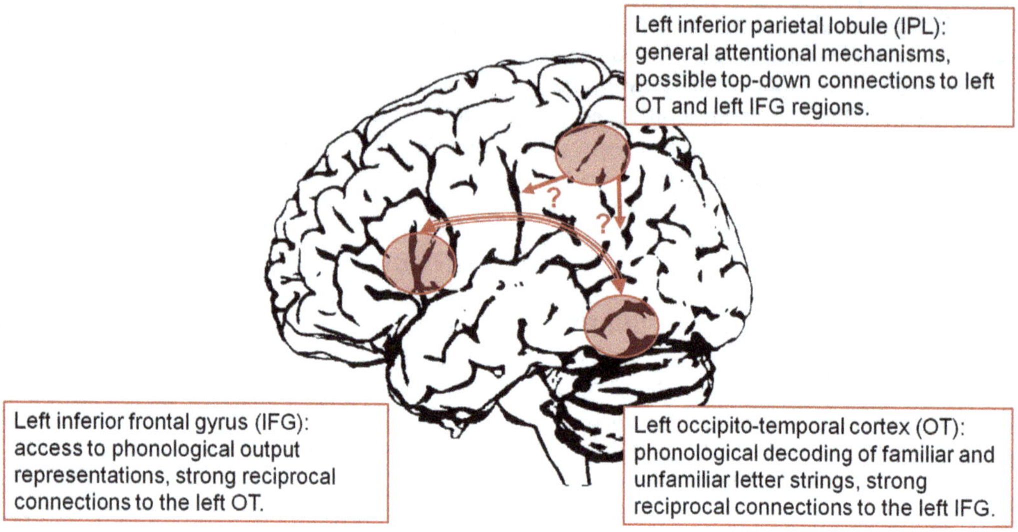

FIGURE 1 | Dysfunction of a left hemisphere reading network in developmental dyslexia.

IFG, and IPL regions is illustrated in **Figure 1**. While there is evidence for strong functional and structural connectivity between left OT and left IFG regions (Catani et al., 2005; Ben-Shachar et al., 2007), connectivity of the left IPL region is less clear. The left OT underactivation was assumed to reflect a deficit in processing of both familiar words and unfamiliar pseudowords. With increasing demands on phonological decoding (i.e., processing of longer pseudowords), the left OT dysfunction of dyslexic readers became even more evident. The same pattern of functional abnormalities was observed for the left IFG. In this region, dyslexic underactivation was interpreted as reflecting a deficit in access to lexical and sublexical phonological representations. When interpreting the left IPL abnormality we can only speculate about possible underlying mechanisms. Assumedly, the function of the left IPL was not specifically related to reading or phonological decoding (as shown by absence of a length effect for pseudowords in non-impaired readers). Rather, it was supposed to be associated with more general mechanisms, as evidenced by engagement in numerical processing and executive functions (Houdé et al., 2010). As suggested by Shaywitz and Shaywitz (2008), the left IPL may be part of a fronto-parietal attention network, which interacts with reading processes via top-down connections. However, the exact mechanisms of this interaction are unclear and should be targeted in future studies, e.g., by means of psychophysiological interactions. Furthermore, one has to keep in mind that the present model is largely based on fMRI studies (with their well-known limitations such as poor temporal resolution). A more comprehensive neuroanatomical model of developmental dyslexia certainly requires the integration of findings from other modalities such as EEG and MEG. However, in contrast to the standard neuroanatomical model (e.g., Pugh et al., 2000), which is based on subjective, narrative review of a limited number of studies, the present model is based on objective, quantitative meta-analysis of a substantially larger number of functional neuroimaging studies on developmental dyslexia. Therefore, it may be viewed as an up-to-date modification of the standard model.

There is an interesting developmental question with respect to the model illustrated in **Figure 1**. In accordance with the phonological deficit explanation, one may assume that a dysfunction of the left frontal component may be specifically critical in the early phase of learning to read, as this component may be engaged by access to phonemes and other sublexical phonological representations. To our knowledge, no evidence for such an early dysfunction of left frontal regions exists. Rather, recent fMRI and EEG studies reported evidence for early left OT engagement in normal reading development and early dysfunction in developmental dyslexia (Maurer et al., 2007; Brem et al., 2010; Bach et al., 2012; Raschle et al., 2012). These findings raise questions about the functional role of the left OT region in reading development. The idea that the left OT functions as a kind of interface area connecting high-level visual representations (or representations from other sensory modalities) to language and conceptual representations (Price and Devlin, 2011) is quite compatible with the finding of an early role of the left OT for learning to read. From this perspective, the aforementioned findings on reduced early left OT engagement in young dyslexic readers may reflect a form of disconnection between visual and phonological representations. This would be consistent with Geschwind's account of dyslexia as a disconnection syndrome (Geschwind, 1965a,b).

ACKNOWLEDGMENTS

I am grateful to Heinz Wimmer, Martin Kronbichler, Matthias Schurz, Benjamin Gagl, Julia Sophia Crone, and Joe Miller for their support. This research was funded by grants of the Austrian Science Foundation (FWF), grant number P18832-B02, and of the 6th Framework Programme of the European Commission (EC), grant number 018696.

REFERENCES

American Psychiatric Association. (2000). *Diagnostic and Statistical Manual of Mental Disorders - DSM- IV-TR.* Washington, DC: American Psychiatric Association.

Bach, S., Richardson, U., Brandeis, D., Martin, E., and Brem, S. (2012). Print-specific multimodal brain activation in kindergarten improves prediction of reading skills in second grade. *Neuroimage* doi: 10.1016/j.neuroimage.2011.07.023. [Epub ahead of print].

Ben-Shachar, M., Dougherty, R. F., and Wandell, B. A. (2007). White mat- ter pathways in reading. Curr. Opin. *Neurobiol.* 17, 258–270.

Brem, S., Bach, S., Kucian, K., Guttorm, T. K., Martin, E., Lyytinen, H., Brandeis, D., and Richardson, U. (2010). Brain sensitivity to print emerges when learn letter-speech sound correspondences. P*roc. Natl. Acad. Sci. U.S.A.* 107, 7939–7944.

Cao, F., Bitan, T., and Booth, J. R. (2008). Effective brain connectivity in children with reading difficul- ties during phonological processing. Brain Lang. 107, 91–101.

Catani, M., Jones, D. K., and ffytche, D. H. (2005). Perisylvian language networks of the human brain. Ann. Neurol. 57, 8–16.

Démonet, J. F., Taylor, M. J., and Chaix, Y. (2004). Developmental dyslexia. Lancet 363, 1451–1460.

Ferrer, E., Shaywitz, B. A., Holahan, J. M., Marchione, K., and Shaywitz, S. E. (2010). Uncoupling of reading and IQ over time: empirical evi- dence for a definition of dyslexia. Psychol. Sci. 21, 93–101.

Geschwind, N. (1965a). Disconnexion syndromes in animals and man. I. Brain 88, 237–294.

Geschwind, N. (1965b). Disconnexion syndromes in animals and man. II. Brain 88, 585–644.

Grande, M., Meffert, E., Huber, W., Amunts, K., and Heim, S. (2011). Word frequency effects in the left IFG in dyslexic and normally read- ing children during picture nam- ing and reading. *Neuroimage* 57, 1212–1220.

Heim, S., Alter, K., Ischebeck, A. K., Amunts, K., Eickhoff, S. B., Mohlberg, H., Zilles, K., von Cramon, D. Y., and Friederici, A.

D. (2005). The role of the left Brodmann's areas 44 and 45 in read- ing words and pseudowords. Brain Res. Cogn. Brain Res. 25, 982–993.

Heim, S., Eickhoff, S. B., and Amunts, K. (2009a). Different roles of cytoarchitectonic BA 44 and BA 45 in phonological and semantic verbal fluency as revealed by dynamic causal modelling. *Neuroimage* 48, 616–624.

Heim, S., Eickhoff, S. B., Ischebeck, A. K., Friederici, A. D., Stephan, K. E., and Amunts, K. (2009b). Effective connectivity of the left BA 44, BA 45, and inferior temporal gyrus during lexical and phonological decisions identified with DCM. *Hum. Brain Mapp.* 30, 392–402.

Heim, S., Wehnelt, A., Grande, M., Huber, W., and Amunts, K. (2012). Effects of lexicality and word frequency on brain activation in dyslexic readers. Brain Lang. doi: 10.1016/j.bandl.2011.12.005. [Epub ahead of print].

Houdé, O., Rossi, S., Lubin, A., and Joliot, M. (2010). Mapping numer- ical processing, reading, and exec- utive functions in the developing brain: an fMRI meta-analysis of 52 studies including 842 children. Dev. Sci. 13, 876–885.

Hu, W., Lee, H. L., Zhang, Q., Liu, T., Geng, L. B., Seghier, M. L., Shakeshaft, C., Twomey, T., Green, D. W., Yang, Y. M., and Price, C. J. (2010). Developmental dyslexia in Chinese and English populations: dissociating the effect of dyslexia from language differences. Brain 133, 1694–1706.

Landerl, K., Wimmer, H., and Frith, U. (1997). The impact of orthographic consistency on dyslexia: a German- English comparison. Cognition 63, 315–334.

Maurer, U., Brem, S., Bucher, K., Kranz, F., Benz, R., Steinhausen, H. C., and Brandeis, D. (2007). Impaired tuning of a fast occipito-temporal response for print in dyslexic chil- dren learning to read. Brain 130, 3200–3210.

McCandliss, B. D., and Noble, K. G. (2003). The development of read- ing impairment: a cognitive neuro- science model. *Ment. Retard. Dev. Disabil. Res. Rev.* 9, 196–204.

Paulesu, E., Démonet, J. F., Fazio, F., McCrory, E., Chanoine, V., Brunswick, N., Cappa, S. F., Cossu, G., Habib, M., Frith, C. D., and Frith, U. (2001). Dyslexia: cultural diversity and biological unity. Science 291, 2165–2167.

Price, C. J., and Devlin, J. T. (2011). The interactive account of ven- tral occipitotemporal contributions to reading. Trends Cogn. Sci. 15, 246–253.

Pugh, K. R., Mencl, W. E., Jenner, A. R., Katz, L., Frost, S. J., Lee, J. R., Shaywitz, S. E., and Shaywitz, B. A. (2000). Functional neuroimag- ing studies of reading and reading disability (developmental dyslexia). *Ment. Retard. Dev. Disabil. Res. Rev.* 6, 207–213.

Raschle, N. M., Zuk, J., and Gaab, N. (2012). Functional characteristics of developmental dyslexia in left- hemispheric posterior brain regions predate reading onset. P*roc. Natl. Acad. Sci. U.S.A.* 109, 2156–2161.

Richlan, F., Kronbichler, M., and Wimmer, H. (2009). Functional abnormalities in the dyslexic brain: a quantitative meta-analysis of neuroimaging studies. *Hum. Brain Mapp.* 30, 3299–3308.

Richlan, F., Kronbichler, M., and Wimmer, H. (2011). Meta- analyzing brain dysfunctions in dyslexic children and adults. *Neuroimage* 56, 1735–1742.

Richlan, F., Sturm, D., Schurz, M., Kronbichler, M., Ladurner, G., and Wimmer, H. (2010). A common left occipito-temporal dysfunc- tion in developmental dyslexia and acquired letter-by-letter read- ing? PLoS One 5:e12073. doi: 10.1371/journal.pone.0012073

Sandak, R., Mencl, W. E., Frost, S. J., and Pugh, K. R. (2004). The neurobiological basis of skilled and impaired reading: recent Findings and new directions. Sci. Stud. Read. 8, 273–292.

Schlaggar, B. L., and McCandliss, B. D. (2007). Development of neu- ral systems for reading. Annu. Rev. Neurosci. 30, 475–503.

Shaywitz, B. A., Skudlarski, P., Holahan, J. M., Marchione, K. E., Constable, R. T., Fulbright, R. K., Zelterman, D., Lacadie, C., and Shaywitz, S. E. (2007). Age-related changes in reading systems of dyslexic children. Ann. Neurol. 61, 363–370.

Shaywitz, S. E., and Shaywitz, B. A. (2005). Dyslexia (specific read- ing disability). Biol. Psychiatry 57, 1301–1309.

Shaywitz, S. E., and Shaywitz, B. A. (2008). Paying attention to read- ing: the neurobiology of reading and dyslexia. Dev. Psychopathol. 20, 1329–1349.

Shaywitz, S. E., Shaywitz, B. A., Fulbright, R. K., Skudlarski, P., Mencl, W. E., Constable, R. T., Pugh, K. R., Holahan, J. M., Marchione, K. E., Fletcher, J. M., Lyon, G. R., and Gore, J. C. (2003). Neural systems for compensa- tion and persistence: young adult outcome of childhood reading disability. Biol. Psychiatry 54, 25–33.

Snowling, M. J. (2000). Dyslexia. Oxford, UK: Blackwell. van der Mark, S., Klaver, P., Bucher, K., Maurer, U., Schulz, E., Brem, S., Martin, E., and Brandeis, D. (2011). The left occipitotemporal system in reading: disruption of focal fMRI connectivity to left inferior frontal and inferior parietal language areas in children with dyslexia. *Neuroimage* 54, 2426–2436.

Vellutino, F. R., and Fletcher, J. M. (2005). "Developmental dyslexia," in *The Science of Reading: A Handbook,* eds M. J. Snowling and C. J. Hulme (Oxford, UK: Blackwell), 362–378.

Wimmer, H. (1993). Characteristics of developmental dyslexia in a regular writing system. *Appl. Psycholinguist.* 14, 1–33.

Wimmer, H., Schurz, M., Sturm, D., Richlan, F., Klackl, J., Kronbichler, M., and Ladurner, G. (2010). A dual-route perspective on poor reading in a regular orthography: an fMRI study. Cortex 46, 1284–1298.

Wolf, M., and Bowers, P. (1999). The double-deficit hypothesis for the developmental dyslexias. J. Educ. Psychol. 91, 415–438.

World Health Organization. (2007). ICD-10 - *International Statistical Classification of Diseases and Related Health Problems.* Geneva, Switzerland: World Health Organization.

Ziegler, J. C., Perry, C., Jacobs, A. M., and Braun, M. (2001). Identical words are read differently in dif- ferent languages. *Psychol. Sci.* 12, 379–384.

Permissions

All chapters in this book were first published by Frontiers; hereby published with permission under the Creative Commons Attribution License or equivalent. Every chapter published in this book has been scrutinized by our experts. Their significance has been extensively debated. The topics covered herein carry significant findings which will fuel the growth of the discipline. They may even be implemented as practical applications or may be referred to as a beginning point for another development.

The contributors of this book come from diverse backgrounds, making this book a truly international effort. This book will bring forth new frontiers with its revolutionizing research information and detailed analysis of the nascent developments around the world.

We would like to thank all the contributing authors for lending their expertise to make the book truly unique. They have played a crucial role in the development of this book. Without their invaluable contributions this book wouldn't have been possible. They have made vital efforts to compile up to date information on the varied aspects of this subject to make this book a valuable addition to the collection of many professionals and students.

This book was conceptualized with the vision of imparting up-to-date information and advanced data in this field. To ensure the same, a matchless editorial board was set up. Every individual on the board went through rigorous rounds of assessment to prove their worth. After which they invested a large part of their time researching and compiling the most relevant data for our readers.

The editorial board has been involved in producing this book since its inception. They have spent rigorous hours researching and exploring the diverse topics which have resulted in the successful publishing of this book. They have passed on their knowledge of decades through this book. To expedite this challenging task, the publisher supported the team at every step. A small team of assistant editors was also appointed to further simplify the editing procedure and attain best results for the readers.

Apart from the editorial board, the designing team has also invested a significant amount of their time in understanding the subject and creating the most relevant covers. They scrutinized every image to scout for the most suitable representation of the subject and create an appropriate cover for the book.

The publishing team has been an ardent support to the editorial, designing and production team. Their endless efforts to recruit the best for this project, has resulted in the accomplishment of this book. They are a veteran in the field of academics and their pool of knowledge is as vast as their experience in printing. Their expertise and guidance has proved useful at every step. Their uncompromising quality standards have made this book an exceptional effort. Their encouragement from time to time has been an inspiration for everyone.

The publisher and the editorial board hope that this book will prove to be a valuable piece of knowledge for researchers, students, practitioners and scholars across the globe.

List of Contributors

Elizabeth G. Conlon, Gry Lilleskaret, Craig M. Wright and Anne Stuksrud
Griffith Health Institute, School of Applied Psychology, Griffith University, Gold Coast, QLD, Australia

Paz Suárez-Coalla, Rrezarta Avdyli and Fernando Cuetos
Department of Psychology, University of Oviedo, Oviedo, Spain

Filippo Gasperini, Daniela Brizzolara, Paola Cristofani, Claudia Casalini and Anna Maria Chilosi
Department of Developmental Neuroscience, IRCCS Fondazione Stella Maris, Pisa, Italy

Katia Lehongre
Research Center of the Brain and Spine Institute (CRICM), Hôpital de la Pitié-Salpêtrière, Paris, France

Benjamin Morillon
Department of Psychiatry, Columbia University Medical Center, New York, NY, USA

Anne-Lise Giraud
Department of Neuroscience, University of Geneva, Geneva, Switzerland

Franck Ramus
Laboratoire de Sciences Cognitives et Psycholinguistique, Ecole Normale Supérieure, EHESS, CNRS, Paris, France

Maria Luisa Lorusso and Chiara Cantiani
Unit of Neuropsychology of Developmental Disorders, Department of Child Psychopathology, Scientific Institute IRCCS "E. Medea", Bosisio Parini, Italy

Massimo Molteni
Developmental Neuropsychology Unit, Istituto Scientifico "E. Medea" di Bosisio Parini, Lecco, Italy
Unit of Neuropsychology of Developmental Disorders, Department of Child Psychopathology, Scientific Institute IRCCS "E. Medea", Bosisio Parini, Italy

Muriel A. Lobier
Laboratoire de Psychologie et NeuroCognition, Université Grenoble Alpes, Grenoble, France
Neuroscience Center, University of Helsinki, Helsinki, Finland

Carole Peyrin, Cédric Pichat and Sylviane Valdois
Laboratoire de Psychologie et NeuroCognition, Université Grenoble Alpes, Grenoble, France
CNRS, Laboratoire de Psychologie et NeuroCognition, UMR5105, Grenoble, France

Jean-François Le Bas
INSERM U836/Université Joseph Fourier – Institut des Neurosciences, Grenoble, France

Trichur R. Vidyasagar
Visual and Cognitive Neuroscience Laboratory, Department of Optometry and Vision Sciences, University of Melbourne, Parkville, VIC, Australia
Melbourne Neuroscience Institute, University of Melbourne, Parkville, VIC, Australia

Victoria Leong and Usha Goswami
Department of Psychology, Centre for Neuroscience in Education, University of Cambridge, Cambridge, UK

Giuseppina Schiavone
Department of Integrative Neurophysiology, Center for Neurogenomics and Cognitive Research, VU University Amsterdam, Amsterdam, Netherlands
Body Area Network, imec/Holst Centre, Eindhoven, Netherlands

Klaus Linkenkaer Hansen and Huibert D. Mansvelder
Department of Integrative Neurophysiology, Center for Neurogenomics and Cognitive Research, VU University Amsterdam, Amsterdam, Netherlands

Natasha M. Maurits
Department of Neurology, University Medical Center Groningen, University of Groningen, Groningen, Netherlands

Anna Plakas
Department of Neurology, University Medical Center Groningen, University of Groningen, Groningen, Netherlands
Research Institute of Child Development and Education, University of Amsterdam, Amsterdam, Netherlands

Ben A. M. Maassen
Center for Language and Cognition Groningen and University Medical Center Groningen, University of Groningen, Groningen, Netherlands

Aryan van der Leij and Titia L. van Zuijen
Research Institute of Child Development and Education, University of Amsterdam, Amsterdam, Netherlands

Maria De Luca
Neuropsychology Unit, IRCCS Fondazione Santa Lucia, Rome, Italy

Maria Pontillo
Department of Psychology, Sapienza University of Rome, Rome, Italy

Silvia Primativo and Pierluigi Zoccolotti
Neuropsychology Unit, IRCCS Fondazione Santa Lucia, Rome, Italy
Department of Psychology, Sapienza University of Rome, Rome, Italy

Donatella Spinelli
Neuropsychology Unit, IRCCS Fondazione Santa Lucia, Rome, Italy
Department of Human Movement Sciences and Health, University of Rome «Foro Italico», Rome, Italy

Jeremy M. Law and Pol Ghesquiere
Faculty of Psychology and Educational Sciences, Parenting and Special Education Research Unit, KU Leuven, Leuven, Belgium

Maaike Vandermosten
Faculty of Psychology and Educational Sciences, Parenting and Special Education Research Unit, KU Leuven, Leuven, Belgium
Laboratory for Experimental ORL, Department of Neuroscience, KU Leuven, Leuven, Belgium

Jan Wouters
Laboratory for Experimental ORL, Department of Neuroscience, KU Leuven, Leuven, Belgium

Simone Gori and Andrea Facoetti
Developmental and Cognitive Neuroscience Laboratory, Dipartimento di Psicologia Generale, Università degli Studi di Padova, Padova, Italy
Developmental Neuropsychology Unit, Istituto Scientifico "E. Medea" di Bosisio Parini, Lecco, Italy

Paolo Cecchini and Anna Bigoni
Ophthalmological Unit, Istituto Scientifico "E. Medea" di San Vito al Tagliamento, Pordenone, Italy

Paul Gimenez, Roeland Hancock and Robert Hendren
Division of Child and Adolescent Psychiatry, Department of Psychiatry, UCSF, San Francisco, CA, USA

Nicolle Bugescu and Emily Kutner
Division of Child and Adolescent Psychiatry, Department of Psychiatry, UCSF, San Francisco, CA, USA
Department of Psychology, Pacific Graduate School of Psychology, Palo Alto University, Palo Alto, CA, USA

Jessica M. Black
Graduate School of Social Work, Boston College, Chestnut Hill, MA, USA

Kenneth Pugh
Haskins Laboratories, Yale University, New Haven, CT, USA

Masanori Nagamine
Division of Child and Adolescent Psychiatry, Department of Psychiatry, UCSF, San Francisco, CA, USA
Division of Behavioral Sciences, National Defense Medical College Research Institute, Tokorozawa, Saitama, Japan

Paul Mazaika
Department of Psychiatry and Behavioral Sciences, Center for Interdisciplinary Brain Sciences Research, Stanford University School of Medicine, Stanford, CA, USA

Bruce D. McCandliss
Department of Psychology and Human Development, Vanderbilt University, Nashville, TN, USA

Fumiko Hoeft
Division of Child and Adolescent Psychiatry, Department of Psychiatry, UCSF, San Francisco, CA, USA
Haskins Laboratories, Yale University, New Haven, CT, USA
Department of Psychiatry and Behavioral Sciences, Center for Interdisciplinary Brain Sciences Research, Stanford University School of Medicine, Stanford, CA, USA
Department of Neuropsychiatry, Keio University School of Medicine, Shinjuku-ku, Tokyo, Japan

Eva Staels and Wim Van den Broeck
Department of Clinical and Lifespan Psychology, Faculty of Psychology and Educational Sciences, Vrije Universiteit Brussel, Brussels, Belgium

Travis White-Schwoch
Auditory Neuroscience Laboratory, Northwestern University, Evanston, IL, USA
Department of Communication Sciences, Northwestern University, Evanston, IL, USA

Nina Kraus
Auditory Neuroscience Laboratory, Northwestern University, Evanston, IL, USA
Department of Communication Sciences, Northwestern University, Evanston, IL, USA
Institute for Neuroscience, Northwestern University, Evanston, IL, USA
Department of Neurobiology and Physiology, Northwestern University, Evanston, IL, USA
Department of Otolaryngology, Northwestern University, Chicago, IL, USA

Paola Angelelli
Department of History, Society and Human Studies, University of Salento, Lecce, Italy

Chiara Valeria Marinelli
Istituto di Ricovero e Cura a Carattere Scientifico (IRCCS) Santa Lucia, Rome, Italy

Cristina Burani
Istituto di Scienze e Tecnologie della Cognizione, Consiglio Nazionale delle Ricerche, Rome, Italy
Department of Life Sciences, University of Trieste, Trieste, Italy

Yvette Kezilas, Saskia Kohnen and Anne Castles
Department of Cognitive Science, ARC Centre of Excellence in Cognition and its Disorders, Macquarie University, Sydney, NSW, Australia

Meredith McKague
Melbourne School of Psychological Science, The University of Melbourne, Melbourne, VIC, Australia

Fabio Richlan
Department of Psychology, Center for Neurocognitive Research, University of Salzburg, Salzburg, Austria

Index

www.ingramcontent.com/pod-product-compliance
Lightning Source LLC
LaVergne TN
LVHW082157200926
848484LV00008B/2174